TAKING SIDES

Clashing Views in

Abnormal Psychology

SIXTH EDITION

D0226179

TAKING·SIDES

Clashing Views in

Abnormal Psychology

SIXTH EDITION

Selected, Edited, and with Introductions by

Richard P. Halgin
University of Massachusetts—Amherst

Mc Graw Hill

Connect
Learn
Succeed™

TAKING SIDES: ABNORMAL PSYCHOLOGY, SIXTH EDITION

Published by McGraw-Hill, a business unit of The McGraw-Hill Companies, Inc., 1221 Avenue of the Americas, New York, NY 10020. Copyright © 2011 by The McGraw-Hill Companies, Inc. All rights reserved. Previous edition(s) © 2009, 2007, and 2005. No part of this publication may be reproduced or distributed in any form or by any means, or stored in a database or retrieval system, without the prior written consent of The McGraw-Hill Companies, Inc., including, but not limited to, in any network or other electronic storage or transmission, or broadcast for distance learning.

Some ancillaries, including electronic and print components, may not be available to customers outside the United States.

Taking Sides® is a registered trademark of the McGraw-Hill Companies, Inc.
Taking Sides is published by the **Contemporary Learning Series** group within the McGraw-Hill Higher Education division.

1 2 3 4 5 6 7 8 9 0 DOC/DOC 1 0 9 8 7 6 5 4 3 2 1 0

MHID: 0-07-805016-2
ISBN: 978-0-07-805016-9
ISSN: 1527-604X (print)
ISSN: 2157-9725

Managing Editor: *Larry Loeppke*
Senior Developmental Editor: *Jill Meloy*
Permissions Coordinator: *DeAnna Dausener*
Senior Marketing Communications Specialist: *Mary Klein*
Senior Project Manager: *Jane Mohr*
Design Coordinator: *Brenda A. Rolwes*
Cover Graphics: *Rick D. Noel*
Buyer: *Nicole Baumgartner*
Media Project Manager: *Sridevi Palani*

Compositor: *MPS Limited, a Macmillan Company*
Cover Image: © Brand X Pictures/Punchstock

Library of Congress Cataloging-in-Publication Data

Main entry under title:
 Taking sides: clashing views in abnormal psychology/selected, edited, and with introductions by Richard P. Halgin. —6th ed.

 Includes bibliographical references.
 1. Psychology, Pathological. I. Halgin, Richard P. *comp*.
                                616.89

Editors/Academic Advisory Board

Members of the Academic Advisory Board are instrumental in the final selection of articles for each edition of TAKING SIDES. Their review of articles for content, level, and appropriateness provides critical direction to the editors and staff. We think that you will find their careful consideration well reflected in this volume.

TAKING SIDES: Clashing Views in

ABNORMAL PSYCHOLOGY

Sixth Edition

EDITOR

Richard P. Halgin
University of Massachusetts—Amherst

Preface

The field of abnormal psychology is inherently controversial because we lack a clear delineation between normal and abnormal behavior. Most phenomena in the realm of abnormal psychology fall along continua; the point on a continuum at which behavior moves from being considered "normal" to being considered "abnormal" varies considerably and is influenced by a number of factors. Consider the example of an active boy's behavior. His running around impulsively and shouting out aimless comments would be viewed as normal behavior on a playground but abnormal behavior in a quiet classroom. In a classroom setting, his behavior might be referred to as impulsive and hyperactive, possibly prompting his teacher to refer him to a mental health professional for therapy and medication to help him settle down and pay attention. Although such referrals are commonplace in American schools, some people contend that we pathologize the normal behavior of children when we view their high levels of energy as mental disorders. This is but one of the debates about which you will read in this book, and it is a good example of the kind of controversy found in the field of mental health.

There are many complex issues that arise in the field of abnormal psychology; in this book you will read about 18 controversial matters with which mental health experts struggle. Unit 1 looks at psychological conditions and treatments about which there has been vehement disagreement in recent years, with some experts expressing intense skepticism about the validity of specific clinical problems and interventions that have been in the spotlight. Unit 2 looks at The Trend Toward Biological Interventions approaches for an array of psychological problems and mental disorders. Unit 3 explores pertinent social issues that interface with the field of abnormal psychology, particularly debates about ethical and legal issues that pertain to the field of mental health.

Most students who enroll in a course in abnormal psychology begin the semester with the belief that they will be learning about problems that affect "other people," rather than themselves. In a short period of time, however, they come to realize that they are reading about conditions that have much more personal salience than they had anticipated. Sooner or later, they recognize conditions that they or someone close to them has experienced, and their interest in the topic intensifies. In all likelihood, you will have a similar reaction as you read this book. To capture the essence of each debate, you will find it helpful to connect yourself in a personal way to the issue under consideration; you might imagine yourself dealing with the issue personally, or as the relative of a client with the particular problem, or even as a professional trying to provide mental health assistance.

Plan of the book   To assist you in understanding the significance of each issue, every issue begins with an *introduction* that provides important background about the issue and summarizes the perspective in each of the pieces. Points and counterpoints are enumerated to help you appreciate the specific areas of disagreement between the two pieces. Each issue concludes with a set of *Challenge Questions* that can serve as the basis for further thought or discussion on the topic as well as a list of suggested additional readings. In addition, Internet site addresses (URLs) have been provided on the *Internet References* page at the beginning of each unit, which should prove useful as starting points for further research on the issues. At the back of the book is a listing of all the *Contributors to This Volume* with a brief biographical sketch of each of the prominent figures whose views are debated here.

Changes to this edition   This sixth edition of *Taking Sides: Clashing Views in Abnormal Psychology* includes some important changes from the fifth edition. This edition includes five new issues, containing a total of 10 new articles. The five new topics address provocative debates which have emerged in recent years. "Is the Use of Aversive Treatment an Inhumane Intervention for Psychologically Disordered Individuals?" (Issue 1) discusses controversial behavior modification techniques for treating individuals who engage in harmful behaviors. "Is Gender Identity Disorder a Mental Illness?" (Issue 2) addresses the debate about the inclusion of this condition in official listings of mental disorders. "Is Addiction a Brain Disease?" (Issue 9) tackles thorny issues about the extent to which drug addicted individuals are responsible for their addictions. "Is It Unethical for Psychologists to Be Involved in Coercive Interrogations?" (Issue 13) addresses the national debate about procedures used for extracting information from suspected terrorists, and the role that psychologists play in the development and administration of coercive interrogation techniques. "Does Research Confirm That Abortion is a Psychologically Benign Experience?" (Issue 18) discusses reviews of the research literature on the psychological effects of abortion, and the extent to which bias influences this field of research.

A word to the instructor   An *Instructor's Resource Guide with Test Questions* (multiple-choice and essay) is available through the publisher for the instructor using *Taking Sides* in the classroom. Instructors will also find a general guidebook, *Using Taking Sides in the Classroom*, which discusses methods and techniques for integrating the pro-con approach into any classroom setting. Online versions of all of these resources, as well as correspondence service for *Taking Sides* adopters can be found on the "instructor" link of the book's Web site at www.mhhe.com/cls.

While article references have not been included in the printed book in order to limit book size, all references for articles appearing in *Taking Sides: Clashing Views in Abnormal Psychology*, 6/e are available on the "student" link of the book's Web site at www.mhhe.com/cls.

Acknowledgments   Very special gratitude goes to the research assistants who contributed to the preparation of this volume by conducting bibliographic research and editing the issues. Ilana Klarman, who played a major role in preparing the fifth edition, contributed to this edition in her work on the chapter entitled "Is Gender Identity Disorder a Mental Illness?" Special thanks also to Alexander Miller who helped prepare the chapter entitled "Is the Use of Aversive Treatment an Inhumane Intervention for Psychologically Disordered Individuals?" and Wilton Dadmun who worked on the topic "Is Addiction a Brain Disease?" Special gratitude also goes to the research assistants whose contributions to previous editions continue to be evident in the sixth edition: Molly Burnett, Rebecca Gray, Joseph Greer, Kerry Halgin, Eric Nguyen, Diana Rancourt, Barbara Sieck, and Justin Smith.

Thanks also to Jill Meloy and the staff at McGraw-Hill. Jill's conscientious oversight and thoughtful direction once again played a major role in the current edition, and I feel especially grateful to have benefited from her editorial guidance.

Richard P. Halgin
University of Massachusetts—Amherst

*To my wonderful wife, Lucille, whose love
and support provide me with immeasurable
amounts of energy, and to our children,
Daniel and Kerry, whose values
and achievements have been
inspiring.*

Contents In Brief

Contents

All references for articles included in *Taking Sides: Clashing Views in Abnormal Psychology, 6/e* can be found on the Web at **www.mhhe.com/cls**.

Laurie Ahern and Eric Rosenthal, writing on behalf of Mental Disability Rights International (MDRI), characterize the intentional infliction of pain at JRC as human rights abuses. Psychologist Matthew Israel, director of the Judge Rotenberg Center (JRC), responds to the MDRI with insistence that JRC is using behavioral methods to save individuals from their treatment-resistant, life-threatening disorders.

The Traditional Values Coalition argues that gender-variant people are psychologically disturbed individuals who need professional help, and that their condition should be viewed as a mental disorder. Kelley Winters asserts that the GID diagnosis imposes the stigma of mental illness upon people who meet no scientific definition of mental disorder.

Attorney Samuel J. Brakel and psychiatrist John M. Davis assert that society has a responsibility to take care of seriously mentally ill individuals who are incapable of making an informed decision about their need for care and treatment. Attorney James B. Gottstein contends that forced treatment of mentally ill citizens represents a curtailment of liberty which leads many people down a road of permanent disability and poverty.

Heather Draper argues that clinicians need to accept the fact that individuals with anorexia nervosa may be competent and may have legitimate reasons for refusing therapy. In such cases, therapists should respect the individual's wishes and should refrain from administering life-sustaining treatment. James L. Werth, Jr. and his colleagues contend that, due to the very nature of anorexia nervosa, individuals with anorexia cannot make rational decisions about nutrition and feeding. Because the behaviors of anorexics have such potential for health damage or even death, clinicians have a duty to protect the lives of their patients, even if it calls for compulsory treatment.

Psychologists Grant J. Devilly and Peter Cotton assert that critical incident stress debriefing (CISD) is poorly defined and has been shown to do more harm than good. They propose alternative approaches for responding to trauma survivors, which they consider more effective. Jeffrey T. Mitchell of the International Critical Incident Stress Foundation (ICISF) argues that Devilly and Cotton have misrepresented important information about psychological debriefing and have confused several aspects of this system of responding to trauma survivors.

Psychologist David H. Gleaves and his colleagues assert that for some people, memories of traumatic events are blocked but may subsequently be recovered. Psychologist John F. Kihlstrom disputes the validity of blocked and recovered memories. He views the phenomenon of "false memories" as a serious problem in contemporary society.

The National Institute of Mental Health views ADHD as a valid disorder affecting between 3 and 5 percent of American children, many of whom will continue to deal with symptoms of this condition into adulthood. According to NIMH, ADHD warrants careful diagnosis and treatment by skilled professionals. Psychologist Rogers H. Wright argues that ADHD has vague diagnostic criteria that lead to overdiagnosis and overmedication of an excessive number of people.

Science writers Robert Mathias and Patrick Zickler argue that MDMA has skyrocketed in popularity and that insufficient attention has been paid to the physical and psychological risks associated with its use. June Riedlinger, an assistant professor of clinical pharmacy, and Michael

Montagne, a professor of pharmacy, contend that the risks associated with MDMA use have been exaggerated and that there are legitimate therapeutic uses for this substance.

UNIT 2 THE TREND TOWARD BIOLOGICAL INTERVENTIONS 203

In the NIDA publication, the argument is made that addiction is indeed a disease, and that scientific information is available about the nature, prevention, and treatment of this disease. Psychiatrist Sally Satel and psychologist Scott O. Lilienfeld object to the brain disease characterization of drug addiction, asserting that addiction is an activity whose course can be altered by its foreseeable consequences.

Law professor Adam J. Kolber supports the use of memory-dampening drugs for survivors of trauma in the belief that some experiences are so horrific that they can stand in the way of traumatized people moving toward happier and healthier levels of functioning. The President's Council on Bioethics, chaired by Dr. Leon Kass, criticizes memory-dampening drugs because they could falsify a person's perception and understanding of the world, making terrible acts seem less terrible than they are.

Physician Peter R. Breggin asserts that Ritalin and similar stimulants are dangerous addictive medications that should not be prescribed to children because they suppress growth and lead to a number of worrisome physical and psychological symptoms. Psychologist and prominent ADHD researcher Russell A. Barkley objects to criticisms of Ritalin and similar stimulants, maintaining that these medications serve as important parts of interventions aimed at helping children increase their attention and concentration.

UNIT 3   SOCIAL ISSUES   281

The American Psychological Association, the American Psychiatric Association, and the National Alliance on Mental Illness collaborated in the preparation of an *amici curiae* brief pertaining to the case of Scott Panetti, who was sentenced to death for murder. In this brief, The argument is made that mentally ill convicts should not be executed if their disability significantly impairs their capacity to understand the nature and purpose of their punishment or to appreciate why the punishment is being imposed on them. An opposing argument is made by Nathaniel Qarterman, who asserts that punishment for murder does not depend on the rational understanding, but rather on the convict's moral culpability at the time the crime was committed.

The APA Task Force (TFMHA) reviewed the empirical literature and concluded that for women who have an unplanned pregnancy, the risk of mental health problems is no greater than the risk for women who deliver an unplanned pregnancy. Professor Priscilla K. Coleman contends that the TFMHA analysis of the evidence reflects politically motivated bias in the selection of studies, analysis of the literature, and the conclusions derived.

Correlation Guide

The *Taking Sides* series presents current issues in a debate-style format designed to stimulate student interest and develop critical thinking skills. Each issue is thoughtfully framed with an issue summary, an issue introduction, and challenge questions. The pro and con essays—selected for their liveliness and substance—represent the arguments of leading scholars and commentators in their fields.

Taking Sides: Clashing Views in Abnormal Psychology, 6/e is an easy-to-use reader that presents issues on important topics such as *psychological conditions and treatments, biological approaches, and social issues.* For more information on *Taking Sides* and other *McGraw-Hill Contemporary Learning Series* titles, visit www.mhhe.com/cls.

This convenient guide matches the issues in **Taking Sides: Clashing Views in Abnormal Psychology,** 6/e with the corresponding chapters in two of our best-selling McGraw-Hill Abnormal Psychology textbooks by Richard P. Halgin/Susan Krauss Whitbourne and Susan Nolen-Hoeksema.

Taking Sides: *Clashing Views in Abnormal Psychology,* 6/e	*Abnormal Psychology, 6/e by* Richard Halgin/Susan Krauss Whitbourne	*Abnormal Psychology Media and Research Update, 5/e by* Susan Nolen-Hoeksema
Issue 1: Is the Use of Aversive Treatment an Inhumane Intervention for Psychologically Disordered Individuals?	**Chapter 11:** Development-Related Disorders **Chapter 15:** Ethical & Legal Issues	**Chapter 2:** Theories and Treatment of Abnormality **Chapter 15:** Health Psychology **Chapter 16:** Mental Health and the Law
Issue 2: Is Gender Identity Disorder a Mental Illness?	**Chapter 2:** Classification & Treatment Plans **Chapter 7:** Sexual Disorders	**Chapter 13:** Sexual Disorders
Issue 3: Is Forced Treatment of Seriously Mentally Ill Individuals Justifiable?	**Chapter 9:** Schizophrenia & Related Disorders **Chapter 15:** Ethical & Legal Issues	**Chapter 2:** Theories and Treatment of Abnormality **Chapter 4:** The Research Endeavor **Chapter 15:** Health Psychology **Chapter 16:** Mental Health and the Law
Issue 4: Should Individuals with Anorexia Nervosa Have the Right to Refuse Life-Sustaining Treatment?	**Chapter 14:** Eating Disorders & Impulse-Control Disorders **Chapter 15:** Ethical & Legal Issues	**Chapter 12:** Eating Disorders
Issue 5: Is Psychological Debriefing a Harmful Intervention for Survivors of Trauma?	**Chapter 5:** Anxiety Disorders	**Chapter 2:** Theories and Treatment of Abnormality **Chapter 5:** Anxiety Disorders
Issue 6: Are Blocked and Recovered Memories Valid Phenomena?	**Chapter 4:** Theoretical Perspectives **Chapter 6:** Anxiety Disorders	**Chapter 2:** Theories and Treatment of Abnormality **Chapter 5:** Anxiety Disorders

(*continued*)

Taking Sides: *Clashing Views in Abnormal Psychology*, 6/e	*Abnormal Psychology*, 6/e by Richard Halgin/Susan Krauss Whitbourne	*Abnormal Psychology Media and Research Update*, 5/e by Susan Nolen-Hoeksema
Issue 7: Is Attention-Deficit/ Hyperactivity Disorder (ADHD) a Real Disorder?	**Chapter 11:** Development-Related Disorders	**Chapter 10:** Childhood Disorders
Issue 8: Should MDMA (Ecstasy) Be Prohibited, Even for Therapeutic Use?	**Chapter 4:** Theoretical Perspectives **Chapter 13:** Substance-Related Disorders	**Chapter 2:** Theories and Treatment of Abnormality **Chapter 14:** Substance-Related Disorders
Issue 9: Is Addiction a Brain Disease?	**Chapter 13:** Substance-Related Disorders	**Chapter 14:** Substance-Related Disorders
Issue 10: Should Memory-Dampening Drugs Be Used to Alleviate the Symptoms of Trauma?	**Chapter 5:** Anxiety Disorders	**Chapter 5:** Anxiety Disorders
Issue 11: Is Ritalin Overprescribed?	**Chapter 11:** Development-Related Disorders	**Chapter 10:** Childhood Disorders
Issue 12: Should Psychologists Prescribe Medications?	**Chapter 2:** Classification & Treatment Plans	**Chapter 2:** Theories and Treatment of Abnormality **Chapter 15:** Health Psychology
Issue 13: Is It Unethical for Psychologists to Be Involved in Coercive Interrogations?	**Chapter 15:** Ethical & Legal Issues	**Chapter 16:** Mental Health and the Law
Issue 14: Is it Ethical to Support the Wish for Healthy Limb Amputation in People with Body Integrity Identity Disorder (BIID)?	**Chapter 6:** Somatoform Disorders, Psychological Factors Affecting Medical Conditions, & Dissociative Disorders **Chapter 15:** Ethical & Legal Issues	**Chapter 6:** Somatoform and Dissociative Disorders **Chapter 16:** Mental Health and the Law
Issue 15: Does Exposure to Media Violence Promote Aggressive Behavior?	**Chapter 10:** Personality Disorders **Chapter 11:** Development-Related Disorders	**Chapter 9:** Personality Disorders **Chapter 10:** Childhood Disorders
Issue 16: Would Legalization of Virtual Child Pornography Reduce Sexual Exploitation of Children?	**Chapter 7:** Sexual Disorders	**Chapter 13:** Sexual Disorders
Issue 17: Must Mentally Ill Murderers Have a Rational Understanding of Why They Are Being Sentenced to Death?	**Chapter 9:** Schizophrenia & Related Disorders **Chapter 15:** Ethical & Legal Issues	**Chapter 8:** Schizophrenia **Chapter 16:** Mental Health and the Law
Issue 18: Does Research Confirm That Abortion is a Psychologically Benign Experience?	**Chapter 5:** Anxiety Disorders **Chapter 8:** Mood Disorders	**Chapter 5:** Anxiety Disorders **Chapter 7:** Mood Disorders and Suicide

Introduction

What's "Abnormal" about Abnormal Psychology?

Richard P. Halgin

The field of abnormal psychology lends itself well to a discussion of controversial issues because of the inherent difficulty involved in defining the concept of "abnormal." The definition of abnormality is contingent on a myriad of influences that include cultural, historical, geographical, societal, interpersonal, and intrapersonal factors. What is considered everyday behavior in one culture might be regarded as bizarre in another. What was acceptable at one point in time might seem absurd in contemporary society. What seems customary in one region, even in one section of a large city, might be viewed as outrageous elsewhere. Even on a very personal level, one person's typical style of emotional expression might be experienced by another person as odd and disruptive. This introductory essay looks at some of the complex issues involved in defining and understanding abnormality and, in doing so, will set the stage for the controversial issues that follow. With this theoretical foundation, you will be better equipped to tackle the thorny issues in this volume and to develop an approach for reaching your own conclusions about these controversies.

Defining Abnormality

One of the best ways to begin a discussion of the complexity of defining abnormality is by considering our own behavior. Think about an outlandish costume that you wore to a Halloween party and the fun you had engaging in this completely normal behavior. Now imagine wearing the same costume to class the following day, and think about the reactions you would have received. What seemed so normal on the evening of October 31 would have been considered bizarre on the morning of November 1. Only a day later, in a different context, you would have been regarded as abnormal, and your behavior would have been viewed as both disturbed and disturbing. Consider another example: Recall a time in which you were intensely emotional, perhaps weeping profusely at a funeral. If you were to display similar emotionality a few days later in a class discussion, your behavior would cause considerable stir, and your classmates would be taken aback by the intensity of your emotions. Now consider a common behavior that is completely acceptable and expected in American culture, such as shaking a person's hand upon meeting. Did you know that in some cultures such behavior is regarded as rude and unacceptable? These simple examples highlight the ways in which the concept of "normal" is contingent on many factors. Because of the wide variability in definitions of what is abnormal, psychologists have spelled out criteria that can be used in determining abnormal human behavior. These criteria fall into four categories: distress, impairment, risk to self or other people, and socially and culturally unacceptable behavior.

Distress

I begin with the most personal criterion of abnormality because the experience of inner emotional distress is a universal phenomenon and a powerful way in which every person at some point in life feels different from everyone around them. Distress, the experience of emotional pain, is experienced in many ways, such as depression, anxiety, and cognitive confusion. When people feel any of these responses to an extreme degree, they feel abnormal, and they typically look for ways to alleviate their feelings of inner pain. Some of the issues in this book illustrate the various ways in which different people respond to similar life events. For example, following the devastating events of September 11, the Asian tsunami, and Hurricane Katrina, many mental health professionals were called upon to intervene with the survivors of these life-threatening traumas. Although providing a therapeutic response in the form of psychological debriefing might seem beneficial, some critics argue that such efforts might make a difficult emotional situation even worse (Issue 5). In recent years efforts have been made to find medications that alleviate the memories associated with the experience of a trauma; Issue 10 addresses the possible benefits as well as the disadvantages of dampening memories of a traumatic experience.

Impairment

People who are intensely distressed are likely to find it difficult to fulfill the everyday responsibilities of life. When people are very depressed or anxious, they typically have a difficult time concentrating on their studies, attending to their work responsibilities, or even interacting with other people. Impairment involves a reduction in a person's ability to function at an optimal or even an average level. Although distress and impairment often go hand in hand, they do not always; a person can be seriously impaired but feel no particular distress. This is often the case with substance abuse, in which people are incapable of the basic tasks of physical coordination and cognitive clarity but feel euphoric. Some of the debates in this book address the issue of impairment and the difficulty in assessing the extent to which people are impaired. For example, Issue 9 focuses on the question of whether addiction is a brain disease. This issue has relevance to issues about the extent to which drug-addicted individuals are capable, physiologically and psychologically, of controlling their self-destructive addictive behaviors.

Risk to Self or Others

Sometimes people act in ways that cause risk to themselves or others. In this context, risk refers to danger or threat to the well-being of a person. In the case of suicide or self-mutilating behavior, the personal risk is evident. In the case of outwardly directed violence, rape, or even emotional exploitation, the risk is to other people. Although the issue of risk to self or others might not seem controversial on the surface, there are many facets of risk that provoke debate. For example, does an individual have the right to engage in self-injurious, perhaps even life-ending, behavior, or does society have a right, even a responsibility, to intervene? As addressed in Issues 3 and 4, do individuals who are at risk of harming other people (i.e., by means of violence) or themselves (i.e., self-starvation) have the right to refuse intervention, or do health professionals have a responsibility to prevent such individuals from engaging in such potentially dangerous behavior? To what extremes should clinicians go in order to behaviorally control the self-injurious, and potentially fatal, behaviors of severely disturbed children and adults? Issue 1 addresses the question of whether harsh aversive treatments are forms of torture or lifesaving interventions. Other potentially harmful behaviors are also discussed, such as pornography involving images of children (Issue 16). Although no reasonable person would defend real child pornography, some argue that virtual images generated by computers are not only legally permissible, but could reduce the victimization of real children by the pornography industry. Critics of that stance argue that pornography involving children, whether virtual or not, increases the likelihood of real-life victimization.

Socially and Culturally Unacceptable Behavior

Another criterion for defining abnormality pertains to the social or cultural context in which behavior occurs. In some instances, behavior that is regarded as odd within a given culture, society, or subgroup is common elsewhere. For example, some people from Mediterranean cultures believe in a phenomenon called *mal de ojo*, or "evil eye," in which the ill will of one person can negatively affect another. According to this belief, receiving the evil eye from a person can cause a range of disturbing physical and emotional symptoms; consequently, individuals in these cultures often take steps to ward off the power of another person's evil eye. Such beliefs might be regarded as strangely superstitious, almost delusional, in American culture, but they are considered common elsewhere. Even more subtle contexts can influence the extent to which a behavior is defined as abnormal, as illustrated by the example of the Halloween costume mentioned previously. This book features issues related to social and cultural variables, such as whether media violence promotes violent behavior in young people (Issue 15). Some people in society view gender-variant behavior as abnormal. At one extreme are those who consider gender identity disorder a mental illness, and at the other end are those who consider such a perspective to represent a stigmatization of mental illness on people who meet no scientific definition of mental disorder.

What Causes Abnormality?

In trying to understand why people act and feel in ways that are regarded as abnormal, social scientists consider three dimensions: biological, psychological, and sociocultural. Rather than viewing these dimensions as independent, however, experts discuss the relative contribution of each dimension in influencing human behavior, and they use the term *biopsychosocial* to capture these intertwining forces. In the context of abnormality, the biopsychosocial conceptualization of human behavior conveys the sense that abnormal behavior arises from a complex set of determinants in the body, the mind, and the social context.

Biological Causes

During the past several decades scientists have made tremendous progress in discovering ways in which human behavior is influenced by a range of biological variables. In the realm of abnormal psychology, the contributions of the biological sciences have been especially impressive, as researchers have developed increasing understanding of the ways in which abnormal behavior is determined by bodily physiology and genetic makeup. As is the case with many medical disorders, various mental disorders, such as depression, run in families. Mental health researchers have made great efforts to understand why certain mental illnesses are passed from one generation to another and also to understand why certain disorders are not inherited even in identical twin pairs when one of the twins has the condition and the other does not.

In addition to understanding the role of genetics, mental health experts also consider the ways in which physical functioning can cause or aggravate the experience of psychological symptoms. Experts know that many medical conditions can cause a person to feel or act in ways that are abnormal. For example, a medical abnormality in the thyroid gland can cause wide variations in mood and emotionality. Brain damage resulting from a head trauma, even a slight one, can result in bizarre behavior and intense emotionality. Similarly, the use of drugs or alcohol can cause people to act in extreme ways that neither they nor those who know them well would have ever imagined (Issue 9). Even exposure to environmental stimuli, such as toxic substances or allergens, can cause people to experience disturbing emotional changes and to act in odd or bizarre ways. Several issues in this book explore conditions in which biology plays a prominent causative role. For example, attention deficit/hyperactivity disorder (ADHD) is regarded as a disorder of the brain that interferes with a person's ability to pay attention or to control behavior (see Issue 7).

Psychological Causes

Biology does not tell the entire story about the causes of mental disorders; many forms of emotional disturbance arise as a result of troubling life experiences. The experiences of life, even seemingly insignificant ones, can leave lasting marks on a person. In cases in which an experience involves trauma, such as rape or abuse, the impact can be emotionally disruptive throughout life, affecting a person's thoughts, behaviors, and even dreams.

In trying to understand the psychological causes of abnormality, social scientists and mental health clinicians consider a person's experiences. Not only do they focus on interpersonal interactions with other people that may have left a mark, but they also consider the inner life of the individual—thoughts and feelings that may cause distress or impairment. Some conditions arise from distorted perceptions and faulty ways of thinking. For example, highly sensitive people may misconstrue innocent comments by acquaintances that cause obsessional worry about being disliked or demeaned. As a result, these people may respond to their acquaintances in hostile ways that perpetuate interpersonal difficulties and inner distress.

For several of the issues in this book, psychological forces play a significant causative role. For example, Issue 6 considers the disturbances of people who have suffered traumatic life experiences and the controversies surrounding the possibility that trauma might be repressed or might cause the development of multiple personalities.

Sociocultural Causes

The term *sociocultural* refers to the various circles of social influence in the lives of people. The most immediate circle is composed of people with whom we interact in our immediate environment; for college students, this includes roommates, classmates, and coworkers. Moving beyond the immediate circle are people who inhabit the extended circle of relationships, such as family members back home or friends from high school. A third circle is composed of the people in our environments with whom we interact minimally and rarely by name, such as residents of our community or campus, whose standards, expectations, and behaviors influence our lives. A fourth circle is the much wider culture in which people live, such as American society.

Abnormal behavior can emerge from experiences in any of these social contexts. Troubled relationships with a roommate or family member can cause intense emotional distress. Involvement in an abusive relationship may initiate an interpersonal style in which the abused person becomes repeatedly caught up with people who are hurtful or damaging. Political turmoil, even on a relatively local level, can evoke emotions ranging from intense anxiety to incapacitating fear.

This book discusses several conditions in which sociocultural factors are significant. For example, Issue 15 discusses the ways in which exposure to media violence may promote aggressive behavior, and Issue 16 addresses the ways in which pornography, even in virtual form, may contribute to the victimization of children.

The Biopsychosocial Perspective

From the discussion so far, it should be evident that most aspects of human behavior are determined by a complex of causes involving an interaction of biological, psychological, and sociocultural factors. As you read about the clinical conditions and mental disorders discussed in this book, it will be useful for you to keep the biopsychosocial perspective in mind, even in those discussions in which the authors seem narrowly focused. For example, a condition may be put forth as being biologically caused, leading the reader to believe that other influences play little or no role. Another condition may be presented as being so psychologically based that it is difficult to fathom the role that biology might play in causing or aggravating the condition. Other issues may be discussed almost exclusively in sociocultural terms, with minimal attention to the roles of biological and psychological factors. An intelligent discussion in the field of abnormal psychology is one that explores the relative importance of biological, psychological, and sociocultural influences. Such a discussion should avoid reductionistic thinking and simplistic explanations for complex human problems.

Why We View Behavior as "Abnormal"

In addition to understanding how to define abnormality and what causes abnormal behavior, it is important to understand how members of society view people who are abnormal and how this view affects people with emotional problems and mental disorders. Many people in our society discriminate against and reject mentally disturbed people. In so doing, they aggravate one of the most profound aspects of dealing with mental disorder—the experience of stigma. A stigma is a label that causes certain people to be regarded as different and defective and to be set apart from mainstream members of society. Today, several decades after sociologist Erving Goffman brought the phenomenon of stigma to public attention, there is ample evidence in American society that people with mental disorders are regarded as different and are often deprived of the basic human right to respectful treatment.

It is common for people with serious psychological disorders, especially those who have been hospitalized, to experience profound and long-lasting emotional and social effects. People who suffer from serious psychological problems tend to think less of themselves because of these experiences, and they often come to believe many of the myths about themselves that are perpetuated in a society that lacks understanding about the nature of mental illness and psychological problems.

Although tremendous efforts have been undertaken to humanize the experiences of people with psychological problems and mental disorders, deeply rooted societal reactions still present obstacles for many emotionally distressed people. Controversies continue to rage about the systems of diagnosis and assessment used by mental health professionals, about the validity of certain clinical conditions, and about the efficacy of various psychotherapeutic and medical interventions. As you read both sides of the debates in this book, it is important that you keep in mind the strong personal beliefs that influence, and possibly bias, the statements of each writer and to consider the ways in which various societal forces are intertwined with the comments of the author.

The most powerful force within the field of mental health during the twentieth century was the medical model, upon which many forms of intervention are based. This book frequently mentions a system of diagnosis developed by the American Psychiatric Association that has been revised several times during the past 50 years. This system is published in a book called the *Diagnostic and Statistical Manual of Mental Disorders*. The most recent version is the fourth edition, which is commonly abbreviated *DSM-IV-TR*. *DSM-V* is scheduled for publication in 2013. In this medical model diagnostic system, mental disorders are construed as diseases that require treatment. There are both advantages and disadvantages to this approach.

Not only does *DSM-IV-TR* rely on the medical model, but it also uses a categorical approach. A categorical approach assumes that diseases fit into distinct categories. For example, the medical disease pneumonia is a condition that fits into the category of diseases involving the respiratory system. In corresponding fashion, conditions involving mood fit into the category of mood disorders, conditions involving anxiety fit into the category of anxiety disorders, and so on. However, as the authors of *DSM-IV-TR* admit, there are limitations to the categorical approach. For one thing, psychological disorders are not neatly separable from each other or from normal functioning. For example, where is the dividing line between normal sadness and clinical depression? Furthermore, many disorders seem linked to each other in fundamental ways. In a state of agitated depression, for example, an individual suffers from both anxiety and saddened mood.

Several of the conditions and interventions discussed in this book have been debated for years. As you read about these issues, it will be helpful for you to keep in mind the context in which these debates have arisen. Some debates arise because of turf battles between professions. For example, psychiatrists may be more inclined to endorse the diagnostic system of the American Psychiatric Association (*DSM-IV-TR*) and to support biological explanations and somatic interventions for mental disorders. Psychologists, on the other hand, may urge mental health professionals to take a broader point of view and to proceed more cautiously in turning to biological explanations and causes.

The Influence of Theoretical Perspective on the Choice of Intervention

Although impressive advances have been achieved in determining why people develop various mental disorders, understanding how best to treat their conditions remains limited and also powerfully influenced by the ideological biases of many clinicians and researchers. For much of the twentieth century, various interventions emerged from markedly different schools of thought, each approach being tied to one of the three major realms—biological, psychological, or sociocultural. But how are biological, psychological, and sociocultural frameworks used in determining choice of intervention?

Within the biological perspective, disturbances in emotions, behavior, and cognitive processes are viewed as being caused by abnormalities in the functioning of the body, such as the brain and nervous system or the endocrine system. Treatments involve a range of somatic therapies, the most common of which is medication, the most extreme of which involves psychosurgery. Several issues in this book focus on debates about reliance on biological explanations and interventions, such as the issue on ADHD (Issue 7), and the issues on medications (Issues 9, 10, 11, and 12).

The realm of psychological theories contains numerous approaches, although three schools of thought emerged as most prominent during the second half of the twentieth century: psychodynamic, humanistic, and behavioral. Proponents of the psychodynamic perspective emphasize unconscious determinants of behavior and recommend the use of techniques involving exploration of the developmental causes of behavior and the interpretation of unconscious influences on thoughts, feelings, and behavior. This is pertinent to the debate over repressed memories (Issue 6), which involves clinicians who believe that people are inclined to "forget" traumatic experiences in order to defend themselves from the disruptive anxiety they would otherwise experience.

At the core of the humanistic perspective is the belief that human motivation is based on an inherent tendency to strive for self-fulfillment and meaning in life. Humanistic therapists use a client-centered approach in which they strive to treat clients with unconditional positive regard and empathy. Mental health professionals are called upon to act in ways that are more client-centered as they deal with issues pertaining to gender identity (Issue 2), trauma (Issue 5), or abortion (Issue 18).

According to the behavioral perspective, abnormality is caused by faulty learning experiences, with a subset of behavioral theory focusing on cognitive functions such as maladaptive thought processes. Because behaviorists and cognitive theorists believe that disturbance results from faulty learning or distorted thinking, intervention focuses on teaching clients more adaptive ways of thinking and behaving. Some of the discussions in this book focus on the ways in which behavioral and cognitive approaches might be preferable to medical approaches to conditions such as ADHD (Issue 7), and the use of aversive techniques for treating self-injurious individuals.

Clinicians working within sociocultural models emphasize the ways that individuals are influenced by people, social institutions, and social forces. According to this viewpoint, psychological problems can emerge from social contexts ranging from the family to society. In a corresponding vein, treatments are determined by the nature of the group. Thus, problems rooted within family systems would be treated with family therapy; societal problems caused by discrimination or inadequate care of the mentally ill would be dealt with through enactment of social policy initiatives. Several issues in this volume touch upon sociocultural influences, such as the effects of pornography (Issue 16), and how best to respond to survivors of life-threatening trauma (Issues 5 and 10).

Keeping the Issues in Perspective

In evaluating the content of the writings in this book, it is important to keep in mind who the writers are and what their agendas might be. Most of the contributors are distinguished figures in the fields of mental health, ethics, and law. They are regarded as clear and influential thinkers who have important messages to convey. However, it would be naive to think that any writer, particularly when addressing a controversial topic, is free of bias.

It is best to read each issue with an understanding of the forces that might influence the development of a particular bias. For example, as physicians, psychiatrists have been trained in the medical model, with its focus on biological causes for problems and somatic interventions. Nonphysician mental health professionals may be more inclined to focus on interpersonal and intrapersonal causes and interventions. Lawyers and ethicists are more likely to be further removed from questions of etiology, focusing instead on what they believe is justified according to the law or right according to ethical standards.

As you read about the issues facing mental health clinicians and researchers, you are certain to be struck by the challenges that these professionals face. You may also be struck by the powerful emotion expressed by the authors who discuss their views on topics in this field. Because psychological stresses and problems are an inherent part of human existence, many discussions about abnormal psychology are emotionally charged. At some point in life, most people have a brush with serious emotional problems, either directly or indirectly. This is a frightening prospect for many people, one that engenders worried expectations and intense reactions. By acknowledging our vulnerability to disruptive emotional experiences, however, we can think about the ways in which we would want clinicians to treat us. As you read the issues in this book, place yourself in the position of an individual in the process of being assessed, diagnosed, and treated for an emotional difficulty or mental disorder.

Before you take a side in each debate, consider how the issue might be personally relevant to you at some point in life. You may be surprised to discover that you respond in different ways to issues that might have special salience to yourself, as opposed to random people somewhere else. By imagining yourself being personally affected by a professional's controversial opinion regarding one or more of the debates in this book, you will find yourself immersed in the discussions about issues for which there is no clear right or wrong.

Internet References . . .

Coalition Against Institutionalized Child Abuse (CAICA)

CAICA is an informational and educational Web site that provides news articles and reports regarding children and teens abused, neglected, and who have died in residential treatment settings.

http://www.caica.org/

The World Professional Association for Transgender Health, Inc.

This Web site offers information on understanding and treating gender identity disorders, along with the organization's compiled standards of care for the medical, psychological, and surgical management of gender identity disorders.

http://www.wpath.org/

Treatment Advocacy Center

A national nonprofit organization dedicated to eliminating barriers to the timely and effective treatment of severe mental illnesses.

http://psychlaws.blogspot.com/

National Eating Disorders Association (NEDA)

NEDA is committed to providing education, resources, and support to people affected by eating disorders.

http://www.nationaleatingdisorders.org/

The Recovered Memory Project

This project collects and disseminates information relevant to the debate over whether traumatic events can be forgotten and then remembered later in life.

http://www.brown.edu/Departments/Taubman_Center/Recovmem/

Centers for Disease Control and Prevention (CDC)—ADHD Web page

The CDC maintains a Web page containing a wealth of information about diagnosis, treatment, and research pertaining to ADHD.

http://www.cdc.gov/ncbddd/adhd/

National Institute on Drug Abuse (NIDA)—MDMA (Ecstasy) Web page

NIDA maintains a Web page containing information about the effects of MDMA on the brain, and research that is being conducted on this drug.

http://www.nida.nih.gov/Infofacts/ecstasy.html

National Center for PTSD

This Web site is sponsored by the U.S. Department of Veterans Affairs for the purpose of advancing science and promoting understanding of traumatic stress.

http://www.ptsd.va.gov/

Psychological Conditions and Treatments

At the heart of abnormal psychology are the psychological conditions and mental disorders for which people need professional treatment. Although most people voluntarily seek professional help for their problems, and willingly participate in the intervention, this is not always the case. For example, some individuals are so severely disturbed that they are incapable of making the decision to participate in treatment, and some behaviors are so dangerous to self or others that extreme forms of intervention are implemented. Questions about human rights emerge in debates about how far society and clinicians can and should go in terms of the approaches they use. Some interventions are controversial because they involve procedures that are regarded by some critics as making a bad situation worse. For example, the process of debriefing following the experience of trauma is helpful for some trauma survivors, but risky for others. The recovery of memories that have long been inaccessible is a process that is controversial in terms of its validity, and of debatable value if and when such recovery takes place in psychotherapy. Some behaviors and conditions engender controversy because questions are put forth about whether some behavioral patterns, such as those considered gender variants, have any place in a list of psychiatric diagnoses. Even commonly diagnosed conditions such as ADHD rouse debate because some view that these conditions are diagnoses being promoted by pharmaceutical companies for the sake of selling more medications.

- Is the Use of Aversive Treatment an Inhumane Intervention for Psychologically Disordered Individuals?

- Is Gender Identity Disorder a Mental Illness?

- Is Forced Treatment of Seriously Mentally Ill Individuals Justifiable?

- Should Individuals with Anorexia Nervosa Have the Right to Refuse Life-Sustaining Treatment?

- Is Psychological Debriefing a Harmful Intervention for Survivors of Trauma?

- Are Blocked and Recovered Memories Valid Phenomena?

- Is Attention-Deficit/Hyperactivity Disorder (ADHD) a Real Disorder?

- Should MDMA (Ecstasy) Be Prohibited, Even for Therapeutic Use?

ISSUE 1

Is the Use of Aversive Treatment an Inhumane Intervention for Psychologically Disordered Individuals?

YES: Laurie Ahern and Eric Rosenthal, from *Torture Not Treatment: Electric Shock and Long-Term Restraint in the United States on Children and Adults with Disabilities at the Judge Rotenberg Center.* (Mental Disability Rights International, 2010)

NO: Matthew L. Israel, from *Aversives at JRC: A Better Alternative to the use of Drugs, Restraint, Isolation, Warehousing, or Expulsion in the Treatment of Severe Behavior Disorders.* (Judge Rotenberg Center, 2010)

ISSUE SUMMARY

YES: Laurie Ahern and Eric Rosenthal, writing on behalf of Mental Disability Rights International (MDRI), characterize the intentional infliction of pain at JRC as human rights abuses.

NO: Psychologist Matthew Israel, director of the Judge Rotenberg Center (JRC), responds to the MDRI with insistence that JRC is using behavioral methods to save individuals from their treatment-resistant, life-threatening disorders.

One of the most heartbreaking experiences for parents of emotionally disordered children is to see these youngsters engage in self-injurious behaviors such as head banging, self-punching, and even manually pulling out teeth. Many of these children are also aggressive, sometimes to the point of life-threatening violence. In these extreme cases, parents desperately seek out solutions so that the well-being of these children can be protected. Traditional therapeutic interventions are customarily the first line of treatment, as parents turn to mental health professionals for therapy for themselves and their children. When talking approaches prove to be of limited value, medications are likely to be recommended. For some children, however, even the most potent of antipsychotic medications may be ineffective in reducing self-destructive behaviors. Feeling exhausted and discouraged, guardians seek out the options of last resort, which sometimes involve behavioral interventions using physical restraints and aversive conditioning. A leader in the application of such procedures is the Judge Rotenberg Center (JRC) in Canton, MA which has been at the center of controversy for the four decades that it has been in operation.

On behalf of Mental Disability Rights International (MDRI), human rights activists Laurie Ahern and Eric Rosenthal prepared a scathing critique of the behavioral techniques used at JRC, which they label "torture" rather than treatment. This report has been submitted to the United Nations (UN) along with a request that the UN initiate an inquiry into what are described as "abusive practices perpetrated against residents of JRC."

Dr. Matthew Israel, founding director of JRC, expresses strong objection to the MDRI claims, citing the fact that JRC has used safe intensive behavioral therapy to treat severe forms of behavioral disorders and has freed hundreds of individuals from disturbing alternatives such as excessive sedation, restraint, seclusion, and institutional warehousing. The claim is made that JRC's 24-hour behavioral system works effectively for individuals for whom every other treatment has failed.

POINT

- No population is more vulnerable to abuse than children with disabilities detained in an institution. For this population, the use of electric shock, long-term restraint, and other aversives by JRC constitutes human rights violations that are even more serious than corporal punishment in a school.

- The Graduated Electronic Decelerator (GED) is used to administer shock for behaviors that are not problematic (i.e., getting out of seat, nagging).

- Aversive interventions such as the GED device are used in children with all kinds of disabilities, many without self-injurious behaviors.

- Behavioral programming at JRC is not sufficiently monitored by appropriate professionals, and in many cases the level of background and preparation of staff are not sufficient for overseeing the intensive treatment of children.

- While the infliction of pain may stop a person from engaging in a specific behavior, aversive treatment cannot treat an underlying emotional disorder or intellectual disability.

COUNTERPOINT

- Under state and federal law, nondisabled individuals have the right to choose aversive therapy to treat behavioral problems such as smoking and drinking. If disabled persons are prevented from being able to avail themselves of aversive therapy for their behavioral problems, this would be an invidious discrimination against disabled persons.

- In treating severe behavioral problems, alternatives to aversives are less effective and can have adverse effects.

- The GED is a supplement to positive-only treatment. It is used infrequently has no significant adverse side effects, and can be discontinued with improvement.

- JRC has been licensed or approved continuously for decades by the state education, developmental disabilities, and child care departments.

- Some students with developmental disabilities, psychiatric problems, and conduct disorders show frighteningly dangerous self-abusive and aggressive behaviors such as gouging out their eyes causing blindness, head banging to the point of causing a stroke, skin scratching, and pulling out all of their teeth.

YES

Laurie Ahern and
Eric Rosenthal

Torture Not Treatment: Electric Shock and Long-Term Restraint in the United States on Children and Adults with Disabilities at the Judge Rotenberg Center

Introduction

The Judge Rotenberg Center (JRC) was founded by psychologist Matthew Israel almost 40 years ago in California when it was known then as the Behavior Research Institute (BRI). According to Israel, the school's philosophy is based on the work of renowned behaviorist B.F. Skinner.[2] In the 1950s, Israel was a student of Skinner's at Harvard University, and today he is a self-proclaimed devotee of radical behaviorism.

In 1981, a 14 year old boy died face down, tied to his bed. JRC (then known as BRI) was not held responsible for the boy's death, but the death resulted in an investigation by California's Department of Social Services. California issued a critical report the following year, citing widespread abuse of children at the facility and the state of California greatly limited the use of punishment as treatment.[3] The facility was then moved to Rhode Island and then again to Canton, Massachusetts, where it is located today.

Today, JRC boasts a main campus with a school and offsite residential apartments with 24 hour staffing. The facility serves as a residential school for children with disabilities, as well as a residential facility for adults. There are approximately 200 children and adults at JRC at any given time,[4] with costs paid for by state and local school districts and state agencies serving adults with disabilities at approximately $220,000 per year, per person. People with disabilities living at the JRC residential center mostly come from New York and Massachusetts, and seven other states.

The Judge Rotenberg Center program

The program of "behavior modification" and "aversive treatment" and the rationale for its use is spelled out on JRC's website. The theory of behavior modification is that every human being responds to positive rewards or negative

From *Mental Disability Rights International* by Laurie Ahern and Eric Rosenthal (Mental Disability Rights International (MDRI), 2010). Copyright © 2010 by Mental Disability Rights International (MDRI). Reprinted by permission.

punishments and that all behavior can be manipulated through a combination of rewards and punishments. Using this approach, "rewards" and "punishments" constitute treatment.[5] Treatment entails the infliction of pain. JRC is clear that this approach "differs markedly" from "traditional approaches" to mental health care.[6] The website boasts that "JRC is probably the most consistently behavioral treatment program in existence."

JRC maintains that the same form of reward and punishment works for anyone, justifying a "near-zero rejection policy" for admission.[7] As a result:

> . . . we really pay relatively little attention to psychiatric diagnosis which are essentially labels for groups of behaviors. . . . Of the first two students we worked with, one was labeled autistic and one was labeled schizophrenic.[8]

The implication of this approach is a highly unorthodox program for treatment and education. All residents, regardless of diagnosis or history, are subjected to the same behavior modification techniques of reward and punishment. The use of traditional psychological therapies and/or medication is virtually non-existent at JRC.[9] Psychotropic medications are rarely used.[10] According to JRC, seventy percent of educational instruction in the school consists of solitary work on a computer referred to by JRC as "self-paced programmed instruction."[11] . . .

Early on, punishments—known as aversives—were used to control the behavior of people who were called severely "mentally retarded" and children with autism. Punishments included pinching, spatula spankings, water sprays, muscle squeezes, forced inhalation of ammonia and helmets which battered the brain with inescapable white noise.[24]

In the late 1980s, JRC began using SIBIS (Self-Injurious Behavior Inhibiting System) machines on students, as an alternative to spanking, squeezing and pinching. The machine, developed in 1985, produced a 0.2 second shock of 2.02 milliamps on the arms or legs of the recipient, with the intention of stopping self-injurious behaviors in children with autism and other developmental disabilities. Controversial from the outset and shunned by advocates, the use of SIBIS was largely abandoned in the 1990s in favor of "positive-based" practices.[25]

Over the years, JRC has found that an individual who responds to low levels of electricity may become "adapted" to pain and "needs a stronger stimulation."[26] The 12 year old nephew of Massachusetts State Representative Jeffrey Sanchez was diagnosed with autism and was a student at JRC in 1989 when JRC began using the SIBIS machine. As described in testimony before the Massachusetts legislature,[27] one day he received more than 5,000 shocks to stop his behaviors—to no avail. When the manufacturer of SIBIS refused JRC's request to provide them with a stronger and more painful shock machine, JRC developed its own mechanism for administering shock, the Graduated Electronic Decelerator (GED). The GED is a remotely controlled device that can be strapped to an individual's back or another part of the body with electrodes attached to the torso, arms, legs, hands and feet. The

GED administers 15.5 milliamps of electricity. A stronger version, the GED-4, subjects an individual to a shock of 45.5 milliamps. Both may be used up to 2.0 seconds. The director of JRC, Matthew Israel, describes the shock as "very painful."[28] Sanchez's nephew is now 31 years old and remains at JRC. According to testimony before the Massachusetts Legislature in November 2009, he is still tethered to the GED shock machine.[29]

JRC also uses physical restraints as a form of aversive treatment, sometimes simultaneously with electric shock.[30] The GED and restraints are sometimes combined because it is necessary to stop a person from ripping the GED pack off his or her body. Other times, physical restraints may be added to the use of the GED when the aversive power of electricity alone is not sufficient. As described on the JRC website, "[T]he safest way to do this is to use mechanical restraint to contain the student, in a prone position, on a flexible plastic restraint platform that has been specially designed for the purpose."[31] It is worth noting that, outside JRC, the use of any "prone" (face down) restraints are widely considered to be inherently dangerous, and many states have banned any form of prone restraints in the mental health context.[32] . . .

Critique of Aversive Treatment from Research and Policy

What's wrong with punishments is that they work immediately, but give no long-term results. The responses to punishment are either the urge to escape, to counterattack or a stubborn apathy.

—B.F. Skinner interview, *The New York Times*, 1987[36]

. . . The NY Psychological Association Task Force, which reviewed NYSED's report, raised particular concerns about the use of aversives at JRC without careful attention to the patients' diagnosis. They point out that for certain children—in particular abuse or trauma survivors—aversives can be particularly dangerous.[45] Other researchers have warned that "restraints and seclusion should never be used with children who present with certain psychological or medical characteristics. . . . Contraindications for the use of seclusion and restraints with children include a history of sexual abuse, physical abuse, or neglect and abandonment."[46]

. . . While the infliction of pain may stop a person from engaging in a specific behavior while being subject to a course of aversive treatment, aversive treatment cannot treat an underlying emotional disorder or intellectual disability. A review of the research found that "the implementation of punishment-based procedures, including those that incorporate noxious stimulation, do not guarantee long-term reductive effects in the treatment of severe disorders."[48] The alleviation of symptoms only takes place while aversives are in place, leaving a person subject to this painful treatment over a long period of time. This is why JRC has had to create increasingly strong systems for administering pain and shock. JRC's website candidly acknowledges that aversives only bring about the temporary alleviation of symptoms. . . .

Findings: The Use of Aversives at JRC

Electric Shock

As described above, JRC's stated reason for the use of electric shocks is behavior modification and punishment.[57] Children and adults at JRC are routinely subject to electric shock, receiving multiple skin shocks on their legs, arms, hands, feet, fingers and torsos for behaviors such as getting out of their seats, making noises, swearing or not following staff directions.[58] The homemade shock devices, invented by the school's founder, Matthew Israel, and manufactured at the school, are carried by students in backpacks with electrodes attached to their skin.[59] The shock is administered remotely by minimally trained staff—some with only two weeks of training.[60] Students never know when they will receive a jolt or where on their body they will be shocked. Some children are subjected to dozens of shocks over the course of a day. The April 2009 report by the Massachusetts Department of Mental Retardation (DMR), found that of the 109 children subjected to electric skin shocks, 48 had been receiving the shocks for 5 years or more.[61] . . .

Restraints

> Some problem behaviors can be controlled and prevented by putting the student into continual manual or mechanical restraint. To manually restrain a vigorous young man can take the efforts of many staff members and is inevitably a dangerous exercise. Putting a student in continuing restraints is much more cruel than changing his/her behavior quickly with a powerful positive reward program that is supplemented with occasional two-second skin shocks.
>
> —JRC website, Frequently Asked Questions

JRC refers to physical restraints as "limitation of movement" (LOM), and this is a core part of its aversive treatment program. According to the JRC website, some students receive shocks while strapped prone to a platform board in 4-point mechanical restraints.[75] Restraints are used in combination with the GED to stop a person from ripping off the GED pack while receiving painful electrical impulses.[76] Restraints may also be used to increase the level of pain and discomfort when electric shock alone is not adequate to produce the behavior changes sought by JRC.[77]

A nurse at the facility is responsible for monitoring abrasions due to restraints, according to the NYSED. Depending on the recommendations of the nurse, "a student may be restrained in a prone, seated, or upright position."[78] As described by the NYSED investigators:

> With mechanical movement limitation the student is strapped into/onto some form of physical apparatus. For example, a four-point platform board designed specifically for this purpose; or a helmet with thick padding and facial grid that reduces sensory stimuli to the ears and eyes. Another form of mechanical restraint occurs when the student

is in a five-point restraint in a chair. **Students may be restrained for extensive periods of time (e.g. hours or intermittently for days)** [emphasis added] when restraint is used as a punishing consequence. Many students are required to carry their own "restraint bag" in which the restraint straps are contained.[79]

MDRI's investigation suggests that restraints may last even longer than reported by the NYSED team. A former patient, a mother, a former teacher at JRC, and an attorney who represented clients at JRC all informed MDRI that children are restrained for weeks and months at a time. . . .

MDRI interviews indicate that students are likely to be restrained after they are admitted and before they go before a court to determine whether they can be subject to Level III aversive treatment. These findings are supported by the findings of the New York State and Massachusetts evaluation teams.[90] These findings raise concerns that restraints may used to pressure or coerce individuals into consenting to the GED. . . .

According to the NYSED evaluation team:

> *It is during this initial restrictive placement at JRC that the frequency of behaviors is documented for purposes of obtaining a substituted judgment for the use of Level III aversive procedures. . . . In this setting, interactions with students involved little to no instruction; staff primarily attended to students' negative behaviors and employed the use of physical and mechanical restraints at a high frequency and for extended periods of time.[91]*

The Massachusetts Certification Team found that restraints were used without being included in treatment plans.[92] According to one observer from the Massachusetts team, "the more JRC used these interventions, the more aggressive the students became."[93] . . .

Provocation of Bad Behavior

One component of treatment at JRC is referred to as the behavioral rehearsal lesson (BRL).[95] Students are restrained and GED administered as the student is forcibly challenged to do the behavior the punishment seeks to eliminate. JRC students are sometimes induced to exhibit a behavior for which they will receive a shock punishment. Students endure surprise mock attacks and threatened stabbings by staff, which compel them to react with aggression, fear or screaming—deemed unacceptable or inappropriate behavior—for which they are subject to more shock for their reactions.

Former students report BRLs as particularly terrifying and some staff describe BRLs as "difficult to participate in and dramatic to watch."[96]

> *It was reported by a JRC staff member that one of the BRL episodes involved holding a student's face still while a staff person went for his mouth with a pen or pencil threatening to stab him in the mouth while repeatedly yelling "You want to eat this?"*

—June 2006 report on JRC by New York State Education Department[97]

The worst thing ever was the BRLs. They try and make you do a bad behavior and then they punish you. The first time I had a BRL, two guys came in the room and grabbed me—I had no idea what was going on. They held a knife to my throat and I started to scream and I got shocked. I had BRL's three times a week for stuff I didn't even do. It went on for about six months or more. I was in a constant state of paranoia and fear. I never knew if a door opened if I would get one. It was more stress than I could ever imagine. Horror.

—MDRI interview with former JRC student[98]

Food Deprivation

In addition to the use of electric shock, restraints, mock stabbings and assaults as a means of punishment, JRC uses dangerous food deprivation techniques to further abuse children, adding to the environment of fear, pain, punishment and control. Collectively known as "Loss of Privileges" or "LOPs," the abuses are masked in clinical sounding terminology. The "Contingent Food Program" (CFP) and the "Specialized Food Program" (SFP) include the systematic with-holding of food as a form of punishment.[99] The CFP "is widely applied and designed to motivate students to be compliant."[100] If children or adolescents exhibit any behaviors not tolerated by JRC staff, a portion of food is with-held during the day. **Food not earned during the day is then given to the child in the evening, "which consists of mashed food sprinkled with liver powder."**[101] The SFP is "more restrictive" for those whose behavior does not improve—there is no make-up food given at the end of the day.[102] . . .

Other LOPs include limitations and restrictions with regard to visits to the school's store, television viewing, bedtime, and permission to talk with other students. And some LOPs result in even harsher consequences. One former student reported that she was forced to eat her dinner tied to a chair, alone in her room, for almost a month—LOPs she earned for talking in class without raising her hand.[105]

When we first visited JRC, she had a beautiful room with a TV and stereo. Within one month, she only had a mattress on the floor.

—MDRI interview with mother of a former JRC student[106]

Stopping work for more than 5 seconds and you would lose points and get LOPs. I sat in front of the computer all day, other than lunch. And we couldn't have a social conversation with any staff member.

—MDRI interview with former JRC student[107]

Creating Social Isolation

To further maintain strict control, socialization among students, between students and staff, and among staff, is also extremely limited.[108] For students, socialization with other peers must be earned. Children spend their school days in classrooms facing the walls and staring at a computer screen. Using self-teaching software, conversations and discussions are virtually non-existent and getting up from a chair or attempting to leave the classroom without permission could result in a shock or other form of punishment. . . .

Additionally, staff is not allowed to carry on any personal conversations with the students and all are under 24 hour video surveillance. Employees must also sign a confidentiality agreement at the beginning of their tenure with JRC, effectively barring them from ever talking about what they observe or participate in at the school—including the use of GEDs—or face legal action against them by the school.[111]

> *You are sworn to secrecy. It is like a secret society. We had to sign a paper that if we said anything that would harm their reputation, they would prosecute you. If you talked bad about the school, everything is taped. If we needed to talk, we had to go outside.*

> —MDRI interview with former JRC employee[112]

Aversives for Harmless Behavior

One of the critiques of the GED identified by the NYSED evaluation team is that it is used on behaviors that "the district did not consider problematic for a student that they had placed at JRC (i.e. getting out of seat, nagging)."[113] Indeed, the NYSED evaluators found that:

> *Many of the students observed at JRC were <u>not</u> exhibiting self-abusive/mutilating behaviors, and their IEP's had no indication that these behaviors existed. However, they were still subject to Level III aversive interventions, including the use of the GED device. The review of the NYS students' records revealed that Level III interventions are used for behaviors including 'refuse to follow staff directions'; 'failure to maintain a neat appearance', 'stopping work for more than 10 seconds', interrupting others','nagging', 'whispering and/or moving conversation away from staff', 'slouch in chair'. . . .[114]*

The observations of the NYSED evaluators were mirrored by a former teacher at JRC.[115] According to this teacher, children are routinely given shock for behaviors as normal or innocuous as reacting in fear when witnessing other students getting shocked; attempting to remove electrodes from their skin; tearing a paper cup; blowing bubbles with saliva; standing up out of a seat without permission; going to the bathroom in one's pants; or asking to go to the bathroom more than five times, which is considered an inappropriate verbal behavior.[116]

MDRI interviewed a teacher and a former JRC student who told similar stories:

> *One girl who was blind, deaf and non-verbal was moaning and rocking. Her moaning was like a cry. The staff shocked her for moaning. Turned out she had broken a tooth. Another child had an accident in the bathroom and was shocked.*

> —MDRI interview with former JRC teacher.[117]

I felt terrible for the kids with autism getting shocked. This one 13 year old girl with autism kept getting the GED. They get it for verbal inappropriate behaviors. They made noises, that's how they communicate. They are non-verbal but they would get more shocks. The poor girl would hurt herself a lot.

—MDRI interview with former JRC student
who was also getting shocked[118]. . .

Deaths and Subsequent Legal Challenges

From the outset, Israel's treatment for children with disabilities was controversial and the focus of much media attention. This was especially true when the magnitude and severity of punishments being perpetrated against children came to light or when an unexplained death occurred at the facility, of which there have been six. As previously described, it was a death at the facility in 1980 that resulted in the virtual ban on the use of aversives in California.

In 1990, the Massachusetts DMR conducted an exhaustive investigation on the horrific death of a 19 year old, a young woman diagnosed with severe mental retardation, who also died at the facility. The report states that the staff and administration committed acts against her that were "egregious" and "inhumane beyond all reason" and violated "universal standards of human decency."[196] The young woman, who was unable to speak, became ill and refused to eat, attempted to vomit and made sounds and noises that were not usual for her. For this she was punished repeatedly as the staff translated her actions as misbehaviors. In the hours leading up to her death from a perforated stomach and ulcers, the investigation found that she endured "8 spankings, 27 finger pinches, 14 muscle squeezes" and was forced to smell ammonia and eat "either vinegar mix, or jalapeno peppers or hot sauce."[197]

Prior to her death, she had been subjected to the school's punishment of withholding food for being unable to do school work on the computer or getting wrong answers, despite having the mental capacity of a pre-schooler. At times she was limited to 300 calories per day.

In the end, DMR concluded that there was not enough evidence to link the punishments to her death.

The Massachusetts Office for Children (OFC) ordered the closure of JRC. The school and its parents sued the OFC and appealed the closure. A state administrative law judge ruled that the school could remain open but limited the use of aversives during the litigation.[198]

In 1986, in the midst of the OFC litigation, JRC (then called the Behavior Research Institute) brought one of its most self-abusive students before the Bristol County Probate Court (MA) and Chief Judge Ernest Rotenberg (for whom the school is now named) for a substituted judgment hearing to allow JRC to use aversive treatments on the student. Judge Rotenberg found in JRC's favor and JRC began to bring each student they felt needed aversives before Judge Rotenberg for approval.

Despite the objections of the OFC, Judge Rotenberg was eventually given judicial authority over all pending legal actions between the OFC, JRC and parents of students and a settlement was reached. In the December 1986 agreement, aversives were permitted with a court-ordered treatment plan, and a monitor must report to the court on the clients' treatment.[199]. . .

New York's Attempts to Limit Use of Aversives

New York State sends more of its children to JRC than any other state. As a result of questions and concerns by NY lawmakers regarding the use of punishment at JRC, specifically electric shock and restraint, the NYSED sent a review team to JRC in April and May 2006. The team included NYSED staff and three behavioral psychologists. One visit was announced; the other was unannounced. The NYSED review team reported a litany of abuses involving the most painful of punishments used by JRC. Following the publication of the NYSED report, New York held public hearings. As a result, NYSED adopted restrictive new regulations that would phase out new cases where aversive treatment would be approved.[206] Before New York could implement these new regulations, parents representing children at the school challenged the regulations in federal court, claiming they have a right to subject their children to Level III aversives. They claim that such treatment is necessary for their children to receive an appropriate education as required by IDEA. The federal court has ordered a stay on the implementation of New York's regulations until the substantive issues under IDEA are heard.[207]

A summary of the NYSED review team findings include:

- Level III punishments are given to children with all kinds of disabilities, many without self-injurious behaviors;
- Level III punishments are given for swearing, nagging and failure to maintain a neat appearance;
- The use of electric shock skin devices raises health and safety concerns;
- The withholding of food as punishment could pose risks affecting growth and development;
- Delayed punishment practices are used so that subjects may not be able to comprehend any relationship between a punishment and a behavior;
- The JRC setting discourages social interactions;
- There is insufficient academic and special education instruction;
- JRC compromises the privacy and dignity of students.[208]

Ultimately, the NYSED's review team concluded that the effects of the punishment on children at JRC are increased fear, anxiety or agression.[209]

One of the findings of the NYSED review team was that "behavioral programming at JRC is not sufficiently monitored by appropriate professionals at the school and in many cases the level of background and preparation of staff is not sufficient to oversee the intensive treatment of children with challenging emotional and behavioral disorders.[210]

The reality is that JRC staff may have had even less training than was represented to the NYSED review team. In May 2006, the Massachusetts Division of Professional Licensure found that JRC had improperly claimed that fourteen JRC clinicians were trained as licensed psychologists. In a consent agreement with the Board of Registration of Psychologists, JRC paid $43,000 in fines.[211] Dr. Matthew Israel, the Director of JRC, was personally fined $29,600 and was reprimanded by the Board.[212]

Recent Incidents of Abuse

In August 2007, an investigation of JRC was conducted by the Massachusetts Department of Early Education and Care (EEC)—the licensing agency for JRC residences—following the unauthorized administering of shock to two boys at their JRC residence. According to the report, one boy received 29 electric shocks, and the other received 77 shocks within a three hour time period.[213] The incident occurred when a former JRC student phoned the residence in the middle of the night, pretending to be a staff person, and ordered the residence staff to use shocks on the sleeping adolescents. EEC investigators interviewed the boys and staff and reviewed video footage and found that both boys had been awoken from their sleep when they received the shock; both boys had additional shocks when they were strapped to a 4-point restraint board; both were in transport restraints (legs and waist) while they were in their beds; and one of the boys did not have the required Level III court approval for restraints in his record. Neither boy was evaluated by any medical staff until the following day after the incident, despite asking for a nurse and complaining of pain.

> *Staff reported that it is not atypical for a resident to say that they have injuries following a GED application. It was reported that typically staff would not call a nurse when a resident voices that he is in pain from a GED application and described it as a pinch.*

The EEC report stated that staff observed that the "skin was off" and there were "fresh marks" on the calf of one of the boys, who complained of leg pain. It was later diagnosed as a stage two ulcer. These wounds were located at the same site that the resident had received the shock.

The EEC investigation further concluded that:

- staff was physically abusive toward the residents;
- the staff was unable to provide for the safety and well being of a child;
- staff lacked necessary training and experience;
- staff used poor judgment;
- staff failed to provide a safe environment;
- staff failed to follow policies regarding medical treatment;
- staff were neglectful in the care of residents.

The incidents of unlawful restraint of the boys at the JRC residence would never have been discovered had EEC not been investigating the unauthorized shock "prank.". . .

Conclusions and Recommendations

. . . No population is more vulnerable to abuse than children with disabilities detained in an institution. This population needs the strongest level of international protection to protect them against abuse. For this population, the use of electric shock, long-term restraint, and other aversives used by JRC constitutes human rights violations that are even more serious than corporal punishment in a school, where children eventually go home to friends and family in the community. The UN Special Rapporteur on Torture has stated that corporal punishment constitutes inhuman and degrading treatment. For a population detained in an institution, such as JRC, the vulnerability is much greater—and the experience of pain and suffering is likely more extreme. Thus, severe pain perpetrated against this population should be viewed as fully tantamount to torture. According to Nowak, "[t]he powerlessness of the victim is the essential criterion which the drafters of the Convention had in mind when they introduced the legal distinction between torture and other forms of ill-treatment."[225] . . .

A flat ban on the use of electricity or long-term use of restraints to treat or modify behavior would be the best way to prevent future abuse. Such a ban would be consistent with federal policy and best practice in the field of behavior modification that strongly supports positive behavioral supports instead of painful aversives. Such a ban would be consistent with what CAT has called for to protect people in custody in a law enforcement context. In 2000, as described above, CAT recommended that the United States "abolish electro-shock stun belts and restraint chairs as methods of restraining those in custody since 'their use almost invariably leads to breaches of article 16 of the Convention [defining inhuman and degrading treatment].'"[226]

This year, CAT will be conducting its fifth periodic review and report of the United States of America and its compliance with the UN Convention against Torture. In its last review of the US in 2006, CAT's report made a number of recommendations to the US government with regard to torture, including a concern they voiced over the use of electro-shock devices: *"restricting it to substitution for lethal weapons and eliminate the use of these devices to restrain persons in custody. . . ."*[227] In this year's review by CAT, in their list of issues of concern, they again bring up the use of electro-shock devices and ask the government if they have restricted its use as a substitution for lethal weapons only, as recommended in CAT's previous observations. And they ask point blank, "Are such devices still used to restrain persons in custody?"[228] CAT has also asked for updated information on steps taken to "address the concern about the conditions of detention of children" with a particular emphasis on the use of excessive force.[229] And finally CAT asks:

> *Please describe steps taken to end the practice of corporal punishment in schools, in particular of mentally and/or physically disabled students.*[230]

This year, the United States human rights record is being scrutinized by the United Nations as part of a process known as "universal periodic review" under all the human rights conventions the United States has ratified. The

United States report to the United Nations should include detailed information on the use of force against children with disabilities at JRC.

Since the United States legal system has failed to protect children and adults with disabilities, **MDRI brings this urgent appeal to the UN Special Rapporteur on Torture and recommends:**

- The UN Special Rapporteur on Torture should demand a full international accounting by the United States government of the abusive practices being perpetrated at the facility;
- The use of electric shock and long-term restraints should be brought to an immediate halt as a form of behavior modification or treatment;
- New federal law should be adopted to completely ban the infliction of severe pain for so-called therapeutic purposes in any context;
- Torture as treatment should be banned and prosecuted under criminal law. . . .

Notes

2. Matthew L. Israel, History of JRC, 1971–1985: Beginnings, Philosophy and Early Growth, *available at* http://www.judgerc.org/history.html. (last visited April 8, 2010).

3. Jennifer Gonnerman, *School of Shock,* 32 Mother Jones, 36,41 (Sept.–Oct. 2007).

4. The number of students is an average taken from a legislative hearing.

5. Matthew L. Israel, Frequently Asked Questions, "Supplementary aversives at JRC—13. How is an aversive defined and which aversives are considered acceptable?" Judge Rotenberg Center, *available at* http://www.judgerc .org/ (last visited April 8, 2010).

6. Matthew L. Israel, *supra* note 2, at 1971–1985: Beginnings, Philosophy and Early Growth.

7. *Id.*

8. *Id.*

9. *Id.*

10. *Id.*, at 1971–1985: Beginnings, Philosophy and Early Growth—No or minimal use of psychotropic medication.

11. Matthew L. Israel, Distinguishing Features of the Judge Rotenberg Center, Judge Rotenberg Center, *available at* http://www/judgerc.org/ (last visited April 20, 2010).

24. Matthew L. Israel, *supra* note 2.

25. Sharon Lohrmann-O'Rourke and Perry A. Zirkel, *The Case Law on Aversive Interventions for Students with Disabilities,* 65 Exceptional Children 101 (Fall 1998).

26. Matthew L. Israel, *supra* note 5, at "Is it true that one of the consequences JRC uses is to administer several GED applications, over a half-hour period during which a student may be restrained on a restraint board?"

27. Patricia Wen, *Showdown over shock therapy testimony moves some critics; new bill would limit, not ban, treatment,* The Boston Globe 1 (Jan. 17, 2008), *available at* http://www.boston.com/news/local/articles/2008/01/17/showdown_ over_shock_therapy/.

28. Paul Kix, *The Shocking Truth,* Boston Magazine Online 3 (2008), *available at* http://www.bostonmagazine.com/articles/the_shocking_truth/.

29. Patricia Wen (2008), *supra* note 27, at 1.

30. Matthew L. Israel, *supra* note 5, at "The use of restraint as an aversive consequence."

31. Matthew L. Israel, *supra* note 5, at "Multiple Applications of GED Combined with Restraint as an Aversive."

32. Gregory D. Kutz, Seclusions and Restraints: Selected Cases of Death and Abuse at Public and Private Schools and Treatment Centers, US Government Accountability Office, GAO-09-719T 4 (2009).

36. Daniel Goleman, *Embattled Giant of Psychology Speaks His Mind,* N.Y. Times, Aug. 25, 1987, at C1 and C3.

45. NY Psychological Association Task Force (2006), *supra* note 37, at 13.

46. *1d.* at 11, *quoting* D. Day, "A review of the literature on restraints and seclusion with children and youth: toward the development of a perspective in practice" (2000), *available at* http://rccp.connell.edu/pdfs/Day.pdf (retrieved July 26, 2006).

48. Frank L. Bird & James K. Luiselli, "Positive behavioral support of adults with developmental disabilities: assessment of long-term adjustment and habilitation following restrictive treatment histories," 31 Journal of Behavior Therapy and Experimental Psychiatry 5, 7 (2000).

57. Matthew L. Israel., Use of Skin Shock as a Supplementary Aversive, Judge Rotenberg Center, para. 1 (2002), *available at* http://www.judgerc.org/ (last visited April 21, 2010).

58. Matthew L. Israel (2002), *supra* note 57, at 1990-date: Development of the GED and GED-4 Devices.

59. *Id.*

60. Certification Team, *Report of the Certification Team on the Application of the Judge Rotenberg Education Center for Level II Behavior Modification Certification,* Commonwealth of Massachusetts, Executive Office of Health & Human Services, Department of Mental Retardation 10 (April 27, 2009) (on file with author).

61. *Id.*

75. Matthew L. Israel, *supra* note 5, at "Is it true that one of the consequences JRC uses is to administer several GED applications, over a half-hour period during which a student may be restrained on a restraint board?" See also, Jennifer Gonnerman (2007), *supra* note 3, at 38.

76. Matthew L. Israel, *supra* note 5, at "Multiple applications of the GED skin shock."

77. Matthew L. Israel, *supra* note 5.

78. NYSED Review Team (2006), *supra* note 17, at 8.

79. *Id.*

90. Certification Team (2009), *supra* note 60, at 32. *See* also, NYSED Review Team (2006), *supra* note 17, at 5.

91. NYSED Review Team (2006), *supra* note 17, at 6.

92. Certification Team (2009), *supra* note 60, at 32.

93. *Id.*

95. Matthew L. Israel, *supra* note 5, at "1. Is it true that at JRC a staff member will sometimes prompt a student to begin to engage in a problem behavior and then arrange an aversive for that? 2. Is there any professional support in the literature for that procedure?"

96. NYSED Review Team (2006), *supra* note 17, at 19.

97. *Id.*

98. MDRI Interview (2009).

99. NYSED Review Team (2006), *supra* note 17, at 10.

100. *Id.*

101. *Id.*

102. *Id.*

105. MDRI Interview (2009).

106. MDRI Interview (2009).

107. MDRI Interview (2009).

108. NYSED Review Team (2006), *supra* note 17, at 24.

111. Jennifer Gonnerman (2007), *supra* note 62, at 46–47.

112. MDRI Interview (2009).

113. NYSED Review Team (2006), *supra* note 17, at 14.

114. *Id.*

115. Greg Miller, *Response to Dr. Matthew Israel's letter entitled "Outrage Over Jennifer Gonnerman's Article, 'School of Shock,"* (Sept. 4, 2007) (posted on Mother Jones comment blog for "School of Shock" article) *available at* http://motherjones.com/politics/2007/08/school-shock?page=4.

116. *Id.*

117. MDRI Interview (2009).

118. MDRI Interview (2009).

196. Letter from Disability Advocates, Addendum to A Call to Action to Eliminate the Use of Aversive Procedures and Other Inhumane Practices, 6 (Sept. 2009), *citing* Coalition for the Legal Rights of People with Disabilities, 6 The Communicator 1 (1995).

197. *Id.*

198. Matthew L. Israel, *supra* note 2, at "1985–1987 Failed Attempt by Office for Children to close JRC."

199. *Behavior Research Institute v. Mary Kay Leonard,* Sup. Ct. Dept. of the Trial Ct., and Prob. and Fam. Ct. of the Dept. of the Trial Ct., Docket No. 86E-0018-GI, Settlement Agreement, (December 12, 1986). Under the settlement agreement, aversive procedures are only permitted with a court-ordered "substituted judgment" treatment plan. In presenting requesting a court-ordered "substituted judgment" treatment plan, the petitioner must show (1) the client's inability to provide informed consent and (2) "target behaviors" to be treated; what procedures will be used to treat the target behaviors; foreseeable adverse side-effects; professional discipline of staff members; prognosis should the procedures be implements; opinions of the client's family; client's previous treatment at BRI or elsewhere; description of appropriate

behaviors; client's IEP. The settlement agreement requires a monitor to report to the court on the client's treatment. The court will also appoint a doctor to oversee BRI's compliance.

206. Rick Karlin, *Regents set to reject use of electric shock,* Albany Times Union, January 9, 2007.

207. *Jeanette Alleyne v. N. Y. State Educ. Dep't,* No. 1:06-cv-00994-GLS (N.D.N.Y 2010) (memorandum-decision and order to the parties).

208. NYSED Review Team (2006), *supra* note 17, at 2–3.

209. *Id.*

210. NYSED Review Team (2006), *supra* note 17, at 11.

211. Massachusetts Office of Consumer Affairs and Business Regulation, "Judge Rotenberg Center clinicians fined $43,000, Consent agreement with Board of Psychologists Reached," Oct. 9, 2006, *available at* http://www.arcmass.org/AversivesPress/tabid/592/Default.aspx#JRCfine

212. Abbie Ruzicka, *Rotenberg Center director fined over clinicians' titles,* The Boston Globe, October 7, 2009.

213. Investigation Report, Massachusetts Department of Early Education and Care 4, November 1, 2007.

225. Nowak & MacArthur (2008), *supra* note 124, at 76–77.

226. Committee Against Torture, Conclusions and Recommendations of the Committee against Torture: United States of America, 15 May 2000, A/55/44, para. 180(c).

227. Committee Against Torture, Conclusions and Recommendations of the Committee Against Torture: United States of America, 18 May 2006, CAT/C/USA/CO/2, para. 35.

228. Committee Against Torture, List of issues prior to the submission of the fifth periodic report of UNITED STATES OF AMERICA 9,20 Jan. 2010, CAT/C/USA/Q/5.

229. *Id.*

230. *Id.*

Matthew L. Israel **NO**

Aversives at JRC: A Better Alternative to the Use of Drugs, Restraint, Isolation, Warehousing or Expulsion in the Treatment of Severe Behavior Disorders[1]

Why Behavior Modification Treatment, Including Aversives in Some Cases, Is Needed

The Judge Rotenberg Educational Center (JRC)[2,3,4], founded in 1971, is a residential education and treatment program in Canton, MA that provides behavior modification therapy, essentially without the use of psychotropic drugs, for 215 special needs children and adults from 7 different states. All of the students have at least one thing in common—they suffer from severe behavior disorders that could not be effectively treated by the many previous treatment programs and psychiatric hospitals they had been in prior to coming to JRC. Because of its zero-rejection, zero-expulsion policy, JRC serves the largest collection of individuals with difficult-to-treat self-abusive, aggressive and severely harmful behaviors in the country. JRC saves individuals from the mental and emotional pain, crippling disabilities, permanent injuries and even death caused by their otherwise untreatable behavior disorders. Before coming to JRC, many students were confined for years in psychiatric or correctional facilities or were living on the streets.

The students who are treated at JRC have shown, prior to admission to JRC, self-abusive behaviors such as: gouging out their eyes, causing near-blindness; smearing feces; head-banging to the point of causing detached retinas and blindness[5] or even stroke[6]; skin scratching to the point of fatal blood and bone infection; pulling out their own adult teeth[7]; running into a street filled with moving cars; or suicidal actions such as attempting to hang oneself, swallowing razor blades, taking a drug overdose, and jumping out of a moving vehicle or off of a building. Some students have shown violent aggression such as biting, hitting, kicking, punching, and head butting others. Some have pushed a parent down a flight of stairs, raped someone, tried to strangle a parent while the parent was driving, and beat a peer so severely that plastic surgery was required. Some have attempted to injure or kill others—for example, by pushing a child into oncoming traffic, smothering a sibling, stabbing a teacher, or slicing a peer's throat. Some have attacked police and therapists. Some have set their homes on fire, lit a fire in school, and lit themselves or family members on fire. Some have engaged in prostitution, been involved in gangs, and assaulted others with weapons such as a machete and chainsaw.

The following letter, which was written by the parents of a student who, prior to her treatment at JRC, had detached both of her retinas through self-abusive head-poking, illustrates what such behavior problems mean to a family. This letter was sent to legislators who were considering a proposed bill in the Massachusetts legislature to ban the use of aversives:

To Whom it May Concern:

We would like to tell you about our daughter, Samantha, and how the Judge Rotenberg School in Canton Massachusetts has saved her life.

We first discovered Samantha was different when she was about 2 years old. She would not relate well to others, had very little speech, and would stare at her hands or small objects for hours at a time. She also had frequent tantrums, and cried often. She began with early intervention, and over the next ten years, she went to four specialized schools for autistic children. In addition to her schooling, numerous therapists, and teachers came to our house to work with Samantha after hours, most of which was paid for out of our own funds. All these schools worked closely with her in small groups, and on a one to one basis, using learning trials, and positive reinforcement. In addition to this, Samantha was under the care of a psychiatrist, and given several different psychotropic medications.

Despite, all these well caring professionals working with our daughter, Samantha progressively deteriorated. Over the years, she became more violent. She would attack us, other children, and her teachers. She would bite, scratch, kick, hit, pinch, and head-butt. In addition she became more self-abusive. She would throw herself on the floor, hit herself, and throw herself against hard objects. She constantly had marks, and bruises on her from her own self abuse. We were also prisoners in our own home, as we could not take her anywhere, due to her behaviors; this had an impact on our other children as well. The final straw came when she hit herself in her head with such force, that she detached both retinas of her eyes, and was virtually blind. This has subsequently required 6 eye surgeries to repair, and her vision is still far from normal. The Anderson School, where she was at the time, told us they could not handle her, and asked us to find another school. This is when we learned about the Judge Rotenberg School (JRC), and the GED device.

Within several weeks of getting treated with the GED device, a miracle happened; Samantha stopped hitting herself, and stopped her violent behavior. She appeared much happier. She was able to be weaned off all of her psychotropic medications.

There was a period of deterioration. In June 2006, aversive treatment became a big issue in New York State. A law was passed prohibiting the use of the GED for antecedent behaviors, leading up to more aggressive behaviors. Samantha became more aggressive, and angry. Some of her old behaviors returned. An injunction to this law was obtained several months later, and the GED was then able to be applied as indicated in the JRC program. Samantha improved, and was happier, and no longer aggressive towards herself or others. This was proof that she needs an ongoing program that includes the GED.

Recently, Samantha had another challenge. Due to a congenital condition, she had to undergo complex orthopedic surgery on both legs to correct a balance problem, and prevent future arthritis. JRC was absolutely wonderful. They accompanied her to all her appointments at the Boston Children's Hospital. She remained in the hospital for 6 days after her surgery. JRC had staff members in her room 24 hours a day, during her entire stay in the hospital. In her post operative period, the staff was with her in her residence at all times, and met her every need. She had to be non-weight bearing for 6 weeks post op, and the JRC staff helped her and transported her to school, and to all her post operative doctor's appointments. One of the most remarkable things about her surgical experience, is through all her pain and all her frustration of not being able to walk, she remained calm, and pleasant. This proves the durability of this program at JRC. If she was anywhere else, surely her old behaviors would have returned, and may have affected her post operative outcome.

Sometimes, we feel that JRC is the most misunderstood place in the world. Samantha has now been at JRC for over 5 years, and we have seen nothing but love and affection for her on the part of the entire staff. They appear to have the same love for all the students at the school. The GED is given only after the failure of positive reinforcement programs, and only after the approval of a judge. It is given carefully, and under strict protocols. Everything done at this school and in the residences is video monitored. The program is 100 percent transparent, and has nothing to hide.

The bottom line is that this program helped, and continues to help our daughter where all other programs have failed. Our daughter is a different person than 5 years ago. She is happy, able to concentrate and learn, and fun to be with. She is on no psychotropic medications.

JRC takes only the most difficult kids that have failed at other programs, and make successes of a large number of them. Many of these children have life threatening behaviors, before arriving at JRC. Everything there is done out of love, not cruelty. We believe our daughter would be dead, or in an institution heavily sedated if it were not for this wonderful school, and caring staff. Many other parents feel the same.

Sincerely,
Mitchell Shear, MD, and Marcia Shear[8]

Fortunately, behavioral psychology has developed a treatment for problematic behaviors such as Samantha's self-abuse. The treatment is called "behavior modification" or "applied behavior analysis." Simply put, this involves analyzing the causes of the problematic behaviors, eliminating events that "trigger" the occurrence of the behaviors, arranging rewards for desired behaviors, and applying corrective consequences (consequences designed to decrease problem behaviors, or *aversives)* for undesired behaviors.

JRC's treatment relies overwhelmingly on the use of positive procedures such as rewards and educational procedures. In fact, JRC has created a unique Yellow Brick Road Reward Area[9] for its students that is found in no other program. However, in the case of 22% of its school-age population (and 41% of its total population), these procedures are not sufficiently effective to treat severe problem behaviors. JRC's experience in this respect is fairly consistent with the scientific literature. Thee major literature reviews show that positive-only procedures are effective in only 50–60% of the cases[10] (JRC's positive programming is able to achieve better results than the literature reports because of JRC's cutting edge reward programs.)

For individuals who do not respond to positive-only procedures, most treatment facilities do the following: administer a cocktail of mind-numbing, sometimes addicting, dangerous, and often ineffective psychotropic drugs; use restraint, take-downs, isolation rooms, and/or warehousing (doing nothing); or expel the student, leaving the parent with no options at all[11]. Instead of using these alternatives, all of which are problematic, JRC employs a corrective consequence ("aversive") in the form of a 2-second shock to the surface of the skin, typically of an arm or leg. This treatment, which feels like a hard pinch, has been extensively validated in the scientific literature (113 published papers since the 1960s[12]), is extremely effective[13], and has no significant adverse side effects[14]. For some individuals it is only required at the beginning of their treatment and can be faded out gradually as their behaviors improve. Even in the minority of cases where it is necessary, it is used rarely (the median number of applications per week at JRC is 0 and the mean is 3), and its use is initiated only after trying positive-only procedures for an average of 11 months. JRC uses this procedure only with an extensive and extraordinary list of safeguards[15]. For example, each individual's treatment program that includes the use of skin shock must be pre-approved by a physician, the parent (who can revoke this consent at any time), included in the student's IEP or IHP, approved by a human rights committee and a peer review committee. It also must be individually pre-approved and reviewed at regular intervals by a Massachusetts Probate Court Judge.[16,17]

JRC has been licensed or approved continuously, throughout its 39-year history, by the state education, developmental disabilities and child care departments of Rhode Island and Massachusetts. The Massachusetts Department of Developmental Services ("DDS") has granted and renewed, ever since 1986, JRC's special certification to use aversive behavioral procedures. More than 15 different judges of the Massachusetts Probate and Family Court have, during the last 25 years, approved individual petitions, by guardians on behalf of incompetent children and adults at JRC, to allow the use of aversive therapy in individual behavior modification treatment programs[18]. Thousands of loving parents—including professors at Harvard and NYU, as well as psychiatrists and pediatricians—have entrusted the care and habilitation of their children to JRC.[19] Former JRC students have voluntarily come before legislative committees to testify that JRC saved their lives.[20]

Certain well-intentioned, but ill-informed advocates object to JRC's use of skin shock and are constantly seeking regulations and legislation to ban the use of aversives. Because JRC is the leading example of a program willing to supplement positive behavioral supports, such as rewards, with skin shock as an aversive, in cases where the person cannot be effectively treated without them, JRC has become the focus of attacks by anti-aversive advocates. Characteristically, these persons are unwilling to rationally weigh the risks or intrusiveness of skin shock aversives against the benefits, and to consider whether using such aversives might be a better choice than the alternatives. They simply ignore the small population of people who cannot be effectively treated with psychotropic drugs and positive behavioral supports alone, and who are being warehoused and drugged into submission. In some cases, these anti-aversives advocates have been so dogmatic that they have contributed to a child's death through self-abuse rather than allow him to receive life-saving therapy that includes aversives[21].

Under state and federal law, non-disabled individuals have the right to choose aversive therapy to treat behavioral problems such as smoking and drinking. To deny persons with developmental or behavior/psychiatric disabilities the same right to treat their behavior problems with aversives would be to impose an invidious form of discrimination against those unfortunate enough to suffer from such disabilities.

The Mental Disabilities Rights International (MDRI) Report

The authors of the MDRI Report have a strong philosophical opposition to aversives. Like other anti-aversive advocates, they are unwilling to use a rational risks-versus-benefits analysis in evaluating the use of aversives. Presumably, even if treatment with behavioral skin shock were the only treatment that could save a child from maiming or killing himself or herself, they would oppose its use. Indeed, Dr. Fredda Brown, one of the key persons who provided information to the authors of the MDRI Report was involved in just such a case.[22] In that case, a young man who was maiming himself through self-abusive scratching until he received effective treatment with behavioral skin shock at JRC. Unfortunately, anti-aversive advocates persuaded his parents that he no longer needed that treatment and could live in a supported apartment where aversives would no longer be available. Without aversives, however, his self-abusive scratching (causing blood and bone infection and eventual paralysis) resumed and caused him a painful and premature death at the age of 25.

Almost all of the persons listed as sources for the information for the MDRI Report have testified in Massachusetts for bills that would, if passed, ban the use of aversives. After trying, unsuccessfully to pass such bills for 24 years, the proponents of these bills now are looking to the United Nations Rapporteur on Torture for help with their political cause.

Because of the authors' strong philosophical opposition to aversives, what they refer to as an "investigation" was simply not that. They never visited

JRC, never sought to discuss their concerns with JRC's clinicians or staff, never spoke to the hundreds of parents who are pleased with what JRC has been able to accomplish for their children, never advised JRC of their investigation or invited JRC to respond to their concerns, and never interviewed current or former students who have been pleased with the results of their treatment at JRC, including the use of aversives.

MDRI's "investigation" consisted largely of the following: finding and using unverified negative accusations available on the internet; taking selective quotations from the JRC website given by parents and students in *support* of JRC's use of aversives, and fraudulently revising those portions to make up false or misleading statements designed to make the authors appear to be *negative* toward JRC's treatment; soliciting information from an individual who, according to an August 29, 2006 police report, claimed to have placed a "whistle blower" inside JRC;[23] soliciting as many negative quotes as possible from persons who are opposed to JRC; accepting and publishing anonymous accusations without researching whether there was any truth to them; taking selective quotations from reports by a state agency that has a philosophical opposition to aversives (and that is currently being sued by a group of JRC parents in the Federal District Court of Northern New York) without any reference to JRC's responses to those accusations, all of which are available on JRC's website; and presenting as facts, outdated, re-hashed, and long—since refuted accusations, some of which are now as much as 30–40 years old.

Here are a few examples of the poorly researched, false and misleading statements in the MDRI Report. More can be found in JRC's full response to the MDRI Report.

1. **"The Judge Rotenberg Center (JRC) was founded . . . in California . . . was then moved to Rhode Island." (p. 6)** This is an example of the shoddiness of the MDRI authors' research, even in simply reporting what they found in JRC's publicly available website. JRC's website clearly states that JRC was started in Cranston, Rhode Island.[24]

2. **"in 1981 [in California], a 14 year-old boy died face down . . ."** [bracketed material supplied] (p. 6) JRC was not operating a program in California in 1981 and was not responsible for this boy's care and treatment.

3. **"What's wrong with punishments is that they work immediately, but give no long-term results . . ." B.F. Skinner interview The New York Times, 1987. (p. 10)** This is another example of MDRI's misleading the reader by providing incomplete misinformation. Subsequent to the interview referred to, Skinner issued a statement on punishment that clarified his position regarding the usefulness of punishment in the treatment of certain behaviors. In this statement he wrote:

> [s]ome autistic children, for example, will seriously injure themselves or engage in other excessive behavior unless drugged or restrained, and other treatment is then virtually impossible. If brief and harmless aversive stimuli, made precisely contingent on self-destructive or other excessive behavior, suppress the behavior and leave the children free to develop in other ways, I believe it can be justified.[25]

4. **"I would be frequently restrained and placed in a small room . . ."
(p. 17 of the full MDRI Report)** Again, MDRI has fraudulently taken
out of context a small part of a longer statement that is very supportive toward JRC and toward the use of the GED skin shock.[26] By
selecting and rearranging words, MDRI makes it seem like a critical
statement. The words as quoted were not what the student actually
said. Notably absent from the words that MDRI chose to quote are
the following words, *"About the GED, it saved my life,"* which appear
as the first sentence in the final paragraph of the letter. The full statement, a letter from a former JRC student, Brian Avery, is re-printed
below. The words taken out of context are indicated by bold font.

> *My name is Brian Avery and I was a student at JRC from Septem-
> ber 1998 to January 2004. Prior to me entering JRC at age 12, I
> was in and out of several psychiatric hospitals and failed in two
> alternative educational settings.*
>
> *My behavioral problems really began to escalate when I was 8
> or 9 years old. I was on several medications including Tegretol,
> Haldol, Ritalin, Risperdal, Depekote, Prozac and Paxil. At age 10,
> my behavior become dangerously out of control. While in school,
> I would climb on furniture, climb under furniture, mouth off at
> the teacher, run out of the classroom and would have to be chased
> down by school staff. I would disrespect authority figures, yell,
> swear, exhibit inappropriate sexual behaviors in school. I would
> even try to stab myself with a pencil. I would become physically
> aggressive with my teachers and would have to be confined in a
> small padded room. In December of 1996 I was moved from a
> co-ed class with a 10:2 student/teacher ratio to another elemen-
> tary school a few towns over and placed in a all male class with
> a 6:2 student/teacher ratio. That change delivered little improve-
> ment in my behavior and academic progress. At home, I spent
> most of my time sleeping or being a couch potato, a debilitating
> side effect of all the medication I was taking. During the time that
> I was awake, I would disrespect my parents, be aggressive towards
> my parents and siblings, throw tantrums, destroy property, and
> would spend hours on end crying. In November of 1996, I spend
> three weeks in a psychiatric hospital. In February of 1998, and
> also in May of that year, I spent another three weeks in a psychiat-
> ric hospital. After my third hospitalization, my parents and school
> district finally came to the conclusion that I needed to be placed
> in a residential school. After visiting numerous schools in New
> York, Pennsylvania, New Jersey, and Massachusetts, my parents
> chose JRC.*
>
> *In September of 1998, I was placed at JRC. Within three months
> of being at JRC, I was taken off all of my medication. My first
> few months at JRC were very depressing. For the first month or so
> of being at JRC, my behavior was much more under control than
> it had been for a very long time. However, once I became accli-
> mated to the program, my behavior began to deteriorate. I would
> once again display the same inappropriate behaviors that I did in*

*public school. **I would be** frequently **restrained and placed in a small room.** JRC would employ an elaborate scheme of behavior contracts and punishments (not the temporary skin shock). Such contracts included earning a small snack and 10 minutes of free time for going an hour without exhibiting inappropriate behaviors, earning a preferred breakfast for completing my morning routine without incident, being able to order take out for going a full day without displaying inappropriate behavior, being able to attend the weekly BBQ and go on field trips for going a week without displaying inappropriate behavior, and so on. Punishments that JRC would employ involve me spending the day in a small room with a staff person whom I was forbidden from socializing with, going to bed at 7 pm, having to do schoolwork or chores on the weekend without being able to socialize with my housemates. Other punishments included being deprived of foods that were rewards. For example, if everyone else were having pizza, I would be served peanut butter and jelly. I would also be put through a ball task, which involved me needing to place 250 foam balls, one at a time, into a trash can while wearing mitts, a task that is very unpleasant. Although I would have occasional bouts of progress (staying on contract for two months at one point), I made no sustainable progress in 1998 through most of 1999. In the fall of 1999, JRC and my parents had decided that it was time to give the GED a try. I reluctantly agreed to the GED and decided not to fight JRC's attempt to place me on the device. I figured that although unpleasant, the GED would deter me from displaying behaviors that would result in me being restrained and losing out on the rewards that came with the program.*

In December of 1999, I was placed on the GED. For the first month or so that I was on the GED, I displayed few inappropriate behaviors, however, once I became acclimated to the fact that I was on the device and was aware of what the GED felt like, I would start displaying lots of more minor behaviors that were not treated with the GED. Once on the GED, instances of me acting out became fewer and more far in between. Although when my contract was broken, I would display lots of inappropriate behaviors, but I would be selective as to not exhibit GED behaviors, although I would occasionally slip up and receive a GED application. By the spring of 2001, it had been several months since my previous major behavioral incident. JRC then began to rapidly fade me off the GED (although the fading process started nearly a year prior, bouts of behavioral episodes impeded the fading process). In July of 2001, I was completely faded from the GED and was moved into a less restrictive residence (apartment), with a student/staff ratio of 4:1. In the apartment, I enjoyed many privileges, such as grocery shopping, going on weekly field trips to the movies, to the arcade, YMCA, local parks etc. I even attended a few sporting events, including the Providence Bruins, Harlem Globetrotters, and even a Red Sox-Yankees game at Fenway Park. I was also given independence to move about the residence and school unsupervised. All of these were privileges I could not even dream of prior to being placed on the GED. From September 2001–September 2002, I would have a few bouts of behavioral incidents and was placed on and off the GED. However, in October of 2002, I was faded from the GED for good. In the fall of 2002, I attended a culinary class at Blue Hills Technical school, and in November I worked in the computer department as an in school job. Also, I began preparing for the New York Regents exams, and in 2003 I began taking the Regents exams. In the fall of 2003, it became clear to JRC, my parents, and school district that I had accomplished all I could while at JRC and in January 2004 I was transitioned back to public school in New York and mainstreamed.

I moved to Florida in August of 2004 and graduated from high school with honors in May 2005. Since then, I took and passed a couple of college courses and had a few jobs, including a seasonal position working for a bank as a data capture specialist, a job that I obtained because of my quick typing skills that I acquired while at JRC.

About the GED, it saved my life. There are lots of opponents to this controversial, yet potentially life-saving treatment, and under-standably so. For someone who has never had the kind of problems I had nor has dealt with anyone who has my kind of problems, when hearing about the GED for the first time, it is only natural to cry torture. However, in reality, being on the GED is a much nicer alternative than being warehoused in a hospital, incarcerated, or being doped up on psychotropic drugs to the point of oblivion. A brief 2-second shock to the surface of the skin sure beats out spending my days restrained and drugged up on drugs and not making any academic progress. I did not like being on the GED when I felt like acting up because it prevented me from being able to do so. But in the end, I'm thankful for the GED because of the enormous progress I made with it and have continued to make once I no longer needed it.

Some people may wind up spending the majority of their life at JRC while being able to enjoy the benefits and privileges the pro-gram has while others, like myself, are able to go on to live an independent life. The bottom line is, if those who opposed the GED had their way, I would currently be locked up and heavily medicate at a hospital or in jail or possibly even dead. So for those who have set out to ban the GED please don't.

Thank you very much

Sincerely,

Brian Avery

5. **"I refused to allow the GED . . ." (p. 18 of the full MDRI Report)**
   This is another example of MDRI fraudulently taking a very positive and supportive statement off of JRC's website and editing it to make it appear to be saying something negative about JRC. This statement

comes from the testimony of Ricardo Mesa, the father of a current JRC student. Mr. Mesa's full testimony is given below.[27] To illustrate how blatantly out of context this quote is, the full testimony is reproduced here and the words taken out of context are shown in bold font. Notably absent from the words that the MDRI Report chose to quote are the words, *"What means something is that I have a daughter who has a life now . . . and is happy."*

> *I have a daughter, Nicole, who went to JRC in 2004. She's still at JRC in the adult services and she was diagnosed with autism and later Landau-Kleffner Syndrom. As the years went by she got progressively worse. She had brain surgery to remove the epilepsy, which helped with her receptive language. But her behavior continued to be extremely severe. To the point that she would constantly punch her eyes like this {demonstrates} constantly. And I used to be a martial Arts instructor and I used to block and there was no way you could block those punches. Those were hard punches to the eyes. She was doing about a thousand a week. We had to pad the entire room, in her bedroom, she lived with us, she still lives with us. We had to, um, we couldn't go anywhere, we couldn't go on vacation, we couldn't. . . . At nights we would hear her banging her head constantly, all night long. She would run out, pinching constantly, her face, her body her breasts, black and blue. You get the picture. She went to the May Center, she went to the LCDC Center, she went to Lighthouse, she went to Perkins School for the Blind, she went to the behavioral program, the neuro-behavioral program at the May Center. These are all excellent programs with very devoted teachers and excellent staff. They couldn't help her. They couldn't stop her. Finally, the Boston School District, the ETL suggested JRC because of some of the progress she had seen from some of the children and I went to see it. We decided to send her over there. And I refused to allow the GED. Because it just, it's so counter-intuitive, I love my daughter, so **I refused to allow it.** And they were fine with it. They allowed me to keep her in the school. They used other methods to try to keep her safe, the restraints, the arm splints and so forth. But Nicole was not making any progress. When she'd come home it was the same story. I agreed after a long time and the hardest day of my life was going before Judge Souten (sp) and asking for them to allow her to use the GED. I told my wife, "We will give them one month. If I don't see immediate progress, she's off it." They put her on the GED, she had a few applications the first day. A few days went by and she had one more. And from that point on she's had an application once every three months, two months and they were usually for very severe behaviors. I don't allow them to use it for any other type of behavior. That contradicts prior testimony {gesturing about someone behind him.} They are fine with it. They have not asked me to take her out of there. Because of that, now she gets one maybe once every year, six months. I mean it's been a long, long time. I can't even recall. She lives at home with us. At home she doesn't wear the GED. It's there in the house and I remind her, that if I see the antecedents, I tell her, "You're going to have to wear*

the GED." She's fine with it. She has to dress well to go to school. She takes really good care of herself. The staff is extremely loving to her. Always has been, that's one of the things I love. I know them well. My wife knows them very well. We've been able to go to a vacation to Florida every year and Virginia Beach, we are able to go to the movies, we are able to go to dinner together, we have a life. And she lives with us. And that's the way I want it. My biggest fear is that we'll lose all of this ground we've made. That she might return to those horrible days, when she was hurting herself so badly. She knocked out my wife a couple of times with headbutts, this was before the GED. And if she were to go back to that stage, it would be just a matter of time before we would have to put her in an institution, or, she wouldn't be able to live with us. So, you know, I really, I know there's a lot of emotion in all of this. A lot of these are articles that have been written, I spoke one time to a reporter all about my daughter and the Boston Globe and the only thing they did, was post "Torture Versus Love." Not one word about what I told them about my daughter was in that article. You can't believe everything you read. And there's a public outcry, against this and exaggerations about what they are doing at the school. I can't speak for anybody else, but I can speak for my daughter and for my life. And I am not a crazy person, or an uninformed person. I am an accountant and I am also an ordained permanent Deacon with the Archdiocese of Boston. I work very closely with Cardinal Law, I mean Cardinal Sean O'Malley. I studied psychology when I was in school. All of that doesn't mean anything. What means something is that I have a daughter who has a life now. I taught her how to ride a bicycle, who can go swimming, who can go on vacation, who goes to school and comes home and is happy.

Particularly disturbing is the authors' willingness to distort testimonial material from JRC's own website, as shown in items 4 and 5 above. The authors took words out of context, made up statements that were not made by the persons who gave the testimonials, and represented the material to be negative comments about JRC and/or skin shock aversives. If the authors were so willing to falsify statements that can be so easily checked—just by going to the JRC website—how much have they distorted the many other accusations in the MDRI Report that were made anonymously and whose accuracy cannot be checked?

In summary, the MDRI Report is a false, misleading, sensationalized, and one-sided account of JRC that is worthy only of a tabloid. It is not a serious or accurate piece of reporting or investigation. One fervently hopes that this Report is an aberration, and not representative of the standards used by MDRI for its other work on both the national and international fronts.

Notes

1. For a more detailed presentation of the material in this document, see pp. 1–50 of JRC's complete Reply to MDRI Report, available at www.judgerc .org/MDRIReportResponse.pdf.

2. JRC's website, at www.judgerc.org, contains a wealth of information. Additional information about aversives can be found at www.effectivetreatment .org.

3. See http://judgerc.org/parents_journey.wmv ("Parents' Journey") for film clips showing some of these types of behavior problems, and giving an overview of how JRC uses positive reward and educational procedures, supplemented with aversives when necessary, in treating these behaviors.

4. JRC's Board of Directors contains five Ph.D. level behavioral psychologists, three of whom are college professors, and one of whom is the President-elect of the Association for Behavior Analysis International, the leading professional organization of behavioral psychologists.

5. JRC currently has such a student who at one point, prior to attending JRC, had detached both retinas due to head-hitting and knee-to-head. Her previous placement, a program that used positive-only treatment procedures, was unable to stop the behavior. Supplementary skin shock at JRC was successful in treating the behavior and thereby enabling the retinas to be re-attached. The young lady is now thriving. See below for photos of this student before and after her treatment at JRC, and for a letter from her parents.

6. JRC currently has a student who is only 16 years old, but who has engaged in head-hitting so forcefully that he has caused himself to have a stroke. His physician has advised JRC that in all probability continued head-banging will cause a fatal brain hemorrhage.

7. JRC currently has a student who has pulled out all but 14 of his adult teeth.

8. This and other letters from JRC parents may be found on the JRC website at http://www.judgerc.org/parentletters.html#letter66.

9. See http://judgerc.org/yellowbrickroad.html.

10. Carr, E. G., Robinson, F., Taylor, J. & Carlson, J. (1990). Positive approaches to the treatment of severe behavior problems in persons with developmental disabilities. In: *National Institutes of Mental Health Consensus Development Conference*, (pp. 231–341). NIH Publication No. 91-2410. And see Carr, E. G., Horner, R. H., Turnbull, A. P., Marquis, J. G., Magito McLaughlin, D., McAtee, M. L., Smith, C. E., Anderson Ryan, K., Ruef, M. B., & Doolabh, A. (1999). *Positive behavior support for people with developmental disabilities: A research synthesis*. Washington, D.C.: American Association of Mental Retardation. Full text available at http://www.judgerc.org/PositiveBehaviorSupport.pdf. And see Horner, R. H., Carr, E. G., Strain, P. S., Todd, A .W., and Reed, H. K. (2002). Problem behavior interventions for young children with autism: A research synthesis. *Journal of Autism and Developmental Disorders*, *32*, 423–445.

11. Israel, M. L., Blenkush, N. A., von Heyn, R. E., and Sands, C. C. Seven Case studies of individuals expelled from positive-only programs (2010). *The Journal of Behavior Analysis of Offender and Victim Treatment and Prevention*, *2* (1), 20–36. Full text available at http://www.judgerc.org/SevenCaseStudies .pdf. See also http://www.judgerc.org/posonlyprograms.pdf (contains documentary proof of the assertion that well-known positive-only programs expel students whose behaviors prove to be too severe to be treated with positive-only treatment procedures).

12. See http://www.effectivetreatment.org/bibliography.html.

13. Israel, M. L., Blenkush, N. A., von Heyn, R. E., & Rivera, P. M. (2008). Treatment of aggression with behavioral programming that includes supplementary skin-shock. *The Journal of Behavior Analysis of Offender and Victim Treatment and Prevention, 1* (4), 119–166. Full text available at http://www.judgerc.org/AggressionPaper.pdf.

14. van Oorsouw, W. M. W. J., Israel, M. L., von Heyn, R. E., & Duker, P. C. (2008). Side effects of contingent shock treatment. *Research in Developmental Disabilities, 29*, 513–523. Full text available at http://www.judgerc.org/SideEffectsContingent.pdf.

15. See "Safeguards for the Use of Aversives with Students at JRC," a paper that may be found in Appendix F in JRC's full response to the MDRI Report, at http://www.judgerc.org/MDRIReportResponse.pdf.

16. In these adversarial hearings, the judge appoints an independent attorney to represent the interests of the student, as distinct from the interests of the parent or JRC. That attorney is given funds to hire an expert who evaluates the student and his/her treatment needs and advises the attorney as to JRC's proposed treatment program. At the hearing, the judge decides whether the student is competent to make his/her own treatment decisions, and whether, if incompetent, he/she would have chosen to use aversives to treat the problem behavior.

17. All programs that educate children with difficult behaviors use aversives but either hide them or give them different names (e.g., "emergency procedures" or "reactive procedures"). If a program administers a "take-down" every time a child is aggressive, this may function as an aversive. The same applies to "time-out" procedures or seclusion procedures that are administered as consistent consequences for certain behaviors. Holding a young autistic child still for 30–60 seconds against his/her will is a frequently used aversive. Physical "redirection" procedures or physical "prompts" that are accompanied with a hard squeeze on the shoulder or arm can also function as "hidden" aversives. A loud shouted "NO!" can be a terrifying aversive for young child. A spank on the buttocks is a common aversive that parents sometimes use. Monetary fines, bad grades, point losses, losses of privileges, ignoring, and signs of disapproval can also function as aversives. It is not the case that JRC uses aversives and other programs do not. Rather, JRC chooses to use a safer and more effective aversive (skin shock) than these other procedures, and is willing to label it for what it really is—an aversive. For an explanation of what aversives are, how and why they are used and the reasons why skin shock is so much more effective than, and preferable to, other aversives, *see* Israel, M. L. (2008). *Primer on Aversives*. Full text available at www.judgerc.org/aversivesprimer.pdf.

18. A brief summary of the legal status of aversives at JRC may be found at http://judgerc.org/LegalBasisAversives.pdf.

19. *See* http://www.judgerc.org/intensivetreatment.html#State_House_Testimonies,_November_2009 and http://www.judgerc.org/Comments/parents_AV.html.

20. *Id.*

21. A young man from New York had been maiming himself through self-abusive scratching until he was placed at JRC where he received effective treatment with behavioral skin shock. Unfortunately, anti-aversive advocates persuaded his parents that he no longer needed that treatment and

could live in a supported apartment where aversives would no longer be available. Without aversives, however, his self-abusive scratching (causing blood and bone infection and eventual paralysis) resumed and caused him a painful and premature death at the age of 25. See Note 5 in JRC's Response to MDRI Report at *persons already enjoy when they use aversives to treat behaviors such as excessive smoking or drinking* http://www .judgerc.org/MDRIReportResponse.pdf.

22. Dr. Brown, a zealous advocate of deinstitutionalization and an anti-aversive supporter, was instrumental in the removal from JRC in the late 1990s of a student named James Velez. James suffered from a debilitating compulsion to scratch and gouge his skin with his fingernails—a behavior that caused serious blood and bone infections and caused him to require a wheelchair. At JRC his behavior improved sufficiently to enable him to get out of the wheelchair. His self-mutilation was drastically reduced, his skin bone infections cleared to the point where he could have some skin grafts, and he was even able to attend classes at a local public high school with having to wear his GED skin shock device. Unfortunately the anti-aversive advocates, advised by Dr. Brown persuaded James' parents that he no longer needed the behavioral structure or aversives of JRC.

James was then removed from JRC against JRC's advice. The advocates who removed him were so hostile to JRC that they refused to even communicate with JRC's medical director about what James' medical needs were, and refused to discuss with JRC's clinicians what his treatment needs were. JRC was unable to even find out where James was living. The anti-aversive advocates were so eager to remove him from JRC that they removed him even before there was a group home or supported apartment ready for him in New York, his home state. As a result he spent 2 years in a ward for developmentally disabled persons at the Brooklyn Development Center.

Eventually James was moved into a supported apartment in Brooklyn operated by an agency that was opposed to the use of aversives. After moving into his apartment, James was invited by the anti-aversive advocates to tell his story at a Boston conference of TASH, an advocacy organization that is strongly opposed to aversives. (Jan Nisbet, one of the other persons providing information for the MDRI Report is a former President of TASH.) James' life story to this point was chronicled in a manner quite sympathetic to the anti-aversive advocates, in four front page articles that ran in the *New York Times* in June and December 1997. Copies of the four *New York Times* articles, James' obituary, and a proposed OpEd piece about James by Dr. Israel are attached hereto in Appendix J. (This Appendix may be found in JRC's full response to the MDRI Report, at www.judgerc.org/ MDRIReportResponse.pdf.)

At his shared apartment James' behavioral consultant was Dr. Brown. Devoid of the behavioral structure and aversives that had served him at JRC, James resumed his scratching, had to use a wheelchair once again, and within about 13 months was hospitalized and nearly died from a leg infection. By February, 1999 he was paralyzed and by October 1999 he was dead at the age of 25, due to infections of the blood and spine caused by the very behaviors JRC had been able to successfully control through the use of skin shock. Characteristically, the anti-aversive advocates showed no remorse over his death or second thoughts as to the wisdom of removing from JRC the one program that had gotten him out of a wheelchair, made him healthy again, and kept him alive. The director of the supervised apartment program in which he died is quoted in his obituary as saying, "Things turned out not to be so simple as we first thought. For the last few years, though, I think that James had the best life that he could have. If that's what this experiment proves, that's a lot. . . . He had the life he wanted . . . James paved the way."

After James' death, when Dr. Brown came to JRC to testify against the use of aversives in the treatment program of another student, Dr. Israel invited her to his office to discuss the case. She refused and marched out of his office when the subject was raised.

23. A copy of the police report may be found in Appendix A of JRC's full response to the MDRI Report, at www.judgerc.org/MDRIReportResponse .pdf. Note that even a fellow JRC-accuser admitted, "I guess we know the whistle blower is not reliable."

24. *See* http://judgerc.org/history.html.

25. Skinner, B. F. A Statement on Punishment. *APA Monitor*, June 1988, p. 22. Full text available at http://www.judgerc.org/Griffin1988Skinner-punishmentstatementAJMR.pdf.

26. Letter from former JRC Student Brian Avery, received June 7, 2009. This statement in its entirety appears on JRC's website at http://judgerc.org/Comments/stultr15.html.

27. Testimony of Father of a JRC Student to Massachusetts Legislative Committee, October 27, 2009. Available in its entirety testimony at: http://judgerc.org/StateHouseTestimonies/42.%20Ricardo%20Mesa%20State%20House%20Testimony%2011.4.09.wmv

CHALLENGE QUESTIONS

Is the Use of Aversive Treatment an Inhumane Intervention for Psychologically Disordered Individuals?

1. In cases in which traditional interventions such as counseling and medication have been ineffective, what options would you recommend to the parents of children who engage in dangerous aggression toward themselves or others?
2. What considerations should be given to the question of how much is too much when it comes to the use of aversive techniques?
3. Imagine that you have been appointed by the governor to conduct an objective evaluation of the ethics of techniques such as those used at JRC. What factors would you include in your evaluation?
4. Assume that you've been awarded a large grant to compare the effectiveness of the JRC techniques to other interventions. What kind of study would you design?
5. What are your thoughts about the emotional effects on the clinicians who administer the aversive techniques to clients?

Suggested Readings

Altiere, M. J., & von Kluge, S. (2009). Searching for acceptance: Challenges encountered while raising a child with autism. *Journal of Intellectual and Developmental Disability*, 34(2), 142–152.

Farrell, J. J. (2009). Protecting the legal interests of children when shocking, restraining, and secluding are the means to an educational end. *St. John's Law Review*, 83(1), 395–426.

Howlin, P. (2010). Evaluating psychological treatments for children with autism-spectrum disorders. *Advances in Psychiatric Treatment*, 16, 133–140.

Matson, J. L. (Ed.) (2009). *Applied behavior analysis for children with autism spectrum disorders*. New York: Springer.

Sailor, W., Dunlap, G., Sugai, G., & Horner, R. (Eds.) (2009). *Handbook of positive behavior support*. New York: Springer.

Weiss, N. R., & Knoster, T. (2008). It may be nonaversive, but is it a positive approach? Relevant questions to ask throughout the process of behavioral assessment and intervention. *Journal of Positive Behavior Interventions*, 10(1), 72–78.

Wood, J., Drahota, A., Sze, K., Har, K., Chiu, A., & Langer, D. (2009). Cognitive behavioral therapy for anxiety in children with autism spectrum disorders: A randomized, controlled trial. *Journal of Child Psychology and Psychiatry*, 50(3), 224–234.

ISSUE 2

Is Gender Identity Disorder a Mental Illness?

YES: Traditional Values Coalition, from "A Gender Identity Disorder Goes Mainstream: Cross-Dressers, Transvestites, and Transgenders Become Militants in the Homosexual Revolution," by Traditional Values Coalition (Washington, DC)

NO: Kelley Winters, from "Diagnosis vs. Treatment: The Horns of a False Dilemma" in GID Reform Weblog (Winter, 2008), and from "Top Ten Problems with the GID Diagnosis" in GID Reform Weblog (Winters, July 1, 2008/July 16, 2008)

ISSUE SUMMARY

YES: The Traditional Values Coalition argues that gender-variant people are psychologically disturbed individuals who need professional help, and that their condition should be viewed as a mental disorder.

NO: Kelley Winters asserts that the GID diagnosis imposes the stigma of mental illness upon people who meet no scientific definition of mental disorder.

$\mathbf{F}$or decades, vehement debates have raged about what is normal and what is abnormal when it comes to human sexual behavior. For much of the twentieth century, homosexuality was regarded as a mental disorder, and was listed in the *Diagnostic and Statistical Manual of Mental Disorders* (*DSM*). In 1973, following great controversy and upheaval within the American Psychiatric Association, homosexuality was deleted from the list of mental disorders. In recent years, similar controversy has emerged about the inclusion of gender identity disorder (GID). Debate has become especially heated in light of the fact that GID continues to be included in the diagnostic nomenclature of *DSM-V*, which is scheduled for publication in 2013.

In *DSM-IV*, GID is characterized as a condition in which a person has a strong and persistent cross-gender identification, which is manifested in a stated desire to be the other sex, frequent passing as the other sex, and the conviction that he or she has the typical feelings and reactions of a person of the other sex. Furthermore, the individual experiences significant distress or impairment, and has persistent discomfort with his or her sex or feels a sense of inappropriateness in the gender role of his or her biological sex.

Those who argue that GID should be viewed as a mental disorder, such as members of the Traditional Values Coalition, assert that transgender people are psychologically disturbed individuals who need professional help, rather than societal approval or affirmation. They contend that maleness and femaleness are unchangeable because they exist in a person's DNA; surgical efforts to change a person's sex result in little other than bodily mutilation.

In a two-part publication, Kelley Winters argues that the GID diagnosis has imposed the stigma of mental illness and sexual deviance upon people who meet no scientific definition of mental disorder. Because of this stigmatization, many gender-variant people fear losing their families, homes, jobs, civil liberties, and access to medical care. The GID diagnosis, Winters argues, implies that the inner identities of gender-variant individuals are not legitimate, but represent perversion, delusion, or immature development.

POINT

- Transgender people are deeply troubled individuals who need professional help, not societal approval or affirmation.

- No person can actually change into a different sex. Maleness and femaleness are in the DNA and are unchangeable.

- A man who has his sex organ removed and takes hormone treatments to grow female breasts is still genetically a male. He is simply a mutilated man, not a woman. This fiction, however, is being perpetrated by a perverted sexual ideology, not by biological facts or science.

- Homosexuals and their transgender allies believe that "gender" is a cultural invention, not a biological reality.

- Gender-confused individuals need long-term counseling, not approval for what is clearly a mental disturbance.

COUNTERPOINT

- The diagnosis of GID in the *DSM* has imposed the stigma of mental illness and sexual deviance upon people who meet no scientific definition of mental disorder. It does not acknowledge the existence of many healthy, well-adjusted transsexual and gender-variant people or justify why they are labeled as mentally ill.

- Identification with the "other sex," meaning other than assigned birth sex, is described as symptomatic regardless of an individual's satisfaction and happiness with that identification.

- The *DSM* diagnosis of GID undermines and even contradicts social transition and the medical necessity of hormonal and surgical treatments that relieve the distress of gender dysphoria, defined here as a persistent distress with one's current or anticipated physical sexual characteristics or current ascribed gender role.

- The current diagnostic criteria are preoccupied with social gender role nonconformity.

- The *DSM* diagnosis of GID fails to distinguish the intrinsic distress of gender dysphoria from that caused by external societal intolerance.

A Gender Identity Disorder Goes Mainstream: Cross-Dressers, Transvestites, and Transgenders Become Militants in the Homosexual Revolution

Lesbian, Gay, Bisexual, and Transgender (LGBT) activists are working to add "sexual orientation," "gender," and "gender identity" to federal legislation. If this legislation is passed, cross-dressers, transsexuals, and drag queens will have federally protected minority status equal to minority groups.

What Is a Transgender?

The term Transgender is an umbrella term coined by transgender activists to describe the following individuals: heterosexual cross-dressers, homosexual transvestites or drag queens, and transsexuals (individuals undergoing so-called sex change operations) and she-males.

Some of these individuals live their lives as she-males with both female and male sexual characteristics. These are deeply troubled individuals who need professional help, not societal approval or affirmation.

A History Lesson: Gender Bill of Rights?

In Houston, in August 1993, at a meeting of the Second International Conference on Transgender Law and Employment Policy, transgender activists passed the "International Gender Bill of Rights."

Here is the text of the Gender Bill of Rights:

> All human beings carry within themselves an ever-unfolding idea of who they are and what they are capable of achieving. The individual's sense of self is not determined by chromosomal sex, genitalia, assigned birth sex, or initial gender role. Thus the individual's identity and capabilities cannot be circumscribed by what society deems to be masculine or feminine behavior.

It is fundamental that individuals have the right to define, and to redefine as their lives unfold, their own gender identity, without regard to chromosomal sex, genitalia, assigned birth sex, or initial gender role.

The Right to Free Expression of Gender Identity—Given the right to define one's own gender identity, all human beings have the corresponding right to free expression of their self-defined gender identity.

The Right to Control and Change One's Own Body—All human beings have the right to control their bodies, which includes the right to change their bodies cosmetically, chemically, or surgically, so as to express a self-defined gender identity.

The Right to Competent Medical and Professional Care—Given the individual right to define one's gender identity, and the right to change one's own body as a means of expressing a self-defined gender identity, no individual should be denied access to competent medical or other professional care on the basis of chromosomal sex, genitalia, assigned birth sex, or initial gender role.

The Right to Freedom from Psychiatric Diagnosis or Treatment—Given the right to define one's own gender identity, individuals should not be subject to psychiatric diagnosis or treatment solely on the basis of their gender identity or role.

The Right to Sexual Expression—Given the right to a self-define gender identity, every consenting adult has a corresponding right to free sexual expression.

The Right to Form Committed, Loving Relationships and Enter into Marital Contracts—Given that all human beings have the right to free expression of a self-defined gender identity, and the right to sexual expression as a form of gender expression, all human beings have a corresponding right to form committed, loving relationships with one another and to enter into marital contracts, regardless of either partner's chromosomal sex, genitalia, assigned birth sex, or initial gender role.

The Right to Conceive or Adopt Children; the Right to Nurture and Have Custody of Children and Exercise of Parental Rights—Given the individual's right to form a committed, loving relationship with another, and to enter into marital contracts with another, together with the right to sexual expression of one's gender identity, all individuals have a corresponding right to conceive or adopt children, to nurture children and to have custody of children, and to exercise parental rights with respect to children, natural or adopted, without regard to chromosomal sex, genitalia, assigned birth sex, or initial gender role.

Transgenders Are Mentally Disordered

The American Psychiatric Association (APA) still lists transsexualism and transvestism as paraphilias or mental disorders in the *Diagnostic and Statistical Manual* (*DSM-IV-TR*). However, homosexual groups such as the Human Rights Campaign (HRC) and GenderPac are pushing hard to have this classification removed from the *DSM*. The objective is to normalize a mental disorder in the same way that homosexuality was normalized in 1973 when psychiatrists removed this sexual dysfunction from the *DSM*. In fact, when the

APA met in May 2003 in San Francisco, Dr. Charles Moser with the Institute for Advanced Study of Human Sexuality argued that sadomasochism, transsexualism/transvestism, and even bestiality (sex with animals) should be removed from the *DSM*. According to Moser, psychiatry no longer has a "base line" to judge what constitutes normal behavior, so these categories should be removed.

Media Is Aiding Transgender Movement

Hollywood and the liberal media are doing their part to normalize this serious mental illness. In 2001, for example, the Los Angeles Times published "Era of the Gender Crosser," that portrayed transgendered individuals as a misunderstood and persecuted minority. According to author Mary McNamara, individuals who believe they are the opposite sex should be treated as if they have a medical condition, not a mental condition.

The Discovery Health Channel repeatedly runs "What Sex Am I?" which questions the reality of male and female.

Hollywood is pushing the transgender agenda in various ways. HBO ran "Normal," in March 2003. This show described a middle-aged married man who decided he was really a woman and sought a sex change. Networks are also running "Brandon Teena," about a poor sexually confused girl who dressed like a boy. She was eventually murdered by two angry young men when they discovered she who she was. Teena Brandon has become a martyr for the transgender cause.

The latest martyr for transgender activists is a boy named Justin Zapata, who dressed like a girl and called himself "Angie."

Justin was brutally murdered in 2008 by a Mexican gang member who briefly "dated" Justin until he found out that "Angie" was actually an 18-year-old boy. The gang member has been sentenced to life in prison without parole—plus an extra sentence for committing a "hate crime" against Zapata.

Hollywood, which is dominated in many areas by homosexual activists, will continue to introduced transgender themes into its movies and TV shows.

Transgender activists are also receiving help from journalists. The National Lesbian and Gay Journalists Association, for example, has distributed to media outlets a "Stylebook Supplement." It encourages journalists to cater to the transgender agenda by referring to transgendered persons by their self-identification, not their actual birth sex.

Psychiatrists and Pediatricians Are Pushing Transgender Confusion on Kids

The transgender movement is also being helped by psychiatrists and pediatricians who are pushing the view that children should be free to choose their own "genders."

In May 2006, the Pediatric Academic Societies held a conference in San Francisco to promote this bizarre viewpoint.

A member of the National Association for Research and Therapy of Homosexuality (NARTH) was an eyewitness at this conference and described what occurred at this conference.

Two of the attendees were Irene N. Sills and Arlene Istar Lev. They presented a paper titled, "Gender-Variant Youth—The Role Of The Pediatrician." They outlined a "non-pathological model for transgender expression" designed to "help identify the gender-variant child as one who simply marches to the beat of a different drummer."

Pro-transgender activists like these are referring to children with serious Gender Identity Disorders as merely "gender variant."

Some pro-transgender pediatricians are actually injecting preteens with hormones to keep them from developing into adult males or females—until these kids "decide" what sex they wish to be.

This is child abuse, yet the transgender agenda is well-advanced in academia and in the medical and mental health professions.

No One Can Change Their Sex

The reality is that no person can actually change into a different sex. Maleness and femaleness are in the DNA and are unchangeable. A man who has his sex organ removed and takes hormone treatments to grow female breasts is still genetically a male. He is simply a mutilated man, not a woman. This fiction, however, is being perpetrated by a perverted sexual ideology—not by biological facts or science.

Homosexual groups such as the Human Rights Campaign and the National Gay and Lesbian Task Force have provided transgender activists with credibility and political power as they pursue their agenda.

The transgender movement's philosophy is based on the writings of several transsexuals. Among them are Nancy Nangeroni, founder of the International Foundation for Gender Education, Martine Rothblatt, and Marxist radical Leslie Feinberg, author of Transgender Warrior, and an editor with the Workers World Party, a Communist splinter group that aligns itself with North Korea.

Nancy Nangeroni claims that Western Civilization is "sick" because it pathologizes any person who wants a sex change operation. Martine Rothblatt is author of *The Apartheid of Sex: A Manifesto on the Freedom of Gender*. According to Rothblatt, our culture's practice of dividing people into two sexes is as evil as racial apartheid. He argues that there are actually several sexes, not just male and female. Those who oppose transgenderism are "transphobic" and intolerant.

The Human Rights Campaign, one of the most aggressive homosexual groups in the United States, is allied with transgender activists and has actually developed workplace guidelines for how businesses should handle men and women who are undergoing sex change operations.

In addition, Parents and Friends of Lesbians and Gays (PFLAG) has a special Transgender Special Outreach Network, which includes coordinators in more than 170 chapters. It also distributed 12,000 copies of "Our Trans Children" to schools and to parents of these sexually confused children.

The leading transgender group is GenderPac, headed by male-to-female transgender Riki Wilchins. He is author of *READ MY LIPS: Sexual Subversion & the End of Gender.* Wilchins works closely with the NGLTF to get the APA to remove transsexualism as a mental disorder. Patricia Ireland, former head of the YWCA, is a member of the board of GenderPac and helps lobby Congress for passage of legislation protecting the "gender identity" of individuals in the workplace and in our culture.

Be Whatever You Wish

Homosexuals and their transgender allies believe that "gender" is a cultural invention, not a biological reality. According to these activists, a person can self-identify and be whatever he or she wishes to be sexually. One pro-transgender activist, Professor Anne Fausto-Sterling, for example, has said that "Complete maleness and complete femaleness represent the extreme ends of a spectrum of possible body types."

Fausto-Sterling published "The Five Sexes: Why Male and Female Are Not Enough," in The Sciences, March/April 1993. In fact, many of these sexually confused individuals decide that they wish to be neither male nor female, but to exist as she-males with female sexual characteristics from the waist up and male sexual characteristics from the waist down.

One of these individuals actually set up a web site to describe herself. Della Grace on her web site "Body Politic," says she is a she-male and former lesbian photographer and visual artist. Grace says she willingly purchased a "one-way ticket" to "no man's land," to inhabit the "nether world" where she is neither male nor female. She calls herself a "pansexual, which means I don't discriminate on the basis of gender or species." She also describes herself as a "gender variant" mutant who has decided against being male or female.

Deconstructing Male and Female

The NARTH has published numerous articles on various Gender Identity Disorders. One is by Dale O'Leary, author of *The Gender Agenda.* In the NARTH paper, "Destabilizing The Categories Of Sex And Gender," O'Leary notes: Patients who suffer from the belief that they are men trapped in the bodies of women (or women trapped in the bodies of men) need real help. . . . The promotion of 'sex changes,' and the normalizing of severe Gender Identity Disorders by radical feminists, pro-same-sex attraction disorder activists, and sexual revolutionaries is part of their larger agenda—namely, the destabilization of the categories of sex and gender."

O'Leary notes that radicals and medical professionals who promote sex change operations are operating under the delusion that one's gender is changeable. One cannot change into a different sex. It is genetically and medically impossible. Gender-confused individuals need long-term counseling, not approval for what is clearly a mental disturbance.

Dr. Martin Silverman, a member of NARTH, has written extensively on Gender Identity Disorders. In a NARTH paper, "Gender Identity Disorder In

Boys: A Complemental Series?" he notes that a boy who has developed a Gender Identity Disorder, such as homosexuality or transvestism, typically comes from a home where the mother is smothering in her love and where the father is passive and feels powerless to overcome his wife's dominance in the family. NARTH has more information on this disorder on its web site: www.narth.com.

What Can Be Done?

If the transgender movement is not already active in your community, it will be. Wherever there are homosexual activist groups, you will find transgendered individuals working alongside them to establish policies and recruitment programs in public schools and to change laws to redefine what it means to be male or female. Here are some suggestions for action:

Monitor city and state legislative proposals that contain the word "gender" in them. Gender is code for cross-dressers, transvestites, and transsexuals. Inform your local politicians of this cultural agenda so they will recognize it when activists attempt to push through legislation.

Oppose Gay Straight Alliance clubs on school campuses. These are recruitment programs to lure children into sexually destructive lifestyles.

These GLSEN-sponsored groups are now promoting cross-dressing for children.

Use TVC, NARTH, and other materials in fighting homosexual/transgenderism.

NO

Part I: Diagnosis vs. Treatment: The Horns of a False Dilemma

The transgender community has been divided by fear that we must choose between access to corrective hormonal and surgical procedures to support transition and the stigma of mental illness imposed by the current diagnosis of Gender Identity Disorder (GID).[1] This schism has allowed little dialogue and no progress on GID reform in nearly three decades. However, the GID diagnosis has failed our community on both points. Transsexual individuals are poorly served by a diagnosis that both stigmatizes us as mentally deficient and sexually deviant *and at the same time* undermines the legitimacy of social transition and medical procedures that are often dismissed as "elective," "cosmetic," or as reinforcing mental disorder.

Gender Identity Disorder in the *Diagnostic and Statistical Manual of Mental Disorders*[2] has imposed stigma of mental illness and sexual deviance upon people who meet no scientific definition of mental disorder.[3] It does not acknowledge the existence of many healthy, well-adjusted transsexual, and gender variant people or justify why we are labeled as mentally ill.

I have heard countless narratives of suffering inflicted by the stereotype of mental illness and "disordered" gender identity, and I have experienced it myself. We lose our families, our children, our homes, jobs, civil liberties, access to medical care, and our physical safety. With each heartbreak, we're almost invariably told the same thing—that we're "nuts," that our identities and affirmed roles are madness and deviance. The following statement by Dr.Robert Spitzer at the 1973 annual meeting of the American Psychiatric Association remains as true today for transgender people as it was for gay and lesbian people then:

> "In the past, homosexuals have been denied civil rights in many areas of life on the ground that because they suffer from a 'mental illness' the burden of proof is on them to demonstrate their competence, reliability, or mental stability."[4]

The current GID diagnosis places a similar burden of proof upon gender variant individuals to prove our competence, with consequences of social stigma and denied civil rights. It harms those it was intended to help. For example,

> "Transsexuals suffer from 'mental pathologies,' are ineligible for admission to Roman Catholic religious orders and should be expelled if they

From *GID Reform Weblog* by Kelley Winters (Kelley Winters, 2008). Copyright © 2008 by Kelley Winters. Reprinted by permission.

have already entered the priesthood or religious life," the Vatican says in new directives."[5]

Simultaneously, GID in the DSM-IV-TR undermines and even contradicts social transition and the medical necessity of hormonal and surgical treatments that relieve the distress of gender dysphoria, defined here as a persistent distress with one's current or anticipated physical sexual characteristics or current ascribed gender role.[6] For example, Paul McHugh, M.D., former psychiatrist-in-chief at Johns Hopkins Hospital, used GID diagnosis as a key reason to eliminate gender confirming surgeries there:

> "I concluded that to provide a surgical alteration to the body of these unfortunate people was to collaborate with a mental disorder rather than to treat it."[7]

Dr. Paul Fedoroff of the Centre for Addiction and Mental Health (formerly the Clarke Institute of Psychiatry) cited the psychiatric diagnosis to urge elimination of gender confirming surgeries in Ontario in 2000,

> "TS [transsexualism, in reference to the GID diagnosis] is also unique for being the only psychiatric disorder in which the defining symptom is facilitated, rather than ameliorated, by the 'treatment.' . . . It is the only psychiatric disorder in which no attempt is made to alter the presenting core symptom."[8]

Paradoxically, the GID diagnosis has been defended as necessary for access to hormonal and surgical transition procedures. It is required by Standards of Care of the World Professional Association for Transgender Health,[9] and GID is cited in legal actions to gain access to these procedures. Attorney Shannon Minter, head counsel for the National Center for Lesbian Rights, was quoted in *The Advocate*,

> "'When we go to court to advocate for transsexual people to get medical treatment in a whole variety of circumstances, from kids in foster care to prisoners on Medicaid,' the GID diagnosis is used to show that treatment is medically necessary."[10]

Dr. Nick Gorton echoed long-standing fears that access to hormonal and surgical procedures would be lost if the GID were removed entirely,

> "Loss of the DSM diagnostic category for GID will endanger the access to care, psychological well being, and in some cases, the very life of countless disenfranchised transgender people who are dependent on the medical and psychiatric justification for access to care."[11]

Gender dysphoric transpeople have therefore assumed that we must suffer degradation and stigma by the current GID diagnosis or forfeit lifesaving medical transition procedures. But has our community been impaled on the horns of a false dilemma?

Are hormonal and surgical procedures available to transitioning individuals because of the current diagnosis of "disordered" gender identity or in spite of it? Because the GID criteria and supporting text are tailored to contradict transition and pathologize birth-role nonconformity[3], affirming and tolerant professionals are burdened to reconstrue GID in more positive and supportive way for transitioning clients. For example, last month the American Medical Association passed a historic resolution, "Removing Financial Barriers to Care for Transgender Patients." It reinterpreted GID to emphasize distress and de-emphasize difference:

> ". . . a persistent discomfort with one's assigned sex and with one's primary and secondary sex characteristics, which causes intense emotional pain and suffering."[12]

The AMA statement is perhaps a model for what the GID diagnosis should become.

The current GID diagnosis and its doctrine of "disordered" gender identity have failed the transcommunity on both issues of harmful psychosexual stigma *and* barriers to medical care access. The DSM-V Sexual and Gender Identity Disorders work group has an opportunity to correct both failures with new diagnostic nomenclature based on scientific standards of distress and impairment rather than intolerance of social role nonconformity and difference from assigned birth sex.

Part I Notes

1. This essay is expanded from K. Winters, "Harm Reduction for Gender Disorders in the DSM-V," Philadelphia Trans Health Conference, May 2008.

2. American Psychiatric Association, *Diagnostic and Statistical Manual of Mental Disorders,* Fourth Edition, Text Revision, Washington, D.C., 2000.

3. K. Winters, "Gender Dissonance: Diagnostic Reform of Gender Identity Disorder for Adults," Sexual and Gender Diagnoses of the Diagnostic and Statistical Manual (DSM), Ed. Dan Karasic, MD, and Jack Drescher, MD, Haworth Press, 2005; co-published in Journal of Psychology & Human Sexuality, vol. 17 issue 3, pp. 71–89, 2005.

4. R. Spitzer, "A Proposal About Homosexuality and the APA Nomenclature: Homosexuality as an Irregular Form of Sexual Behavior and Sexual Orientation Disturbance as a Psychiatric Disorder," *American Journal of Psychiatry,* Vol. 130, No. 11, November 1973, p. 1216.

5. N. Winfield, Associated Press, "Vatican Denounces Transsexuals," *Newsday,* Jan 2003.

6. Working definition of Gender dysphoria by Dr. Randall Ehrbar and I following our panel presentations at the 2007 convention of the American Psychological Association. It is defined in glossary of the DSM-IV-TR as "A persistent aversion toward some of all of those physical characteristics or social roles that connote one's own biological sex." (p. 823)

7. P. McHugh, "Surgical Sex," *First Things* 147:34–38, http://www.firstthings.com/ftissues/ft0411/articles/mchugh.htm, 2004.

8. J. Fedoroff, "The Case Against Publicly Funded Transsexual Surgery," *Psychiatry Rounds,* Vol 4, Issue 2, April 2000.

9. World Professional Association for Transgender Health (formerly HBIGDA), "Standards of Care for The Hormonal and Surgical Sex Reassignment of Gender Dysphoric Persons," http://wpath.org/Documents2/socv6.pdf, 2001.

10. S. Rochman, "What's Up, Doc?" *The Advocate,* http://www.advocate.com/issue_story_ektid50125.asp, Nov 2007.

11. R.N. Gorton, "Transgender as Mental Illness: Nosology, Social Justice, and the. Tarnished Golden Mean," www.Nickgorton.org/misc/work/private_research/transgender_as_mental_illness.pdf, 2006.

12. American Medical Association, "Resolution 122, Removing Financial Barriers to Care for Transgender Patients," http://www.ama-assn.org/ama1/pub/upload/mm/16/a08_hod_resolutions.pdf, June 2008.

Part II: Top Ten Problems with the GID Diagnosis

What are the problems with the Gender Identity Disorder diagnosis in the *Diagnostic and Statistical Manual of Mental Disorders* (DSM)[1]? How are overarching issues of psychiatric stigma and access to medical transition procedures related to specific flaws in the diagnostic criteria[2] and supporting text? The philosopher Jiddu Krishnamurti said

> If we can really understand the problem, the answer will come out of it, because the answer is not separate from the problem.[3]

This is my personal list of the most egregious problems with the current Gender Identity Disorder diagnosis. While far from comprehensive, it is perhaps a starting point for dialogue about how harm reduction of gender nomenclature might be possible in the DSM-V.

1. **Focus of pathology on nonconformity to assigned birth sex in disregard to the definition of mental disorder, which comprises distress and impairment.**
   Recent revisions of the DSM increasingly target gender identity and expression that differ from natal or assigned sex as disordered. The current diagnostic criteria for GID in the DSM-IV-TR are preoccupied with social gender role nonconformity, especially for children. Identification with the "other sex," meaning other than assigned birth sex, is described as symptomatic regardless of our satisfaction and happiness with that identification [p. 581].

2. **Stigma of mental illness upon emotions and expressions that are ordinary or even exemplary for nontransgender children, adolescents and adults.**

   Criterion A for Gender Identity Disorder highlights a desire to be treated as, or "frequently passing as," our affirmed gender as pathological. For children, criteria A and B stress ordinary masculine or feminine expression in clothing, play, games, toys, and fantasy as symptoms of mental "disturbance" [p. 581]. The supporting text disparages innocent childhood play as disorder, including Barbie dolls, playing house, Batman and "rough-and-tumble" activity, if they violate stereotypes of assigned birth sex [pp. 576–577]. Incredulously, knitting is implicated as a focus of sexual perversion for adult transwomen in the supporting text [p. 579].

3. **Lacks clarity on gender dysphoria, defined here as clinically significant distress with physical sex characteristics or ascribed gender role.**[4]

   The distress of gender dysphoria that necessitates medical intervention is inadequately described in criterion B of the GID diagnosis in the DSM-IV-TR as "discomfort" or "inappropriateness." For children, this often-debilitating pain is obfuscated in the diagnostic criterion, which emphasizes nonconformity to gender stereotypes of assigned birth sex rather than clinically significant distress. Adolescents and adults who believe that we were "born in the wrong sex" meet criterion B on the basis of their belief, even if our gender dysphoria has been relieved by transition or related medical procedures [p. 581].

4. **Contradicts transition and access to hormonal and surgical treatments, which are well proven to relieve distress of gender dysphoria.**

   Social role transition, living and passing in our affirmed gender roles, and desiring congruent anatomic sex characteristics are listed as "manifestation" of mental pathology in criterion A of Gender Identity Disorder. Requests for hormonal or surgical treatment to relieve gender dysphoria are disparaged as "preoccupation" in criterion B and supporting text rather than medical necessity [p. 581]. Evidence of medical transition treatment, such as breast development for transwomen or chest reconstruction for transmen, is described in a negative context as "associated features and disorders" of mental illness in the supporting text [p. 579].

5. **Encourages gender-conversion therapies, intended to change or shame one's gender identity or expression.**

   The DSM is intended as a diagnostic guide without specific treatment recommendations [p. xxxvii]. Nevertheless, the current GID diagnostic criteria are biased to favor punitive gender-conversion "therapies." For example, gender variant youth, adolescents or adults who have been shamed into the closet, forced into concealing our inner gender identities, no longer meet the diagnostic criteria of Gender Identity Disorder and are emancipated from a label of mental illness.

6. **Misleading title of "Gender Identity Disorder," suggesting that gender identity is itself disordered or deficient.**

   The name, Gender Identity Disorder, implies "disordered" gender identity—that the inner identities of gender variant individuals are not legitimate but represent perversion, delusion or immature development. In other words, the current GID diagnosis in the DSM-IV-TR implies that transwomen are nothing more than mentally ill or confused "men" and vice versa for transmen.[5]

7. **Maligning terminology, including "autogynephilia," which disrespects transitioned individuals with inappropriate pronouns and labels.**

   Maligning language labels gender variant people by our assigned birth sex in disregard of our gender identity. In other words, affirmed or transitioned transwomen are demeaned as "he" and transmen as "she." It appears throughout the diagnostic criteria and supporting text of the GID diagnosis in the current DSM-IV-TR, where affirmed roles are termed "other sex" [p. 581], transsexual women are called "males" and "he" [p. 577], and transsexual men as "females" [p. 579]. Such demeaning terms deny our social legitimacy and empower defamatory social stereotypes like "a man in a dress," in the press, the courts, our workplace, and our families.

8. **False positive diagnosis of those who are no longer gender dysphoric after transition and of gender nonconforming children who were never gender dysphoric.**

   There is no exit clause in the diagnostic criteria for individuals whose gender dysphoria has been relieved by transition, hormones or surgical treatments, regardless of how happy or well adjusted with our affirmed gender roles. The diagnosis is implied "to have a chronic course" for adults [p. 580], despite transition status or absence of distress. Children may be diagnosed with Gender Identity Disorder, solely on the basis of gender role nonconformity, without evidence of gender dysphoria. Criterion A requires only four of five listed attributes, and four of those describe violation of gender stereotypes of assigned birth sex, The fifth, describing unhappiness with birth sex, is not required to meet criterion A. Criterion B may be met by "aversion toward rough-and-tumble play and rejection of male stereotypical toys . . ." for natal boys and "aversion toward normative feminine clothing" for natal girls [p. 581].

9. **Conflation of impairment caused by prejudice with distress intrinsic to gender dysphoria.**

   Criterion D of the GID diagnosis, the clinical significance criterion [p. 581], was intended to require clinically significant distress or impairment to meet the accepted definition of mental disorder [p. xxxi]. Unfortunately, it fails to distinguish intrinsic distress of gender dysphoria from that caused by external societal intolerance. Lacking clarity in criterion D, prejudice, and discrimination can be misconstrued as psychological impairment for gender variant individuals who are not distressed by our physical sex characteristics or ascribed gender roles.

10. **Placement in the class of sexual disorders.**
    In 1994, Gender Identity Disorders were moved from the class of "Disorders Usually First Evident in Infancy, Childhood or Adolescence," to the section of sexual disorders in the DSM-IV, renamed "Sexual and Gender Identity Disorders".[6] This reinforces stereotypes of sexual deviance for gender variant people.

The DSM-V Task Force has an opportunity to address these shortcomings in the current GID diagnosis. I hope that this list can help provide a way to evaluate proposals for less harmful diagnostic nomenclature in the fifth edition of the DSM.

Part II Notes

1. American Psychiatric Association, *Diagnostic and Statistical Manual of Mental Disorders,* Fourth Edition, Text Revision, Washington, D.C., 2000, pp. 576–582.

2. DSM-IV-TR Diagnostic criteria for Gender Identity Disorder of Adults and Adolescents are available online at http://www.gidreform.org/gid30285.html and for children at http://www.gidreform.org/gid3026.html

3. "Krishnamurti Quotes," http://www.krishnamurti.org.au/articles/krishnamurti_quotes.htm

4. Working definition of Gender dysphoria by Dr. Randall Ehrbar and I, following our panel presentations at the 2007 convention of the American Psychological Association. It is defined in glossary of the DSM-IV-TR as "A persistent aversion toward some of all of those physical characteristics or social roles that connote one's own biological sex." (p. 823)

5. K. Winters, "Gender Dissonance: Diagnostic Reform of Gender Identity Disorder for Adults," *Sexual and Gender Diagnoses of the Diagnostic and Statistical Manual (DSM),* Ed. Dan Karasic, MD. and Jack Drescher, MD., Haworth Press, 2005; co-published in *Journal of Psychology & Human Sexuality,* vol. 17, issue 3, pp. 71–89, 2005.

6. American Psychiatric Association, *Diagnostic and Statistical Manual of Mental Disorders,* Fourth Edition, 1994.

CHALLENGE QUESTIONS

Is Gender Identity Disorder a Mental Illness?

1. To what extent should the mental health profession be concerned about personal issues of gender identity, particularly in people who do not view themselves as psychologically disturbed?
2. Assuming that GID is included in *DSM-V,* the assumption would be that this is a "treatable condition." What kind of "treatment" should be recommended?
3. How would you go about designing a research study of the psychological difficulties experienced by gender-variant individuals?
4. If you were designing an educational program to inform the public about gender-variant individuals, what message would you want to convey?
5. The authors of *DSM-V* have proposed the diagnosis "Gender Identity Disorder in Children." What issues should be considered before assigning this diagnosis to a child?

Suggested Readings

Ault, A. & Brzuzy, S. (2009). Removing gender identity disorder from the Diagnostic and Statistical Manual of Mental Disorders: A call for action. *Social Work, 54*(2), 187–189.

Hill, D., Rozanski, C., Carfagnini, J., & Willoughby, B. (2007). Gender identity disorders in childhood and adolescence: A critical inquiry. *International Journal of Sexual Health, 19*(1), 57–75.

Lawrence, A. A. (2008). Gender identity disorder in adults: Diagnosis and treatment. In Rowland, D. L. & Incrocci, L. (eds.): *Handbook of Sexual and Gender Identity Disorders* (423–456). Hoboken, NJ: John Wiley & Sons, Inc.

Singh, D., Deogracias, J., Johnson, L., Bradley, S., Kibblewhite, S., Owen-Anderson, A., et al. (2010). The gender identity/gender dysphoria questionnaire for adolescents and adults: Further validity evidence. *The Journal of Sex Research, 47*(1), 49–58.

Singh, D. (2008). *Psychometric assessment of gender identity/gender dysphoria and recalled sex-typed behaviour in childhood: A comparison of adolescents and adults with gender identity disorder and clinical controls.* University of Toronto.

Winters, K. (2009). *Gender madness in American psychiatry: Essays from the struggle for dignity.* BookSurge Publishing.

Zucker, K. J., & Cohen-Kettenis, P. T. (2008). Gender identity disorder in children and adolescents. In Rowland, D. L. & Incrocci, L. (eds.): *Handbook of*

Sexual and Gender Identity Disorders (376–422). Hoboken, NJ: John Wiley & Sons, Inc.

Zucker, K., & Lawrence, A. (2009). Epidemiology of gender identity disorder: Recommendations for the standards of care of the World Professional Association for Transgender Health. *International Journal of Transgenderism, 11*(1), 8–18.

ISSUE 3

Is Forced Treatment of Seriously Mentally Ill Individuals Justifiable?

YES: Samuel J. Brakel and John M. Davis, from *Overriding Mental Health Treatment Refusals: How Much Process Is "Due"?* (Saint Louis University Law Journal)

NO: James B. Gottstein, from "How the Legal System Can Help Create a Recovery Culture in Mental Health Systems," *Leading the Transformation to Recovery* (2005)

ISSUE SUMMARY

YES: Attorney Samuel J. Brakel and psychiatrist John M. Davis assert that society has a responsibility to take care of seriously mentally ill individuals who are incapable of making an informed decision about their need for care and treatment.

NO: Attorney James B. Gottstein contends that forced treatment of mentally ill citizens represents a curtailment of liberty which leads many people down a road of permanent disability and poverty.

The deinstitutionalization movement which began in the final quarter of the twentieth century was regarded as an important positive trend in the treatment of seriously mentally ill people. Although some patients who were transferred to community programs and halfway houses thrived in a less restrictive environment, other patients became lost in the maze, with many becoming homeless and destitute. In response to the social crisis following deinstitutionalization, some social critics have called for more aggressive efforts to reach out to seriously mentally ill people so that they can be provided with badly needed care, even if these individuals resist such solicitous efforts. A controversy has raged about whether therapeutic treatment should be forced upon seriously mentally ill people.

In the first reading, Attorney Samuel Brakel and psychiatrist John M. Davis argues that many citizens with profound mental illness are incapable of caring for themselves, and will resist treatment because they do not view themselves as mentally ill. Without treatment many individuals will not only be at risk, but will be deprived of experiencing a better quality of life. These authors believe that mental health professionals should be allowed to initiate treatment over a patient's objection in instances involving seriously ill individuals who cannot be convinced to accept treatment voluntarily.

In the second reading, Attorney James Gottstein argues vehemently against the idea of forcing treatment upon unwilling citizens. He argues that myths about mental illness need to be debunked, while efforts are made to provide more humane, effective, recovery-oriented, and noncoercive interventions. Gottstein contends that it is easier for the system to lock people up and drug them into submission than it is to engage them in a much more humane process of recovery.

POINT

- Without drugs as the base treatment for schizophrenia and other psychotic disorders, there is no hope for improvement. Talk and behavior therapy, by themselves, are useless treatment methods for schizophrenia.

- Many people suffering from psychosis have a neurological inability to appreciate that they are sick and need treatment (a condition called anosognosia). These people will resist treatment because they do not view themselves as mentally ill.

- Antipsychotic drugs used in treatment are highly efficacious and without the purported negative side effects portrayed by antipsychiatry alarmists.

- If a patient cannot be convinced to accept prescribed treatment, the physician should be allowed to initiate treatment over the patient's objection with minimal legal interference.

- Patients who adhere to continued drug treatment benefit on virtually all important personal and social measures and have lower rates of rehospitalization, criminal recidivism, and violent behavior.

COUNTERPOINT

- It is far easier for the system to lock people up and drug them into submission than it is to spend the time with them to develop a therapeutic relationship, and thus be able to engage troubled individuals with voluntary humane alternatives leading to recovery.

- Mental patients are not by definition incapable of making rational decisions, nor are they necessarily less competent than nonmentally ill medical patients.

- Forced drugging simply cannot be scientifically proven to be in a person's best interest; information is lacking about the long-term effectiveness or the possible harm associated with these drugs.

- As posited by the United States Supreme Court, involuntary commitment does nothing to enhance autonomy, but rather represents a "massive curtailment of liberty."

- Rather than providing remarkable opportunities for growth and autonomy, the system of forced psychiatry leads a tremendous number of people down a road to permanent disability and poverty.

YES Samuel J. Brakel and John M. Davis

Overriding Mental Health Treatment Refusals: How Much Process Is "Due"?

Abstract

Getting mental health treatment to patients who need it is today a much belegaled enterprise. This is in part because law makers have a skewed view of the enterprise, in particular the treatment of patients with antipsychotic medications. The properties and uses of these medications are misunderstood by many in the legal community, while the drugs' undesirable side-effects are typically overstated and the remedial effects undersold when not outright ignored. One specific legal effect has been to accord to mental patients a substantively outsized right to refuse treatment that comes with a correspondingly action-stifling dose of procedural safeguards, this despite the patients' frequent lack of capacity to exercise the right wisely and the bad personal and systemic consequences that flow from that. The purpose of this article is to provide better balanced and accurate evidence of the properties of antipsychotic drugs so as to convince law makers and advocates for the mentally disabled that it is safe to roll back some of the more counterproductive legal strictures on the effort to provide mental health treatment. . . .

I. Introduction

In 1991 the above listed authors published an article in the *Indiana Law Review* titled "Taking Harms Seriously: Involuntary Mental Patients and the Right to Refuse Treatment."[1] In it we argued that the extension to involuntarily committed mental health patients of a legal right to refuse mental health treatment (at least in the sense of its being protected by potentially multiple judicial hearings), was a legal/logical anomaly and one that had bad consequences for those patients who exercised the right, not to mention their fellow patients, the hospital doctors and the institutions in which the patients were (ware) housed. We felt, somewhat naively perhaps, that the reason the law was askew stemmed from the lack of good medical information on the part of lawyers, judges and legislators and that rectifying the situation required the presentation in an appropriate legal forum of such information. Everyone's eyes would be opened and the law would change in the direction warranted

From *bepress Legal Series,* Year 2007 Paper 1964, 2007. Reprinted with permission of the Saint Louis University Law Journal © 2008 St. Louis University School of Law, St. Louis, Missouri.

by our confidence in the medical facts—*i.e.*, that the antipsychotic drugs predominantly used in treatment were highly efficacious and without anywhere near the negative side-effects profiles portrayed by antipsychiatric alarmists. There has been some success in the realization of this hope, though pinning much or any of it on the publication/dissemination of a legal academic article would be presumptuous.[2] There has been progress in the law in the sense that the cases and statutes today are somewhat more likely than a decade or so ago to reflect an appropriate appreciation of what the medications can do (and what they won't do), in multiple contexts. Whether the issue is civil commitment and treatment (inpatient or outpatient), or treatment in the criminal justice-mandated context of competency commitments (whether pretrial or presentence) or post-conviction treatment in the prison setting, medical authority to medicate unwilling patients has overall expanded while judicial review has been relegated to a lesser and later ("postdeprivation") role—a realignment of power that one would surmise has much to do with better knowledge of the (large) benefits vs. (relatively small) costs in potential negative consequences of the medications.

At the same time, however, there has been some jurisprudential back-sliding as well, including at the U.S. Supreme Court level, (p. 5) . . . where a small number of decisions have been handed down and some language articulated that seems to give new life to what one had hoped was the moribund view of psychotropic drugs as predominantly harmful and the accompanying disbelief in the competence and integrity of doctors to appropriately prescribe them.

Given the thus still uneven, not to say precarious, lay of the legal landscape on treatment refusals, we feel it is timely to do a reprise of sorts of our 1991 article and to present once again what we believe is a true picture of the risks and benefits of antipsychotic medications. It is a picture that in many respects is and can be more optimistic than before, consistent with another set of major advances over the last 10–15 years in psychiatric medicine (in particular, the development of the so-called atypicals, a new line of antipsychotic drugs with higher benefit potential and fewer risks than the "old" medications, and continuing improvement in their usage). . . .

We will begin by presenting the new medical data because (1) it is the most significant (new) element in the debate on the matter of treatment rights, including the right to refuse it and (2) it immediately makes more intelligible what that debate is about as well as what our preferences/biases as authors are and from where these derive. We will present the research and anecdotal results documenting the heightened efficacy and the reduced possibility of untoward effects of the new antipsychotic drugs. This section of the paper will include information, new information to the extent it has been developed, on the harms, both personal and institutional, that result from withholding for legal reasons treatment that is medically indicated—in short we will present some indication at least of the costs of an inefficient legal treatment refusal regime, one that makes any conscientious and medically justified attempt to override the patient's resistance to treatment cumbersome to the point of impractical, if not impossible. . . .

II. Of Typicals and Atypicals: The Old and New Medical Data

We begin this section on the new medical data by summarizing what we said in the old article. Under the heading "Separating Myth from Reality" we first reported on a review we conducted of the legal literature on the use of psychotropic drugs—law journals as well as judicial opinions—concluding that the vast bulk of it was woefully, even willfully, misinformed about the both the drugs' risks and benefits.[3] The prevalence and severity of negative (side-) effects were almost uniformly overstated, alleged misuse of "drugging" by state physicians was played up as rampant if not the norm (embellishments/ inventions ranging from the charge that drugs were administered mostly for administrative convenience or punishment to the suggestion by analogy that it might be or at least risked being done to suppress political dissent), while the huge health benefits of proper drug usage for people with serious mental illness got no play at all (the whole helping rationale behind psychiatric treatment being simply ignored).[4] We wrote of the characteristic internal referencing aspect of this legal literature where reliance for authority was not on original medical publications but almost exclusively on a few biased analyses written by non-physicians or one or two radical antipsychiatry doctors, leading to an inevitable repetition of false information and myth or even, as in the legal cases ruled by common law precedent, the outright transformation of medical myth into legal fact.[5] . . .

One area where the law needs to adjust is the treatment of patients with antipsychotic drugs. When these drugs were first discovered in the early 1950's they were referred to as tranquilizers. The first antipsychotic drug, chlorpromazine, did have considerable sedative properties. Thence came the charge that the drugs "dulled the senses" or that they were a convenient chemical straightjacket. But even the early drugs did not act by sedation. Like the newer drugs their action is to counteract psychosis by blocking excessive dopamine in the brain, a hormone-like substance whose release in abnormal quantities is associated with "positive" psychiatric symptoms such as hallucinations and delusions.[6] While the drugs may quiet a highly agitated and excited patient, they also help restore apathetic, affect-less patients.[7] The restoration is in the nature of a regaining of cognitive skills, ideally as close as possible to normal premorbid thinking and functioning. . . .

Treatment with antipsychotic drugs is the hallmark of psychiatric treatment of patients suffering from schizophrenia and other major mental disorders. In no institution today, whether the remaining state facilities, private general hospitals or specialized facilities, the medical schools, or for that matter in the doctor's office, is psychological or psychosocial treatment alone provided. Treatment is always given with drugs. It is not true that wealthy patients get verbal psychotherapy while poor patients are drugged. The wealthy get drugs *plus* psychotherapy. Medication dispensation and management have become primary aspects of psychiatric treatment for mentally ill patients of all classes and cultures. What is seen by unknowing critics as an orgy of pill pushing is no more than a reflection of the reality that without drugs as the base treatment for schizophrenia and other psychotic disorders there is no hope for improvement. Talk and behavior therapy are still provided, but such therapy builds on the substantial degree of cognitive and emotional restoration that can be achieved with medication. Often its focus is on developing the patient's and even the family's coping skills, to sharpen recognition of the onset of an episode of the conditions, stresses that signal vulnerability, and what to do in the face of them. . . . By themselves however these treatment methods are useless for schizophrenia, potentially harmful even, particularly if used to the exclusion of needed pharmacology.[8]

Prior to the early 1950s most schizophrenic patients spent much of their life in state insane asylums. Since schizophrenia's onset is typically in adolescence, the illness took away most of the patients' normal lives. In the early 1950s, 50% of the hospital beds in the country were in massive state mental facilities located in rural areas.[9] Up to half a million mental patients filled these beds.[10] When chlorpromazine was discovered in 1953 its use spread quickly throughout the world in two or three years. Violence in state hospitals in the United States dropped by 90% almost overnight.[11] The number of patients in hospitals began to drop year by year with comparable alacrity. Today the total [number] of patients in state mental hospitals throughout the United States is less than 10% of what it was in the mid-1950s and the facilities themselves have almost completely disappeared, been restructured for new use or torn down.[12]

When good care is available and patients take their medication the majority of them can return to work or school and be productive members of society. Unfortunately, many schizophrenic patients do not have access to high quality care. The emptying of the state hospitals was accompanied by the realization that much of the treatment burden would now fall on community, mostly outpatient, programs. But the will or wherewithal to create a community treatment system equal to the task never materialized. The result is that the hope of full social rehabilitation, a theoretical possibility for many schizophrenic patients, is realized in all too few cases. For other patients it is worse than that. They may get brief treatment in a hospital or, more likely today, in a jail but they will stop taking their medication once released. Their lives will spiral downward to where episodes of active schizophrenia grow more frequent and worse and recovery is less complete with each episode. Eventually the disease process may flatten out but by then too often alcoholism, drug abuse and homelessness will have become dominant if not permanent features of the patient's existence.[13] What used to be the back wards of hospitals for these patients have today become the back streets and jails. As presently structured, the law and the courts provide little in the way of relief from this pattern.

Schizophrenia is not normally thought of as a fatal illness. The average life expectancy of schizophrenic patients is lower than that of the normal population, but many live into old age. Much of the shorter life span is attributable to a high suicide rate among people suffering from schizophrenia, as well as accidental death and the negative lifestyle effects of those who are not well cared for. In that respect, it is relevant to note that schizophrenic patients not receiving drugs die at a rate ten times higher than patients on medication.[14] . . .

[T]here is today a great deal more documented evidence of the concept of anosognosia.[15] More than just an assertion that mentally ill people sometimes lack full awareness of or adequate insight into their illness and distinct from denial as a psychologically-based defense tactic, the term is meant to describe a "biologically-based" or even "neurological" inability on the part of the sick person to appreciate that he/she is sick and needs treatment, which is a characteristic of the illness itself. It is said to afflict some 47%–57% of schizophrenic patients[16] with implications not just for health and behavior (as mentioned, untreated mental illness is strongly related to psychiatric deterioration and violence) but of course also the law's assessment of a treatment refuser's 'competence' and the desirability/wisdom of honoring his or her wishes. . . .

We also wrote of the costs of treatment delayed or denied because of the law's overprotections: individual clinical costs such as mental deterioration and the inability to recapture such psychiatric loss; institutional costs and harms on the order of increased violence in hospitals on the part of untreated patients and its effect on compliant patients and care givers; and the direct financial costs of warehousing patients before they can be treated, as well as legal process expenditures in judicially or administratively resolving treatment refusal disputes.[17]

Finally, we wrote of the "true risks of side effects" of the antipsychotic drugs (the first-generation drugs of that time), noting that on the one hand all drugs have side effects, and on the other, that as measured by both their efficacy (high but underappreciated) and their asserted bad effects (grossly overstated as to seriousness, general prevalence and particular risk to the patient or patient class) the antipsychotics predominantly used were relatively benign.[18] (p. 13) . . . [T]he risk of death from untreated psychosis, drawn from hospital studies documenting large numbers of deaths from lethal catatonia, suicide, accidents, infection and other harms that used to befall chronically psychotic patients in predrug days, was infinitely larger than from the antipsychotic drugs, a situation we analogized to the benefits of penicillin which exponentially increased medical survival rates in homes, hospitals and on the battle fields despite the fact that an allergic reaction to the drug can on occasion be fatal.[19] (p. 13) . . . To anticipate arguments about autonomy or (even) free speech, we emphasized, as we do today, the restorative properties of the drugs; that the evidence of cognitive/perceptual restoration to premorbid "normal" mental processing was substantial for many patients treated with the drugs; and the bearing this in turn should have on which of the patient's choices in what mental state to honor.[20]

This was the state of the medication treatment art in regard to what have since been called the "typicals" (*i.e.*, haloperidol, chlorpromazine, thioridazine, fluphenazine, perphenazine), the "old," "conventional" antipsychotic drugs that in the early 1990s began to be replaced by a newer line of pharmaceuticals called (of course) the "atypicals" (the forerunner clozapine and later olanzapine, quetiapine, risperidone, ziprasidone, and aripiprazole). Trials and other research on the atypicals tended to show substantial efficacy gains as well as a marked reduction in the prevalence and seriousness of undesirable side effects. . . .

The evidence also continues to accumulate and solidify that all drugs, old or new, produce major gains and help safeguard against psychiatric loss which occurs in the absence of treatment and cannot be recouped even after treatment is initiated. Recent studies document disturbingly high percentages of untreated mental illness or treatment that is interrupted against medical advice (this, in a context where the law's preoccupation continues, anachronistically, to be with alleged unneeded and unwanted treatment). A 2001 report of a National Comorbidity Survey conducted between 1990 and 1992 found that fewer than 40% of a cohort of seriously mentally ill patients received stable treatment, with the primary reason for failure to seek treatment or failing to continue being the subjects' unwillingness or inability to see the need.[21] The prognosis for these patients is a diminishing chance of amelioration or recovery as relapses mount and symptoms increase in acuity, severity (negative symptoms in particular) and resistance to remediation.[22] At the same time, studies on adherence to drug treatment, many conducted in the context of attempts to evaluate the merits of so-called outpatient commitment (OPC),[23] show the benefits of treatment and especially *continued* treatment (even for the minimally symptomatic) on virtually all important personal and social measures: *i.e.,* reduced hospital recidivism and reduced criminal recidivism/violent behavior,[24] as well as reduced victimization;[25] quality of life improvements such as measured by reduced psychiatric symptomatology and better functioning;[26] and systemic gains in terms of less discordant and more appropriate use of the mental health and correctional systems, respectively, for mentally ill people who come into contact with the law as well as appreciable gains in housing situations (reductions in homelessness).[27]

Finally, as mentioned, new findings and confirmation of older study results on anognosia, which document the relationship between schizophrenia and lack of insight as one of the latter being a neurological function/symptom of the former,[28] provide strengthening support for a best-medical-interests decision making model in mental health matters. The implications of the concept of anognosia for treatment adherence/compliance are self-evident. A person who believes he is not sick will resist treatment at all stages and levels. To the extent the implications for the person's mental health (negative, as they would be for most any untreated somatic illness) are not equally self-evident, they have been described and documented in studies such as those cited in the preceding paragraph. Last, while the details may ultimately bedevil some or many, we believe no spelling out is required of anognosia's implication *in principle* regarding the need for and propriety of the option of (legal) coercion in mental health treatment. Much as we might want, desirable as it may seem, we cannot afford to limit mental health treatment to its entirely voluntary provision and acceptance.

These then are the contemporary medical facts against whose backdrop we proceed with the analysis in the remainder of the paper.

III. Once Again: What Is the Legal Debate About?

. . . All patients have a legally, even constitutionally, protected right to refuse treatment. There is no disagreement on this and need not be. Nor, despite its constitutionally protected status, is there any doubt that this right of a patient

(p. 17) . . . in some situations must yield to superior interests, in particular the interests of treating doctors and/or those they represent. The "issue" is how much/what kind of process must be observed to override the patient's refusal, should that be considered medically necessary. This is where opinions, both legal and lay, diverge. And the legal/medical context in which the refusal is asserted will have everything to do with what the answer is or, better, as there is no consensus here, what we think the answer ought to be. This is the crux of the matter[.] . . .

VI. Legislative Process and Progress

Reports by groups favoring psychiatric intervention when needed such as the Treatment Advocacy Center (TAC)[29] suggest that in regard to inpatient commitment observable strides have been made nationally—*i.e.*, jurisdiction by jurisdiction—to impart a more medically-oriented/*parens patriae* perspective and, if not replace, to at least supplement the danger-to-others/police power focus of the earlier statutes. This has been accomplished via a revival of the need for treatment standard to suffice for commitment and an accompanying refocus of the legal lens on indicators such as psychiatric treatment history, recent decompensation, deterioration or destabilization, or even mere risk of such—all of which avoid, conceptually, the implicit emergency/police power strictures that dominate the dangerousness formulation, and should help us move away in practice from the consequent futile pattern of repetitive one-at-a-time, typically post-crisis, interventions.

As for outpatient commitment statutes, the concept underlying them is not new, but they have over the past few years swept the country in terms of increased visibility and use.[30] The objective of these laws, at least partly met according to early studies,[31] is to ensure treatment for those who otherwise resist, avoid, stop, slip-through-the-cracks-of, and "recycle" through the mental health and criminal justice systems, to their own as well as their fellow citizens' detriment. More, and especially earlier, treatment for more people who need it is the aspiration here, as is the continuation of treatment already begun given the proven benefits of adherence/compliance and the well-documented negatives associated with the interruption or cessation of the treatment regimen. The concept's ancillary virtue . . . "is that it is and has been correctly perceived by many as a lesser infringement on patients' liberty than having the treatment need met by inpatient hospitalization (or the 'police need' for segregation met by incarceration)." In other words, it is a concept on which people of differing political/philosophical persuasion and orientation—*i.e.*, those on opposite sides of the traditional advocacy divide—should be able to agree.[32] . . .

A. Increased Treatment Focus in Commitment Statutes

1. Persistence of Dangerousness as the Sole Commitment Criterion (and Four Deviations)

It is the view, correct in our opinion, that for determining the need for psychiatric intervention it is both apposite and sufficient to use psychiatric standards and terms, and not those of law enforcement. The law is not asking a secondary question here such as it does in the context of, say, the insanity defense, where the psychiatric input is meant to address cognitive or volitional capacity so as to help resolve the ultimate legal issue of accountability/culpability, or any of a number of issues where the law seeks psychiatric consultation as it were via testimony on so-called penultimate issues.[33] This is direct and ultimate: it is about treatment and treatability. The question can both be posed and answered directly, in medical terms.[34] . . .

[A] growing number of states are passing statutory provisions that premise involuntary hospitalization on a finding by the committing court that the individual proposed therefore lacks capacity to make treatment decisions . . . Such laws collapse the inquiry into need for hospitalization with the (to us, self-evident) need to be treated once hospitalized and thereby avoid the anomaly of legally sustainable treatment refusals . . .

B. Outpatient "Commitment" Laws

The judicial power to order treatment outside the institutional context has today been formalized in the laws of all but eight states in the U.S. with the passages of what are generally, if oxymoronically, known as outpatient commitment statutes.

VII. The ADA, *Olmstead* and the "Conversion" of Justice Kennedy

It must be remembered that for the person with severe mental illness who has no treatment, the most dreaded of confinements can be the imprisonment inflicted by his own mind, which shuts reality out and subjects him to the torment of voices and images beyond our powers to describe. . . . It is a common phenomenon that a patient functions well with medication, yet, because of the mental illness itself, lacks discipline or capacity to follow the regime the medication requires.[35] . . .

Conclusions

We believe that for civil commitment . . . and commitment for restoration to trial competence both the substantive standards and procedures can and should be medical. As we said at the outset, every patient or proposed patient has a right to refuse treatment if he/she does not want it. That is to say, patients as other citizens should be able to articulate their objection to prescribed treatment and that objection, if made, should be heard. Moreover, the physician who is responsible for treating the patient should try to convince the patient that the course prescribed is best for him/her or propose another course or courses that the patient finds more palatable but that, despite perhaps being suboptimal, still work(s). In short, we support the kind of therapist/patient dialogue about therapy that we will presume takes place in any hospital, community treatment center or doctor's office to the extent the patient's mental condition permits.[36]

However, if the patient cannot be convinced to accept the prescribed treatment, rejecting it and any plausible alternative courses (including trial and error), the physician should be allowed to initiate treatment over the patient's objection with minimal legal interference. That is, the only substantive criterion that need or should inform the physician's decision to proceed to treat is medical need/propriety. Inquiries into the patient's dangerousness, the government's (compelling) interest in prosecuting or any similarly diversionary issues should not be required. Procedurally, in-house medical review of the initial treatment decision should suffice to allow the primary physician to go ahead. The purpose after all of each of these commitments, simply stated even if not always simple to achieve, is to restore mental health and functioning as much and as quickly as possible[.] . . .

Judges cannot be and should not be the baseline decision makers in any of these institutional (or non-institutional), post-legal judgment phases of the treatment process. Forced treatment can begin once the medical reviewer has approved the treating physician's recommendation. Post-deprivation judicial review, after treatment has been initiated and limited by the professional judgment rule, is all the law should call for at this juncture.[37]

Notes

1. Samuel J. Brakel & John M. Davis, *Taking Harms Seriously: Involuntary Mental Patients and the Right to Refuse Treatment*, 25 *IND. L. REV.* 429 (1991).

2. Indeed, it would be demonstrably wrong. (1) What success there is has been slow in coming and uneven. (2) The article has not been cited with great frequency, its appeal apparently being limited mostly to the already converted. And (3) the achievement of significant legal change tends to require a combination of many factors and forces, among which academic writings may play a role but not usually a prominent one. . . .

3. Brakel & Davis, *supra*, note 1, at 437–438 and notes.

4. *Ibid.*

5. *Id.* at 438–440, especially note 33, citing *In re* the Mental Commitment of M.P., 510 N.E. 2d 645 (IN 1987) and *In re* Orr, 531 N.E. 2d 64 (IL 1988) as textbook examples. The earlier Indiana case had made reference to a "virtually undisputed allegation that a person medicated with antipsychotic drugs has a 50% risk of contracting tardive dyskinesia." This in fact highly disputable, if not plain erroneous (the much less alarming facts were not widely known at the time), allegation was then cited by the Illinois court in a subsequent decision as a "fact" "found" by the Indiana Supreme Court. . . .

6. There are imaging data today from living schizophrenic patients that show excessive dopamine release in the brain when the patient is having hallucinations and delusions, as well as of the blocking effect on dopamine receptors when antipsychotics are administered. *See* A. Abi-Dargam, R.Gil, J. Krystal *et al.*, *Increased Striatal Dopamine Transmission in Schizophrenia: Confirmation in a Second Cohort*, 155 *AM. J. PSYCHIATRY* 761 (1998); A. Bartolomeis, D.R. Weinberger, N. Weisenfeld *et al.*, *Schizophrenia Is Associated with Elevated Amphetamine-Induced Synaptic Dopamine Concentrations: Evidence from a Novel Positron Emission Tomography Method*, 94 *PROC. NAT'L. ACAD. SCI. U.S.A.* 2569 (1997).

7. The amotivational, apathetic, poor social skills aspects of schizophrenia are its so-called negative symptoms. Combined with cognitive/executive defects, these deficits contribute greatly to poor social and vocational functioning among people with the illness. But today's drugs can go a long way toward remedying these deficits and we have an understanding, albeit imperfect, of how they work. S. R. Marder, J.M. Davis & G. Chouinard, *The Effects of Risperidone on the Five Dimensions of Schizophrenia Derived by Factor Analysis: Combined Results of the North American Trial*, 58 *J. CLIN. PSYCHIATRY* 538 (1997); J.M. Davis & N. Chen, *Clinical Profile of an Atypical Antipsychotic: Risperidone*, 28 *SCHIZOPHRENIA BULLETIN* 43 (2002). . . .

8. It is less a matter of psychosocial treatments having no place or a lesser place in the treatment of severe mental illness today than that the treatments are entirely different. They *capitalize* today on the gains in thinking and functioning that can be achieved by the medications, as distinct from trying the impossible, which is to achieve these gains directly through verbal or behavioral therapy. *See Osherhoff v. Chestnut Lodge, Inc.* 62 Md. App. 519, 490 A.2d 720 (1985) for an early case—the reported court case merely affirms an arbitration award for allegedly negligent treatment that took place in 1979—involving the recognition that verbal therapy as such is ineffective in treating mental illness with substantial biological components, in this instance a psychotic depressive reaction, and that the failure on the part of the defendant to initiate psychopharmacologic treatments may constitute negligence. The defendant institution, Chestnut Lodge, was a facility famous for furthering psychoanalytic theory and practice, having trained a number of prominent American psychiatrists of this school, a fact which seems to have influenced the diagnosis its staff made of the plaintiff's mental health problems as much as the treatment course that was pursued in the face of unmistakable evidence that the patient was getting worse rather than better.

9. E. FULLER TORREY, *OUT OF THE SHADOWS* (1997).

10. *Ibid. See* also, H. Brill & R.E. Patton, *Population Fall in New York State Mental Hospitals in First Year of a Large-Scale Use of Tranquilizing Drugs*, 114 *AM. J. PSYCHIATRY* 509 (1957).

11. See Brill & Patton, *supra*, note 28.

12. *See OUT OF THE SHADOWS, supra*, note 27. The lawyer author of this paper conducted social/legal research in the early 1970's at Kankakee State Hospital 30 miles south of Chicago at a time when it housed some 4,000 patients. Within a few years the hospital was a relic, empty of mentally ill patients and in the process of being converted, to the extent possible, to other uses.

13. The neuropsychological deficits and the loss of grey matter seem to get worse after the patient's first psychotic episode and there is strong evidence that failure to treat the first episode with antipsychotic drugs leads to substantially worse outcome, in terms of repeat episodes and recovery therefrom, in the following five years. There is beginning evidence that at least some of the second-generation drugs in particular are effective in blocking the progression of these deficits and losses. K. Kasai, M.E. Shenton *et al., Progressive Decrease of Left Superior Temporal Gyrus Grey Matter Volume in Patients with First-Episode Schizophrenia*, 160 *AM. J. PSYCHIATRY* 156

(2003); W. Cahn, H.E. Hulshoff Poll *et al., Brain Volume Changes in First-Episode Schizophrenia: A One-Year Follow-Up Study,* 59 ARCH. GEN. PSYCHIATRY 1002 (2002). Moreover, a large study carried out in Finland, based on that country's central register, found that the risk of untreated schizophrenic patients dying was 10 times higher than that of patients on medication. J. Tiihonen, K. Wahlbeck *et al., Effectiveness of Antipsychotic Treatments in a Nationwide Cohort of Patients in Community Care after First Hospitalization Due to Schizophrenia and Schizoaffective Disorder: Observational Follow-Up Study,* 333 BRITISH MED. J. 224 (2006).

14. *Ibid.* . . .

15. Researchers most prominently identified with the concept of anosognosia, through studies conducted in the early 1990s, are psychologist Xavier Amador at Columbia University in New York and psychiatrist Anthony David at the Institute of Psychiatry in London (UK). Psychiatrist Joseph McEvoy of the University of Pittsburgh however first explicitly linked the characteristic to the illness in the 1980s. Joseph P. McEvoy *et al., Why Must Some Schizophrenic Patients Be Involuntarily Committed? The Role of Insight,* 30 COMPR. PSYCHIATRY 13 (1989); Joseph P. McEvoy *et al., Measuring Chronic Schizophrenic Patients' Attitudes Toward Their Illness and Treatment,* 32 HOSP. COMMUNITY PSYCHIATRY 856 (1981).

16. Xavier Amador *et al., Awareness of Illness in Schizophrenia and Schizoaffective and Mood Disorders,* 51 ARCHIVES GEN. PSYCHIATRY 826 (1994); Xavier Amador *et al., Awareness Deficits in Neurological Disorders and Schizophrenia* (abstract), 24 SCHIZOPHRENIA RES. 96 (1997). . . .

17. *Id.* at 453–461, under "Research Findings on the Harms Resulting from Delayed Treatment."

18. *Id.* at 461–467. . . .

19. *Ibid.* . . .

20. *Id.* at 465. . . .

21. Ronald C. Kessler, Patricia A. Berglund, Martha L. Bruce *et al., The Prevalence and Correlates of Untreated Serious Mental Illness,* 36 HEALTH SERVICES RESEARCH 978 (2001).

22. *E.g.,* Diana O. Perkins, Hongbin Gu, Kalina Boteva & Jeffrey A. Lieberman, *Relationships Between Duration of Untreated Psychosis and Outcome in First-Episode Schizophrenia: A Critical Review and Meta Analysis,* 162 AM. J. PSYCHIATRY 1785 (2005); D.A.W. Johnson, G. Pasterski, L. Ludlow *et al., The Discontinuance of Maintenance Neuroleptic Therapy in Chronic Schizophrenic Patients: Drug and Social Consequences,* 67 ACTA. PSYCHIATR. SCAND. 339 (1983); Charles M. Beasley, Jr., Virginia K. Sutton, Cindy C. Taylor *et al., Is Quality of Life Among Minimally Symptomatic Patients with Schizophrenia Better Following Withdrawal or Continuation of Antipsychotic Treatment?* 26 J. OF CLINICAL PSYCHOPHARMACOLOGY 40 (2006).

23. See section on this topic *infra* at pp.– of this paper.

24. Jeffrey W. Swanson, Randy Borum, Marvin S. Swartz, Virginia A. Hiday *et al., Can Involuntary Outpatient Commitment Reduce Arrests Among Persons with Severe Mental Illness?* 28 CRIM. JUSTICE AND BEHAVIOR 156 (2001); Jeffrey W. Swanson, Marvin S. Swartz, Randy Borum, Virginia A. Hiday *et al., Involuntary Outpatient Commitment and Reduction of Violent Behaviour in*

Persons with Severe Mental Illness, 176 *BRITISH J. OF PSYCHIATRY* 324 (2000); Marvin S. Swartz, Jeffrey W. Swanson, H. Ryan Wagner, Barbara J. Burns *et al.*, *Can Involuntary Outpatient Commitment Reduce Hospital Recidivism?: Findings from a Randomized Trial with Severely Mentally Ill Individuals*, 156 *AM. J. PSYCHIATRY* 1968 (1999).

25. Virginia A. Hiday, Marvin S. Swartz, Jeffrey W. Swanson, Randy Borum & H. Ryan Wagner, *Impact of Outpatient Commitment on Victimization of People with Severe Mental Illness*, 159 *AM. J. PSYCHIATRY* 1403 (2002).

26. Jeffrey W. Swanson, Marvin S. Swartz, Eric B. Elbogen *et al.*, *Effects of Involuntary Outpatient Commitment on Subjective Quality of Life in Persons with Severe Mental Illness*, 21 *BEHAV. SCIENCES AND THE LAW* 473 (2003).

27. Haya Ascher-Svanum, Douglas E. Faries, Baojin Zhu *et al.*, *Medication Adherence and Long-Term Functional Outcomes in the Treatment of Schizophrenia in Usual Care*, 67 *J. OF CLINICAL PSYCHIATRY* 453 (2006).

28. See Amador and McEvoy articles, *supra.* Also, Joseph P. McEvoy, Paul S. Appelbaum, L. Joy Apperson *et al.*, *Why Must Some Schizophrenic Patients Be Involuntarily Committed? The Role of Insight*, 30 *COMPR. PSYCHIATRY* 13 (1989); Anthony S. David, *Insight and Psychosis*, 156 *BRITISH J. OF PSYCHIATRY* 798 (1990); Xavier F. Amador, David H. Strauss, Scott A. Yale & Jack M. Gorman, *Awareness of Illness in Schizophrenia*, 17 *SCHIZOPHRENIA BULLETIN* 113 (1991); Faith B. Dickerson, John J. Boronow, Norman Ringel & Frederick Parente, *Lack of Insight Among Outpatients with Schizophrenia*, 48 *PSYCHIATRIC SERVICES* 195 (1997); Xavier F. Amador & Regina A. Seckinger, *The Assessment of Insight: A Methodological Review*, 27 *PSYCHIATRIC ANNALS* 798 (1997); Graig Goodman, Gabriella Knoll, Victoria Isakov & Henry Silver, *Insight into Illness in Schizophrenia*, 46 *COMPR. PSYCHIATRY* 284 (2005).

29. See the *CATALYST* (Newsletter of the Treatment Advocacy Center) Spring/ Summer 2004. TAC also maintains a website, www.psychlaws.org, on which it provides, *i.e.*, updates on the latest legislative reforms. TAC advocates refer to the process as "assisted outpatient treatment" (AOT) which apart from deemphasizing the nonconsensual aspects of "outpatient commitment" also has the advantage of avoiding its oxymoronic quality, the term commitment being associated with confinement in an institution, *i.e.*, being an *in*patient.

30. *Ibid.*

31. *CATALYST,* Spring/Summer 2005 at 7 and 15. The latter page presents "real-world results" on New York's Kendra's law under the title "Kendra's Law families and participants laud program: Report shows sharp reductions in hospitalizations, incarcerations, homelessness." The TAC group points to a number of other studies supporting the notion that the outpatient commitment laws have achieved their intended effects: Guido Zanni & Leslie deVeau, *Inpatient Stays Before and After Outpatient Commitment*, 37 *HOSP. & CMTY PSYCHIATRY* 941 (1986); M.R. Munetz *et al.*, *The Effectiveness of Outpatient Civil Commitment*, 47 *Psychiatric Services* 1251 (1996); B.M. Rohland, *The Role of Outpatient Commitment in the Management of Persons with Schizophrenia*, IOWA CONSORTIUM FOR MENTAL HEALTH SERVICES, TRAINING, AND RESEARCH (1998); and Gustavo A. Fernandez & Sylvia Nygard, *Impact of Involuntary Outpatient Commitment on the Revolving-Door*

Syndrome in North Carolina, 41 *HOSP. & CMTY PSYCHIATRY* 1001 (1990). Later studies in North Carolina have been especially persuasive in documenting positive effects of mandated outpatient treatment in various respects. *See* (the titles are indicative) Marvin S. Swartz, Jeffrey W. Swanson, H. Ryan Wagner *et al., Can Involuntary Outpatient Commitment Reduce Hospital Recidivism?* 156 *AM. J. PSYCHIATRY* 1986 (1999); Jeffrey W. Swanson, Marvin S. Swartz, R. Borum *et al., Involuntary Outpatient Commitment and Reduction in Violent Behaviour in Persons with Severe Mental Illness,* 176 *BRIT. J. PSYCHIAT.* 224 (2000); Jeffrey W. Swanson, R. Borum, Marvin S. Swartz *et al., Can Involuntary Outpatient Commitment Reduce Arrests among Persons with Severe Mental Illness?* 28 *CRIM. JUSTICE & BEHAVIOR* 156 (2001); Virginia A. Hiday, Marvin S. Swartz, Jeffrey W. Swanson *et al., Impact of Outpatient Commitment on Victimization of People with Severe Mental Illness,* 159 *AM. J. PSYCHIAT.* 1403 (2002). . . .

32. **In theory at least.** A recent article by Richard J. Bonnie and John Monahan, *From Coercion to Contract: Reframing the Debate on Mandated Community Treatment for People with Mental Disorders,* 29 *LAW AND HUMAN BEHAVIOR* 485 (2005), confirms (by the title alone) that there is much less agreement on the value of the concept than its proponents once optimistically believed. See also note 277, *supra.* . . .

33. The law has gone back and forth on whether it is appropriate for mental health experts to offer testimony on ultimate legal issues, with the post-Hinckley reforms following the acquittal by reason of insanity of President Reagan's would-be assassin, enacted in 1984 for the federal courts, leading the way toward the currently dominant position of disallowing it.

34. It has been pointed out innumerable times by both judges and legal commentators that commitment is a social/legal decision rather than a medical one, but this does not alter the fact that medical criteria and medical facts are what that social/legal decision should be heavily based on. . . .

35. *Id.* at 609–610.

36. The law is allowed to, should in fact, assume basic medical/institutional realities including such that there ordinarily is communication about treatment prospects and plans between therapist and patient. As distinct from case law drawn from litigation where worst-case evidence is introduced, the statutory or regulatory law ordinarily need not and should not be written based on worst-case scenarios. *Cf.* the discussion of *Rennie v. Klein* in the text, *supra,* at pp.– where we reproduce the administrative regulation—presumptively a codification of practices—guiding doctors in New Jersey on how to approach patients who resist prescribed treatment. Substantively, the regulation in fact incorporates the least intrusive/least restrictive principle and its procedural mandates suggest abundant deference to the patient's preferences via the physician's stated obligation to discuss alternatives with the patient, to try make the patient understand and to encourage voluntary acceptance (with the help of relatives and friends if so indicated) before seeking approval from the hospital medical director to proceed over the patient's objections. . . .

37. Postdeprivation judicial review should suffice because (1) judges have no expertise in medical matters and therefore should not be baseline (first-instance) decision makers and (2) the costs in time and treatment foregone, deflection of resources, and institutional bad effects of the judiciary's failing to show proper deference to medical professionals are large.

James B. Gottstein **NO**

How the Legal System Can Help Create a Recovery Culture in Mental Health Systems

Summary

The purpose of this paper is to show how strategic litigation can and should be a part of efforts to transform mental health systems to a culture of recovery. Currently, involuntary commitment and forced drugging are by far the "path of least resistance" when society is faced with someone who is disturbing and their thinking does not conform to society's norms.[1] In other words, it is far easier for the system to lock people up and drug them into submission, than it is to spend the time with them to develop a therapeutic relationship and thus able to engage the person with voluntary humane alternatives leading to recovery.[2] I estimate that 10% of involuntary commitments in the United States and none of the forced drugging under the *parens patriae* doctrine[3] are legally justified. This presents a tremendous opportunity to use litigation to "encourage" the creation of voluntary, recovery-oriented services.[4]

In my view, though, in order to be successful various myths of mental illness need to be debunked among the general public and humane, effective recovery oriented, noncoercive alternatives must be made available. . . . The thesis of this paper is that strategic litigation (and public education) are likely essential to transforming the mental health system to one of a recovery culture. . . .

For example, debunking the myth among the general public that people do not recover from a diagnosis of serious mental health illness can encourage the willingness to invest in recovery-oriented alternatives. Similarly, having successful, recovery-oriented alternatives will help in debunking the myth that people don't recover from serious mental illness. In like fashion, judges and even counsel appointed to represent psychiatric defendants believe the myth "if this person wasn't crazy, she would know these drugs are good for her" and therefore don't let her pesky rights get in the way of doing the "right thing," i.e., forced drugging. The myth of dangerousness results in people being locked up. In other words, the judges and lawyers reflect society's views and to the extent that society's views change, the judges and lawyers' responses will change to suit. That leads to taking people's rights more seriously. The converse is true as well. Legal cases can have a big impact on public views. *Brown v. Board of Education,*[5] which resulted in outlawing segregation is a classic example of this. Finally, the involuntary mental illness system[6] operates largely illegally, including through its failure to offer less restrictive alternatives.[7] Thus, litigation can force the creation of such alternatives. At the same time, as a practical matter, the availability of acceptable (to the person) recovery-oriented alternatives are necessary for anyone to actually be able to get such services when faced with involuntary commitment and forced drugging.

The Involuntary Mental Illness System Operates Largely Illegally

Involuntary "treatment"[8] in the United States largely operates illegally in that court orders for forced treatment are obtained without actual compliance with statutory and constitutional requirements. One of the fundamental constitutional rights that is ignored in practice is that of a "less restrictive alternative."[9] Thus, enforcement of this right through the courts can be instrumental in bringing about change. First, I will discuss the key constitutional principles. . . .

Constitutional Limits on Involuntary Commitment

The United States Supreme Court has recongnized for a long time that involuntary civil commitment is a "massive curtailment of liberty"[10] requiring substantive due process protection:

> Freedom from bodily restraint has always been at the core of the liberty protected by the Due Process Clause from arbitrary governmental action. "It is clear that commitment for any purpose constitutes a significant deprivation of liberty that requires due process protection."[11]

Constitutional Limits on Forced Drugging

The United States Supreme Court has also held a number of times that being free of unwanted psychiatric medication is a fundamental constitutional right.[15] In the most recent case, *Sell,* the United States Supreme Court reiterated:

> [A]n individual has a "significant" constitutionally protected "liberty interest" in "avoiding the unwanted administration of antipsychotic drugs."[16] . . .

The Massachusetts Supreme Judicial Court has held people have the absolute right to decline medication unless they are incompetent to make such a decision and if they are incompetent they cannot be medicated against their will except by a court made Substituted Judgment Decision that includes the following factors:

1. The patient's expressed preferences regarding treatment.
2. The strength of the incompetent patient's religious convictions, to the extent that they may contribute to his refusal of treatment.

3. The impact of the decision on the ward's family—this factor being primarily relevant when the patient is part of a closely knit family.
4. The probability of adverse side effects.
5. The prognosis without treatment.
6. The prognosis with treatment.
7. Any other factors which appear relevant." . . .

[I]n *Rivers v. Katz*,[24] decided strictly on common law and constitutional due process grounds, New York's highest court held a person's right to be free from unwanted antipsychotic medication is a constitutionally protected liberty interest:

[I]f the law recognizes the right of an individual to make decisions about . . . life out of respect for the dignity and autonomy of the individual, that interest is no less significant when the individual is mentally or physically ill.

We reject any argument that the mere fact that appellants are mentally ill reduces in any manner their fundamental liberty interest to reject antipsychotic medication. We likewise reject any argument that involuntarily committed patients lose their liberty interest in avoiding the unwanted administration of antipsychotic medication.

If . . . the court determines that the patient has the capability to make his own treatment decisions, the State shall be precluded from administering antipsychotic drugs. If, however, the court concludes that the patient lacks the capacity to determine the course of his own treatment, the court must determine whether the proposed treatment is narrowly tailored to give substantive effect to the patient's liberty interest, taking into consideration all relevant circumstances, including the patient's best interests, the benefits to be gained from the treatment, the adverse side effects associated with the treatment and any less intrusive alternative treatments. The State would bear the burden to establish by clear and convincing evidence that the proposed treatment meets these criteria. . . .

[I]n practice, people's rights are not being honored.[25] There are other states which have just as good legal rights and some that don't under state law, but the common denominator in all of them is whatever rights people have, they are uniformly ignored." . . .

In *Sell*, decided in 2003, the United States Supreme Court held someone could not be force drugged to make them competent to stand trial unless:

1. The court finds that *important* governmental interests are at stake.

2. The court must conclude that involuntary medication will *significantly further* those concomitant state interests.
3. The court must conclude that involuntary medication is *necessary* to further those interests. The court must find that any alternative, less intrusive treatments are unlikely to achieve substantially the same results.
4. The court must conclude that administration of the drugs is *medically appropriate*, i.e., in the patient's best medical interest in light of his medical condition. The specific kinds of drugs at issue may matter here as elsewhere. Different kinds of antipsychotic drugs may produce different side effects and enjoy different levels of success.

(italics in original) These are general constitutional principles and should apply in the civil context. Thus, for example, while in *Sell*, the "*important* governmental interest" is in bringing a criminal defendant to trial, the governmental interest in the civil context is (supposedly) the person's best interest, i.e., the *parens patriae* doctrine.[26]

With respect to the second requirement that the forced drugging "will *significantly further*" those interests, the question in the competence to stand trial context is whether the forced drugging is likely to make the person competent to stand trial, while in the civil context, the question is whether it is in the person's best interest or is the decision the person would make if he or she were competent.

The third requirement that the forced drugging must be *necessary* and there is no less restrictive alternative is hugely important in the civil context because it is a potential lever to require less restrictive (i.e., non-drug, recovery-oriented alternatives). It is important to note here that failure to find these alternatives does not give the government the right to force drug someone. If a less restrictive alternative could be made available, the forced drugging is unconstitutional.[27] . . .

The fourth requirement is also very important because it essentially requires the state to prove the drugging is in the person's best interest and not merely recite "professional judgment."

The take-away message is, in my view, people are constitutionally entitled to noncoercive, nondrugging, recovery-oriented alternatives before involuntary commitment and forced drugging can occur and even then forced drugging can only constitutionally occur if it is in the person's best interest. There are a couple of ways to look at this since the reality is so far from what the law requires. One is to see it as a tremendous opportunity to improve the situation. The other is that there are forces operating to totally defeat people's rights. Both are true and this paper suggests there are actions that can be taken to have people's rights honored that can play a crucial part in transforming the mental health system to one of a recovery culture.

Proper Procedures and Evidentiary Standards

Mentioned above are the United States Supreme Court rulings that involuntary commitment can occur only pursuant to proper procedures and evidentiary standards. In contrast to this legal requirement, involuntary commitment and forced drugging proceedings can quite fairly be characterized as a sham, a farce, Kangaroo Courts, etc., in the vast majority of cases.[29] . . .

Proper Procedures . . .

Proper evidentiary standards.   . . . [I]involuntary commitment is constitutionally permissible only if the person is a harm to self or others as a result of a "mental illness." In *Addington v. Texas*[33] the United States held that this has to be proven by "clear and convincing evidence," which is less than "'beyond a reasonable doubt,'" but more than the normal "preponderance of the evidence"[34] standard in most civil cases. . . .

The truth is psychiatric testimony as to a person's dangerousness is highly unreliable with a high likelihood of overestimating dangerousness.

> The voluminous literature as to the ability of psychiatrists (or other mental health professionals) to testify reliably as to an individual's dangerousness in the indeterminate future had been virtually unanimous: "psychiatrists have absolutely no expertise in predicting dangerous behavior—indeed, they may be less accurate predictors than laymen—and that they usually err by overpredicting violence."[37]

This is the primary reason why I estimate only 10% of involuntary commitments are legally justified. If people were only involuntarily committed when it can be shown, by clear and convincing evidence, under scientifically reliable methods of predicting the requisite harm to self or others, my view is 90% of current commitments would not be granted.

With respect to forced drugging, one of the prerequisites is the person must be found to be incompetent to decline the drug(s). Here, too, psychiatrists, to be kind, overestimate incompetence.

> [M]ental patients are not always incompetent to make rational decisions and are not inherently more incompetent than nonmentally ill medical patients.[38] . . .

The reason why I believe no forced drugging in the civil context is legally justified is it simply cannot be scientifically proven it is in a person's best interest.[40] It would make this paper even more too long than it already is to fully support this assertion, but some will be presented. First, there is really no doubt the current overreliance on the drugs is at least doubling the number of people becoming defined by the system as chronically mentally ill with it recently being estimated it has increased the rate of disability due to "mental Illness" six-fold.[41] In the case where we litigated the issue in Alaska, the trial court found:

> The relevant conclusion that I draw from [the evidence presented by the Respondent's experts] is that there is a real and viable debate among

qualified experts in the psychiatric community regarding whether the standard of care for treating schizophrenic patients should be the administration of antipsychotic medication.

_◦✦◦_

[T]here is a viable debate in the psychiatric community regarding whether administration of this type of medication might actually cause damage to her or ultimately worsen her condition.[42]

A recent study in Ireland concluded the already elevated risk for death in schizophrenia due to the older neuroleptics was doubled with the newer, so-called "atypical" neuroleptics, such as Zyprexa and Risperdal.[43] More information on these drugs can be found on PsychRights' website. . . .

In sum, my view is the state can never (or virtually never) actually meet its burden of proving forced drugging is in a person's best interest (assuming that is required) because of the lack of long-term effectiveness and great harm they cause. Again, this raises the question of why forced drugging is so pervasive and what might be done about it. In other words, it is an opportunity for strategic litigation playing a key role in a transformation to a recovery-oriented system.

Corrupt Involuntary Mental "Treatment" System

As set forth above, people are locked up under judicial findings of dangerousness and force drugged based on it being in their best interests without any legitimate scientific evidence of either dangerousness or the drugs being in a person's best interests. As Professor Michael Perlin has noted:

[C]ourts accept . . . testimonial dishonesty, . . . specifically where witnesses, especially expert witnesses, show a "high propensity to purposely distort their testimony in order to achieve desired ends." . . .

Experts frequently . . . and openly subvert statutory and case law criteria that impose rigorous behavioral standards as predicates for commitment. . . .

This combination . . . helps define a system in which (1) dishonest testimony is often regularly (and unthinkingly) accepted; (2) statutory and case law standards are frequently subverted; and (3) insurmountable barriers are raised to insure that the allegedly "therapeutically correct" social end is met. . . . In short, the mental disability law system often deprives individuals of liberty disingenuously and upon bases that have no relationship to case law or to statutes.[44]

In other words, testifying psychiatrists lie,[45] the trial (but generally not appellate) courts don't care, and lawyers assigned to represent defendants in these cases, are "woefully inadequate—disinterested, uninformed, roleless, and often hostile. A model of "'paternalism/best interests'" is substituted for a traditional legal advocacy position, and this substitution is rarely questioned."[46]

Counsel appointed to represent psychiatric defendants is more often than not, actually working for the other side, or barely put up even a token defense, which amounts to the same thing.[47]

No one in the legal system is taking psychiatric defendants' rights seriously, including the lawyer appointed to represent the person. There are two reasons for this: The first is the belief that "if this person wasn't crazy, she'd know this is good for her." The second is the system is driven by irrational fear. All the evidence shows people who end up with psychiatric labels are no more likely to be dangerous than the general population and that medications increase the overall relapse rate, yet society's response has been to lock people up, and whether locked up or not, force them to take these drugs.[48] . . .

The Requirement and Necessity of Alternatives

Hopefully it is apparent from the foregoing that people should be allowed (less restrictive) alternatives when they are faced with forced drugging. The same is basically true of involuntary commitment.[55] These alternatives, I suggest, should primarily include noncoercive, for sure, and nondrug alternatives that are known to lead to recovery for many people.[56] The reality is likely a "which came first, the chicken or the egg?" situation, because judges will be reluctant to deny petitions for forced drugging on the basis that a less restrictive alternative could be made available, but in fact is not available. Thus, the actual availability of alternatives is important. However, where sufficient legal pressure is applied, the courts will simply not be able to order forced drugging. I know these are contradictory statements, but that is why they reinforce each other as set forth above (and below).

[A]s set forth above, everyone has the absolute constitutional right to decline psychiatric drugs, with one exception, which is if they are incompetent to do so. Currently, the competency determinations are not legitimate and Advance Directives are ignored. One reason I would posit, is that the system simply does not know what else to do with people so the system deals with it by finding people incompetent when they are not. . . .

The Importance of Public Opinion

It is perhaps easier to see how Public Education and the Availability of Alternatives reinforce each other. Alternatives to the hopelessness driven, medication only, stabilization-oriented system are not available because our society believes it is the only possibility, in spite of all kinds of evidence to the contrary. Thus, to the extent effective alternatives become known to society in general, these alternatives will become desired by society because they produce much more desired outcomes. Not only do people get better, but huge amounts of money will be saved by more than halving the number of people who become a permanent ward of government. At the same time, having successful Alternatives will show society that they are viable. Thus, as with the Availability of Alternatives and Honoring Legal Rights, they reinforce each other. . . .

Interplay Between Public Education and Honoring Legal Rights

As set forth above, the judges and even the lawyers representing people facing forced psychiatry accept the current societal view that people need to be locked up and forcibly drugged for society's and the person's own safety and best interests. To the extent society becomes aware this is not true, the judicial system will reflect that and be much more willing to honor people's rights. . . .

Requirements for Successful Litigation— Attorneys & Expert Witnesses

The building blocks for mounting successful strategic litigation are recruiting attorneys who will put forth a serious effort to discharge their ethical duties to their clients and expert witnesses who can prove the junk science behind current "treatment" and the effectiveness of recovery-oriented alternatives.

Types of Legal Actions . . .

Establishing the Right to Effective Assistance of Counsel

If people's rights were being honored, the problem of forced psychiatry would be mostly solved and this would absolutely force society to come up with alternatives—hopefully recovery oriented. Thus, challenges to the effectiveness of counsel should be made. In light of the current state of affairs, there seems little downside to trying to get the United States Supreme Court to hold it is a right under the United States Constitution. I also believe that ethics complaints should be brought against the attorneys who do not discharge their duty to zealously represent their clients. If every involuntary commitment and forced drugging hearing were zealously represented, each case should take at least half a day. In my view it takes that long to fully challenge the state's case and present the patient's. This, in itself, would encourage the system to look for alternatives (the "path of least resistance" principle).

Challenges to State Proceedings

States that proceed under the "professional judgment" rule should be challenged. The right to state paid expert witnesses should be pursued. The right to less restrictive alternatives should be pursued. Challenges to "expert witness" opinion testimony regarding dangerousness and competence should be made. Challenges to *ex parté* proceedings should be made. There are a myriad of challenges that can be made in the various states, depending on the statutes and procedures utilized in them.[58] . . .

Public Attitudes

Even though this paper is about the court's potential role in transforming mental health systems to a recovery culture, it seems worthwhile to also make a few comments about changing public attitudes. There is an historic opportunity right now to make substantial inroads against the Psychopharmacology/Psychiatric hegemony because of the revelations in the media regarding dangerous, ineffective drugs, but this must be seized or it will be lost. **A serious public education program must be mounted.**

An Effective Public Relations Campaign

In the main, perhaps unduplicated for any other issue, the power of the Psychopharmacology/Psychiatric hegemony has so controlled the message that the media tends not to even acknowledge there is another side. For most issues, the media will present at least one spokesperson from each side. However, when the latest questionable breakthrough in mental illness research or "treatment" is announced, the other side is not even presented. One might want to pass this off as Big Pharma advertising money infecting the news departments, but I think that is way too simplistic and perhaps even largely untrue. . . .

Alternatives

It also seems worthwhile to spend a little bit of space here on creating alternatives. Ultimately, in order to be successful, alternatives need to be funded by the public system.[75] One argument in its favor that should be attractive to government (but has not heretofore been) in the current system is breaking the bank. As Whitaker has shown, the disability rate for mental illness has increased six-fold since the introduction of Thorazine.[76] Making so many people permanently disabled and financially supported by the government, rather than working and supporting the government, is not only a huge human tragedy, but is also a massive, unnecessary governmental expense.

One of the simplest, but very important things that should be done is to compile a readily accessible, accurate, list of existing alternatives and efforts to get them going. I have seen lists of alternatives, but then I hear that this program or that is really not a true nondrugging and/or noncoercive alternative. It would be extremely helpful for there to be a description of each such program with enough investigation to know what is really happening. . . .

Conclusion

A final word about the importance of the potential role of the courts and the forced psychiatry issue. While it is true that many, even maybe most, people in the system are not under court orders at any given time, it is my view that the forced psychiatry system is what starts a tremendous number of people on the road to permanent disability (and poverty) and drives the whole public system. Of course, coercion to take the drugs is pervasive outside of court orders too, but again I see the legal coercion as a key element. If people who are now being dragged into forced psychiatry were given, noncoercive, recovery-oriented options, they would also become available for the people who are not subject to forced psychiatry. I hope this paper has conveyed the role that strategic litigation can play in transforming mental health systems to a culture of recovery.

Notes

1. By phrasing it this way, I am not disputing that people become psychotic. I have been there. . . . However, there are lots of degrees—a continuum, if you will—and there are different ways of looking at these unaccepted ways of thinking, or altered states of consciousness. So, what I mean by this terminology is that people are faced with involuntary commitment and forced drugging when two conditions exist: One, they are bothering another person(s), including concern about the risk of suicide or other self-harm, and two, they are expressing thoughts that do not conform to those accepted "normal" by society. Of course, this ignores the reality that a lot of both are often trumped up, especially against people who have previously been subjected to the system.

2. The system believes it is also less expensive, but the opposite is actually true. The overreliance on neuroleptics and, increasingly, polypharmacy, has at least doubled the number of people who become permanently reliant on government transfer payments. In *Anatomy of an Epidemic: Psychiatric Drugs and the Astonishing Rise of Mental Illness in America,* which is available at . . . Robert Whitaker demonstrates the rate of disability has increased six-fold since the introduction of Thorazine in the mid '50s. The Michigan State Psychotherapy Project demonstrated extremely more favorable long-term outcomes for those receiving psychotherapy alone from psychotherapists with *relevant* training and experience. The short-term costs were comparable to the standard treatment and the long-term savings were tremendous. This study can be found at. . . .

3. "Parens Patriae" is legal Latin, literally meaning "parent of his or her country." *Black's Law Dictionary,* seventh edition defines it as "the state in its capacity as provider of protection to those unable to care for themselves." It is invoked with respect to minors and adults who are deemed incompetent to make their own decisions. In the context of forced drugging under the *parens patriae* doctrine, it basically is based on the notion, "If you weren't crazy, you'd know this was good for you."

4. At the same time there are impediments to doing so, primarily the lack of legal resources.

5. U.S. 294, 75 S.Ct. 753, 99 L.Ed. 1083 (1955).

6. In light of the system basically creating massive numbers of people who become categorized as chronically mentally ill, I call it the mental illness system, rather than the mental health system.

7. By saying the mental illness system operates largely illegally I mean that to the extent people are locked up and forcibly drugged when the statutory and constitutional requirements are not being met, that is illegal. Of course, this is done by filing paperwork and getting court orders, which looked at another way, makes it legal.

8. "Treatment" is in quotes because it is both (1) pretty clear the current, virtually exclusive reliance on psychiatric drugs by the public mental illness system hinders recovery for the vast majority of people, and (2) if it isn't voluntary, it isn't treatment.

9. *See*, e.g., *Sell v. United States*, 539 U.S. 166 (2003). However, not everyone agrees with my legal analysis of the right to the least restrictive alternative.

10. *Humphrey v. Cady*, 405 U.S. 504 (1972).

11. *Addington v. Texas*, 441 U.S. 418 (1979).

15. *Mills v. Rogers*, 457 U.S. 291 (1982); *Washington v. Harper*, 494 U.S. 210 (1990; *Riggins v. Nevada*, 504 U.S. 127 (1992); and *Sell v. United States*, 539 U.S. 166 (2003).

16. *Sell v. United States*, 539 U.S. 166, 177-8 (2003), citing to the Due Process Clause, U.S. Const., amend. 5, and *Washington v. Harper*, 494 U.S. 210, 110 S.Ct. 1028 (1990).

24. *Rivers v. Katz*, 495 N.E.2d 337, 341-3 (NY 1986).

25. *See*, Mental Hygiene Law Court Monitoring Project: Part 1 of Report: Do Psychiatric Inmates in New York Have the Right to Refuse Drugs? An Examination of Rivers Hearings in the Brooklyn Court, which can be accessed on the Internet at. . . .

26. I say, "supposedly," because in truth, controlling the person's behavior is a primary interest. "Police power" justification, which actually is based on controlling dangerous behavior, has also been used to justify forced drugging. *See*, *Rivers v. Katz*, 495 N.E.2d 337, 343 (NY 1986). However, the behavior presumably has to be very extreme to invoke "police power" and is not normally the stated basis for seeking forced drugging orders. It has been suggested there is an important government interest in ending indeterminate commitment and returning the individual to society, which can be done most effectively if the person is required to take the prescribed drugs. However, this is not the basis normally asserted and I would argue it is not a sufficient interest to override a person's rights to decline the drugs, particularly in light of the physical harms they cause.

27. There are likely limits on this, such as there being no requirement for Herculean efforts or where the cost is prohibitive. *See*, e.g., *Mathews v. Eldridge*, 424 U.S. 319, 334–35 (1976). . . .

29. An example is described in the recent Alaska Supreme Court brief we filed in *Wetherhorn v. Alaska Psychiatric Institute*, which can be found on the Internet at. . . .

33. 441 U.S. 418 (1979).

34. "Preponderance of the evidence," means more likely than not or, put another way, it only requires the balance to be slightly more on one side than the other. Yet another way to look at it is it just has to be more than 50% likely. . . .

37. Michael L. Perlin, *Mental Disability Law: Civil and Criminal*, §2A-4.3c, p. 109 (2d. Ed. 1998), footnotes omitted. *See*, also, Morris, Pursuing Justice for the Mentally Disabled, 42 San Diego L. Rev. 757, 764 (2005) ("Recent studies confirm [] that psychotic symptoms, such as delusions or hallucinations, currently being experienced by a person, do not elevate his or her risk of violence.")

38. Perlin, "And My Best Friend, My Doctor/Won't Even Say What It Is I've Got: The Role And Significance Of Counsel In Right To Refuse Treatment Cases," 42 *San Diego Law Review* 735, 746–7 (2005), citing to Thomas Grisso & Paul S. Appelbaum, *The MacArthur Treatment Competence Study. III: Abilities of Patients to Consent to Psychiatric and Medical Treatments*, 19 *Law & Hum. Behav.* 149 (1995). . . .

40. While I believe this is true in the forced drugging context in terms of meeting the legal burden of justifying overriding a person's right to decline the medications, and I know this paper comes off as a polemic against psychiatric drugs, I absolutely believe people also have the right to choose to take them. I do think people should be fully informed about them, of course, which is normally not done, but that is a different issue. Not surprisingly, in a study of people who have recovered after being diagnosed with serious mental illness, those who felt the drugs helped them, used them in their recovery and those that didn't find them helpful, didn't use the drugs in their recovery. "How do We Recover? An Analysis of Psychiatric Survivor Oral Histories," by Oryx Cohen, in *Journal of Humanistic Psychology*, Vol. 45, No. 3, Summer 2005, 333–35, which is available on the Internet at. . . .

41. Anatomy of an Epidemic: Psychiatric Drugs and the Astonishing Rise of Mental Illness in America, by Robert Whitaker, *Ethical Human Psychology and Psychiatry*, Volume 7, Number I: 23–35 Spring 2005, which can be accessed on the Internet at. . . .

42. Order, in *In the Matter of the Hospitalization of Faith Myers,* Anchorage Superior Court, Third Judicial District, State of Alaska, Case No. 3AN-03-277 PR, March 14, 2003, pp. 8, 13, which can be accessed on the Internet at. . . .

43. Prospective analysis of premature mortality in schizophrenia in relation to health service engagement: a 7.5-year study within an epidemiologically complete, homogeneous population in rural Ireland, by Maria G. Morgan, Paul J. Scully, Hanafy A. Youssef, Anthony Kinsellac, John M. Owensa, and John L. Waddingtona, *Psychiatry Research* 117 (2003) 127–135, which can be found on the Internet at. . . .

44. *The ADA and Persons with Mental Disabilities: Can Sanist Attitudes Be Undone? Journal of Law and Health,* 1993/1994, 8 *JLHEALTH* 15, 33–34.

45. "It would probably be difficult to find any American Psychiatrist working with the mentally ill who has not, at a minimum, exaggerated the dangerousness of a mentally ill person's behavior to obtain a judicial order for commitment." Torrey, E. Fuller. 1997. *Out of the Shadows: Confronting America's Mental Illness Crisis*, New York: John Wiley and Sons, page 152. Dr. Torrey goes on to say this lying to the courts is a good thing. Of course, lying in court is perjury. Dr. Torrey also quotes psychiatrist Paul Applebaum as saying when "confronted with psychotic persons who might well benefit from treatment, and who would certainly suffer without it, mental health professionals and judges alike were reluctant to comply with the law," noting that in "'the dominance of the commonsense model,' the laws are sometimes simply disregarded."

46. Perlin, *"And My Best Friend, My Doctor/Won't Even Say What It Is I've Got": The Role And Significance Of Counsel In Right To Refuse Treatment Cases*, 42 *San Diego Law Review* 735, 738 (2005).

47. This is a violation of professional ethics. For example, the Comment to the Model Rules of Professional Conduct for attorneys, Rule 1.3, includes, "A lawyer should pursue a matter on behalf of a client despite opposition, obstruction or personal inconvenience to the lawyer, and take whatever lawful and ethical measures are required to vindicate a client's cause or endeavor. A lawyer must also act with commitment and dedication to the interests of the client and with zeal in advocacy upon the client's behalf."

48. "Kendra's Law" in New York is a classic example of this. There a person who had been denied numerous attempts to obtain mental health services pushed Kendra in front of a moving subway and when he was grabbed, said something like "now maybe I will get some help." The response was to pass an outpatient commitment law requiring people to take psychiatric drugs or be locked up in the hospital. This is a characterization, but when this was challenged, New York's high court ruled Kendra's Law didn't require people to take the drugs; that all it did was subject people to "heightened scrutiny" for involuntary commitment if they didn't. *See, In the Matter of K.L.*, 806 N.E.2d 480(NY 2004). . . .

55. Many state statutes certainly require it, and I would suggest it is constitutionally required as well.

56. *See*, Effective Non-Drug Treatments, which can be found on the Internet at. . . .

58. For example, I have identified a lot of things under Alaska law where I think valid challenges to what is going on can and should be made. . . .

75. However, I am also in favor of non-system alternatives.

76. *See*, Anatomy of an Epidemic: Psychiatric Drugs and the Astonishing Rise of Mental Illness in America, which is available at. . . .

CHALLENGE QUESTIONS

Is Forced Treatment of Seriously Mentally Ill Individuals Justifiable?

1. What legal protections can be put in place, and what specific procedures followed, to protect the right of individuals to make choices affecting their psychological and physical well-being?
2. What arguments can be made to support the idea that mental health professionals should be accorded the legal right to administer treatments against the will of a mentally ill person?
3. To what extent should family members of a seriously mentally ill individual be given the right to approve treatment for a loved one who is resisting such intervention?
4. In cases in which an involuntarily treated patient begins to recover from symptoms, how should decisions be made by mental health professionals to respect the prerogative of the patient to stop the treatment?
5. How would you go about designing a study to evaluate the psychological impact on individuals for whom treatment has been involuntarily administered?

Suggested Readings

Bassman, R. (2005). Mental illness and the freedom to refuse treatment: Privilege or right. *Professional Psychology: Research and Practice, 36*(5), 488–497.

Fritz, M. (2006, February 1). A Doctor's fight: More forced care for the mentally ill. *The Wall Street Journal*, p. A1.

Torrey, E. F. (2007, April 27). Commitment phobia. *The Wall Street Journal*, p. A17.

Treatment Advocacy Center (Spring, 2006). *Catalyst*. Arlington, VA: Treatment Advocacy Center.

ISSUE 4

Should Individuals with Anorexia Nervosa Have the Right to Refuse Life-Sustaining Treatment?

YES: Heather Draper, from "Anorexia Nervosa and Respecting a Refusal of Life-Prolonging Therapy: A Limited Justification," *Bioethics* (April 1, 2000)

NO: James L. Werth, Jr., Kimberley S. Wright, Rita J. Archambault, and Rebekah J. Bardash, from "When Does the 'Duty to Protect' Apply with a Client Who Has Anorexia Nervosa?" *The Counseling Psychologist* (July 2003)

ISSUE SUMMARY

YES: Heather Draper argues that clinicians need to accept the fact that individuals with anorexia nervosa may be competent and may have legitimate reasons for refusing therapy. In such cases, therapists should respect the individual's wishes and should refrain from administering life-sustaining treatment.

NO: James L. Werth, Jr. and his colleagues contend that, due to the very nature of anorexia nervosa, individuals with anorexia cannot make rational decisions about nutrition and feeding. Because the behaviors of anorexics have such potential for health damage or even death, clinicians have a duty to protect the lives of their patients, even if it calls for compulsory treatment.

Health practitioners have long debated the ethics of treating individuals against their will. When an individual engages in behavior that may lead to self-harm, and possible death, it is assumed that professionals have an obligation to intervene. In the case of suicide, most would support hospitalization, with or without that person's consent. However, consider instances in which the individual may lack the competence to evaluate the extent to which a behavior is self-damaging, or instances in which the individual may reject medical assistance, regardless of medical recommendations. People with anorexia nervosa fall into this latter category. It is unclear whether a person in the throes of starvation and gross weight loss can make a competent decision about feeding and nutrition, even though this individual seems to demonstrate competence in other areas of life. Professionals trying to treat such individuals face an ethical dilemma about a "duty to protect." In other words, they confront decisions about whether to take actions to protect a patient, regardless of the patient's preference to be left to his or her own choices.

Heather Draper argues that mental health professionals need to consider the possibility that individuals with anorexia nervosa can make competent decisions about their treatment. Draper makes the case that professionals should respect the individual's refusal of therapy, especially when the refusal is grounded in arguments about the quality of life and the burden of therapy. Furthermore, Draper questions the effectiveness of forced feeding; it may save the life of the individual but does nothing to alleviate the underlying condition. Ultimately, it is the individual who is responsible for the consequences of his or her decisions, even if death is possible.

James L. Werth, Jr. and his colleagues assert that individuals with anorexia nervosa may experience significant harm and possible death as a result of behaviors related to the disorder. Due to this risk, Werth argues that there exists an obligation to take action when anorexia-related behavior progresses to the point at which it poses serious danger to the individual. Werth and his colleagues conclude that, while maintaining the individual's autonomy is indeed important to the success of the therapeutic process, health professionals have a duty to protect an anorexic client, even when this client refuses therapy.

POINT

- Some sufferers of anorexia nervosa may be competent to refuse therapy. In such cases, it would be wrong and unlawful to force them to undergo therapy that they choose to refuse.

- Mental health professionals should respect an individual's autonomy. This includes respecting the individual's refusal of therapy and accepting that the patient is responsible for the consequences of decisions, even if it may result in death.

- While forced feeding may save the life of the individual, it does nothing for the underlying condition and may actually worsen the situation.

- Patients may be better off when the clinician agrees to work within their frame of reference. Agreeing with them that they may be better off anorexic is often a new experience for them and may allow them to proceed with much more confidence.

COUNTERPOINT

- The pattern of thinking demonstrated by an individual with anorexia nervosa can be considered to be a thought disturbance. Since the individual secretly thrives on the results of starvation, a reinforcing loop exists that prevents competent decisions about food intake.

- Experts in the treatment of anorexia state that clients are not competent to make decisions regarding treatment, and that they are often grateful for medical intervention once they are no longer in the downward spiral of the disorder.

- Once a person's weight is stabilized, the benefits of psychological and pharmacological treatment are more likely to accrue and be appreciated by the patient.

- Allowing patients to make their own decisions about treatment may facilitate the therapeutic relationship, but it also increases the risk of serious health deterioration. Clients are more likely to be grateful for the intervention once they are medically and psychologically stable.

YES

Heather Draper

Anorexia Nervosa and Respecting a Refusal of Life-Prolonging Therapy: A Limited Justification

Introduction

The eating disorder anorexia nervosa results in the death of between 20–30[%] patients per year in the UK[1] and death rates internationally are reported to be between 4–20%.[2] This death rate would undoubtedly be higher if anorexics were not force-fed once their weight became dangerously low. Force-feeding (feeding without consent) has been recognised in the UK by the Mental Health Commission as a legitimate therapy to give under section 63 of the UK Mental Health Act 1983,[3] and the legitimacy of force-feeding in conjunction with other therapies is also supported in case law.[4] Force-feeding may take the form of literally forcing a patient to eat; coercing her to eat by putting her under pressure to feed herself; or, by tube feeding. Feeding alone is thought to be ineffective—unless it is done simply to restore the patient sufficiently to enable her to participate in other psychiatric therapies. Sectioning for feeding should, therefore, only be considered as an adjunct to other therapies if it is to be justified by appeals to best interest. It is also thought likely that repeated episodes of force-feeding—particularly of the literally forcing food into the mouths of sufferers—decrease the chances of long-term recovery and it is doubtful that it is actually in the best interests of a patient to be subjected to a regime of force-feeding on more than a few occasions.[5] Nevertheless, medical practitioners are understandably reluctant not to force-feed by one method or another when a patient is dying for want of nutrition. A recent article[6] suggesting that there might be a role for a palliative approach for patients who are both long-term sufferers and refusing therapy, attracted more criticism than support from practitioners, and the possibility of respecting a sufferer from anorexia's decision not to proceed with therapy—whatever the circumstances—has been described as collusion.[7] It is asserted that sufferers from anorexia are not competent to make any decisions that relate in any way to food, and withdrawing therapy or treating palliatively effectively entails withdrawing feeding. On one level this assertion may be pointing out the obvious—someone who is on the point of starving to death, has uncontrollable (non) eating behaviour and a completely distorted body image is not likely to be competent. Such an assertion, however, assumes that incompetence is a description of an individual

From *Bioethics*, vol. 14, issue 2, April 2000, pp. 261–278. Copyright © 2000 by Blackwell Publishing, Ltd. Reprinted by permission.

(broad or global incompetence) rather than an assessment of the capacity of the individual to make a specific decision (narrow incompetence). Some anorexics may indeed be incompetent as individuals (be broadly incompetent): for example, those on the point of starving to death. Others are certainly not broadly incompetent; they are studying for school leaving exams, or degrees, or are running their own financial affairs, others are professionals working in demanding jobs. It is because incompetence is also task specific (narrow) that it is accepted that a patient who is sectioned for compulsory treatment for a specific mental disorder cannot be treated on an involuntary basis for any other health problem, however life-threatening it is thought to be.[8] Thus, sufferers from anorexia cannot be involuntarily subjected to any therapies unrelated to their eating disorder. But could an anorexic competently decide to withdraw from therapy not on the grounds that she didn't want to eat, nor that she was 'fat' but because the quality of her life was so poor that the therapy was no longer of benefit to her, or that it was on balance more of a burden than a benefit?

In this paper, it is argued that whilst it is generally legitimate to detain and treat sufferers from anorexia against their will, under some circumstances there is a failure to respect their competent refusal of therapy; namely where those who are refusing have been afflicted beyond the natural cycle of the disorder (which is between one and eight years); have already been force-fed on previous occasions; are competent to make decisions concerning their quality of life; have insight into the influence which their anorexia has over some aspects of their lives, and are not at death's door (they may, for instance, have just been released from a section for compulsory treatment). It will be argued that in these cases, the decision to refuse therapy is on a par with other decisions to refuse life-prolonging therapy made by sufferers of debilitating chronic, or acute onset terminal illness and that in such cases palliation might justifiably replace aggressive therapy. In order to do this the paper will first revisit the distinction between competent refusal of therapy and passive euthanasia and the distinction between incompetent and irrational decisions. Both distinctions will then be applied to decision to refuse food. Finally, the extent to which sufferers from anorexia nervosa can be categorised as either incompetent or irrational will be examined. It is against this background that it will be argued that at least some of those who suffer from anorexia should have their refusals of therapy respected, even if they may die as a result.

The Distinction Between Passive Euthanasia and Competent Refusal of Life-Prolonging Therapy

A distinction is drawn in many jurisdictions between passive euthanasia—which may be viewed as murder or a similar crime and respecting a competent patient's decision to refuse lifesaving or life-prolonging therapy—which is part of respecting the right to consent. This distinction can also be important in ethics where passive euthanasia is considered wrong, but respecting a patient's decision to withdraw or withhold therapy is not only permissible but may be required.[9] Clearly the distinction is irrelevant for those who think that euthanasia can be permissible, but for those who disagree, it is perceived to form the boundary between acceptable and unacceptable withdrawal of therapy. The distinction will be used in this paper to argue that whilst it might be wrong for clinicians to give up on anorexics, and therefore for them to decide to withdraw therapy, it is acceptable for the anorexic herself to make a decision to withdraw from therapy, under certain circumstances and for reasons which will be addressed in the second half of this paper. So, can the distinction between passive euthanasia and competent withdrawal from therapy be defended?

In passive euthanasia, therapy is withdrawn or omitted with the intention that the patient will die as a result. To be euthanasia, the omission or withdrawal must be thought to be in the patient's best interests, whether or not the patient is party to this decision.[10] The final judgement about whether or not to omit therapy rests with the clinician and not the patient, even when the patient is party to the decision, or even when the patient goes to considerable lengths to persuade the clinician of her point of view. . . . However, if the patient simply said that she withdrew her consent for the therapy to continue, the clinician would have to comply but would comply without compromising his view that her life was worth living. When a competent patient refuses therapy—whether or not she has a terminal illness or a poor quality of life or will die as a result—professional carers are ethically and legally bound to accept this refusal.

The moral difference between passive euthanasia and competent refusal of therapy lies in who makes the final decision. Euthanasia is something which one person gives to another—whether or not it is voluntary. Withdrawing from therapy is something which one does to, or for, oneself. Respecting autonomy means that we bound to take our own moral decisions and others are bound not to interfere; but it also means that we are responsible for the decisions which we make. There is, then, a strong sense in which clinicians are responsible for decisions to give euthanasia, and patients are responsible for decisions which they make to withdraw from therapy.[11,12]

Distinction Between Irrational Decisions and Incompetent Decisions

Patients can refuse therapy for a variety of reasons. They may have religious objections to some procedures which are lifesaving (like Jehovah's Witnesses do to blood transfusions); they may have moral objections (perhaps a strongly held view that it is wrong to terminate the life of the unborn even to save one's own life); they may be objecting on economic moral grounds (believing that the money which is to be spent on them would be put to better use saving someone else); they may hold the personal belief (whether or not well founded) that they have become too much of a burden upon their family; or, they may consider that the burden of the therapy has become too great so that even though they would rather live, they would rather risk dying than continue with this therapy. None of these reasons requires us to be convinced that it is in the patient's best interests to be dead—as would be necessary in passive euthanasia—but any of these reasons given by a competent patient would be sufficient to suppose that her decision should be respected.

Of course, we might want to argue that it is irrational to put religious beliefs before life itself—particularly when the religious belief is based on a literal interpretation of the bible. We might argue that it is irrational to prefer to save the life of an unborn child to one's own, particularly if the unborn child may die anyway as a result of one's own death. We might argue that it is irrational to give up one's own chance of life when one has no control over where the resources will be spent instead. We might argue that it is irrational to perceive oneself as a burden to relatives because burdensomeness is in the eye of the beholder. But we should be wary of confusing irrational reasons with reasons with which we simply do not agree. Furthermore, we should be wary of confusing either irrationality or strong disagreement with incompetence. . . .

To summarise, a competent decision to refuse therapy can be made on rational or irrational grounds, or even no grounds at all. A request for voluntary, passive euthanasia, however, must, in addition to being competent, be rational to the extent that the doctor concerned can be persuaded to become party to the decision. But the doctor can also refuse to be party to the decision not because it is an incompetent one, nor because it is an irrational one, but because he disagrees that euthanasia is the appropriate clinical or moral option under the circumstances. At least two things follow from this distinction. The first is that patients who might otherwise request passive euthanasia could instead refuse all therapy necessary to sustain or save life. If food is considered to be a therapy,[13] then no competent patient is without the means to end her life since she simply has to refuse to eat and decline her consent to tube feeding. The advantage of so doing is that it is not necessary for the patient to make the clinician an accomplice to her decision. This does not mean that she has to conceal her desire for death from her clinician—indeed, this desire is likely to be discussed when any patient makes such a request. Rather it means that the patient remains in control, since it is her decision, rather than that of her clinician, which is the decisive one. The second is that since it is already legal for competent patients to refuse therapy, there is no need, in addition, to legalise voluntary, passive euthanasia in order to give patients autonomy over their own bodies. Both these arguments may meet some of the ethical problems with euthanasia previously outlined.[14]

Refusal of Feeding

But can these distinctions between voluntary, passive euthanasia and competent refusal of consent be applied to feeding? It certainly seems so, for a decision to withhold/withdraw tubefeeding from an incompetent patient on the grounds that their interests were best served by being dead would certainly be euthanasia,[15] whilst competent decisions to refuse food (whether by tube or other means) are not.

Once more, the distinction seems to turn upon who makes the final decision, the doctor (in euthanasia) or the patient (in refusal of food). Moreover, a decision to commence (tube) feeding once a patient is so weak that they become incompetent is at odds with the judgement that Jehovah's Witnesses carrying cards saying they do not want to receive blood products cannot be given transfusions—even if they are unconscious upon arrival at hospital.[16] . . .

Anorexia Nervosa and the Decision to Refuse Food

The condition which challenges these distinctions is anorexia nervosa where food is refused because the patient is completely obsessed with the idea of weight loss, or maintaining weight at a level incompatible with active life or even any life at all. Here the lack of distinction between providing food and therapy is even more marked because nutrition is very definitely part of the therapy required to restore the anorexic to 'health'.

Inverted commas around health are necessary here because anorexia nervosa is commonly, but often uncomfortably, described as an illness—a mental illness. The ambivalence with which this categorisation is viewed by treating clinicians is very evident in Crisp's textbook *Anorexia Nervosa: Let me be*.[17] Crisp—widely recognised as an international expert on eating disorders—claims in the first chapter that in his opinion the condition is an illness. His theory is that anorexia is a psychological adaptive stance operating through biological mechanisms, as the sufferer tries either to avoid puberty or return to a prepubescent state.[18] Nevertheless, he almost invariably puts 'illness' in inverted commas when referring to anorexia and frequently compares it to alcoholism, another state that is only uncomfortably described as an illness.

The anorexic's determination to starve in the face of abundance is essentially seen as irrational—whatever psychological theory is used to explain this behaviour. As has already been indicated, whether it is a sufficiently irrational obsession to be categorised as a mental illness cannot be taken for granted, but even if it is, it is far from obvious that simply being classed as suffering from a mental illness is necessarily an indication that one is an incompetent individual. Nor is it obvious that anorexics refusing therapy are sufficiently irrational to be classed as incompetent to make decisions regarding their food intake.

There are two justifications for associating irrationality with incompetence in the case of anorexia. One is that the desire not to eat undermines an even stronger desire not to die. Another is that the desire not to eat might itself be an involuntary one, grounded in some other deeply held, but false, belief about their body image—usually that they are 'fat'.

It is interesting that although the irrational nature of their beliefs is often cited (alongside the desire to prevent them from dying) as a reason to overrule their refusal of food, working with this irrational belief is also perceived to be a valuable clinical option. For instance, Crisp writes:

> '. . . a statement that he (the therapist) agrees that the patient is probably better off, all things considered, remaining anorexic, can be the most helpful and often totally new experience for the anorexic. She can approach the task of limited weight gain with much more confidence under such circumstances.'[19]

This suggests that therapists are prepared to work within the anorexic's frame of reference, provided that the anorexic is making decisions, which are life-promoting rather than decisions that are likely to result in her death. Of course, it is rational for the therapist to do this because it achieves his aim of preventing his patient's death. This does not, however, make the anorexic's beliefs any more rational. Accordingly, either the relationship is still one of the clinician's proxy determination of the best therapy for his patient (her wishes just happen to coincide with the therapy he has chosen for her); or, if the patient is considered to be competent to decide for herself, she is only as competent as she was when she decided to refuse food[20]—which makes any previous decision to override her wishes and force-feed her highly paternalistic and even a battery, however well motivated. There is always a danger in clinical relationships that competence is more likely to be questioned when the patient disagrees with the judgement of the clinician. This questioning itself highlights the ease with which assessments about a patient's competence can be muddied by disagreements over the relative value of deep-seated beliefs.[21]

It is at this point that the clinical management of eating disorders begins to challenge the established view that competent refusals of consent must be respected. Let us return to one example and introduce yet another. Earlier, the point was made that it would be deemed unacceptable for clinicians to forcibly prevent from eating those whose over-eating was life-threatening. One reason for this is that overeating is not considered to be a mental disorder. Yet, neither is the vast majority of under-eating—namely that which is done for the sake of current fashion and in conformity with current trends about body image and healthy living. Anorexia nervosa differs from this kind of under-eating in two important respects. First, the diagnosis is usually only made once the under-eating threatens life and health. Second, it is believed that the compulsion not to eat is somehow involuntary or beyond the control of the sufferer. If this is the case, then there are good grounds for supposing that in regard to eating, sufferers from anorexia are not competent. There is no one universal explanation for this disorder but it is often associated with other psychological problems such as low self-esteem, a sense of having no control over one's lives, or a history of sexual abuse. . . .

The second example concerns those women who refuse to undergo radical breast surgery when they are diagnosed with breast cancer, because they consider that their breasts are so integral to their identity and/or quality of life that they would rather die with their breasts intact, than live without them. This is a view that attracts a great deal of sympathy, despite the fact that it seems irrational to give greater weight to one's body image than to one's life expectancy. But provided that she is competent and understands the dangers of refusing to consent, such a patient would never be compelled to undergo surgery. In this case, competence and irrationality are clearly differentiated.

But what of the sufferer from anorexia who refuses therapy, not because she thinks that her condition is not life-threatening, nor because she refuses to accept that she has a problem at all, but because for her too the burden of therapy and the side-effects of successful therapy—in terms of the body with which she will be left—are such that she prefers to take her chances with death? Such a sufferer would not be a typical case (any more than a woman who refuses surgery for breast cancer would). However, what we need to be mindful of at this point is that some sufferers from anorexia nervosa are never cured, not even to the extent that they are able to live with their disorder by maintaining an abnormally low but constant, life-sustaining body weight.[22] Granted that the received wisdom is that of an illness with a natural cycle of anywhere between one and eight years, under discussion here is someone who has endured a decade or more of repeated painful weight loss and traumatic weight gain. The stress of living with anorexia nervosa prompted Crisp to write:

> (m)any anorexics feel constantly like alcoholics, that they are just one step away from disaster. When suicide occurs it is often within this context. The individual is seeking relief from the endless terror and the exhaustion of a battle to maintain her position.[23]

Crisp acknowledges that the tension between the desire to eat and fear of the consequences of eating is a constant battle; one that can leave the sufferer from anorexia feeling so battle-weary that death becomes a viable and preferred option. If this is true for those sufferers from anorexia who decide to take their own lives, why can it not also be true for some of those sufferers from anorexia who refuse the therapy which will save their lives?

[S]ome refusals of consent by sufferers from anorexia may actually be voluntary. It was noted earlier that many sufferers are not broadly incompetent. Granted that broad competence is intact,[24] we should be open to the possibility that sufferers are actually as competent as anyone else to make decisions about the quality of their lives, and to assess the relative value of their lives in the light of its quality. For this reason, it is proposed that it may be wrong, as well as unlawful, to force patients to comply with therapy simply because they are anorexic.

It is undoubtedly awful to watch someone—possibly a young someone—die when they can so easily be saved. However, if justice is to be given to those sufferers who can neither live with their anorexia nor live without it, we must listen carefully to their refusals of therapy. The first step on this road is to accept that at least some sufferers from anorexia may be competent to refuse therapy—even if this is only a tiny minority. To do this we will have to listen to the reasons that they give for their refusal, not to determine whether or not these reasons are rational per se, but to hear whether these reasons reflect the burden that life with anorexia and therapy has become. We need to bear in mind that there is a difference between saving the life of a sufferer and curing them of their anorexia. Whilst feeding may be lifesaving, it does nothing for the underlying condition—indeed it may even worsen it. Accordingly, we may also have to be open to the possibility that some sufferers from anorexia will never be cured, and that offering palliative care in such cases should not be dismissed as collusion with a mental illness. Rather it should be seen as offering the same services to incurable anorexics as are available to others who cannot be cured.

There is a wider danger in rejecting the possibility that some refusals of therapy by sufferers from anorexia are actually about quality of life and not involuntary refusals of food. This danger is that of weakening of the distinction between passive euthanasia and competent refusal of lifesaving therapy. If we exclude the possibility of a competent refusal being made for reasons which we cannot endorse—which I am suggesting may be happening in a minority of anorexia cases—there is a danger that a refusal of life-prolonging therapy will need to become as convincing to a physician as a request for passive euthanasia needs to be. Respecting a patient's autonomy is not simply about letting her make some decisions, or even all decisions. It is also about accepting that it is the patient who is responsible for the consequences of her decisions, and not the person who records this refusal of consent in the patient's medical notes.

Notes

1. Crisp, *Anorexia Nervosa: Let Me Be* (Baillere Tindell, London, 1990), p. 31.

2. The death rate varies according to study and length of follow up. For instance, see Phillip W. Lang. The Harvard Mental Health Letter, Oct./Nov. 1997 who also cites a prevalence for anorexia nervosa of 0.10.6% in the general population in the USA (a figure which he claims is several times higher amongst adolescent girls).

3. Mental Health Act Commission Guidance Note 3: Guidance on the Treatment of Anorexia Nervosa Under the Mental Health Act 1983 (Issued August 1997).

4. See *Riverside Health NHS Trust v. Fox* [1994] 1 FLR and *B v. Croydon H.A.* [1995] 1 AUER 683.

5. This argument was made very forcefully by Penny Lewis 'Feeding anorexic patients who refuse food,' *Medical Law Review*, 7, 1, (1999), pp. 21-37.

6. J. O'Neill, *American Journal of Hospice and Palliative Care* Nov./Dec. 1994 pp. 36-8. In 1998, the *British Medical Journal* 18 July 1998 pp. 195-197 also addressed the issue of palliation in its 'Education and Debate' section. In this discussion, C. J. Williams, L. Pieri, & A. Sims, argued that patients should always be treated actively, whilst L. Russon, & D. Alison, argued that there was a case for extending palliative care to anorexics.

7. Janet Treasure speaking at 'Food, Glorious Food?', Kings College, London, 4th July 1997.

8. In one dramatic example a patient, who was sectioned for treatment for paranoid schizophrenia, refused to have his leg amputated even though medical advice was that the gangrene would otherwise kill him. A court upheld his fight to refuse treatment on the grounds that he was competent to do so. Re C (refusal of medical treatment) [1994] 1 All ER 819 (FD).

9. For instance, it might be argued that whilst it is acceptable to take one's own life, it is wrong to enlist the help of others in so doing, or that it is wrong for doctors to take life, or that permitting any form of euthanasia is the first step on a dangerous slippery slope.

10. For more on the definition of euthanasia and distinctions between euthanasia and other forms of killing—including self-killing—see Heather Draper's 'Euthanasia' in *Encyclopaedia of Applied Ethics,* ed. R. Chadwick (Academic Press, San Diego, 1997). pp. 175-187.

11. Though, as one of the referees for this paper helpfully pointed out, there is a sense in which a patient who goes to great lengths to persuade a clinician to perform euthanasia upon her, shares some of the responsibility for her own death. More generally this point is well taken because otherwise we would be able to avoid responsibility for any action by persuading an accomplice to undertake it for us.

12. Obviously, some people would want to argue that voluntary euthanasia also respects the autonomous decision of the patient.

13. In the UK, it was established that tube-feeding was a medical intervention in *Airedale NHS Trust v. Bland* [1993] 3 WLR 316.

14. See the points made in footnote 9.

15. This point is well made by James Rachels 'Active and Passive Euthanasia' in Applied Ethics, ed. Peter Singer (Oxford University Press, Oxford, 1986) pp. 29-35.

16. See for instance the Canadian case *Malette v. Shulman* NW Ont CA (1009) 67 DLR (4th) 321.

17. Crisp, *Anorexia Nervosa: Let Me Be.*

18. This is, of course, only one view about the origins of the disorder. For an excellent critique of Crisp and outlines and critiques of other theories, see Morag MacSween's *Anorexic Bodies* (Routledge, London and New York, 1996), Chapters Two and Three.

19. Crisp, *Anorexia Nervosa: Let Me Be,* p. 146.

20. Competent in a general sense. I do not, of course, mean an incompetent refusal of food on the point of near death. A patient who has been force-fed under a section, who is released from the section and then requests that this cycle is not repeated would qualify for the kind of consideration I am suggesting here.

21. There are many examples of this in practice, particularly where patients refuse lifesaving therapy. The issue is discussed in Heather Draper, 'Consent and Midwifery' in *ed. Frith, L. Ethics and Midwifery* (Butterworth Heinemann, Oxford, 1994). pp. 17-33; and Heather Draper, "Women, reproductive responsibilities and forced caesareans', *Journal of Medical Ethics,* 22, 6 (1996), pp. 327-333.

22. Statistics for recovery vary. Lang, *The Harvard Medical Letter* cites a recovery rate of between 50-70% over ten years. E. D. Eckert, et al., 'Ten year follow-up of anorexia nervosa: clinical course and outcome', *Psychological Medicine,* 25 (1995), pp 143-156, suggest a 24% full recovery rate and just under 50% benign outcome. Obviously, taken together these sources suggest a failure rate of between 25-50% over ten years.

23. Crisp, *Anorexia Nervosa: Let Me Be,* p. 81.

24. Which, again, would exclude those on the point of starving to death.

James L. Werth, Jr., Kimberly
S. Wright, Rita J. Archambault,
and Rebekah J. Bardash

 NO

When Does the "Duty to Protect" Apply with a Client Who Has Anorexia Nervosa?

• • • **W**hile the literature abounds with protocols that will assist the counselor in case conceptualization and treatment (see Stein et al., 2001), a minimally addressed issue is the ethical and legal quagmire that ensues as the health of clients with eating disorders, particularly those with anorexia nervosa, declines. For the therapist, the task is to balance the therapeutic needs of these clients, particularly autonomy, with concerns about the person's health. Allowing clients to make their own decisions about treatment and recovery may facilitate the therapeutic relationship but may increase the risk of medical deterioration. Maintaining the balance between respecting the client's autonomy and protecting the client's health is especially challenging. It is within this context that practitioners, trainers, and supervisors could benefit from a discussion of their ethical, legal, and clinical obligations when a client with anorexia is in medical jeopardy (i.e., her or his life is in danger).

The purposes of this article are to (a) discuss the intersection between the duty to protect (i.e., an obligation to take some action when a person is engaging or considering engaging in a behavior that may lead to self-harm) and the treatment of people with eating disorders, specifically anorexia nervosa; and (b) provide some general guidelines for intervention. To determine whether there may be an essentially heretofore neglected duty to protect in the case of counseling with people who have certain eating disorders, this article first provides a brief overview of anorexia nervosa and then reviews the incidence of mortality in people with this condition. The next section outlines the duty to protect in instances of self-harm and discusses legal options when a person is considered to be at risk. Then, based on the information about anorexia and the ethical and legal issues associated with the duty to protect, the question of when this duty applies with clients who have anorexia is examined. The article concludes with implications of this analysis.

Anorexia Nervosa

Cognitive Functioning

Unfortunately, the *DSM-IV-TR* is silent about how anorexia can affect cognitive functioning beyond mentioning comorbid mental disorders. Experts on anorexia (e.g., Goldner, 1989; Goldner, Birmingham, & Smye, 1997; Kluge, 1991) and forensics (e.g., Appelbaum & Rumpf, 1998; Dresser, 1984a, 1984b; Dresser & Boisaubin, 1986) have noted that self-starvation can interfere with conceptualization, perceptions, and decision making. These cognitive deficits can impact the person's ability to realistically assess her situation and then impair judgment to the point that she is legally incompetent, specifically in areas related to eating and receiving treatments designed to increase weight and/or become medically stable. "The question of competence for individuals with anorexia nervosa centers on their specific ability to make rational decisions about nutrition, refeeding, and other medical treatments" (Goldner et al., 1997, p. 454). In other words, the disorder itself impairs judgment. Because they are often high functioning in other areas, the lack of severe delusions or other psychotic features in these clients can deceive some clinicians, attorneys, and judges (see Gutheil & Bursztajn, 1986). Depending on the course of the condition, these deficits may be apparent in standardized psychological and neuropsychological testing (Bowers, 1994; Hamsher, Halmi, & Benton, 1981; Watson, Bowers, & Andersen, 2000). In more severe cases, the inability to care for self as well as the person's medical jeopardy will be evident to observers (Appelbaum & Rumpf, 1998; Dresser, 1984a, 1984b).

Although not a cognitive deficit in and of itself, the pattern of thinking by the person with anorexia can be considered to be a thought disturbance. Importantly, it is the ego-syntonic dimension of this thought disturbance that negatively affects help seeking, treatment compliance, and retention in therapy (Stein et al., 2001). Despite their obvious physiological decline, these clients refuse to acknowledge the extent of their disorder and are secretly pleased with their emaciation. Unlike those with other conditions, clients with anorexia value and seek the symptoms of their disorder (i.e., thinness and starvation). Because clients with anorexia rely on and value their symptoms to organize and manage their lives, there is little or no incentive for change, especially given their almost delusional capacity to ignore their emaciation. There is, then, a synergy between the ego-syntonic dimension of the disorder and the physiological-cognitive response to starvation. These cognitive factors create a reinforcing loop that fuels and maintains the need for personal control, to control food intake, and to resist change (and therefore treatment).

Mortality

The *DSM-IV-TR* indicates that the long-term mortality for individuals with anorexia admitted to university hospitals is 10%; death usually results from the effects of starvation, an electrolyte imbalance, or suicide. These conclusions were likely based on several studies and reviews that have been conducted in the past 20 years on the causes and rate of mortality of those who exhibit the condition (e.g., Crow, Praus, & Thuras, 1999; Deter & Herzog, 1994; Eckert, Halmi, Marchi, Grove, & Crosby, 1995; Herzog et al., 2000; Neumarker, 1997, 2000; Nielsen et al., 1998; Ratnasuriya, Eisler, Szmukler, & Russell, 1991; Schwartz & Thompson, 1981; Theander, 1985). After reviewing this research, Sullivan (1995) recounted this list of comparisons:

> The aggregate annual mortality rate associated with anorexia nervosa is more than 12 times higher than the annual death rate due to all causes of death for females 15–24 years old in the general population . . . and more than 200 times greater than the suicide rate in the general population. . . . The annual mortality rate associated with anorexia nervosa is more than twice that of a national study group of female psychiatric patients. (p. 1074)

This led Sullivan to conclude, "These data highlight the status of anorexia as a serious psychiatric disorder with a substantial risk of mortality" (p. 1074). More succinctly, Neumarker (2000, p. 181) stated that "it is clear that anorexia nervosa has the highest mortality rate of all the psychiatric illnesses" (see also Griffiths & Russell, 1998; Harris & Barraclough, 1998; Herzog et al., 2000; Nielsen et al., 1998; Vitiello & Lederhendler, 2000). . . .

Ethical and Legal Issues When a Client May Be at Risk of Self-Harm

Ethical Considerations

An integral part of the psychotherapeutic process is the client's understanding and belief that what is discussed with the therapist will remain confidential. Although what a client says in the therapy room is considered confidential and is also protected by law (i.e., it is privileged communication) in most situations, there are situations where the counselor is legally and ethically able (or obligated, in some cases) to divulge what the client said (Kitchener, 2000).

One of the limitations to confidentiality occurs when a person is perceived to be at risk of self-harm. Although harm-to-self is often discussed in the context of suicide, a close examination reveals that it is not the *intent* to die or to cause harm to one's being that is the key; it is that the behavior itself, or the inability to manage one's behavior, has the potential of causing significant damage or death (Appelbaum & Rumpf, 1998). Therefore, whether a client has suicidal ideation, expressed intent to kill herself or himself, or taken actions that could be interpreted as suicidal is not the issue; the outcome is the key point (Werth & Rogers, 2003). In such situations, a therapist must exercise reasonable care to prevent foreseeable harm or danger that may result from a client's mental or physical incapacity (Bongar, 2002). This is an example of the "duty to protect" applied to self-harm as opposed to harm to others (see *Bellah v. Greenson,* 1978). Thus, although the duty to protect grew from case law related to harming others (i.e., *Tarasoff v. Regents of the University of*

California, 1976), it has since been expanded to become an ethical and clinical standard of care and to encompass other client actions (Bongar, 2002; Vande-Creek & Knapp, 2001). . . .

Ethical Meta-Principles

The ethical meta-principles such as autonomy, beneficence, nonmaleficence, justice, and fidelity have been discussed as important aspects of ethical decision making in counseling psychology for nearly two decades (Kitchener, 1984; Kitchener & Anderson, 2000). Although the interpretations of these principles are culture-bound and potentially problematic (see, e.g., Blackhall, Murphy, Frank, Michel, & Azen, 1995; Carrese & Rhodes, 1995), the principles are relevant in this context, and the interplay between them contributes to the dilemma faced by the clinician (Goldner et al., 1997). For example, many authors have emphasized that autonomy (i.e., control) is such an important issue for individuals with anorexia (e.g., Russell, 2001; Stein et al., 2001) that a desire may exist to maximize this principle; however, beneficence and nonmaleficence may conflict with autonomy, given that death may result, and therefore may temporarily override autonomy (Griffiths & Russell, 1998). Thus, the question for the counselor may revolve around when, if ever, the client's autonomy should give way to the therapist's interpretation of what constitutes beneficence and nonmaleficence.

Legal Considerations

For the purposes of this analysis, three important legal issues are germane: (a) whether state law mandates intervention when a counselor believes a person may harm himself or herself, (b) when involuntary hospitalization (i.e., civil commitment) is possible in situations involving self-harm, and (c) when treatment can and cannot be refused. These matters are discussed in turn.

Just as some psychologists may erroneously believe the APA ethics code (2002) mandates breaking confidentiality (or some other intervention) when a person is believed to be at risk of self-harm, some may think that state laws require intervention in such situations. However, with only a few exceptions, this is mistaken. Most state laws related to potential harm-to-self are similar to the APA ethics code in that they allow, but do not mandate, action (Werth, 2001; see also Barret et al., 2001). The intervention discussed in state laws related to self-harm is involuntary hospitalization.

In terms of civil commitment related to self-harm, a person can be judged to be a danger to herself or himself to a degree that legally allows for intervention in two ways: The self-harm must be the result of (a) a mental illness or (b) grave disability (Appelbaum & Rumpf, 1998; Werth, 2001). Although the mental illness criterion is typically vaguely defined in laws, a *DSM* Axis I disorder would likely suffice. Grave disability, in essence, means that judgment is so impaired that the individual cannot take care of herself or himself: One example of this may be intentional malnutrition (Appelbaum & Rumpf, 1998).

However, even if involuntarily hospitalized, a person has a right to refuse treatment unless (a) declared legally incompetent or (b) competency is in question and a life-threatening emergency arises. In the latter case, after stabilization, competence must be reassessed, and treatment refusal may take place unless a court declares the person incompetent (Appelbaum & Rumpf, 1998; Dresser 1984a, 1984b; Dresser & Boisaubin, 1986). If deemed incompetent, a person with anorexia can be force-fed; this situation is referred to as *compulsory treatment*.

Summary

Psychologists who have a client in danger of self-harm must practice up to the standards of care, which means that they have a duty to protect the client. Many interventions may satisfy the duty, and both the APA ethics code (2002) and most state laws allow for (but do not mandate) the breaking of confidentiality and attempts at involuntary hospitalization in certain situations. However, except in rare circumstances, the client has the right to refuse treatment.

Is There a Duty to Protect with Clients Who Have Anorexia?

The preceding discussion on anorexia and on the duty to protect leads to the following key points:

- Anorexia is a diagnosable mental condition in both the *DSM-IV-TR* and the *ICD-10* (World Health Organization, 1992).
- People with anorexia have a high mortality rate because of medical complications associated with the disorder and because of suicide.
- An ethical duty to protect exists when a client is a potential harm-to-self (although the actual intervention is dependent on the standard of care for that clinical situation).
- The APA (2002) ethics code permits the breaking of confidentiality to protect a person from self-harm.
- Possibilities exist for involuntary hospitalization of a person whose self-harm is not necessarily intentional but is the result of a mental disorder or grave disability.
- Involuntarily hospitalized persons can refuse treatment unless declared incompetent.

It is in this context that the counselor may be faced with the clinical, ethical, and legal dilemma of how to protect a client with anorexia from the life-threatening impact of the disorder while maintaining the client's autonomy (which is especially significant given that control typically is such an important issue for individuals with eating disorders).

If a client with anorexia is explicitly suicidal, then a duty to protect likely exists (for studies specifically on suicidality among people with eating disorders, see Bulik, Sullivan, & Joyce, 1999; Favaro & Santonastaso, 1996, 1997; and Viesselman & Roig, 1985). However, the issue to be examined next is the broader one of whether the eating-related behaviors associated with anorexia nervosa *in and of themselves* activate the duty to protect. In other words, in the discussion that follows, we are *not* saying that client behaviors associated with severe anorexia amount to suicidality but rather that the client's disorder-related actions may at some point put her health at significant risk and this is what engenders the duty to protect.

Given that low-burden standard interventions (e.g., increasing session frequency, adding a therapeutic modality) are not likely to be controversial, the focus here is on the most forceful actions: involuntary hospitalization and compulsory treatment. These must be discussed, even if these interventions are used relatively rarely, because (given the arguments made above) a duty to protect exists with clients who have anorexia, and the counselor must be willing to implement any ethically and legally acceptable intervention to meet that duty and protect the client.

Because the possibility that the behaviors of clients with anorexia nervosa may engender a duty to protect requiring extreme intervention has been discussed more frequently outside the United States (Appelbaum & Rumpf, 1998), we review this literature first. Analysis specific to the United States follows, along with responses to concerns about these interventions.

International Perspectives

In the international literature, the issue of what to do when faced with a client whose anorexia is quite severe is usually examined in terms of compulsory treatment. Distinguishing between involuntary hospitalization and compulsory treatment is important. In the treatment of eating disorders, *involuntary hospitalization* refers to the client's being placed into a restrictive environment where she is able to partake of the same treatment program as voluntary clients. *Compulsory treatment* is more specific and may include forced or nasogastric feeding. This distinction is not always made clear in the literature, but it is significant in the United States because of the assumption that a person is competent, and therefore able to refuse treatment, unless proven otherwise in court.

Therapists and physicians in the United Kingdom and Australia have been the most attentive to the issue of compulsory treatment. Tiller, Schmidt, and Treasure (1993; see also Lanceley & Travers, 1993) considered whether compulsory treatment for anorexia nervosa was compassion or coercion. They mentioned the case of a 16-year-old female who had appealed to an English court to refuse treatment for her anorexia (see also Brahams, 1997; Dolan, 1998). Tiller and colleagues said that given the mortality rate for anorexia, they found it hard to understand why compulsory treatment was so controversial. They concluded that compulsory treatment should be considered when the person is at a BMI below 13.5 (e.g., 5'5" and 81 pounds) and has considerable physical complications and concomitant psychiatric diagnoses. Serfaty and McCluskey (1998) reviewed instances of people receiving compulsory treatment in their specialty unit, and they, too, used the criteria of a BMI below 13.5 and serious physical complications.

English researchers Ramsay, Ward, Treasure, and Russell (1999) examined the conditions associated with compulsory inpatient treatment. They compared 81 compulsory patients (16% of all admissions), virtually all of whom had anorexia nervosa, with 81 voluntary patients. The investigators gave four reasons for compulsory treatment:

(i)   Detention was necessary in the interest of the patient's health, for example by virtue of extreme weight loss and persistent avoidance of food;
(ii) Detention was in the interest of the patient's safety, for example he or she was making suicidal plans or had already attempted self-harm;
(iii) The detention was in the interest of both health and safety;
(iv) Other reasons (e.g., aggression or violence), (p. 148)

Note that both anorexic behaviors in and of themselves as well as specific plans for self-harm were considered acceptable reasons for compulsory treatment. Ramsay's team found that those individuals who received compulsory treatment did not significantly differ from the voluntary patients in admission weight or BMI, but the members of the compulsory group were significantly more likely to have a history of childhood physical/sexual abuse, prior admissions, longer hospitalizations, and explicit self-harm. . . .

United States

The literature in the United States has also attended to the dangers associated with anorexia, but the focus has been on mandatory withdrawal from a university (e.g., Glenn, Pollard, Denovchek, & Smith, 1986; Pavela, 1985) and involuntary hospitalization (Appelbaum & Rumpf, 1998; Dresser, 1984a, 1984b; see also Goldner et al., 1997). Of special relevance to counseling psychologists who work on college campuses, Pavela (1985) asserted that students with eating disorders made up one of three groups that may warrant involuntary withdrawal from a university because of the effects of the condition on the person, the impact on the university community, or the fact that the student could not receive adequate treatment on campus (the other groups were suicidal students and students with mental disorders who commit offenses without awareness of the nature of their actions). He stated that after other measures have been tried, "Unresponsive patients with potentially life threatening complications should be committed to a medical facility for prompt intervention, if necessary" (p. 60); but he did not indicate when such action would be "necessary." Glenn and colleagues (1986) provided four levels of interventions for students with eating disorders. The highest-level intervention is warranted when a student is "behaving in ways that are a threat to the life or health of self or others" (p. 164). They reported that there were two instances at their university where intervention began at the highest level because of the severity of the students' behavior.

Recently, Appelbaum and Rumpf (1998; see also Dresser, 1984a; Dresser & Boisaubin, 1986; Fost, 1984) discussed the prospect of involuntary hospitalization for people with anorexia. These authors explicitly stated that civil commitment in the case of anorexia is analogous to "other areas of mental health practice, involving the treatment of overtly suicidal patients or those so gravely disabled as to be unable to meet their basic needs" (p. 225). Yet the authors noted that it appears rare for people with anorexia to be involuntarily hospitalized (see also Fost, 1984), perhaps because many therapists do not consider a client with anorexia, who is not explicitly suicidal, to be a harm-to-self and, therefore, do not consider attempting involuntary hospitalization if other interventions fail. However, as previously reviewed, neither overt suicidality nor intent to harm oneself is necessary for the duty to protect to apply. Furthermore, given the mortality data previously cited, it should be clear that.

> the effect of anorexic behavior can be fully as lethal as the more direct suicidal actions of a severely depressed patient. Thus, the focus on expressed intent is misleading and potentially harmful to the patient. . . . Even without the intent to end their lives, anorexics often act in ways that make that outcome likely. (p. 227)

As a result, Appelbaum and Rumpf concluded, therapists should consider involuntary hospitalization if a client's anorexia-related behaviors are severe enough to suggest that the individual's life is in jeopardy.

Objections to Involuntary Hospitalization

Although a few authors have made the case that some individuals with anorexia may be acting in ways, or have progressed far enough in their disease process, to warrant strong interventions, others object to the consideration of involuntary treatment for these clients. Reasons most often cited include potential violation of client rights, questionable efficacy of enforced treatment, and the likely deterioration of the therapeutic relationship.

One of the primary concerns regarding the use of involuntary hospitalization or compulsory treatment is that this imposition violates the client's right to decide for herself—her autonomy is taken away. This violation of client rights is seen as running counter to good therapeutic practice and believed to be counterproductive in both the short and long run (Dresser, 1984a, 1984b; Rathner, 1998). Although this may be true in principle, experts in anorexia indicate that clients are often grateful for such intervention once they are not in the downward spiral of the disorder (Fost, 1984; Goldner et al., 1997; Griffiths & Russell, 1998).

Experts have also suggested that involuntary hospitalization serves the temporary purpose of medical stabilization but does not actually treat the eating disorder because this requires the cooperation of the client (Rathner, 1998). Although short-term results are positive, the long-term success rates of involuntary treatment have been less clear. Only three studies to date have assessed the outcome of involuntary treatment (Griffiths et al., 1997; Ramsay et al., 1999; Watson et al., 2000). Although the investigations were not directly comparable, Russell (2001) summarized the results of research from these three outcome studies (one each in Australia, London, and Iowa). All three indicated that the involuntary patients experienced successful refeeding, although the results took longer than with the voluntary patients (mean 113 days compared to mean 88 days, respectively). Long-term follow-up was not done, but mortality comparisons were made with the London data. At an average of 5.7 years postadmission, the involuntary patients had a higher mortality rate (10 of 70 involuntary patients had died compared with 2 of the 70 voluntary patients). This was believed to be the result of the more severe pathology of the involuntary patients (Russell, 2001). How many deaths were prevented by the hospitalization, however, is unknown. More research is required to determine the long-term therapeutic impact of involuntary hospitalization.

Another concern about involuntary treatments is that such efforts could irreparably damage the therapeutic relationship and make it less likely that the client would seek treatment in the future (Richmond, 2001). There are no data to suggest that this is true, however, and some authors offer anecdotal evidence that clients are more likely to be grateful for the intervention once they are medically and psychologically stable (Andersen, Bowers, & Evans, 1997; Fost, 1984). Furthermore, it is argued, mere admission does not mean the person will necessarily improve (Dresser, 1984a), and if all that is achieved through hospitalization is medical stabilization without treatment for the actual disorder(s), positive treatment outcome is less likely. Once a person's weight is stabilized, however, the benefits of psychological and pharmacological treatment are more likely to accrue. A recent study (Watson et al., 2000) comparing voluntary and involuntary in-patients with eating disorders demonstrated that treatment outcomes were not significantly different and that the involuntary patients were just as likely to benefit from the treatment as were the voluntary patients. Long-term follow-up is still needed to determine whether these positive outcomes are sustained.

Objections to Applying the Duty to Protect with Clients Who Have Anorexia

Although we have attempted to make the case that counselors have a duty to protect with clients who have anorexia and that discharging this duty may even lead to attempts at involuntary hospitalization and compulsory treatment, readers may object to this line of reasoning. Some may argue that because the incidence of anorexia is lower than that of other mental disorders, even a mortality rate of 10% represents a relatively small number of deaths compared to those associated with other conditions. However, the number of deaths associated with anorexia is not the issue; the *probability* of death is the key. Because anorexia will lead to death if the course is not interrupted, the clinician has a duty to intervene if the course has progressed far enough (i.e., to the point of medical jeopardy). . . .

Implications for Practice

Based on the foregoing, we contend that there is a duty to protect with clients who have anorexia and, therefore, the counselor must be prepared to attempt involuntary hospitalization with clients whose conditions warrant extreme intervention. Regardless of whether a therapist considers the behaviors associated with anorexia nervosa to be overtly suicidal or to be the result of a condition that has compromised the ability to think clearly and care for oneself, it would appear obvious that such behaviors are dangerous and the counselor needs to intervene in some way. How to intervene is shaped, in part, by whether a duty to protect exists. Because the diagnosis of anorexia nervosa alone is not sufficient, the duty to protect applies when the client's behaviors have become extreme or are associated with significant health risks. The uninterrupted course of anorexia will inevitably lead to medical jeopardy and death. The goal of treatment is to slow the progression of symptoms until the client is able to develop healthy coping mechanisms. Depending on the client's response, decisions will need to be made about whether to maintain the current course of treatment or to develop a more aggressive plan, which would include more protective measures.

An example of how the physical and psychological decompensation of a client with anorexia can lead to (a) significant health concerns, (b) consideration as to whether the duty to protect applies and, if so, (c) decisions about what interventions are necessary illustrates the dilemma for the counselor.

Jan was an 18-year-old first-year student at a large university. She had been treated for eating disorder behaviors in an outpatient clinic during high school and, although not fully recovered, she was attending college 1,500 miles from home. She lived in the residence hall on campus. Despite her best intentions to maintain her progress, she started restricting her food intake shortly after classes began in the fall. Initially friendly, she began to withdraw from her new friends and roommates, particularly avoiding activities that involved meals. By late fall, her roommates expressed their concern about Jan's avoidance and declining weight to the resident assistant. The residence hall staff referred her to the campus counseling center. She began counseling and medical monitoring through student health services as part of a multidisciplinary treatment team and remained stable through winter break. After returning to campus in the spring semester, her weight continued to drop. Although she agreed to have her parents notified that she was in counseling, she denied the extent of her decline both medically and psychologically. She had developed a strong therapeutic relationship with her counselor but was terrified of making any changes in her eating behavior. In an attempt to maintain her autonomy and avoid a power struggle, treatment options were discussed with her, but she refused inpatient treatment and refused to leave school voluntarily. Despite her weakened condition, she was seen by acquaintances exercising excessively. She had alienated her friends and had reduced her contact with her family.

The treatment team worked carefully to maintain Jan's engagement and cooperation in the treatment process. Although she maintained her counseling and medical appointments, her disorder continued to progress. Her mood became more dysphoric, she had little energy, and her memory showed impairment. Furthermore, her weight had fallen to 95 pounds (given her height of 5'5", this equated to a BMI of 15.8), so her therapist and physician constructed a behavioral contract that included more frequent counseling sessions, nutritionist appointments, weight expectations and monitoring, and activity restrictions. She signed the contract to avoid being involuntarily withdrawn from school, although she continued to claim that she was medically stable and functioning well. Jan felt some pressure to sign the contract, but by allowing the team physician to monitor the medical consequences, the counselor was able to maintain an empathic connection and address Jan's fears. As a result, the therapeutic relationship did not seem to suffer by implementing the contract.

By spring break, Jan had been taken to a local emergency room twice: once for rehydration after fainting and once because of cardiac dysrhythmia. Her treatment team had already escalated interventions in response to her physical and psychological condition and, again, determined that more aggressive treatment was necessary to preserve her life. As outpatient treatment on campus proved insufficient in reversing the course of her disorder, and her BMI dropped to 15 (90 pounds), they decided to call her parents to make arrangements for more intensive treatment, with or without Jan's consent.

Although counselors routinely intensify treatment with clients who are decompensating, it is unclear in the literature when counselors engage in an assessment of the need to protect the client from the probable death associated with continued anorexic behavior. Although no one has specifically identified a set of criteria that would implicate the duty to protect when a client, such as Jan, has anorexia nervosa, a tentative list of conditions may be generated based on the research and analysis associated with compulsory treatment in the United Kingdom and Australia (Griffiths et al., 1997; Griffiths & Russell, 1998; Ramsay et al., 1999; Serfaty & McCluskey, 1998), the reviews of civil commitment in the United States (Appelbaum & Rumpf, 1998; Dresser, 1984a, 1984b; Goldner et al., 1997), and discussions of the physical complications associated with and treatments for anorexia nervosa (American Psychiatric Association, 2000a; Andersen et al., 1997; Becker, Grinspoon, Klibanski, & Herzog, 1999; Brotman & Stern, 1983; Casper & Davis, 1977; Garner & Needleman, 1997; J. E. Mitchell, Pomeroy, & Adson, 1997; see also Stein et al., 2001). Unfortunately, the rate of progression toward medical danger in anorexia is difficult to predict. Death in these cases is often the result of a cardiac event for which there was no warning (Birmingham, 1989; Brotman & Stern, 1983).

Given the medical risk associated with this disorder, the therapist must work closely with medical personnel or as part of a multidisciplinary treatment team in evaluating the health risk of the individual patient (Kalodner, 1998). In fact, the American Psychiatric Association (2000b) guidelines prescribe that eating disorder treatment decisions be made by a multidisciplinary team. The American Psychiatric Association guidelines also highlight certain characteristics that would warrant immediate hospitalization: increase in pulse of greater than 20 beats per minute (bpm) or a drop in blood pressure of greater than 20 mm Hg/minute standing, bradycardia less than 40 bpm, tachycardia greater than 110 bpm, or inability to sustain body core temperature above 97.0 degrees. Having no motivation for recovery is also cited as an indicator for inpatient hospitalization. Short of these emergent physical signs, the risk factors listed below indicate more protective/ aggressive treatment strategies are necessary, which may include behavioral contracts, intensive outpatient treatment, and, ultimately, voluntary or involuntary hospitalization.

High-risk indicators include

1. BMI below 15 (e.g., 5'2" and 82 pounds; 5'5" and 90 pounds; 5'8" and 98 pounds)
2. Any of the following medical conditions: cardiac arrhythmia, seizures, syncopol episodes, organic brain syndrome, bradycardia (less than 40 bpm), exercise-induced chest pain, reduced exercise tolerance, dysrhythmias, renal dysfunction, tetany, blood volume depletion
3. Abnormalities in electrolyte levels
4. Rapid weight loss into dangerous weight range for height
5. Comorbid psychiatric conditions (e.g., major depression, obsessive-compulsive disorder, bipolar disorder, posttraumatic stress disorder, substance abuse)
6. History of self-harm or prior hospitalizations
7. Cognitive impairment that interferes with judgment to the point that the person is incompetent or gravely disabled

The clinician who has a client meeting one or more of the above criteria (in particular, 1, 2, or 7) should consider herself or himself to have an affirmative duty to take explicit action to protect the health of the client (if the client is a minor, special duties apply; see Dresser, 1984a, 1984b, for a discussion of these). Any combination of the above risk factors should alert the clinician that more aggressive treatment is warranted. Because the progression of symptoms is typically gradual, it will be the cumulative clinical judgment of the treatment team that determines whether a duty exists to intensify the interventions. In general, the counselor might proceed from establishing a behavioral contract, to using intensive outpatient treatment, to instituting partial hospitalization or day treatment. When these efforts have failed to bring about sufficient change, voluntary or involuntary hospitalization should be considered.

Appelbaum and Rumpf (1998; see also Gutheil & Bursztajn, 1986) made a compelling case that the most aggressive form of intervention—civil commitment—is a possible course of action for therapists working with clients whose health is in jeopardy because of the behaviors associated with anorexia nervosa. Although framed within the auspices of the duty to protect, Appelbaum and Rumpf did not discuss other, less extreme, interventions that may be both appropriate and necessary under this duty. Ideally, the therapist should proceed from the least restrictive (e.g., verbal contract) to more restrictive treatment options (e.g., breaking confidentiality) and only consider involuntary hospitalization when other treatment attempts have failed or medical risks necessitate (Andersen et al., 1997). . . .

Conclusion

To practice up to the standard of care when working with clients who are at risk of self-harm, psychologists must take some action to protect the person (Bongar, 2002). We have asserted that when a counselor is seeing a client with anorexia, the therapist may eventually have a duty to take action to protect the client's health even if the client is not explicitly suicidal and is not engaging in anorexic behaviors with the explicit intent of self-harm. The specific diagnosis is not the key; the behaviors associated with the diagnosis are what trigger the duty. For example, just as a diagnosis of major depression does not automatically require intervention to protect the well-being of the client unless the behaviors or potential behaviors associated with the depression (e.g., suicidal ideation with a plan or attempt) signaled that significant harm was believed likely, the diagnosis of anorexia in and of itself is not sufficient. However, if the behaviors associated with the condition are such that the therapist, after medical consultation, perceives the client's life to be in danger, then the duty would apply.

The goal of this article is to make explicit what may have been implicit: At times, there is a duty to protect with clients who have anorexia nervosa. The medical danger associated with this condition invokes the ethical and legal responsibility to protect clients in an acute state of the disorder. Counseling psychologists and trainees would benefit from an increased understanding of the overlap of clinical and ethical dimensions of decision making and treatment planning with clients with anorexia. We hope that this article will prompt others to examine this issue and that researchers will work to further define the conditions under which the duty to protect applies. Until then, counselors are reminded that even if their clients with anorexia nervosa are not explicitly suicidal, the behaviors associated with this condition do put these clients at risk of significant self-harm and death, and the therapist therefore may have an affirmative duty to protect clients with anorexia.

All references for articles included in *Taking Sides: Clashing Views in Abnormal Psychology, 6/e* can be found on the Web at www.mhhe.com/cls.

CHALLENGE QUESTIONS

Should Individuals with Anorexia Nervosa Have the Right to Refuse Life-Sustaining Treatment?

1. To what extent do you agree with James L. Werth and his colleagues that medical providers have a duty to protect the patient when the individual's behaviors pose a serious threat to health? In what kind of situations, if any, should the medical professional put aside the obligation to protect?
2. Consider the situation in which an individual does not refuse treatment outright but expresses a resistance to intervention. If you were the treating clinician, how would you deal with such an individual?
3. Werth presents a fictional case about a college student named Jan who suffers from anorexia. If Jan were a friend of yours, at what point should you intervene if concerned about the possibility of this individual engaging in self-injurious behaviors related to anorexia nervosa? What "duty to protect" does a friend or relative have in such situations?
4. Heather Draper makes the comparison between individuals with anorexia and individuals with breast cancer. She contends that a competent individual may base her decision to refuse therapy on arguments about the burden of therapy and the side effects of successful treatment. Just as a breast cancer patient may not want to undergo a mastectomy, an individual with anorexia may not want to live with a larger body. What similarities and differences pertain to these medical conditions?
5. How should one go about making the determination about a client's competency to make decisions about treatment options? Who should make the assessment about competency—clinicians, lawyers, or judges?

Suggested Readings

Couturier, J., & Mahmood, A. (2009). Meal support therapy reduces the use of nasogastric feeding for adolescents hospitalized with anorexia nervosa. *Eating Disorders: The Journal of Treatment & Prevention, 17*(4), 327–332.

Grilo, C.M., & Mitchell, J.E. (2010). *The treatment of eating disorders: A clinical handbook*. New York: Guilford Press.

Johnson, S.L. (2009). *Therapist's guide to posttraumatic stress disorder intervention*. San Diego, CA: Elsevier.

Ogden, J. (2010). *The psychology of eating: From healthy to disordered behavior* (2nd ed.). Wiley-Blackwell.

Thiels, C., & Curtice, M. (2009). Forced treatment of anorexic patients: Part 2. *Current Opinion in Psychiatry, 22*(5), 497–500.

ISSUE 5

Is Psychological Debriefing a Harmful Intervention for Survivors of Trauma?

YES: Grant J. Devilly and Peter Cotton, from "Psychological Debriefing and the Workplace: Defining a Concept, Controversies and Guidelines for Intervention," *Australian Psychologist* (July 2003)

NO: Jeffrey T. Mitchell, from "A Response to the Devilly and Cotton Article, 'Psychological Debriefing and the Workplace . . .,'" *Australian Psychologist* (March 2004)

ISSUE SUMMARY

YES: Psychologists Grant J. Devilly and Peter Cotton assert that critical incident stress debriefing (CISD) is poorly defined and has been shown to do more harm than good. They propose alternative approaches for responding to trauma survivors, which they consider more effective.

NO: Jeffrey T. Mitchell of the International Critical Incident Stress Foundation (ICISF) argues that Devilly and Cotton have misrepresented important information about psychological debriefing and have confused several aspects of this system of responding to trauma survivors.

Immediately following the September 11 terrorist attacks, thousands of well-meaning people descended upon Ground Zero in New York with the intention of consoling and aiding the survivors of that harrowing trauma. Some of these helpers had the goal in mind of offering their "debriefing" services to traumatized individuals who had just barely escaped death. Psychological debriefing is an intervention process in which survivors are urged to recount and relive the incident in order to avoid long-term consequences and traumatic stress responses. Experts in the field of psychology and crisis intervention, however, debate the efficacy of psychological debriefing and, more specifically, critical incident stress debriefing (CISD). While some professionals insist that CISD can be greatly beneficial, others contend that this approach can do more harm than good.

Grant J. Devilly and Peter Cotton assert that CISD and critical incident stress management (CISM) are poorly defined responses to traumatized individuals, which at their worst are noxious and at their best are ineffective. They cite examples of research suggesting that generic psychological debriefing has almost no effect on trauma victims and that CISD can actually provoke more negative symptoms in those who undergo the debriefing.

Jeffrey T. Mitchell criticizes the article by Devilly and Cotton, arguing that they have not done adequate research and contends that they make several glaring errors, including the erroneous presentation of CISD and CISM as synonymous. Mitchell explains that CISD is a 7-step, small-group crisis intervention process, while CISM is a comprehensive, systematic, and multicomponent system. Mitchell also asserts that the research studies upon which Devilly and Cotton rest their aguments involve instances in which the specifics of CISD are not properly applied, and do not reflect true efficacy of stress debriefing.

POINT

- The philosophy and techniques associated with psychological debriefing represent little more than "emotional first aid" for survivors of life-threatening trauma.

- Good intentions and the passion to help following a trauma may result in paradoxical effects, particularly if the tools being used to aid are cursorily understood, dogmatically applied, and the peer-reviewed research literature is ignored.

- Current expert consensus and meta-analytic reviews suggest that CISD is possibly noxious, that generic psychological debriefing is probably inert, and that more emphasis should be placed on the screening for, and providing, early intervention to those who go on to develop pathological reactions.

- It appears that CISD and CISM are indistinguishable. We can only conclude that CISD may or may not be one component of CISM, or CISD may be equivalent to CISM, and CISM may or may not have a definite procedure.

- Debriefing is widely and routinely practiced and is increasingly turned to as a first resort when disasters strike. Following harrowing experiences, psychological debriefing providers frequently advise organizations to use their services, asserting a number of claims about the effectiveness of debriefing.

COUNTERPOINT

- Crisis intervention is not intended to be a substitute for psychotherapy, but rather an effective provision of support following life-threatening trauma.

- There is ample justification for having unequivocal confidence in the group CISD process when it is properly applied according to acceptable standards of practice, and by people who have been properly trained in applying the model.

- Devilly and Cotton cannot legitimately state that "CISD is possibly noxious." The studies they use to support this comment never actually evaluated CISD processes that were provided by properly trained personnel adhering to acceptable standards of care.

- The most prominent of the many glaring errors of Devilly and Cotton is the treatment of a specific, structured, 7-step, small-group crisis intervention process called CISD as if it were one and the same as a comprehensive, systematic, and multicomponent program called CISM.

- Although Devilly and Cotton assert that psychological debriefing is the first resort when disasters strike; in fact, debriefings are not recommended for several weeks or longer after a disaster. The only people who would resort first to debriefing after a disaster are those who are untrained and apparently unaware of what is needed before debriefing.

YES

Grant J. Devilly and
Peter Cotton

Psychological Debriefing and the Workplace: Defining a Concept, Controversies and Guidelines for Intervention

Critical incident stress debriefing (CISD), a specific form of psychological debriefing, has gained widespread acceptance and implementation in the few short years since it was first proposed (Mitchell, 1983). However, there has been recent doubt cast on this practice and confusion regarding the terminology used. This article explores the claims frequently made by proponents regarding its use, counterclaims of ineffectiveness by its detractors, and general consensus regarding its specific use and the use of more generic psychological debriefing. We conclude that the recently introduced critical incident stress management (CISM) and its proposed progenitor, CISD, are currently poorly defined and relatively indistinct in the treatment-outcome literature and should be treated similarly. Current expert consensus and meta-analytic reviews suggest that CISD is possibly noxious, generic psychological debriefing is probably inert and that more emphasis should be placed on screening for, and providing, early intervention to those who go on to develop pathological reactions. A set of generic guide lines for the minimisation and management of workplace traumatic stress responses is also proposed.

⋅⊙⋅

During times of organisational upheaval and personal and interpersonal crisis, organisations frequently access the services of psychologists to help mitigate the long-term consequences of these occurrences. Indeed, the provision of "debriefing" services to organisations is now a multi-million dollar industry. For example, after the tragedy of the World Trade Centre terrorist attacks in New York (2001) newspaper articles reported that thousands of "debriefers" attended the area, advocating and offering debriefing services (Kadet, 2002). This also involved many of the organisations associated with the World Trade Center being contacted and offered such debriefing services. The primary aims of this article are to evaluate the need for "psychological debriefing," to define the terms currently being used and to determine whether such an intervention is useful or can, in

From *Australian Psychologist*, vol. 38, no. 2, July 2003, pp. 144–150. Copyright © 2003 by Taylor & Francis Journals. Reprinted by permission.

fact, be counterproductive. Our secondary goal is to extrapolate from what we do know from the literature and provide some general guidelines for organisations and psychologists, based on our current state of knowledge.

Psychological debriefing has been recently placed under the scientific microscope (van Emmerik, Kamphuis, Hulsbosch, & Emmelkamp, 2002), and it has been argued that good intentions and the passion to help following a trauma may carry with it paradoxical effects, particularly if the tools being used to aid are cursorily understood, dogmatically applied and the peer-reviewed research literature left untouched (Gist & Devilry, 2002). Yet debriefing is widely and routinely practised and appears to be increasingly turned-to as a first resort when disasters strike. Following harrowing experiences psychological debriefing providers frequently advise organisations to utilise their services, asserting a number of claims about the effectiveness of debriefing. The rationale typically includes the following:

- Debriefing will be seen as a gesture of support by the employer, concerned with the psychological welfare of their employees.
- Psychological debriefing will help mitigate long-term poor functioning, which otherwise is "likely" to occur and is a "foreseeable" consequence of the event.
- This will, therefore, also protect the organisation from litigation for not fulfilling their workplace, health and safety obligations.
- And, lastly, with employees less likely to suffer long-term psychological consequences following the debriefing, the workforce will be healthier—and a healthy workforce is a more productive workforce.

With these claims in mind, it is fitting that we present working definition of our terms. Frequently, and particularly in applied contexts, terms are being used without operational definitions and are often used interchangeably. This makes inspecting the evidence behind the claims a murky and very difficult task.

Definitions

"Psychological debriefing" is a generic term that has been suitably equated with "emotional first-aid" following trauma. To our knowledge the term was first referenced in the Australian literature by Raphael (1984) who noted that some psychological debriefing programs "usually involved the rapid mobilisation of skilled staff to interview and work with the victims to assist them with the psychological response to the disaster and its aftermath, frequently in direct outreach to the disaster sites and the victims' homes" (p. 303). More recently, in a meta-analytic review of psychological debriefing (PD), Rose, Wessely and Bisson (2001) defined PD as "any brief psychological intervention that involves some reworking/reliving/recollection of the trauma and subsequent emotional reactions." However, for the sake of being comprehensive, yet not at the price of specificity, Devilly Gist, and Cotton (2002) describe PD as:

> . . . the generic term for immediate interventions following trauma (usually within 3 days) that seek to relieve stress with the hopeful intent of

mitigating or preventing long term pathology . . . [and that . . . PD relies predominantly on ventilation/catharsis, normalisation of distress, and psycho-education regarding presumed symptoms] (p. 4).

This is to be contrasted with the proprietary-based term critical incident stress debriefing (and, more recently, critical incident stress management). This is a specific variety of PD, frequently utilised with groups, and developed by Mitchell (1983) as a structured approach with seven aspects. These steps include:

1. the introductory phase (where the rules, process and goals are outlined)
2. the fact phase (serial clarification of what the participants saw, did, heard etc.)
3. the thoughts phase (what the participants' first thoughts were/are following the event)
4. the reaction phase (exploration of individuals emotional reactions)
5. the symptoms phase (global assessment of physical or psychological symptoms)
6. the teaching/information phase (educating the participants about possible, common, or even "likely" stress responses)
7. the re-entry phase (referral information provided for future follow-up).

More recently, and with evidence against the use of CISD becoming more and more convincing, Everly and Mitchell (1999) proposed that CISD had been superseded by Critical Incident Stress Management (CISM), and these authors have since offered two reviews of CISM (Everly, Flannery & Mitchell, 2000; Everly, Flannery, & Eyler, 2002). But what is CISM and does it significantly and operationally differ from CISD?

A review of the CISM literature offered by Everly et al. (2000) described it as "a new generation of intervention technologies" (p. 23) and, in keeping with a 7-step formula, offered the following definition:

CISM represents seven core integrated elements: (a) pre-crisis preparation (both individual and organisational); (b) large scale demobilisation procedures for use after mass disasters; (c) individual acute crisis counselling; (d) brief small group discussions, called defusings, designed to assist in acute symptom reduction; (e) longer small group discussions, called Critical Incident Stress Debriefing (CISD), designed to assist in achieving a sense of psychological closure post-crisis and/or facilitate the referral process; (f) family crisis intervention techniques; and (g) follow-up procedures, and/or referral for psychological assessment or treatment (p. 24).

It would seem, therefore, that by 2000 CISD had been somewhat redefined and incorporated into a larger and more encompassing approach, although it should be stressed that there is no empirical support for any of the newly proposed steps. However, of interest in the review is that in support of CISM, studies which used only CISD were cited. It, therefore, begs the question of whether CISD and CISM are distinguishable.

In fact, in supporting the use of CISM, one of the studies Everly et al. (2000) cite is an Australian report (Leeman-Conley, 1990). This study details a management-wide intervention for dealing with trauma following violent bank hold-ups in the Commonwealth Banking Corporation. However, the term CISM is never referred to in this study, the procedure appears to differ significantly from that outlined by Everly et al. (2000), and outcome was assessed by comparing compensation costs and absenteeism in the year following the introduction of the intervention to the previous year's costs (i.e., not a randomised trial and open to untold influence from many other organisational and non-specific changes that may have occurred, e.g., improved security, improved health plans, fewer hold-ups, change in seasonal illnesses, changes in absenteeism practices).

By 2002, Everly et al. describe CISM as "an integrated multicomponent crisis intervention system"(p. 171, Everly et al., 2002). It is unclear exactly how to interpret this, but the authors claim that CISD "was designed to be only one component of a comprehensive multicomponent crisis intervention program referred to as Critical Incident Stress Management" (p. 174) and then cite Everly and Mitchell (1999) in support of this. It is difficult to see how this can be the case since the term CISM did not even enter the debriefing lexicon until the mid-1990s and CISD was advocated as a method for mitigating the effects of trauma back in the early 1980s (Mitchell, 1983).

The review by Everly et al. (2002) of CISM also needs further analysis. Firstly, the authors claimed that "CISD was never designed to be implemented as a single intervention outside of the multicomponent CISM program" (p. 174) and provide a 1999 reference to support this. As alluded to above, there appears to be an element of historical revisionism characterising this account, which is further weakened through citing such recent references. Notwithstanding, there are three further factors which are of even greater concern.

First, no operational definition of the facets integral to CISM, and necessary or sufficient to qualify as CISM, were incorporated into the review. Rather, studies were included which were "purporting to specifically assess interventions consistent with the CISM formulation" (p. 177). Second, of the eight studies that met this criteria, six were studies by the directors of the International Critical Incident Stress Foundation (ICISF) who are also the originators of CISD/M. This is important because meta-analyses typically draw on a range of studies delivering conclusions that are less likely to be disproportionately weighted by methodological weaknesses and/or researcher allegiance. Out of the two studies by other authors, one (Busuttil et al., 1995) had incorporated PD within a group therapy program aimed at *treating* posttraumatic stress disorder (PTSD) and no explicit mention of CISM is made, and the other (Richards, 1999) was a presentation at an ICISF conference and, therefore, not easily accessible for review.

Third, the authors of this review included into the same analysis studies using different domains of outcome measurement. Some of the studies were termed "Assault Staff Action Programs" and the outcome measure was the number of times staff (psychiatric hospital staff or community care staff) were assaulted following the intervention compared to before the intervention.

Other studies utilised diagnostic interviews/psychometric assessment of distress levels of workers with PTSD and traumatic reactions. As mentioned, some of the studies were aimed at treating *trauma reactions* (and sometimes many months following the trauma; Busuttil et al., 1995; Mitchell, Schiller, Eyler, & Everly, 1999) and others were aimed at mitigating further distress or number of assaults (Flannery Hanson, Penk, Flannery, & Gallagher, 1995; Flannery et al., 1998; Flannery Penk, & Corrigan, 1999; Flannery, Anderson, Marks, & Uzoma, 2000). Such a fundamental methodological flaw undermines the validity of any conclusions based on the meta-analysis of this group of studies.

For now, we can only conclude that CISD may or may not be one component of CISM, or CISD may be equivalent to CISM, and CISM may or may not have a definite procedure. Until the necessary and sufficient conditions for what counts as CISD and/or CISM are clarified CISM must be regarded as an unfalsifiable intervention system, and the two terms should for now be treated synonymously.

More broadly, it is important to differentiate debriefing from early intervention. Devilly (2002) suggested that early intervention "is the provision of what could be called 'restorative treatment' to individuals who *request* psychological help following crime/trauma and have a *clinically significant* presentation" (p. 4). The notion here is that whilst the individuals report pathological functioning (2 days to 4 weeks following the event), the goal of early intervention is to prevent long-term, psychological and functional impairment. Interventions at this level are goal orientated, explicit and evidence based. Such an example would be interventions for Acute Stress Disorder (ASD). Untreated, about 80% of individuals with ASD go on to develop PTSD by 6 months, and 75% maintain this presentation up to 2 years later (Bryant & Harvey, 2000). However, cognitive-behavioural treatments (CBT) based upon exposure principles have demonstrated efficacy to the point where only 8% at post-treatment (17% at 6 months) meet the criteria for PTSD, which is contrasted to supportive counselling strategies which show that 83% at posttreatment (and 67% at 6 months) meet criteria for PTSD (Foa, Hearst-Ikeda, & Perry, 1995; Bryant, Harvey, Dang, Sackville, & Basten, 1998; Bryant, Sackville, Dang, Moulds, & Guthrie, 1999). Likewise, CBT treatment for PTSD has shown exceptional efficacy with between 80% [and] 90% of those treated no longer meeting criteria at post-treatment and maintaining this presentation to 3 months and even 12 months follow-up (e.g., Devilly & Spence, 1999; Foa et al., 1999; Foa, Rothbaum, Riggs, & Murdoch, 1991). Current research in this paradigm is now focussing on improving the attrition rates during treatment and factors associated with treatment tolerance (see Devilly & Foa, 2001, and Tarrier, 2001, for a discussion of measurement issues relating to this and Foa, Zoellner, Feeny, Hembree, & Alvarez-Conrad, 2002, for a discussion of predictors of attrition during exposure therapy).

It should be clear that the basis of the distinction between CISD and early intervention goals appears to be that while the former aims to mitigate short- and long-term negative reactions through preventative intervention immediately following an event, the latter aims to actively treat pathology with the goal of restoring the individual to pre-trauma functioning.

Consensus: Mitigation of Long-Term Poor Functioning?

At the beginning of this article, we outlined some arguments frequently posited by those promoting the use of PD. Perhaps the most important of these from a psychologist's perspective is the promise that psychological debriefing will help mitigate poor long-term functioning, which otherwise may occur, or even worse is "likely" to occur, and is a "foreseeable" consequence of the event.

Turning to the second half of this statement first, while it can be convincingly argued that there is the *possibility* of poor long-term functioning following a trauma, this is not equivalent to claiming that it is *likely and foreseeable*. In the Australian National Morbidity Study, Creamer, Burgess, and McFarlane (2001) found an estimated 12-month, PTSD prevalence rate of 1.3% in the community, with 64.6% of males and 49.5% of females having ever experienced at least one traumatic event. However, of those who had experienced any trauma, 1.9% of men and 2.9% of women met criteria for PTSD over the previous 12 months. Notwithstanding specific categories of trauma, such as rape, which evidences a *12-month* PTSD prevalence rate of 9.2% in women (Creamer et al., 2001), lifetime prevalence rates of PTSD for the whole community is estimated at 7.8% (10.4% for women, 5.0% for men; Kessler, Sonnega, Bromet, Hughes, & Nelson, 1995). Hence, in the light of this epidemiological evidence, it is specious to assert that PTSD is likely and foreseeable following exposure to a specific stressful event.

Further, PTSD is not the only, or even the most likely pathological outcome from experiencing traumatic events. Studies have demonstrated that a history of trauma is in itself a risk factor for depression (Zlotnick, Warshaw, Shea, & Keller, 1997) with one study (Lopez, Piffaut, & Seguin, 1992) reporting that 71% of raped women suffered from major depression whilst 37.5% developed chronic PTSD that lasted from 1 to 3 years. Given that proponents of CISD have claimed that it aims to mitigate long-term distress, one needs to also investigate whether it has demonstrated potency in domains other than PTSD.

As part of the Cochrane Collaboration, Rose et al. (2001) conducted a meta-analytic review of the psychological debriefing literature. Their inclusion criteria were that the studies utilised psychological debriefing (which employed normalisation and ventilation), was administered as a single session within one month of the trauma, and relied upon a randomised design. This elicited only eight studies in all, two of which had uninterpretable statistics (Bunn & Clarke, 1979; Bordrow & Porritt, 1979). Unfortunately, the randomisation requirement, though scientifically rigorous and laudable, also meant that no group-based interventions were included in the review. This is problematic because group-based debriefing is the usual method of delivery for this type of intervention. Nevertheless, of the six studies that were interpretable, all either found no benefit of PD or—and worryingly—that PD increased the likelihood of developing PTSD compared to no intervention. Rose et al. (2001) concluded that compulsory debriefings should cease immediately and that resources would be better utilised by focusing on those individuals who develop recognisable disorders.

The thrust of this sentiment is shared in a recent meta-analysis by van Emmerik et al. (2002). These authors likewise conducted a literature search to find studies which had used debriefing within 1 month following a trauma, and where symptoms were assessed pre- and post-debriefing using psychometrically acceptable assessment instruments. Seven studies met their criteria, five of which used CISD as one intervention, six used no-intervention control conditions, and three used conditions of other PD interventions (i.e., "30-minute counselling," "education," and "historical group debriefing"). The results suggested that while people have a disposition to improve over time when they received no intervention (on both measures of PTSD and other trauma-related domains), if they received non-CISD based interventions this made no significant difference to the outcome. However, those who received CISD did not improve over time on either PTSD symptoms or on other symptom dimensions. In summary, these authors found that while some generic PD made no significant difference to long-term outcome, CISD would seem to *hinder* recovery.

These findings and conclusions contrast dramatically with the review of CISD/CISM by Everly et al. (2000) and a statistical meta-analysis by Everly and Boyle (1997). The meta-analytic review stated that it only included studies that explicitly used CISD and group debriefings. They concluded that CISD achieved a treatment effect size of Cohen's $d = 0.86$ (i.e., a large, positive effect). However, when one looks at the studies included, it is interesting to note that not one of them was included in either of the reviews outlined above (Rose et al., 2001; van Emmerik et al., 2002). It should also be stressed that none of the studies used a randomised, controlled design and some of the studies were unavailable for inspection. Furthermore, of those that were available, Devilly et al. (2002) were unable to equate the reported effect size in Everly and Boyle (1997) with the original data presented in two of the available three articles. Additionally, if CISD was never designed to be used as a stand-alone intervention, but rather as one aspect of a "multicomponent CISM program" (Everly et al., 2002), then it is puzzling why a meta-analysis of CISD was performed and acts as the bedrock to base claims for CISD/M effectiveness.

For now, one can only conclude that there has never been a randomly controlled trial of group CISD/M and, therefore, its effectiveness has not been demonstrated. On the other hand, a consensus of randomised controlled trial ssuggests that individual debriefings using the CISD/M system are noxious, and that generic PD has little or no prophylactic effect.

One anomaly characterising PD, though, is the replicated finding that people typically report high satisfaction ratings following involvement in PD (e.g., Matthews, 1998; Robinson & Mitchell, 1993). However, it has been argued that while this is one outcome domain, it is not necessarily the best upon which to make decisions regarding treatment implementation (Devilly, 2002). Additionally, Hart and Cotton (2003) have suggested an alternative explanation in terms of the possible impact of PD not on employee distress levels but on employee positive affective responses. In other words, PD may be more of a "morale maintenance" intervention qua gesture of employer support, rather than a clinical intervention influencing distress and clinical symptomatology. This line of enquiry is promising and warrants further investigation.

Of further interest are the findings that those who are offered PD yet decline to be involved are the most likely to be unaffected by the event in the long term (Matthews, 1998), and those who are most distressed by the event are the very same people who are most likely to be adversely affected by debriefing (Mayou, Ehlers, & Hobbs, 2000). Such results do not make good bedfellows with enforced practice following employee exposure to a major stressor.

Protection from Litigation

As mentioned above, an argument is frequently made for PD that reminds organisations that they have obligations under workplace health and safety commitments to provide for their staff when traumatic incidents occur in the workplace. Putting aside possible issues related to "terminology slippage" and the definition of what could count as a traumatic event—which has been and is still an issue of great debate (e.g., see Bryant, 1996, and Dobson & Marshall, 1998)—the basis of this claim needs to be scrutinised. Perhaps the most famous case in Australia is that of *Howell v. the State Rail Authority of New South Wales* (1997; S6/1997). On 4th December 1992, a female suicided by jumping in front of a train, the result of which was that some 42 different body parts lay on the track and surrounding area. A rail worker (Mr Howell) was called from a nearby station to secure the scene while emergency service workers were called for, and during this time he witnessed the horrendous outcome of the suicide. A psychologist, contracted by the rail authority to follow-up on their worker, telephoned Mr Howell at home later that night and asked whether he would like to speak about how the event had affected him. Mr Howell reported that he did not wish to do so and the psychologist arranged to follow-up again a few days later. On the second contact, Mr Howell again refused help and the psychologist submitted a report and remit for payment to the rail authority. In a case which came to a close in 1997, Mr Howell sued the rail authority for breach of duty, having developed PTSD as a result of the incident. Mr Howell was first awarded $514,000 ($130,000 damages for non-economic loss, $115,000 for past economic loss, $200,000 for future economic loss, $15,000 for superannuation loss, $16,000 in past medical expenses, $18,000 for future medical costs, and $20,000 relating to topping-up received workers compensation). However, after various presentations and appeals, this sum was eventually increased to $750,000.

Naturally, such a hefty award has made many employers anxious to mitigate the effects of trauma that occur in the workplace. Indeed, a cursory search of Australian websites quickly demonstrates how this case is currently being used as a reason why debriefing should always be advocated, particularly by the providers of Employee Assistance Programs. Furthermore, in answer to Bledsoe (2002) who warns of possible liability *for providing* debriefing, the ICISF recently used this decision as further evidence for the use of CISD (Robinson, 2002). However, this decision needs to be inspected more closely.

First, it was implicitly accepted by the trial judge that debriefing would have improved the status of Mr Howell and acted as a mitigating force in long-term pathology. In light of hindsight and the more recent evidence, as cited above, such a decision would now seem ill-advised. Secondly, the rail authority handbook stipulated that Critical Incident Stress Debriefing (note that CISD was used and not generic PD) be provided in such cases within 48 hours. The fact that this was not followed leant heavily on the decision that the authority had breached their duty and acted negligently. Naturally, such practices need to be amended in keeping with the first point above. Thirdly, the trial judge decided that the psychologist either knew or should have known that "by 12.30 p.m. on Saturday 5 December 1992 . . . that the plaintiff was showing signs of Post-traumatic Stress Disorder." This is indeed a bold claim and in direct contradiction to research evidence and our current method of classification. Acute Stress Disorder (outlined above), as a method of early detection for PTSD, is sensitive but not specific as it currently stands (Harvey & Bryant, 1998) and even then cannot be diagnosed until at least 2 days following the event. However, and of further interest to psychologists, was the judge's explicitly declared low opinion of the psychologist. The judge decided that this psychologist was negligent in not conducting a face-to-face interview with Mr Howell and had:

> . . . seriously suggested in an initial report to the Railways that he had, in fact, had interviews, which would infer that he had conducted face to face interviews with the plaintiff at least on 7 December and 9 December . . . and [therefore] that there had been a misreporting by the psychologist as to what he had done.

It is thought that such a disparaged view of a psychologist may have tempered the final decision and detracted from the substantive point of whether the debriefing would have actually helped or not.

In an appeal that challenged this implicit assumption of debriefing as effective, the awarded sum was actually further increased to $750,000. However, it appears that this was mainly because it was testified by a prominent psychiatrist that had ASD been diagnosed, then early intervention could have been instituted based upon CBT procedures, which would increase the likelihood of recovery. This is a different argument to looking at debriefing effectiveness and appropriateness. Furthermore, this argument appears to be utilising information that was not available to either the organisation or the psychological community in 1992.

In fact, in light of the available evidence it is, in our opinion, more likely that at some point in the future a company may be litigated against where they compel employees to attend CISD rather than omit to provide it. This opinion is being taken more seriously in the literature (e.g., Bledsoe, 2002; in press), and one can only sympathise with organisations who must feel that they are trapped between a rock and a very hard place. Irrespective of vulnerability to litigation, expert traumatic stress panels have warned against such well-intentioned care and, for example, after the World Trade Centre Terrorist attack on 11th September 2001, a letter signed by 14 eminent psychologists from around the world appeared in the New York Times and the American Psychiatric Association's newsletter, *The Monitor,* (Herbert et al., 2001) warning of the dangers of "debriefers" flocking to the area. In fact, this practice of armies of debriefers descending upon war-torn or devastated parts of the world has received the moniker, somewhat cynically, of "Trauma Tourism" (Gist & Lubin, 1999).

A Healthy Workforce Is a Productive Workforce

A review of the organisational behaviour and work psychology literature suggests that limited progress has been made in linking workplace-oriented clinical interventions to organisational performance outcomes (Hart & Cooper, 2001; Wright & Cropanzano, 2000). However, there are indications that increasing employee-positive affective responses contributes towards increasing discretionary performance (Borman & Motowildo, 1993) as well as reducing absenteeism (George, 1989, 1996) and workers compensation costs (Hart & Cotton, 2003).

Accordingly, a healthy workforce may well be a more productive workforce, but the most reliable method of avoiding a sick workforce after a traumatic event is still open to debate. Nevertheless, given our current state of knowledge, it is possible to delineate some general guidelines to be used in organisational practice.

General Guidelines

Below we have outlined a very brief summary of suggested intervention principles:

Organisational policy. An organisation's critical incident management policy should be regularly updated and be consistent with developments in the research literature. To facilitate this, an organisation might contract a recognised expert in this field to review their policy documentation.

Facilitate access to immediate practical and social support. It is not possible to specify all the kinds of practical support that are viable in all situations. For example, following mass trauma events, such as bushfires and floods, governments provide facilities such as access to information, places of safety, bedding, food and sanitation. Organisations after events, such as a workplace fatality, may provide such facilities as help with funeral arrangements, transport for work colleagues, and general changes in workplace conditions that may facilitate a sense that the employer cares about their plight. This may include making available a "veteran" in their area of work who has a wealth of experience and is willing to talk to those who witnessed the event or are concerned regarding how to cope. This use of a respected veteran that workers know and trust is discussed in greater detail by Bledsoe (in press) and Devilly et al. (2002). Contact from the exposed individuals' immediate manager to express concern and support is also helpful, as is the availability of contact with peers. The type of social support referred to here is the (non-clinical) everyday expression of care and listening to the individual's concerns.

Offer access to employee assistance services for those who request it.   In Australia, organisations have a non-delegable duty of care in relation to workplace health. Providing access to appropriately qualified mental health service providers, for *face-to-face* emotional support and follow-up, also provides an important gesture of employer support. Additionally, accessing employee assistance programs provides an opportunity to screen for individuals who may go on to develop post-trauma reactions. The provision of "comfort" *may* also appease general and non-diagnosable distress. However, at this point it should not be regarded as a clinical intervention, but more as a socially supportive intervention and an opportunity to screen for individuals who may require more substantive support and treatment.

Provide factual information and normalise reactions (not "symptoms"). Without doubt, most frequently the first need of victims of crime or surviving members of a trauma (or related family and friends) is the need for information. This information can include the need to know who has been hurt, how far investigative processes have progressed, which documentation should be completed and when, and how to access facilities. At a national level, this need is frequently met by the use of a well-informed telephone help-line, and at an organisational level this can be accomplished by regular, frequent and official meetings with all those involved.

Some authors recommend educating the client at various points about reactions to stressors (e.g., Litz, Gray, Bryant, & Adler, 2002) and others suggest that psycho-education regarding possible reactions should be done as a matter of course (e.g., Mitchell, 1983). However, we have argued elsewhere (Devilly et al., 2002) that this may in fact be counterproductive and may actually prime participating individuals to develop the very problems we wish them to avoid. However, educating people about *possible* reactions is very different to normalising problems that they report to be *already* experiencing. The latter is the more appropriate focus in post-incident follow-up. In the past, however, such intervention has been mandatory and did not take into account individual coping styles and reflect the wishes of the individuals involved. We suggest that this form of intervention can be conducted in either a group meeting or on an individual basis. The point, however, is that the delivery not be compulsory.

Terminology slippage.   Frequently the types of "critical events" that psychologists are brought in to provide services for are not of a "traumatic" nature. "Debriefing" following, for example, workplace bullying or in reaction to a member of a team being dismissed, has become increasingly frequent and the terminology used during these interventions are often inappropriate. It is our view that the available evidence suggests that in these cases the responsible course is to recommend referral to a specialist in organisational psychology and, frequently, an expert in organisational change or mediation.

Promote proactive problem-solving.   Proactivity increases a sense of mastery over situations and increases a sense of self-efficacy It is suggested that employees be encouraged to devise coping strategies that make sense to their specific situation. No specific coping strategies should be mandated (apart from discouraging counter-productive coping strategies such as increased alcohol consumption).

Monitor staff to identify at-risk individuals.   Following the provision of "comfort" and the facilitation of immediate needs being met, a follow-up for individuals of between 4 days and 2 weeks subsequent to the incident would offer the appropriate window of opportunity to screen for symptoms of depression, excessive arousal, avoidance behaviours, intrusive phenomena and dissociation.

Monitoring can be conducted collaboratively between employee assistance providers, managers and Human Resource professionals. The psychologist or EAP provider can consult with workplace personnel, to support them in identifying possible at-risk individuals, who can then be specifically followed up.

Provide access to early intervention for individuals who report enduring distress.   Access to early intervention psychological treatment has been shown to mitigate long-term pathology. More specifically these interventions are specific and structured, and rely on cognitive-behavioural strategies, and predominantly on exposure treatment. These interventions should not be confounded with more generic supportive counselling which has no demonstrated impact on the course of post-traumatic incident recovery. Moreover, the effective delivery of these interventions requires specialised clinical training. Given the wide range of training and skill levels characterising employee assistance professionals, it is important for an organisation to ensure that any contracted Employee Assistance Providers possess the relevant specialist skills in this area. We note that in our own profession, a wide range of interventions are currently advocated, and not all of these are evidenced-based. Reliance on anecdotal reports or personal commitment to support the application of an intervention is inappropriate. Given that we know that early intervention cognitive-behavioural based interventions have demonstrated effectiveness, we suggest that we are now entering a time where serious ethical concerns may arise in circumstances where exposed individuals are initially offered other types of interventions.

Ensure appropriate organisational liaison and feedback occurs.   This may also require that the psychologist feedback to the organisation ideas, concepts and remedies [are] suggested by the employees. However, caution should be taken during this process to ensure that the psychologist does not actively collude with any dissatisfaction with the organisation that may be expressed by the workers, but rather acts as a facilitative conduit between the organisational floor and management. It is important that service providers avoid confounding post-incident distress with any pre-existing industrial discontent. In effect, the service provider should carefully balance "dual-client" considerations and not become an advocate for the individual and should carefully differentiate incident-related concerns from other industrial preoccupations.

The above guidelines should not be seen as prescriptive but rather suggestive of approaches that may act as a template to be adapted to the specific needs of the organisation and event.

Conclusion

What we hope to have highlighted in this paper is that claims of CISD/M being able to mitigate long-term pathology are not proven and this intervention system may, in fact, result in paradoxical outcomes. Specifically, this appears to be the case for individual CISD. To our knowledge, there are currently no randomised group debriefing studies in existence and hence the efficacy of such approaches is unproven. We also conclude that CISD and CISM, as terms currently used in the research literature, have not been sufficiently differentiated to be used independently. Further, it is our opinion that research and practice in this area of psychological debriefing (or "psychological first-aid"), if not in its embryonic stage, has yet to reach adolescence.

All references for articles included in *Taking Sides: Clashing Views in Abnormal Psychology, 6/e* can be found on the Web at www.mhhe.com/cls.

Jeffrey T. Mitchell

 NO

A Response to the Devilly and Cotton Article, "Psychological Debriefing and the Workplace..."

"**P**sychological Debriefing and the Workplace: Defining a Concept, Controversies and Guidelines for Intervention" appeared in *Australian Psychologist*, 38(2), 144–150. The article is replete with inaccuracies, misinterpretations and distortions. Furthermore, it gives the impression that both peer and editorial review processes were inadequate.

The most prominent of the many glaring errors in the article is the treatment of a specific, structured, 7-step, small group crisis intervention process called the Critical Incident Stress Debriefing (CISD) as if it were one and the same as a comprehensive, systematic and multicomponent program called Critical Incident Stress Management (CISM).

The CISM program includes many tactics and techniques, but it is not limited to:

- crisis assessment services and strategic planning programs
- family support services
- individual, peer-provided crisis intervention services
- pre-crisis education programs
- large group crisis interventions
- the provision of food and fluids to work crews
- rotation and resting of work crews
- advice to command staff and supervisors
- small group crisis interventions
- follow-up services and referral services
- post-crisis education
- and many other services

The authors demonstrate a drastic lack of familiarity with the literature in the field of CISM. There is a substantial body of CISM literature not referred to by the authors. Even a cursory reading of these many publications would certainly have clarified the definitions in the CISM field and most likely would have eliminated the need for this confusing and inaccurate article.

The conclusion that a specific, 7-step group crisis intervention tool is equivalent to an entire multifaceted program defies logic and reason. Likewise,

From *Australian Psychologist*, vol. 39, no. 1, March 2004, pp. 24–28. Copyright © 2004 by Taylor & Francis Journals. Reprinted by permission.

equating a broad spectrum of different crisis intervention tools and psychological counselling techniques, as if they were one and the same, is not only imprecise, it is clinically and academically illegitimate.

Crisis intervention is a support service, not psychotherapy or a substitute for psychotherapy. It is an opportunity for assessment to see if people need additional services including referrals for therapy such as cognitive-behavioral therapy. Comparing supportive "psychological first aid" with psychotherapy is a misguided endeavour which creates further confusion. Therapy does not substitute for crisis intervention. Likewise, crisis intervention does not substitute for psychotherapy.

On page 145, there is a colossal misrepresentation of the facts. Devilly and Cotton say, "More recently, and with evidence against the use of CISD becoming more and more convincing, Everly and Mitchell (1999) proposed that CISD has been superceded by Critical Incident Stress Management (CISM)." The statement is very far from the truth.

In 1983, I wrote the first article ever written on Critical Incident Stress Debriefing ("When Disaster Strikes . . . The Critical Incident Stress Debriefing Process," *Journal of Emergency Medical Services, 13*(11), 36–39). I stated then, "There are many methods to deal with a stress response syndrome" (p. 37). The following items were listed as part of a comprehensive systematic and multicomponent program:

- ". . . strenuous physical exercise . . .
- . . . special relaxation programs . . .
- . . . individual or group meetings . . .
- . . . assessment by the facilitator of the intensity of the stress response in the workers . . .
- . . . support and reassurance from the facilitator . . .
- . . . information is provided . . .
- . . . a plan of further action may be designed . . .
- . . . referrals, if necessary, are made . . .
- The initial defusing . . .
- The *Formal CISD* . . .
- . . . *Follow-up*. . . ." (pp. 37–38)

Keep in mind that in the "When Disaster Strikes . . ." article the concepts were new, the thought processes were new and the wording may not have been perfect. A core of systematic interventions was present, however, and the specific CISD group process (then known at the "formal CISD") was not thought of as a stand alone intervention.

As in any field of human endeavour, imperfect initial efforts go through refinements and elaborations over time. More clearly defined systems and specific procedures emerge. This dynamic growth certainly occurred in the CISM field.

Shortly after the first article was published, it was recognised that "CISD" was being used as an umbrella term to cover the entire field as well as a label for a specific group crisis intervention process. The dual use of the term "CISD" was confusing. The error was corrected in numerous publications subsequent to the 1983 article. For example, the first issue of *Life Net,* the official publication of the International Critical Incident Stress Foundation, referred to "Critical Incident Stress Management Teams" (1990, pp. 1–2). In the same issue, the use of the term "Critical Incident Stress Management (CISM) teams" was encouraged in an article entitled "CISM vs. CISD" (p. 5). Subsequent issues of *Life Net* contained articles that suggested a clarification and proper utilisation of the terms Critical Incident Stress Management (CISM) for the field and Critical Incident Stress Debriefing (CISD), previously known as the "formal CISD," for the specific group process. In 1998, the following quote appeared on the International Critical Incident Stress Foundation's website and in several of its training workbooks:

> Admittedly, some of the confusion surrounding this point was engendered by virtue of the fact that in the earlier expositions, the term CISD was used to denote the generic and overarching umbrella program/system, while the term "formal CISD" was used to denote the specific 7-phase group discussion process. The term CISM was later used to replace the generic CISD and serve as the overarching umbrella program/system . . . (Everly & Mitchell, 1997)

Again in 2001 the correction was made:

> Originally Mitchell (1983) used the term Critical Incident Stress Debriefing, or CISD, as an overarching label to refer to a strategic multi-componential approach to crisis intervention. . . . As can be imagined, the author's use of the term CISD to denote both the entire strategic approach to crisis intervention and the "formal" 6-phase small group discussion process that was part of it, led to significant confusion, which persists even today. In a direct effort to undo the confusion created by the dual usage of the term CISD and, more importantly, by the inferred, but erroneous, tacit endorsement of CISD (the small group discussion) as a stand-alone crisis intervention, the use of the term Critical Incident Stress Debriefing as the label for the cumulative strategic crisis intervention system was abandoned in favor of the term Critical Incident Stress Management. (Everly, Flannery, Eyler, & Mitchell, 2001)

Let me be perfectly clear, the change in terminology described in the paragraphs above had nothing to do with Devilly and Cotton's suggestion that "mounting evidence" against the use of CISD caused the change. In fact, we still have unequivocal confidence in the group CISD process when it is properly applied according to acceptable standards of practice and by people who have been properly trained in applying the model. Their perception of the reason for the change is, therefore, grossly mistaken.

On page 147 of their article, the authors make reference to an Australian legal case *(Howell v. the State Rail Authority of New South Wales, 1997)* and then state ". . . the ICISF recently used this decision as further evidence for the use of CISD." *This is a blatant misrepresentation of the facts.* ICISF *did not* and *would not* use such a case to support the utilisation of the group crisis intervention process known as CISD. First of all, ICISF is not a source of legal guidance.

Second, ICISF is not knowledgeable about the case and would not choose to use it in recommending any kind of service. Third, the case was about an individual and ICISF would never recommend that a CISD be provided to an individual because the CISD is a group process. In any case, my personal opinion on the little I know of that particular legal case is that the CISD would, by commonly accepted standards of practice, have been the wrong intervention to apply.

It is troubling to see a disregard for studies that evaluate CISM and present positive results just because those studies do not refer to the "brand name" of CISM. Such is the case when the authors discuss Dr Raymond Flannery's studies. The authors say that his work is not about CISM because he calls his program the "Assaulted Staff Action Program (ASAP)." One does not have to look very far to see the misinformation that those authors are distributing. On the back cover of Dr Flannery's 1998 book, *The Assaulted Staff Action Program: Coping with the Psychological Aftermath of Violence,* he states "ASAP is a Critical Incident Stress Management approach that includes individual crisis counseling, group debriefings, an employee victims' support group, employee victim family outreach, and professional referrals, when needed." On page 37 of his book, Flannery states:

> It was clear to me that no one intervention, no matter how effective in its own right, could address the differing needs of the employee victims in this facility. These differing situations suggested the need for a CISM approach (Everly & Mitchell, 1997), and led to my developing the *Assaulted Staff Action Program* (ASAP). (Flannery, 1998, p. 37)

Flannery defines his *Assaulted Staff Action Program* as ". . . a voluntary, systemwide, peer help, CISM crisis intervention program for employee victims of patient assault" (1999, pp. 103–108).

Furthermore, Devilly and Cotton say that Dr Flannery used the wrong dependent variable and that he only reports on violence reduction which is not a goal of CISM. They simply skip the other findings that Dr Flannery reports. Those findings demonstrate the effectiveness of his ASAP program which he clearly states is a CISM program. Take a look at what Dr Flannery actually says:

> ASAP, the most widely researched program of its kind in the world, is associated with providing needed support to employee victims and with sharp reductions in the frequency of violence in many of the facilities, where it is fielded. ASAP programs pay for themselves by means of sustained productivity, less medical and legal expense and reduced human suffering.

Again, this quote is on the back cover of his ASAP book. A reading of his actual articles will reveal greater details on the findings this eminent Harvard researcher and clinician has discovered which clearly demonstrate that CISM, even if called by another name, is a successful crisis intervention program.

The point about misinterpretation of Flannery's work has been made. However, I have found no less than eight other articles in peer reviewed journals in which he carefully defines CISM and then directly links CISM and his

ASAP program (Flannery, 2001). Again Devilly and Cotton have demonstrated a significant lack of familiarity with the literature in the CISM field.

The authors cannot legitimately state that "CISD is possibly noxious" as they do in the first paragraph of their article (p. 144). The studies they use to support this comment never actually evaluated CISD processes that were provided by properly trained personnel who adhered to acceptable standards of care. In fact, there has never been a negative outcome study of the actual CISD when properly trained personnel adhered to the commonly accepted standards of practice that are used by 700 CISM teams in 28 countries around the world.

The majority of criticisms against debriefing have been levelled at a process called "single session debriefing" which *in no way resembles* the specific group crisis intervention process of CISD. This is so even in light of the fact that some of studies evaluating the single session debriefing erroneously use the term "CISD." The studies were not measuring the same things. Yet the authors glibly intermingle the terms throughout the article as if they were one and the same. ICISF has never recommended the single session debriefings. They are considered a clear violation of the standards of CISM practice. It should be noted that no other organisation which provides crisis services has ever recommended the "single session debriefings." That includes the International Red Cross, the American Red Cross, the National Organisation of Victim Assistance, the American Academy of Experts in Traumatic Stress, the Salvation Army or the Association of Traumatic Stress Specialists. When primary victims are receiving truncated, poorly designed and badly executed services that call themselves "debriefings," "psychological debriefings," or "CISD," but do not follow the standards of care in the CISM field, it is of no surprise that they would generate negative outcomes. But the authors cannot, with legitimacy, say that those studies are evaluating the same things as a study on the specific group crisis process of CISD.

As a point of fact, the negative outcome studies represent a hodgepodge of different types of interventions which do not equate to the actual CISD but which loosely use the terminology "CISD." Each of those studies is seriously flawed. Such a prejudicial statement about CISD being possibly noxious so early on in an article without substantiating evidence implies an author bias. It is suggested that the readers of this response review the "Crisis Intervention and CISM Research Summary" which appears on the International Critical Incident Stress Foundation website. . . . That article outlines both sides of the controversy and counteracts the unsubstantiated comments of the authors of the article under discussion here.

On page 144, Devilly and Cotton state that psychological debriefing is "first resort when disasters strike." The only people who would resort first to debriefing after a disaster are those who are untrained and apparently unaware that many other things need to be done before a debriefing is provided. Debriefings are not recommended for several weeks or longer after a disaster. The reader should be aware that disaster response is only a tiny percentage of the activity of a CISM team. Most of the Devilly and Cotton argument against CISM seems to be focused on disaster response. At least that is the most sensational (and erroneous) material they bring out in their article.

In proportion to stress management education, individual peer support, family support, defusings, referrals, planning, protocol development, consultation with administration and supervisor staff, and responses to daily small scale emergencies, the number of times that CISM services are used at a disaster is rather small.

Likewise, the number of small group, 7-phase CISD processes actually utilised by any CISM team is minute. The proportion of one-on-one peer support services to CISDs is about 1000 to 1. We have witnessed among the many CISM teams a decline in the number of CISDs when stress education, defusing services and one-on-one crisis intervention services are pursued by CISM teams. Much of that work is provided by trained para-professionals called "peer support personnel."

I would question whether administrations of emergency services organisations are willing to substitute expensive therapy programs run exclusively by mental health professionals when trained peer support personnel have been very successful running these programs for nearly 30 years. My personal experience and that of the nearly 7000 members of the International Critical Incident Stress Foundation which includes over 2500 mental health professionals, is that peer support personnel are absolutely vital to the success of a CISM program and mental health professionals are usually kept at an arm's length from the operations personnel even when they are known and trusted people who have provided valuable services in the past.

The following items are of further concern within the Devilly and Cotton article:

- Paragraph number 2 on page 144 is sensational but not backed up by the actual numbers. The term "multimillion dollar industry" is very questionable. ICISF coordinates over 700 CISM teams and they almost all offer their services free of charge and largely on a "by request" basis. The average call out for a team is less than once a month. No fees are charged for services provided to emergency services personnel. So where is the "multimillion dollar industry?"
- Reports about the World Trade Center that thousands of "'debriefers' attended the area, advocating and offering debriefing services" (p. 144) are greatly exaggerated. First, who were they? Did they come in under some official body designated to provide disaster support services or by themselves? If they came in by themselves, then why would Devilly and Cotton attempt to lay the blame for this abnormal and inappropriate response in the CISM camp? Second, what did they offer? Third, what is the definition of a "debriefing?" It seems that many unauthorised people may have offered a plethora of good and bad services. But these people were not functioning under auspices of a CISM team or any official disaster response organisation such as the Red Cross and the field of CISM should not be blamed for their poor behavior.
- At *the request* of the New York Police Department, ICISF coordinated a response of 1500 CISM trained police officers, police psychologists and police chaplains. It took over *a year and a half* to cycle these people through New York. They went in 7 to 12 at a time, depending on specific

local needs and they stayed for a 7-day commitment. Critical Incident Stress Debriefings (specific, 7-stage, group process provided by a trained team of personnel and following well publicised standards of practice) were rarely held. They were only provided when homogeneous groups with roughly equal exposure to specific traumatic events were finished with their long-term disaster assignments. For some that was months after the event. The greatest emphasis in New York was on individual crisis intervention support. Does this organised, appropriate, free of charge, and requested level of support need to be painted with the same brush that Devilly and Cotton use to condemn the thousands who descended like an army of "trauma tourists" on New York City? Professional articles should, in my opinion, stick to verifiable facts and not degenerate into name calling and fantastic, but unsubstantiated rhetoric.

- On page 145, the authors state that two of the authors of some of the studies in one of the meta-analyses are "directors" of the International Critical Incident Stress Foundation. *That is not the truth.* Dr Everly and I are not the directors of ICISF. Please, let's everyone stick to the facts. The innuendo, of course, is that the authors of the meta-analyses cannot be trusted because they developed the program. It disregards their professional credentials and status and their actual qualifications to evaluate material with which they are most familiar. That is a rather bizarre position to hold and it smacks of an ad hominem argument.

- Toward[s] the end of the article, they describe a program that offers many of the same types of services that a CISM program offers. I must ask "Why is their program any more acceptable than a program that has been functioning well for nearly 30 years?" It appears inappropriate to criticise one program only to offer a similar program with the exception that theirs is based in psychotherapy and mental health professional control instead of crisis intervention with peer support personnel in control. If the Devilly and Cotton are recommending a therapy program, such as cognitive-behavioral therapy, that is just fine. It would appear to me that they would make better progress by extolling the benefits of their program without trying to diminish the value of another program. Should their program not stand on its own without attacking another?

Scientific articles should serve to clear up confusion and misunderstandings. The Devilly and Cotton article, unfortunately, only adds to the cacophony of misinformation about crisis intervention and the field of Critical Incident Stress Management.

All references for articles included in *Taking Sides: Clashing Views in Abnormal Psychology*, 6/e can be found on the Web at www.mhhe.com/cls.

CHALLENGE QUESTIONS

Is Psychological Debriefing a Harmful Intervention for Survivors of Trauma?

1. Mitchell claims that only untrained people would resort to psychological debriefing as a first resort after a disaster. Why is it important to wait as long as several weeks or months before using psychological debriefing services?
2. Imagine that you are a clinician who is treating a person who has survived a life-threatening trauma. How would you go about assessing the extent to which you would have the client relive the details of the trauma?
3. If you were a researcher interested in studying the extent to which psychological debriefing helps or harms survivors of trauma, how would you go about studying this question?
4. Some would argue that following the experience of trauma, it makes more sense to try to avoid recollections of the harrowing event. What arguments would support this viewpoint, and how realistic is it to put such troubling memories out of mind?
5. The positions regarding psychological debriefing taken by the authors in the two pieces you read are quite vehement. What are your thoughts about the reasons such strong viewpoints are expressed on this topic?

Suggested Readings

Doka, K. J. (2003). *Living with grief: Coping with public tragedy.* New York: Brunner-Routledge.

Johnson, S. L. (2009). *Therapist's guide to posttraumatic stress disorder intervention.* San Diego, CA: Elsevier.

Mitchell, J. T., & Everly, George S. (2001). *Critical incident stress debriefing: An operations manual for CISD, defusing and other group crisis intervention services.* Ellicott, MD: Chevron Publishing Company.

Phillips, B. D. (2009). *Disaster recovery.* Boca Raton, FL: Auerbach.

Precin, P. (Ed.) (2004). *Surviving 9/11: Impact and experiences of occupational therapy practitioners.* Binghamton, NY: The Haworth Press.

Thompson, R. (2004). *Crisis intervention and crisis management: Strategies that work in schools and communities.* New York: Brunner-Routledge.

ISSUE 6

Are Blocked and Recovered Memories Valid Phenomena?

YES: David H. Gleaves, Steven M. Smith, Lisa D. Butler, and David Spiegel, from "False and Recovered Memories in the Laboratory and Clinic: A Review of Experimental and Clinical Evidence," *Clinical Psychology: Science and Practice* (Spring 2004)

NO: John F. Kihlstrom, from "An Unbalanced Balancing Act: Blocked, Recovered, and False Memories in the Laboratory and Clinic," *Clinical Psychology: Science and Practice* (Spring 2004)

ISSUE SUMMARY

YES: Psychologist David H. Gleaves and his colleagues assert that for some people, memories of traumatic events are blocked but may subsequently be recovered.

NO: Psychologist John F. Kihlstrom disputes the validity of blocked and recovered memories. He views the phenomenon of "false memories" as a serious problem in contemporary society.

Most people have had an experience in life that has been so traumatic that they strive to avoid any memories of the harrowing event. In such instances, this response is a coping strategy that enables people to move on with life despite a horrible event. There is no controversy about the process associated with active efforts to suppress or avoid intrusive recollections of the trauma. But, are there instances in which a survivor unconsciously "blocks" the memory of the traumatic event? And, can these blocked memories at some point be "recovered"? For decades, clinicians and researchers have engaged in vigorous debate about the validity of the phenomena of blocked and recovered memories.

David H. Gleaves and his colleagues assert that under certain circumstances, severe distress can lead to suppression or blocking of memory, and then to a reemergence or recovering of the memory. These scholars reject the notion of a "false memory syndrome" in which individuals reportedly experience memories of a traumatic event that did not occur. They acknowledge that, while researchers have reported that some individuals do indeed believe that they have memories of events that did not occur, these "memories" usually pertain to ordinary and nonstressful topics that can be experimentally "implanted."

John F. Kihlstrom systematically refutes the claims of Gleaves regarding the validity of blocked and recovered memories. Rather, he points to the impact of persuasive therapists and popular culture in perpetuating myths that memories of trauma are commonly blocked and can be recovered. He rejects the assertion that there is a history of recovered memories that gives the concept credibility, and he cites methodological inconsistencies and flaws associated with claims that these are valid phenomena.

POINT

- Clinicians have recognized the phenomena of blocked and recovered memories for two centuries in soldiers, holocaust survivors, and victims of civilian violence or childhood abuse.

- Memories that are blocked, and subsequently recovered, are often a response to what the DSM characterizes as an event "usually of a traumatic or stressful nature"; furthermore, the inability to remember is "too extensive to be explained by normal forgetfulness."

- While it has been proven that false memories about ordinary and non-stressful topics can be successfully implanted, people are unlikely to develop false memories about traumatic situations.

- Attempts to substantiate claims of false memories come not from empirical data, but from anecdotal reports, often from those who assert that they were wrongly accused of perpetrating sexual abuse or from "retractors" (persons who once reported memories of sexual abuse that they subsequently came to recognize as false).

- While there is support for the phenomenon of false memories, there is little professional support for the notion of "false memory syndrome," a concept that is primarily used in efforts to discredit those who make accusations of sexual abuse.

COUNTERPOINT

- Claims of blocked and recovered memories emerge primarily from "clinical folklore" rather than scientific studies and evidence. While memory loss is not disputed, the assertion that its cause is trauma has not been proven.

- Given that emotional arousal leads to the release of stress hormones that actually improve memory, it follows that trauma should result in a more vivid memory—not a repressed one.

- Therapists who believe in both the traumatic etiology of syndromes and the theory of repression will likely communicate these ideas to the patient, who may already share them because of exposure to the popular media. The result may be beliefs about unsubstantiated trauma that seem quite plausible.

- While much of the evidence supporting false memories comes in the form of anecdotal case reports published in the popular press, that is not a reason to discount them. "Anecdotal" does not mean invalid. In fact, journalists or other lay-people who report incidents of false memory are held to a higher level of corroborative accountability than psychotherapists who claim to assist in recovering blocked memories.

- False memory syndrome involves more than a person's individual false memory. Instead, it occurs when a person uses a false memory to construct an entirely different identity and personality based on that memory. There have been several documented cases of the false memory syndrome.

YES ↵ David H. Gleaves, Steven M. Smith, Lisa D. Butler, and David Spiegel

False and Recovered Memories in the Laboratory and Clinic: A Review of Experimental and Clinical Evidence

Blocked and recovered memories of traumatic events have long been regarded as real phenomena by the mental health profession, our legal system, and the public at large. These phenomena originally were studied by Pierre Janet and Sigmund Freud, and Freud's (1896/1962) "Aetiology of Hysteria" is perhaps the best known early discussion of this topic. In this now famous 1896 address, Freud presented his "Seduction Theory" in which he argued that "hysteria" resulted from repressed memories of childhood sexual trauma. Freud further argued that bringing these memories into consciousness would lead to the alleviation of the hysterical symptom.

Freud subsequently abandoned his seduction theory in favor of his theory of childhood sexual fantasy at a time when he was trying to develop a more general theory of psychopathology designed to account for disorders other than hysteria such as obsessive-compulsive neurosis (Freud, 1955) and schizophrenia. However, the concept of repressed memories of trauma continued to receive attention, particularly in the literature on wartime trauma. For example, Sargant and Slater (1941) described a World War II account of 1000 consecutive admissions to a neurological unit. Over 14% of the sample exhibited amnesia, with the severity of amnesia appearing to be associated with the severity of trauma (e.g., 35% of those exposed to severe stress exhibited significant amnesias). Retrieval of these memories of trauma was seen as essential to recovery and was accomplished through the use of psychotherapy, hypnosis (Kardiner & Spiegel, 1947), or even drugs such as sodium pentothal (see also Grinker & Spiegel, 1945).

More recently, reported amnesia and/or subsequent recovery of memories have been found to be relatively common in studies of clinical populations that experienced childhood sexual and physical abuse (e.g., Briere & Conte, 1993; Feldman-Summers & Pope, 1994; Herman & Schatzow, 1987; Loftus, Polonsky & Fullilove, 1994; L. Williams, 1994, 1995; for a recent review, see D. Brown, Scheflin, & Whitfield, 1999).

From *Clinical Psychology: Science and Practice,* vol. 11, issue 1, pp. 3–28, March 2004 (excerpts). Copyright © 2004 by Society of Clinical Psychology/APA. Reprinted by permission of Wiley-Blackwell.

Despite these clinical data, other researchers, clinicians, or journalists have questioned the existence of repressed and recovered memories (e.g., Holmes, 1994; Loftus, 1993; Ofshe & Watters, 1993; H. Pope & Hudson, 1996), challenging the academic community to provide objective evidence of these phenomena and at times going so far as to claim that there is no scientific support for the phenomena (e.g., Ofshe & Watters, 1993). Some have also questioned whether "recovered" memories might actually be confabulated or false memories (e.g., Lindsay, Read, & Sharma 1998; Loftus, 1993). Empirical evidence from controlled laboratory studies of nonpatient populations reliably demonstrates the reality of false memories (e.g., Brewer & Treyens, 1981; Loftus, Miller, & Burns, 1978; McDermott, 1996; Loftus & Palmer, 1974; Payne, Elie, Blackwell, & Neuschatz, 1996; Read, 1996; Roediger & McDermott, 1995), providing support for this alternative explanation.

The debate over false and recovered memories has polarized the academic and mental health communities into camps that endorse one phenomenon or the other (see Pezdek & Banks, 1996 for a balanced review). The controversy also affects the legal system in that it has seen lawsuits based on alleged repressed and recovered memory as well as lawsuits based on alleged implantation of false memories of abuse (see Bowman & Mertz, 1996a, 1996b; Brown, Scheflin & Whitfield, 1999).

In the present paper we take the position described by Pezdek and Banks (1996) as well as others (e.g., Brewin, 1996; Butler & Spiegel, 1997; J. J. Freyd, 1996; Knapp & VandeCreek, 2000; Smith, 1995a). We acknowledge that under certain circumstances both false and genuine recovered memories may exist. We describe laboratory analogues for both types of experiences. Assuming that both types of phenomena are possible, we suggest that the critical questions are (a) how common is each type of memory phenomenon, (b) what factors lead to the occurrence of each (including under what conditions are each possible and/or likely to occur), and perhaps most importantly, (c) can these two types of memories be distinguished from each other? Toward these goals, we review experimental and clinical data relevant to answering these questions and propose and describe an empirical research protocol that can not only demonstrate both phenomena, but that can also compare the two. Such comparisons can help to determine the causes of these phenomena, discover factors that influence the two, and hopefully reveal signature variables that could provide telltale signs differentiating false memories from recovered ones.

Theoretical Accounts and Evidence of False Memories

The Logic of False Memories

A number of researchers have found evidence of "false memories," defined as experiences that to rememberers seem to be memories of events that took place within experiments, but which do not correspond to experimentally presented stimuli (e.g., McDermott, 1996; Payne et al., 1996; Read, 1996; Robinson & Roediger, 1997; Roediger & McDermott, 1995). A false memory is not simply any memory error. The term refers to cases in which one appears to experience a memory of an event that did not occur. Memory errors that do not constitute false memories include, for example, retrieval failures, omission errors in recall, and recognition failures. Rather than the absence of memory that is characteristic of omission errors, a false memory involves an experience of remembering a relatively complete episode that did not in fact occur. The difference between accurate and false memories is in the correspondence or noncorrespondence of the memory with objective reality.

Human memories constitute evidence of prior experiences, but currently there may be no guarantee of accuracy, however authentic the memories may seem to the rememberer. Studies of the relation between subjective metacognitive assessments of one's memory accuracy and objective measures of accuracy have often shown weak or even nonexistent correlations (e.g., Wells & Loftus, 1984). Even when such correlations are strong, they are by no means perfect, indicating that the accuracy of memories can be misjudged (Lindsay, Read, & Sharma, 1998).

Clinical Evidence for False Memories

Despite recent claims that false memories of sexual abuse and a false-memory syndrome reached epidemic proportions in the 1990s (e.g., P. Freyd, 1999; Goldstein & Farmer, 1992; Pendergrast, 1995), we found no empirical clinical research to support such a claim (for further discussion of this topic see K. S. Pope, 1996, 1997; for a critique, see Kihlstrom, 1997). The primary clinical evidence for the existence of false memories of trauma comes mainly from anecdotal reports by either persons who claim to have been falsely accused of sexual abuse or from persons known as "retractors" or "recantors," persons who once reported having had memories of sexual abuse that they now believe to be false. In addition, there are clinical reports (particularly with respect to dissociative identity disorder) that describe admixtures of true and false traumatic memories being recounted by the same patient (e.g., Kluft, 1998). Reports of the first type have appeared as books published in the popular literature (e.g., Goldstein & Farmer, 1992; Pendergrast, 1995) and have been described in review papers published in the scientific literature. For example, Loftus (1993) described having received numerous letters from persons claiming to have been falsely accused of sexual abuse. Anecdotal and case reports of recantors have also recently been published in the popular and scientific literature (de Rivera, 1997, 2000; Gavigan, 1992; Lief & Fetkewicz, 1995; McElroy & Keck, 1995; Nelson & Simpson, 1994; Pasley, 1994).

In addition, there have been published discussions of "high profile" cases in which persons claimed that false memories of abuse had been suggested or implanted. One such case occurred in *Ramona v. Ramona* (also *Ramona v. Isabella;* see Bowman & Mertz, 1996a; H. Pope & Hudson, 1996) in which a man whose daughter allegedly recovered memories of abuse by him successfully sued his daughter's therapist (against the daughter's wishes) for suggesting or reinforcing false memories. Another often cited case is that of Paul Ingram, a man serving time after confessing to raping his daughters repeatedly. Writers who have cited his case as an example of false memories (e.g., Loftus, 1993; Ofshe, 1992) argue that Ingram's confessions were based on false memories created during interrogation (see Kassin, 1997 for a discussion of "internalized false confession"). Thus, in this case, both the alleged victim and the alleged perpetrator are said to have had false memories of nonexistent sexual abuse.

Experimental Evidence of False Memories

Despite the lack of clinical evidence for a false-memory syndrome epidemic, several lines of experimental research support the conclusion that subjects can be made to report remembering events that did not occur. These include studies of the misinformation effect (e.g., Loftus & Palmer, 1974), hypnotic pseudomemory (e.g., Laurence & Perry, 1983), failures of reality monitoring (e.g., Johnson & Raye, 1981), intrusions in schema-guided recall (e.g., Brewer & Treyens, 1981), and intrusions in recall of list words (e.g., Roediger & McDermott, 1995). The putative causes of the false memories in these studies have included overwriting of the original memory trace, which inextricably integrates accurate and inaccurate information, and source monitoring failures that involve such factors as misattributions of familiarity or failures to distinguish perceived events from imagined ones.

The misinformation effect, similar to retroactive interference effects, is generated in three basic steps that include presentation of the original events, intervening events intended to mislead the participant, and a memory test. For example, the participant might witness a videotaped sequence of events, followed by a postevent question that contained a misleading inference. On a later test many participants remember the inferred events as having actually occurred.

In a particularly interesting example of the misinformation effect, the subject is convinced by family members that a fabricated event occurred during the subject's childhood, at which point the subject may report remembering details of what is a fabricated event (e.g., Hyman, Husband, & Billings, 1995; Loftus & Ketchum, 1994). Although the validity of Loftus' "lost in the mall study" has been seriously questioned (e.g., D. Brown, 1995), in part because the misinformation was of a relatively common, plausible, and nontraumatic experience, Pezdek and colleagues (Pezdek, Finger, & Hodge, 1997) replicated the finding to the extent that three of 20 subjects accepted a similar suggestion. However, when a suggestion of a more unusual and possibly traumatic memory analogous to sexual abuse (a rectal enema) was given, none of the subjects adopted the suggestion.

The original explanation of misinformation effects was based upon the notion that related events are not stored faithfully, independently, and veridically, but rather the individual events are used to construct an integrated memory trace that represents the gist or general meaning of the episode (e.g., Bransford & Franks, 1972). This constructed memory supposedly includes inferences, not only from the original events, but potentially from intervening misleading suggestions. Furthermore, according to this explanation, original events cannot be distinguished from the potentially false inferences in a memory representation. In this view, false memories could include retrieval of false suggestions or inferences, or retrieval of blends of original and intervening (false) information (e.g., Loftus & Hoffman, 1989). Alternative explanations of misinformation effects are based upon the presumption that parallel and independent memory traces of original and intervening events are both stored in memory, thereby allowing at least the possibility of later distinguishing original events from inaccurate suggestions and inferences (e.g., Estes, 1997; Zaragoza & Koshmider, 1989). This theoretical debate has not yet been resolved.

Another experimental methodology for creating and demonstrating false memory, which is a variant of the misinformation approach, involves hypnotically created pseudomemory (Barnier & McConkey, 1992; Laurence & Perry, 1983; Lynn, Weekes, & Milano, 1989). In Laurence and Perry's experiment, they hypnotically regressed subjects to a night during the previous week and suggested their having awakened from sleep upon hearing a loud noise. Approximately half of the highly hypnotizable subjects reported the suggested memory as real (although some reported being unsure; also see below discussion for alternative interpretations from Spanos & McLean, 1985–1986, of these results). Barnier and McConkey (1992) extended this line of research by determining that it was hypnotizability rather than induction of a hypnotic trance that better predicted the report of pseudomemory. Dywan and Bowers (1983) illustrated another nonhypnotic component that affects findings in studies of hypnotic "misinformation." They found that the use of hypnosis increased conviction that recalled information was correct, but not its accuracy. Accuracy was a product of recall effort: the more information produced, the less likely it was to be accurate, indicating that the increase in productivity occurs at the expense of the strictness of the response criterion (Erdelyi & Goldberg, 1979). On the one hand, the best recollection is usually not the first one; repeated recall trials produce more accurate information (Erdelyi & Kleinbard, 1978), meaning that at least some accurate information is not immediately available to conscious recall. On the other hand, pressure to recall more information about an event may result in lower overall accuracy of recall.

Another experimental methodology that has been used to demonstrate false memory effects is the reality-monitoring paradigm (e.g., Johnson & Raye, 1981). Reality monitoring refers to the ability (or inability) to distinguish between memories that were generated from internal and those from external events. In this procedure, participants might be asked to view a mixed list of pictures and words and to form mental images of the referents of the words. On a later memory test the participants are often unable to distinguish between pictures they were shown and those that they generated through mental imagery (although see Johnson & Raye, 1981 for a discussion of the conditions under which participants *are* able to discriminate the two). This phenomenon has its corollary in the hypnotic phenomenon of "source amnesia," in which an individual will recall some information implanted during hypnosis but will be unable to recall, or will misrepresent, the source, for example it as coming from a prior store of information rather than the recent hypnotic suggestion (Evans, 1988).

Johnson, Hashtroudi, and Lindsay (1993) have explained failures of reality monitoring as examples of more general source-monitoring failures. Source monitoring refers to the ability to correctly attribute the source of a memory. A number of attributes of memories, including contextual, semantic, or perceptual features, potentially can be used to discriminate among different sources of the memories. Johnson et al. claimed that most memory illusions, such as misattributed familiarity (e.g., Jacoby, 1991), cryptamnesia (e.g., A. S. Brown & Murphy, 1989), and confabulation (e.g., Loftus & Palmer, 1974) are due to source monitoring failures. Jacoby's (1991) explanation of misattributed familiarity is based upon a distinction between two types of memory, an automatic, unconscious familiarity response, and an intentional, deliberate type of remembering that is under conscious control. When a memory is automatically stimulated without an accompanying conscious respecification of its source, the resultant familiarity might be attributed to an inappropriate source.

Another approach to the study of false memories has been to observe schema-guided recall and recognition (e.g., Brewer & Treyens, 1981; Rabinowitz & Mandler, 1983). For example, Brewer and Treyens (1981) examined false recognition of objects that fit an episodic schema. They found that schema-consistent memories were more likely to be falsely recalled and recognized than schema-inconsistent responses. This is similar to Pezdek et al.'s (1997) finding that plausibility and script-relevant knowledge determine the extent to which events can be suggestively implanted in memory.

List-learning techniques have also been used to study false memories (e.g., McDermott, 1996; Payne et al., 1996; Read, 1996; Robinson & Roediger, 1997; Roediger & McDermott, 1995). Participants in these paradigms are typically presented with a list of words that are all associatively related to a single nonpresented target word. The critical nonpresented target word is often falsely recalled even though it does not appear on the memorized list. For example, a list might have words associated with the word *spider,* such as *web, insect,* and *arachnid,* but not the word *spider.* Participants often claim to recall *spider* even when they are admonished not to report words that were not on the list. In one variant of this procedure, participants are given a categorized list that contains the most common members of a category except for the most typical category member, which is omitted from the list. Participants often falsely recall the nonpresented category member, and the effect is even stronger if the number of associates is increased (Robinson & Roediger, 1997) or the critical nonpresented word is primed on an unrelated task (Smith et al., 1996).

Theoretical accounts of false memories generated in list-learning paradigms include explanations involving implicit associative responses, misattributed source memory, and fuzzy memory traces. The first of these explanations is that when people study a list of words they implicitly think of associates of those words, and memories of the implicit associates are later mistaken for memories of actual list members (e.g., Kirkpatrick, 1894; Roediger & McDermott, 1995). This explanation is related to the source-monitoring explanation of false memories in that it supposes that memories of implicit associative responses are not adequately distinguished from memories of physical stimuli. The source monitoring explanation is also useful for explaining primed false memories (Smith et al., 1996); memories of primed words are not adequately distinguished from memories of correct list words.

Another theory, the fuzzy-trace explanation of false memories in list-word recall, is that both verbatim and gist memory traces are stored during learning, and false recall can result if memory relies on the inaccurate memory trace representing the gist of the event (e.g., Reyna & Brainerd, 1995). Reliance on fuzzy-gist memory traces rather than veridical verbatim traces, according to this theory, is increased by longer retention intervals, a prediction supported by the results of list-learning studies of false memories (e.g., McDermott, 1996). In addition, when memory tests emphasize memory for substance (i.e., meaning), then things that were not previously studied may be easier to endorse on recognition tests than things that were (Brainerd & Reyna, 1998).

Conclusions and Limitations of Conclusions about False Memory Research

The clinical and experimental research on false memory, each has its own strengths and limitations. The most glaring limitation of some *clinical* reports on false memory is that they provide no way of determining if the memories are in fact false. In many cases, the credibility of the source of information needs to be considered. For example, Rubin (1996) noted that when the source of information is the parent accused of the abuse, there are numerous alternative interpretations of what may have actually occurred. Rubin noted that "Denial, dynamics of secrecy in incestuous families, behavioral reenactments of childhood victimization, alcohol-induced blackouts, and outright lying" (p. 447) may explain some claims that persons have been falsely accused of abuse. When the data come from a "retractor" they may be more convincing. However, persons with verifiable histories of abuse are known to vacillate between accepting and denying the reality of their memories of abuse and may be vulnerable to suggestions (by family members or lawyers) that their memories are false (Gleaves, 1994). It is inconsistent to assume that a memory is credible when someone claims not to have been abused, and to assume that a memory is not credible when someone claims the opposite (Schooler, 1996, sic). However, there are reports in which the history of abuse has been documented, such as L. M. Williams' study in which the episodes were identified through hospital emergency room records of assessment and treatment for abuse (L. M. Williams, 1994, 1995).

There are also severe limitations regarding the "high profile" cases that have been presented in the scientific literature. Numerous authors (Gleaves, 1994; Olio, 1994; Olio & Cornell, 1994, 1998; Peterson, 1994, sic) have noted that claims regarding the Ingram case are contradicted by the actual facts. For example, there is testimony from those who initially interviewed Ingram, that he confessed to the sexual abuse the first time he was confronted with the charges, rather than after months of interrogation, suggestions, and pressure, as some commentators (e.g., Loftus, 1993; Kassin, 1997) have suggested. Olio and Cornell (1998) have . . . observed that the uncritical acceptance and parroting of the alleged facts of the Ingram case have become "an academic version of an urban legend" (p. 1195). Similarly, regarding the *Ramona v. Isabella* case, we refer the reader to Bowman and Mertz's (1996a) indepth discussion of the case to determine to what degree it should be regarded as evidence supporting the reality of false memories of abuse. This type of data suffer from the same limitation as the clinical data described above; there is not convincing evidence that the memories in question are in fact false.

Another limitation of the clinical data on false memories is that the possible occurrence of such phenomena does not imply the existence of a false-memory syndrome (FMS). The current *Diagnostic and Statistical Manual of Mental Disorders* (*DSM-IV;* American Psychiatric Association, 1994) defines a syndrome as "a grouping of signs and symptoms, based on their frequent co-occurrence, that may suggest a common underlying pathogenesis, course, familial pattern, or treatment selection" (p. 771). Currently there are few or no empirical data supporting the claim that false-memory syndrome exists (Gleaves & Freyd, 1997; K. Pope, 1996, 1997), mainly because so little research on this issue has been conducted. In one published empirical study that we found, Hovdestad and Kristiansen (1996, sic) concluded that, "In sum, the weak evidence for the construct validity of the phenomenon referred to as FMS, together with the finding that few women with recovered memories satisfied the criteria and that women with continuous memories were equally likely to do so, lends little support to the FMS theory" (p. 330). More recently, Dallam (2001) concluded that "in the absence of any substantive scientific support, 'False memory Syndrome' is best characterized as a pseudoscientific syndrome that was developed to defend against claims of child abuse" (p. 10).

Although these conclusions illustrate that data in support of false-memory syndrome are still lacking, objection to the term is not new among the scientific community. As early as 1993, numerous researchers published a formal objection to the term being used in this context arguing that the term false-memory syndrome was really "a non-psychological term originated by a private foundation whose stated purpose is to support accused parents." They urged, "For the sake of intellectual honesty, let's leave the term 'false memory syndrome' to the popular press" (Carstensen et al., 1993, p. 23).

Kihlstrom (1998) has more recently attempted to defend the use of the term. Basically his argument was that numerous other writers have used the term "syndrome" in nonscientific context (e.g., the "Lolita syndrome," "sissy boy syndrome," and "China syndrome," p. 17); thus there is no reason to question its use in this case. A related defense (noted by a reviewer of this article) is that criticism of use of the term "syndrome" is simply a red herring, and the critical matter is whether memories are accurate or inaccurate. Although we in general agree with the justification here (that accuracy per se is what is critical), the issue is not a red herring because clearly FMS is being described (a) *as if* it is a scientific diagnosis and form of psychopathology, and (b) as being an entity above and beyond the simple issue of the accuracy of a memory. One needs to look no further than the definition from Kihlstrom quoted on the False Memory Syndrome Foundation web site. He described FMS as a form of psychopathology above and beyond the simple issue of the accuracy of memory. Kihlstrom wrote:

> Note that the syndrome is *not* characterized by false memories as such. We all have memories that are inaccurate. Rather, the *syndrome* may be *diagnosed* when the memory is so deeply ingrained that it orients the

individual's entire personality and lifestyle, in turn disrupting all sorts of other adaptive behavior. The analogy to *personality disorder* is intentional. [emphasis added]

Clearly false-memory syndrome is being described as if it is a form of psychopathology much above and beyond the issue of the accuracy of memory. The fact that mental health professionals have even testified in court that plaintiffs in sexual abuse cases suffered from "FMS" is further evidence that the term is being misused. Although research may someday suggest that FMS actually exists, current data do not. Thus, it is at best premature to use the term "false memory syndrome" and we recommend that the term not be used. To thoroughly discuss this issue is beyond the scope of the present paper (see Dallam, 2001; K. S. Pope, 1996, 1997 for a more detailed discussion).

Regarding the experimental research on false memories, these studies make it clear that some persons can be made to report remembering events that did not occur (or objects that were not observed) in settings in which the consequences of a mistake are relatively minor. Reported false memories can be reliably and predictably evoked and studied with a variety of laboratory procedures. Furthermore, the occurrence of false memories does not appear to rely on extraordinary affective states or special cognitive processes; rather, they seem to be produced by the same cognitive mechanisms that produce accurate remembering. However, there are a number of limitations to the conclusions and inferences that can be made from experimental research on false memories. One limitation concerns the degree to which reported false memories reflect genuine alterations in memory (or belief in memory) versus reporting biases (Barnier & McConkey, 1992; Murrey, Cross, & Whipple, 1992; Spanos & McLean, 1985–1986). That is, do research participants reporting false memories really believe that what they are reporting are memories, or are their reports due to the demand characteristics of the research? In their study of hypnotizability and pseudomemory, Lynn, Weekes, and Milano (1989) asked subjects about reported pseudomemories in more than one way. When asked in open-ended style, 11.5% of subjects reported actually remembering the suggested event (a phone ringing). However, when actually required (in a forced-choice format) to indicate whether they had heard an actual phone ring or if the ring was suggested, none of the participants exhibited pseudomemory. The findings led the authors to conclude that "Although hypnotic suggestions produce shifts in awareness and attention, subjects are not deluded by suggestions into confusing fantasy with reality" (p. 143).

Similar results were obtained by Barnier and McConkey (1992), who showed participants slides of a purse snatching and then suggested false aspects of the event in the slides (that the attacker wore a scarf and helped the victim pick up flowers). The authors tested for false memories in both formal and informal contexts using high-and low-hypnotizable subjects. Although a sizeable number of the highly hypnotizable subjects reported remembering the false aspects of the events when tested in a formal setting, the majority (13 out of 15 for one memory and 14 out of 15 for another) did *not* exhibit pseudomemory when tested in an informal setting. The authors also collected qualitative data regarding participants' behaviors. Some indicated behavioral compliance. For example, one noted: "I knew he didn't have a scarf. I felt pressured, so I put a scarf on him to give an answer" (p. 525). Response bias does not seem to explain all of the experimental research on false memory, but the degree to which it does should not be minimized and has not been completely determined.

Another limitation of published empirical work concerns the degree to which this research can be generalized and applied to cases of false memories of child sexual abuse (Butler & Speigel, 1997; J. J. Freyd & Gleaves, 1996) or naturally occurring traumatic events. The reliability of producing certain laboratory phenomena, such as optical illusions, is no assurance that the phenomena are common, naturally occurring events. Indeed, Mook (1983; see also Butler & Spiegel, 1997) suggests that laboratory research best illuminates "what *can* happen, rather than what typically *does*" (p. 384). When the purpose is to predict or explain behavior in the real world, then the generalizability concerns as to the comparability of populations, settings, manipulations, and measurement must be considered (Butler & Spiegel, 1997; Campbell & Stanley, 1967). At issue is the fact that the vast majority of the laboratory research on false memories has involved suggesting memories of schema-consistent, mundane events or objects to nonclinical subjects—events which are, in many cases, corroborated by family members—and eliciting false reports with no long-term personal consequences, such as family disruption or a jail term for a family member. In the only study with adult subjects in which the investigators attempted to implant a memory remotely similar to child sexual abuse (Pezdek et al., 1997), they were unsuccessful in doing so.

There are also many ways in which false memory research fails to parallel what may happen in psychotherapy, thus limiting the generalizability of the results. For example, in Loftus's "lost in the mall" study, it was actually the family member, rather than the experimenter, who convinced the subjects of the false childhood memories. The generalizability depends on what this finding actually demonstrates. Is it that therapists can have powerful influence over clients or that parents or other family members can deceive their children? If it is the latter, such results do not support the position that false memories frequently occur in therapy.

In another line of recent laboratory research that more closely mimics a possible psychotherapy situation, Loftus and Mazzoni (1998) exposed subjects to a 30-min brief-therapy simulation in which an expert clinician analyzed a dream report that the subject offered. The clinician proposed an interpretation (an "expert personalized suggestion") that the dream indicated that the subject had probably experienced a given event in early childhood (either being lost or being in a dangerous situation). The theme of the interpretation was determined by random assignment, however, the interpretation was personalized to build on the dream material that the subject had provided. Results indicated that the majority of subjects were more confident at four-week follow-up that they had experienced these childhood events. It is unknown, however, whether participants also developed false memories of the events that corresponded to their increased confidence.

This distinction between increasing confidence that something has happened and increasing the production of false memories of the event is a potential limitation to the relevance of the recent "imagination inflation" literature to the understanding of false-memory creation. In these studies, having subjects simply imagine events increases their confidence that the events have indeed occurred (e.g., Garry, Manning, Loftus, & Sherman, 1996; reviewed in Garry & Polaschek, 2000). However, changing beliefs about the likelihood of the events does not necessarily create memories of the event. In one false-memory study, however, coupling imagination with authoritative suggestion (for an event confirmed by family members) increased false-memory creation over authoritative suggestion alone (Hyman & Pentland, 1996), confirming that imagination can facilitate false-memory creation.

For a different reason, laboratory research may *underestimate* the degree of influence and suggestion that may occur in therapy. Contact between experimenter and research participant is generally brief compared to therapist–client contact. In Hyman et al.'s (1995) study of false childhood memories, participants only reported false memories after two or three sessions but never did in the first. In the Loftus and Mazzoni study (1998) only one experience was interpreted. The possible effects of several weeks or even months of suggestion, or of multiple converging suggestions/interpretations, have not been studied experimentally. Of relevance to the former possible effect, Zaragoza and Mitchell (1996) found that repeated exposure to suggestion can increase confidence in and conscious recollections of false memories of witnessing an event.

Experimental studies have not yet determined whether false memories could occur for bizarre or affectively charged events, important concerns to clinical psychologists. It is not yet known whether bizarreness in a memory identifies it as a false memory or an accurate one. The limitation of our understanding of false memories that is most relevant to the present paper is whether accurate and false memories can be distinguished from one another, either by the subject who is remembering, or by an observer. Whether or not there are experiential or behavioral "signatures" that indicate the likelihood that a memory is false or accurate is a critical question that has not been thoroughly addressed by empirical research. To date, findings suggest that memories for true events tend to be described with more words, contain greater clarity of perceptual details, and are held with greater confidence than are false memories (for reviews see Oakes & Hyman, 2000; Pezdek & Taylor, 2000). The sensory detail results are similar to those found when experimenters compare remembered versus imagined autobiographical childhood events (Johnson, Foley, Suengas, & Raye, 1988) or childhood events that subjects *remember* happening rather than simply *know* happened (Hyman, Gilstrap, Decker, & Wilkinson, 1998).

To summarize, the empirical findings of false memories provide an alternative explanation for memories recovered in therapy, casting some doubt as to the accuracy or reality of the memories. However, the circumstances under which false memories can or are likely to occur have yet to be determined. Furthermore, the existence of false memories does not imply the existence of a syndrome nor does it contradict the possibility that blocked and accurately recovered memories can also occur. We now consider evidence concerning blocked and recovered memories.

Empirical Evidence and Theories of Memory Blocking and Recovery

Defining Blocked and Recovered Memories

What we refer to as blocked and recovered memories are cases in which established memories are rendered inaccessible for some period of time, after which the essentially intact memories are retrieved. Memory blocks and the potential recovery of memories are directly relevant to clinical disorders such as post-traumatic stress disorder and the dissociative disorders. Our operational definition of blocked and recovered memories specifies three criteria: (a) There must be corroborating evidence that the event in question was actually experienced by the person, (b) At some later time it must be found that the event cannot be recalled, and (c) After the period of inaccessibility, it must be found that the event can be successfully recalled. Criteria similar to these have also been used by Haber and Haber (1996) and Schooler and colleagues (Schooler & Fiore, 1995; Schooler, Ambadar, & Bendiksen, 1997).

Clinical Evidence of Blocked and Recovered Memories: Dissociative Amnesia

In the current *DSM* (APA, 1994), dissociative amnesia is defined as "a reversible memory impairment in which memories of personal experience cannot be retrieved in verbal form" (p. 478). The events that cannot be recalled are "usually of a traumatic or stressful nature" (p. 478) and the inability to remember is "too extensive to be explained by normal forgetfulness" (p. 478) (see also Gleaves, 1996; Loewenstein, 1991; or van der Hart & Nijenhuis, 1995 for more extensive reviews).

Although there have been claims that dissociative amnesia is a recently recognized (or invented) phenomenon (e.g., Ofshe & Singer, 1994), it has been recognized by clinicians since the beginning of the 19th century (Nemiah, 1979; Prince 1906). Dissociative (or psychogenic or hysterical) amnesia was studied and described extensively by Pierre Janet in the 1880s as well as by Freud in some of his early writings. There are also numerous descriptions of dissociative amnesia in the early and recent literature on combat and war trauma (e.g., Bremner, Steinberg, Southwick, Johnson, & Charney, 1993; Grinker & Spiegel, 1945; Kardiner & Spiegel 1947; Kolb, 1988; Sargant & Slater, 1941) and civilian violence (e.g., Kaszniak, Nussbaum, Berren, & Santiago, 1988). Modai (1994) also described total amnesia for childhood in a survivor of the holocaust. In many of these reports, the authors also described how memory for the traumatic experiences of war could be retrieved through therapy, hypnosis, or even narcosynthesis. These authors did sometimes caution that what was retrieved was often a mixture of accurate memory and fantasy (e.g., Kolb, 1988; Sargant & Slater, 1941).

    More recent research has focused on the presence of amnesia and/or recovered memory for experiences of child sexual abuse (CSA). Recently reported anecdotal, legal, and clinical cases (e.g., Bull, 1999; Cheit, 1998; Corwin & Olafson, 1997; Dalenberg, 1996, 1997; Duggal & Sroufe, 1998; Schooler et al., 1997) of amnesia and memory recovery offer compelling "existence proof" for these phenomena. D. Brown, Scheflin, and Whitfield (1999) recently reviewed the clinical research in this area. They concluded that "In just this past decade alone, 68 research studies have been conducted on naturally occurring dissociative or traumatic amnesia for childhood sexual abuse. Not a single one of the 68 data-based studies failed to find it" (p. 126). Similar conclusions were reached by van der Hart and Nijenhuis (1995) and Scheflin and D. Brown (1996) in their earlier review of the literature. Critics of these conclusions may point to the report of H. G. Pope, Hudson, Bodkin, and Oliva (1998), who reviewed 63 different studies of victims of non-CSA types of trauma and claimed that they "could not find any clear and unexplained occurrences of amnesia for the traumatic events" (p. 213), though some of the evidence and conclusions presented in this review were disputed by D. Brown et al. (1999). More recently, some of D. Brown and colleagues' own evidence and conclusions have also been vigorously challenged (Piper, Pope, & Borowiecki, 2000). Nonetheless, collectively the clinical evidence does seem to suggest that varying degrees of amnesia for traumatic experiences and subsequent recovery of memory are real phenomena.

Experimental Evidence for Blocked and Recovered Memory

Critics or skeptics of the concept of recovered memory (e.g. Ofshe & Watters, 1993; Wakefield & Underwager, 1994) often claim that there is no experimental (or laboratory) evidence for the concept of recovered memory. Almost invariably, the reference cited for such statements is a literature review by Holmes (1990) who concluded that "despite over sixty years of research . . . at the present time there is no controlled laboratory evidence supporting the concept of repression" (p. 96). To thoroughly discuss Holmes's conclusions and the relevance to the recovered memory/false memory controversy would be beyond the scope of this article (see Gleaves, 1996 or Gleaves & Freyd, 1997 for more extensive discussions). The critical point is that Holmes only reviewed evidence for one possible mechanism of memory blocking and recovery (repression), defined in a very specific form.

    In reality, empirical evidence of memory blocking (or inhibition) and recovery has come from several experimental paradigms, including spontaneous recovery from retroactive interference (e.g., Wheeler, 1995), tip-of-the-tongue (TOT) research (e.g., Jones, 1989; Read & Bruce, 1982; Smith, 1994b), blocking in implicit memory (e.g., Lustig & Hasher, 2001; Smith & Tindell, 1997), recovery from posthypnotic amnesia (e.g., Kihlstrom, 1987), output interference and recovery (e.g., J. Brown & Smith, 1992; Roediger, 1974; Smith & Vela, 1991), retrieval-induced forgetting (e.g., Anderson, Bjork & Bjork, 1994), directed forgetting and recovery (e.g., Bjork & Bjork, 1996), and memory inhibition through executive control (Anderson & Green, 2001). In each of these cases the memory blocks are more enduring than a few seconds, as is the case with many other empirical findings of temporary inaccessibility, such as negative priming effects (e.g., Tipper, 1985), Stroop interference tasks (e.g., MacLeod, 1991), or inhibitory orthographic priming (e.g., Grainger, 1990). We will briefly review each of these areas of empirical research that documents memory blocking and recovery (for a more extensive review of interference and inhibition effects in memory retrieval see Anderson & Bjork, 1994; Anderson & Neely, 1996).

Retroactive interference and spontaneous recovery. Retroactive interference has been one of the longest standing topics of interest in the experimental study of human memory. When experiences similar to an event in question are stored in memory after the target event, the resultant forgetting of the target event is referred to as retroactive interference. Lengthening the retention interval, however, causes recovery of the forgotten material (e.g., A. S. Brown, 1976), suggesting either that associations weakened by retroactive interference somehow recover their strength, or that original associations remain intact and interference only causes temporary inaccessibility. Consistent with the notion that original memories remain intact after retroactive interference are findings from associative-matching tests that show retention of original memories (e.g., Postman, Stark, & Fraser 1968), as well as evidence that original and interfering memories are independent entities (e.g., Martin, 1971). Spontaneous recovery effects in verbal learning and memory have been found with paired associate learning tasks, serial recall, and free recall (Wheeler, 1995). These findings show that whatever the mechanisms involved, it is nonetheless clear that learned associations can become temporarily inaccessible and can be recovered at a later time.

Output interference and reminiscence. Memory blocking and recovery can be used to explain another interesting conundrum, the question of what causes hypermnesia and reminiscence (Payne, 1987). Hypermnesia is a net improvement in recall when repeated recall tests are given without extra practice sessions. Reminiscence, a very similar concept, refers to the recovery of unrecalled material, independently of the amount forgotten from one test to the next. These phenomena defy the notion that forgetting increases over time, because more is remembered on later tests.

Hypermnesia and reminiscence can be explained as recovery from initial blocking in recall. That is, when people recall a list of words or pictures, the act of recalling some of the items on the list has the effect of blocking other items that have not yet been recalled (e.g., Roediger, 1974). This inhibition or interference has been termed *output interference* (e.g., Rundus, 1973). Thus, hypermnesia and reminiscence may occur on a later test because blocks caused by output interference weaken over time, in accordance with predictions of stimulus fluctuation theory (e.g., Estes, 1955; Mensink & Raaijmakers, 1988). The theory predicts that delaying a second recall test should allow more time for output interference to weaken, and therefore should increase recovery. This prediction was supported by the finding of incubated reminiscence and hypermnesia effects (Smith & Vela, 1991).

Output interference is caused not only by one's own recall efforts, but also by experimenter-provided items from a learned list. The procedure in which the experimenter provides some of the list items as cues on a recall test is called part-list or part-set cueing. Surprisingly, part-list cueing inhibits or interferes with recall of the remainder of the list (e.g., Rundus, 1973; Nickerson, 1984).

If part-list cueing causes output interference, and if greater initial output interference leads to greater recovery and hypermnesia, then using part-list cues on an initial recall test should increase the hypermnesia observed on a retest. Experiments reported by Basden and Basden (1995), Basden, Basden, and Galloway (1977), and J. M. Brown and Smith (1992) supported this prediction; part-list cues caused memory blocking on an initial recall test, and increasing recovery (reminiscence) on a later recall test. An exaggerated version of this part-list cueing procedure constitutes an essential component of the comparative memory paradigm that we report in the present study.

Directed forgetting.   The directed forgetting paradigm (e.g., Bjork, 1972) has been used successfully to impair the accessibility of experimentally presented materials. In one version of the directed forgetting paradigm, the list method, experimental participants are told that they can forget the list of words they had just been trying to memorize because, they are told, they will not need to remember that list on a later memory test (e.g., Basden, Basden, & Gargano, 1993; Bjork & Bjork, 1996). Instead, participants are told, they should concentrate on memorizing a second list of words, which are then presented. In the control condition, participants are not given this *forget* instruction. The typical directed forgetting effect is evidenced by two results: (a) the first list is recalled more poorly if forget instructions are given, and (b) the second list is recalled better if the forget instruction is given, presumably due to decreased proactive interference from the forgotten first list.

Bjork and Bjork (1996) found that the inaccessibility caused by directed forgetting can be eradicated if experimental participants are reexposed to some of the forgotten material on a recognition test. In this study Bjork and Bjork found that if they included a few forgotten list-1 words on an intervening recognition test, then directed forgetting effects were not seen on a final recall test. This result constitutes another finding of recovery of memories that had been made inaccessible.

Posthypnotic amnesia and hypermnesia.   Perhaps the strongest experimental support for blocked and recovered memories comes from the research on hypnotic (or posthypnotic) amnesia and hypermnesia (e.g., Clemes, 1964; Evans, 1988; Kihlstrom, 1979; Kihlstrom & Evans, 1979). This body of research shows that when hypnotizable participants are given suggestions during hypnosis to forget some events they have already experienced, memories of those events appear to be blocked or inaccessible. Although the degree of forgetting induced by hypnotic suggestion is often great, it has also been found that the "lost" memories can be largely recovered if the participant is given a prearranged signal to cancel the suggested amnesia. As noted by Evans (1988), "When the experimenter administers a prearranged cue, the critical memories appear to flood back into awareness, and the hitherto amnesic subject is now able to remember the events and experiences clearly and without difficulty" (p. 161).

It is this reversibility of amnesia that makes the hypnotic phenomenon most analogous to blocked and recovered memories of naturally occurring traumatic events (for an examination of the parallels between formal hypnotic and pathological dissociative states, see Butler, Duran, Jasiukaitus, Koopman, & Spiegel, 1996). Furthermore, experimental tests of implicit memory suggest that during their period of inaccessibility, memories may indirectly affect experiences and behavior (Kihlstrom & Barnhardt, 1993) in the same sense that dissociated memories are allegedly assumed to affect behavior even though one may have no explicit memory of the events.

Another aspect of posthypnotic amnesia that makes it a good laboratory model for dissociative amnesia concerns Bowers and Woody's (1996) study of hypnotic amnesia and the "paradox of intentional forgetting." This paradox refers to the fact that, in many instances, when someone tries to forget some learned material, the result is an intrusion of the to-be-forgotten material (see Wegner's 1989 study of forgetting white bears). As noted by Bowers and Woody and known by many clinicians, the very intention to *not* think about something paradoxically can bring the material to mind (cf. Anderson & Green, 2001).

This paradox of intentional forgetting in some ways parallels what is observed with victims of psychological trauma. That is, most put great effort into not thinking about the events in question (Koutstaal & Schacter, 1997), but frequently still (or perhaps consequently) experience intrusive thoughts (Horowitz, 1986). In fact, the *DSM-IV* (APA, 1994) diagnostic criteria for post-traumatic stress disorder include both avoidance (e.g., trying to avoid thinking about the event, amnesia for the experience) and reexperiencing/intrusive symptoms (e.g., intrusive thoughts, nightmares, flashbacks). The fact that many persons with PTSD seem to exhibit this paradoxical inability to forget has led some critics of dissociative amnesia to argue that it is totally inconsistent with what is observed in actual victims of trauma (i.e., actual trauma victims cannot forget). For example, in describing her experiences at a conference for the False Memory Syndrome Foundation, Wylie (1993) wrote, "People remember their traumas, speakers point out again and again; their problem is not that they've lost their memories, but that they can't get rid of them—they intrude relentlessly into their daily lives and always have" (p. 22). However, this analysis suggests a fundamental lack of understanding of the clinical phenomenon. The problem in PTSD is not simply a paucity *or* a flooding of memories. Rather it is poor modulation of these emotionally charged memories, such that they are sometimes overwhelming and at other times avoided (Horowitz, 1986). Their intrusive strength invites withdrawal, and their reappearance is experienced as an unbidden reinflicting of the trauma, analogous to the effect of the traumatic event itself, now recapitulated through the nature of its reappearance in memory (Horowitz, 1986; Spiegel, 1997). As Widiger and Sankis (2000) noted, explaining why PTSD is more similar to the dissociative disorders than the anxiety disorders, "difficulty forgetting (or letting go of) a horrifying experience may simply be the opposite side of the same coin of difficulty remembering (accepting or acknowledging) a horrifying experience" (p. 391).

In Bowers and Woody's (1996) study, however, they found that hypnotic amnesia was *not* associated with paradoxical effects. They noted that the majority of high-hypnotizable individuals showed no intrusions when administered suggestions for amnesia and concluded that "thought suppression and hypnotic amnesia represent quite different processes" (p. 381). This distinction may be the laboratory analogue of what happens to some victims of trauma. The clinical data on dissociative disorders, some of which we reviewed above, suggest that some persons *are* able to block out trauma memories to varying degrees. Furthermore, the diagnostic criteria for PTSD actually include amnesia. Thus, the above assertion that all trauma victims cannot "get rid of " their traumatic memories appears inaccurate. It would be more accurate to say that victims of trauma experience varying degrees of intrusive memories versus amnesias for the events. A diathesis-stress model has been proposed in which the level of hypnotizabilty (or a related trait) interacts with the nature of the traumatic event to the degree to which memories intrude or are blocked at any given point in time (Butler, et al., 1996). The level of motivation and the forgetting strategy the person uses (Bower, 1990; L. M. Williams, 1995) may also be factors in determining memory accessibility. . . .

Theoretical Explanations for Blocked and Recovered Memories

Our brief review of theoretical mechanisms that could cause memory blocking and recovery reveals a number of potential causes of these phenomena that can occur even in simple laboratory situations. Although we make no definitive claims as to which of these mechanisms are at work in naturally occurring cases, it is nonetheless clear that there already exist several possible explanations of blocking and recovery that have been used to explain experimental findings. Theoretical mechanisms that could be used to explain blocked and recovered memories include explanations of hypermnesia, recovery from retrieval inhibition, state-dependent memory, arousal effects, and a special emotion mechanism.

Repression and hypermnesia.   Erdelyi and Goldberg (1979) defined repression as a tendentious rejection from awareness of aversive memories for the purpose of avoiding the painful feelings associated with the rejected memories. This rejection from awareness may or may not occur as a result of unconscious mechanisms, depending upon one's theoretical outlook. The best evidence of the existence of repression, according to Erdelyi and Goldberg, is hypermnesia, a lifting or recovery from the amnesia that is symptomatic of repression. Citing evidence from a broad array of clinical and nonclinical sources, they conclude that most people experience such hypermnesias, recalling events that had previously excluded from consciousness to avoid psychic pain. An alternative explanation, that hypermnesia effects are not due to memory, but rather to a reporting bias, was not supported by the results of Roediger and Payne (1985), who found that the observed level of hypermnesia was not affected by a relaxed reporting criterion, or even by "forced recall" instructions that required experimental participants to guess at to-be-recalled memories once intentional attempts to recall had been exhausted. Although the cognitive mechanisms that give rise to hypermnesia have not yet been conclusively determined, it is conceivable that laboratory-induced and clinically observed hypermnesias have the same causes.

State dependence. Mood-dependent memory, sometimes seen as a type of contextual dependence (e.g., Smith, 1988, 1995c), refers to findings that show that memory of events can be enhanced by reinstating the affective state present when the events were initially experienced (e.g., Bower, 1981; Eich, 1989, 1995). Mood-dependence could be one of the reasons that traumatic memories become blocked from conscious awareness. That is, if the critical events were associated with an extreme or unusual affective state, then dissociation could occur, or become exacerbated, by the low likelihood of reentering that mood state. Bower (1994) has proposed this as a possible model of how some memories and identity information could remain inaccessible at times for patients with dissociative identity disorder.

Interference, inhibition, and spontaneous recovery. Interference, a classic issue of interest in the experimental study of memory (e.g., McGeoch, 1933; Melton & Irwin, 1940; Postman & Underwood, 1973), is forgetting caused by the presence of material in memory that is similar to the target of one's memory search. Mechanisms that have been proposed as underlying interference effects include response competition, occlusion, inhibition, and unlearning. Whereas unlearning (Melton & Irwin, 1940) refers to a loss of material from memory, response competition, occlusion, and inhibition refer to temporary memory failures. Response competition (e.g., McGeoch, 1942) occurs when the retrieval of one associated response impedes or delays retrieval of another associated response. Occlusion (e.g., Anderson & Bjork, 1994; Anderson, Bjork, & Bjork, 1994) is similar to competition and refers to forgetting that depends upon the strength of competing associations.

Inhibition, a theoretical mechanism analogous to neural inhibition, refers to a temporary deficiency in one's ability to retrieve material stored in memory. Retrieval inhibition has been suggested as the mechanism responsible for a number of forgetting phenomena, including posthypnotic amnesia, directed forgetting (e.g., Geiselman et al., 1983; but see Kihlstrom, 1983; Kihlstrom & Barnhardt, 1993), retrieval-induced forgetting, part-list cueing effects (e.g., Anderson & Bjork, 1994), and memory suppression (e.g., Anderson & Green, 2001). In the Anderson and Green study, both associative interference and unlearning of the cue-target association were ruled out as the mechanisms underlying the observed retrieval impairment, providing strong support in this case for the existence of an inhibitory control mechanism inhibiting the unwanted memory itself.

Recovery from interference (or inhibition), sometimes called spontaneous recovery, constitutes the best evidence that interference does not necessarily render memories permanently inaccessible. A theoretical model that explains recovery from retroactive interference originated with Estes' (1955) stimulus-sampling theory, and has been developed by several other theoreticians, including Bower (1972), Glenberg (1979), and Mensink and Raaijmakers (1988). The general form of this model states that interfering memories, which are cue-dependent, are rendered inaccessible over time or with contextual changes because temporal/contextual change leads to altered encodings of memory cues. Decreasing the accessibility of competing memories makes the originally blocked memories less inaccessible, thereby increasing the chances of recovering the original memories (see Smith, 1994a). This research is consistent with the notion that conflicting memories regarding abusive parents that emerge from victimization and continued dependence on the same people may hamper episodic memory retrieval (Freyd, 1996). This type of model can also be used to explain recovery of memories in other experimental paradigms (Smith, 1995b).

Mechanisms related to emotion and arousal.   Approaches to repression as forgetting of emotionally traumatic experiences focus more on the traumatic aspects of the phenomenon rather than the resultant amnesia. Experimental evidence of such a putative emotional mechanism is understandably sparse. However, in studies by Loftus and Burns (1982) and Christianson and Nilsson (1984), both of which used material that was perhaps as stressful as ethically possible, both found that amnesia was associated with trauma. Although Loftus and Burns concluded that their results suggested that "mentally shocking episodes" (p. 318) possibly disrupt processes related to storage of information in memory (p. 318), Christianson and Nilsson found amnesia on tests of recall but not recognition, indicating that retrieval rather than storage was affected by the traumatic experience.

Conclusions and Limitations of Conclusions Regarding Blocked and Recovered Memory

As with the reviewed research on false memory, there are many limitations associated with the clinical and experimental research on blocked and recovered memory. Many of the clinical reports suffer from limitations of retrospective research. In many instances, the alleged events of abuse were not corroborated. When they were, the type of corroborating evidence was sometimes not described (e.g., Feldman-Summers & Pope, 1994) and thus is not open to objective evaluation. In some of the research, especially the report by L. M. Williams (1994), one cannot be certain that failure to report memory is due to failure to remember or that failure to remember is due to anything other than normal forgetting, although the documented intensity of the trauma and resulting injury make this explanation less plausible.

Nonetheless, there is an accumulating, if small, store of corroborated and well-documented case studies (e.g., Bull, 1999; Cheit, 1998; Corwin & Olafson, 1997; Dalenberg, 1996, 1997; Duggal & Sroufe, 1998; Schooler et al., 1997; L. M. Williams, 1995) that may help illuminate the phenomena and inform future research. In fact, in one clinical case study (Corwin & Olafson, 1997) the initial memory recovery event was videotaped and has been examined and evaluated by a variety of commentators (e.g., Ekman, 1997; Neisser, 1997;

Putnam, 1997). Additionally, clinical studies of the circumstances and triggers of memory recovery (e.g., Andrews et al., 2000; Herman & Harvey, 1997) have helped to further describe the nature of amnesia and memory recovery in the case of real traumatic memories.

Some of the laboratory research also suffers from limitations. For the same ethical reason that one cannot try to induce false memories of actual sexual trauma, one cannot subject participants to truly traumatic experiences to determine the degree to which persons can block or "repress" these memories. Thus, the degree to which research on blocking and recovery of memory can be generalized to memories of trauma cannot be directly determined.

Some researchers (e.g., Coe, 1978; Spanos, 1986) have argued that findings of posthypnotic amnesia are limited no less than are findings of hypnotic pseudomemories. It is not clear to what degree reports of amnesia are due to compliance, role playing, or strategic enactment, although these studies rarely take hypnotizability into account and overemphasize subjects' motivation to "behave like a hypnotized person." As with the research on hypnotically induced false memory, these factors do not appear to account for all of the findings of posthypnotic amnesia (Evans, 1988). . . .

Conclusions and Future Directions

When memories of traumatic events appear to be recovered, do such experiences reflect truly recovered memories that are essentially accurate, or are such events likely to be false memories of events that never happened? Although no immediate resolution of this important question is at hand, in the present paper we acknowledge and demonstrate the reality of both recovered and false memories. That is, the conclusion that we want to convey is that there is a wealth of data related to both sides of this controversial coin. Recurrent claims that no data exist that support either of these phenomena are, in our opinion, contradicted by the actual data. Furthermore, we believe that it is also inaccurate to paint this debate (as has been done both in the popular and scientific media) as being the academics against the clinicians with only the clinical data supporting the recovered memory position and the experimental data supporting the false memory position. Research from numerous bodies of experimental research supports the reality of memory blocking and recovery.

The issues that are truly debatable concern what inferences can be drawn from the available data. All of the data are limited to some degree. For ethical reasons, research that would perhaps definitively resolve this controversy cannot be conducted. It is noteworthy that the same ethical limitation applies to both aspects of this topic. That is, it would be unethical to subject research participants (particularly children) to the types of events allegedly associated with dissociative amnesia (i.e., physical and/or sexual traumas). However, it would also be unethical to attempt to create false memories of horrific events in research participants. We are then left with different bodies of research that, each in its own way, are limited in terms of what inferences can be drawn.

Pezdek and Banks (1996) described the unavoidable dialectic of "control versus applicability" (p. 1) or that of internal versus external validity. Often the research that has the highest of the former has the least of the latter (or vice-versa), and this appears to be the case when it comes to false versus recovered memory research. We urge researchers to exercise appropriate cautions and to consider seriously both types of validity when interpreting research. We also suggest that there is much room for improvement in terms of finding a balance of the different types of validity. That is, we believe that the external validity of research can be improved without necessarily sacrificing internal validity. Pezdek et al.'s (1997) study of the limits of what types of memory can be suggested is an example of a step in the correct direction. Applying controlled experimental paradigms to clinical samples (rather than simply undergraduate students) is another.

Another step in the correct direction was Smith et al.'s (2003) attempt to study both false and recovered memories within a single experimental procedure, allowing for the possibility of directly comparing the two phenomena. We believe that the greatest advancements will be made by researchers with interests in studying both phenomena. Unfortunately, few researchers seem interested in doing so. Smith et al. (2003) were indeed able to discriminate between false and recovered memories on the basis of metacognitive reports, including confidence ratings (Experiments 1 and 2) and remember/know judgments (Experiment 2). To our knowledge, this was the first experimental attempt to make such a discrimination. Two variables measuring response latencies did not prove to be useful in discriminating the two types of memories. One of the major goals of future research on this topic should be to experimentally test other variables (e.g., emotionality of events, affective states, retention intervals, and personality factors) that might discriminate the two types of memory phenomena.

By exploring these naturalistic phenomena in controlled experimental settings we can learn more about the mechanisms that underlie them. The same signatures that occur in experimental paradigms could be investigated in naturally occurring cases. Retrospective accounts of individuals with histories of memory dissociation and of therapists who have treated such individuals could be examined as a function of evidence that corroborates or falsifies the reality of the recovered memories (similar to the methodology of Dalenberg, 1996, 1997). The clearest cases of recovered and false memories, as determined by corroborating evidence, would hopefully display the same signatures that can be observed in controlled laboratory studies. Thus, only by returning our attention to those naturalistic contexts, looking for the same patterns identified experimentally, will we learn whether or not the mechanisms we identify in the laboratory are relevant to real life cases of memory blocking and recovery.

All references for articles included in *Taking Sides: Clashing Views in Abnormal Psychology,* *6/e* **can be found on the Web at www.mhhe.com/cls.**

John F. Kihlstrom

 NO

An Unbalanced Balancing Act: Blocked, Recovered, and False Memories in the Laboratory and Clinic

In their paper, Gleaves, Smith, Butler, and Spiegel [2004] draw on clinical and laboratory research to persuade the reader that traumatic memories can be repressed, that recovered memories of trauma are valid, and that false memories of trauma are not too important, thus supporting both the trauma-memory argument and recovered-memory therapy. Although the authors adopt an ostensibly balanced position that "both false and genuine recovered memories may exist" (p. 4), their actual presentation is seriously unbalanced. As a result, the reader is encouraged to discount laboratory evidence of false memories while accepting laboratory evidence of repression and recovered memories, and to discount clinical evidence of false memories while accepting clinical evidence of repression and recovered memories.

Clinical Studies of False Memories

With respect to false memories, Gleaves et al. (2004) discuss the clinical evidence in a little over a page of text. While it may be true that much of this evidence comes in the form of anecdotal case reports published in the popular press, that is no reason to discount them. Journalists, lawyers, judges, and other "laymen" can read and reason too, as exemplified by Frederick Crews, the literary critic whose articles on the "memory wars" did so much to bring our attention to the problems raised by the recovered memory movement (Crews, 1995), and Dorothy Rabinowitz, the *Wall Street Journal* columnist who won a 2001 Pulitzer Prize in part for her critical commentaries on the "Kelly Michaels" and "Amirault" cases of preschool child sex-abuse allegations (Rabinowitz, 2003). At least responsible journalists are required to confirm their sources before their stories are published. Psychotherapists—or at least psychotherapists of a certain kind—are content with "narrative" or "personal" truth, regardless of the fact of the matter (Spence, 1982, 1994). It took a journalist interviewing a psychiatrist for a literary journal to expose Sybil as, shall we say, misdiagnosed (Borch-Jacobsen, 1997).

From *Clinical Psychology: Science and Practice,* vol. 11, issue 1, pp. 34–41, March 2004. Copyright © 2004 by Society of Clinical Psychology/APA. Reprinted by permission of Wiley-Blackwell.

   What really matters, of course, is not the professional affiliation of the investigator, or the means by which the investigation was published, but the actual evidence produced by the investigation. On this score, Gleaves et al. (2004) have remarkably little to say. They do not confront Moira Johnston's (1997) account of the Ramona case, a landmark court decision in which practitioners paid heavy penalties and lost their licenses for implanting false memories and which established the precedent, entirely new in tort law, that third parties can sue practitioners for damages caused by malpractice. And although we can quibble about the details of who said what, when, and under what circumstances, can anyone read Lawrence Wright's (1994) account of the Paul Ingram case and not come away wondering whether he really participated in hundreds of episodes of ritual infanticide and cannibalism, including the rape of his own children by his poker buddies while their mother watched? Unfortunately, neither of these book-length analyses is even cited by the authors, much less discussed.

   Turning to the "professional" literature, Gleaves et al. (2004) cite Williams' (1994) study as evidence that self-reports of abuse have been independently "documented" (p. 8). But this is something of a red herring because the issue is not whether Williams' survey respondents had been abused. The issue is whether any of them showed trauma-induced amnesia for their abuse. On that matter, Williams' study is simply unconvincing (Kihlstrom, 1995, 1996, 1997, 1998). It is more likely that the events in question were subject to normal forgetting processes or to infantile and childhood amnesia. It is also likely that many informants were simply unwilling to disclose their histories to the interviewer, a common and well-known problem with crime reports of any type (Widom & Morris, 1997; Widom & Shepard, 1996).

   To my knowledge, nobody has ever claimed that all adult memories of childhood sexual abuse are false, so it should come as no surprise that some such memories can be corroborated. But what are we to do with those self-reports that are not corroborated? Should we simply accept them at face value? Just because some memories are valid does not mean that all memories are valid. But that seems to be the implication of the authors' argument. When therapists speculate that their patients' current problems are causally linked to events in childhood, it would seem that they incur some obligation to determine whether the alleged events actually occurred. But apparently therapists rarely seek independent corroboration of their patients' autobiographical narratives (Shobe & Kihlstrom, 2002). If indeed there is an absence of clinical literature bearing on the problem of false memory, to a great extent this may be attributed to a sort of "pact of ignorance" between patients, who do not wish to have their self-narratives challenged, and therapists, who have no wish to challenge them.

   People can also quibble forever about the scientific status of "false memory syndrome," but no one who uses such concepts as "battered woman syndrome" (Walker, 1988, 1991) or "Stockholm syndrome" (Graham, Rawlings, & Rimini, 1988; Graham et al., 1995) in clinical discourse should have any principled objection to the term. Still, Gleaves et al. (2004) are quite right that the essence of the syndrome is not merely the existence of a false memory.

Rather, the syndrome refers to the re-orientation of an individual's identity and personality around a mental representation of his or her personal past—in other words, a memory—that is objectively false. Consider, for example, the well-documented case of Binjamin Wilkomirski, author of the award-winning Holocaust "memoir" *Fragments* (Eskin, 2002; Gourevitch, 1999; Lappin, 1999; Mächler & Wilkomirski, 2001). *Fragments* now appears to have been the work of an author who was actually born in neutral Switzerland to an unmarried Protestant woman and raised and schooled there by foster parents who died before he published his book. Apparently, Wilkomirski incorporated details of the Holocaust gleaned from his voluminous reading into what is essentially a work of the imagination, but one in which he himself devoutly believed. Following a detailed investigation, Wilkomirski's publisher withdrew *Fragments* from publication. Yet, when confronted with the facts, the author angrily replied, "I *am* Binjamin Wilkomirski!" In an interesting twist, at one point a woman who claimed to have been in the camps as a child herself, and to have known Wilkomirski there ("He's my Binje!"), was found to have been born in Tacoma in 1941 and raised in Washington as a foster child by devout Presbyterians.

Laboratory Studies of False Memories

In stark contrast to their relatively brief overview of the clinical evidence of false memories, Gleaves et al. (2004) provide a detailed analysis of laboratory studies of false memories—but one that is written in such a way as to blunt the impact of the laboratory findings and convey the impression that they are not too important for clinicians. For example, the reader is informed that there are several different explanations for both the postevent misinformation effect (Loftus & Palmer, 1974) and the associative-memory illusion (Roediger & McDermott, 1995)—as if that mattered, given that both effects are so robust that they can be demonstrated under classroom conditions. In the final analysis, it is the robust nature of these and similar effects that should give clinicians pause, because the effects are created by the very forces that go on in recovered-memory therapy: the presentation and discussion of themes related to incest, sexual abuse, and the like (Shobe & Kihlstrom, 2002). In fact, the clinical situation may be even more conducive to the formation of illusory memories than the laboratory.

Instead, we are reassured that because laboratory phenomena do not necessarily occur in the real world, we do not have to worry about them after all. The authors barely mention studies indicating that people with histories of self-reported childhood sexual abuse and other traumas show elevated levels of the associative-memory illusion (Bremner, Shobe, & Kihlstrom, 2000; Clancy, Schacter, McNally, & Pitman, 2000). Moreover, they push the conclusion that false memories for unusual or infrequent events are difficult to implant (Pezdek, Finger, & Hodge, 1997), without any mention of later studies that show otherwise (Mazzoni, Loftus, & Kirsch, 2001; Porter, Yuille, & Lehman, 1999). In a psychotherapeutic context, a therapist who believes in both the traumatic etiology of syndromes like anxiety, depression, and eating disorders, as well as the theory of repression, will very likely communicate these ideas to the patient, who may already share them by virtue of exposure to the popular media. Under such circumstances, repressed childhood sexual abuse may become quite plausible indeed.

Despite the authors' efforts to blunt the impact of the laboratory evidence, everything we know about memory from laboratory research suggests that false memories can be a real problem in the clinic, and in the courtroom as well, as indicated, for example, by the extensive literature on false eyewitness identification (Loftus, 1979; Wells & Olsen, 2003). This body of memory research is supplemented by a wealth of literature on persuasion, conformity, and other aspects of social influence that are relevant to the therapeutic situation (Forgas & Williams, 2001; Zanna, Olson, & Herman, 1987). Psychotherapy, including psychiatry and clinical psychology, must be the only part of healthcare where basic laboratory research is routinely dismissed when inconvenient. Maybe that's why psychotherapy is in the shape it's in.

Clinical Studies of "Blocked" and "Recovered" Memories

Turning to clinical evidence for "blocked and recovered" memories, Gleaves et al. (2004) begin by offering an argument from authority that blocked memories have been recognized by clinicians since the beginning of the 19th century. Unfortunately, they fail to distinguish between clinical folklore, which indeed contains abundant references to repression and other forms of trauma-induced amnesia, and the evidentiary basis for this folklore. While it is true that functional (psychogenic, dissociative) amnesia, fugue, and multiple personality disorder (dissociative identity disorder) have long been recognized in the psychiatric nosology, the evidence for a traumatic etiology in these rarely observed syndromes is remarkably thin (Kihlstrom, 2001a; Kihlstrom & Schacter, 2000). The term "dissociative," as applied to these disorders, is better construed as a descriptive label (referring to loss of conscious access to memory) than any pathological process instigated by trauma.

Gleaves et al. (2004) also make reference to the clinical literature on combat trauma—a good rhetorical device, because amnesia has been part of the folklore of war neurosis, and a staple of many movies, since World War I. But this evidence is totally unanalyzed. How well were the clinicians able to rule out brain insult, injury, and disease as causal factors? How well were the clinicians able to independently corroborate the combat memories ostensibly recovered by their patients after hypnosis or narcosynthesis? They also cite the widely discussed case study of Jane Doe (Corwin & Olafson, 1997) as a compelling "existence proof" of recovered memory, despite subsequent evidence that the alleged abuse might not have occurred at all and that Jane Doe's alleged recovery of abuse memories may have been nothing more than her remembering *what she said,* rather than what she experienced, 11 years previously (Loftus & Guyer, 2002a, 2002b).

Going beyond anecdotal case evidence, Gleaves et al. (2004) attempt to bolster their case for trauma-induced amnesia by referring to studies of amnesia for childhood sexual abuse (CSA) reviewed by Brown, Scheflin, and Whitfield

(1999), and they quote approvingly those authors' statement that "Not a single one of the 68 databased studies failed to find it" (manuscript, pp. 19–20). Unfortunately, re-examination of this body of evidence, as well as of studies of trauma other than CSA, shows the facts to be otherwise (Piper, Pope, & Borowiecki, 2000; Pope, Hudson, Bodkin, & Oliva, 1998; Pope, Oliva, & Hudson, 2000). All too often, researchers in the area of trauma and memory fail to obtain independent corroboration of the traumatic event in question. Or, when the trauma has been satisfactorily documented, they fail to distinguish memory failure from reporting failure. Or, in cases of genuine forgetting, they fail to distinguish functional amnesia induced by psychological trauma, and presumably mediated by processes such as repression and dissociation, from other causes of forgetting, including normal forgetting over a long retention interval, the effects of infantile and childhood amnesia, and "organic" amnesia associated with brain insult, injury, or disease. Nor, in cases where trauma was forgotten and subsequently remembered, do they distinguish memories recovered by the lifting of repression or breaching of dissociation from other causes of remembering, including the normal effects of shifting retrieval cues, reminiscence, and hypermnesia. Nor is there any distinction drawn between the recovery of a forgotten memory of trauma and a reinterpretation of an event that had always been remembered.

These are serious methodological problems, and one or more of them infect every one of the studies in this body of literature. In a particularly revealing exchange, Brown et al. (1999) offered nine studies "in favor of the existence of traumatic amnesia" (p. 28), only to have each of these studies systematically dismantled by Piper et al. (2000). Nevertheless, Gleaves et al. (2004) conclude that, "collectively the clinical evidence does seem to suggest that varying degrees of amnesia for traumatic experiences and subsequent recovery of memory are real phenomena" (p. 12). It would be more accurate to say that this entire body of research has failed to uncover even a single convincing instance of repressive or dissociative amnesia for trauma.

Laboratory Studies of "Blocked" and "Recovered" Memories

Turning to laboratory evidence for "blocked and recovered" memory, Gleaves et al. (2004) attempt to bolster clinical claims of repression and recovered memory by listing a number of experimental paradigms that show either the blocking or the recovery of memory or both, including spontaneous recovery from retroactive inhibition and the tip-of-the-tongue phenomenon. The fact is that nobody has ever argued that people cannot intentionally forget things, nor has anybody ever argued that people cannot forget something they once remembered and then remember it again later. The real question is whether the laboratory evidence of "blocked and recovered" memories cited by Gleaves et al. (2004) supports the idea that traumatic memories can be blocked by such psychological processes as repression and dissociation (however broadly defined), or that recovered-memory therapy can generate valid memories of traumatic events.

Consider, for example, the authors' statement that studies by Loftus and Burns (1982) and Christianson and Nilsson (1984) "both found that amnesia was associated with trauma" (p. 17). In fact, they found nothing of the sort. In the Loftus and Burns study, for example, subjects in the violent condition showed an average recall of 75.6% correct across the 17 items tested, compared to 80.9% in the nonviolent control group. Both studies did find impairments of memory for peripheral details of an event, in line with the Yerkes-Dodson law (Anderson, 1990; Revelle & Loftus, 1992). But none of the subjects forgot central details, just as no trauma victim who was old enough to remember (and not brain damaged) was amnesic for his or her experiences in the clinical studies reviewed earlier (Piper et al., 2000; Pope et al., 2000).

Omitted from this discussion is the wealth of laboratory research, including studies of nonhuman animals employing more stressful conditions than can be used with humans, showing conclusively that emotional arousal leading to the release of stress hormones actually improves memory, at least so far as the central details of the arousing event are concerned (e.g., Cahill & McGaugh, 1998). The well-known relation between arousal and memory can easily account for the "un-forgettable" memories suffered by those with post-traumatic stress disorder, but it cannot account for the repressive and dissociative amnesias claimed by some patients and their therapists (Kihlstrom, 2001b; Shobe & Kihlstrom, 1997).

Consider, too, the authors' favorable discussion of the study by Anderson and Green (Anderson & Green, 2001), which has also been touted elsewhere as evidence for Freud's concept of repression (Anderson & Levy, 2002; Conway, 2001; Levy & Anderson, 2002). In fact, it is woefully inadequate for this purpose (Kihlstrom, 2002). The memories in this study were pairs of innocuous words, deliberately suppressed by the subjects at the request of the experimenter. But even after 16 suppression trials, the average subject still recalled more than 70% of the targets. There was no evidence presented of persisting unconscious influence of the suppressed items, and there was no evidence that the "amnesia" could be "reversed." Moreover, it is extremely doubtful that any of the subjects were induced to forget that they had participated in a laboratory experiment. The fact is, as the clinical research cited above documents convincingly, the vast majority of trauma victims remember what happened to them all too well. The Anderson and Green study is an interesting contribution to an already extensive literature on the self-regulation of memory (Kihlstrom & Barnhardt, 1993), but as support for Freudian repression its reach far exceeds its grasp.

Gleaves et al. (2004) also review a laboratory study that combined the Anderson and Green (Anderson & Green, 2001) retrieval-inhibition paradigm with the Roediger and McDermott (Roediger & McDermott, 1995) false-memory paradigm in an attempt to uncover features that might discriminate between continuously remembered, blocked but accurately recovered, and false-created memories (S. M. Smith et al., 2003). Of course, the clinically important issue is not the nomothetic question of how these classes of memories might be distinguished statistically in the aggregate. Rather, it is the idiographic question of whether any discriminanda are reliable enough to be used to evaluate individual memories in the absence of independent corroboration.

In this respect, previous attempts to distinguish memories that are the product of experience from those that are the product of imagination (e.g., Johnson, Hashtroudi, & Lindsay, 1993; Johnson & Raye, 1981) hold out little hope. In any event, the principal conclusion from this research was that continuous and recovered memories were associated with higher confidence levels than false memories (dichotomous remember-know judgments are highly correlated with confidence). But surely the authors cannot be suggesting that clinicians use confidence levels as a proxy for accuracy in memory. The weakness of the relationship between accuracy and confidence is one of the best-documented phenomena in the 100-year history of eyewitness memory research (Bothwell, Deffenbacher, & Brigham, 1987; Busey, Tunnicliff, Loftus, & Loftus, 2000; Read, Lindsay, & Nicholls, 1998; V. L. Smith, Kassin, & Ellsworth, 1989; Sporer, Penrod, Read, & Cutler, 1995; Wells & Lindsay, 1985; Wells & Murray, 1984). If confidence were an adequate criterion for validity, Binjamin Wilkomirski might have gotten a Pulitzer Prize for history.

The irony of this last section should not go unnoticed: Gleaves himself was among the first to complain (Freyd & Gleaves, 1996) when Roediger and McDermott (1995) suggested that their laboratory paradigm had any bearing on the problem of recovered memories in the clinic (for a reply, see Roediger & McDermott, 1996). If Gleaves et al. (2004) are going to discount and dismiss laboratory evidence of false memories, as they seek to do earlier in their paper, why are they so ready to accept laboratory evidence of "blocked and recovered" memories later? The bottom line is that, more than 100 years after Janet and Freud, the proponents of the trauma-memory argument and recovered-memory therapy can point to only a handful of clinical cases to support their views, and even these cases are ambiguous. Theirs is a laboratory model in search of a clinical phenomenon. The irony goes even further, because Gleaves et al. (2004) call on researchers and theorists to "[return] our attention to . . . naturalistic contexts" and "real life cases of memory blocking and recovery" (p. 39), as if the laboratory research they have reviewed at such length, including their own, is irrelevant after all.

Memory in Science and in Practice

The fact is, there has been plenty of attention to naturalistic contexts in research on trauma and memory (McNally, 2003). Unfortunately, the clinical research purporting to demonstrate the blocking and recovery of traumatic memories is fatally flawed, in many cases due to a failure to demonstrate either that the events in question actually occurred or that the person was actually amnesic. Moreover, research on actual trauma victims has produced hardly a shred of evidence for psychogenic amnesia covering the traumatic event itself. Perhaps, after more than 100 years, we should simply declare the trauma-memory argument bankrupt and recovered-memory therapy passé. This would allow us to break the Freudian death-grip on clinical practice once and for all and move psychotherapy into the here and now, where patients' problems actually exist, and where their problems must be resolved. Because the status and autonomy of clinical psychology rest on the assumption that its principles and methods are scientifically validated, continued reliance on clinical folklore with respect to trauma, memory, and repression can only serve to undermine the profession.

All references for articles included in *Taking Sides: Clashing Views in Abnormal Psychology, 6/e* can be found on the Web at **www.mhhe.com/cls.**

CHALLENGE QUESTIONS

Are Blocked and Recovered Memories Valid Phenomena?

1. Both articles accept that examples of false memories most often emerge anecdotally and from the popular press, rather than through clinical experiments. David H. Gleaves and his colleagues use this information to discredit those who say there is a prevalence of false memories in today's world. John F. Kihlstrom, however, asserts that anecdotal evidence can be just as compelling as statistically significant research. What are the strengths of an argument that relies on anecdotal evidence? What are the weaknesses?
2. Gleaves and his colleagues assert that while mundane false memories are relatively easy to create, it is much more difficult to convince a person that a trauma or an event occurred, when in fact it has not. Thus, these authors contend that those who recover memories of trauma can usually be viewed as truthful. To what extent do you agree with this notion? What are your thoughts about the possibility that popular culture has pushed people to accept the phenomenon of false memories?
3. How would you develop a research study that would shed more light on the validity of blocked and recovered memories? What ethical challenges would you face in conducting this kind of research?
4. What recommendations would you make to clinicians treating clients who report that they have recovered a formerly blocked memory?
5. Usually it is not possible to confirm the reality or accuracy of memories that have been blocked and then recovered. In a clinical situation, how should therapists proceed with clients who reportedly recover memories that would implicate another person in criminal behavior, such as perpetrating the abuse of children?

Suggested Readings

Arnold, M., & Lindsay, D. (2002). Remembering remembering. *Journal of Experimental Psychology: Learning, Memory and Cognition, 28,* 521–529.

Lindsay, D., Hagen, L., Read, J., Wade, K., & Garry, M. (2004). True photographs and false memories. *Psychological Science, 15,* 149.

Loftus, E. (2004). Memories of things unseen. *Current Directions in Psychological Science, 13,* 145–147.

McNally, R.J., & Garaerts, E. (2009). A new solution to the recovered memory debate. *Perspectives on Psychological Science, 4*(2), 126–134.

Peace, K., & Porter, S. (2004). A longitudinal investigation of the reliability of memories for trauma and other emotional experiences. *Applied Cognitive Psychology, 18,* 1143–1159.

Schacter, D. L. (2001). *The seven sins of memory: How the mind forgets and remembers.* Boston: Houghton Mifflin.

Hovdestad, W.E., & Kristiansen, C.M. (1996). A field study of false memory syndrome: Construct validity and incidence. *Journal of Psychiatry & Law, 24,* 299–338.

ISSUE 7

Is Attention-Deficit/Hyperactivity Disorder (ADHD) a Real Disorder?

YES: National Institute of Mental Health, from *Attention Deficit Hyperactivity Disorder* (NIH Publication No. 3572) (U.S. Department of Health and Human Services, 2006)

NO: Rogers H. Wright, from "Attention Deficit Hyperactivity Disorder: What It Is and What It Is Not," in Rogers H. Wright and Nicholas A. Cummings, eds., *Destructive Trends in Mental Health: The Well Intentioned Path to Harm* (Routledge 2005)

ISSUE SUMMARY

YES: The National Institute of Mental Health views ADHD as a valid disorder affecting between 3 and 5 percent of American children, many of whom will continue to deal with symptoms of this condition into adulthood. According to NIMH, ADHD warrants careful diagnosis and treatment by skilled professionals.

NO: Psychologist Rogers H. Wright argues that ADHD has vague diagnostic criteria that lead to overdiagnosis and overmedication of an excessive number of people.

Some children who show a constellation of behaviors characterized by inattention and hyperactivity are referred to by teachers and special educators as having attention-deficit/hyperactivity disorder (ADHD), as described in *DSM-IV-TR*. Their inattention is evidenced by a range of behaviors, including carelessness, distractibility, forgetfulness, and difficulty following through on tasks or organizing themselves. Their hyperactivity is characterized by restlessness, running around, difficulty playing with others, excessive talk, and other behaviors.

In the following section, the National Institute of Mental Health (NIMH) takes a stand in endorsing ADHD as a biologically caused condition affecting between 3 and 5 percent of American children. Between 30 and 70 percent of children with ADHD continue to exhibit symptoms in their adult years. In differentiating ADHD from commonplace forms of heightened activity, inattention, or impulsivity, NIMH contends that a valid diagnosis must take into consideration the extent to which the behavior is inappropriate for the person's age, and the degree to which the behaviors cause a real handicap. Diagnosis and treatment of people with ADHD should be done by specialists who understand the causes, symptom picture, and most effective interventions.

In the second selection, Rogers H. Wright asserts that ADHD is a fad diagnosis, which has moved beyond the confines of childhood and adolescence, and is now a diagnosis that has invaded adulthood as well. Wright points out that the diagnostic criteria for the "so-called" disorder include symptoms that normal children and adults experience on a day-to-day basis. He acknowledges that there are some extreme cases for which a comprehensive evaluation by several specialists might provide evidence of neurological involvement; in such cases, if medication is indicated, it would be of a type quite different from what is so widely prescribed to people with the condition known as ADHD.

POINT

- Scientists are finding more and more evidence that ADHD is a diagnosable condition that stems from biological causes. Studies indicate that ADHD is strongly influenced by genetics, and that children with ADHD show brain differences compared with children who do not have ADHD.

- Although all children can experience hyperactivity, distractibility, poor concentration, or impulsivity, for children with ADHD, such behaviors often affect their performance in school, social relationships, or their life at home.

- To assess whether someone has ADHD, specialists compare the person's pattern of behavior against a set of criteria and characteristics of the disorder as listed in the *DSM-IV-TR*.

- Research shows that medication, ideally in combination with behavioral treatment, is the most effective remedy for ADHD. While the brains of non-medicated ADHD children have abnormally small volumes of white matter, once medicated, the white matter brain volume in these children does not differ from that in non-ADHD children.

- People who believe that they may have ADHD should consult with a professional with expertise in the diagnosis of this condition.

COUNTERPOINT

- ADHD is just another fad diagnosis that doesn't exist, not unlike the former fad label "minimal brain syndrome."

- Hyperactivity and distractibility are behaviors that are most commonly symptoms of excessive fatigue or stress, rather than signs of a psychological disorder.

- A major disservice caused by the elevation of nonspecific symptoms, and then diagnoses of ADHD, is that we lump together individuals with very different needs and problems and then attempt to treat the problems with a single entity, resulting in a one-pill-fits-all response.

- Treatment interventions focused primarily on medication, and based on such ethereal and universal symptoms, promise an instant "cure" for a patient who now does not have to confront possible unhappiness or stress.

- Whether or not someone has ADHD is a judgment that is best made only after exhaustive study by pediatrics, psychology, neurology, and perhaps, last of all, psychiatry, which so often seems too eager to overmedicate.

Attention Deficit Hyperactivity Disorder

Attention Deficit Hyperactivity Disorder (ADHD) is a condition that becomes apparent in some children in the preschool and early school years. It is hard for these children to control their behavior and/or pay attention. It is estimated that between 3 and 5 percent of children have attention deficit hyperactivity disorder (ADHD), or approximately 2 million children in the United States. This means that in a classroom of 25 to 30 children, it is likely that at least one will have ADHD.

A child with ADHD faces a difficult but not insurmountable task ahead. In order to achieve his or her full potential, he or she should receive help, guidance, and understanding from parents, guidance counselors, and the public education system.

Symptoms

The [principal] characteristics of ADHD are inattention, hyperactivity, and impulsivity. These symptoms appear early in a child's life. Because many normal children may have these symptoms, but at a low level, or the symptoms may be caused by another disorder, it is important that the child receive a thorough examination and appropriate diagnosis by a well-qualified professional. Symptoms of ADHD will appear over the course of many months, often with the symptoms of impulsiveness and hyperactivity preceding those of inattention that may not emerge for a year or more. Different symptoms may appear in different settings, depending on the demands the situation may pose for the child's self-control. A child who "can't sit still" or is otherwise disruptive will be noticeable in school, but the inattentive daydreamer may be overlooked. The impulsive child who acts before thinking may be considered just a "discipline problem," while the child who is passive or sluggish may be viewed as merely unmotivated. Yet both may have different types of ADHD. All children are sometimes restless, sometimes act without thinking, sometimes daydream the time away. When the child's hyperactivity, distractibility, poor concentration, or impulsivity begin to affect performance in school, social relationships with other children, or behavior at home, ADHD may be suspected. But because the symptoms vary so much across settings, ADHD is not easy to diagnose. This is especially true when inattentiveness is the primary symptom.

From *National Institute of Mental Health,* NIH Publication No. 3572, 2006. Published by The National Institute of Mental Health. www.nimh.nih.gov

According to the most recent version of the Diagnostic and Statistical Manual of Mental Disorders (DSM-IV-TR), there are three patterns of behavior that indicate ADHD. People with ADHD may show several signs of being consistently inattentive. They may have a pattern of being hyperactive and impulsive far more than others of their age. Or they may show all three types of behavior. This means that there are three subtypes of ADHD recognized by professionals. These are the predominantly hyperactive-impulsive type (that does not show significant inattention); the predominantly inattentive type (that does not show significant hyperactive-impulsive behavior) sometimes called ADD—an outdated term for this entire disorder; and the combined type (that displays both inattentive and hyperactive-impulsive symptoms).

Hyperactivity-Impulsivity

Some signs of hyperactivity-impulsivity are:

- Feeling restless, often fidgeting with hands or feet, or squirming while seated
- Running, climbing, or leaving a seat in situations where sitting or quiet behavior is expected
- Blurting out answers before hearing the whole question
- Having difficulty waiting in line or taking turns.

Inattention

The DSM-IV-TR gives these signs of inattention.

- Often becoming easily distracted by irrelevant sights and sounds
- Often failing to pay attention to details and making careless mistakes
- Rarely following instructions carefully and completely losing or forgetting things like toys, or pencils, books, and tools needed for a task
- Often skipping from one uncompleted activity to another

Is It Really ADHD?

Not everyone who is overly hyperactive, inattentive, or impulsive has ADHD. Since most people sometimes blurt out things they didn't mean to say, or jump from one task to another, or become disorganized and forgetful, how can specialists tell if the problem is ADHD?

Because everyone shows some of these behaviors at times, the diagnosis requires that such behavior be demonstrated to a degree that is inappropriate for the person's age. The diagnostic guidelines also contain specific requirements for determining when the symptoms indicate ADHD. The behaviors must appear early in life, before age 7, and continue for at least 6 months. Above all, the behaviors must create a real handicap in at least two areas of a person's life such as in the schoolroom, on the playground, at home, in the community, or in social settings. So someone who shows some symptoms but whose schoolwork or friendships are not impaired by these behaviors would not be diagnosed with ADHD. Nor would a child who seems overly active on the playground but functions well elsewhere receive an ADHD diagnosis.

To assess whether a child has ADHD, specialists consider several critical questions: Are these behaviors excessive, long-term, and pervasive? That is, do they occur more often than in other children the same age? Are they a continuous problem, not just a response to a temporary situation? Do the behaviors occur in several settings or only in one specific place like the playground or in the schoolroom? The person's pattern of behavior is compared against a set of criteria and characteristics of the disorder as listed in the DSM-IV-TR.

Diagnosis

Professionals Who Make the Diagnosis

If ADHD is suspected, to whom can the family turn? What kinds of specialists do they need?

Ideally, the diagnosis should be made by a professional in your area with training in ADHD or in the diagnosis of mental disorders. Child psychiatrists and psychologists, developmental/behavioral pediatricians, or behavioral neurologists are those most often trained in differential diagnosis. Clinical social workers may also have such training. The family can start by talking with the child's pediatrician or their family doctor. Some pediatricians may do the assessment themselves, but often they refer the family to an appropriate mental health specialist they know and trust. In addition, state and local agencies that serve families and children . . . can help identify appropriate specialists.

Within each specialty, individual doctors and mental health professionals differ in their experiences with ADHD. So in selecting a specialist, it's important to find someone with specific training and experience in diagnosing and treating the disorder.

Whatever the specialist's expertise, his or her first task is to gather information that will rule out other possible reasons for the child's behavior. Among possible causes of ADHD-like behavior are the following:

- A sudden change in the child's life—the death of a parent or grandparent; parents' divorce; a parent's job loss.
- Undetected seizures, such as in petit mal or temporal lobe seizures
- A middle ear infection that causes intermittent hearing problems
- Medical disorders that may affect brain functioning
- Underachievement caused by learning disability
- Anxiety or depression

Next the specialist gathers information on the child's ongoing behavior in order to compare these behaviors to the symptoms and diagnostic criteria listed in the DSM-IV-TR. This also involves talking with the child and, if possible, observing the child in class and other settings.

The child's teachers, past and present, are asked to rate their observations of the child's behavior on standardized evaluation forms, known as behavior rating scales, to compare the child's behavior to that of other children [of] the same age.

The specialist interviews the child's teachers and parents, and may contact other people who know the child well, such as coaches or babysitters. Parents are asked to describe their child's behavior in a variety of situations. They may also fill out a rating scale to indicate how severe and frequent the behaviors seem to be.

In most cases, the child will be evaluated for social adjustment and mental health. Tests of intelligence and learning achievement may be given to see if the child has a learning disability and whether the disability is in one or more subjects.

The specialist then pieces together a profile of the child's behavior.

A correct diagnosis often resolves confusion about the reasons for the child's problems that lets parents and child move forward in their lives with more accurate information on what is wrong and what can be done to help. Once the disorder is diagnosed, the child and family can begin to receive whatever combination of educational, medical, and emotional help they need. This may include providing recommendations to school staff, seeking out a more appropriate classroom setting, selecting the right medication, and helping parents to manage their child's behavior.

What Causes ADHD?

One of the first questions a parent will have is "Why? What went wrong?" "Did I do something to cause this?" There is little compelling evidence at this time that ADHD can arise purely from social factors or child-rearing methods. Most substantiated causes appear to fall in the realm of neurobiology and genetics. This is not to say that environmental factors may not influence the severity of the disorder, and especially the degree of impairment and suffering the child may experience, but that such factors do not seem to give rise to the condition by themselves.

The parents' focus should be on looking forward and finding the best possible way to help their child. Scientists are studying causes in an effort to identify better ways to treat, and perhaps someday, to prevent ADHD. They are finding more and more evidence that ADHD does not stem from home environment, but from biological causes. Knowing this can remove a huge burden of guilt from parents who might blame themselves for their child's behavior.

Genetics.   Attention disorders often run in families, so there are likely to be genetic influences. Studies indicate that 25 percent of the close relatives in the families of ADHD children also have ADHD, whereas the rate is about 5 percent in the general population. Many studies of twins now show that a strong genetic influence exists in the disorder.

Researchers continue to study the genetic contribution to ADHD and to identify the genes that cause a person to be susceptible to ADHD. Since its inception in 1999, the Attention-Deficit Hyperactivity Disorder Molecular Genetics Network has served as a way for researchers to share findings regarding possible genetic influences on ADHD.

Recent Studies on Causes of ADHD.   Some knowledge of the structure of the brain is helpful in understanding the research scientists are doing in searching for a physical basis for attention deficit hyperactivity disorder. One part of the brain that scientists have focused on in their search is the frontal lobes of the cerebrum. The frontal lobes allow us to solve problems, plan ahead, understand the behavior of others, and restrain our impulses. The two frontal lobes, the right and the left, communicate with each other through the corpus callosum, (nerve fibers that connect the right and left frontal lobes).

The basal ganglia are the interconnected gray masses deep in the cerebral hemisphere that serve as the connection between the cerebrum and the cerebellum and, with the cerebellum are responsible for motor coordination. The cerebellum is divided into three parts. The middle part is called the vermis.

All of these parts of the brain have been studied through the use of various methods for seeing into or imaging the brain. These methods include functional magnetic resonance imaging (fMRI), positron emission tomography (PET), and single photon emission computed tomography (SPECT). The main or central psychological deficits in those with ADHD have been linked through these studies. By 2002 the researchers in the NIMH Child Psychiatry Branch had studied 152 boys and girls with ADHD, matched with 139 age- and gender-matched controls without ADHD. The children were scanned at least twice, some as many as four times over a decade. As a group, the ADHD children showed 3–4 percent smaller brain volumes in all regions—the frontal lobes, temporal gray matter, caudate nucleus, and cerebellum.

This study also showed that the ADHD children who were on medication had a white matter volume that did not differ from that of controls. Those never-medicated patients had an abnormally small volume of white matter. The white matter consists of fibers that establish long-distance connections between brain regions. It normally thickens as a child grows older and the brain matures.

The Treatment of ADHD

Every family wants to determine what treatment will be most effective for their child. This question needs to be answered by each family in consultation with their health care professional. To help families make this important decision, the National Institute of Mental Health (NIMH) has funded many studies of treatments for ADHD and has conducted the most intensive study ever undertaken for evaluating the treatment of this disorder. This study is known as the Multimodal Treatment Study of Children with Attention Deficit Hyperactivity Disorder (MTA).

The MTA study included 579 (95–98 at each of treatment sites) elementary school boys and girls with ADHD, randomly assigning them to one of four treatment programs: (1) medication management alone; (2) behavioral treatment alone; (3) a combination of both; or (4) routine community care.

In each of the study sites, three groups were treated for the first 14 months in a specified protocol and the fourth group was referred for community treatment of the parents' choosing. All of the children were reassessed regularly throughout the study period. An essential part of the program was the cooperation of the schools, including principals and teachers. Both teachers and parents rated the children on hyperactivity, impulsivity, and inattention, and symptoms of anxiety and depression as well as social skills.

The children in two groups (medication management alone and the combination treatment) were seen monthly for one-half hour at each medication visit. During the treatment visits, the prescribing physician spoke with the parent, met with the child, and sought to determine any concerns that the family might have regarding the medication or the child's ADHD-related difficulties. The physicians, in addition, sought input from the teachers on a monthly basis. The physicians in the medication-only group did not provide behavioral therapy but did advise the parents when necessary concerning any problems the child might have.

In the behavior treatment-only group, families met up to 35 times with a behavior therapist, mostly in group sessions. These therapists also made repeated visits to schools to consult with children's teachers and to supervise a special aide assigned to each child in the group. In addition, children attended a special 8-week summer treatment program where they worked on academic, social, and sports skills, and where intensive behavioral therapy was delivered to assist children in improving their behavior.

Children in the combined therapy group received both treatments, that is, all the same assistance that the medication-only received as well as all of the behavior therapy treatments.

In routine community care, the children saw the community-treatment doctor of their parents' choice one to two times per year for short periods of time. Also, the community-treatment doctor did not have any interaction with the teachers.

The results of the study indicated that long-term combination treatments and the medication-management alone were superior to intensive behavioral treatment and routine community treatment. And in some areas—anxiety, academic performance, oppositionality, parent–child relations, and social skills—the combined treatment was usually superior. Another advantage of combined treatment was that children could be successfully treated with lower doses of medicine, compared with the medication-only group.

Medications

For decades, medications have been used to treat the symptoms of ADHD.

The medications that seem to be the most effective are a class of drugs known as stimulants.

Some people get better results from one medication, some from another. It is important to work with the prescribing physician to find the right medication and the right dosage. For many people, the stimulants dramatically reduce their hyperactivity and impulsivity and improve their ability to focus, work, and learn. The medications may also improve physical coordination, such as that needed in handwriting and in sports.

The stimulant drugs, when used with medical supervision, are usually considered quite safe. . . . [T]o date there is no convincing evidence that stimulant medications, when used for treatment of ADHD, cause drug abuse or dependence. A review of all long-term studies on stimulant medication and substance abuse, conducted by researchers at Massachusetts General Hospital and Harvard Medical School, found that teenagers with ADHD who remained on their medication during the teen years had a lower likelihood of substance use or abuse than did ADHD adolescents who were not taking medications.

The stimulant drugs come in long- and short-term forms. The newer sustained-release stimulants can be taken before school and are long-lasting so that the child does not need to go to the school nurse every day for a pill. The doctor can discuss with the parents the child's needs and decide which preparation to use and whether the child needs to take the medicine during school hours only or in the evening and weekends too.

About one out of ten children is not helped by a stimulant medication. Other types of medication may be used if stimulants don't work or if the ADHD occurs with another disorder. Antidepressants and other medications can help control accompanying depression or anxiety.

Side Effects of the Medications

Most side effects of the stimulant medications are minor and are usually related to the dosage of the medication being taken. Higher doses produce more side effects. The most common side effects are decreased appetite, insomnia, increased anxiety and/or irritability. Some children report mild stomach aches or headaches.

When a child's schoolwork and behavior improve soon after starting medication, the child, parents, and teachers tend to applaud the drug for causing the sudden changes. Unfortunately, when people see such immediate improvement, they often think medication is all that's needed. But medications don't cure ADHD; they only control the symptoms on the day they are taken. Although the medications help the child pay better attention and complete school work, they can't increase knowledge or improve academic skills. The medications help the child to use those skills he or she already possesses.

Behavioral therapy, emotional counseling, and practical support will help ADHD children cope with everyday problems and feel better about themselves.

Facts to Remember about Medication for ADHD

- Medications for ADHD help many children focus and be more successful at school, home, and play. Avoiding negative experiences now may actually help prevent addictions and other emotional problems later.
- About 80 percent of children who need medication for ADHD still need it as teenagers. Over 50 percent need medication as adults.

The Family and the ADHD Child

Medication can help the ADHD child in everyday life. He or she may be better able to control some of the behavior problems that have led to trouble with parents and siblings. But it takes time to undo the frustration, blame, and anger that may have gone on for so long. Both parents and children may need special help to develop techniques for managing the patterns of behavior. In such cases, mental health professionals can counsel the child and the family, helping them to develop new skills, attitudes, and ways of relating to each other. In individual counseling, the therapist helps children with ADHD learn to feel better about themselves. The therapist can also help them to identify and build on their strengths, cope with daily problems, and control their attention and aggression. Sometimes only the child with ADHD needs counseling support. But in many cases, because the problem affects the family as a whole, the entire family may need help. The therapist assists the family in finding better ways to handle the disruptive behaviors and promote change. If the child is young, most of the therapist's work is with the parents, teaching them techniques for coping with and improving their child's behavior.

Several intervention approaches are available. Knowing something about the various types of interventions makes it easier for families to choose a therapist that is right for their needs.

Psychotherapy works to help people with ADHD to like and accept themselves despite their disorder. It does not address the symptoms or underlying causes of the disorder. In psychotherapy, patients talk with the therapist about upsetting thoughts and feelings, explore self-defeating patterns of behavior, and learn alternative ways to handle their emotions. As they talk, the therapist tries to help them understand how they can change or better cope with their disorder.

Behavioral therapy (BT) helps people develop more effective ways to work on immediate issues. Rather than helping the child understand his or her feelings and actions, it helps directly in changing their thinking and coping and thus may lead to changes in behavior. The support might be practical assistance, like help in organizing tasks or schoolwork or dealing with emotionally charged events. Or the support might be in self-monitoring one's own behavior and giving self-praise or rewards for acting in a desired way such as controlling anger or thinking before acting.

Social skills training can also help children learn new behaviors. In social skills training, the therapist discusses and models appropriate behaviors important in developing and maintaining social relationships, like waiting for a turn, sharing toys, asking for help, or responding to teasing, then gives children a chance to practice. For example, a child might learn to "read" other people's facial expression and tone of voice in order to respond appropriately. Social skills training helps the child to develop better ways to play and work with other children.

Attention Deficit Hyperactivity Disorder in Adults

Attention Deficit Hyperactivity Disorder is a highly publicized childhood disorder that affects approximately 3 to 5 percent of all children. What is much less well known is the probability that, of children who have ADHD, many will still have it as adults. Several studies done in recent years estimate that between 30 percent and 70 percent of children with ADHD continue to exhibit symptoms in the adult years.

Typically, adults with ADHD are unaware that they have this disorder— they often just feel that it's impossible to get organized, to stick to a job, to keep an appointment. The everyday tasks of getting up, getting dressed and ready for the day's work, getting to work on time, and being productive on the job can be major challenges for the ADD adult.

Diagnosing ADHD in an Adult

Diagnosing an adult with ADHD is not easy. Many times, when a child is diagnosed with the disorder, a parent will recognize that he or she has many of the same symptoms the child has and, for the first time, will begin to understand some of the traits that have given him or her trouble for years—distractability, impulsivity, [and] restlessness. Other adults will seek professional help for depression or anxiety and will find out that the root cause of some of their emotional problems is ADHD. They may have a history of school failures or problems at work. Often they have been involved in frequent automobile accidents.

To be diagnosed with ADHD, an adult must have childhood-onset, persistent, and current symptoms. The accuracy of the diagnosis of adult ADHD is of utmost importance and should be made by a clinician with expertise in the area of attention dysfunction. For an accurate diagnosis, a history of the patient's childhood behavior, together with an interview with his life partner, a parent, close friend, or other close associate, will be needed. A physical examination and psychological tests should also be given. Comorbidity with other conditions may exist such as specific learning disabilities, anxiety, or affective disorders.

A correct diagnosis of ADHD can bring a sense of relief. The individual has brought into adulthood many negative perceptions of himself that may have led to low esteem. Now he can begin to understand why he has some of his problems and can begin to face them.

All references for articles included in *Taking Sides: Clashing Views in Abnormal Psychology*, 6/e can be found on the Web at www.mhhe.com/cls.

Attention Deficit Hyperactivity Disorder: What It Is and What It Is Not

It is almost axiomatic in the mental health field that fads will occur in the "diagnosis" and treatment of various types of behavioral aberrations, some of which border on being mere discomforts. Although the same faddism exists to some degree in physical medicine, its appearance is not nearly as blatant, perhaps in part because physical medicine is more soundly grounded in the physical sciences than are diagnoses in the mental health field. These fads spill over into the general culture, where direct marketing often takes place. One has to spend only a brief period in front of a television set during prime time to discover ADHD (Attention Deficit Hyperactivity Disorder), SAD (Social Anxiety Disorder), or IBS (Irritable Bowl Syndrome). Even when purporting to be informational, these are more or less disguised commercials, inasmuch as they posit a cure that varies with the drug manufacturer sponsoring the television ad.

The other certainty is that these "diagnoses" will fall from usage as other fads emerge, as was the case a decade or so ago with the disappearance of a once-common designation for what is now sometimes called ADHD. That passing fad was known as minimal brain syndrome (MBS) and/or food disorder (ostensibly from red dye or other food additives). From this author's perspective, these fad "diagnoses" don't really exist. Other writers in this volume (e.g., Cummings, Rosemond, and Wright) have commented on the slipperiness of these "diagnoses"—that is, the elevation of a symptom and/or its description to the level of a disorder or syndrome—and the concomitant tendency to over-medicate for these nonexistent maladies.

Children and ADHD

Certainly, there are deficiencies of attention and hyperactivity, but such behavioral aberrancies are most often indicative of a transitory state or condition within the organism. They are not in and of themselves indicative of a "disorder." Every parent has noticed, particularly with younger children, that toward the end of an especially exciting and fatiguing day children are literally "ricocheting off

From *Destructive Trends In Mental Health: The Well Intentioned Path To Harm,* by Rogers H. Wright and Nicholas A. Cummings, eds., 2005, pp.129–141. Copyright © 2005 by Taylor & Francis Books, Inc. Reprinted by permission via the Copyright Clearance Center.

the walls." Although this behavior may in the broadest sense be classifiable as hyperactivity, it is generally pathognomonic of nothing more than excessive fatigue, for which the treatment of choice is a good night's sleep. Distractibility (attention deficit) is a frequent concomitant of excessive fatigue, particularly with children under five years of age and can even be seen in adults if fatigue levels are extreme or if stress is prolonged. However, such "symptoms" in these contexts do not rise to the level of a treatable disorder.

Conversely, when distractibility and/or hyperactivity characterize the child's everyday behavior (especially if accompanied by factors such as delayed development, learning difficulties, impaired motor skills, and impaired judgment), they may be indicative of either a neurological disorder or of developing emotional difficulties. However, after nearly fifty years of diagnosing and treating several thousand such problems, it is my considered judgment that the distractibility and hyperactivity seen in such children is not the same as the distractibility and hyperactivity in children currently diagnosed as having ADHD. Furthermore, the hyperactivity/distractibility seen in the non-ADHD children described above is qualitatively and quantitatively different, depending on whether it is caused by incipient emotional maldevelopment (functional; i.e., nonorganic) or whether it is due to neurological involvement.

It is also notable that most children whose distractibility and/or hyperactivity is occasioned by emotional distress do not show either the kind or degree of learning disability, delayed genetic development, poor judgment, and impaired motor skills that are seen in children whose "distractibility/hyperactivity" is occasioned by neurological involvement. Only in children with the severest forms of emotional disturbance does one see the kind of developmental delays and impaired behavioral controls that are more reflective of neurological involvement (or what was known as MBS until the ADHD fad took hold). Differentiating the child with actual neurological involvement from the child that has emotionally based distractibility is neither simple nor easy to do, especially if the behavioral (as opposed to neurological) involvement is severe.

A major and profound disservice occasioned by the current fad of elevating nonspecific symptoms such as anxiety and hyperactivity to the level of a syndrome or disorder and then diagnosing ADD/ADHD is that we lump together individuals with very different needs and very different problems. We then attempt to treat the problem(s) with a single entity, resulting in a one-pill-fits-all response. It is also unfortunately the case that many mental health providers (e.g., child psychiatrists, child psychologists, child social workers), as well as many general care practitioners (e.g., pediatricians and internists), are not competent to make such discriminations alone. Therefore, it follows that such practitioners are not trained and equipped to provide ongoing care, even when an appropriate diagnosis has been made.

To add to an already complicated situation, the symptom picture in children tends to change with time and maturation. Children with neurological involvement typically tend to improve spontaneously over time, so that the symptoms of distractibility and hyperactivity often represent diminished components in the clinical picture. Conversely, children whose distractibility and hyperactivity are emotionally determined typically have symptoms that tend to intensify or be accompanied/replaced by even more dramatic indices of emotional distress.

Management of Children Exhibiting "ADHD" According to Etiology

It is apparent that somewhat superficially similar presenting complaints (i.e., distractibility and hyperactivity) may reflect two very different causative factors, and that the successful treatment and management of the complaint should vary according to the underlying causation. Neurological damage can stem from a number of causative factors during pregnancy or the birth process, and a successful remedial program may require the combined knowledge of the child's pediatrician, a neuropsychologist specializing in the diagnosis and treatment of children, and a child neurologist. In these cases, appropriate medication for the child is often very helpful.

Psychotherapy for the child (particularly younger children) is, in this writer's experience, largely a waste of time. On the other hand, remedial training in visual perception, motor activities, visual–motor integration, spatial relations, numerical skills, and reading and writing may be crucial in alleviating or at least diminishing the impact of symptoms. Deficits in these skills can be major contributors to the hyperactivity and distractibility so frequently identified with such children. Counseling and psychotherapeutic work with the parents is very important and should always be a part of an integrated therapeutic program. Such children need to be followed by an attending pediatrician, a child neurologist, a child neuropsychologist, and an educational therapist, bearing in mind that treatment needs change throughout the span of remediation. For example, medication levels and regimens may need to be adjusted, and training programs will constantly need to be revised or elaborated.

It is also noteworthy that so-called tranquilizing medication with these children typically produces an adverse effect. This writer remembers a situation that occurred early in his practice, a case he has used repeatedly to alert fledgling clinicians to the importance of a comprehensive initial evaluation and ongoing supervision in the development of neurologically involved children.

John, a two-and-a-half-year-old boy, was referred by his pediatrician for evaluation of extreme hyperactivity, distractibility, and mild developmental delay. The psychological evaluation elicited evidence of visual perceptual impairment in a context of impaired visual motor integration, a finding suggestive of an irritative focus in the parietal-occipital areas of the brain. This finding was later corroborated by a child neurologist, and John was placed on dilantin and phenobarbital. A developmental training program was instituted, and the parents began participation in a group specifically designed for the parents of brain-injured children. Over the next couple of years, the patient's progress was excellent, and his development and learning difficulties were singularly diminished. The parents were comfortable with John's progress and with their ability to manage it, so they decided to have a long-wanted additional child. In the meantime, the father's work necessitated moving to another location, leading to a change of obstetrician and pediatrician.

The second pregnancy proceeded uneventfully and eventuated in the birth of a second boy. Shortly after the mother returned home with the new infant, John began to regress, exhibiting a number of prior symptoms such as hyperactivity and distractibility as well as problems in behavioral control. The new pediatrician referred the family to a child psychiatrist, who promptly placed John on a tranquilizer. Shortly thereafter, John's academic performance began to deteriorate dramatically, and his school counseled the parents about the possibility that he had been promoted too rapidly and "could not handle work at this grade level."

At this point, the parents again contacted this writer, primarily out of concern for John's diminished academic performance. Because it had been more than two years since John had been formally evaluated, I advised the parents that another comprehensive evaluation was indicated. The parents agreed, and a full diagnostic battery was administered to John, the results of which were then compared to his prior performance. It immediately became apparent that he was not functioning at grade level, and that the overall level of his functioning had deteriorated dramatically.

In his initial evaluation, John's functional level had been in the Bright Normal range (i.e., overall IQ of 110 to 119), whereas his current functioning placed him at the Borderline Mentally Retarded level (IQ below 60). The history revealed nothing of significance other than the behavioral regression after the birth of the sibling and the introduction of the new medication. I advised the parents that I thought the child was being erroneously medicated, with consequent diminution of his intellectual efficiency, and that the supposition could be tested by asking the attending child psychiatrist to diminish John's medication to see if the child's performance improved.

The attending child psychiatrist was quite upset by the recommendations and the implications thereof and threatened to sue me for "practicing medicine without a license." I informed the physician that I was not practicing medicine but rather neuropsychology, along with deductive reasoning known as "common sense," which we could test by appropriately reducing John's dosage level for a month and then retesting him. Faced with the alternative of a legal action for slander or libel for having accused this neuropsychologist of a felony, the child psychiatrist agreed.

Upon retesting a month later, the child's performance level had returned to Bright Normal, and his academic performance and behavior in school had improved dramatically. By this time approximately six to eight months had elapsed since the birth of the sibling, and John had become accustomed to his new brother. All concerned agreed that the medication had not been helpful and that the child should continue for another three to six months without medication. Subsequent contact with the parents some six months later indicated that John was doing well at school. The parents were quite comfortable with the behavioral management skills they had learned, which enabled them to handle a child with an underlying neurological handicap.

As noted earlier, the marked distractibility and/or hyperactivity in children with neurological involvement tends to diminish through adolescence, especially after puberty, as do many of the other symptoms. As a consequence, these children present a very different clinical picture in adolescence and adulthood. Typically, they are characterized by impulsivity, at times poor judgment, and excessive fatigability. It is generally only under the circumstances of extreme fatigue (or other stress) that one will see fairly dramatic degrees of distractibility and hyperactivity. Thus, an appropriate diagnosis leading to productive intervention is difficult to make.

Conversely, children who exhibit the symptoms of distractibility and hyperactivity on an emotional basis typically do not show the diminution of symptomatology with increasing age. In fact, the symptoms may intensify and/or be replaced by even more dramatic symptoms, especially during puberty and adolescence (Myklebust, 1973). It should also be emphasized that the kind of distractibility and hyperactivity exhibited by the emotionally disturbed youngster is very different in quality and quantity from that of a youngster whose hyperactivity and distractibility has a neurological basis (Myklebust, 1973; Ochroch, 1979). Unfortunately, it is also frequently the case that a youngster with a neurological handicap may have significant emotional problems overlaying the basic neurological problems, making diagnosis even more complicated (Small, 1980). But the overriding problem confronting parents today is the misdiagnosis of emotionally based symptoms that brings the recommendation of unwarranted medication.

In the largest study of its kind, Cummings and Wiggins (2001) retrospectively examined the records of 168,113 children and adolescents who had been referred and treated over a four-year period in a national behavioral health provider operating in thirty-nine states. Before beginning treatment, sixty-one percent of the males and twenty-three percent of the females were taking psychotropic medication for ADD/ADHD by a psychiatrist, a pediatrician, or a primary care physician. Most of them lived in a single-parent home and lacked an effective father figure or were subjected to negative and frequently abusive male role models. Behavioral interventions included a compassionate but firm male therapist and the introduction of positive male role models (e.g., fathers, Big Brothers, coaches, Sunday school teachers, etc.) into the child's life. Counseling focused on helping parents understand what constitutes the behavior of a normal boy.

After an average of nearly eleven treatments with the parent and approximately six with the child, the percentage of boys on medication was reduced from sixty-one percent to eleven percent, and the percentage of girls on medication went from twenty-three percent to two percent. These dramatic results occurred despite very strict requirements for discontinuing the medication, which seems to point to an alarming overdiagnosis and overmedication of ADD/ADHD and greater efficacy of behavioral interventions than is generally believed to be the case by the mental health community.

Adult ADHD

The wholesale invasion of ADHD in childhood and adolescence is accompanied by a concurrent explosion of such diagnoses into adulthood. One cannot watch television without being bombarded by the direct marketing that asks: "Do you find it difficult to finish a task at work? Do you frequently find yourself daydreaming or distracted? You may be suffering from ADD. Consult your physician or WebMD." Of course, adult ADD exists; children with real ADD will grow into adulthood. But the symptoms described in this aggressive TV marketing are more reflective of boredom, the mid-day blahs, job dissatisfaction, or stress than a syndrome or disorder requiring treatment.

Unfortunately, treatment interventions focused primarily on medication and based on such ethereal and universal symptoms promise an instant "cure" for the patient who now does not have to confront possible unhappiness or stress. Such simple solutions also find great favor with the insurers and HMOs that look for the cheapest treatment. Persons exhibiting "symptoms" are more likely to benefit from a variety of behavioral interventions ranging from vocational counseling for job dissatisfaction and marital counseling for an unhappy marriage, to psychotherapy for underlying emotional stress, anxiety, or depression. Such interventions tend to be time-consuming and costly, with the consequence that the patients may inadvertently ally themselves with managed care companies devoted to the principle that the least expensive treatment is the treatment of choice.

Distractibility and hyperactivity of the type that we have called the "real ADHD" does exist in adults. However, in general, symptoms are much more subtle and, in many if not most cases, overshadowed by other symptoms. Thus, if mentioned at all, distractibility and hyperactivity are rarely significant presenting complaints. Such things as poor judgment, behavioral difficulties, forgetting, difficulties in reading/calculating, and getting lost are typically preeminent in the adult patient's presenting complaints. These usually become apparent in adulthood after an accident, strokes (CVA), infections of the brain, and other such events. The very drama of the causative factor typically makes the diagnosis apparent, and treatment providers are "tuned in" to anticipate sequellae secondary to neurological damage: intellectual and/or judgmental deficits, behavioral change, impulsivity, and motor impairment.

It should be emphasized that hyperactivity and distractibility, although present, are less dramatic symptoms that are understandably of less concern to the patient. Furthermore, they often diminish rapidly in the first eighteen months following the neurological event. Even then, the major constellation of symptoms may not be sufficiently dramatic to alert attending medical personnel as to the primary cause of the patient's complaints. This is particularly true of contrecoup lesions occurring most frequently in auto accidents.

Although circumstances resulting in contrecoup damage are frequent and often missed, there are also other, even more significant, types of neurological involvement that may also pass unnoticed. These include early-onset Alzheimer's disease beginning at age fifty and cerebral toxicity resulting from inappropriate medication in the elderly, which is usually misdiagnosed as incipient Alzheimer's. Expectation can unfortunately contribute not only to a misdiagnosis, but also failure to order tests that might elicit the underlying condition. In addition, the converse may infrequently occur: Neurological involvement may be anticipated but is not demonstrable and does not exist. Three illustrative cases follow.

Case 1

Bill, a young construction worker, received notice of his imminent induction into the armed services. Right after lunch on a Friday afternoon, a large section of 2×4 lumber dropped from the second story of a work site, striking him butt-first in the right anterior temporal region of the head. He was unconscious for a short period of time, quickly recovered consciousness, and showed no apparent ill effects from the blow. He refused hospitalization and was taken by his employer to his home.

On the following Monday, Bill phoned his employer saying that he was still "not feeling too good," and given the imminence of his induction into the Army, he "was just going to goof off" until he was "called up." The employer had no further contact with Bill, who was inducted into the Army, where he almost immediately began to have difficulty, primarily of a behavioral type. Throughout his basic training, he tended to be impulsive and to use poor judgment, and he was constantly getting into fights with his companions. He barely made it through training and was shipped overseas where he was assigned to a unit whose primary duty was guard duty.

Throughout his training and his subsequent duty assignment, Bill was a frequent attendee at sick call with consistent complaints of headache, earning him the reputation of "goof-off." His military career was terminated shortly after an apparently unprovoked attack on the officer in charge of the guard detail to which Bill was assigned. After a short detention in the stockade, he was discharged from the Army. His headaches and impulsivity continued into civilian life and prompted Bill to seek medical assistance through the Veterans Administration. The VA clinic's case study included neurological screening tests that were strongly suggestive of brain involvement. Consequently, he was given a full psychological work-up, which revealed intellectual impairment attendant to temporal lobe damage.

Subsequent neurological and encephalographic studies were consistent with the neuropsychological conclusions, and indicated a major focus in the anterior temporal area of the brain. A careful and detailed history was taken, and the incident of the blow to the head was elicited. This case suggests that even though Bill refused hospitalization, because of the severity of the blow it would have been prudent for the employer to insist on a thorough evaluation.

Case 2

James, a man in his late forties, was the son of a Southern sharecropper. Upon graduation from high school, he attended the Tuskegee Institute for a short period before he was drafted into the armed forces. James had a productive military career and upon his discharge moved to California, got married, and proceeded to raise his family. He had trained himself as a finish carpenter and cabinetmaker. His work was highly regarded, and his annual income was well above the average for his field. One of his three children was a college graduate, a second was well along in college, and the third was graduating from high school. James owned his own home and enjoyed a fine reputation as a contributing citizen of his community.

While at work installing a complicated newel post and banister, James became disoriented and tumbled from a stair landing, falling some five feet, and landing primarily on his head and shoulders but experiencing no apparent loss of consciousness. He was taken to a hospital for evaluation but was released with no significant findings. Almost immediately thereafter, he began to have difficulty at work. He would become disoriented, could not tell left from right, and made frequent mistakes in measuring, sawing, and fitting even simple elements. Before the accident he seldom if ever missed work, but now he became a frequent absentee. The quality of his work deteriorated and his income plummeted. He sought medical advice and was given a small stipend under the Workers Compensation program.

Over several weeks, he demonstrated no progress, and the attending neurologist and neurosurgeon referred him for neuropsychodiagnostic evaluation as a possible malingerer. The neuropsychologist noted that James' current status was completely at odds with his prior history, and not at all consistent with malingering. For example, the evaluation revealed that this highly skilled cabinetmaker, to his embarrassment, could no longer answer the question, "How many inches are there in two and a half feet?" The neuropsychological finding of pervasive occipital-parietal involvement was subsequently corroborated by electroencephalographic study.

Case 3

An airline captain driving along Wilshire Boulevard in Los Angeles lost consciousness when he experienced a spontaneous cerebral hemorrhage. He was immediately taken to a nearby major hospital where he received immediate and continuing care. Subsequently, a subdural hematoma developed, requiring surgical intervention. The captain recovered and showed no clinically significant signs of neurological involvement. An immediate postrecovery issue was the possibility of being returned to flight status. The attending neurosurgeon referred the patient for a comprehensive neuropsychological evaluation that found no indication of residual neurological deficit. Consequently, the neuropsychologist and the attending neurosurgeon recommended return to flight status.

In summary, in none of the foregoing situations was attention deficit or hyperactivity a significant presenting complaint, although the presence of both was clinically demonstrable at various times in the posttraumatic period. Yet the failure to recognize their presence would not have had a negative impact on treatment planning and or management in any of the three cases. Conversely, if excessive focus on the possible "attention deficits and/or hyperactivity disorder" dictated the nature of the therapeutic intervention, a significant disservice to each of these patients would have resulted.

Traditionally when distractibility and/or hyperactivity are prominent parts of the presenting complaint, the mental health provider directs diagnostic energies toward ascertaining the underlying source of these dysphoric experiences. The distractibility and hyperactivity would have been viewed as secondary symptoms to be tolerated, if possible, until the resolution of the underlying problem resulted in their alleviation. In situations where the symptoms were so extreme as to be significantly debilitating, the mental health provider might reluctantly attempt to provide some symptom relief. However, in such cases this was done with the certain knowledge that it was an expedient and was not addressing causation.

Times have changed dramatically, reflecting the interaction of a number of factors such as competition and cost controls. With the emergence of a plethora of mental health service providers, psychiatry opted to "remedicalize," essentially abandoning what it refers to as "talk therapy" in favor of medicating questionable syndromes and disorders. Psychology, pushed by its academic wing, could never decide what level of training was sufficient for independent mental health service delivery (i.e., master's versus doctoral degrees), and graduate-level training programs began to turn out hordes of master's-level providers in counseling, social work, education, and school psychology.

Meanwhile, the inclusion of mental health benefits in prepaid health programs broadened consumption and brought about managed care as a means of reducing consumption of all kinds of health services, including behavioral health services. When the American public's impatience with time-consuming processes is added to managed care's limiting of services in the context of a glut of mental health providers the scene is set for considerable mischief. Add to this brew the fact that psychiatry holds a virtual medication-prescribing monopoly in mental health and that drug manufacturers are constantly developing and marketing new magic pills, it all adds up to an environment that encourages the "discovery" of yet another syndrome or disorder for which treatment is necessary.

Summary

When hyperactivity and/or distractibility is truly one of the presenting symptoms, it is indicative of a complex situation that warrants extensive and thoughtful evaluation, and, more often than not, complex and comprehensive treatment planning from the perspective of a variety of specialists. In situations where the attention deficit and/or hyperactivity reflects problems in parenting, chemotherapeutic intervention for the child is likely to be, at best, no more than palliative and, at worse, may succeed in considerably complicating the situation. In this writer's experience, chemotherapeutic intervention for emotionally disturbed children is a last resort and of minimal value in addressing the overall problem. Psychotherapeutic intervention with the parents, which may or may not include the child, is more often than not the treatment of choice. This is a judgment that is best made only after exhaustive study by pediatrics, psychology, neurology, and perhaps, last of all, psychiatry, which so often seems all too eager to overmedicate. . . .

Where the presenting complaints of hyperactivity and distractibility are in a context of delayed development, excessive fatigability, learning deficits, and other such signs, the complexity of the diagnostic problem is substantially increased. In such circumstances, it is absolutely not in the child's best interest to limit the diagnostic evaluation to a single specialty. With the increasing evidence that neurological involvement can follow any number of prenatal and postnatal exposures, wise and caring parents will insist on a comprehensive evaluation by specialists in pediatrics, child neurology, and child neuropsychology. More often than not, if medication is indicated, it will be of a type quite different than what is used in the management of so-called ADHD.

Furthermore, treatment intervention and case management will likely involve skilled educational training of the specialized type developed for use with the brain-injured child (see Myklebust, 1973, 1978; Ochroch, 1979; Small, 1980, 1982; Strauss & Kephart, 1955). In the case of a friendly pediatrician, a concerned psychologist, or a caring child psychiatrist, any or all attempting unilaterally to diagnose and/or manage the treatment regimen, the concerned and caring parent is well advised to promptly seek additional opinions. For a comprehensive description of the type of evaluation that is most productive in the management of children of this kind, see Small (1982).

All references for articles included in *Taking Sides: Clashing Views in Abnormal Psychology, 6/e* can be found on the Web at **www.mhhe.com/cls**.

CHALLENGE QUESTIONS

Is Attention-Deficit/Hyperactivity Disorder (ADHD) a Real Disorder?

1. To what extent should conditions involving inattention and hyper-activity be regarded as medical, as opposed to emotional, disorders?
2. What are the minimal behavioral criteria that should be met before recommending that an inattentive and easily distracted individual should be prescribed medication?
3. What might motivate some individuals to want to be diagnosed with the ADHD label?
4. How would you go about designing a research study aimed at differentiating normal characteristics such as occasional inattentiveness from diagnosable conditions such as ADHD?
5. A common style in contemporary society is to multitask, in which attention is divided among several simultaneous tasks (e.g., word processing, instant messaging, telephone conversations, and interpersonal chats). To what extent does multitasking cause people to believe that they have ADHD because they feel unable to process all the information coming their way?

Suggested Readings

O'Regan, F. (2008). *Understanding AD/HD: Frequently asked questions*. London: Jessica Kingsley Publishers.

Pauc, R. (2006). *The learning disability myth: Understanding and overcoming your child's diagnosis of dyspraxia, Tourette's Syndrome of childhood, ADD, ADHD or OCD*. London: Virgin Books.

Phillips, C. B. (2006). Medicine goes to school: Teachers as sickness brokers for ADHD. *PLOS Medicine, 3(4)*, from http://medicine.plosjournals.org/perlserv/?request=get-document&doi=10.1371%2Fjournal.pmed.0030182.

Zeigler Dendy, C. A. (2006). *Teenagers with ADD and ADHD: A guide for parents and professionals* (2nd ed.). Bethesda: Woodbine House.

ISSUE 8

Should MDMA (Ecstasy) Be Prohibited, Even for Therapeutic Use?

YES: Robert Mathias and Patrick Zickler, from "NIDA Conference Highlights Scientific Findings on MDMA/Ecstasy," *NIDA Notes* (December 2001)

NO: June Riedlinger and Michael Montagne, from "Using MDMA in the Treatment of Depression," in Julie Holland, ed., *Ecstasy: The Complete Guide* (Park Street Press, 2001)

ISSUE SUMMARY

YES: Science writers Robert Mathias and Patrick Zickler argue that MDMA has skyrocketed in popularity and that insufficient attention has been paid to the physical and psychological risks associated with its use.

NO: June Riedlinger, an assistant professor of clinical pharmacy, and Michael Montagne, a professor of pharmacy, contend that the risks associated with MDMA use have been exaggerated and that there are legitimate therapeutic uses for this substance.

MDMA, popularly known as "Ecstasy," was first synthesized at the beginning of the twentieth century when a pharmaceutical company was trying to develop a medication to stop bleeding. However, this product was abandoned because of its dramatic psychoactive properties. MDMA resurfaced in the 1980s when some psychotherapists proposed that it be used to enhance communication in patients. The drug also began appearing on college campuses and in nightclubs, where users were enthralled by its euphoria-inducing effects. Although the Drug Enforcement Agency outlawed MDMA in 1985, the use of this substance continued to grow dramatically throughout the 1990s, as partygoers attending dance marathons known as raves craved MDMA as their recreational drug of choice.

By the late 1990s, the rave party scene had caught the attention of the media and law enforcement authorities because of the increasing number of medical emergencies associated with the uncontrolled use of substances such as MDMA. For example, in 1994, there were 253 MDMA-related emergency room incidents, but by the year 2000 the number had risen to 4,511 individuals being rushed to hospitals because they were suffering from dehydration, hyperthermia, and seizures caused by MDMA. As Robert Mathias and Patrick Zickler assert in the following selection, in addition to the immediate physical risks associated with MDMA, there are long-term emotional and cognitive costs. For instance, chronic users of MDMA show evidence of impairment in learning and memory as well as an increased likelihood of developing serious psychological conditions later in life.

In the second selection, June Riedlinger and Michael Montagne acknowledge the potential for adverse effects and neurotoxicity associated with MDMA, but they urge more thoughtful attention to the haphazard ways in which MDMA has been taken by recreational users. They also argue that there are some potentially useful ways in which this substance might be prescribed to treat certain psychological problems, such as depression, for which traditional medications have considerable limitations and side effects. In responding to harsh criticisms of MDMA, Riedlinger and Montagne contend that the problems are attributable to the lack of pharmaceutical regulation; if MDMA were professionally manufactured such that samples of known purity were distributed, most adverse reactions would be avoidable.

POINT

- Even small doses of MDMA can greatly reduce the body's ability to metabolize the drug. Increased toxic effects can lead to harmful reactions, such as dehydration, hyperthermia, and seizures.
- In clinical studies, MDMA users have shown massive impairment on tests of learning, memory, and general intelligence when compared to nonusers.
- Exposure to MDMA is associated with damage to brain cells that release serotonin.
- Compared with nonusers, current and former users of MDMA have drastically higher measures of psychopathology, such as impulsivity, anxiety, and depression.
- Many Ecstasy-related emergencies occur because tablets are frequently laced with other drugs.

COUNTERPOINT

- Reports of adverse reactions have been sensationalized. Most adverse reactions and neurotoxicity can be avoided if the lowest effective therapeutic doses are used.
- Most clinical studies that allege neurotoxicity have recruited volunteers with histories of excessive and prolonged use. No study has been published that assesses individuals with histories of infrequent oral dosing.
- MDMA works to enhance serotonergic function and heightens mood in a matter of hours.
- MDMA is, in fact, effective in treating psychopathology. It facilitates psychotherapy and helps to alleviate feelings of hopelessness.
- If MDMA were regulated and samples of known purity were used, most adverse reactions would be avoidable.

YES

**Robert Mathias
and Patrick Zickler**

NIDA Conference Highlights Scientific Findings on MDMA/Ecstasy

In the face of worldwide increase in the use of MDMA, or ecstasy, particularly among teens and young adults, NIDA convened an international array of scientists at the National Institutes of Health in Bethesda, Maryland, in July [2001] for a conference on "MDMA/Ecstasy Research: Advances, Challenges, Future Directions." MDMA researchers from Australia, Europe, and all regions of the United States detailed the latest findings on patterns and trends of MDMA abuse, its complex acute effects on the brain and behavior, and the possible long-term consequences of its use.

In opening remarks, Dr. Glen Hanson, director of NIDA's Division of Neuroscience and Behavioral Research, noted the tremendous interest of the scientific community and the general public in MDMA and its effects. The soldout conference drew an audience of 565 people with a broad range of interests and perspectives. They included scientists, drug abuse prevention and treatment practitioners, clinicians, educators, high school counselors, and representatives from Federal and local public health departments and agencies.

A public health perspective on MDMA by James N. Hall, of the Up Front Drug Information Center in Miami, Florida, provided a sharp contrast to the prevailing public view of MDMA as an innocuous drug. MDMA use began to expand rapidly in the United States in 1996 with "more pills going to younger populations," Mr. Hall said. This upsurge in use led to an increase in drug-related problems. For example, MDMA-related hospital emergency room incidents increased from 253 in 1994 to 4,511 in 2000, according to recent data from the Substance Abuse and Mental Health Services Administration's Drug Abuse Warning Network. "Most of these emergency room mentions are multiple-drug cases," Mr. Hall said, "as polydrug use has become the norm."

The common practice of using MDMA in conjunction with other drugs was just one of several recurring themes sounded during a conference session on current trends and patterns of MDMA use. Other significant themes were:

- MDMA now is being used in urban, suburban, and rural areas throughout the country;
- MDMA continues to be used in its traditional settings of all-night dance parties, called "raves," and nightclubs; use also is common now on college campuses and at small group gatherings, such as house parties;

From *NIDA Notes*, vol. 16, no. 5 (December 2001).

Figure 1

MDMA-Related Hospital Emergency Room Incidents—1994–2000

- MDMA is used by all ages but still mainly by adolescents and young adults; use has increased sharply in this population in recent years;
- MDMA users are predominantly white, but ethnically and racially diverse groups of people are now using the drug; and
- MDMA's euphoric effects can lead to unplanned or unwanted sexual contact that increases the risk of transmitting HIV/AIDS and other infectious diseases.

Acute Effects of MDMA

A session on MDMA's acute effects presented the latest findings on how the drug works in the brain and body to produce its perceptual and physiological impact. The session explored the interaction of underlying biological and behavioral factors and mechanisms that may contribute to the possibly harmful effects of MDMA use.

Animal studies have indicated that MDMA increases extracellular levels of the chemical messengers serotonin and dopamine. In laboratory studies to understand how these increases affect humans, Dr. Manuel Tancer of Wayne State University in Detroit asked participants to compare MDMA's effects to those produced by compounds that stimulate serotonin alone and dopamine alone. MDMA's effects were reported to resemble some features of both compounds, noted Dr. Tancer. This indicates that both the dopamine and serotonin systems play a role in producing MDMA's subjective effects in humans.

MDMA also has powerful acute physiological effects in humans that increase with larger doses, according to several presentations. MDMA's cardiovascular effects include large increases in blood pressure, heart rate, and myocardial oxygen consumption, noted Dr. John Mendelson of the University of California, San Francisco. MDMA's elevations of heart rate and blood pressure were comparable to those produced by a maximal dose of dobutamine, a cardiovascular stimulant used in stress tests to evaluate patients for coronary artery disease, he said. However, unlike dobutamine, MDMA did not increase the heart's pumping efficiency. Thus, MDMA-induced heart rate and blood pressure increases may lead to an unexpectedly large increase in myocardial oxygen consumption, which can increase the risk for a cardiovascular catastrophe in people with preexisting heart disease, he said.

Even small increases in MDMA dose can greatly reduce the body's ability to metabolize the drug. This means MDMA is not processed and removed from the body quickly and remains active for longer periods. "As a result, plasma levels of the drug and concomitant increases in toxicity may rise dramatically when users take multiple doses over brief time periods. Increased toxic effects can lead to harmful reactions such as dehydration, hyperthermia, and seizures," Dr. Mendelson said. Drugs such as methamphetamine that are commonly abused in conjunction with MDMA also may increase the cardiovascular effects of MDMA, he said.

MDMA tablets often contain other drugs, such as ephedrine, a stimulant, and dextromethorphan, a cough suppressant that has PCP-like effects at high doses, that also can increase its harmful effects. In addition, drugs sold as MDMA may actually be substances that are much more dangerous, according to Dr. Rodney Irvine of the University of Adelaide in Australia. For example, the hallucinogen PMA (4-methoxyamphetamine), which is similar in some respects to MDMA, has even more severe toxic effects on the cardiovascular system, particularly as dosage increases. The drug has been sold as MDMA in Australia and has been associated with a number of deaths. PMA is now being distributed in the United States and has been linked to deaths in Chicago and Central Florida, according to the Federal Drug Enforcement Administration.

Long-Term Effects of MDMA

During the second day of the conference, researchers from the United States and other countries described current investigations of ecstasy's long-term effects. Introducing the day's program, Dr. Hanson summarized the mechanisms thought to be responsible for MDMA's toxic effects on the brain's serotonin system. In tests of learning and memory, he noted, MDMA users perform more poorly than nonusers on tasks associated with brain regions affected by MDMA. Higher doses of MDMA appear to be associated with more profound effects, and the consequences may be long-lasting.

Dr. Charles Vorhees of Children's Hospital Medical Center in Cincinnati, Ohio, has found that, in rats, exposure to MDMA during a period of brain development that corresponds to human brain development during the trimester before birth is associated with learning deficits that last into adulthood. "The impairment, which affects the rate at which the animals learn new tasks, increases in severity as the dose of MDMA increases and is more pronounced as the tasks become more complex," Dr. Vorhees said.

These findings of MDMA's effects on brain development are limited to studies involving rats, but there is a growing body of research suggesting that—in adult primates—MDMA can cause long-lasting damage. At the Johns Hopkins University School of Medicine in Baltimore, Drs. Una McCann, George Ricaurte, and other investigators have found that exposure to MDMA is associated with damage to brain cells that release serotonin; this damage persists for at least 7 years in nonhuman primates. In humans, the researchers have found that MDMA use is associated with verbal and visual memory

Figure 2

Effects of MDMA Use on Tryptophan Utilization

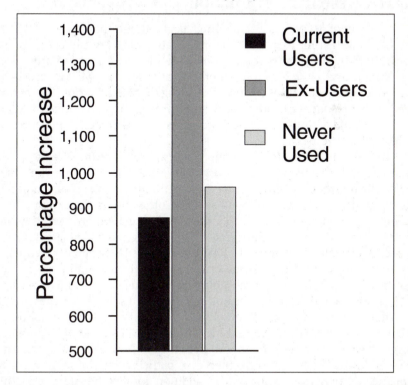

Note: MDMA disrupts brain processes that use the amino acid tryptophan to make the neurotransmitter serotonin, which affects memory and mood. Five hours after drinking a tryptophan supplement, ex-users of MDMA showed greater elevations of their blood tryptophan levels than did current users or nonusers, indicating that less of the amino acid had been converted to serotonin.

problems in individuals who have not used the drug for at least 2 weeks. "We see a relationship between the dose of MDMA and the severity of the effects. In animals, MDMA-induced damage is extensive and long-lasting and we do not yet know if it is reversible," Dr. Ricaurte said. "A person who takes enough of the drug to feel its effects is taking enough to be at serious risk of similar damage to the brain and to memory and learning."

Dr. Linda Chang, a scientist at the Brookhaven National Laboratory in Upton, New York, reported on research using brain imaging techniques to evaluate the effects of occasional use of MDMA. She and her colleagues Dr. Charles Grob and Dr. Russell Poland at the University of California, Los Angeles, used single photon emission computed tomography to evaluate blood flow to the brain—which is regulated in part by serotonin—in 21 MDMA users who had taken the drug at least 6 times per year for more than 1 year (on average, a total of 75 times), but had not used the drug in at least 2 weeks (4 months average abstinence). The participants then were given MDMA in two sessions over the course of a week. Two weeks later, brain images showed decreased blood flow compared to the earlier images. The decrease was greater in those individuals who had higher total use of the drug.

MDMA Research in Europe

The popularity of MDMA as a "club drug" began in Europe in the late 1980s—roughly 5 years earlier than in the United States—and researchers there have studied the drug's effects in populations with a longer history of drug use. In Great Britain and Germany researchers have found that MDMA users—and even former users who have not taken the drug for at least 6 months—perform more poorly on some tests of memory and learning than do nonusers. MDMA also is associated with psychological problems such as anxiety and depression, this research suggests.

The learning and memory functions that appear to be impaired by MDMA in animal and human studies are associated with the brain's serotonin system. The specific effects of MDMA can be evaluated directly in animal studies, but in humans nearly all MDMA users also use other drugs such as marijuana, cocaine, and alcohol. In an effort to more fully understand how MDMA affects polydrug users, Dr. Valerie Curran and her colleagues at University College London investigated the effect of MDMA use on the body's ability to use tryptophan, an amino acid that is one of the chemical building blocks for serotonin. The research involved three groups of polydrug users: some were current MDMA users, some had stopped using the drug, and some had never used it.

The researchers first measured blood levels of tryptophan and found that current and ex-users of MDMA had higher blood levels than did nonusers and that the levels were elevated in proportion to the total amount of drug the participants had used. The investigators then gave participants drinks that contained augmented amounts of tryptophan in addition to all other necessary amino acids. Five hours later they measured blood levels of the amino acid. Ex-users of MDMA showed far higher levels of tryptophan in their blood than did nonusers or current users, Dr. Curran said. "Tryptophan should cross the blood–brain

Figure 3

Effect of MDMA Use on Impulsivity

Note: The airplane figure at top is exactly matched by only one of six similar figures below. When asked to find the correct match, current and ex-users of MDMA made quicker choices and made more wrong choices before identifying the correct match than participants who used drugs other than MDMA or who used no drugs at all.

Figure 4

Long-Term Effects of MDMA Use on Memory

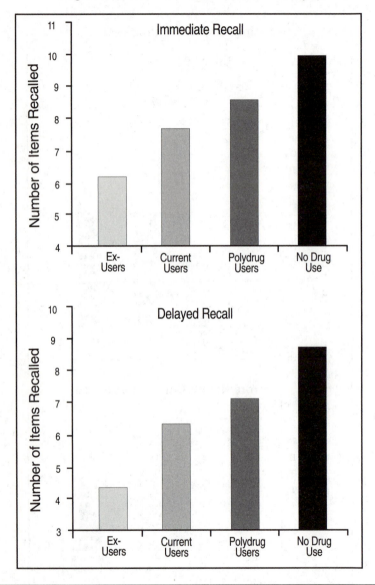

Note: In tests of MDMA effects on memory, ex-users and current users performed worse than participants who used drugs other than MDMA or used no drugs. Ex-users, in particular, showed greatly impaired memory.

barrier to be incorporated into the biosynthesis of serotonin, but in ex-users, significantly higher levels of tryptophan remained in the blood," she said.

In memory tests, current users did more poorly than did nonusers; ex-users—who had not taken MDMA for an average of 2 years—had the poorest performance. The reason for such poor performance among the ex-users is uncertain, Dr. Curran said. One possibility is that these were people who developed particularly severe adverse effects and quit using the drug because of them. "Whatever the reason, there is a clear correlation between a biological marker (blood levels of tryptophan), a functional deficit (poor performance on tests of memory), and the total dosage and length of time these people used MDMA before they stopped," Dr. Curran said.

Dr. Euphrosyne Gouzoulis-Mayfrank of the University of Technology in Aachen, Germany, also described research involving MDMA's effects on poly-drug users. She and her colleagues compared cognitive performance in three groups of participants age[d] 18 to 30. One group included MDMA users with a typical pattern of recreational use (at least twice per month within the preceding 2 years) who also used marijuana (at least once per month over a 6-month period), a second group who did not use MDMA but whose marijuana use roughly matched that of the MDMA users, and a third group who had never used either drug. "Ecstasy users showed no impairment in tests of alertness," she said, "but performed worse than one or both control groups in more complex tasks of attention, in memory and learning tasks, and in tasks reflecting aspects of general intelligence."

Dr. Michael Morgan of the University of Sussex in Great Britain described research that suggests a relationship between marijuana use, MDMA use, and psychological problems and memory deficits. Dr. Morgan and his colleagues studied the effects among groups of current MDMA users, ex-users, polydrug users who did not use MDMA, and participants who had never used drugs.

The researchers found that the psychological measures were more closely associated in the polydrug population with current marijuana use than with past MDMA use. "Overall, however, current and ex-users of MDMA have dramatically higher measures of psychopathology such as impulsivity than nonusers," Dr. Morgan said. Like Dr. Curran, Dr. Morgan found cognitive deficits associated with rates of past MDMA use. In tests of memory, both current and ex-users performed more poorly than nonusers. He also found that on some tests ex-users performed worse than did current users, although he noted that the reasons for poorer performance by ex-users could not clearly be linked exclusively to MDMA use. "Nonetheless, as a practical matter, ex-users show massively impaired memory. Not only had they not recovered, they were actually worse than current users," Dr. Morgan said.

June Riedlinger and
Michael Montagne

 NO

Using MDMA in the Treatment of Depression

Introduction

In this [selection], we discuss the use of the substance MDMA [ecstasy] for the treatment of depression. The first author's personal experience and work as a clinical pharmacist in psychiatry was the foundation for the hypothesis that MDMA could be a healing agent for the life-threatening illness of depression. Before discussing how MDMA may be beneficial in treating depression, a brief review of the medical criteria for the condition is warranted. . . .

Biochemical Basis of Depression

The possibility that some forms of human depression are based on central nervous system deficiencies of the neurotransmitter serotonin (5-hydroxytryptamine, or 5-HT) was first suggested by van Praag (1962) and then reinforced by the findings of other researchers (Coppen 1967; Lapin and Oxenburg 1969). Based on his later research, van Praag (1982) concluded that serotonin disorders are implicated most clearly in a subgroup of approximately 40 percent of patients afflicted with depression. He also emphasized that serotonin disorders probably play a causative, rather than a secondary, role in depression. This is suggested by the fact that serotonin-potentiating compounds, such as the precursors 5-hydroxytryptophan (5-HTP) and L-tryptophan, an essential amino acid, can have a therapeutic effect in depression (van Praag 1981).

It is significant that many of the drugs prescribed for treatment of depression have serotonergic activity. The newest class of antidepressants, the serotonin reuptake inhibitors (Prozac, Zoloft, Paxil, Celexa, and others) and, to varying degrees, the tricyclic antidepressants prevent the recycling of serotonin back into presynaptic nerve endings. Monoamine oxidase (MAO) inhibitors prevent the breakdown of serotonin by the enzyme MAO. In either case, more serotonin is available for binding to receptors (Spiegel and Aebi 1983). The specific mechanism of action of these drugs, however, is still not clear.

There is an entire class of psychoactive drugs that almost certainly derives its main effect from serotonin mediation (Freedman et al. 1970; Haigler and Aghajanian 1973; Anden et al. 1974; Winter 1975; Meltzer et al. 1978). These drugs, the psychedelics, are reported to have positive effects in the treatment of various psychological disorders, including depression. We present and discuss the value of psychedelic agents, with a focus on clinical reports and theoretical explanations for one specific drug, MDMA, that may become an efficacious treatment for depression in the future.

Psychedelic Psychotherapy

The possibility that psychedelic drugs could help facilitate the modern psychotherapeutic process was virtually ignored in the United States and Europe until about 1950. Between then and the mid-1960s, more than one thousand clinical papers describing forty thousand patients who had taken part in psychedelic therapy or other research trials were published as well as several dozen related books; six international conferences on psychedelic drug therapy were held (Grinspoon and Bakalar 1983). Two different types of psychedelic psychotherapy were described (Grinspoon and Bakalar 1979). One emphasized a mystical or conversion experience and its after-effects (psychedelic therapy); using high doses of LSD (more than 200 mcg) was thought to be especially effective in reforming alcoholics and criminals. The other type explored the unconscious in the manner of psychoanalysis (psycholytic therapy); it focused on the treatment of neuroses and psychosomatic disorders using low doses of LSD (100–150 mcg) as well as other psychedelic drugs.

By the mid-1950s, it was recognized that psychedelics function as nonspecific amplifiers, drugs that project into consciousness (amplify) memories, fears, and other subjectively varying (nonspecific) psychological material that had been repressed, or was unconscious. Among the first announcements of this highly significant finding was a report entitled "Ataractic and Hallucinogenic Drugs in Psychiatry," written by a team of international experts convened by the World Health Organization. This report challenged the prevailing idea that psychedelic drugs are psychotomimetic, that is, capable of inducing a model of temporary psychosis. Instead, the team concluded, "It may be a gross oversimplification to speak of drug-specific reactivity patterns. On the contrary, experience suggests that the same drug, in the same dose, in the same subject may produce very different effects according to the precise interpersonal and motivational situation in which it was given" (World Health Organization, 1958). Thus, it was made clear that the issues of set (the users' expectations) and setting (the environment for the drug experience) . . . must be taken into account when using psychedelics.

Another important issue to consider in a discussion of drug-assisted psychotherapy is this: at present, psychiatrists prescribe doses of mood elevators or stabilizers with which patients must comply on a daily basis. There is no currently accepted model of one-time or infrequent dosing of medications to alleviate psychic suffering. Thus, Grinspoon and Bakalar (1986) have emphasized: "It is a misunderstanding to consider psychedelic drug therapy as a form of chemotherapy, which must be regarded in the same way as prescribing lithium or phenothiazines." Instead, it is more like "a hybrid between pharmacotherapy and psychotherapy" (Grinspoon and Bakalar 1990) that incorporates features of both. . . .

MDMA's Role in the Treatment of Depression

That MDMA is apparently serotonergic was first noted by Nichols and associates (1982), who introduced it in vitro to homogenized rat brains and then measured the release of serotonin from the synaptosomes (vesicles in the synapses that store neurotransmitters). Elevated levels were detected, suggesting that serotonin release may play a role in MDMA's pharmacological activity. Subsequent research described in Peroutka (1990) appears to confirm the drug's serotongenicity. As with serotonergic antidepressant drugs, however, the specific mode of action is uncertain. . . .

In any case, MDMA's use in psychotherapy to stimulate positive feelings, such as openness and empathy, would seem to recommend it for a possible clinical role in treating depression. Riedlinger (1985) first proposed this in a discussion of MDMA's positive isomer activity and consequent release of serotonin in the brain. Because it is a potent releaser of serotonin into the synapse, and because of its short duration of effect, MDMA seems to be both effective and efficient as a drug for the medical treatment of depression. It works to enhance serotonergic function and mood in a matter of hours instead of weeks (as is the case for most prescription antidepressants), and it is effective when administered infrequently, perhaps in weekly or monthly dosing intervals. This compares favorably to the multiple daily dosing required for most of the currently available drugs that can be prescribed for treating depression (such as tricyclic antidepressants, MAO inhibitors, serotonin reuptake inhibitors). The other drugs often take several days or even weeks to produce antidepressant effects and frequently cause lasting troublesome side effects (appetite and sleep changes, sexual dysfunction, sweating, nausea, and headaches). Compassion for the victims of depression, in addition to the evidence of MDMA's serotonin-releasing effect, should compel further research to establish clearly whether MDMA is indeed an alternative antidepressant.

Treating Suicidal Depression with MDMA

The notion that MDMA might be useful in treating suicidal depression is based on a comparison of psychological patterns in suicidal people and MDMA's psychoactive effects. Psychological characteristics of suicidal people tend to vary between different age groups, cultures, economic classes, and gender (Hendin 1982; American Psychiatric Association 1994). Many cases seem to be manifestations of alienation. The anguish of the suicidal person is frequently that of a person in exile. He or she feels totally isolated, singled out by fate to suffer hardships and endless frustrations alone. Such people often find it hard to deal with the conflicts and demands of interpersonal relationships. They withdraw into a private, lonely world. Their justification might be that they feel unworthy of love or that others have abandoned them unfairly. In either case, the isolation typically starts to feel irreversible. There seems to be no possibility of ever establishing meaningful contact with other human beings.

According to the *Harvard Medical School Mental Health Letter* ("Suicide," 1986), "Among the immediate motives for suicide, not surprisingly, despair is most common. In one long-term study, hopelessness alone accounted for most of the association between depression and suicide, and a high level of hopelessness was the strongest signal that a person who had attempted suicide would try again. Intense guilt, psychotic delusions, and even the severity of the depression were much less adequate indicators." The study referred to in the *Mental Health Letter,* by Beck and colleagues (1985), reported that high ratings on the Beck Hopelessness Scale successfully predicted 90.9 percent of eventual cases of suicide in a sample of 165 hospitalized suicide ideators (people who initially went to the doctor with thoughts of suicide) who were followed for five to ten years after taking the test. A subsequent report regarding the study affirmed that "because hopelessness can be reduced fairly rapidly by specific therapeutic interventions . . . the assessment of hopelessness can potentially improve the prevention as well as the prediction of suicide" (Beck et al. 1989). Hopelessness itself might mediate the relationship between dysfunctional attitudes and psychopathology, especially depression.

Interpersonal attitudes related to depression, not hopelessness per se, also may be the root cause of suicide. To that extent, suicide might be considered an act of interpersonal frustration that seeks to communicate misery and break out of isolation ("Suicide," 1986). This goal may be reached, alternatively and more safely, by means of guided psychotherapy. The recalcitrance of suicidal people, however, is a problem for conventional psychotherapy. For therapy to work, a positive, dynamic interaction must take place between the patient and the therapist (Henry et al. 1990; Talley et al. 1990; Strupp 1993). The patient must be willing to communicate what is going on inside. Someone who is consumed by strong feelings of alienation and hopelessness is likely to resist interpersonal contact and open discussion. Of course, it is frequently true that patients hesitate to talk about personal problems at the start of psychotherapy and need several sessions before they warm up to the therapist. Time is often a luxury that suicidal patients cannot afford, however. They may be treatable over the long term with conventional psychotherapy, but first they must be stabilized or otherwise prevented from taking their own lives. Usually this means hospitalization, keeping a suicide watch on such patients, and even actively restraining them if necessary.

Here is where MDMA can perhaps play a viable role, based on certain effects and ramifications for guided psychotherapy succinctly described in an issue of the *Harvard Medical School Mental Health Letter* (Grinspoon and Bakalar 1985): Although MDMA has no officially approved medical or psychiatric application, a few psychiatrists and other therapists had been using it as an aid to psychotherapy for more than fifteen years, in the 1970s and [19]80s. It has now been taken in a therapeutic setting by hundreds, if not thousands, of people with few reported complications. It is said to fortify the therapeutic alliance by inviting self-disclosure and enhancing trust. Some patients also report changes that last several days to several weeks or longer—improved mood, greater relaxation, heightened self-esteem, and enhanced relations with others. Psychiatrists who have used MDMA with patients suggest that it might be helpful, for example, in marital counseling, in diagnostic interviews, or as a catalyst for insight in psychotherapy. Reports of therapeutic results are so far unpublished and anecdotal and cannot be properly evaluated without more systematic study.

Anecdotal reports by the hundreds of people who have taken MDMA in therapeutic settings are not irrelevant. Their testimonies indicate that certain psychological effects occur consistently across a broad spectrum of usage. This is evident in Adamson's (1985) collection of about fifty such testimonies. The foreword, by Ralph Metzner, observes that these firsthand accounts include such words as "ecstasy, empathy, openness, acceptance, forgiveness, and emotional bonding" in reference to MDMA's effects. These are the opposite terms often used to describe the psychological distress of suicidal people: anguish, alienation, recalcitrance, rejection, blame, guilt, and emotional withdrawal. Eisner (1989) also describes several cases of MDMA-assisted psychotherapy in which depression is mentioned specifically as one of the symptoms that is alleviated.

The value of MDMA is that it does not make its users feel better by transporting them into a naive state of bliss. They are aware of the fact that their lives have been burdened by negative thinking, have been based on fears and anxieties. MDMA seems to lend them a different perspective for several hours by minimizing their defensiveness and fear of emotional injury (Greer 1985; Greer and Tolbert 1986, 1990). It stimulates a process by which they are able to look at their problems more objectively and thus transcend a feeling of hopeless entrapment. At the same time, they feel more in touch with their positive emotions. This sustains them as the therapeutic process takes its course. The drug gives them the courage to confront their emotional problems and the strength to work them out, often by enhancing their desire to communicate constructively. Numerous examples of this process are described in Adamson's book (1985).

The particular value of MDMA for suicidal patients and, by extension, for patients with less severe forms of depression is twofold. First, it might be useful as an interventional medicine. By providing the relief from overwhelmingly dark emotions, MDMA likely can help forestall the act of suicide or otherwise alleviate the patient's sense of hopelessness. This buys time for the drug's second major effect, facilitating psychotherapy by helping to enhance the patient's trust and by inviting self-analysis and disclosure. As previously noted, the result is a fortifying of the therapeutic alliance between patient and therapist. Furthermore, MDMA does so in a relatively short time. According to Metzner in Adamson's book (1985): "One therapist has estimated that in five hours of one Adam [MDMA] session clients could activate and process psychic material that would normally require five months of weekly sessions." Needless to say, such accelerated therapeutic healing can mean the difference between life and death for people in imminent danger of suicide.

Risks of MDMA Use

There has been concern about neurotoxicity and other possible health risks from MDMA use. Most of these adverse reactions appear to be avoidable, if samples of known purity are administered in the lowest effective therapeutic dose range and frequency, after carefully screening patients for risk factors. This is consistent with the view of Grob and colleagues (1990) that fears of

MDMA neurotoxicity may have been exaggerated and that rigorous clinical trials of the drug in psychotherapy should be resumed.*

Animal research with MDMA seems to indicate that even its high-dose neurotoxic effects can be minimized by the concurrent administration of fluoxetine (Schmidt 1987; Schmidt et al. 1987). One report by McCann and Ricaurte (1993) suggested that fluoxetine pretreatment, at doses of 20 to 40 mg, does not compromise MDMA's therapeutic effects and, furthermore, decreases postsession insomnia and fatigue. A cautionary editorial by Price and colleagues (1990) maintains that it is premature to pursue clinical trials of MDMA in conditions that are not life-threatening. Both sides would be served by exploring the possible use of MDMA as an intervention drug for the stabilization and subsequent treatment of patients afflicted with severe and perhaps suicidal depression.

Conclusions

Central nervous system deficiency of 5-hydroxytryptamine (serotonin) has been implicated as a biochemical basis of at least some forms of depression. Existing drug treatments for depression include some with serotonergic effects. Studies suggest that psychedelic drugs are also serotonergic, which may indicate that there is a role for psychedelics in the treatment of depression. Such treatment has been attempted using psychedelic drugs in both the indoleamine and phelylalkylamine categories. Encouraging results recommend further research, with special emphasis on drugs in the group called entactogens or empathogens, which cause substantially less distortion of normative consciousness than classic psychedelics, such as LSD or mescaline. They could be assimilated more easily into existing psychotherapy approaches, where their function would be to accelerate and enhance the normal psychotherapeutic process rather than to serve as a maintenance medication. Their usefulness in such an application would be mainly at the start of psychotherapy. The goals would be to reduce the client's fear response, which often inhibits the ability to deal with repressed traumatic material; to facilitate the client's interpersonal communications with the therapist, spouse, or significant others; and to accelerate the formation of a therapeutic alliance between client and therapist.

---

* [Most articles that allege neurotoxicity have recruited volunteers with histories of excessive and prolonged use. No study has been published that examines infrequent, single oral dosing.—Ed.]

CHALLENGE QUESTIONS

Should MDMA (Ecstasy) Be Prohibited, Even for Therapeutic Use?

1. As spokespersons for the federal government, Robert Mathias and Patrick Zickler present compelling arguments against the use of MDMA based on extensive research. What are some of the social issues associated with the government's aggressive efforts to reduce MDMA use?
2. June Riedlinger and Michael Montagne object to anti-MDMA arguments, which they view as biased and exaggerated. How could one justify the regulated production of MDMA by pharmaceutical companies?
3. Concerns about the detrimental side effects of MDMA use have been downplayed by those who say that such problems are found only in chronic heavy users, rather than occasional recreational users. How could researchers investigate the validity of this argument?
4. Some social critics assert that it is the right of the individual to make choices about substance use and that such choices should not be the concern of the government. What are your thoughts about this viewpoint?
5. Much controversy has emerged in recent years about the medical use of substances such as marijuana to alleviate chronic pain. What are some arguments for and against the use of MDMA for the alleviation of psychological distress such as depression?

Suggested Readings

Cukor, J., Spitalnick, J., Difede, J., Rizzo, A., & Rothbaum, B. (2009). Emerging treatments for PTSD. *Clinical Psychology Review, 29*(8), 715–726.

Degenhardt, L., & Hall, W. (Eds.) (2010). The health and psychological effects of "ecstasy" (MDMA) use. National Drug and Alcohol Research Centre. University of New South Wales, Sydney. NDARC Monograph No. 62.

Holland, J. (Ed.). (2001). *Ecstasy: The complete guide: A comprehensive look at the risks and benefits of MDMA.* South Paris, ME: Park Street Press.

Johansen, P. O., & Krebs, T. S. (2009). How could MDMA (ecstasy) help anxiety disorders? A neurobiological rationale. *Journal of Psychopharmacology, 4,* 389–391.

Levert, S. (2004). *The facts about Ecstasy (drugs).* New York: Benchmark Books.

Parrott, A. C. (Ed.). (2000). *MDMA (Methylenedioxymethamphetamine).* Farmington, CT: S. Karger Publishing.

Internet References . . .

National Institute on Drug Abuse

This Web site, home to the NIDA, contains a wealth of information on topics related to drugs in society. The Web site contains wide range of information for young people, parents and teachers, health professionals, and researchers. Detailed information is provided about the most commonly abused drugs in society.

http://www.nida.nih.gov/

Baldwin Research Institute

The Web site for the Baldwin Research Institute contains articles and links pertinent to the proposition that addiction is not a brain disease, but rather a choice. The Web site has links to sites aimed at helping people recover from substance addiction, as well as information about the "Baldwin Research Project," an initiative to disprove that addiction is a brain disease.

http://www.baldwinresearch.com/

The Center for Anxiety and Traumatic Stress Disorders, Massachusetts General Hospital

The CATSD at Massachusetts General Hospital conducts state-of-the-art research aimed at improving the standard of care for people suffering from anxiety disorders such at PTSD.

http://www2.massgeneral.org/allpsych/anxiety/

VA-Yale Clinical Neurosciences PTSD Research Program

The VA-Yale program investigates the neurobiology of traumatic stress, PTSD, and resilience to stress. The program aims to develop new biological approaches for the treatment of trauma-related disorders.

http://www.psychiatry.yale.edu/research/programs/clinical_people/ptsd.aspx

Clinical and Research Programs in Pediatric Psychiatry and Adult ADHD at Massachusetts General Hospital

This Web site provides information about current research and clinical endeavors pertaining to pharmacological interventions for children and adults with ADHD.

http://www2.massgeneral.org/allpsych/pedipsych/home.html

The Mayo Clinic

The Mayo Clinic provides extensive information about diagnosis, treatment, and research pertaining to many psychological disorders including ADHD.

http://www.mayoclinic.com/health/adhd/ds00275/dsection=treatments-and-drugs

The Prescribing Psychologists Information Page

This Web site provides information about education, training, and legislation related to prescription privileges for psychologists.

http://www.prescribingpsychologist.com

The Trend Toward Biological Interventions

*A*lthough the medical model has been prominent in the field of mental health for the past century, in recent years the trend toward biological explanations and interventions for psychological problems has been more evident. For example, debate has intensified about the extent to which drug addiction should be viewed as a disease of the brain or a maladaptive behavior pattern under volitional control. The field of psychopharmacology has mushroomed to such an extent that billions of dollars are spent each year on medications for a wide array of emotional and behavioral problems. Medications are being tried in ways that would have been regarded as quite unlikely only a decade ago, as is the case in the use of drugs to dampen the memories of a traumatic experience and thereby reduce the likelihood of developing post-traumatic stress disorder. Many psychologists have expressed interest in becoming more central players in the medical sphere by pursuing the right to prescribe medications, an option regarded as objectionable by many physicians and of questionable wisdom by many psychologists.

- Is Addiction a Brain Disease?
- Should Memory-Dampening Drugs Be Used to Alleviate the Symptoms of Trauma?
- Is Ritalin Overprescribed?
- Should Psychologists Prescribe Medication?

ISSUE 9

Is Addiction a Brain Disease?

YES: **National Institute on Drug Abuse**, from *Drugs, Brain, and Behavior: The Science of Addiction*, revised ed., Washington, DC: National Institute on Drug Abuse (2008)

NO: **Sally Satel and Scott O. Lilienfeld**, from "Singing the Brain Disease Blues," *AJOB Neuroscience* (vol. 1, no. 1, pp. 46, 47, January, 2010)

ISSUE SUMMARY

YES: In the NIDA publication, the argument is made that addiction is indeed a disease, and that scientific information is available about the nature, prevention, and treatment of this disease.

NO: Psychiatrist Sally Satel and psychologist Scott O. Lilienfeld object to the brain disease characterization of drug addiction, asserting that addiction is an activity whose course can be altered by its foreseeable consequences.

For quite some time, American people have been given the message that drug addiction is not a moral failing, but rather a medical disease. In other words, it is not the fault of addicts that they are unable to control irresistible urges to consume drugs any more than it is the fault of a person who struggles with the debilitating symptoms of diabetes. This premise has been supported by the American Medical Association which endorses the ideas that drug dependencies, including alcoholism, are diseases, and that their treatment is a legitimate component of medical practice. Thousands of Web sites that promote treatment programs for substance-dependent individuals characterize addiction as a disease, and treated by health professionals.

A common misconception exists that Alcoholics Anonymous (AA) promotes the view that alcoholism is a disease. However, AA has no opinion on controversial issues such as the nature of alcoholism. They state merely that alcoholism "is an illness which only a spiritual experience will conquer." Words such as these would certainly not be applicable to medical diseases such as diabetes or asthma. Interestingly, it seems that the disease model of drug addiction has been promulgated most vehemently by agencies of the U.S. government such as the National Institute on Drug Abuse (NIDA) and the Substance Abuse and Mental Health Services Administration (SAMHSA). Although these agencies provide valuable services, social observers question whether promotion of the disease model is to acquire funding for research.

Addiction is indeed a disease supported by scientific information according to the NIDA publication. NIDA promotes the idea that it is important for scientists to study the effects that drugs have on the brain and on behavior, so that this information can be used to develop drug abuse prevention and treatment programs. NIDA highlights the fact that, although the initial decision to take drugs is voluntary, over time drug-addicted individuals show physical changes in areas of the brain that are critical to judgment and behavior.

Satel and Lilienfeld contend that drug users should be viewed in terms of their capacity for self-governance, rather than as helpless individuals incapable of changing their behavior. Further, the brain disease model erroneously suggests that the brain is the most useful level of analysis for understanding and treating addiction. These authors point out that repetitive drug use is reduced or stopped altogether when the adverse consequences of drug use exceed its rewards.

POINT

- Addiction is a chronic, relapsing brain disease that is characterized by compulsive drug seeking and use despite harmful consequences.

- Pleasurable activities become less pleasurable with continuous drug use, and drug abuse becomes necessary for abusers to simply feel "normal." Drug abusers reach a point where they seek and take drugs despite the consequences. Some users may feel the need to take higher or more frequent doses, even in the early stages of their drug use.

- The initial decision to take drugs is mostly voluntary. However, when abuse takes over, one's ability to exert self-control can become impaired. Brain imaging studies from drug-addicts show physical changes in areas of the brain that are critical to judgment, decision making, learning and memory, and behavior control.

- The overall risk for addiction is influenced by the biological makeup of the individual. It can even be influenced by gender or ethnicity, developmental stage, and social environment.

- Scientists study the effects that drugs have on the brain and on behavior. Information is used to develop prevention and recovery programs.

COUNTERPOINT

- Addiction can be defined in any way the definer thinks fit. However, if one's purpose is providing psychosocial treatment and devising policy, then the "neurocentric" view doesn't help much.

- The capacity for self-governance is the key to the most promising treatments for addiction. This fact is often obscured . . . [and] the state of "addiction" is taken to mean that the desire to use is unmalleable and beyond the reach of environmental contingencies. Therefore, addicted individuals are believed to be helpless to change their behavior.

- Addiction is an activity whose course can be altered by its foreseeable consequences. No amount of reinforcement or punishment can alter the course of an entirely autonomous biological condition.

- The mechanical simplicity of the "brain disease" rhetoric has a seductive appeal that obscures the considerable degree of choice in addiction.

- The brain disease model implies erroneously that the brain is necessarily the most important and useful level of analysis for understanding and treating addiction.

YES ↩ National Institute on Drug Abuse

The Science of Addiction

Drug Abuse and Addiction

What Is Drug Addiction?

Addiction is defined as a chronic, relapsing brain disease that is characterized by compulsive drug seeking and use, despite harmful consequences. It is considered a brain disease because drugs change the brain—they change its structure and how it works. These brain changes can be long lasting, and can lead to the harmful behaviors seen in people who abuse drugs.

Is Continued Drug Abuse a Voluntary Behavior?

The initial decision to take drugs is mostly voluntary. However, when drug abuse takes over, a person's ability to exert self control can become seriously impaired. Brain imaging studies from drug-addicted individuals show physical changes in areas of the brain that are critical to judgment, decision making, learning and memory, and behavior control. Scientists believe that these changes alter the way the brain works, and may help explain the compulsive and destructive behaviors of addiction.

Why Do Some People Become Addicted to Drugs, While Others Do Not?

As with any other disease, vulnerability to addiction differs from person to person. In general, the more risk factors an individual has, the greater the chance that taking drugs will lead to abuse and addiction. "Protective" factors reduce a person's risk of developing addiction.

What Factors Determine If a Person Will Become Addicted?

No single factor determines whether a person will become addicted to drugs. The overall risk for addiction is impacted by the biological makeup of the individual—it can even be influenced by gender or ethnicity, his or her developmental stage, and the surrounding social environment (e.g., conditions at home, at school, and in the neighborhood).

Published by *National Institutes of Health*, NIH Pub no. 07-5605, April 2007, pp. 5, 7, 8, 10, 15–20.

Which Biological Factors Increase Risk of Addiction?

Scientists estimate that genetic factors account for between 40 and 60 percent of a person's vulnerability to addiction, including the effects of environment on gene expression and function. Adolescents and individuals with mental disorders are at greater risk of drug abuse and addiction than the general population.

The Brain Continues to Develop into Adulthood and Undergoes Dramatic Changes During Adolescence

One of the brain areas still maturing during adolescence is the prefrontal cortex—the part of the brain that enables us to assess situations, make sound decisions, and keep our emotions and desires under control. The fact that this critical part of an adolescent's brain is still a work-in-progress puts them at increased risk for poor decisions (such as trying drugs or continued abuse). Thus, introducing drugs while the brain is still developing may have profound and long-lasting consequences.

Drugs and the Brain

Introducing the Human Brain

The human brain is the most complex organ in the body. This three-pound mass of gray and white matter sits at the center of all human activity—you need it to drive a car, to enjoy a meal, to breathe, to create an artistic masterpiece, and to enjoy everyday activities. In brief, the brain regulates your basic body functions; enables you to interpret and respond to everything you experience, and shapes your thoughts, emotions, and behavior.

The brain is made up of many parts that all work together as a team. Different parts of the brain are responsible for coordinating and performing specific functions. Drugs can alter important brain areas that are necessary for life-sustaining functions and can drive the compulsive drug abuse that marks addiction. Brain areas affected by drug abuse—

- *The brain stem* controls basic functions critical to life, such as heart rate, breathing, and sleeping.
- *The limbic system* contains the brain's reward circuit—it links together a number of brain structures that control and regulate our ability to feel pleasure. Feeling pleasure motivates us to repeat behaviors such as eating—actions that are critical to our existence. The limbic system is activated when we perform these activities—and also by drugs of abuse. In addition, the limbic system is responsible for our perception of other emotions, both positive and negative, which explains the mood-altering properties of many drugs.
- *The cerebral cortex* is divided into areas that control specific functions. Different areas process information from our senses, enabling us to see, feel, hear, and taste. The front part of the cortex, the frontal cortex or forebrain, is the thinking center of the brain; it powers our ability to think, plan, solve problems, and make decisions.

How Does the Brain Communicate?

The brain is a communications center consisting of billions of neurons, or nerve cells. Networks of neurons pass messages back and forth to different structures within the brain, the spinal column, and the peripheral nervous system. These nerve networks coordinate and regulate everything we feel, think, and do.

- *Neuron to Neuron*
  Each nerve cell in the brain sends and receives messages in the form of electrical impulses. Once a cell receives and processes a message, it sends it on to other neurons.
- *Neurotransmitters—The Brain's Chemical Messengers*
  The messages are carried between neurons by chemicals called neurotransmitters. (They transmit messages between neurons.)
- *Receptors—The Brain's Chemical Receivers*
  The neurotransmitter attaches to a specialized site on the receiving cell called a receptor. A neurotransmitter and its receptor operate like a "key and lock," an exquisitely specific mechanism that ensures that each receptor will forward the appropriate message only after interacting with the right kind of neurotransmitter.
- *Transporters—The Brain's Chemical Recyclers*
  Located on the cell that releases the neurotransmitter, transporters recycle these neurotransmitters (i.e., bring them back into the cell that released them), thereby shutting off the signal between neurons.

How Do Drugs Work in the Brain?

Drugs are chemicals. They work in the brain by tapping into the brain's communication system and interfering with the way nerve cells normally send, receive, and process information. Some drugs, such as marijuana and heroin, can activate neurons because their chemical structure mimics that of a natural neurotransmitter. This similarity in structure "fools" receptors and allows the drugs to lock onto and activate the nerve cells. Although these drugs mimic brain chemicals, they don't activate nerve cells in the same way as a natural neurotransmitter, and they lead to abnormal messages being transmitted through the network.

Other drugs, such as amphetamine or cocaine, can cause the nerve cells to release abnormally large amounts of natural neurotransmitters or prevent the normal recycling of these brain chemicals. This disruption produces a greatly amplified message, ultimately disrupting communication channels. The difference in effect can be described as the difference between someone whispering into your ear and someone shouting into a microphone.

How Do Drugs Work in the Brain to Produce Pleasure?

All drugs of abuse directly or indirectly target the brain's reward system by flooding the circuit with dopamine. Dopamine is a neurotransmitter present in regions of the brain that regulate movement, emotion, cognition, motivation, and feelings of pleasure. The overstimulation of this system, which rewards our natural behaviors, produces the euphoric effects sought by people who abuse drugs and teaches them to repeat the behavior.

How Does Stimulation of the Brain's Pleasure Circuit Teach Us to Keep Taking Drugs?

Our brains are wired to ensure that we will repeat life-sustaining activities by associating those activities with pleasure or reward. Whenever this reward circuit is activated, the brain notes that something important is happening that needs to be remembered, and teaches us to do it again and again, without thinking about it. Because drugs of abuse stimulate the same circuit, we learn to abuse drugs in the same way.

Why Are Drugs More Addictive Than Natural Rewards?

When some drugs of abuse are taken, they can release 2 to 10 times the amount of dopamine that natural rewards do. In some cases, this occurs almost immediately (as when drugs are smoked or injected), and the effects can last much longer than those produced by natural rewards. The resulting effects on the brain's pleasure circuit dwarfs those produced by naturally rewarding behaviors such as eating and sex. The effect of such a powerful reward strongly motivates people to take drugs again and again. This is why scientists sometimes say that drug abuse is something we learn to do very, very well.

What Happens to Your Brain If You Keep Taking Drugs?

Just as we turn down the volume on a radio that is too loud, the brain adjusts to the overwhelming surges in dopamine (and other neurotransmitters) by producing less dopamine or by reducing the number of receptors that can receive and transmit signals. As a result, dopamine's impact on the reward circuit of a drug abuser's brain can become abnormally low, and the ability to experience any pleasure is reduced. This is why the abuser eventually feels flat, lifeless, and depressed, and is unable to enjoy things that previously brought them pleasure. Now, they need to take drugs just to bring their dopamine function back up to normal. And, they must take larger amounts of the drug than they first did to create the dopamine high—an effect known as tolerance.

How Does Long-Term Drug Taking Affect Brain Circuits?

We know that the same sort of mechanisms involved in the development of tolerance can eventually lead to profound changes in neurons and brain circuits, with the potential to severely compromise the long-term health of the brain. For example, glutamate is another neurotransmitter that influences the reward circuit and the ability to learn. When the optimal concentration of glutamate is altered by drug abuse, the brain attempts to compensate for this change, which can cause impairment in cognitive function. Similarly, long-term drug abuse can trigger adaptations in habit or nonconscious memory systems.

Conditioning is one example of this type of learning, whereby environmental cues become associated with the drug experience and can trigger uncontrollable cravings if the individual is later exposed to these cues, even without the drug itself being available. This learned "reflex" is extremely robust and can emerge even after many years of abstinence.

What Other Brain Changes Occur with Abuse?

Chronic exposure to drugs of abuse disrupts the way critical brain structures interact to control behavior—behavior specifically related to drug abuse. Just as continued abuse may lead to tolerance or the need for higher drug dosages to produce an effect, it may also lead to addiction, which can drive an abuser to seek out and take drugs compulsively. Drug addiction erodes a person's self-control and ability to make sound decisions, while sending intense impulses to take drugs.

Sally Satel and Scott O. Lilienfeld **NO**

Singing the Brain Disease Blues

Well over a decade ago, the National Institute on Drug Abuse began advancing the idea that addiction is a "brain disease." Over the years, the concept has become orthodoxy—a dubious achievement that has justifiably prompted Buchman and his colleagues (2010) to call for a more nuanced perspective on addiction. In this peer commentary we challenge the validity of the brain disease model of addiction and discuss its adverse implications for treatment.

Let us begin with the concept of brain disease. "That addiction is tied to changes in brain structure and function is what makes it, fundamentally, a brain disease," wrote a former director of the National Institute on Drug Abuse in a seminal 1997 *Science* article (Leshner 1997). What does this statement really mean? Surely, drugs operate at the level of the brain (Hyman 2007). No dispute there. Regular, heavy use of alcohol, nicotine, heroin, cocaine, and other substances produces brain changes (reward centers are "hijacked," as it is commonly put) that, in turn, influence the urge to use drugs and the struggle to quit. Brain-related differences among users influence the rapidity with which they develop addiction, their subjective experience of the drug, the potency of their craving, and the severity of their withdrawal symptoms.

That said, why should this make addiction a brain disease as opposed to, say, a molecular disease, a psychological disease, or a sociocultural disease? All are equally valid perspectives for different purposes. As psychologist Nick Heather wisely asserted, "Addiction can be defined in any way the definer thinks fit. . . . The crucial issue is how useful the definition is for specific purposes" (Heather 1998). So, for example, if one's purpose is to investigate dopamine circuitry, then viewing addiction as as brain-based phenomenon makes sense. But if one's purpose is providing psychosocial treatment and devising policy, then the "neurocentric" view doesn't help much.

The mechanical simplicity of the "brain disease" rhetoric has a seductive appeal that obscures the considerable degree of choice in addiction, as Buchman and colleagues note. Consider the daily routine of addicts. They rarely spend all of their time in the throes of an intense neurochemical siege. Most heroin addicts, for example, perform some kind of gainful work between administrations of the drug. In the days between binges, cocaine addicts make many decisions that have nothing to do with drug-seeking. Should they try to find a different job? Kick that freeloading cousin off their couch? Attend a Narcotics Anonymous meeting, enter treatment if they have private insurance, or register at a public clinic if they don't? These decisions are often based on personal meaning. Many autobiographical accounts by former addicts reveal that they were startled into quitting by a spasm of self-reproach (Lawford 2008): "My God, I almost robbed someone!" or "What kind of mother am I?"

Most important, knotty philosophical issues of free will versus determinism aside, addiction is an activity whose course can be altered by its foreseeable consequences. No amount of reinforcement or punishment can alter the course of an entirely autonomous biological condition. Imagine bribing an Alzheimer's patient to keep her dementia from worsening, or threatening to impose a penalty on her if it did. It won't work. But incentives do work in addicted patients, as clinical trials of a strategy called "contingency management" show. The standard trial compares addicts who know they will receive a reward for submitting drug-free urines with matched addicts not offered rewards (Silverman et al. 2001). In general, the groups that are eligible to be rewarded with, for example, cash, gift certificates, or services are about two to three times more likely to turn in drug-free urines compared with similar counterparts who were not able to work for such incentives. In drug courts (a jail-diversion treatment program for nonviolent drug offenders), offenders are sanctioned for continued drug use (perhaps a night or two in jail) and rewarded for cooperation with the program. The judge holds the person, not his or her brain, accountable for setbacks and progress.

Even without formal incentives or sanctions, users perform their own mental calculations all the time. Repetitive drug use is reduced or stopped altogether when the adverse consequences of drug use exceed its rewards. An addict might reason, for example, "Heroin quells my psychic pain and soothes withdrawal, but it is costing my family too much." In a choice model, according to psychologist Gene Heyman (2009), addiction is the triumph of feel-good local decisions ("I'll use today") over punishing global anxieties ("I don't want to be an addict tomorrow"). As the relative value of costs and benefits of addiction change over time (yes, benefits: people use drugs and maintain addictions for psychological reasons—a reality obfuscated by the brain disease model), users become less ambivalent about quitting.

Whether powered by changes in meaning or incentives, the capacity for self-governance is the key to the most promising treatments for addiction. This fact is often obscured, however, by a semantic glitch whereby the state of "addiction" is taken to mean that the desire to use is unmalleable and beyond the reach of environmental contingencies. In circular fashion, then, addicted individuals are believed to be helpless to change their behavior. And, if so, it is wrong to expect them to respond to sanctions.

This was the destructive logic employed by the opponents of Proposition 36 in California, a 2001 referendum on the state's jail diversion program for nonviolent drug offenders (Urada et al. 2008). They prevailed and within a few years treatment program staff began clamoring for permission to use modest penalties and incentives—without them, the staff had no leverage. Similarly, drug courts and probationary programs have been hampered by ideological resistance to imposing consequences for positive urine tests because, after all, victims of a brain disease cannot be held accountable for their behavior; what's more, they are "supposed" to relapse.

The brain disease model implies erroneously that the brain is necessarily the most important and useful level of analysis for understanding and treating addiction. Like Buchman and colleagues, we believe that it is far more productive to view addiction as a behavior that operates on several levels, ranging from molecular function and structure to brain physiology to psychology to psychosocial environment and social relations (see also Kendler 2005; Lilienfeld 2007). The lower levels of explanation, particularly the brain, are merely among them—and not necessarily the most informative for practical purposes. Indeed, an "eliminative" or "greedy" (to use philosopher Daniel Dennett's apt term) reductionistic view—which posits that lower levels of analysis render higher levels superfluous—leads to ambivalence about the importance of holding addicts accountable and, in turn, undermines the most effective behavioral treatments available (Dennett 1995). Fortunately for addicts, their behavior can be modified by contingencies. Official rhetoric does them a disservice when it implies they are merely helpless victims of their own hijacked brains.

All references for articles included in *Taking Sides: Clashing Views in Abnormal Psychology, 6/e* **can be found on the Web at www.mhhe.com/cls.**

CHALLENGE QUESTIONS

Is Addiction a Brain Disease?

1. Imagine that you are a researcher who initiated a study assessing the relative contributions of biology and personality to the development of drug addiction. How would you go about studying this complex question?
2. Put yourself in the place of a clinician who is beginning to treat a drug-addicted individual. What questions would you ask in order to assess the extent to which the client is taking personal responsibility for the addiction?
3. Imagine that you are an educator with the goal of helping young people understand why drugs can be so addictive. Which points would you emphasize in your lecture?
4. What are the pros and cons of viewing drug addiction as a brain disease?
5. If unlimited funds were available for a program designed to reduce drug addiction, what initiatives would you imagine as the most effective?

Suggested Readings

Heyman, G. M. (2009). *Addiction: A disorder of choice.* Cambridge: Harvard University Press.

Hoffman, J. (2007). *Addiction: Why can't they just stop? New knowledge. New treatments. New hope.* Emmaus, PA: Rodale Books.

Mate, G. (2010). *In the realm of hungry ghosts: Close encounters with addiction.* Berkeley, CA: North Atlantic Books.

Nace, E. P., & Tinsley, J. A. (2007). *Patients with substance abuse problems: Effective identification, diagnosis, and treatment.* New York: W.W. Norton.

Vale, P.H. (2010). Addiction—and rational choice theory. *International Journal of Consumer Studies, 34*(1), 38–45.

ISSUE 10

Should Memory-Dampening Drugs Be Used to Alleviate the Symptoms of Trauma?

YES: Adam J. Kolber, from "Therapeutic Forgetting: The Legal and Ethical Implications of Memory Dampening," *Vanderbilt Law Review* (2006)

NO: The President's Council on Bioethics, from *Beyond Therapy: Biotechnology and the Pursuit of Happiness* (October 2003)

ISSUE SUMMARY

YES: Law professor Adam J. Kolber supports the use of memory-dampening drugs for survivors of trauma in the belief that some experiences are so horrific that they can stand in the way of traumatized people moving toward happier and healthier levels of functioning.

NO: The President's Council on Bioethics, chaired by Dr. Leon Kass, criticizes memory-dampening drugs because they could falsify a person's perception and understanding of the world, making terrible acts seem less terrible than they are.

It is understandable that people who have survived a trauma would go to great lengths to reduce their symptoms and alleviate their profound distress. Preliminary research has pointed to the possibility that the drug propranolol can dampen the memory of trauma, thereby making life more bearable for some trauma survivors. Controversy has arisen about whether this intervention is really as beneficial as it sounds.

Law professor Adam J. Kolber asserts that a memory-dampening drug such as propranolol can alleviate the suffering of millions of people, and that government restriction is inappropriate. Kolber contends that people have the right to control their own memories and believes that the debate about memory dampening raises fundamental questions about who owns memories. Rather than representing an unfortunate loss of one's life narrative through the process of memory dampening, trauma survivors can make life transformations that they would have otherwise been incapable of making.

The President's Council on Bioethics, chaired by Dr. Leon Kass, criticizes the use of memory-dampening drugs to treat the symptoms of trauma by asking, "What kind of society are we likely to have when the powers to control memory, mood, and mental life through drugs reach their full maturity?" The Council asserts that identities are formed by what people do and what they undergo or suffer. Escaping painful memories would necessarily result in a change in the identity of person as well as the person's perception and understanding of significant life events.

POINT

- So long as physicians who prescribe propranolol explain to their patients the potential costs and benefits of the treatment, the fact that the treatment involves making a decision based on the probability (as opposed to certainty) of different outcomes is otherwise irrelevant.

- It seems quite plausible that one could craft a coherent life narrative that is punctuated by periods of dampened memories, and it is open to debate how important it is that one's life story be coherent or otherwise neatly packaged.

- Memory-dampening drugs may enable traumatized people to make life transformations that they would be incapable of making without these drugs.

- What makes the retention of a traumatic, socially relevant memory significant is that the person who bears the traumatic memory has chosen to identify with it in some way. In fact, memory-dampening drugs, by giving us the opportunity to consciously choose to keep a memory intact, may actually facilitate our identification with it.

- If memory dampening does make some trauma *seem* less horrible, this happens in part because memory dampening can *actually make* trauma less horrible. That is, much of what is bad about traumatic experience is that it traumatizes those who survive it.

COUNTERPOINT

- Since the drugs in question appear to be effective only when administered during or shortly after a traumatic event, we would have to make a prospective judgment as to which traumatized individuals should be treated.

- As we reminisce from greater distance and with more experience, even our painful experiences can often acquire for us a meaning that we did not foresee when the experiences occurred.

- Our identities are formed both by what we do and by what we undergo or suffer. Although we may regret the shadows that unchosen memories cast over our pursuit of happiness, we cannot simply escape them while remaining who we really are.

- Those who endure bad memories should not use the new biotechnical powers to ease the psychic pain of bad memories. Using such medications does not preserve the memories' truth, but attempts instead to make the problem go away, and with it the truth of the experience in question.

- Altering the formation of emotionally powerful memories risks falsifying our perception and understanding of the world, making shameful acts seem less shameful, or terrible acts less terrible.

YES

Adam J. Kolber

Therapeutic Forgetting: The Legal and Ethical Implications of Memory Dampening

In this article, . . . I describe the ethical concerns raised by the President's Council on Bioethics and argue that they are insufficient to justify broad government interference with our ability to dampen memories.[1]

If I am right that memory dampening has the potential someday to ease the suffering of millions of people and that heavy-handed government restriction of memory dampening is inappropriate, it follows that we should have some limited right to therapeutically forget. I will suggest that this right is just a small part of a larger bundle of rights to control our own memories that I call our "freedom of memory." This bundle of rights will become increasingly important as neuroscientists develop more powerful ways to manipulate human memory.

I. Memory-Dampening Technology

In this [p]art, I provide background on PTSD, the disorder that has sparked the quest for a means of therapeutic forgetting. I describe how traumatic experiences are believed to generate the painful, recurrent memories that characterize PTSD and how drugs like propranolol may prevent these memories from imprinting as strongly as they would in the absence of the drug. By weakening the emotionality of our reactions to arousing experiences, drugs like propranolol may, in effect, dampen emotional, and perhaps even factual, aspects of memory.

According to a recent, large-scale study, approximately 7% of Americans are expected to develop PTSD within their lifetimes.[2] It is estimated that "a person with PTSD will endure 20 years of active symptoms and will experience almost 1 day a week of work impairment, perhaps resulting in a $3 billion annual productivity loss in the United States."[3] Rates of attempted suicide among those with PTSD have been reported to be "as high as 19%."[4] According to the DSM, rates of PTSD are particularly high among survivors of rape, combat, and genocide.[5] Approximately one-third to one-half of those in these at-risk populations have or will develop the disorder.[6]

First published in *Vanderbilt Law Review*, vol. 59, 2006, pp. 1521–1626 (excerpts). Copyright © 2006 by Adam J. Kolber. Reprinted by permission of the author and Vanderbilt University Law School.

PTSD can be quite debilitating. Those with PTSD have been described as "stuck" on their trauma, "reliving it in thoughts, feelings, actions, or images."[7] They may become physiologically hyperaroused or develop a sense of helplessness, symptoms that can "permanently change how a person deals with stress, alter his or her self-concept, and interfere with his or her view of the world as a manageable place."[8] Usually, PTSD is associated with "vivid intrusions of traumatic images and sensations,"[9] although some upsetting experiences can lead to a loss of recall.[10]

Current treatments for PTSD rely on antidepressants[11] and a variety of forms of psychotherapy.[12] A common form of therapy gradually exposes patients to stimuli associated with their traumatic experiences in a controlled manner in hopes of easing their responses.[13] Despite such efforts, however, PTSD is difficult to treat, and the search continues for new therapies. Treatments under investigation include d-cycloserine,[14] MDMA (commonly known as "ecstasy"),[15] transcranial magnetic stimulation,[16] and memory-dampening drugs that are the subject of this article.[17]

II. Legal Issues

[M]emory dampening using propranolol is currently thought most likely to be effective in the first six hours after a traumatic event while the memory is still in the process of consolidating.[18] During this period, however, we cannot accurately predict whether a given patient will eventually develop PTSD or otherwise develop severe traumatic memories. This means that doctors would have to prescribe propranolol and seek informed consent to the treatment before they can predict with confidence whether a particular patient would go on to develop PTSD in the absence of the drug.

Despite these concerns, . . . we frequently use preventative medicines on people who are unlikely to develop the illnesses we seek to prevent. We make such decisions by weighing expected costs and benefits, even when these decisions dramatically alter people's lives. For example, some women with a known genetic predisposition to develop breast cancer opt for preventative mastectomies even though many of them would never have actually developed the disease.[19] Part of the role of physicians is to inform patients of the costs and benefits of medical interventions, particularly when the outcome of a proposed intervention is uncertain. Thus, physicians prescribing propranolol have obligations to obtain their patients' consent after describing the probabilistic costs and benefits of treatment. Assuming they do so, the fact that the treatment involves probabilistic decision making is otherwise irrelevant.

Furthermore, while it is true that many of those asked to consent to memory dampening, having just recently suffered emotional trauma, will not have the full benefit of their faculties of contemplative reflection, we ordinarily require no such thing before commencing serious medical treatments. For example, suppose a person is severely injured in a motor vehicle accident and is rushed to the emergency room, conscious and aware but emotionally shaken. Suppose further that the patient must decide whether to have part of a limb amputated to reduce the probability of amputating the entire limb later on.

Despite the patient's emotional turmoil, both from the accident itself and the prospect of amputation, if the patient satisfies rather minimal standards of competence,[20] health professionals will seek the patient's consent to the operation.[21]

Assume now that this same patient must decide not only whether to amputate but also whether to dampen his memory of the accident. If he can consent to the amputation by making a probabilistic determination after recently suffering trauma, then he can make the same sort of determination about memory dampening.[22]

III. Ethical Issues

The President's Council on Bioethics was established by executive order in November 2001 to "advise the President on bioethical issues that may emerge as a consequence of advances in biomedical science and technology."[23] In October 2002 and again in March 2003, the Council held hearings on ethical issues raised by memory-altering drugs.[24] Not surprisingly, part of these hearings concerned efforts to increase memory retention, either to help those with memory disorders, like Alzheimer's disease, or to give healthy people extraordinary powers of recall.[25] More importantly for our purposes, the Council also heard testimony concerning the current state of research on memory dampening and the direction it may take in the future.[26]

By and large, however, the tone of the Council's report is skeptical of the benefits of technologies that go beyond therapy, including memory dampening.[27]

1. Specific Responses to the Prudential Concerns

The Tough Love Concern

The Council claims that memory dampening, by offering us a solution in a bottle, allows us to avoid the difficult but important process of coming to terms with emotional pain. There are two ways to understand the concern. The first is that there is something false or undeserved about the manner in which memory dampening eases distress. Gilbert Meilaender makes this point in his essay on memory dampening where he claims that, rather than erasing traumatic experiences, "it might still be better to struggle—with the help of others—to fit them into a coherent story that is the narrative of our life."[28] "Our task," according to Meilaender, "is not so much to erase embarrassing, troubling, or painful moments, but, as best we can and with whatever help we are given, to attempt to redeem those moments by drawing them into a life whose whole transforms and transfigures them."[29]

People have divergent views, however, about what it means to transform and transfigure our experiences into "a coherent story."[30] It seems quite plausible that one could craft a coherent life narrative that is punctuated by periods of dampened memories. Moreover, it is open to debate how important it is that one's life story be coherent or otherwise neatly packaged.

Furthermore, even if one shares Meilaender's preference to redeem and transform our experiences without memory dampeners, two additional responses are suggested. First, many experiences are simply tragic and terrifying, offering virtually no opportunity for redemption or transformation. For example, after a 1978 plane crash in San Diego, desk clerks and baggage handlers were assigned to retrieve dead bodies and clean up the crash site.[31] Emotionally unprepared for this task, many of them were so distraught that they were unable to return to work.[32] In such cases, it seems unlikely that the traumatized employees should, in Meilaender's words, "redeem those moments by drawing them into a life whose whole transforms and transfigures them."[33] Most would agree that such employees should not have participated in the cleanup in the first place, and, hence, they should not be required or expected to bear the emotional burden of having done so.[34]

Second, even if it is better to weave traumatic events into positive, life-affirming narratives, many people are never able to do so. Memory-dampening drugs may enable such people to make life transformations that they would be *incapable* of making in the absence of the drugs. For others, pharmaceuticals may drastically shorten the time it takes to recover from a traumatic experience. Suppose a person spends ten years coming to terms with a traumatic event that he could have come to terms with in two years with pharmaceutical assistance. While he might be viewed as heroic by Meilaender, others might view him as extremely obstinate. Therefore, even in those instances when positive human transformation should accompany traumatic experience, there may well be a role for memory dampening to facilitate the process.

As the Council acknowledges, "individuals 'naturally' edit their memory of traumatic or significant events—both giving new meaning to the past in light of new experiences and in some cases distorting the past to make it more bearable."[35] In fact, such selective reconstruction of our lives seems to be at the very heart of the creation of a coherent life story that Gilbert Meilaender advocates.[36] Nevertheless, we do not worry whether our better-feeling naturally reconstructed selves remain the same as before.

It is, thus, not at all clear why we ought to revere the selective rewriting of our lives that we do without pharmaceuticals, yet be so skeptical of pharmaceutically assisted rewriting.[37] In fact, memory dampening may strengthen our sense of identity. By preventing traumatic memories from consuming us, memory dampeners may allow us to pursue our own life projects, rather than those dictated by bad luck or past mistakes. As David Wasserman has noted, "pharmacologically assisted authorship may strengthen rather than reduce narrative identity,"[38] by allowing one to "edit his autobiography, instead of having it altered only by the vagaries of neurobiology."[39] Thus, to the extent that people voluntarily make changes to their mental processes, such changes may be perceived as bolstering self-identity. In fact, many people who begin taking antidepressants report feeling like themselves for the first time.[40] This suggests that some deliberate shifts in identity may not seem alienating at all.

The Genuine Experiences Concern

The Council also worries that a memory-dampened life, chemically altered as it is, is somehow a less genuine life.[41] According to the Council, "we might

often be tempted to sacrifice the accuracy of our memories for the sake of easing our pain or expanding our control over our own psychic lives. But doing so
means, ultimately, severing ourselves from reality and leaving our own identity behind."[42] This, according to the Council, "risks making us false, small, or
capable of great illusions."[43] It also risks making us "capable of great decadence
or great evil."[44]

Unfortunately, the Council never explains what makes a life genuine and
truthful (nor how leading a life that is otherwise makes us capable of great
evil). Is a memory-dampened life thought less genuine simply because some
of the memories associated with it decay at a faster rate than they otherwise
would have? Given that memories never precisely replicate our past experiences, do undampened memories provide a standard of genuineness? How
important is it to lead a "genuine" life, whatever that means?[45]

In the case of those who are emotionally traumatized, memories of the
trauma can be overwhelming and trigger exaggerated responses to harmless
stimuli associated with a traumatic memory. Such overreactions are themselves divorced from reality. Memory dampeners, by preventing people from
being overtaken by trauma, may actually make them more genuine, more true
to what they take their lives to be, than they would be if they were gripped by
upsetting memories.

Furthermore, we are not always troubled by discrepancies between our
perceptions and the world as it "genuinely" is.

At a March 2003 hearing, then-Council member Michael Sandel raised a
related example.[46] At a class on child-bearing, Sandel was told that the memory women have of the pain of childbirth is dulled through natural processes
and that because of this, women are less likely to be deterred from having
children in the future.[47] Whether or not this folklore is true,[48] Sandel suggested (and most would agree) that if it were true, we would not be troubled
by this natural process of memory dampening, even if the memory of the
pain were, in some sense, less representative of the pain as it was actually
experienced.[49]

No doubt, as a general life strategy, we do well to firmly commit ourselves
to reality and to discovering the truth about ourselves and the world around
us. Yet, such a strategy might, at times, be worse for us all things considered; or,
at least, the Council has not shown otherwise. To make the case that memory-
dampening drugs will harmfully affect our lives, the Council must be much
more specific about what makes a life genuine, how these drugs make lives less
genuine, and why that should matter so much to us that we ought to suffer in
distress to preserve our unadulterated memories.

Each of the concerns presented reflects a bias for our natural, pharmaceutical-
free mechanisms of responding to trauma. The Council implicitly or explicitly
defended: (1) our natural ability to surmount difficult life obstacles, (2) our
natural memories as the desirable basis for our sense of identity, and (3) our
natural memories as more genuine and more desirable than those that are
pharmaceutically altered.

[W]e clearly hold people responsible for failing to remember. For
example, we blame those who forget an important birthday or anniversary,

and we penalize those who forget to file a timely tax return.[50] Some of the most tragic instances of failed memory occur when parents unintentionally cause the death of their young children by leaving them stranded in the backseats of automobiles on hot days,[51] sometimes leading to criminal punishment.[52]

Even if we can have obligations to remember, however, it is easy to overestimate the strength of these obligations. Perhaps the Council does so when it states that it may have been inappropriate for those with firsthand experiences of the Holocaust to dampen their traumatic memories:

> Consider the case of a person who has suffered or witnessed atrocities that occasion unbearable memories: for example, those with firsthand experience of the Holocaust. The life of that individual might well be served by dulling such bitter memories, but such a humanitarian intervention, if widely practiced, would seem deeply troubling: Would the community as a whole—would the human race—be served by such a mass numbing of this terrible but indispensable memory? Do those who suffer evil have a duty to remember and bear witness, lest we all forget the very horrors that haunt them?[53]

There is something harsh about expecting trauma sufferers to bear the additional burden of carrying forward their traumatic memories for the benefit of others. The Council, recognizing this, goes on to soften its perspective somewhat, stating that "we cannot and should not force those who live through great trauma to endure its painful memory *for the benefit of the rest of us.*"[54] Yet, even for those who suffer from the most tragic of memories, the Council is ambivalent about the ethics of pharmaceutical dampening:

> [A]s a community, there are certain events that we have an obligation to remember—an obligation that falls disproportionately, one might even say unfairly, on those who experience such events most directly. What kind of people would we be if we did not "want" to remember the Holocaust, if we sought to make the anguish it caused simply go away? And yet, what kind of people are we, especially those who face such horrors firsthand, that we can endure such awful memories?[55]

According to the Council, we are sometimes obligated to remember some person or set of events because doing so pays respect to that person or set of events.[56] For example, we may have obligations to remember great sacrifices that others make on our behalf, not because these memories will guide our actions, but rather because retaining the memory demonstrates a kind of respect or concern for these others.

The case for legally restricting memory dampening is particularly weak when it comes to such "homage" memories. What makes the retention of a traumatic homage memory significant is that the person who bears the traumatic memory has chosen to identify with it in some way. In fact, memory-dampening drugs, by giving us the opportunity to consciously choose to keep a memory intact, may actually facilitate our identification with it. On the other hand, if an individual retains an homage memory simply because he has no choice—because the tragic memory was indelibly imprinted into his brain by stress hormones or because memory dampening has been prohibited—the holding of the homage memory loses much of its significance. Such memories are not truly homages at all.[57]

Coarsening to Horror

The Council also expressed concern that memory dampening will coarsen our reactions to horror and tragedy. If we see the world from a chemically softened, affect-dulled perspective, we may grow inured to trauma and its associated distress, "making shameful acts seem less shameful, or terrible acts less terrible, than they really are."[58] As an example, the Council describes a hypothetical witness to a violent crime who dampens his memory and eventually perceives the crime as less severe than he would have without pharmaceutical assistance:

> Imagine the experience of a person who witnesses a shocking murder. Fearing that he will be haunted by images of this event, he immediately takes propranolol (or its more potent successor) to render his memory of the murder less painful and intrusive. Thanks to the drug, his memory of the murder gets encoded as a garden-variety, emotionally neutral experience. But in manipulating his memory in this way, he risks coming to think about the murder as more tolerable than it really is, as an event that should not sting those who witness it. For our opinions about the meaning of our experiences are shaped partly by the feelings evoked when we remember them. If, psychologically, the murder is transformed into an event our witness can recall without pain—or without any particular emotion—perhaps its moral significance will also fade from consciousness.[59]

One concern . . . is that memory dampening will coarsen our feelings and make us less willing to respond to tragic situations. Along these lines, one can imagine a would-be-famous civil rights leader in the 1960s who, in order to combat the memory of childhood injustices, would have gone on to revolutionize our social institutions but, due to his use of memory dampeners, instead pursues a more mundane life plan and is never so much as mentioned in the history books.

Not only might our coarsened emotions disincline us to take positive action, it has been suggested that memory dampeners could reduce our inhibitions to engage in socially destructive action. Thus, violent criminals could use memory dampeners to ease feelings of guilt, making them more likely to recidivate.[60] In addition, it has been claimed, memory-dampened soldiers, freed from burdens of conscience, may be more effective at killing.[61] Council member Paul McHugh asks, "If soldiers did something that ended up with children getting killed, do you want to give them beta blockers so that they can do it again?"[62] The question is lacking in some important details but, more importantly, these examples suggest that fear and remorse or expectations of fear and remorse inhibit certain antisocial behaviors and that memory dampening may interfere with this desirable control mechanism. While this concern is far from universal,[63] it may warrant studying whether any proposed memory-dampening agent actually has such effects.

Even if there is some empirical basis for these concerns, however, it is important not to overstate their importance. For even if memory dampening does make some trauma seem less horrible, this happens in part because memory dampening can *actually make* trauma less horrible. That is, much of what is bad about traumatic experience is that it traumatizes those who survive it. So, for example, to the extent that we can ease the traumatic memories of those involved in military conflict (without leading to a significant increase in total military conflict), then memory dampening makes combat somewhat better than it would otherwise be. Furthermore, when soldiers are injured in battle, we heal their physical wounds using advanced technology, even if doing so makes war seem less horrible; so it is unclear why their emotional wounds should be treated any differently.[64]

While the coarsening concern is far from overwhelming, it at least shows how the widespread use of memory dampeners can potentially affect the lives of those who do not use them. Nevertheless, this concern cannot alone justify broad restrictions on memory dampening, at least not if such restrictions are consistent with our typical policies of drug regulation. For example, people consume alcohol to relieve themselves of the pain of traumatic events. Whether or not this leads to some general inurement to tragedy in society (which seems doubtful), most would not address the problem with a comprehensive prohibition of alcohol. Similarly, even if antidepressants are used for relief from the pain of traumatic experiences, we would not generally prohibit them for fear that society will be less compassionate. Likewise, the world may benefit from the inspired artwork of a Vincent van Gogh, yet few would deprive a tortured soul of antidepressants in order to foster artistic creation.

We likely permit the use of such drugs, despite whatever minimal effects they may have on our reactions to tragedy, because their costs are outweighed by other benefits. So even if data someday support the Council's concern that memory-dampening drugs can have negative effects on soldiers' battlefield reactions or on societal reactions more generally, we can surely tailor limits on their use in particular contexts.

While memory dampening has its drawbacks, such may be the price we pay in order to heal intense emotional suffering.

Freedom of Memory

I have argued that concerns over memory dampening are insufficient to justify broad restrictions on the therapy. Furthermore, having the choice to dampen memories supports our interests in self-determination and in avoiding mental illness and upset, and, as noted, enables us to identify more strongly with memories that we decide to keep. Given the potential that memory dampening has to ease the pain of so many people, and that, at a minimum, memory dampening ought not be entirely prohibited, it follows that we should have some right to dampen our memories.

Conclusion

The mere possibility of memory dampening raises fundamental questions about who owns our memories and how we should balance the rights of memory-holders against society as a whole.

Notes

1. Because our understanding of memory dampening is still in its early stages, I do not attempt to draw the line between a broad restriction on memory dampening, which I disfavor, and more narrow restrictions on its use in particular contexts, which I readily entertain. Prohibiting any kind of possession of memory-dampening drugs is an example of the former, but requiring that such drugs be prescribed by a physician is an example of the latter. I am content to allow finer gradations to be determined in the future.

2. Ronald C. Kessler et al., *Lifetime Prevalence and Age-of-Onset Distributions of* DSM-IV *Disorders in the National Comorbidity Survey Replication,* 62 ARCHIVES OF GEN. PSYCHIATRY 593, 595 (2005); *cf.* Davidson, *supra* note 32, at 584 ("In the US population, lifetime prevalence rates are in the range of 8%, with women affected twice as often as men. However, studies from other countries and studies of high-risk populations have reported widely ranging prevalence rates from a low of 1.3% in Germany to 37.4% in Algeria."). *But cf.* [Richard J. McNally], REMEMBERING TRAUMA 282-85 (2003) (discussing controversy as to whether PTSD is, in part, a "social construction"); Benedict Carey, *Most Will Be Mentally Ill at Some Point, Study Says,* N.Y. TIMES, June 7, 2005, at A18 (noting that some experts believe that the data cited in the text rely on overly-inclusive diagnostic standards).

3. Davidson, *supra* note 32, at 584.

4. *Id.*

5. DSM IV-TR, *supra* note 33, at 466.

6. *Id.; see also* Ronald C. Kessler et al., *Posttraumatic Stress Disorder in the National Comorbidity Survey,* 52 ARCHIVES OF GEN. PSYCHIATRY 1053 (1995) ("Sixty-five percent of men and 45.9% of women who reported [being raped] as their most upsetting trauma developed PTSD.").

7. Bessel A. van der Kolk et al., *A General Approach to Treatment of Posttraumatic Stress Disorder* [hereinafter Bessel A. van der Kolk et al., *A General Approach*], in TRAUMATIC STRESS: THE EFFECTS OF OVERWHELMING EXPERIENCE ON MIND, BODY, AND SOCIETY 417, 419 (Bessel A. van der Kolk et al. eds., 1995) [hereinafter TRAUMATIC STRESS].

8. *Id.*

9. Bessel A. van der Kolk, *Trauma and Memory, in* TRAUMATIC STRESS, *supra* note 39, at 279, 283.

10. *Id.; see also* [McNally], *supra* note 34, at 186–228 (discussing the nature of traumatic amnesia); Alison Motluk, *Memory Fails You After Severe Stress,* 182 NEW SCIENTIST 14, 14 (2004) (reporting a study finding that military personnel subject to intense physiological stress during mock interrogations

had great difficulty identifying their mock interrogators a day after the exercise). Though I know of no research on the matter, if drugs like propranolol can help patients avoid extreme forgetting (or perhaps extreme repression), then propranolol could actually have a memory-enhancing effect. For the time being, I disregard this possibility.

11. Jonathan R. Davidson & Bessel A. van der Kolk, *The Psychopharmacological Treatment of Posttraumatic Stress Disorder, in* TRAUMATIC STRESS, *supra* note 39, at 510, 516–20.

12. Bessel A. van der Kolk et al., *A General Approach, supra* note 39, at 417–18.

13. *See id.* at 430, 434-35 (describing controlled exposure methods of treatment).

14. U. Heresco-Levy et al., *Pilot-Controlled Trial of D-Cycloserine for the Treatment of Post-Traumatic Stress Disorder*, 5 INT'L J. NEUROPSYCHOPHARMACOLOGY 301, 301-07 (2002).

15. The FDA has approved use of MDMA (methylenedioxymethamphetamine) in medical experiments investigating PTSD treatment. David Adam, *Ecstasy Trials for Combat Stress*, GUARDIAN, Feb. 17, 2005, at 6; *see also* National Institutes of Health, *A Test of MDMA-Assisted Psychotherapy in People with Posttraumatic Stress Disorder.* . . .

16. Miller, *supra* note 12, at 35.

17. Whether we should treat or seek to prevent PTSD with memory dampening will, of course, depend on the relative efficacy, financial costs, and side effects of the technology compared to the alternatives.

18. *See supra* note 87 and accompanying text.

   [87. See [McGaugh], *supra* note 54, at 68 ("Immediately after learning, the brain is in a state that allows either disruption (retrograde amnesia) or enhancement of the consolidation of the long-term memory."); *see also* Janine Rossato et al., *Retrograde Amnesia Induced by Drugs Acting on Different Molecular Systems*, 118 BEHAVIORAL NEUROSCIENCE 563, 563 (2004) (recognizing research in animals demonstrating that "[m]emories can be modified by pharmacological treatments not only in the immediate posttraining period, but also several hours after training" (citations omitted)).]

19. Timothy R. Rebbeck et al., *Bilateral Prophylactic Mastectomy Reduces Breast Cancer Risk in BRCA1 and BRCA2 Mutation Carriers: The PROSE Study Group*, 22 J. CLINICAL ONCOLOGY 1055, 1055 (2004); *see also* Carl T. Hall, *Surgery Cuts Risk of Breast Cancer: Study Supports Use of Preventive Mastectomies*, S.F. CHRON., Feb. 24, 2004, at A2 ("The first major study of preventive breast-removal surgery in women with a high genetic risk for breast cancer showed the radical step may reduce cancer risk by 90 percent.").

20. "[N]o general agreement exists concerning the appropriate legal standard for ascertaining competency to provide informed consent." WINICK, *supra* note 96, at 349. "Some courts simply describe a valid choice as 'informed,' 'reasoned,' or 'rational,' without specifying any particular decisionmaking process. Most courts, however, do indicate that the patient must understand essential information." Elyn R. Saks, *Competency to Refuse Treatment*, 69 N.C. L. REV. 945, 978 (1991) (footnotes omitted); *see also In re Schiller*, 372 A.2d 360, 367 (N.J. Super. Ct. Ch. Div. 1977) (stating that "[t]he mental capacity to give consent to a surgical procedure is the same as that

required to enter into a contract," requiring examination of whether a patient "possesses sufficient mind to understand, in a reasonable manner, the nature, extent, character, and effect of the act or transaction in which he is engaged.").

21. Similarly, parents who are emotionally traumatized from witnessing their children's traumatic injuries can ordinarily still give informed consent to their children's medical treatment.

22. As Bruce Winick has noted:

    [I]f the decision process is sufficiently free of coercion and undue influence, a patient . . . who receives sufficient information concerning the possible risks and side effects of a proposed therapy and alternative approaches, and who is sufficiently competent and intelligent to comprehend the information, may choose whether to participate in the proposed treatment. Such an informed consent allows treatment to be administered and constitutes a defense to any subsequent legal action asserting violation of the right to refuse treatment. WINICK, *supra* note 96, at 346.

23. Exec. Order No. 13237, 66 Fed. Reg. 59851 (Nov. 28, 2001), . . .

24. *See supra* note 17 and accompanying text.

25. *See* Hearings, Part 1, *supra* note 17.

26. *See id.*; Hearings, Part 2, *supra* note 17; Hearings, Part 3, *supra* note 17.

27. *See id.* at 299–300 (summarizing the Council's concerns about enhancement technologies and stating that our efforts to obtain human perfection "may turn out to be at best but passing illusions, at worst a Faustian bargain that could cost us our full and flourishing humanity").

28. Meilaender, *supra* note 11, at 21–22.

29. *Id.* at 22.

30. *Id.* at 21.

31. This example was raised by James McGaugh at the Council's Hearing. See Hearings, Part 2, *supra* note 17, at 23–24; *see also* James N. Butcher & Chris Hatcher, *The Neglected Entity in Air Disaster Planning*, 43 AM. PSYCHOLOGIST 724, 728 (1988) (describing the incident).

32. Hearings, Part 2, *supra* note 17, at 23 (comments of James McGaugh).

33. Meilaender, *supra* note 11, at 22.

34. The Council acknowledges that if "bitter memories are so painful and intrusive as to ruin the possibility for normal experience of much of life and the world," the "impulse" to dampen those memories is "fully understandable." BEYOND THERAPY, *supra* note 97, at 230. The Council quickly retreats, however, adding: "And yet, there may be a great cost to acting compassionately for those who suffer bad memories, if we do so by compromising the truthfulness of how they remember." *Id.*

35. BEYOND THERAPY, *supra* note 97, at 217 n.*

36. *See supra* text accompanying notes 190–91.

37. *The Council's preference for natural changes in memory can be seen in the following:*

    [We] live through memorable experiences that we would never have chosen—experiences we often wish never happened at all. To some extent, these unchosen

memories constrain us; though we may regret the shadows they cast over our pursuit of happiness, we cannot simply escape them while remaining who we really are. And yet, through the act of remembering—the act of discerning and giving meaning to the past as it really was—we can shape, to some degree, the meaning of our memories, both good and bad.

BEYOND THERAPY, *supra* note 97, at 216.

38. Wasserman, *supra* note 11, at 14.

39. *Id.*

40. Peter Kramer quotes a patient who, after starting the SSRI antidepressant Prozac, said she felt "as if I had been in a drugged state all those years and now I am clearheaded." PETER KRAMER, LISTENING TO PROZAC 8 (1993). Eight months after beginning Prozac, the same patient stopped the treatment and said she felt like "I am not myself." *Id.* at 18. Some have argued that SSRI antidepressants have little, if any, efficacy that cannot be explained as a placebo effect. *See* Joanna Moncrieff & Irving Kirsch, *Efficacy of Antidepressants in Adults*, 331 BMJ 155, 157 (2005). Whatever personality changes Prozac patients experience, however, whether caused by placebo pathways or serotonin pathways, these patients frequently identify more closely with their pharmaceutically- or placebo-influenced new selves than their former selves.

41. *See* BEYOND THERAPY, *supra* note 97, at 213 ("[B]y disconnecting our mood and memory from what we do and experience, the new drugs could jeopardize the fitness and truthfulness of how we live and what we feel . . .").

42. *Id.* at 233–34.

43. *Id.* at 234.

44. *Id.*

45. Robert Nozick's famous "experience machine" thought experiment is often taken to show that we want our lives to be closely connected to reality. *See* ROBERT NOZICK, ANARCHY, STATE, & UTOPIA 42–45 (1974). Nozick asked us to imagine that:

Superduper neuropsychologists could stimulate your brain so that you would think and feel you were writing a great novel, or making a friend, or reading an interesting book. All the time you would be floating in a tank, with electrodes attached to your brain. Should you plug into this machine for life, preprogramming your life's experiences? . . . Of course, while in the tank you won't know that you're there; you'll think it's all actually happening.

Id. at 42–43. According to Nozick, we would not choose to spend our lives connected to such a machine because we value not just particular experiences but particular *genuine* experiences. *Id.* at 4–45. At best, however, Nozick's example only shows that we value *some* connection to the real world, not that we are opposed to having *any* illusory beliefs or perceptions (for example, the drug-induced, trauma-relieving perception that one has not witnessed some atrocity that, in fact, one has).

Furthermore, even Nozick's limited conclusion that we value some connection to the real world is not robustly demonstrated by the thought experiment. The thought experiment would be more convincing if those already connected to an experience machine would also choose to disconnect from it in order to lead more genuine but substantially less enjoyable lives than they do while connected. Consistent with all available evidence, we might be connected to experience machines right now, yet I question whether we would choose to disconnect from the simulacra of our current lives, if given the choice. As I argue elsewhere, the fact that we are more willing to remain connected to an experience machine than to connect in the first place suggests that our initial intuitions about the experience machine may not be entirely trustworthy. *See* Adam Kolber, *Mental Statism and the Experience Machine*, 3 BARD J. SOC. SCI. 10 (Winter 1994/1995).

46. Hearings, Part 3, *supra* note 17, at 17.

47. *Id.*

48. *See* Catherine A. Niven & Tricia Murphy-Black, *Memory for Labor Pain: A Review of the Literature*, 27 BIRTH 244, 248–49, 252 (2000) (finding little scientific evidence to support folklore that memory of labor pain is quickly forgotten); C.A. Niven & E.E. Brodie, *Memory for Labor Pain: Context and Quality*, 64 PAIN 387, 388 (1996) (characterizing several studies as "reveal[ing] that the accuracy of memory for the intensity of labor pain is modest in accord with conclusions relating to memory for pain of diverse aetiology").

49. Sandel notes:

    [T]he objection to altering memory, whether to blot out traumatic memories or to increase our ability to remember certain things on either direction might be seen as part of what we do anyhow when we take in the world, and it might be odd to think that the way we just happen to take in the world unaltered from either direction is the past. . . . Why should we think that that's necessarily going to lead us to the truest life story?

    Hearings, Part 3, *supra* note 17, at 4.

50. *See* 26 U.S.C. § 6651 (2006) (setting forth penalties for failure to file a timely tax return). Of course, one may fail to file a timely tax return for reasons other than forgetfulness.

51. *See* Minerva Canto, *Kids' Death in Hot Cars Is a Curse for Parents*, ORANGE COUNTY REGISTER (Oct. 5, 2004). . . . Suzette Hackney, *County Won't Charge Father: Neglect Not Criminal in Son's Death in Van*, DETROIT FREE PRESS, July 28, 1999, at A1.

52. Before pursuing such cases, prosecutors generally require an extreme kind of forgetfulness that evidences gross negligence. *See, e.g.*, Kelly v. Commonwealth, 592 S.E.2d 353, 355-57 (Va. Ct. App. 2004) (affirming the manslaughter conviction of a father who left his 21-month-old daughter unattended in a hot van for approximately seven hours where there was evidence that the father had stranded children in automobiles in the past).

53. BEYOND THERAPY, *supra* note 97, at 230–31 (footnotes omitted).

54. *Id.* at 231.

55. *Id.* (footnotes omitted). The Council fears that memory dampening will encourage a shallow kind of human solidarity:

    [T]hose who suffer terrible things cannot or should not have to endure their own bad memories alone. If, as people, we have an obligation to remember certain terrible events truthfully, surely we ought to help those who suffered through those events to come to terms with their worst memories. Of course, one might see the new biotechnical powers, developed precisely to ease the psychic pain of bad memories, as the mark of such solidarity. . . . But such solidarity may, in the end, prove false: for it exempts us from the duty to suffer-with (literally, to feel *com*-passion for) those who remember; it does not demand that we preserve the truth of their memories; it attempts instead to make the problem go away, and with it the truth of the experience in question.

> *Id.* at 231–32.

56. *See id.*

57. The analysis is complicated, however, by the inability to recover a previously dampened or erased memory. At one point in time, a particular memory could be merely homage-like, held only because one has no choice. With age and understanding, perhaps, the memory could become a genuine homage if the individual voluntarily identifies with the memory. By allowing people to erase homage-like memories, we cut off the subsequent opportunity to embrace the memory. This is a variation of the view described earlier by Gilbert Meilaender. *See supra* Part III.B.1.

58. *See supra* Part II.A.1.

58. BEYOND THERAPY, *supra* note 97, at 228.

59. *Id.* at 229.

60. *Cf.* BEYOND THERAPY, *supra* note 97, at 224 (noting that memory dampeners could be used "to dull the sting of one's own shameful acts").

61. *See id.* at 154 (describing the remorse-free soldier as a "killing machine"). At the Council's hearings, James McGaugh testified that "stimulants have been given to soldiers for years to make them implicitly, and I think explicitly in some cases, to make them better soldiers." Hearings, Part 1, *supra* note 17, at 13.

62. Mundell, *supra* note 5 (quoting McHugh).

63. *Id.* (quoting psychiatrist Margaret Altemus as saying, "I think Dr. McHugh may have been assuming that what prevents soldiers from committing atrocities is this overwhelming fear. . . . I've never been in a war, but my guess is that they do these things because they are really angry, or through some group attitude.").

64. James McGaugh, speaking of a hypothetical injured soldier who has killed during battle, asks: Do you just let him lie there and bleed to death because he needs to suffer the consequences of having killed another human being in battle? We give him first aid, pain medication, we do everything we can. But if he's having an emotional disturbance because of that trauma, we can't do anything about that because that would change the nature of who they are. Doesn't losing a leg change the nature of who they are? Jeanie Lerche Davis, *Forget Something? We Wish We Could*, WebMD, Apr. 9, 2004, . . . (quoting McGaugh).

Beyond Therapy: Biotechnology and the Pursuit of Happiness

Chapter Five

Who has not wanted to escape the clutches of oppressive and punishing memories? Or to calm the burdensome feelings of anxiety, disappointment, and regret? Or to achieve a psychic state of pure and undivided pleasure and joy? The satisfaction of such desires seems inseparable from our happiness, which we pursue by right and with passion.

In these efforts at peace of mind, human beings have from time immemorial sought help from doctors and drugs. In a famous literary instance, Shakespeare's Macbeth entreats his doctor to free Lady Macbeth from the haunting memory of her own guilty acts:

> *Macbeth.*   Canst thou not minister to a mind diseas'd,
>   Pluck from the memory a rooted sorrow,
>   Raze out the written troubles of the brain,
>   And with some sweet oblivious antidote
>   Cleanse the stuff'd bosom of that perilous stuff
>   Which weighs upon the heart?
>
> *Doctor.*   Therein the patient
>   Must minister to himself.

Ministering to oneself, however, is easier said than done, and many people have found themselves unequal to the task without some outside assistance. For centuries, they have made use of external agents to drown their sorrows or lift their spirits.

The burgeoning field of neuroscience is providing new, more specific, and safer agents to help us combat all sorts of psychic distress. Soon, doctors may have just the "sweet oblivious antidote" that Macbeth so desired: drugs (such as beta-adrenergic blockers) that numb the emotional sting typically associated with our intensely bad memories[.]

To be sure, these agents—and their better versions, yet to come—are, for now at least, being developed not as means for drug-induced happiness but rather as agents for combating major depression or preventing posttraumatic stress disorder (PTSD). Yet once available for those purposes, they could also be used to ease the soul and enhance the mood of nearly anyone.

From the *President's Council on Bioethics*, October 2003.

By using drugs to satisfy more easily the enduring aspirations to forget what torments us and approach the world with greater peace of mind, what deeper human aspirations might we occlude or frustrate? What qualities of character may become less necessary and, with diminished use, atrophy or become extinct, as we increasingly depend on drugs to cope with misfortune? How will we experience our incompleteness or understand our mortality as our ability grows to medically dissolve all sorts of anxiety? Will the availability of drug-induced conditions of ecstatic pleasure estrange us from the forms of pleasure that depend upon discipline and devotion? And, going beyond the implications for individuals, what kind of a society are we likely to have when the powers to control memory, mood, and mental life through drugs reach their full maturity and are widely used?

I. What are "Happy Souls"?

Because the happiness we seek we seek for *ourselves*—for *our* self, not for someone else's, and for our *self* or embodied soul, not for our bodies as material stuff—our happiness is bound up with our personhood and our identity. We would not want to attain happiness (or any other object of our desires) if the condition for attaining it required that we become someone else, that we lose our identity in the process.

The importance of identity for happiness implies necessarily the importance of memory. If experiencing our happiness depends on experiencing a stable identity, then our happiness depends also on our memory, on knowing who we are in relation to who we have been.

But if enfeebled memory can cripple identity, selectively altered memory can distort it. Changing the content of our memories or altering their emotional tonalities, however desirable to alleviate guilty or painful consciousness, could subtly reshape who we are, at least to ourselves. With altered memories we might feel better about ourselves, but it is not clear that the better-feeling "we" remains the same as before. Lady Macbeth, cured of her guilty torment, would remain the murderess she was, but not the conscience-stricken being even she could not help but be.

[A]n unchecked power to erase memories, brighten moods, and alter our emotional dispositions could imperil our capacity to form a strong and coherent personal identity. To the extent that our inner life ceases to reflect the ups and downs of daily existence and instead operates independently of them, we dissipate our identity, which is formed through engagement with others and through immersion in the mix of routine and unpredictable events that constitute our lives.

II. Memory and Happiness

Our identity or sense of self emerges, grows, and changes. Yet, despite all the changes, thanks to the integrating powers of memory, our identity also, remarkably, persists *as ours*.

We especially want our memories to be not simply a sequence of disconnected experiences, but a narrative that seems to contain some unfolding purpose, some larger point from beginning to end, some aspiration discovered, pursued, and at least partially fulfilled.

Memory is central to human flourishing, in other words, precisely because we pursue happiness in time, as time-bound beings. We have a past and a future as well as a present, and being happy through time requires that these be connected in a meaningful way. If we are to flourish as ourselves, we must do so without abandoning or forgetting who we are or once were. Yet because our lives are time-bound, our happiness is always incomplete—always not-yet and on-the-way, always here but slipping away, but also always possible again and in the future. Our happiest experiences can be revivified. And, as we reminisce from greater distance and with more experience, even our painful experiences can often acquire for us a meaning not in evidence when they occurred.

The place of memory in the pursuit of happiness also suggests something essential about human identity, a theme raised in various places and in different ways throughout this report: namely, our identities are formed both by what we do and by what we undergo or suffer. We actively choose paths and do deeds fit to be remembered. But we also live through memorable experiences that we would never have chosen—experiences we often wish never happened at all. To some extent, these unchosen memories constrain us; though we may regret the shadows they cast over our pursuit of happiness, we cannot simply escape them while remaining who we really are. And yet, through the act of remembering—the act of discerning and giving meaning to the past as it really was—we can shape, to some degree, the meaning of our memories, both good and bad.

The capacity to alter or numb our remembrance of things past cuts to the heart of what it means to remember in a human way, and it is this biotechnical possibility that we focus on here. Deciding when or whether to use such biotechnical power will require that we think long and hard about what it means to remember truthfully, to live in time, and to seek happiness without losing or abandoning our identity. The rest of this discussion of "memory and happiness" is an invitation to such reflection.

Good Memories and Bad

[T]he significance of past events often becomes clear to us only after much rumination in light of later experience, and what seems trivial at one time may appear crucial at another. Neither can an excellent memory be one that remembers only what we *want* to remember: sometimes our most valuable memories are of events that were painful when they occurred, but that on reflection teach us vital lessons.

Biotechnology and Memory Alteration

It is a commonplace observation that, while some events fade quickly from the mind, emotionally intense experiences form memories that are peculiarly vivid and long-lasting. Not only do we recall such events long after they happened, but the recollection is often accompanied, in some measure, by a recurrence of the emotions aroused during the original experience.

When a person experiences especially shocking or violent events (such as a plane crash or bloody combat), the release of stress hormones may be so intense that the memory-encoding system is over-activated. The result is a consolidation of memories both far stronger and more persistent than normal and also more apt, upon recollection, to call forth the intense emotional response of the original experience. In such cases, each time the person relives the traumatic memory, a new flood of stress hormones is released, and the experience may be so emotionally intense as to be encoded as a new experience. With time, the memories grow more recurrent and intrusive, and the response—fear, helplessness, horror—more incapacitating. As we shall see, drugs that might prevent or alleviate the symptoms of PTSD are among the chief medical benefits that scientists expect from recent research in the neurochemistry of memory formation.

In fact, the discovery of hormonal regulation of memory formation was quickly followed up by clinical studies on human subjects demonstrating that memory of emotional experiences can be altered pharmacologically. In one particularly interesting series of experiments, Larry Cahill and his colleagues showed that injections of beta-blockers can, by inhibiting the action of stress hormones, suppress the memory-enhancing effects of strong emotional arousal.

[T]aking propranolol appears to have little or no effect on how we remember everyday or emotionally neutral information. But when taken at the time of highly emotional experiences, propranolol appears to suppress the normal memory-enhancing effects of emotional arousal—while leaving the immediate emotional response unaffected. These results suggested the possibility of using beta-blockers to help survivors of traumatic events to reduce their intrusive—and in some cases crippling—memories of those events.

[A]lthough the pharmacology of memory alteration is a science still in its infancy, the significance of this potential new power—to separate the subjective experience of memory from the truth of the experience that is remembered—should not be underestimated. It surely returns us to the large ethical and anthropological questions with which we began—about memory's role in shaping personal identity and the character of human life, and about the meaning of remembering things that we would rather forget and of forgetting things that we perhaps ought to remember.

Memory-Blunting: Ethical Analysis

If we had the power, by promptly taking a memory-altering drug, to dull the emotional impact of what could become very painful memories, when might we be tempted to use it? And for what reasons should we yield to or resist the temptation?

At first glance, such a drug would seem ideally suited for the prevention of PTSD, the complex of debilitating symptoms that sometimes afflict those who have experienced severe trauma. These symptoms—which include persistent reexperiencing of the traumatic event and avoidance of every person, place, or thing that might stimulate the horrid memory's return[1] can so burden mental life as to make normal everyday living extremely difficult, if not impossible.[2] For those suffering these disturbing symptoms, a drug that could separate a painful memory from its powerful emotional component would appear very welcom[ing] indeed.

Yet the prospect of preventing (even) PTSD with beta-blockers or other memory-blunting agents seems to be, for several reasons, problematic. First of all, the drugs in question appear to be effective only when administered during or shortly after a traumatic event—and thus well before any symptoms of PTSD would be manifested. How then could we make, and make on the spot, the *prospective* judgment that a particular event is sufficiently terrible to warrant preemptive memory-blunting? Second, how shall we judge *which* participants in the event merit such treatment? After all, not everyone who suffers through painful experiences is destined to have pathological memory effects. Should the drugs in question be given to everyone or only to those with an observed susceptibility to PTSD, and, if the latter, how will we know who these are? Finally, in some cases merely witnessing a disturbing event (for example, a murder, rape, or terrorist attack) is sufficient to cause PTSD-like symptoms long afterwards. Should we then, as soon as disaster strikes, consider giving memory-altering drugs to all the witnesses, in addition to those directly involved?

If the apparent powers of memory-blunting drugs are confirmed, some might be inclined to prescribe them liberally to all who are involved in a sufficiently terrible event. After all, even those not destined to come down with full-blown PTSD are likely to suffer painful recurrent memories of an airplane crash, an incident of terrorism, or a violent combat operation. In the aftermath of such shocking incidents, why not give everyone the chance to remember these events without the added burden of painful emotions? This line of reasoning might, in fact, tempt us to give beta-blockers liberally to soldiers on the eve of combat, to emergency workers en route to a disaster site, or even to individuals requesting prophylaxis against the shame or guilt they might incur from future misdeeds—in general, to anyone facing an experience that is likely to leave lasting intrusive memories.

Yet on further reflection it seems clear that not every intrusive memory is a suitable candidate for prospective pharmacological blunting. As Daniel Schacter has observed, "attempts to avoid traumatic memories often backfire":

> Intrusive memories need to be acknowledged, confronted, and worked through, in order to set them to rest for the long term. Unwelcome memories of trauma are symptoms of a disrupted psyche that requires attention before it can resume healthy functioning. Beta-blockers might make it easier for trauma survivors to face and incorporate traumatic recollections, and in that sense could facilitate long-term adaptation. Yet it is also possible that beta-blockers would work against the normal process of recovery: traumatic memories would not spring to mind with the kind of psychological force that demands attention and perhaps intervention. Prescription of beta-blockers could bring about

an effective trade-off between short-term reductions in the sting of traumatic memories and long-term increases in persistence of related symptoms of a trauma that has not been adequately confronted.[3]

The point can be generalized: in the immediate aftermath of a painful experience, we simply cannot know either the full meaning of the experience in question or the ultimate character and future prospects of the individual who experiences it. We cannot know how this experience will change this person at this time and over time. Will he be cursed forever by unbearable memories that, in retrospect, clearly should have been blunted medically? Or will he succeed, over time, in "redeeming" those painful memories by actively integrating them into the narrative of his life? By "rewriting" memories pharmacologically we might succeed in easing real suffering at the risk of falsifying our perception of the world and undermining our true identity.

Finally, the decision whether or not to use memory-blunting drugs must be made in the absence of clearly diagnosable disease. The drug must be taken right after a traumatic experience has occurred, and thus before the different ways that different individuals handle the same experience has become clear. In some cases, these interventions will turn out to have been preventive medicine, intervening to ward off the onset of PTSD before it arrives—though it is worth noting that we would lack even post hoc knowledge of whether any particular now-unaffected individual, in the absence of using the drug, would have become symptomatic.[4] In other cases, the interventions would not be medicine at all: altering the memory of individuals who could have lived well, even with severely painful memories, without pharmacologically dulling the pain. Worse, in still other cases, the use of such drugs would inoculate individuals in advance against the psychic pain that *should* accompany their commission of cruel, brutal, or shameful deeds. But in all cases, from the defensible to the dubious, the use of such powers changes the character of human memory, by intervening directly in the way individuals "encode," and thus the way they understand, the happenings of their own lives and the realities of the world around them.

Remembering Fitly and Truly

Altering the formation of emotionally powerful memories risks severing what we remember from how we remember it and distorting the link between our perception of significant human events and the significance of the events themselves. It risks, in a word, falsifying our perception and understanding of the world. It risks making shameful acts seem less shameful, or terrible acts less terrible, than they really are.

Imagine the experience of a person who witnesses a shocking murder. Fearing that he will be haunted by images of this event, he immediately takes propranolol (or its more potent successor) to render his memory of the murder less painful and intrusive. Thanks to the drug, his memory of the murder gets encoded as a garden-variety, emotionally neutral experience. But in manipulating his memory in this way, he risks coming to think about the murder as more tolerable than it really is, as an event that should not sting those who witness it. For our opinions about the meaning of our experiences are shaped partly by the feelings evoked when we remember them. If, psychologically, the murder is transformed into an event our witness can recall without pain—or without *any* particular emotion—perhaps its moral significance will also fade from consciousness. If so, he would in a sense have ceased to be a genuine witness of the murder. When asked about it, he might say, "Yes, I was there. But it wasn't so terrible."

This points us to a deeper set of questions about bad memories: Would dulling our memory of terrible things make us too comfortable with the world, unmoved by suffering, wrongdoing, or cruelty? Does not the experience of hard truths—of the unchosen, the inexplicable, the tragic—remind us that we can never be fully at home in the world, especially if we are to take seriously the reality of human evil? Further, by blunting our experience and awareness of shameful, fearful, and hateful things, might we not also risk deadening our response to what is admirable, inspiring, and lovable? Can we become numb to life's sharpest sorrows without also becoming numb to its greatest joys?

There seems to be little doubt that some bitter memories are so painful and intrusive as to ruin the possibility for normal experience of much of life and the world. In such cases the impulse to relieve a crushing burden and restore lost innocence is fully understandable: If there are some things that it is better never to have experienced at all—things we would avoid if we possibly could—why not erase them from the memory of those unfortunate enough to have suffered them? If there are some things it is better never to have known or seen, why not use our power over memory to restore a witness's shattered peace of mind? There is great force in this argument, perhaps especially in cases where children lose prematurely that innocence that is rightfully theirs.

And yet, there may be a great cost to acting compassionately for those who suffer bad memories, if we do so by compromising the truthfulness of how they remember. We risk having them live falsely in order simply to cope, to survive by whatever means possible.

The Obligation to Remember

Having truthful memories is not simply a personal matter. Strange to say, our own memory is not merely our own; it is part of the fabric of the society in which we live. Consider the case of a person who has suffered or witnessed atrocities that occasion unbearable memories: for example, those with firsthand experience of the Holocaust. The life of that individual might well be served by dulling such bitter memories,[5] but such a humanitarian intervention, if widely practiced, would seem deeply troubling: Would the community as a whole—would the human race—be served by such a mass numbing of this terrible but indispensable memory? Do those who suffer evil have a duty to remember and bear witness, lest we all forget the very horrors that haunt them?

Surely, we cannot and should not force those who live through great trauma to endure its painful memory *for the benefit of the rest of us*. But as a community, there are certain events that we have an obligation to remember—an obligation that falls disproportionately, one might even say unfairly, on those who experience such events most directly.[6] What kind of people would we be if we did not "want" to remember the Holocaust, if we sought to make the anguish it caused simply go away? And yet, what kind of people are we, especially those who face such horrors firsthand, that we can endure such awful memories?

The answer, in part, is that those who suffer terrible things cannot or should not have to endure their own bad memories alone. If, as a people, we have an obligation to remember certain terrible events truthfully, surely we ought to help those who suffered through those events to come to terms with their worst memories. Of course, one might see the new biotechnical powers, developed precisely to ease the psychic pain of bad memories, as the mark of such solidarity: perhaps it is our new way of meeting the obligation to aid those who remember the hardest things, those who bear witness to us and for us. But such solidarity may, in the end, prove false: for it exempts us from the duty to suffer-with (literally, to feel *com*-passion for) those who remember; it does not demand that we preserve the truth of their memories; it attempts instead to make the problem go away, and with it the truth of the experience in question.

The Soul of Memory, the Remembering Soul

[W]e might often be tempted to sacrifice the accuracy of our memories for the sake of easing our pain or expanding our control over our own psychic lives. But doing so means, ultimately, severing ourselves from reality and leaving our own identity behind; it risks making us false, small, or capable of great illusions, and thus capable of great decadence or great evil, or perhaps simply willing to accept a phony contentment. We might be tempted to alter our memories to preserve an open future—to live the life we wanted to live before a particular experience happened to us. But in another sense, such interventions assume that our own future is not open—that we cannot and could never redeem the unwanted memory over time, that we cannot and could never integrate the remembered experience with our own truthful pursuit of happiness.

To have only happy memories would be a blessing—and a curse. Nothing would trouble us, but we would probably be shallow people, never falling to the depths of despair because we have little interest in the heights of human happiness or in the complicated lives of those around us. In the end, to have only happy memories is not to be happy in a truly human way. It is simply to be free of misery—an understandable desire given the many troubles of life, but a low aspiration for those who seek a truly human happiness.

Notes

1. These symptoms are observed especially among combat veterans; indeed, PTSD is the modern name for what used to be called "shell shock" or "combat neurosis." Among veterans, PTSD is frequently associated with recurrent nightmares, substance abuse, and delusional outbursts of violence. There is controversy about the prevalence of PTSD, with some studies finding that up to 8 percent of adult Americans have suffered the

disorder as well as a third of all veterans of the Vietnam War. See Kessler, R. C., et al., "Post-Traumatic Stress Disorder in the National Comorbidity Survey," *Archives of General Psychiatry* 52(12): 1048–1060, 1995; Kulka, R. A., et al., *Trauma and the Vietnam War Generation: Report of Findings from the National Vietnam Veterans Readjustment Study*, New York: Brunner/Mazel, 1990.

2. There is already ongoing controversy about excessive diagnosis of PTSD. Many psychotherapists believe that a patient's psychic troubles are generally based on some earlier (now repressed) traumatic experience which must be unearthed and dealt with if relief is to be found. True PTSD is, however, generally transient, and the search for treatment is directed against the symptoms of its initial (worst) phase—the sleeplessness, the nightmares, the excessive jitteriness.

3. Of course, many Holocaust survivors managed, without pharmacological assistance, to live fulfilling lives while never forgetting what they lived through. At the same time, many survivors would almost certainly have benefited from pharmacological treatment.

4. There is no definitive diagnostic criterion for PTSD, but the core symptoms are thought to include persistent re-experiencing of the traumatic event, avoidance of associated stimuli, and hyperarousal. See *Diagnostic and Statistical Manual of Mental Disorders, Fourth Edition, text revision*, Washington, D.C.: American Psychiatric Association, 2000, pp. 463–486.

5. Schacter, D., *The Seven Sins of Memory: How the Mind Forgets and Remembers*, New York: Houghton Mifflin, 2001, p. 183.

6. For a discussion of memory-altering drugs and the meaning of "bearing witness," see the essay by Cohen, E., "Our Psychotropic Memory," *SEED*, no. 8, Fall 2003, p. 42.

CHALLENGE QUESTIONS

Should Memory-Dampening Drugs Be Used to Alleviate the Symptoms of Trauma?

1. Assuming that memory-dampening drugs become available to the public, who should be given responsibility for determining the appropriateness of such a drug for an individual? For example, should it fall on the shoulders of a physician to make such a determination?
2. What specific criteria should be used in determining the appropriateness of such a drug prescription? Should prescriptions be limited to survivors of life-threatening traumas? What about victims of sexual assault? What about those who have been psychologically terrorized? What about people who are distressed as a result of profound humiliation?
3. What would be the youngest age at which memory-dampening drugs could be considered, and why?
4. What kind of research study could be designed to assess the costs and benefits of taking memory-dampening drugs?
5. In recent years, researchers have been investigating a phenomenon called "posttraumatic growth" in which trauma survivors speak about ways in which life became better for them as a result of having lived through a trauma. In what ways can the experience of a trauma be viewed as a beneficial event in a person's life? Give some examples.

Suggested Readings

Dupree, C. (2004). Cushioning hard memories. *Harvard Magazine, 106*(6). http://www.harvardmagazine.com/on-line/070467.html/

Fletcher, T. (2005). A case of reemergent post-traumatic stress disorder arrested by propranolol intervention: Does a stitch in time save nine? In Corales, T. A. (ed.), *Focus on posttraumatic stress disorder research* (37–49). Hauppauge, NY: Nova Science Publishers.

Kindt, M., Soeter, M., & Vervliet, B. (2009). Beyond extinction: Erasing human fear responses and preventing the return of fear. *Nature Neuroscience, 12*(3), 256–258.

Marvasti, J. A., & Pascal, B. (2004). Pharmacotherapy for victims of trauma. In Marvasti, J. A. (ed.), *Psychiatric treatment of victims and survivors of sexual trauma: A neuro-bio-psychological approach* (113–131). Springfield, IL: Charles C. Thomas Publisher.

Roberts, J. (2006). The trauma tamer: Easing the emotional strain of crippling memories. *Headway, 2*(1). http://www.mcgill.ca/headway/fall2006/ newwave/

Rosenwald, M. (May, 2006). The spotless mind: A routine heart drug shows promise as a way to blunt bad memories. Popsci.com. http://www. popsci.com/popsci/medicine/7001525ad18aa010vgnvcm1000004eecbccdrcrd.html/

ISSUE 11

Is Ritalin Overprescribed?

YES: Peter R. Breggin, from *The Ritalin Fact Book: What Your Doctor Won't Tell You about ADHD and Stimulant Drugs* (Perseus, 2002)

NO: Russell A. Barkley, from *Taking Charge of ADHD: The Complete, Authoritative Guide for Parents* (Guilford, 2000)

ISSUE SUMMARY

YES: Physician Peter R. Breggin asserts that Ritalin and similar stimulants are dangerous addictive medications that should not be prescribed to children because they suppress growth and lead to a number of worrisome physical and psychological symptoms.

NO: Psychologist and prominent ADHD researcher Russell A. Barkley objects to criticisms of Ritalin and similar stimulants, maintaining that these medications serve as important parts of interventions aimed at helping children increase their attention and concentration.

Fifteen years ago it would have been unfathomable to imagine a school-aged child entering a school and gunning down classmates, yet such images have become indelibly marked in the minds of Americans. Such alarming events have caused educators, parents, and mental health professionals to increasingly focus their attention on the behavior of young people, look for ways to help underachievers reach their potential, and make sure troubled youth get the help they need. Children with attention deficit hyperactivity disorder (ADHD) have been of particular concern because of the psychological problems they experience and also because of the disruption they cause at school, at home, and in the community.

ADHD is a disorder involving inattentiveness and hyperactivity-impulsivity, and it is a condition that is usually evident early in life. Even during the toddler years, children with this condition show a range of problematic behaviors, including defiance, resistance, and hostility. Many of them are incessant in their hyperactivity, incapable of paying attention even briefly. Their lives usually involve impaired relationships and serious inner distress. The most common interventions for ADHD involve behavioral techniques and medication, particularly stimulants such as Ritalin (methylphenidate). Proponents of medication express relief about the fact that such an effective intervention is available to help young people who need it; opponents are distressed by the increasing tendency to rely on a chemical for controlling active children rather than on methods that have been used for generations.

Peter R. Breggin, who is widely known and respected for his critical analysis of trends in psychiatry, is appalled by the extensive use of Ritalin-like medications. Breggin raises serious concerns about the physical dangers and psychological risks associated with these medications, and argues that the literature supporting their effectiveness is limited and biased.

Russell A. Barkley, who has established an international reputation as a researcher and expert on ADHD, views behavior disorders such as ADHD as serious conditions of brain dysfunction that warrant medical intervention; he asserts that stimulant medication helps ADHD children improve their attention and concentration, and therefore succeed academically.

POINT

- Like amphetamines, stimulants have a high potential for abuse and can cause potentially serious withdrawal symptoms.

- The growth of many children is suppressed or even stunted by stimulants.

- Drug-company propaganda has led the public to believe that psychiatric drugs correct biochemical imbalances; in fact, these drugs disrupt normal brain function.

- There is no evidence that stimulant drugs actually improve academic performance. Drug-induced impairments cannot make children wiser; they can only make children sit down, shut up, and do what they are told.

- There are hundreds of cases documenting Ritalin-induced psychiatric reactions, including agitation, hostility, depression, psychosis, and other troubling conditions.

COUNTERPOINT

- There are no reported cases of addiction or serious drug dependence on these medications, nor does research support the notion that children taking these drugs are at greater risk of abusing other substances during their teenage years.

- It is a myth to suggest that stimulant medications stunt children's growth; recent studies have shown that this is not as much of a problem as once thought.

- ADHD is largely a genetic disorder associated with deficiencies in brain functioning; stimulant medication helps normalize functioning in most cases.

- Stimulant medication's ability to improve children's attention span, resistance to distraction, and concentration is beneficial to their academic performance.

- Although stimulant medications can produce temporary symptoms of psychosis at very high doses, such reactions are very rare at low doses; such reactions occur in fewer than 1% of cases and last only until the dose wears off.

YES

Peter R. Breggin

The Ritalin Fact Book: What Your Doctor Won't Tell You about ADHD and Stimulant Drugs

Of Cages and Creativity—How Stimulants Work

If you are considering the use of stimulant drugs for yourself or your children, you probably want answers to the following questions:

> Do stimulants really help children?
> How do they work?
> Are they dangerous?

In response to these questions, too many doctors tell parents and patients that stimulants work well and have few if any serious risks. They may also explain that the drugs work by "correcting biochemical imbalances" or "improving focus and attention." . . .

Observing Children in the Classroom

The effectiveness of stimulant drugs is often "proven" by asking teachers to rate the behavior of children in a classroom setting. The teachers will be given checklists to fill out for the children containing items that are used in the official diagnostic manual to determine if a child has ADHD. This *Diagnostic and Statistical Manual of Mental Disorders, IV* is published by the American Psychiatric Association (1994). It contains items such as "often fidgets with hands or feet or squirms in seat," "often leaves seat in classroom," "often blurts out answers," "has difficulty awaiting turn," and "often does not seem to listen."

Teachers and parents almost always report a reduction of these kinds of behaviors in children given stimulants. The teachers and parents have not been told that this involves a suppression of spontaneous behavior with enforced submissiveness and so they fail to recognize that the drugs are suppressing or dulling the children.

Teachers are especially likely to find that the children are "improved" because they are asked to rate behaviors such as "blurts out answers" or "leaves seat" that are especially reduced when overall spontaneity is crushed. The reduction in spontaneous behavior, as well as the enforced submissiveness, makes the children less talkative, less likely to leave their seats, and less likely to socialize with their neighbors. These reductions in overall spontaneous behavior make it easier for teachers to run their classrooms without having to pay attention to the individual child.

Exactly as in the animal studies, stimulants also make children more compulsive. For the chimpanzees, this means sitting by themselves while they groom one small spot on the arm or play endlessly with a pebble. For our children, this drug-enforced compulsivity makes them focus on previously unendurable boring tasks such as copying from the board or writing something down ten times. These children often become so compulsive that they bear down too hard on the paper as they write or persist at the task even when asked to stop. Studies describe them as abnormally overfocused. However, teachers and parents are likely to mistake such behavior for a genuine "buckling down" on schoolwork and homework.

Table 1 is entitled "Harmful Stimulant Drug Reactions Commonly Misidentified as 'Therapeutic' or 'Beneficial.'" When children are given Ritalin, Adderall, and other stimulant drugs, they frequently develop these kinds of reactions. Unfortunately, researchers, doctors, teachers, and parents routinely misinterpret these toxic effects as improvements in the children.

Do the children learn better? Are their scholastic abilities improved? Of course not. Drug-induced impairments cannot make a child wiser, more thoughtful, or better informed. They can only make children sit down, shut up, and do what they are told. As we shall see, there is no evidence that stimulant drugs actually improve academic performance. But they do sometimes

---

Table 1

Harmful Stimulant Drug Reactions Commonly Misidentified as "Therapeutic" or "Beneficial," Selected from 20 Controlled Clinical Trials Involving Children Diagnosed with ADHD

Obsessive-Compulsive Effects	Social Withdrawal Effects	Behaviorally Suppressive Effects
Compulsive persistence at meaningless activities (called stereotypical or perseverative behavior)	Social withdrawal and isolation	Compliant in structured environment; socially inhibited, passive, and submissive
Increased obsessive-compulsive behavior (e.g., repeating chores endlessly and ineffectively)	General dampened social behavior	Somber, subdued, apathetic, lethargic, dopey, dazed, and tired
Mental rigidity (called cognitive perseveration)	Reduced communication and socialization	Bland, emotionally flat, humorless, not smiling, depressed, and sad with frequent crying
Inflexible thinking	Decreased responsiveness to parents and other children	Lacking in initiative, spontaneity, curiosity, surprise, or pleasure
Overly narrow or excessive focusing	Increased solitary play and diminished overall play	

Modified from Breggin (1999b, 1999c). References to the 20 clinical trials provided in Breggin (1999b, 1999c).

lead to improved grades because many teachers will reward more submissive, unobtrusive behavior with better grades.

Some of the staunchest advocates of stimulants for children have in effect admitted that the drugs work by enforcing blind obedience. Russell Barkley, one of the most widely published Ritalin/ADHD advocates, uses the term "compliance" to describe this improved behavior. Stimulant drugs do indeed tend to make children more compliant, that is, more manageable and obedient. They do so at the expense of their imaginations, their creativity, their capacity to generate activity, and their overall enthusiasm for life.

"Correcting Biochemical Imbalances"

Recently I gave a lecture to students and professionals at a medical center. Initially, some of them were surprised when I explained that all psychoactive drugs disrupt normal brain function. They, too, had been misled by drug-company propaganda to believe that psychiatric drugs correct biochemical imbalances. However, several were immediately able to see the truth once I reminded them about the facts.

Research on psychoactive drugs almost always begins with animal studies. As a first step, a series of animal brains will be examined to measure the normal activity of a specific function, such as the rate of firing of a particular type of brain cell (neuron). Tiny electrodes may be inserted into the brains to measure the activity of the cells. Or the animal brain may be removed in order to determine the normal amount of a specific chemical in the region.

Next, a new series of animals will be given the stimulant drug, such as Ritalin or Adderall. Then their brains will be examined to determine how the drug changes these normal functions. For example, the brain cells may begin to fire more rapidly than normal for a while and then, later on, more slowly than normal. Or the specific chemical messenger may increase above normal in amount for a while and then decrease below normal later on.

The pharmacological action of any psychoactive drug is demonstrated by how it disrupts the normal function of an animal's brain. That disruption is the basis of the psychoactive effect. The researchers, the drug company, the FDA, and everyone else involved in the field will then assume that the drug disrupts human brain function in exactly the same fashion. When textbooks or reviews discuss the drug's "mode of action," they will simply describe what has been learned from research on how the drug interferes with the functioning of the normal animal brain.

However, when the drug company and its experts get ready to present this information to the medical profession and the public, they will perform remarkable verbal sleights of hand. The known fact that the drug disrupts normal brain function will be ignored and instead the drug will be falsely promoted as correcting biochemical imbalances. The claim about correcting biochemical imbalances is a deliberate deception to make the drugs look positive. Similarly, the known fact that the drug suppresses behavior will be ignored, and in the case of the stimulants, nothing at all will be said about it. How the drug actually works will remain shrouded in mystery. . . .

How Stimulants Cause Psychiatric Disorders

Stimulants are powerful psychoactive substances that impact the brain and mind. We have already seen that their primary or therapeutic impact involves flattening all spontaneous behavior, enforcing submissiveness, and causing obsessive focus on rote activities. Therefore, it should be no surprise that they can cause a variety of other mental abnormalities.

In reviewing adverse drug reaction reports made to the FDA concerning Ritalin, I found hundreds of cases of Ritalin-induced psychiatric reactions. Children taking Ritalin were most commonly reported to develop—in the following order—agitation, hostility, depression and psychotic depression, abnormal thinking, hallucinations, psychosis, and emotional instability (called "lability"). There were many reports of overdose, intentional overdose, and suicide attempts, confirming the risk of depression and potential suicide. . . .

I have taken several approaches to summarizing the overall adverse effects of stimulants. Table 1 . . . uses data from twenty clinical trials to describe adverse psychiatric effects such as apathy, depression, and overfocusing that are commonly mistaken for improvements in children's behavior.

Table 2, "Toxic Reactions to Stimulants: Usually in Overdose and Occasionally at Low Doses," is drawn entirely from the "Overdose" sections of

Table 2

Toxic Reactions to Stimulants: Usually in Overdose and Occasionally at Low Doses

Agitation	Elevated heart rate
Tremors	Palpitations
Increased neurologic reflexes	Cardiac arrhythmias
Muscle twitching	Hypertension
Convulsions	Enlarged pupils
Coma	Dry mouth, nose, and eyes
Euphoria	Increased respiration[a]
Confusion	Nausea, vomiting, diarrhea,
Hallucinations	and cramps[a]
Delirium	Muscle breakdown[a]
Sweating	Hypotension, shock, and
Flushing	circulatory collapse[a]
Headache	Panic states[a]
High fever	Assaultiveness[a]

---

[a]Indicates the item was taken from the FDA-approved overdose section of the labels for Dexedrine, Adderall, and Adderall XR, but not Ritalin. The remainder was taken from the Ritalin label with some overlap. The Dexedrine and Adderall labels both state that "individual patient response to amphetamines varies widely" and "toxic symptoms occasionally occur as an idiosyncrasy at doses as low as 2 mg." The Adderall XR label also states that patient responses "vary widely" and "toxic symptoms" may occur "at low doses." *Most of the symptoms can occur with any of the stimulants at routine clinical doses.*

the official FDA-approved labels for Ritalin, Dexedrine, Adderall, and Adderall XR. Almost any adverse reaction that occurs in overdose can also occur at lower doses.

For an overview of stimulant effects taken from a broader variety of medical sources other than the drug labels, see Table 3, "Overview of Harmful Reactions to Stimulant Drugs: Ritalin, Dexedrine, Adderall, Concerta, and Metadate."

Tables 1, 2, and 3 cover most of the adverse effects of stimulants that are likely to show up in routine clinical use. They are compiled from standard or mainstream sources that tend to approve or advocate the use of stimulant drugs. There is a great tendency in the medical literature to minimize adverse drug effects in order to support or promote the use of medications in general. Therefore, the individual sources are not as comprehensive as the data that I have compiled in this book from all of the sources. *In addition, few if any sources*

Table 3

Overview of Harmful Reactions to Stimulant Drugs: Ritalin, Dexedrine, Adderall, Concerta, and Metadate

Brain and Mind Function	Gastrointestinal Function	Endocrine and Metabolic Function
Obsessive-compulsive behavior	Anorexia	Pituitary dysfunction, including growth hormone and prolactin disruption
Zombie-like (robotic) behavior with loss of emotional spontaneity	Nausea, vomiting, bad taste	
	Stomachache	Weight loss
Drowsiness, "dopey," reduced alertness	Cramps	Growth suppression
	Dry mouth	Disturbed sexual function
Abnormal movements, tics, Tourette's	Constipation, diarrhea	**Cardiovascular Function**
	Liver dysfunction	
Nervous habits (picking at skin, pulling hair)	**Withdrawal and Rebound Reactions**	Hypertension
Convulsions		Abnormal heartbeat
Headache	Insomnia	Heart disease
Stroke	Excessive sleep	Cardiac arrest
Mania, psychosis	Evening crash	**Other Functions**
Visual and tactile hallucinations	Depression	Blurred vision
Agitation, anxiety, nervousness	Rebound worsening of ADHD-like symptoms	Hair loss
Insomnia	Overactivity and irritability	Dizziness
Irritability, hostility, aggression		Hypersensitivity reaction with rash
Depression, suicide, easy crying, social withdrawal		
Confusion, mental impairments (decreased cognition and learning)		
Stimulant addiction and abuse		

Modified from Breggin (1999a, 1999c).

fully address the brain damage and dysfunction produced by these drugs, including strong evidence for stimulant-induced brain shrinkage, cell death, and persistent biochemical changes. . . .

Stimulants Commonly Cause Mental Disorders

Stimulants commonly cause a variety of serious emotional disturbances. I am not alone in drawing this conclusion. A handbook frequently used by physicians lists the . . . rates of adverse mental effects caused by stimulants [in Table 4].

The rates in [Table 4] are drawn from clinical studies. Not many parents would expose their children to these drugs if they were aware of the frequency with which the drugs can impair a child's mental life.

The studies are usually conducted by advocates for drugs and tend to minimize adverse drug reactions. Therefore, most of the rates are actually higher than reported in [Table 4]. While the rates for these adverse effects vary widely from study to study, the main point is inescapable: Stimulants frequently harm the brain and mind.

As a part of my scientific presentation at the NIH Consensus Development Conference on the Diagnosis and Treatment of Attention Deficit Hyperactivity Disorder in 1998, I reviewed eight representative controlled clinical trials to estimate the frequency of adverse effects. All of the studies were conducted by advocates of stimulants and aimed at proving that the drugs are safe and effective. I have reviewed them in the scientific literature and in *Talking Back to Ritalin* (rev. ed., 2001a). Based on these studies, I estimate that the reported rate of serious adverse reactions in children was as high as 10–20 percent or more. The real rate in clinical practice would be even higher.

In reviewing Table 4, it is important to realize that symptoms such as "irritability," "agitation," and "confused" are related to each other. They reflect gross underlying brain dysfunctions that then become manifested in varying ways. When brain function is disrupted in such a global or generalized way, almost any mental abnormality or mixture of abnormalities can result. . . .

Table 4

Rates of Adverse Mental Effects Reported in Stimulant Clinical Trials

Adverse Stimulant Effect	Amphetamines (Dexedrine, Adderall)	Methylphenidate (Ritalin, Concerta, Metadate ER)
Drowsiness, less alert	5.5%	5.7%
Confused, "dopey"	10.3% (8–12%)	3.9% (2–10%)
Depression	39%	8.7%
Agitation, restlessness	More than 10%	6.7% (3.3% to more than 10%)
Irritability, stimulation	25% (17–29%)	17.3% (11–19%)

The data are from Maxmen and Ward (1995, p. 366). The numbers are percentages of patients reported in studies to suffer from the adverse effects. Numbers in parentheses represent the range reported in studies.

My clinical experience confirms the data in Table 4: Children taking stimulants frequently become very depressed and even suicidal. Their doctors often fail to recognize the source of the depression. Instead of stopping the stimulant medication, they add an antidepressant, causing even greater emotional disturbances in the child.

How common is stimulant-induced depression? Very common! . . .

How Stimulants Harm the Child's Body

. . . From the heart to the skin, stimulants can also harm a variety of other organs of the body. By interfering with normal growth-hormone production, stimulants impair and even stunt the growth of the entire body.

Some harmful effects on the body result indirectly from the disruption of brain function, some result more directly from toxic effects on the organs themselves, and some result from both. . . .

Stunting Growth

In many cases, the growth of children is obviously suppressed or even stunted by stimulants. Some of the children look skinny and unhealthy as if starving, while others seem normal. Most will rebound with an unbelievably rapid growth in height and weight—if the drugs are stopped while the child is still growing. In one study, Ritalin reduced the expected monthly weight gain by 25 percent. When the drug was stopped, weight gain accelerated far above the normally expected rate.

When children seem to be growing well while taking stimulants, some doctors or parents will observe, "John's very big; the stimulants haven't hurt him." Unfortunately, we don't know how tall or large Johnny might have become without the drug, and the fact that he's achieved an even above-average size says little about the drug's actual effect on his unique genetic endowment for growth.

Too many doctors are misled into believing that growth suppression is a relatively harmless problem that results from a child losing his or her appetite. However, there's more to it than the mere loss of appetite. The stimulants cause marked dysfunction in the production of growth hormone. Specifically, they cause an abnormal increase in growth hormone during the day and then an abnormal compensatory suppression of the hormone at night, when it most significantly affects growth.

The impact on growth hormone is so dramatic that researchers have observed that growth-hormone levels can be used as a marker for whether or not children are taking their medication. If the growth-hormone cycle isn't disrupted, then the children are not taking the medication. Because stimulants always impair growth-hormone production, we should assume that there is always some impairment of growth, even if it remains grossly undetectable.

Some doctors used to tell parents not to worry about growth suppression because there is a compensatory growth spurt when the drugs are stopped. While the body does try to catch up when the stimulant is stopped, the phase of accelerated growth is abnormally rapid and not necessarily altogether healthy. In addition, there's no guarantee that irreversible harm hasn't been done along the way during weeks or months of stimulant treatment. Furthermore, nowadays children are kept on stimulants for months or years at a time, so the body is given no opportunity to go through a growth spurt.

The disruption of growth hormone should be viewed as an ominous finding. It means that all growth processes are being impaired, including the growth of the brain, heart, and lungs. The entire body relies on growth hormone to regulate its developmental processes. Citing many research reports, a respected research team wrote:

> Research reveals that methylphenidate stimulates daytime release of growth hormone, disrupting the usual nocturnal release. This is troublesome since disturbances in the normal release of growth hormone may not only influence height velocity but may also impair other critical aspects of physical development such as sexual maturation.

The researchers should also have emphasized the threat to the growth of the brain and hence the mind.

The authors of a medical textbook suggest that the growth lag caused by stimulants is temporary "in most cases." This assumes that the children are given regular drug vacations in order to catch up. Although these authors are staunch advocates of stimulants for children, they go on to recognize that "the effects on growth that the long-term use of stimulants has on children leads some physicians to believe that this drug should never be prescribed for children." This observation—like many others in this book—should give strength to parents who believe, as I do, that children should never be given these drugs for "ADHD" or the control of behavior.

Despite decades of sophisticated research demonstrating that stimulants disrupt growth hormone, cause growth suppression, and lead to accelerated growth spurts when stopped, some drug advocates have tried to demonstrate that there are no significant effects on growth. In my experience, the doctors who make these claims typically go to extremes in order to convince professionals and parents that it's safe to use these drugs. One such study was published in 1996 in an attempt to undermine a large, consistent body of research demonstrating growth suppression. However, the new study used only one measurement of height and weight for each child and attempted to draw conclusions from it. The researchers did not use consecutive measures on the same child to show the effect of the drug; they took one measure on every child and attempted to compare that one measurement to a similar measure in a control group of children who were not drug treated. Using these dubious methods as well as a badly flawed control group and questionable statistics, the authors leaped from one single measurement to a conclusion about the long-term effect of stimulants on growth. By contrast, many other studies have used multiple measurements to show a definite inhibition of growth.

As a result of disrupting pituitary function, stimulants also interfere with the normal cycles of prolactin production. Prolactin can be found throughout the body, but its functions are poorly understood. It does, however, participate in the regulation of sexual development, yet another fact that should raise caution in regard to giving stimulants to children and adolescents.

Causing Heart Problems

As already noted, stimulants produce a combined assault on the heart, first by overstimulating heart rate and blood pressure, and then by weakening the muscles of the overstressed organ. Palpitations are one signal that the heart is beating irregularly.

What's the result?

My review of spontaneous reports of adverse Ritalin effects made to the FDA disclosed a very large number of Ritalin-induced cases of cardiovascular disease. Many concerned the well-known problem of stimulant-caused hypertension. Most of them involved arrhythmias and conduction problems that sometimes cause sudden cardiac arrest. There were more than a dozen reports of cardiac arrest or heart failure. This was a relatively small portion of the 2,821 reports made during the period of time (1985 through early 1997) but presents an important signal of danger.

I have been consulted in several cases in which stimulant drugs have caused fatal cardiac arrhythmias in children. In one case, the child's heart on autopsy showed a pattern of deterioration that the coroner compared to changes he had observed in chronic cocaine addicts.

A number of animal studies confirm that stimulants such as Ritalin weaken heart muscle and reduce its function. Stimulants also cause high blood pressure, a special concern among African-American boys, who are especially prone to develop severe hypertension as relatively young adults. Weakened heart muscle combined with hypertension is, of course, a hazard for any human being.

Causing Strokes

Ritalin, Adderall, and all stimulants can cause strokes (cerebral vascular accidents). These potentially catastrophic events can result from bleeding or inflammation of the blood vessels in the brain. Hypertension probably plays a key role in many of these disasters. Physicians sometimes seem particularly unaware of stimulant-induced strokes, probably leading to underreporting of the problem.

Bleeding in the brain in association with oral amphetamine use has been reported in the literature since 1970. There are reports of strokes after a "single low dose exposure," but most reports have been made in association with stimulant abuse.

A report in *Lancet* in 1988 described the first published case of stroke involving Ritalin in a boy receiving the drug for hyperactivity. The author observed, "Physicians who prescribe methylphenidate [Ritalin] for long-term use should be aware of this potential complication and specifically question patients regarding symptoms of cerebral ischaemia [reduced blood flow], including headache." Remember that Ritalin and amphetamine both produce gross reductions in blood flow to the brain, thereby creating the conditions for stroke.

A report in 2000 in the *Journal of Child Neurology* describes the case of an eight-year-old boy who developed vasculitis and stroke after taking Ritalin for one and one-half years for hyperactivity. These authors also issue a warning: "We draw your attention to the risk of using methylphenidate [Ritalin] for a long period of time."

Overall, stimulants pose serious cardiovascular hazards. Individuals suffering from or at risk of experiencing hypertension, heart disease, or strokes should especially avoid stimulants. . . .

How Stimulants Cause Withdrawal, Addiction, and Abuse

The following remarkable warning appears in capital letters in a boxed section as the first item to be read in the Adderall and the Dexedrine labels:

> AMPHETAMINES HAVE A HIGH POTENTIAL FOR ABUSE. ADMINISTRA-TION OF AMPHETAMINES FOR PROLONGED PERIODS OF TIME MAY LEAD TO DRUG DEPENDENCE AND MUST BE AVOIDED.

Although it does not appear with the same strength in the Ritalin label, this statement is equally true for Ritalin and all of the other stimulants commonly used to treat children. It should also be taken as a warning that all of these drugs cause potentially severe withdrawal reactions.

Much of the medical profession acts as if it has never been admonished that stimulant administration for prolonged periods of time "must be avoided." Instead, long-term use of stimulants is often encouraged, and parents are told to keep their children on amphetamines for months and years.

If the medical profession were prescribing rationally, the forewarning to avoid long-term administration and the lack of evidence for any long-term efficacy would utterly prevent the prescription of stimulants to children or adults for more than a few weeks' duration.

Withdrawal Reactions and Worsening Behavior

Symptoms of withdrawal can take place a few hours after the last dose of a stimulant, so that children commonly begin to go into withdrawal by the evening or the next morning. If a child's behavior appears to get worse or to deteriorate in any way a few hours or more after taking a stimulant drug, there's a high probability that the child is undergoing a withdrawal reaction.

Teachers often observe, "I can tell when Johnny hasn't taken his medication," meaning that they can see his behavior become more distressed or distressing. They don't realize that this is typically caused by a withdrawal reaction rather than by Johnny's own problems.

Parents and teachers sometimes believe that a child needs stimulants because the child's behavior deteriorates when one or two doses are missed. Such abrupt changes in a child are more likely due to withdrawal symptoms than to a child's inherent need for the drug. If we thought of alcohol or narcotics in the same way, we would think that alcoholics and narcotics addicts "needed" their drugs in order to be normal. In fact, they need to get free of their drugs in order to have a hope of becoming normal or healthy human beings.

The Ritalin label confirms, however inadequately, the danger of serious withdrawal problems. In a boxed section labeled "Drug Dependence," it states, "Careful supervision is required during drug withdrawal, since severe depression as well as the effects of chronic overactivity can be unmasked." The sentence is marred by spin doctoring that suggests that the symptoms are somehow being "unmasked" rather than directly caused by the Ritalin withdrawal. The label then states, "Long-term follow-up may be required because of the patient's basic personality disturbances." Again, this is spin doctoring of the fact that long-term exposure to these drugs, followed by withdrawal, can leave the patient with "basic personality disturbances" that the individual never had before taking stimulants. . . .

Russell A. Barkley with George J. DuPaul and Daniel Connor

NO

Taking Charge of ADHD: The Complete, Authoritative Guide for Parents

Medication is probably the most widely publicized, most hotly debated treatment for ADHD. As a whole, the hundreds of studies conducted indicate that stimulants, certain antidepressants, and clonidine (a drug used to treat high blood pressure in many adults) can be of great help to those with ADHD. The stimulants, the drugs most commonly used, have been shown to be effective in improving behavior, academic work, and social adjustment in anywhere from 50% to 95% of children with ADHD. How well your child responds may, however, depend on the presence of other problems, and the truth is that medication does not help everyone. For that reason—and because medication is no exception to the rule that misinformation about ADHD abounds—you should gather as much background knowledge as you can before agreeing to a trial of medication for your child. This article gives the most up-to-date information available on the stimulant medications. The brand names of these medications (with generic names in parentheses) include Ritalin (methylphenidate), Dexedrine (*d*-amphetamine), Adderall (*d*- and *l*-amphetamine combination), and Cylert (pemoline). . . .

Stimulant Drugs Are Dangerous and Should Not Be Taken by Any Child

During the 1980s and again in the mid- to late 1990s, an inaccurate and regrettably successful media propaganda campaign against the use of stimulants, particularly Ritalin (methylphenidate), with children was waged by a fringe religious group, causing a dramatic rise in media coverage of this medication. The 1990s campaign was fueled by the release of misleading, alarmist, and biased information about stimulant medication abuse in the United States by the Drug Enforcement Administration as part of an effort to prevent Ritalin from being reclassified as a nonaddictive drug—a change that would have made prescribing this medication more convenient for physicians. As a consequence, the use of these medications for children with ADHD continues to be controversial in the public's mind, although there is absolutely no controversy among the scientific community as to the safety and effectiveness of these medications.

Stimulants Just Cover Up the "Real Problem" and Do Not Deal Directly with the Root Causes of the Child's ADHD

Many parents come to us with the concern that stimulants do not treat the "real problems," but it is simply untrue. Critics of these medications mistakenly assume that a child's ADHD symptoms stem from purely social causes, such as poor discipline or lack of love at home. . . . [T]here is no scientific evidence that purely social causes are at the root of a child's ADHD. We now know that ADHD is largely a genetic disorder associated with deficiencies in the functioning of certain regions in the brain related to inhibition, attention, and self-control. The stimulants deal directly with the part of the brain that is underactive and gives rise to the outward symptoms of ADHD, as explained later in this [article]. In this sense, the stimulants are no different from using insulin for a child with diabetes. Unfortunately, like insulin, stimulants have only a temporary effect, which leads some people to believe they're masking the problem rather than helping it. Like a diabetic who needs insulin, your child may have to take stimulant medicine daily for a long time, but these drugs are a way of tackling the problem directly. *Stimulants are the only treatment to date that normalizes the inattentive, impulsive, and restless behavior in children with ADHD.* However, even though the stimulants do *improve* the behavior of 70–90% of all children with ADHD, the stimulants do not *normalize* the behavioral problems of all of these children who respond positively to medication. For approximately 30–45% of children with ADHD, their behavior will be significantly improved but not normalized by this medication.

Stimulants Make Children "High," as Other Drugs Do, and Are Addictive

You may have heard that adults who take stimulants often have a sense of elevated mood, euphoria, or excessive well-being. While this does happen, it is not common, and in children it is rare. Some children do describe feeling "funny," "different," or dizzy. Others actually become a little bland in their mood, and a few even report feelings of sadness. These mood changes occur a few hours after the medicine is taken and occur more often among children treated with higher doses. In most children, these changes are very minor.

Parents are often also quite concerned about the risk of addiction to stimulants and about an increased risk of abusing other drugs when the children become teenagers. There are no reported cases of addiction or serious drug dependence to date with these medications, and the several studies that have examined whether children on these drugs are more likely than those not taking them to abuse other substances as teenagers suggest that they are not. Indeed, several recent studies conducted by Dr. Timothy E. Wilens and colleagues at Massachusetts General Hospital (Harvard Medical School), and by Drs. Howard Chilcoat and Naomi Breslau at Henry Ford Hospital in Detroit, found that taking stimulants during childhood did not predispose children with ADHD to an increased risk of substance use or abuse as teenagers. In fact, Dr. Wilens's study found that adolescents with ADHD who had remained on their medication during the teen years had a significantly lower likelihood of substance use or abuse than did children with ADHD who were not taking medications during adolescence. Thus the scientific literature to date should reassure parents that they are not predisposing their children to the potential for later substance use or abuse by giving stimulants to their children for the management of ADHD. Parents should know that the most important factors in determining a child's risk for adolescent substance use or abuse are (1) early onset of conduct disorder or antisocial behavior in the child, (2) poor monitoring by parents of the child's or teen's whereabouts in the community, (3) the affiliation of the child or teen with other teens who are using or abusing illegal substances, and (4) the degree to which the parents may also be using alcohol or tobacco products or illegal substances.

Stimulant Medications Stunt Children's Growth, and Their Use Is Strictly Limited by Age

Some studies in the early 1970s seemed to suggest that children taking these medicines might be stunted in their height and weight gain. More recent and better studies have shown that this is not as much of a problem as was once thought. Your child's eventual adult height or skeletal size is not going to be affected by taking the medicine, and the effects on your child's weight are also likely to be minimal, resulting in a loss of one or two pounds during the initial year of treatment. Any weight lost should return by the second or later years of treatment. Keep in mind that children respond very differently to these medicines, some experiencing no weight change and others losing more than just a few pounds. Your child should be followed by your physician to make sure that any weight loss is not serious.

The initial belief in the 1970s that stimulants might stunt the growth of children with ADHD led to the common practice by physicians of recommending that children take these medications only for school days and stop taking them on weekends, on school holidays, and during summer vacations. Because we now know that the risk of growth problems arising from these medications is much less than was originally believed, it is not necessary that all children taking stimulants have such drug holidays. Many can continue to take medication throughout the weekends and summers. They will derive benefits from doing so in their relations with peers; their participation in organized clubs, sports, and summer programs; and their general behavior at home. Parents whose children experience significant behavioral problems during these and other weekend and summer activities, and whose children are not having growth problems from the medication, should discuss with the children's physicians the possible value of continuing the children's stimulant medication during these periods. . . .

Stimulants Do Not Result in Lasting Benefits to a Child's Academic Achievement

The argument that stimulants have no lasting positive effects on academic achievement is a misleading one, concocted as part of broader efforts to dissuade parents from considering the use of stimulants for their children with ADHD. If one takes a simplistic view of the term academic achievement and expects stimulants to directly increase the amount of academic knowledge and skill in a school subject matter that a child acquires, then of course the stimulants will disappoint. The pills do not contain any knowledge that is automatically placed in a child's brain when consumed. A child with ADHD who does not know her multiplication tables today, while not taking any medication, will not automatically know them tomorrow after taking a dose of stimulant medication. To expect this kind of change would be silly and demonstrates the flaws in this criticism of stimulants.

What the stimulants do is help the child with ADHD show what she knows during performance of school assignments by improving the child's attention span, concentration, resistance to distraction, and thoughtful, reflective behavior. They also make the child more available to learn what is being taught in school by reducing the child's off-task, disruptive, and otherwise inattentive behavior. Given these gains, several years of medication may very well leave the child with more academic knowledge than she would have had without medication, but unfortunately no studies have examined this issue beyond 14 to 18 months of medication use. We simply don't know about the long-term benefits to academic knowledge or skills from continued use of medication over several years or more of schooling.

If we view the term *academic achievement* more broadly, as how well the child is behaving at school, getting along with peers, following classroom rules and teacher directions, completing assignments, and completing them accurately, the evidence is overwhelming that the stimulant medications produce significant improvements. Even if the stimulants do not increase a child's academic knowledge, the fact that they result in improvements in many other areas of school functioning is sufficient justification for parents to consider the possible use of these medications with their children. Such changes not only can boost self-confidence and self-esteem in the classroom setting, but can make the child more likable to the peer group and therefore give him more opportunities to make or keep classmates as friends. They can also reduce the amount of censure, punishment, and rejection the child experiences at school from both peers and teachers, and may well preclude the child from needing to be retained in grade due to substandard academic achievement. For all of these reasons, the improvements in school adjustment and success that result from the stimulants are frequently the most common reasons for prescribing these medications for children with ADHD. . . .

The Side Effects

There are many side effects that children can experience when taking these medicines, but the vast majority are minor. Again, keep in mind that if any of these are bothersome enough to warrant stopping the medication, they will likely go away once the medicine "washes out" of a child's body—within 24 hours. Most of these side effects are clearly related to the dose of medicine the child is taking: Higher doses produce more side effects. It has been estimated, however, that from 1% to 3% of children with ADHD cannot tolerate *any* dose of *any* stimulant medication.

It's impossible to predict whether your child will have any of the side effects discussed here, but we do have some revealing test findings: Over half of children with ADHD we tested in our clinic showed decreased appetite, insomnia, anxiousness, irritability, or proneness to crying. *However many of these side effects (especially those associated with mood) were* present *when the children took a fake pill (called a placebo). This means that these side effects may represent problems that are associated with ADHD rather than with the medicine.* In most cases the actual side effects were quite mild. Stomachaches and headaches were reported in about a third of the children, but these were also mild. . . .

All of the stimulants seem to reduce a child's appetite to some degree—temporarily and mainly in the late morning or early afternoon, which explains why over half of all children on these drugs may eat little of their lunch while on the medicine. For many children their appetite comes back (sometimes with a vengeance!) by evening. That is why you should make sure that a child who is on this medicine has a chance to eat adequate types and amounts of food each day to grow well. . . .

Your physician may find that your child's heart rate and blood pressure increase a little while taking these medicines. These changes are minor and do not place most children with ADHD at any risk. However, if your child is one of the rare children who has high blood pressure already, you should make sure your doctor takes this into consideration. Cylert may be less likely to produce these effects on heart rate and blood pressure. . . .

Nearly half of all children placed on medication may notice that it is harder to fall asleep at bedtime after taking these medicines during the day. Most children fall asleep within an hour or so after their typical bedtime. If not, and this is a problem for your child, tell your physician so that the dose can be lowered. . . .

All of the stimulant medications can produce temporary symptoms of psychosis (thought disorganization, rapid speech, skin hallucinations, extreme anxiety, supersensitivity to noises, etc.) at very high doses. In very rare cases this can happen at low doses. Such reactions occur in fewer than 1% of the cases and last only until the dose wears off. . . .

CHALLENGE QUESTIONS

Is Ritalin Overprescribed?

1. Some people argue that parents and teachers play a prominent role in causing and maintaining problematic behaviors in children, because they fail to set limits or follow through with consequences for misbehavior. Taking this viewpoint, enumerate some dysfunctional styles that might contribute to children acting out of control.
2. Breggin contends that stimulants suppress spontaneous behavior with enforced submissiveness, thus dulling children. How would you go about differentiating spontaneous energy from disruptively annoying behaviors?
3. Some social critics have expressed alarm about the extent to which people are managing problems with medications such as Ritalin and Prozac. Discuss the extent to which medication provides a treatment for the basic problem (neurochemical dysfunction) or serves as a temporary method for alleviating symptoms of a more deeply rooted emotional nature.
4. Imagine that you are a psychiatrist being consulted by parents of a five-year-old boy who is reportedly "acting up" in kindergarten. They request a prescription of Ritalin for him. What kind of information would you want to have before making your decision about the prescription, and what kind of preliminary steps would you recommend before going along with the parents' request?
5. Imagine that you are a researcher who has been given research support to study different methods of intervening in a class composed of 20 "hyperactive" boys. What research methods would you use to compare the effectiveness of Ritalin to behavioral methods aimed at reducing the activity level of these boys?

Suggested Readings

Barkley, R. A. (2010). *Attention deficit hyperactivity disorder in adults: The latest assessment and treatment strategies.* Sudbury, MA: Jones and Bartlett Publishers.

Glasser, H. (2005). *101 reasons to avoid Ritalin like the plague.* Tucson, AZ: Nurtured Heart Publications.

Meijer, W. M., Faber, A., van den Ban, E., & Tobin, H. (2009). Current issues around the pharmacotherapy of ADHD in children and adults. *Pharmacy World and Science, 31*(5), 509–516.

Tait, G. (2009). The logic of ADHD: A brief review of fallacious reasoning. *Studies in Philosophy and Education, 28*(3), 239–254.

ISSUE 12

Should Psychologists Prescribe Medication?

YES: Robert Resnick, from "To Prescribe or Not to Prescribe—Is That the Question?" *The Psychologist* (April 2003)

NO: William N. Robiner, et al., from "Prescriptive Authority for Psychologists: A Looming Health Hazard?" *Clinical Psychology: Science and Practice* (Fall 2002)

ISSUE SUMMARY

YES: Psychologist Robert Resnick endorses the recommendation that psychologists be given prescription privileges in order to expand psychopharmacological availability to people needing medication.

NO: Psychologist William N. Robiner and his colleagues object to the notion of granting prescription privileges to psychologists, and express several concerns pertaining to training and competence.

During the past three decades, tremendous advances have been made in understanding biologically based causes and treatments for a wide array of emotional and behavioral disorders. The introduction of selective serotonin reuptake inhibitors in the 1980s began a revolution in the treatment of depression and several other serotonin-related conditions such as obsessive-compulsive disorder. During the past three decades, medications such as Ritalin and similar stimulants have become increasingly prescribed not only for children with attention-deficit/hyperactivity disorder, but also for adults with attentional problems. Psychopharmacological interventions have become so common and accepted in society that commercials and advertisements are found in all the media boasting about the effectiveness of these medications. As mental health professionals have increasingly endorsed the prescription of medications, questions have arisen about the possibility of permitting nonphysician professionals to prescribe these medications for their patients.

Psychologist Robert Resnick asserts that there is ample justification for giving prescription privileges to psychologists. He cites the social benefit for patients in underserved areas of the United States who would be able to turn to professionals other than physicians for psychopharmacological prescriptions.

Resnick contends that well-trained psychologists would be able to provide a comprehensive service in which they offer a range of services including, assessment, consultation, therapy, and medication.

Psychologist William N. Robiner and his colleagues express serious objections to the proposal to give prescription privileges to psychologists. Concern is expressed about the fact that the medically relevant training of psychologists differs markedly from that received by physicians and by other professionals with prescription privileges. Robiner and his colleagues criticize the arguments that have been put forth by those advocating prescription privileges for psychologists, noting that prescribing psychologists are not especially likely to relocate to underserved geographical regions, nor will they necessarily be able to respond to the needs of patients who seem to prefer obtaining their prescriptions from physicians.

POINT

- In many areas of the United States, people have urgent and unmet health needs that can be alleviated by professionals who can provide both psychotherapy and, when needed, medication.

- Prescribing psychologists will offer patients better options and more knowledgeable referrals. Of concern is the fact that 85 percent of prescriptions used to treat mental problems are written by physicians who have little or no training in psychiatry.

- As evidenced by a program initiated in 1991 by the U.S. Department of Defense, psychologists can be successfully trained to prescribe; after several years and thousands of prescriptions written by this small number of military psychologists, there has not been one inappropriate use, missed physical diagnosis or complication, or one untoward outcome.

- Giving psychologists prescribing privileges would make it easier for patients to obtain quality and accessible mental health care in a timely fashion and at the lowest cost; it is much more efficient to see one professional rather than two.

COUNTERPOINT

- There is little reason to believe that psychologists with prescriptive authority would relocate to areas lacking other prescribers, or would focus their practices to address the needs of underserved populations.

- There are several reasons why nonpsychiatric physicians account for the majority of psychotropic prescriptions written, including the fact that (1) some patients are more comfortable seeing their primary care physician than a mental health professional and (2) managed care companies recommend such treatment by primary care physicians over referrals to specialist mental health professionals.

- It is not known how well the successes of these 10 military prescribing psychologists, who were trained in a military medical setting, and whose care was confined to a patient population largely screened for health and other factors, would generalize to independently practicing psychologists working in a diversity of settings.

- As an alternative to giving psychologists prescription privileges, efficiency of service delivery in the mental health system can be enhanced by taking steps to improve collaboration between psychologists and medical personnel who prescribe medications.

YES

Robert Resnick

To Prescribe or Not to Prescribe— Is That the Question?

A patient is speaking to the doctor, relating several months of sadness, loss of appetite and sleep, irritability and just plain 'feeling lousy.' After further discussion the doctor concludes the patient is experiencing significant depression and decides upon a course of treatment: psychotherapy and the short-term use of an antidepressant. The doctor takes out a pad, writes a prescription for one of the newer antidepressant medications, and arranges to start psychotherapy with the patient next week while monitoring the response to the medication. A psychiatrist? No, a psychologist in the State of New Mexico. In March 2002, New Mexico became the first state in the United States to permit psychologists, with additional training, to prescribe medication for nervous, emotional and mental problems.

While New Mexico is the first of the 50 states to obtain the legal right to prescribe medications used in mental health practices, it is not alone. Eleven other states will be introducing proposed modifications in their state laws to permit psychologists to prescribe medications. An additional 20 states have groups of psychologists laying the groundwork to introduce such legislative change.

Why do psychologists want to prescribe? The answer is a bit complicated. Physicians have historically been the only professionals permitted to prescribe, but in the last 50 years, in addition to dentists and podiatrists (who can prescribe medications but are not medical doctors) many other health-care professionals have added this service through changes in state law. Nurses and optometrists are permitted to prescribe medications in all states, physician assistants and pharmacists in many. For psychology it is not a case of 'me too' or 'monkey see, monkey do.' It is about quality care, and it is about accessible care.

To illustrate: I am a specialist in attention deficit disorder, and frequently medication is used as part of the overall treatment plan. Recently, a 10-year-old child was referred to me. Jason had significant problems with inattention and hyperactivity, and was failing in school. His parents had tried everything they could to get him to pay attention in school and complete homework. After the evaluation and a diagnosis of attention deficit hyperactivity disorder, I decided upon a four-part plan: work with Jason to develop better coping mechanisms for his behaviour; help his parents develop different ways

From *The Psychologist*, vol. 16, no. 4, pp. 184–186, April 2003. Copyright © 2003 by British Psychological Society. Reprinted by permission.

of parenting and relating to him; establish school-based strategies aimed at reducing classroom distraction and ensuring that homework and classwork were completed; and the use of a medication known to be effective in reducing the impulsivity and hyperactivity. The first three parts of the treatment plan were put in place within the first 24 to 48 hours. However, it took six weeks (with another report card grading period ending) before Jason and his parents were able to get an appointment with their paediatrician who would prescribe the medicine. Then, a four-week wait to see the paediatrician again for follow-up and adjustment of the medication towards the correct dose. If, as a psychologist, I had the right to prescribe medication, as I was seeing Jason and his parents weekly in psychotherapy, this part of the treatment plan would have been 'on board' within 24 hours as well. Lest the reader believe the paediatrician should have been involved earlier, the referral came from the paediatrician! This is not an uncommon experience among psychologists who see, and are referred, patients who need both psychotherapy and medication management. Frequently these referrals come from physicians who are ill equipped or trained to diagnose and treat psychological and mental issues.

There is clear evidence in the US that there are very grave and urgent unmet mental health needs. These needs could be met by professionals who can provide both psychotherapy and, when needed, medication. For example, there are over 450 counties in the United States with no psychiatrists in residence. An additional concern is that only about a third of the psychiatry training positions (residencies) are filled with American medical school graduates, with the majority of the remaining residency position being filled by physicians whose first language is not English. Language problems make it very difficult to work with minorities, inner-city families, Native Americans and rural communities. To illustrate the concern: A foreign-trained psychiatry resident whose English comprehension was passable but not extensive, admitted a man for 'being crazy,' 'because he talks to animals.' After I evaluated him the next morning, he was released with apologies. This was a African-American jazz musician who, when speaking about his band members told the resident 'I says to this cat, and the cat says to me.' Talks to animals! Right!

Also of concern is the fact that 85 per cent of prescriptions used to treat mental problems are written by physicians who have little or no training in psychiatry (Zimmerman & Wienckowski, 1991). The average psychiatric training is less than seven weeks and the average number of instructional hours in psychiatric medications is only 99 in the four years of US medical school training. . . . Thus another component of the complicated answer would include the ability of families to obtain quality and accessible mental health services in a timely fashion and at the lowest cost. It is much more efficient (in terms of time lost from work or school) and more cost-effective to see one professional rather than two.

Can psychologists be trained to be psychologist prescribers? They already have been! Many psychologists in medical schools and government agencies have either written prescriptions 'under the table' or did everything but sign them, seeking out a physician who would simply add his or her name. This has been going on for decades, though most of the training was self-taught and some by 'osmosis.' In 1991, however, the US Department of Defense began a four-year demonstration programme, to determine if psychologists who were in the military could be trained to prescribe medications. Several years later and thousands of prescriptions written, there has not been one inappropriate use, missed physical diagnosis or complication; nor has there been one untoward outcome. Clearly, psychologists can be trained to provide medication management at a very high level of competence as well as to provide high-quality psychotherapy.

The demonstration project was modified, over time, and evolved into a two-year postdoctoral programme. The first year is didactics, and the second on-the-job clinical experience. How is this training different from medical school? Prescribing psychologists embrace a more integrative or psychological model of prescribing. Psychological training is a health model focusing on strengths first then weaknesses, rather than the disease model of medical school. As a consequence psychologists are less likely to 'knee-jerk' a medication to treat symptoms. Indeed, the experience of the military psychologists has demonstrated this point over and over again.

We in the psychologist prescription movement acknowledge two truths that are—or should be—self-evident: medications are indeed effective for some patients, and current prescription writing practices are inadequate and dangerous, especially for underserved populations. We also recognise a very important 'treatment' given to prescribing psychologists: the authority to discontinue medications that have been prescribed by other professionals. Particularly with mental problems, there has been a tendency to practise 'polypharmacy'— prescribing more and more medications to treat newly created symptoms. In part, this is due to the problems cited earlier in psychiatric and medical training. A quick example: A depressed patient is given an antidepressant then gets the side-effect of sleep problems. Now a sedative is prescribed, but there are side-effects of morning drowsiness and fatigue. When a stimulant is added to provide 'alertness,' extrapyramidal symptoms such as severe dry mouth and lip-smacking develop and an anticholinergic drug is added. So the right to prescribe is also the right to *stop* inappropriate medications. You should note that over 7000 people a year die from legally prescribed medications (Kohn *et al.*, 2000: . . .

For almost a hundred years American psychology has debated the expansion of its competence and scope of practice. While never achieving unanimity, it has matured as a healthcare profession and will continue to do so. Clearly, a larger scope of practice will enable a psychologist to offer comprehensive services, including assessment, consultation, psychotherapy and, yes, when needed, medication. As psychology, like other professions, began the quest for independent prescriptive authority, organised medicine and some psychologists ominously warned of health hazards. In each instance the woeful predictions of wrongly treated patients flocking to hospitals and thousands of deaths never materialised.

Finally, I would argue that the best reason for psychologists having the ability to prescribe medication is not that it is good for psychology, but that it is good for the consumers. Psychologists have not entered this area of practice quickly or impulsively, but did so with deliberation and debate beginning in 1984. As a result, the additional training required for psychologists to prescribe medications has crucial differences from medical school training. Our training model is not disease-based. We include intensive and extensive training in the interaction of psychotherapy and medication, stressing when one is therapeutically superior to the other and when the use of both is in the best interest of the patient. In the final analysis, isn't this what this should be about? Isn't it what is best for the individuals, families and public we serve? It should be.

All references for articles included in *Taking Sides: Clashing Views in Abnormal Psychology, 6/e* can be found on the Web at **www.mhhe.com/cls.**

William N. Robiner, et al. **NO**

Prescriptive Authority for Psychologists: A Looming Health Hazard?

Advances in neuroscience, the development of safer, efficacious drugs such as the SSRIs, and changing realities in health care economics are transforming the delivery of mental health services. As these unfold, and as the use of psychotropics increases (Pincus et al., 1998), psychologists' interest in obtaining prescriptive authority for psychotropic medication has also increased (Ax, Forbes, & Thompson, 1997; Brentar & McNamara, 1991a, 1991b; Burns, DeLeon, Chemtob, Welch, & Samuels, 1988; Cullen & Newman, 1997; DeLeon, Folen, Jennings, Wilkis, & Wright, 1991; DeLeon, Fox, & Graham, 1991; DeLeon & Wiggins, 1996; Fox, 1988; Sammons, 1994). In this article we address a range of issues related to prescriptive authority for psychologists, including training, accreditation, regulation, and other topics raised by proponents of the prescriptive agenda, and discuss our concerns about it. . . .

Department of Defense Psychopharmacology Project

The controversy surrounding psychologists' prescription privileges was heightened by the Department of Defense (DoD) Psychopharmacology Demonstration Project (PDP). The PDP ultimately trained ten psychologists to prescribe in military health care settings (U.S. General Accounting Office, 1999). The initial PDP participants undertook some preparation in chemistry and biochemistry before completing a majority of first-year medical school courses. During their first full-time year at the Uniformed Services University of the Health Sciences, they worked with the Psychiatry-Liaison service and assumed night call with second-year psychiatry residents. In the second full-time year, they completed core basic science courses and continued psychopharmacology training and clinical work. After 2-day written and oral examinations, they had a third year of supervised clinical work at Walter Reed Army Medical Center or Malcolm Grow Medical Center. The PDP curriculum underwent subsequent iterations, streamlining training to 1 year of coursework and a year of supervised clinical practice (Sammons & Brown, 1997; Sammons, Sexton, & Meredith, 1996). For example, the didactic hours decreased by 48% in the second iteration. Most PDP graduates have functioned as prescribing psychologists in branches of the military. One graduate went on to medical school.

The PDP was discontinued after the first few years. Advocates of psychologist prescription privileges argue that the successes of the small sample of PDP participants justify extending prescriptive authority to other psychologists who undergo training consistent with the American Psychological Association (APA) (Council of Representatives [COR], 1996) model, even though that training model and the likely resources available for the training differ substantially from the PDP. It is not known how well the successes of the 10 PDP psychologists, who were trained within a military medical school and military hospital settings, and whose care was confined to a patient population largely screened for health and other factors, would generalize to the potentially thousands of psychologists who might wish to obtain psychopharmacology training and to practice independently across the spectrum of clinical or counseling settings with diverse populations (Bieliauskas, 1992a; Kennedy, 1998). If the clinical psychopharmacology training psychologists obtain elsewhere is less rigorous or is based on more limited access to medical populations than the PDP, the outcomes of the PDP potentially would overestimate outcomes of such training.

Additional skepticism seems warranted especially in light of the concerns about certain limitations of the PDP fellows' clinical proficiencies, such as in treating medically complex patients (Kennedy, 1998). The Final Report of the American College of Neuropsychopharmacology (1998) on the PDP assessed graduates as weaker medically and psychiatrically than psychiatrists. The report indicated that graduates only saw patients ages 18–65, some had limited formularies, and some continued to have dependent prescriptive practice (i.e., supervised by a physician). Moreover, the PDP graduates advised against "short-cut" programs and considered that a year of intensive full-time clinical experience, including inpatient care, was essential. Some of the program's psychiatrists, physicians, and graduates expressed doubts about the safety and effectiveness of psychologists prescribing independently outside of the interdisciplinary team of the military context. This latter concern has been echoed in a survey of military psychiatrists, nonpsychiatric physicians, and social workers (Klusman, 1998). Given the likelihood that other programs would lack some of the advantages of the PDP, and would provide less training than some of the PDP graduates received, we question how well the conditions of the PDP would be duplicated. Despite the positive experiences of PDP graduates, these concerns justify wariness about prescribing psychologists relative to other prescribers, especially for populations not included or emphasized in the PDP. We believe that more complete disclosure and consideration of the limitations and problems noted in the PDP are needed, both in the dialogue within the profession as well as in terms of public policy reviews of the prescriptive agenda. . . .

Quality of Care: The Central Concern about Psychologist Prescribing

Our primary concern is the risk of suboptimal care if psychologists undertake prescribing that could arise from their limited breadth and depth of knowledge about human physiology, medicine, and related areas. This risk would be compounded by psychologists' limited supervised physical clinical training experiences. Such knowledge and skills are fundamental to competent prescribing but have been limited or absent in training professional (i.e., clinical, counseling, school) psychologists. In one survey, more than two thirds of psychologists in independent practice described their training related to psychopharmacological issues as poor (APA, 1992b, p. 50). This is not surprising given the limited psychopharmacology training in doctoral programs and psychology internships (APA, 1992b).

Although advocates of prescription privileges readily acknowledge that additional training is needed to prepare psychologists to prescribe, the central questions are these. How much training is needed? Is it possible to attain adequate knowledge and skill through abbreviated training, such as proposed in models by the APA (CoR, 1996) or the California Psychological Association-California School of Professional Psychology Blue Ribbon Panel (1995)? How would psychologists who undergo the proposed training measure up to other prescribers? The concern is that abbreviated "crash courses" are inadequate to make up for psychologists' deficits in medical education (Bieliauskas, 1992a; Bütz, 1994).

At times, advocates for psychologist prescription privileges gloss over the complexity of knowledge sets inherent in competent prescribing (Kennedy, 1998; Kingsbury, 1992; Pies; 1991). For example, Patrick DeLeon, PhD, JD, Past President of the APA, contends that "prescription privileges is no big deal. It's like learning how to use a desk-top computer" (Roan, 1993). Related speculation that technological advances, such as computer-assisted learning (DeLeon & Wiggins, 1996), or prescriptive algorithms, could abbreviate the education necessary to prescribe competently strikes even proponents of prescription privileges as naïve (Pachman, 1996). Similarly, it seems unlikely that relying on more active roles of pharmacists or computerized systems for administration of drugs would compensate adequately for gaps in prescribers' medical knowledge. Ultimately, competence in prescribing demands adequate understanding not just of psychology and psychopharmacology but also of other domains of medical knowledge (e.g., human physiology, pathophysiology, biochemistry, clinical medicine) and clinical proficiencies (e.g., physical examination, interpretation of laboratory data) that historically have been excluded from the education and training of psychologists. More specifically, thorough understanding and proficiency related to two broad medical domains are required: understanding patients' medical status prior to and concurrent with prescribing and their medical status during and after treatment (i.e., their physiological responses to prescribed medications) (Pies, 1991; Robiner, 1999; see Table 1).

Table 1

Knowledge Base and Clinical Proficiencies Required for Prescribing

Psychopathology and Psychological Issues	Medical Status Prior to Prescribing	Response to Treatments
Primary psychiatric conditions	Comorbid medical conditions	Knowledge of adverse reactions 1. Side effects 2. Toxic effects
Comorbid psychiatric conditions	Contraindications	Ability to recognize, diagnose, and treat adverse reactions
Prevalence and course of psychiatric conditions	Medical effects of concurrent treatments 1. Drug interactions 2. Other treatments (e.g., dialysis, plasmaphoresis)	Ability to differentiate between physical and psychiatric effects of psychoactive agents and concurrent medications
Knowledge of nonpharmacologic treatment options	Long-term effects of medications History of medication use	Other issues related to monitoring, titrating, or discontinuing prescribed medications

Note: The education of psychologists typically addresses column 1, but neglects columns 2 and 3.

There are scant data regarding how well prepared psychologists are to prescribe. Anecdotally, psychologists' confidence in diagnosing patients and providing other types of psychological treatment, combined with limited psychopharmacology training and informal exposure to medications, may provide some sense that they have much of the knowledge related to prescribing. Thus far, however, little is known about how well the combination of doctoral training in psychology and relatively brief, focused training in psychopharmacology would develop psychologists' knowledge base and clinical proficiency for managing patients' medications, especially long-term and in diverse settings. Noteworthy differences exist between pharmacotherapy and current aspects of psychologists' clinical practice. As one psychologist turned psychiatrist observes:

> *The effects of medications on the kidney, the heart, and so forth is important for the use of many medications. Managing these effects is often crucial and has more to do with biochemistry and physiology than with psychology. I was surprised to discover how little about medication use has to do with psychological principles and how much of it is just medical. (Kingsbury, 1992, p. 5)*

Training for Prescribing

Proponents have construed prescriptive authority for psychologists as an "evolutionary" or "logical" step (DeLeon, Folen, et al., 1991; Fox, 1988) or even a "right" (Brentar & McNamara, 1991a) that is consistent with the trend in other health care disciplines towards broadened scopes of professional practice, including prescribing.

The first premise is debatable, especially given its fundamental departure from psychology's historic training paradigms and conceptualizations of psychopathology and intervention. The education and training for a doctoral degree in psychology largely neglects key topics relevant to prescribing (i.e., the biological and physical sciences, physical examination). Also, psychology historically has questioned, de-emphasized, or even eschewed the "medical model" (Matthews, 1998; May & Belsky, 1992). Pursuing prescriptive authority reflects a profound change in the direction toward embracing the medical model. Adding prescribing to psychology's scope of practice might more realistically be characterized as "revolutionary" or "radical," requiring major shifts in focus; marked expansions of training and continuing education in key areas; reformulation of accreditation criteria; modification of regulatory structure, domains, and processes; expanded ethical guidelines; and uniform requirements that at least part of psychologists' training occur within health care settings.

The second premise, that psychologists' scope of practice should broaden because some nonphysicians such as physician assistants (PAs) and advanced practice nurses (APNs) prescribe also is dubious. This seems to be based on the notion that the overall length of doctoral training that psychologists undergo might justify prescribing despite the limited relevance to prescribing of much of their actual training. Disparities in training between psychology and other professions with prescriptive authority challenge the notion that those professions' scopes of practice justify expanding psychologists' scope of practice to incorporate prescription privileges. Other professions' training models are much closer to that of physicians than to that of psychologists, and their clinical practice is more focused on physical functioning, including medication effects. Comparing the boundaries of other professions' scope of practice with psychology's is inappropriate given the differences in training between those other disciplines and psychology. . . .

The comparisons that advocates draw between psychology's and other disciplines' scope of practice compel closer inspection of the entry requirements and training models for psychology and other prescribing disciplines (McCabe & Grover, 1999). As outlined below, the differences in emphasis and structure are noteworthy. Since prescribing psychologists would probably be compared most closely with psychiatrists, our emphasis is on these two groups.

Undergraduate Training

The APA task force (Smyer et al., 1993) noted that other health professions (e.g., nursing, allied health professions) require undergraduate preparation in anatomy, biology, inorganic and organic chemistry, pharmacology, human physiology (and some require physics); undergraduate psychology degrees and admission to psychology graduate school do not. The biological sciences and related course work is the educational foundation for knowledge and conceptual understanding related to prescribing safely. Hence, the APA task force envisioned that students with strong undergraduate, postbaccalaureate, or early graduate biological backgrounds would be admitted to psychopharmacology training (Smyer et al., 1993). The problem is that such backgrounds are rare. A survey of psychology graduate students revealed that only 27% thought they had the undergraduate preparation to undertake training to prescribe (Tatman et al., 1997). Only 7% had completed the recommended undergraduate biology and chemistry prerequisites (APA, 1992b; Smyer et al., 1993). Robiner et al. (2001) found that psychologists generally had taken fewer than five courses in the biological and physical sciences during their undergraduate and graduate education. . . .

Unlike medical school applicants and medical students, whose mastery of these areas is reflected through a competitive selection process (e.g., based on grades in biological and physical science courses, MCAT scores) and screened again in objective measures (i.e., national board scores such as steps one, two, and three of the United States Medical Licensing Examination [USMLE]; specialty board examinations following residency), entry into proposed psychopharmacology training programs for psychologists would not require standardized, objective indices of applicants' understanding of the biological and physical sciences. It is not known whether competitive performance in biological and physical science courses with laboratory prerequisites would play any role in determining eligibility for psychologists' psychopharmacology training. In summary, the discrepancies between physicians' and psychologists' education in the biological and physical sciences, and objective mechanisms verifying that general scientific knowledge has been acquired (i.e., psychology has none), begin at the undergraduate level.

The APA College of Professional Psychology in conjunction with Professional Examination Services developed an examination for psychologists who have undergone training in clinical psychopharmacology, the Psychopharmacology Examination for Psychologists (PEP). Other groups have developed other tests (e.g., Veritas Assessment Systems). Within the APA (1996) model, psychologists seeking prescription privileges would be expected to pass one of these written tests. Such testing is an important safeguard, but may be limited, especially in an era when commercial courses have been designed to prepare individuals for tests. Whereas proponents would argue that passage of that examination demonstrates adequate knowledge for prescribing, it seems questionable that a single 3-hour, 150-item test on psychopharmacology could assure adequate knowledge of the broad spectrum of medical issues beyond clinical psychopharmacology per se that are relevant to prescribing safely or knowledge and clinical skill sets comparable to that of other prescribers (e.g., physicians, nurse practitioners).

Graduate Training

Educational discrepancies between psychologists and physicians widen at the graduate level. The training of physicians and other doctoral providers (e.g., dentists) entails coursework in anatomy, biochemistry, cell biology, immunology, microbiology, pathology, pharmacology, physiology, as well as laboratory experiences in the biological and physical sciences and physical, clinical training. Doctoral-level psychology education never has (see APA Office of Program

Consultation and Accreditation, 1996). Rather, graduate education in psychology has been characterized as comprising "vastly differing models of study and practice" with "no effort to standardize the training of psychologists" (Klein, 1996). Programs vary in how much training is provided in the biological and physical sciences (Sammons et al., 1996), but it is generally quite limited for degrees in professional psychology. Some types of psychology degrees, (e.g., school psychology) have relatively limited exposure to psychopathology and psychological treatments, let alone the physical sciences (DeMers, 1994; Moyer, 1995) or medical environments. . . .

Surveys suggest that only 25% of psychology graduate students had courses in psychopharmacology (Tatman et al., 1997) and 36% of licensed psychologists indicated that their graduate programs offered psychopharmacology courses (Ferguson, 1997). Presumably fewer had courses in pharmacology or pathophysiology, which are intrinsic to prescribing safely (i.e., due to potential interactions and adverse effects). These limitations are of greater concern than the limitations identified in medical students' psychiatric training (Zimmerman & Wienckowski, 1991) or estimates that medical school students receive only approximately 100 hours of pharmacology instruction (Association for Medical School Pharmacology [1990] cited by the APA Task Force [APA, 1992b]); physicians' other didactics are relevant to prescribing and their lengthy supervised training across a continuum of settings and supervisors includes wide exposure to related topics and patient populations.

By the time psychologists obtain doctorates, most have obtained relatively little training that overlaps with that of physicians or other prescribers. Moreover, there are no objective quality assurance processes to ensure that the biological and physical sciences are well understood by entrants to psychology graduate school or by entrants to proposed postdoctoral psychopharmacology training programs. Even the Examination for the Professional Practice of Psychology (EPPP), the written test required for licensure in psychology, minimally queries knowledge of the biological and physical sciences (e.g., biochemistry) (Association of State and Provincial Psychology Boards, 2000).

Proposed Postdoctoral Level Psychopharmacology Training

. . . The APA (CoR, 1996) emphasizes that the proposed training is "unique to the needs of the practicing psychologist, and does not simply follow traditional medical practices." We question whether such condensed training overcomes current shortcomings to achieve knowledge and clinical proficiency equivalent to that of other prescribers, especially psychiatrists, and ensure competent prescribing that the public should reasonably expect of its doctors. Furthermore, it seems incumbent upon proponents of the prescriptive agenda to fully inform legislators and the public precisely how the psychopharmacology training proposed by the APA differs from "traditional medical practices." . . .

Proponents of prescription privileges recognize that the supervised practice in proposed psychopharmacology training "essential for effective, safe, ethical and practical incorporation of drugs into a psychological practice . . . is a substantive matter" (Fox et al., 1992, p. 218). Curiously, despite recognition of this substantiveness, the scope and requirements for supervised pharmacotherapeutic practice are not fully delineated in the APA model, so it is not possible to evaluate how adequate the supervised practice would be. Consistent with the APA model, training programs are designed for trainees to see a series of patients (e.g., $100) for psychopharmacologic management. The APA model fails to specify minimal criteria for (a) the breadth of patients' mental health conditions; (b) the duration of treatment (i.e., to allow for adequate monitoring and feedback) or requirements for outpatient or inpatient experiences; (c) exposure to adverse medication effects; or (d) exposure to patients with comorbid medical conditions and complex drug regimens. Also, the qualifications for supervisors are vague. Whereas the CPA-CSPP Panel (1995) recommended an 18-month practicum, the APA model does not specify any length. That the didactic and practical training would be abbreviated relative to the PDP, and less likely to occur in organized, academic health care settings with lengthy track records of providing medical or psychiatric training, raises questions about how comparable such programs would be to the PDP.

We doubt that the proposed models of training in psychopharmacology for psychologists (APA, 1996; CPA/CSPP, 1995; Fox et al., 1992) would prepare them to provide care equivalent to that provided by psychiatrists or other health professionals. Not only would they obtain less didactics in relevant areas, but the supervised pharmacologic care of patients would be considerably less comprehensive and less well organized than training within psychiatric residencies. . . .

Regulatory and Legal Issues

. . . A number of legal issues also would arise if psychologists were granted prescriptive authority. This includes the level of independence versus dependence of this authority, potential restrictions on their prescriptive practices (e.g., limited formulary and duration of treatment; specific settings), and the most appropriate standard of care to which psychologists would be held. Would psychologists be compared with other "reasonably prudent" psychologists who have undergone the proposed psychopharmacology training, or with other prescribers, such as psychiatrists, who have greater training and experience related to medication management and who have set the standard for prescribing psychoactive medications thus far? From the consumer's perspective, it seems likely that a standard of care closer to that provided by psychiatrists would promote accountability and afford greater protections and legal remedies than an unknown, less stringent, evolving standard based on psychologists who might gain prescriptive authority based on training that is less intensive than that of other prescribers. In addition, formulation of ethical guidelines relevant to prescribing, which are beyond the current APA (1992a) Ethical Principles of Psychologists and Code of Conduct, would be needed (Buelow & Chafetz, 1996) to address a range of ethical challenges associated with prescribing (Heiby, 1998).

Proponents' Focus on Peripheral Issues

In essentially waging a campaign for prescriptive authority, proponents tend to focus on certain provocative issues to promote their cause and divert attention away from the inadequacies in psychologists' education, knowledge, and skills in areas critical to prescribing. For example, DeLeon and Wiggins (1996) decry problems of current prescribers as if psychologists (who would have less extensive physical science backgrounds and more limited supervised prescriptive practical training) would avoid developing problematic patterns if they prescribe. Alternative strategies, such as enhancing the ability of current prescribers through such means as education and redesign of prescribing systems (Lesar, Briceland, & Stein, 1997), or enhancing psychologists' collaborative practices, as proposed in the APA task force's (Smyer et al., 1993) Level 2 training, might address such problems without requiring that psychologists prescribe.

Similarly, underserved populations (e.g., rural populations, the seriously and persistently mentally ill [SPMI], the elderly) have been invoked to frame prescriptive authority as a policy response to meet pressing societal needs (DeLeon, Sammons, & Sexton, 1995; Hanson et al., 1999). This line of reasoning is flawed in failing to consider the similar access patterns to psychologists and psychiatrists across the urban-rural continuum (Hendryx, Borders, & Johnson, 1995; Holzer, Goldsmith, & Ciarlo, 1998) and the APA task force's expectation that only "a small . . . minority of psychologists" (APA, 1992b, p. 106) would seek Level 3 psychopharmacology training. Such data and predictions, along with the virtual absence of any concrete plan to redistribute prescribing psychologists to meet the actual needs of underserved populations (May & Belsky, 1992), render broadening psychologists' scope of practice to include prescriptive authority an indirect, needlessly risky, and highly inefficient public policy response to rural areas' shortage of psychopharmacologic prescribers. . . .

Ultimately, there is little reason to assume that psychologists with prescriptive authority actually would relocate to areas lacking other prescribers, or would focus their practices to address the needs of other types of underserved populations (Adams & Bieliauskas, 1994; Bieliauskas, 1992a, 1992b). Even some proponents of prescriptive privileges concede that psychologists may not be more inclined than psychiatrists to work with underserved groups (Hanson et al., 1999).

Attempts to garner support for the prescriptive agenda on the basis of underserved populations also ignores efforts by the American Psychiatric Association to enhance psychiatric consultation to primary care providers ("APA board takes action," 1998) and the potential benefits of expanded use of telehealth technology to supplement the expertise of primary care practitioners in areas underserved by psychiatrists. Similarly, it ignores data that psychiatrists see significantly more SPMI and socially disadvantaged patients than do psychologists (Olfson & Pincus, 1996), which brings into question whether prescriptive authority would have a major impact in expanding care to SPMI populations. Pursuing prescriptive authority may distract focus from important opportunities for psychologists to improve their collaborations with primary care providers to collectively address needs as suggested by groups such as the National Depressive and Manic-Depressive Association (Hirschfeld et al., 1977) or the National Alliance for the Mentally Ill (NAMI). . . .

Another rationale of proponents of prescription privileges is that many mental health services, including prescriptions of psychotropic medications, are provided by nonpsychiatric physicians who have little psychiatric training (DeLeon & Wiggins, 1996). Indeed, the general medical sector is an essential component of the mental health system, serving an estimated 40–50% of people with mental disorders according to the utilization data of the Epidemiologic Catchment Area (ECA) study (Narrow, Regier, Rae, Manderscheid, & Locke, 1993). Similarly, data from the National Ambulatory Medicare Care Survey (NAMCS) reveal that outpatient appointments with primary care physicians and medical specialists account respectively for 48% and 19% of all appointments involving psychoactive prescription drugs: More than the appointments with psychiatrists (33%) (Pincus et al., 1998). General physicians provide somewhat more of the nation's outpatient mental health services (35%) than either psychologists (31%) or psychiatrists (27%) (Olfson & Pincus, 1996).

According to DeLeon and Wiggins (1996), an estimated 135.8 million prescriptions for psychoactive medications were written in 1991, of which only 17.3% were by psychiatrists. Such statistics, albeit interesting, do *not* indicate how many of these physician interactions for prescriptions are enhanced by consultations involving psychiatrists, psychologists, or other mental health professionals, or how many truly need mental health consultation. There are no benchmarks for how many prescriptions nonpsychiatric physicians should write or what percentage of them ought to be informed by collaborations with mental health professionals. It is possible that the large number of prescriptions written by nonpsychiatric physicians reflect that consultation with mental health professionals may be necessary only for subgroups of patients, or that adequate consultation already occurs related to many patients who might need medication. Moreover, despite focus on such patterns (DeLeon & Wiggins, 1996), the numbers neither reveal anything about problematic patterns of prescribing by physicians nor do they persuade that psychologists should prescribe. They probably do reflect several factors, such as (1) some people are more comfortable seeing their primary care physician than a mental health professional (Geller & Muus, 1997; Murstein & Fontaine, 1993), and (2) managed care organizations and capitated systems encourage primary care physicians to treat mental disorders rather than refer to specialist mental health professionals (Pincus et al., 1998). Such systems of health care delivery are similar to the service delivery models in other countries (e.g., Great Britain), where lower per capita rates of psychiatrists reflect psychiatrists' roles as specialist consultants to nonpsychiatric physicians who play primary roles in the psychopharmacological management of most patients' care (Scully, 1999).

The widespread prescription of psychoactive agents by nonpsychiatrist physicians reflects the significant opportunities for psychiatrists and psychologists (especially those with Level 2 training) to collaborate and consult about psychopharmacology. The data confirm the importance of continuing the ongoing efforts to enhance psychopharmacology training of nonpsychiatric physicians and other prescribers. Such trends do not, however, indicate a need or justification for psychologists to prescribe.

Medication Adverse Effects and Errors

Prescribers even of limited formularies necessarily assume some responsibility for the broader health status of their patients (Heiby, 1998; Kingsbury, 1992). Psychoactive medications have been described as presenting more complex drug interactions and adverse effects than any other class of drug (Hayes, 1998). Many people who take psychoactive medications also take other medications that complicate their care. Fewer than 30% who take an antidepressant take no other medications, so it is important to understand the comorbid conditions and other medications that patients concurrently experience (Preskorn, 1999). In primary care and psychiatric settings, more than 70% of patients prescribed an antidepressant take at least one other drug and a third take at least three other drugs (Preskorn, 1999). Polypharmacy rates are often higher with the elderly and medically ill, and in more specialized clinics (e.g., HIV). . . .

The timing of the intensification of psychologists' lobbying for prescriptive authority is ironic in light of growing national concern about errors in prescribing medication (Classen, Pestotnik, Evans, Lloyd, & Burke, 1997). Nationally, medication errors are estimated to lead to as many as 7,000 deaths annually (Phillips, Christenfeld, & Glynn, 1998). The Federal Drug Administration currently receives 235,000 reports per year about adverse drug events (Institute of Medicine Committee on Quality of Health Care in America, 1999). This could increase as medication options expand, requiring constant upgrades in knowledge of the entire pharmaceutical spectrum. In 1998, the FDA approved 90 new drugs, 30 new molecular entities, 124 new or expanded use of agents, and 344 generic drugs, not counting over the counter and orphan drugs (FDA, 1999). That nearly half of the drugs currently marketed have become available in the last decade (Shatin, Gardner, & Stergachis, 1999) suggests that the knowledge base for prescribing is becoming even more complex, requiring yet more extensive scientific understanding. Between 1970 and 1997, the annual number of publications on drug-drug interactions increased fivefold (Preskorn, 1999), reflecting factors such as increased use of medications for chronic conditions and an aging society with more medical problems and more complex medication regimens. Such trends underscore the need for strong basic education in medicine and pharmacology to prepare prescribers to understand medical conditions in integrating pharmacologic developments into their practice.

Among the many contributing factors to medication errors are *inadequate knowledge* and use of knowledge regarding drug therapy and *inadequate recognition* of important patient factors (e.g., impaired renal function, drug allergies) (Lesar et al., 1997). The influence of other factors that require more sophisticated scientific understanding, such as genetic variation in drug metabolism and uptake, is increasingly likely to affect prescribing. Along with other recommendations, Lesar et al. (1997) recommended *improved prescriber education*. There have not been calls from outside of psychology to create a new category of prescribers with relatively *less* training (as psychologist prescribers would be).

Given the paucity of education and training directly related to prescribing throughout undergraduate and graduate training in psychology (Robiner et al., 2001), the scant data about psychologists' proficiency in managing medications, which is limited to relatively few individuals, as well as inadequacies in psychologists' knowledge related to psychopharmacology (Robiner et al., 2001), we doubt that abbreviated psychopharmacology training for psychologists would be sufficient to ensure adequate competence in prescribing. Moreover, we are concerned that psychologists would lack the medical expertise to recognize, assess (e.g., all relevant hematological assays), and understand adverse effects and initiate proper medical care.

Short cuts in education seem likely to undermine patient care and contribute to medication errors along the patterns outlined by Lesar et al. (1997). Such training, especially if paired with independent prescriptive authority, risks generating a wave of suboptimal medication management and potentially avoidable adverse drug events. In addition to potentially hazardous consequences for patients, problems associated with psychologist prescribing would present regulatory conundrums, provide a new basis for litigation, and ultimately could detract from the public's esteem of psychologists in general.

Closing Considerations

We appreciate the important roles psychologists play within the delivery of health care broadly and mental health care in particular. Our findings and conclusions in no way belittle psychologists' knowledge or proficiencies in other areas. We agree with the APA task force (APA, 1992b) that it would be beneficial to promote psychologists' psychopharmacology knowledge so as to inform and enhance their collaborations with primary care providers and psychiatrists in providing care to patients who need medications. However, achieving the APA task force's goals for enhancing the care of patients needing medications does not require prescriptive authority for psychologists. Instead, we recommend that the APA refocus its energies to better educate psychologists about psychopharmacology to enhance the psychological services that psychologists provide and their collaborations with prescribers. This is a type of training that most psychology graduate students need and would welcome (Tatman et al., 1997). Also, survey data suggest that most (90%) licensed psychologists feel that psychologists should pursue a minimum of the collaborative practice level of training and most (79%) would be personally willing to pursue it (Ferguson, 1997). Moreover, most (85%) applied psychologists already consult regularly with physicians, so such training would enhance services that already are provided (Barkley, 1991).

Unfortunately, if psychologists prescribe, medically complex patients (e.g., older patients taking multiple medications) would probably be most vulnerable to the adverse consequences that potentially could derive from shortcomings in psychologists' scientific and medical training (Hayes & Heiby, 1996; Klein, 1996). Promoting psychologists' collaborative practices with prescribers rather than psychologists' prescription privileges would preclude new risks to patients associated with a potentially suboptimal level of care. Collaboration would avoid further confusion about psychologists' identities (Ax et al., 1997), skills, scope of practice, and the differentiation between psychology and psychiatry (Murstein & Fontaine, 1993; Wood, Jones, & Benjamin, 1986). . . .

As psychologists, educators of psychologists, and related health professionals, the authors have actively supported psychology's many other advances (e.g., Medicare reimbursement, licensure, provision of nonpharmacologic interventions), including appropriate, innovative roles of psychologists in health care (Schofield, 1969). We caution against framing the debate about prescription privileges as a chapter in the saga of struggles between psychology and psychiatry (DeLeon & Wiggins, 1996). Rather, at its core it is a controversy about the education and training necessary to promote safe and effective treatment that limits unnecessary risks to patients.

We have doubts that the shortcomings in psychologists' education and knowledge related to prescribing can be surmounted through abbreviated training, such as that currently advocated by the APA. Our skepticism that these gaps can be overcome within such a shorter time frame than is involved in the training of other prescribers leads us to urge psychologists to resist the temptation to venture into aspects of health care (i.e., prescribing and its related clinical activities) for which they would not be well-prepared. As legislators and regulators are lobbied about psychologists' prescriptive privileges agenda, they need to weigh judiciously any hoped-for benefits against the potential risks associated with the inadequacies in psychologists' preparation to prescribe, even after they may have obtained the psychopharmacology training in accordance with the model recommended by the APA (CoR, 1996).

Acknowledgment

The authors appreciatively acknowledge the editorial guidance and other contributions of William Schofield, PhD, and Irving I. Gottesman, PhD, in the preparation of this article.

All references for articles included in *Taking Sides: Clashing Views in Abnormal Psychology, 6/e* can be found on the Web at **www.mhhe.com/cls**.

CHALLENGE QUESTIONS

Should Psychologists Prescribe Medication?

1. Imagine that you are suffering from an intense degree of anxiety or depression for which medication has been shown to be an effective intervention. From whom would you want to seek a prescription, and what factors would influence your choice?
2. An argument has been made that giving psychologists the right to prescribe medications would address the fact that there are many regions in which prescribing mental health professionals are not available. Discuss the strengths and weaknesses of this argument.
3. In recent years, increased attention has been given to the aggressive marketing of psychotropic medications. Of particular concern are practices in which physicians are lavishly indulged with gifts or expensive dinners in order to "learn about" a pharmaceutical company's product. Discuss the ethical issues involved in such practices, and consider ways in which objectionable marketing practices could be changed.
4. Imagine that you are a researcher with a grant to evaluate effectiveness and satisfaction associated with psychologists being given prescription privileges. What factors would go into designing a study on this topic?
5. Consider the fact that the majority of prescriptions for mental health conditions are written by nonpsychiatric physicians. Discuss the benefits and problems associated with this practice.

Suggested Readings

Fox, R., DeLeon, P., Newman, R., Sammons, M., Dunivin, D., & Baker, D. (2009). Prescriptive authority and psychology: A status report. *American Psychologist, 64*(4), 257–268.

Heiby, E.M. (2009). Concerns about substandard training or prescription privileges for psychologists. *Journal of Clinical Psychology, 66*(1), 104–111.

Hobson, J. A., & Leonard, J. A. (2001). *Out of its mind: Psychiatry in crisis.* Boston: Perseus.

Johnstone, L. (2003). Back to basics. *The Psychologist, 16*(4), 186–187.

Long, J. E., Jr. (2005). Power to prescribe: The debate over prescription privileges for psychologists and the legal issues implicated. *Law and Psychology Review, 29*, 243–260.

Muse, M., & McGrath, R.E. (2009). Training comparison among three professions prescribing psychoactive medications: psychiatric nurse practitioners, physicians, and pharmacologically trained psychologists. *Journal of Clinical Psychology, 66*(1), 96–103.

Sternberg, R. J. (2001). Prescription privileges for psychologists: A view from academe. *The California Psychologist, 34*(10), 16–17.

Internet References . . .

Web site of Dr. Ken Pope

This site provides resources on ethical and professional issues, including a section on detainee interrogations.

http://kspope.com/index.php

The Society for the Psychological Study of Social Issues (SPSSI)

This site provides research on the psychological aspects of important social issues and public policy solutions.

http://www.spssi.org/

The Body Image Program at Rhode Island Hospital

This site provides research and clinical services pertaining to body image disturbances such as body dysmorphic disorder.

http://www.rhodeislandhospital.org/rih/services/mentalhealth/bodyimage/

Media Psychology Division of the American Psychological Association

This APA Division promotes research into the impact of media on human behavior.

http://www.apa.org/divisions/div46/

Against Pornography

This Web site aims to raise awareness about the harms of pornography.

https://againstpornography.org/

American Constitution Society for Law and Policy

This nonprofit legal organization focuses on issues of human dignity, equality, individual rights, liberties, and access to justice.

http://www.acsblog.org

Crime and Consequences

This Web site is dedicated to ensuring that criminals are punished quickly and in accord with the Constitution.

http://www.crimeandconsequences.com

American Psychological Association

This Web site contains information on issues pertaining to the science and practice of psychology, including topics such as the psychological aftereffects of abortion.

http://www.apa.org

afterabortion.com

This Web site contains "neutral, nonjudgmental, nonreligion based, nonpolitically affiliated online support, information, help and healing."

http://www.afterabortion.com/

UNIT 3

Social Issues

*M*any issues in the field of abnormal psychology interface with social issues, with heated debate emerging about topics pertaining to balancing the protection of personal rights while also responding to societal concerns. For example, during the decade following the 9/11 terrorist attacks, psychologists have been called upon to participate in the development and administration of coercive interrogation techniques, a role that some consider as unethical for helping professionals. Other examples of ethical quandaries include the questions of whether it is acceptable to yield to individuals with extremely unusual or socially unacceptable wishes. Should society support (both ideologically and financially through insurance coverage) a person's wish to amputate a healthy limb? Should pornographic images of children that are generated by computers be protected by the First Amendment? How much psychological and social disturbance is attributable to out-of-control media images of violence? The role of mental health professionals in several of these debates is quite complex. What role should clinicians play in end-of-life decisions? What voice should be expressed in cases involving seriously mentally ill murderers who are sentenced to death, but who may not understand the rationale for their execution? What kinds of bias might be evident in the research of psychologists who study controversial social phenomena, such as questions about the impact of abortion on a woman's mental health?

- Is It Unethical for Psychologists to Be Involved in Coercive Interrogations?
- Is It Ethical to Support the Wish for Healthy Limb Amputation in People with Body Integrity Identity Disorder (BIID)?
- Does Exposure to Media Violence Promote Aggressive Behavior?
- Would Legalization of Virtual Child Pornography Reduce Sexual Exploitation of Children?
- Must Mentally Ill Murderers Have a Rational Understanding of Why They Are Being Sentenced to Death?
- Does Research Confirm That Abortion is a Psychologically Benign Experience?

ISSUE 13

Is It Unethical for Psychologists to Be Involved in Coercive Interrogations?

YES: Mark Costanzo, Ellen Gerrity, and M. Brinton Lykes, from "Psychologists and the Use of Torture in Interrogations," *Analyses of Social Issues and Public Policy (ASAP)* (December 2007)

NO: Kirk M. Hubbard, from "Psychologists and Interrogations: What's Torture Got to Do with It?" *Analyses of Social Issues and Public Policy (ASAP)* (December 2007)

ISSUE SUMMARY

YES: Psychologists Mark Costanzo, Ellen Gerrity, and M. Brinton Lykes assert that the involvement of psychologists in enhanced interrogations is a violation of fundamental ethical principles.

NO: Psychologist and intelligence expert Kirk M. Hubbard asserts that psychologists can assist in developing effective, lawful ways to obtain actionable intelligence in fighting terrorism and can bring a wealth of knowledge to the administration of interrogations.

Since the September 11 terrorist attacks, many Americans fear that other assaults could happen at any time. On the international scene, the "war against terror" escalated, as potential terrorists were tracked down, apprehended, and held in various places around the globe and were interrogated, at times through means that many would regard as inhumane violations of the Geneva Convention. These "enhanced interrogation techniques" were designed to extract information from detainees and included procedures such as forced nudity, painful stress positions, sleep deprivation, and waterboarding (provokes the sensation of being drowned).

Psychologists were called upon by various sectors of the U.S. government to develop effective techniques for eliciting information from detainees. Some of these techniques were based on the "learned helplessness" theory of the prominent research psychologist Martin Seligman. For much of the decade, the American Psychological Association (APA) debated whether it was unethical for psychologists to use their scientific knowledge and clinical expertise for the development and implementation of enhanced interrogation techniques.

Although many vocal critics argued that such participation was tantamount to participating in torture, opponents of this view saw the potential for psychologists to play a major role in protecting national security by assisting government personnel in obtaining information about potential threats.

The debate about the involvement of psychologists in controversial activities such as enhanced interrogation techniques culminated in a 2010 decision by the APA to amend its Ethics Code to address potential conflicts among professional ethics, legal authority, and organizational demands. Previously, the Ethics Code implied that if psychologists could not resolve such conflicts, they could adhere to the law or to demands of an organization without further consideration. The 2010 amendments to the Ethics Code were intended to affirm APA's long-standing policy that psychologists may never violate human rights, regardless of demands placed upon them.

Psychologists Mark Costanzo, Ellen Gerrity, and M. Brinton Lykes argue strongly that psychologists should not be involved in interrogations that involve forms of inhumane treatment. They assert that the involvement of psychologists in such interrogations is a violation of fundamental ethical principles.

Psychologist and intelligence expert Kirk M. Hubbard asserts that psychologists from various subdisciplines can bring a wealth of knowledge to the administration of legal interrogations. He contends that if the psychological profession does not like the use of coercion to obtain actionable information, then the profession should step up and suggest effective alternatives.

POINT

- Psychologists should be forbidden from participating in interrogations that involve the use of any form of inhuman treatment of human beings.
- Coercive interrogations are ineffective in extracting reliable information. Many survivors of torture report that they would have said anything to "make the torture stop."
- There is irrefutable evidence that techniques *less coercive* than torture have produced verifiably false confessions.

- Psychologists' involvement in coercive interrogations is a violation of ethical principles and international and domestic law.
- Torture produces severe and lasting trauma and other negative consequences for individuals and societies that support it.

COUNTERPOINT

- It is objectionable to think that it is unfair to use what is known about psychological science to protect and defend American lives and culture.
- Costanzo et al. create a scenario that is not grounded in current knowledge of terrorism, and they attempt to (mis)lead readers into thinking that legal interrogations do not yield actionable intelligence.
- The assertion that rapport and liking are the keys to obtaining information ignores the coercive pressures inherent in the circumstances. For terrorists who do not care if they live or die, there is little or no incentive to work with interrogators.
- There is no reason why psychologists cannot assist in developing effective, lawful ways to obtain actionable intelligence in fighting terrorism.
- The case of Jose Padilla (who was planning to detonate a "dirty bomb" in apartment buildings) is a prime example of how a legal interrogation of a known terrorist led to the prevention of an attack.

YES

Mark Costanzo, Ellen Gerrity, and M. Brinton Lykes

Psychologists and the Use of Torture in Interrogations

This article argues that psychologists should not be involved in interrogations that make use of torture or other forms of cruel, inhumane, or degrading treatment. The use of torture is first evaluated in light of professional ethics codes and international law. Next, research on interrogations and false confessions is reviewed and its relevance for torture-based interrogations is explored. Finally, research on the negative mental health consequences of torture for survivors and perpetrators is summarized. Based on our review, we conclude that psychologists' involvement in designing, assisting with, or participating in interrogations that make use of torture or other forms of cruel, inhumane, or degrading treatment is a violation of fundamental ethical principles, a violation of international and domestic law, and an ineffective means of extracting reliable information. Torture produces severe and lasting trauma as well as other negative consequences for individuals and for the societies that support it. The article concludes with several recommendations about how APA and other professional organizations should respond to the involvement of psychologists in interrogations that make use of torture or other forms of cruel, inhumane, or degrading treatment.

The United States and its military should immediately ban the use of torture, and psychologists should be expressly prohibited from using their expertise to plan, design, assist, or participate in interrogations that make use of torture and other forms of cruel, inhumane, or degrading treatment. The use of torture as an interrogation device is contrary to ethical standards of conduct for psychologists and is in violation of international law. Torture is ineffective as a means of extracting reliable information, and likely leads to faulty intelligence. Torture has long-term negative consequences for the mental health of both survivors and perpetrators of torture. The use of torture has far-reaching consequences for American citizens: it damages the reputation of the United States, creates hostility toward our troops, provides a pretext for cruelty against U.S. soldiers and citizens, places the United States in the company of some of the most oppressive regimes in the world, and undermines the credibility of the United States when it argues for international human rights.

From *Analyses of Social Issues and Public Policy*, 7(1), pp. 7–16, December 2007. Copyright © 2007 by The Society for the Psychological Study of Social Issues. Reprinted by permission of Wiley-Blackwell.

1. Torture as a Violation of Professional Codes of Conduct

The American Psychological Association's *Ethical Principles of Psychologists and Code of Conduct* encourages psychologists to, " . . . strive to benefit those with whom they work and take care to do no harm." These guidelines incorporate basic *principles* or *moral imperatives* that guide behavior as well as specific *codes of conduct* describing what psychologists *can* or *cannot* do and are, therefore, directly applicable to the participation of psychologists in torture or in inter-rogation situations involving harm. Psychologists, physicians, and other health and mental health professionals are also guided by international and inter-professional codes of ethics and organizational resolutions, such as the 1985 joint statement against torture issued by the American Psychiatric Asso-ciation and the American Psychological Association. In 1986, the American Psychological Association passed a *Resolution against Torture and Other Cruel, Inhuman, or Degrading Treatment*. Both statements "condemn torture wherever it occurs."

The International Union of Psychological Science (IUPsyS), the Inter-national Association of Applied Psychology (IAAP), and the International Association for Cross-Cultural Psychology (IACCP) are collaborating in the development of a Universal Declaration of Ethical Principles for Psychologists. They have identified "principles and values that provide a common moral framework . . . [to] "guide the development of differing standards as appro-priate for differing cultural contexts". . . . An analysis of eight current ethical codes identified across multiple continents revealed five cross-cutting prin-ciples: (1) respect for the dignity and rights of persons, (2) caring for others and concern for their welfare, (3) competence, (4) integrity, and (5) profes-sional, scientific, and social responsibility. Sinclair traced the origins of these eight codes to 12 documents including the Code of Hammurabi (Babylon, circa 1795–1750 BC), the Ayurvedic Instruction (India, circa 500–300 BC), the Hippocratic Oath (Greece, circa 400 BC), the (First) American Medical Associa-tion Code of Ethics (1847 AD), and the Nuremberg Code of Ethics in Medical Research (1948 AD). Among the ethical principles proposed as universal for all psychologists is that they "uphold the value of taking care to do no harm to individuals, families, groups, and communities."

A wide range of declarations, conventions, and principles govern the conduct of doctors and all health professionals in the context of torture (e.g., the World Medical Association's (1975) Tokyo Declaration), including the establishment of international standards for medical assessments of allega-tions of torture (e.g., the *Manual on the Effective Investigation and Documenta-tion of Torture and Other Cruel, Inhuman or Degrading Treatment or Punishment (Istanbul Protocol)*, United Nations, 1999). Specific restrictions prohibiting the participation of medical personnel in torture and degrading interrogation practices were established in the 1982 United Nations' *"Principles of Medical Ethics* (United Nations, 1982)." The World Medical Association has also estab-lished that it is not ethically appropriate for physicians or other health profes-sionals to serve as consultants or advisors in interrogation.

Psychologists can find themselves in contexts where expected professional and ethical conduct and the protection of human rights conflict with compliance with government policies and practices. A 2002 report of Physicians for Human Rights described this "dual loyalty" now confronting a growing number of health professionals within and outside of the Armed Forces. This tension is particularly acute when such policies and practices run counter to international declarations, laws, and conventions that protect human rights (see, for example, the report of Army Regulation-15, 2005).

2. Torture as a Violation of Law

As citizens, psychologists in the United States are required to observe a wide range of international and national treaties, conventions, and laws that prohibit torture. The *Universal Declaration of Human Rights* (United Nations, 1948) and the *International Covenant on Civil and Political Rights* (United Nations, adopted in 1966, entered into force, 1976), alongside six other core international human rights treaties, constitute an international "bill of human rights" that guarantees freedom from torture and cruel, inhuman, or degrading treatment (see Article 5 of the Universal Declaration on Human Rights).

Article 1 of the UN *Convention against Torture and other Cruel, Inhuman or Degrading Treatment (CAT),* (United Nations, 1984, 1987), which was signed by the United States in 1988 and ratified in 1994, defines torture during interrogation as:

Any act by which severe pain or suffering, whether physical or mental, is intentionally inflicted on a person for such purposes as obtaining from him or a third person information or a confession . . . when such pain or suffering is inflicted by or at the instigation of or with the consent or acquiescence of a public official or other person acting in an official capacity.

Article 2 (2) of the Convention outlines specific additional prohibitions and obligations of states that: "No exceptional circumstances whatsoever, whether a state of war or a threat of war, internal political instability or any other public emergency, may be invoked as a justification of torture." . . .

Multiple U.S. laws and resolutions, including the U.S. Bill of Rights, the U.S. Constitution, and the joint congressional resolution opposing torture that was signed into law by President Reagan on October 4, 1984 (United States Congress, 1984), prohibit cruel, inhuman, or degrading treatment or torture. Other conventions to which the United States subscribes prohibit any form of torture as a means of gathering information in times of war (see, for example, the *Geneva Conventions* (1949) and the *European Convention (1989)*) relative to the treatment of prisoners of war and to the prevention of torture. In this tradition, Senator John McCain's Amendment (section 1403 of H.R. 1815), approved by the U.S. Congress and signed by President Bush at the end of 2005, prohibits torture and cruel, inhumane, and degrading treatment. However, President Bush's less widely publicized accompanying "signing statement" indicated that he would interpret the law in a manner consistent with his presidential powers, re-igniting debate in many circles within and beyond government. The inconclusiveness of debates among branches of government, and the condemnation of the United States's treatment of prisoners at Guantánamo and Abu Ghraib by foreign governments as well as the UN Committee Against Torture, underscore the urgent need to clarify ethical guidelines for psychologists.

3. Research on Interrogations and the Utility of Torture as an Interrogation Tool

Although the primary purpose of torture is to terrorize a group and break the resistance of an enemy, the use of torture is frequently justified as an interrogation device. However, there is no evidence that torture is an effective means of gathering reliable information. Many survivors of torture report they that would have said anything to "make the torture stop." Those who make the claim that "torture works" offer as evidence only unverifiable anecdotal accounts. Even if there are cases where torture may have preceded the disclosure of useful information, it is impossible to know whether less coercive forms of interrogation might have yielded the same or even better results.

Because torture-based interrogations are generally conducted in secret, there is no systematic research on the relationship between torture and false confessions. However, there is irrefutable evidence from the civilian criminal justice system that techniques *less coercive* than torture have produced verifiably false confessions in a surprising number of cases. An analysis of DNA exonerations of innocent but wrongly convicted criminal suspects revealed that false confessions are the second most frequent cause of wrongful convictions, accounting for 24% of the total. . . . In a recent large-scale study, Drizin and Leo identified 125 proven false confessions over a 30-year period. Two characteristics of these known false confessions are notable. First, they tended to occur in the most serious cases—81% confessed to the crime of murder, and another 9% confessed to the crime of rape. Second, because only *proven* false confessions were included (e.g., cases where the confessor was exonerated by DNA evidence or cases where the alleged crime never occurred), the actual number of false confessions is likely to be substantially higher. Military action based on false information extracted through the use of torture has the potential to jeopardize the lives of military personnel and civilians.

The defining feature of an interrogation is the presumption that a suspect is lying or withholding vital information. If torture is an available option, interrogators are likely to resort to torture when they believe a suspect is lying about what he or she knows or does not know. However, there is no reason to believe that interrogators are able to tell whether or not a suspect is lying. Indeed, there is considerable research demonstrating that trained interrogators are *not* accurate in judging the truthfulness of the suspects they interrogate. Overall, people with relevant professional training (e.g., interrogators, polygraphers, customs officers) are able to detect deception at a level only slightly above chance. Moreover, some researchers have identified a troubling perceptual bias among people who have received interrogation training—an increased tendency to believe that others are lying to them. In addition, although specialized training in interrogation techniques does not improve the ability to discern lying, it does increase the confidence of interrogators in their ability to tell whether a suspect is lying or withholding information. The presumption that a suspect is lying, in combination with the overconfidence produced by interrogation training, leads to a biased style of questioning which seeks to confirm guilt while ignoring or discounting information that suggests that a suspect is being truthful. There is also evidence that interrogators become most coercive when questioning innocent suspects, because truthful suspects are regarded as resistant and defiant. Thus, interrogators may be especially likely to resort to torture when faced with persistent denials by innocent suspects. Under such conditions, torture may be used to punish a suspect or as an expression of frustration and desperation on the part of the interrogator. More broadly, there is substantial evidence that judgments about others are influenced by conscious and nonconscious stereotyping and prejudice. Prejudice may lead interrogators to target suspects for torture based on physical appearance, ethnicity, or erroneous stereotypes about behavioral cues.

Unless local authorities (e.g., commanders in charge of a military detention facility) explicitly prohibit the use of torture in interrogations, the risk of torture will be unacceptably high. Decades of research by social psychologists has demonstrated that strong situational forces can overwhelm people's better impulses and cause good people to treat others cruelly. These forces include the presence of an authority figure who appears to sanction the use of cruelty, and a large power disparity between groups, such as the disparity that exists between prisoners and guards. In addition, the dehumanization and demonization of the enemy that occurs during times of intense group conflict—particularly during times of war—reduce inhibitions against cruelty. All of these conditions, combined with the stresses of long-term confinement, appear to have been present at Abu Ghraib. The well-documented reports of torture at the Abu Ghraib and Guantanamo Bay facilities serve as disturbing reminders that it is essential for military authorities to issue clear directives about unacceptable practices in the interrogation of prisoners. These directives need to be combined with effective monitoring of military detention facilities, especially during times of war.

In an effort to circumvent ethical concerns and the lack of evidence about the effectiveness of torture, advocates of the use of torture often resort to hypothetical arguments such as the "ticking time bomb scenario." This frequently used justification for the use of torture as an interrogation tactic presupposes that the United States has in its custody a terrorist who has knowledge of the location of a time bomb that will soon explode and kill thousands of innocent people. Embedded in this implausible scenario are several questionable assumptions: that it is known for certain that the suspect possesses specific "actionable" knowledge that would avert the disaster; that the threat is imminent; that only torture would lead to the disclosure of the information; and that torture is the fastest means of extracting valid, actionable information. Of course, this scenario also recasts the person who tortures as a principled, heroic figure who reluctantly uses torture to save innocent lives. While this scenario might provide a useful stimulus for discussion in college ethics courses, or an interesting plot device for a television drama, we can find no evidence that it has ever occurred and it appears highly improbable.

4. The Effects of Torture on Survivors and Perpetrators

Torture is one of the most extreme forms of human violence, resulting in both physical and psychological consequences. It is also widespread and occurs throughout much of the world. Despite potentially confounding variables, including related stressors (such as refugee experiences or traumatic bereavement), and comorbid conditions (such as anxiety, depression, or physical injury), torture itself has been shown to be directly linked to posttraumatic stress disorder (PTSD) and other symptoms and disabilities. The findings from both uncontrolled and controlled studies have produced substantial evidence that for some individuals, torture has serious and long-lasting psychological consequences.

Most trauma experts—including survivors of torture, mental health researchers, and therapists—agree that the psychiatric diagnosis of PTSD is relevant for torture survivors. However, these same experts emphasize that the consequences of torture go beyond psychiatric diagnoses. Turner and Gorst-Unsworth highlighted four common themes in the complex picture of torture and its consequences: (1) PTSD as a result of specific torture experiences; (2) depression as a result of multiple losses associated with torture; (3) physical symptoms resulting from the specific forms of torture; and (4) the "existential dilemma" of surviving in a world in which torture is a reality. The 10th revision of the *International Classification of Diseases* includes a diagnosis of "Enduring Personality Change after Catastrophic Experience" as one effort to capture the long-term existential consequences of the tearing up of a social world caused by torture. The profound psychological and physical consequences of torture are also evident in several carefully written personal accounts of the experience of torture.

Comprehensive reviews of the psychological effects of torture have systematically evaluated research with torture survivors, examining the unique consequences associated with torture and the complex interaction of social, environmental, and justice-related issues. As noted in these reviews, the psychological problems most commonly reported by torture survivors in research studies include (a) psychological symptoms (anxiety, depression, irritability or aggressiveness, emotional instability, self-isolation or social withdrawal); (b) cognitive symptoms (confusion or disorientation, impaired memory and concentration); and (c) neurovegetative symptoms (insomnia, nightmares, sexual dysfunction). Other findings reported in studies of torture survivors include abnormal sleep patterns, brain damage, and personality changes. The effects of torture can extend throughout the life of the survivor affecting his or her psychological, familial, and economic functioning. Such consequences have also been shown to be transmitted across generations in studies of various victim/survivor populations and across trauma types.

Studies conducted over the past 15 years strongly suggest that people who develop PTSD may also experience serious neurobiological changes, including changes in the body's ability to respond to stress (through alterations in stress hormones), and changes in the hippocampus, an area in the brain related to contextual memory. Thus, the development of PTSD has direct and long-term implications for the functioning of numerous biological systems essential to human functioning.

For survivors, having "healers" participating in their torture by supporting interrogators or providing medical treatment in order to prolong torture can erode future recovery by damaging the legitimate role that physicians or therapists could provide in offering treatment or social support, essential components in the recovery of trauma survivors. For these reasons, numerous medical associations, including the American Psychiatric Association and the World Medical Association, include as part of their ethical and professional standards a complete prohibition against participation of their members in interrogation, torture, or other forms of ill treatment. Similarly, the South African Truth and Reconciliation Commission documented how health providers were at times complicit in human rights abuses under apartheid, and through their report, hoped to shed light on this worldwide phenomenon and work toward an international effort to prevent such abuses from occurring.

Research that focuses directly on the participation of health professionals in torture and interrogation has documented important contextual issues for understanding how such participation can occur. Robert Lifton interviewed Nazi doctors who participated in human experimentation and killings, and found them to be "normal professionals" who offered medical justifications for their actions. In studies of physicians and other health providers who are involved in forms of military interrogation, Lifton elaborates on "atrocity-producing" environments in which normal individuals may forsake personal or professional values in an environment where torture is the norm. Furthermore, these same health care professionals may, through their actions, transfer legitimacy to a situation, supporting an illusion for all participants that some form of therapy or medical purpose is involved.

Other studies of those who torture have provided details about the step-by-step training that can transform ordinary people into people who can and will torture others, by systematically providing justifications for actions, professional or role authority, and secrecy. Participation in torture and other atrocities has been shown to have long-term negative psychological consequences for perpetrators, even in situations where professional or environmental justifications were offered to them in the context of their actions. . . .

Therefore, we urge APA and other scholarly and professional associations of psychologists to:

1. Unambiguously condemn the use of torture and other forms of cruel, inhuman, or degrading treatment as interrogation devices and call upon the U.S. government and its military to explicitly ban the use of such treatment and enforce all laws and regulations prohibiting its use.

2. Conduct an independent investigation of the extent to which psychologists have been involved in using torture or other cruel, inhuman, or degrading treatment as interrogation tools. If psychologists are found to have participated in the design or conduct of interrogations that have made use of torture, they should be appropriately sanctioned by APA and other professional organizations.
3. Expressly forbid psychologists from planning, designing, assisting, or participating in interrogations that involve the use of torture and any form of cruel, inhuman, or degrading treatment of human beings.
4. Develop specific guidelines and explicit codes of conduct for psychologists working in contexts of war and imprisonment. These guidelines should be consistent with international treaties and human rights covenants as well as guidelines developed for health professionals. Such guidelines should include meaningful enforcement, processes for the investigation of violations, and professional and legal consequences for violations.

Kirk M. Hubbard

 NO

Psychologists and Interrogations: What's Torture Got to Do with It?

In an article that has been endorsed by SPSSI, Costanzo, Gerrity, and Lykes (2007) argue that "psychologists should not be involved in interrogations that make use of torture or other forms of cruel, inhumane, or degrading treatment" (doi: 10.1111/j.1530-2415.2007.00118.x). Their statement is ironic, for torture is illegal in the United States. But even more importantly, it seems to come from and apply to a world that no longer exists, and that simplifies issues so that they can be as one might like them to be. As recent events in England illustrate (August 2006), Islamic militants seek to kill us and undermine if not destroy our way of life. We have only to listen to what they say and watch their actions in order to know that regardless of how we would like things to be, they mean us harm. We also know from findings of the 9/11 commission that this problem did not start, nor will it likely finish, with the current presidential administration. An important point that is illustrated is that we no longer live in a world where people agree on what is ethical or even acceptable, and where concern for other humans transcends familial ties. When adolescents carry bombs on their bodies and plan suicides that will kill others, we know that shared values no longer exist. In the words of Scottish comedian Billy Connolly, "It seems to me that Islam and Christianity and Judaism all have the same god, and he's telling them all different things."

A prominent challenge for psychologists is determining how narrowly or broadly the field should prescribe what is acceptable behavior for professionals working with diverse populations, for increasingly psychologists come from differing backgrounds and hold varying beliefs. Effective practice with one population may be totally ineffective with another; we as a profession have not yet thoughtfully addressed how we balance what one culture defines as ethical against what another could view as necessary to be successful. The comment by Costanzo et al., and its rejoinders, provide a good illustration, namely, how does one balance standards of behaviors against results. What if, hypothetically, Middle Eastern psychologists told us that in order to successfully obtain information from suspected terrorists we would have to use approaches that we found inappropriate or unethical? I reject the idea that it is somehow unfair to use what we know about psychological science to protect our families and defend our lives and culture. Many areas of psychology

From *Analyses of Social Issues and Public Policy*, 7(1), pp. 29–33, December 2007. Copyright © 2007 by The Society for the Psychological Study of Social Issues. Reprinted by permission of Wiley-Blackwell.

owe their advancement in large part to research conducted under the auspices of the military and supported by it. Clinical psychology has roots in the military and the OSS, and many psychologists have proudly defended their country with honor. In this context, the SPSSI policy statement by Costanzo et al. is both unnecessary and gratuitous. It is unnecessary because torture is already illegal in the United States. It is gratuitous because it feeds the egos of those who endorse it. It gives the illusion of possessing a higher moral ground, when in fact what is left unsaid and readable between the lines reveals it to be ideological and political. As parallels, SPSSI might put out policy statements against rape and murder, for those also are illegal, and we would not want our members participating in such behaviors. But murder and rape occur despite being illegal, and similarly, behaviors that are classified as torture may periodically occur. But that does not mean that torture is a government-sanctioned tool for conducting interrogations or even acceptable to use. There are specific and strict federal guidelines regarding what constitutes a legal and acceptable interrogation. I submit that there is no evidence that psychologists were involved in cases of torture—certainly not at Abu Ghraib prison.

A second issue of import is whether or not psychologists should be involved in legal interrogations. Again, the position of the authors is too simplistic. I take exception to the suggestion that all psychologists should be banned from assisting in legal interrogations. It is one thing to "ban" psychologists who are members of APA from engaging in torture, but quite another to prohibit them from consulting or advising during legal interrogations. First, there are many types of psychologists (social psychologist, industrial/organizational psychologists, and experimental psychologists, for example) who are not licensed mental health professionals and therefore should not be bound by the doctor/patient relationship code of ethics. Yet they bring information from their fields that help exert influence. Second, I object to the "psychocentric" and seemingly arrogant position that receiving training in psychology trumps all other roles a person may choose to pursue, or because of circumstances, are obliged to fulfill. Is it not possible for someone to receive training in psychology and then decide to pursue a career in law enforcement and engage in legal interrogations? Should being a psychologist as well as a law enforcement agent prohibit their participation if psychologists are prohibited? And, third, how is psychology accountable to society—should it withhold information about ways in which to protect our population or to influence terrorists to disclose information? What does psychology owe society? Should we focus exclusively on individuals with whom psychologists come in contact? What about helping to protect communities from terrorism? I simply do not believe that at a policy level we should decide that the "rights" of an individual count more than the rights and safety of society. APA and SPSSI should do something positive to fight terrorism rather than merely sit on the sidelines and criticize others who are trying to protect the United States from another senseless 9/11 attack. Honorable men and women are at war with those who seek to harm us, and the rest of us are at risk from terrorists. If psychology wants to make a positive contribution, the profession should accept that it is sometimes necessary to get information from those who would harm us and are intentionally withholding information that could stop attacks. If we as a profession do not like the use of coercion to obtain actionable information, then we as a profession should be willing to step up to the plate and suggest reliable and effective alternatives that do not rely on psychological or physical coercion. Have we as professional organizations of psychologists committed resources to develop ethical, nonpunishing approaches that improve the quality of information that we can extract from individuals who are not willing to share it?

I also find it ironic that SPSSI can so readily become exercised about cruel and degrading treatment of suspected terrorists, yet conduct only limited research on similar behaviors that are manifested all too frequently in military boot camps, in legal police interrogations, in U.S. prisons, and government psychiatric hospitals. Indeed, even college fraternities and schoolyard bullies engage in cruel and degrading behavior. Why is it so easy for SPSSI to react so adamantly about illegal interrogations, yet do so little about domestic kinds of cruel and degrading treatment?

I also wonder how Costanzo et al. would feel if the "ticking time bomb scenario" that they attempt to render as "implausible" were to occur. Would they feel responsible for telling U.S. citizens that it won't ever happen? The "ticking bomb" scenario may be implausible for many APA members, but it was very real for those individuals interrogating Khalid Sheik Mohammed or Abu Zubayadh. Instead of focusing on decades old research that may no longer be relevant, Constanzo et al. might have cited the Jose Padilla case that was covered by the press. As readers may recall, Jose Padilla was a trained al Qaeda operative who was arrested as he tried to enter the United States in Chicago on May 8, 2002. He had accepted an assignment to destroy apartment buildings and had planned to detonate a radiological device commonly referred to as a "dirty bomb." As reported by CNN (June 11, 2002) and *Time* (June 16, 2002), Padilla was arrested directly as a result of an interrogation of captured senior al Qaeda member Abu Zubaydah. The Padilla case is a prime example of how a legal interrogation of a known terrorist led to the prevention of another terrorist attack.

Similarly, imagine that al Qaeda leader Abu Mussib al Zarqawri has been captured alive in Iraq rather than killed by bombings. Is there anyone who believes that he would have no potentially worthwhile knowledge of attacks planned to occur in the days following his capture? Costanzo et al. create a scenario that is not grounded in current knowledge of terrorism in general and terrorists in particular when they attempt to (mis)lead us into thinking legal interrogations do not yield actionable intelligence.

The prototypical "expert" on interrogation asserts that information is more reliable when voluntarily given rather than coerced. Well, of course it is. The expert then may assert that the way to elicit voluntary provision of information is to build a relationship with the terrorist so that the terrorist likes you or to appeal to common values so the terrorist sees your interests as converging with his/hers, and then the terrorist will tell you what you need to know. Such reasoning ignores the demand characteristics of both the prototypical law enforcement interrogation and the terrorist's values and operational intent. Are we to think the terrorist has the following thoughts: "You know, nobody has ever been as nice to me as these people—I'm going to turn my back on my God and my life's work and tell them what they what to know." Alternatively, maybe the terrorist will think "What a clever way of asking that question. Now that they put it that way, I have no choice but to tell them what they need to know to disrupt my plans." Unfortunately, it is difficult to envision scenarios where useful information will be forthcoming.

For many Westerners caught after committing a crime, the psychological pressure of trying to influence whether or not they are charged, what they are charged with, and the kind of punishment they are likely to receive coerces them into working with the person who seems to understand them to make the best deal in a bad set of circumstances. The "experts'" assertion that rapport and liking are the keys to obtaining information, ignore the coercive pressures inherent in the circumstances. To pretend that these coercive pressures are not present does not make them go away. For terrorists who do not care if they live or die and have no fear of prison, there is little or no incentive to work with interrogators. And, to our discredit, we as psychologists have contributed little to increasing our understanding of circumstances like these and techniques of persuasion that might be effective.

Lastly, I found the call for an independent investigation of the extent to which psychologists have been involved in using torture or other cruel, inhuman, or degrading treatment during an interrogation unwarranted. Costanzo et al. present virtually no evidence that psychologists have been involved in even a single case. APA/SPSSI has no authority by which to sanction nonmembers. Many psychologists are choosing not to join APA or to allow their memberships to lapse, believing that it does not represent their interests and values. In my opinion, APA and some of its divisions have drifted from a being a professional organization advancing the science of psychology and translating research to action and policy, to a point where they are promoting a social and political agenda.

I am opposed to torture. But I endorse the use of interrogation when used consistently with current federal law and conducted by trained interrogators. And I certainly see no reason why psychologists cannot assist in developing effective, lawful ways to obtain actionable intelligence in fighting terrorism. If the information can be obtained noncoercively, all the better. Social psychology taught us how to use social influence in getting people to do things they ordinarily would not do and buy things they often do not need or want. In my view, it is common sense that you would want psychologists involved in the interrogation of known terrorists. As psychologists, rather than decrying illegal use of cruel and inhumane treatment to obtain information, we should work to develop reliable noncoercive ways to get people to tell us about terrorist activity of which they have knowledge and are attempting to withhold. We need to take a proactive stance in saving lives and preventing acts of terror. The Costanzo et al. article does not appreciably help psychology to move forward, for it limits opportunities for psychologists to gain first-hand knowledge of the nature of the challenges interrogators face, and focuses on current approaches rather than on developing new ones that apply and improve current psychological knowledge.

CHALLENGE QUESTIONS

Is It Unethical for Psychologists to Be Involved in Coercive Interrogations?

1. What variables should be considered in drawing the line between interrogation techniques that are inhumane and those that are effective, but not cruel?
2. How might participation in enhanced interrogation techniques affect the psychological well-being and functioning of the interrogators?
3. Imagine that you are a psychologist who is being hired to develop effective techniques for extracting critical information from suspected terrorists. With whom would you consult to ensure that the techniques are not in violation of human rights?
4. What kind of responsibility does society have for detainees who have been coercively interrogated, but then released when it becomes apparent that they lack useful information?
5. Some social observers contend that as the years have passed since the 9/11 attacks, feelings of vulnerability among Americans have lessened, while critiques of government efforts to protect national security have escalated. What are your thoughts on this observation?

Suggested Readings

Freedman, A.M. (2009). The work of psychologists in the U.S. intelligence community. *Consulting Psychology Journal: Practice and Research, 61*(1), 68–83.

Halpern, A.L., Halpern, J.H., & Doherty, S.B. (2008). "Enhanced" interrogation of detainees: Do psychologist and psychiatrists participate? *Philosophy, Ethics, and Humanities in Medicine, 3,* 21.

Kalbeitzer, R. (2009). Psychologists and interrogations: Ethical dilemmas in times of war. *Ethics and Behavior, 19*(2), 156–168.

Pope, K.S., & Gutheil, T.G. (2009). Contrasting ethical principles of physicians and psychologists concerning interrogation of detainees. *BMJ, 338,* b1653.

Soldz, S. (2008). Healers or interrogators: Psychology and the United States torture regime. *Psychoanalytic Dialogues, 18*(5), 592–613.

ISSUE 14

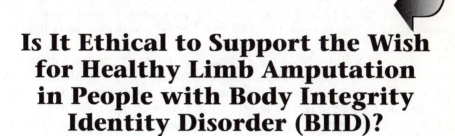

Is It Ethical to Support the Wish for Healthy Limb Amputation in People with Body Integrity Identity Disorder (BIID)?

YES: Tim Bayne and Neil Levy, from "Amputees by Choice: Body Integrity Identity Disorder and the Ethics of Amputation," *Journal of Applied Philosophy* (vol. 22, no. 1, 2005)

NO: Wesley J. Smith, from "Secondhand Smoke: Blog of Wesley J. Smith (2007)

ISSUE SUMMARY

YES: Authors Tim Bayne and Neil Levy argue that people with body integrity identity disorder are in emotional pain because of their experience of incongruity between their body image and their actual body. Such individuals should be accorded with their prerogative to have a healthy limb amputated.

NO: Author Wesley J. Smith objects to the notion of acquiescing to the wishes for healthy limb amputation in people whom he views as severely mentally disturbed. Smith asserts that these people need treatment, not amputation.

$\mathbf{A}$lthough millions of people undergo elective cosmetic surgery each year, very little controversy has arisen about the ethics. In contrast, a different response emerges when the topic turns to elective amputation of healthy limbs. People with body integrity identity disorder (BIID) have a form of body dysmorphic disorder so extreme that they feel compelled to seek amputation of a healthy body part, claiming that they are so psychologically pained by the discrepancy between their actual body and their body image that they live a life of torment. The question arises, then, about whether it is appropriate for health professionals to acquiesce to the wishes of people with BIID (who refer to themselves as "wannabes") to amputate a healthy limb, with the aim of satisfying the wish of these individuals to enhance psychological well-being.

Tim Bayne and Neil Levy argue that surgeons should accede to the requests of people with BIID requesting healthy limb amputation. These authors sympathize with the plight of people who have spent much of their lives with a nonstandard sense of embodiment. Bayne and Levy believe that would-be amputees are likely to persist in their desire for amputation and might actually take matters into their own hands, risking extensive injury or death in doing so.

Wesley J. Smith views would-be amputees as severely mentally disturbed individuals who need treatment, not amputation. In light of the fact that amputation is an irreversible procedure, insufficient thought is given to the likelihood of postamputation regret. Smith contends that these individuals should be protected from harming themselves, and he critiques the notion of "choice" in such matters. Physicians who collude with emotionally unstable individuals in such situations are failing to adhere to their oath to do no harm.

POINT

- People with BIID have a nonstandard sense of embodiment, and their experience of themselves has been built around this sense. To require them to change it is, to some extent, to require them to change who they are.
- Many would-be amputees will take matters into their own hands, risking extensive injury or death in doing so. Surgery may be the least of all evils.

- A would-be amputee can have a reasonable understanding of what life as an amputee would be like before becoming an amputee.
- An individual's conception of his or her own good should be respected in medical decision-making contexts.
- In the case of at least some would-be amputees, the limb in question is not as healthy as it might appear: in an important sense, a limb that is not experienced as one's own is not in fact one's own.

COUNTERPOINT

- Only a severely mentally disturbed person would want a healthy leg, arm, hand, or foot cut off. Such people need treatment, not amputation.

- Physicians are duty-bound to "do no harm," and thus should refuse to provide harmful medical services to patients—no matter how earnest the request. A physician who accedes to a patient's request to be mutilated would essentially be abandoning the patient.
- Once a limb is gone, it is gone for good. What if the patient has regrets?

- Would-be amputees need to be protected from harming themselves.

- If we allow doctors to remove healthy limbs, what is next? Helping people who want to cut themselves, slice themselves repeatedly? Or, helping people who want to burn themselves do so safely?

YES

Tim Bayne and Neil Levy

Amputees by Choice: Body Integrity Identity Disorder and the Ethics of Amputation

In 1997, a Scottish surgeon by the name of Robert Smith was approached by a man with an unusual request: he wanted his apparently healthy lower left leg amputated. Although details about the case are sketchy, the would-be amputee appears to have desired the amputation on the grounds that his left foot wasn't part of him—it felt alien. After consultation with psychiatrists, Smith performed the amputation. Two and a half years later, the patient reported that his life had been transformed for the better by the operation.[1] A second patient was also reported as having been satisfied with his amputation.[2]

Smith was scheduled to perform further amputations of healthy limbs when the story broke in the media. Predictably, there was a public outcry, and Smith's hospital instructed him to cease performing such operations. At present, no hospital offers healthy limb amputations. Would-be amputees—or 'wannabes', as they refer to themselves—would appear to number in the thousands. They have their own websites and are the subject of a recent documentary.[3]

In this paper, we are concerned with two basic questions. First, what would motivate someone to have an apparently healthy limb amputated? Second, under what conditions is it reasonable for doctors to accede to such requests? We believe that the first question can shed significant light on the second, showing that, on the evidence available today, such amputations may be morally permissible.

What Is It Like to Be a Wannabe?

What motivates someone to desire the amputation of a healthy limb? One possibility is that wannabes suffer from Body Dysmorphic Disorder (BDD), a condition in which the individual believes, incorrectly, that a part of their body is diseased or exceedingly ugly.[4] This belief can be a matter of intense concern for the individual and is resistant to evidence against it. BDD appears to be closely akin to anorexia nervosa, in that both appear to be monothematic delusions that are sustained by misperceptions of one's own body.[5] Perhaps wannabes desire amputation in order to rid themselves of a limb that they believe to be diseased or ugly.

A second explanation is that wannabes have a sexual attraction to amputees or to being an amputee.[6] On this account, the desire for amputation would stem from apotemnophilia, which is a kind of paraphilia—a psychosexual disorder. Apotemnophiles are sexually attracted to amputees, and sexually excited by the notion that they might become amputees themselves.

A third explanation is that there is a mismatch between the wannabe's experience of their body and the actual structure of their body. On this view, there is a mismatch between their body and their body as they experience it—what we might call their phenomenal (or subjective) body. On this view, which is increasingly gaining favour, wannabes suffer from Body Integrity Identity Disorder (BIID), also known as Amputee Identity Disorder (AID).[7]

The BIID account can be developed in different ways depending on the type of bodily representation that is thought to be involved. On the one hand, one could conceive of BIID in terms of a mismatch between the patient's body and their body *schema*. The body schema is a representation of one's body that is used in the automatic regulation of posture and movement.[8] It operates sub-personally and sub-consciously, guiding the parts of one's body to successful performance of action. The body schema is a dynamic structure, providing a moment-by-moment sense of how one's body parts are articulated.

Mismatches between a person's body schema and their actual body are not uncommon. Individuals who lose (or have never had) a limb often experience a phantom limb: they feel as though the limb is still there, and in some cases attempt to employ it in order to carry out actions—such as answering the telephone. Whereas the body schema of individuals with phantom limbs includes body parts that they lack, other patients have no body schema for body parts they have. Patients who have undergone deafferentation from the neck down lose any proprioceptive sense of how their limbs are currently positioned, and rely on visual cues to control action.[9]

Perhaps wannabes also have a body schema that fails to incorporate the full extent of their bodies. Although we do not want to dismiss this suggestion, the evidence we have to date weighs against this account. As far as we know, wannabes do not exhibit any of the impairments in control of movement that one would expect in a person with a distorted or incomplete body schema. Further, wannabes who have had the amputation they desire seem, as far as we can tell, to be content to use a prosthesis. This suggests that the problem they suffer from is not primarily a conflict between their body and their body schema.

A more plausible possibility is that BIID involves a mismatch between the wannabe's body and their body *image*. One's body image is a consciously accessible representation of the general shape and structure of one's body. The body image is derived from a number of sources, including visual experience, proprioceptive experience, and tactile experience. It structures one's bodily sensations (aches, pains, tickles, and so on), and forms the basis of one's beliefs about oneself.[10]

Discrepancies between a person's body and their body image occur in a wide range of cases, known as asomatognosias. Asomatognosia can occur as a result of the loss of proprioception, in post-stroke neglect, and in the context of depersonalisation.[11] In many of these cases, the patient in question has become delusional and denies either the existence of the affected limb or their ownership of it. In a condition known as somatoparaphrenia, patients will even ascribe ownership of their limbs to another person.[12]

Other forms of asomatognosia concern only the patient's perception of their body and leave the doxastic component of their body image intact. Oliver Sacks eloquently describes his own experience of this condition:

> In that instant, that very first encounter, *I knew not my leg*. It was utterly strange, not-mine, unfamiliar. I gazed upon it with absolute non-recognition [. . .] The more I gazed at that cylinder of chalk, the more alien and incomprehensible it appeared to me. I could no longer feel it as mine, as part of me. It seemed to bear no relation whatever to me. It was absolutely not-me—and yet, impossibly, it was attached to me—and even more impossibly, continuous with me.[13]

Sacks did not become delusional—he knew that the leg in question was his—but he no longer experienced it as his own. Perhaps BIID involves a similar form of nondelusional somatic alienation. If so, then there might be a very real sense in which the limb in question—or at least, the neuronal representation of it—is not healthy.

It is also tempting to draw parallels between BIID and the discrepancy between body image and the person's actual body that characterizes anorexia nervosa and bulimia nervosa.[14] Of course, there are also important differences between these conditions: Whereas the person with anorexia or bulimia fails to (fully) recognize the discrepancy between her body and her body image, the wannabe is all too aware of this discrepancy.

None of the three explanations of the desire for amputation that we have outlined attempts to provide *complete* models of the phenomenon: the BDD model does not attempt to explain why wannabes might regard the limb in question as diseased or ugly; the apotemnophilia model does not attempt to explain why wannabes might be sexually attracted to a conception of themselves as amputees; and the BIID model does not attempt to explain why wannabes might fail to incorporate the limb into their body image. Clearly these models can, at best, provide only a first step in understanding why someone might become a wannabe. Nevertheless, even though these models are incomplete, we can make some progress in evaluating them.

A first point to make is that these models may not be exclusive. It could be that there are two or three bases for the desire for amputation, with some patients suffering from BDD, others suffering from a paraphilia, and others suffering from a form of BIID. Some individuals might even suffer from a combination of these disorders. Perhaps, for example, the sexual element is better conceived of as a common, though not inevitable, element of asomatognosia. Sexuality is, after all, an essential ingredient in most people's sense of identity. Elliott reports that at least one wannabe (who is also a psychologist) characterizes their desire for amputation as indissolubly a matter of sex *and* identity.[15] Like Gender Identity Disorder, BIID might be importantly sexual without ceasing to be essentially concerned with identity.

However, although each of the three models might play some role in accounting for the desire for healthy limb amputation, we can also ask which model best fits most wannabes. The initial media stories and a subsequent BBC documentary, *Complete Obsession*, identified Robert Smith's patients as suffering from BDD. However, there seems good reason to doubt whether any of these individuals suffered from BDD, strictly speaking. Neither of the two individuals featured in *Complete Obsession* appears to find their limbs diseased or ugly. Instead, they feel in some way alienated from them. Further evidence against the BDD hypothesis is provided by recent research by Michael First.[16] First conducted in-depth anonymous interviews with 52 wannabes, nine of whom had either amputated one of their limbs themselves or had enlisted a surgeon to amputate it. Only one of the 52 individuals interviewed cited the ugliness of the limb as a reason for wanting the amputation.

What about the suggestion that the desire for amputation stems from apotemphilia? First's study provides limited grounds for thinking that the desire for amputation might have a sexual basis in some cases. 15% (n = 8) of First's interviewees cited feelings of sexual arousal as their primary reason for desiring amputation, and 52% cited it as their secondary reason. Further, 87% of his subjects reported being sexually attracted to amputees. Additional support for the apotemenophilia hypothesis stems from the fact that there is a large overlap between the classes of devotees (acrotomophiles: people sexually attracted to amputees), pretenders (people who consciously fake a disability) and wannabes. More than 50% of devotees are also pretenders and wannabes, suggesting a common cause for all three syndromes.[17] Because of this overlap, the data researchers have gathered on devotees may be relevant to the desire for amputation.

Devotees are apparently more sexually attracted to the *idea* of amputation than to amputees themselves. Though many have had sexual relations with amputees, few go on to establish long-term relationships with particular individuals. As Riddle puts it, for the acrotomophile, 'No amputee is the right amputee'.[18] Bruno suggests that this fact is evidence that acrotomophilia essentially involves projection: the wannabe imagines themselves in place of the amputee. Acrotomophilia is apotemnophilia displaced, projected onto others. If apotemnophilia is essentially a body integrity disorder, Bruno seems to think, it could not be displaced so easily. But it seems just as plausible to interpret the acrotomophile's lack of interest in the individual amputee as evidence that it is a concern with his *own* body that motivates the devotee.

In any case, although First's study provides some support for thinking that the desire for amputation can have a sexual component in some instances, it offers little support for the paraphilia hypothesis as the best explanation of the disorder. After all, only 15% of wannabes identified sexual arousal as the primary motivation for amputation: this leaves 85% unaccounted for.

First's data provides equivocal support for the third model, on which the desire for amputation derives from the experience of a gulf between one's actual body and one's subjective or lived body. The leading primary reason First's subjects gave for wanting an amputation was to restore them to their true identity (63%, n = 33). Participants said such things as, 'I feel like an amputee with natural prostheses—they're my legs, but I want to get rid of them—they don't fit my body image', and, 'I felt like I was in the wrong body; that I am only complete with both my arm and leg off on the right side'. First suggests that this data supports the view that most wannabes suffer from BIID, which he considers akin to Gender Identity Disorder.

There is reason for caution here. For one thing, only 37% (n = 19) of First's participants said that the limb in question felt different in some way, and only 13% (n = 7) said that the limb felt like it was not their own. In addition, we know of no evidence that wannabes suffer from the kinds of sensory and attentional impairments—such as neglect—that tend to accompany, and perhaps underlie, standard forms of asomatognosia.

Perhaps the notion of body image that First's subjects have in mind is closer to that of the self-image of the person who wants cosmetic surgery, say, for breast enlargement. She knows that she has small breasts, but her idealised image of herself is of someone with large breasts. She does not feel comfortable—at home—in her own body.

Although more research needs to be done about the nature and aetiology of the desire for amputation of a healthy limb, the foregoing suffices to put us in a position to make an initial foray into the ethical issues raised by such requests. We turn now to an examination of three arguments in favour of performing the requested amputations.

Harm Minimization

The first and perhaps weakest of the three arguments is familiar from other contexts. Whether wannabes are correct in thinking that their disorder requires surgery or not, we must recognize that a significant proportion of them will persist in their desire for amputation, even in the face of repeated refusals, and will go on to take matters into their own hands. The Internet sites run by wannabes often discuss relatively painless and safe ways of amputating limbs, or damaging them sufficiently to ensure that surgeons have no choice but to amputate. Six of the 52 participants in First's study had amputated a limb themselves, utilizing dangerous means including a shotgun, a chainsaw and a wood chipper. Other patients have turned to incompetent surgeons after competent doctors refused to treat them. In 1998, a seventy-nine year old man died of gangrene after paying $10,000 for a black-market amputation.[19]

Given that many patients will go ahead with amputations in any case, and risk extensive injury or death in doing so, it might be argued that surgeons should accede to the requests, at least of those patients who they (or a competent authority) judge are likely to take matters into their own hands. At least so long as no other treatments are available, surgery might be the least of all evils. This raises familiar practical and ethical issues to do with participation in a practice of which we might disapprove and our inability to confidently distinguish those patients for whom the desire for an amputation might be transient from those who will persist in their demand. Because these issues are familiar and have been extensively treated elsewhere, we will not dwell on them here.

Autonomy

It is well-entrenched maxim of medical ethics that informed, autonomous desires ought to be given serious weight. An individual's conception of his or her good should be respected in medical decision-making contexts. Where a wannabe has a long-standing and informed request for amputation, it therefore seems permissible for a surgeon to act on this request.

As an analogy, consider the refusal of life-saving treatment on religious grounds. Although such decisions might result in the death of the patient, they are accorded significant weight in the context of medical decision making. If we ignore the informed and repeated wishes of the Jehovah's Witness who refuses the blood-transfusion needed to save her life, we fail to respect her as an autonomous moral agent who is living her life according to her conception of the good. If it is permissible (or even obligatory) to respect informed and autonomous rejections of life-saving treatment, it is also permissible to act on informed and autonomous requests for the amputation of a healthy limb.

Of course, the parallel between the Jehovah's Witness who refuses life-saving treatment and the wannabe who requests the amputation of a limb is not exact: the first case involves an omission but the second case involves an action. This is a difference, but whether or not it is morally relevant depends on what one makes of the act/omission distinction. We are doubtful that the distinction can do much moral work in this context, but to make the case for this position would take us too far away from our present concerns.

We shall consider two objections to the argument from autonomy. The first is that wannabes are not fully rational, and that therefore their requests should not be regarded as autonomous. As Arthur Caplan put it: 'It's absolute, utter lunacy to go along with a request to maim somebody', because there is a real question whether sufferers 'are competent to make a decision when they're running around saying, "Chop my leg off".'[20]

It is clear that some individuals who might request the amputation of healthy limbs are not rational. Neither the schizophrenic patient who believes that God is telling her to amputate her leg nor the patient with somatoparaphrenia who attempts to throw his leg out of bed because he thinks it is not his own is rational. To what extent wannabes are also incompetent depends on what kinds of wannabes they are.

There is a prima facie case to be made for thinking that wannabes suffering from BDD are not competent to request surgery. There are grounds for regarding BDD as a monothematic delusion, akin to, say, Capgras' delusion (the delusion that a close relative has been replaced by an impostor) or Cotard's delusion (the delusion that one is dead). After all, individuals with BDD appear to satisfy the DSM definition of a delusion: they have beliefs that are firmly sustained despite what almost everyone else believes and despite incontrovertible and obvious proof or evidence to the contrary.[21]

Of course, the circumscribed and monothematic nature of this delusion problematizes the charge of incompetence. These patients are not globally irrational. One might argue that despite the fact that their beliefs about the affected limb have been arrived at irrationally, their deliberations concerning what to do in the light of these beliefs are rational, and hence ought to be respected. One might draw a parallel between the position of the person who requests amputation as a result of BDD and the person who refuses life-saving treatment on the grounds of strange religious beliefs. One might argue that in both cases the agent has arrived at their beliefs irrationally, but they may have chosen a reasonable course of action given their beliefs. And—so the argument continues—one might argue that competence is undermined only by unreasonable practical reasoning, not by impaired belief-fixation or theoretical reasoning.

There is obviously much more that could be said about whether or not individuals with BDD are competent to request surgery, but we will not pursue these issues, for—as we have already pointed out—First's data suggest that few wannabes are motivated by the belief that their healthy limb is diseased or exceedingly ugly. Instead, most wannabes appear to have some form of BIID: they appear to be motivated to achieve a fit between their body and their body image. Are wannabes with BIID delusional?

We have already suggested that they are not. Although wannabes seem not to experience parts of their body as their own, they do not go on to form the corresponding belief that it is alien. The wannabe with BIID clearly recognizes that the leg is hers: she does not identify it as someone else's leg, nor does she attempt to throw it out of bed, in the way that patients with somatoparaphrenia sometimes do.

One might argue that the wannabe's response to her somatic alienation demonstrates a form of irrationality. One might think that the rational response to a conflict between one's subjective experience of embodiment and one's body would be to change one's experience of embodiment rather than change the structure of one's body. The claim is correct but irrelevant: the wannabe's desire for amputation appears to be born out of an inability to change the way in which she experiences her body. Of course, it may be that some wannabes would rather change their actual body to fit their experienced body than vice versa. Is someone with such a desire set competent to make a request for amputation? They certainly challenge our notions of autonomy and competency, but it is far from obvious that they ought to be regarded as incompetent. It is important to bear in mind that they have spent many years—perhaps even decades—with a non-standard sense of embodiment. (Most wannabes report having had a feeling of somatic alienation since childhood.) Their experience of themselves has been built around this sense, and to require them to change it is, to some extent, to require them to change who they are. The case is not dissimilar to a situation in which an elderly person, blind from an early age, is suddenly presented with the opportunity to regain her sight. The decision to decline such an offer can be understood as an exercise of rational agency.

A useful angle on the question of whether the requests of wannabes could be competent is provided by contrasting wannabes with people who desire cosmetic surgery (where the surgery is not for the treatment of disfigurement). While one can certainly argue on feminist grounds that such people are not fully competent, these arguments have left many people unmoved.[22] We allow individuals to mould their body to an idealized body type, even when we recognize that this body image has been formed under the pressure of non-rational considerations, such as advertising, gender norms, and the like. If this holds for the individual seeking cosmetic surgery, what reason is there to resist a parallel line of argument for those seeking amputation? Of course, the latter individual is seeking to mould their body to an ideal that few of us aspire to, and one that has been formed under conditions that are far from perfect, but why should these facts cut any moral ice? In fact, one might think that the desire for cosmetic surgery (and gender-reassignment surgery) is *more* problematic than the desire for amputation. Men who believe that they are really women 'trapped in a man's body'—and the overwhelming majority of transsexuals are male-to-female—typically reinforce a stereotyped view of femininity, and contribute, however unwittingly and obliquely, to gender inequality.[23] The essential woman they seek to be is weak and helpless, obsessed by appearance, and so on.[24] There are related feminist grounds (and not only feminist grounds) on which to criticize cosmetic surgery: it reinforces a very unfortunate emphasis on appearance over substance. It is hard to see that the desire for amputation could be criticized upon grounds of these kinds, since it goes against the grain of our culturally endorsed ideals of the body.

A second objection to the argument from autonomy is that the wannabe is not in a position to give informed consent to the surgery, for he or she does not—and cannot—know what it is like to be an amputee without first becoming an amputee.

We think that this objection is weak. First, it is not at all obvious that the wannabe cannot know what it will be like to be an amputee without becoming an amputee. Arguably, there is a sense in which the wannabe *already* knows what it is like to be an amputee. We might also note that at least some wannabes pretend to be amputees—they spend their weekends in a wheelchair, and so on. To some degree, it seems that a wannabe can know what it is like to be an amputee.

But a more important point to be made here is that the objection appears to set the bar for autonomy too high.[25] Autonomy demands only that one have an adequate understanding of the likely consequences of an action, and one can have a reasonable understanding of what life as an amputee would be like without first becoming an amputee. Arguably, the wannabe is in a better position to appreciate the consequences of the desired surgery than is the person who seeks cosmetic surgery, the would-be surrogate mother, or the person desiring gender reassignment surgery.

Therapy

A third argument in favour of operating appeals to the therapeutic effects promised by such operations. The argument rests on four premises: (i) wannabes endure serious suffering as a result of their condition; (ii) amputation will—or is likely to—secure relief from this suffering; (iii) this relief cannot be secured by less drastic means; (iv) securing relief from this suffering is worth the cost of amputation. This argument parallels the justification for conventional amputations.

There is some reason to endorse (i). First, the lengths to which wannabes go in an effort to amputate their own limbs suggest that their desires are strong and unrelenting. Even when wannabes do not take active steps to secure an amputation, their feeling of bodily alienation seems to cause severe disruption to their everyday lives. 44% of First's subjects reported that their desire interfered with social functioning, occupational functioning, or leisure activities.

Some writers suggest that (ii) is problematic. Bruno and Riddle claim that the desire for amputation has its origins in attention-seeking sparked by the deprivation of parental love.[26] On this hypothesis, though it is *possible* that satisfying their wish for an amputation might give the wannabe the attention and kindness they seek, it is unlikely. Though amputees are treated with a certain degree of solicitude in many situations, the daily frustrations and difficulties caused by their condition almost certainly more than overbalance this care. Moreover, it is quite likely that the wannabe will not be satisfied with the solicitude of strangers. Instead she will seek ongoing commitment from particular individuals, and there is little reason to think that she is more likely to get this than are non-amputees. Finally, it might be that even the love of particular others will not suffice: it may be that literally nothing can stand in for the love of which she was deprived as a child. Bruno suggests that psychotherapy is the appropriate response to the disorder, not surgery. The patient needs to develop insight into the real source of her problems before she can solve them.

Bruno's proposal is empirically testable: we can evaluate whether the desire for amputation responds to psychotherapy, and whether amputation simply leads to the displacement of the patient's symptoms. What little data we have to date suggests that Bruno is wrong on both counts. We know of no systematic study of the effects of psychotherapy on the desire for amputation, but First's study suggests that it is not particularly effective. Of the 52 individuals he interviewed, 18 had told their psychotherapist about their desire for amputation, and none reported a reduction in the intensity of the desire following psychotherapy.

On the other hand, on the scant evidence available, wannabes who succeed in procuring an amputation seem to experience a significant and lasting increase in well-being. Both of Robert Smith's patients were reported as having been very happy with their operations, and the nine subjects in First's study who had had an amputation also expressed satisfaction with the results.[27] As far as we can tell, such individuals do not develop the desire for additional amputations (in contrast to individuals who have had cosmetic surgery). Nor, as far as we know, do such patients develop (unwanted) phantom limbs. Of course, it may be that the sample to which researchers have had access is self-selecting: adherents of the BIID account are motivated to come forward to adduce evidence in favour of their theory, while those who have had more unhappy experiences simply lose interest in the debate, or are too depressed to motivate themselves to take any further part. In any case, the sample sizes are too small to be statistically significant. Unfortunately, it is hard to see how it will be possible to collect sufficient data of the required sort. We can of course follow the fortunes of those who have arranged non-medical amputations for themselves, but a controlled study would presumably require medical amputations, and ethical approval for performing such operations is unlikely to be forthcoming without this very data.[28]

We turn now to (iii): can the wannabe secure relief from their suffering by less drastic means than amputation? Again, the jury is out on this. First's study suggests that psychotherapy is not a particularly effective form of treatment, but psychotherapy is not the only alternative to amputation. Some form of cognitive behavioural therapy might prove effective, perhaps in combination with psychotropic drugs. But it might also be that some wannabes cannot be helped by available drugs or talking therapy whatever the aetiology of the disorder. After all, the phantom limb phenomenon is resistant to these forms of treatment. For at least some patients, there may be no treatment available other than amputation.

Finally, we turn to (iv): is securing relief from this suffering worth the cost of amputation? This, of course, will depend on the degree of suffering in question and the costs of amputation. We have already noted that there is reason to think that wannabes often experience significant misery from their condition. But what should we say about the costs of amputation? These, of course, will vary from case to case, depending on the financial and social circumstances of the individual, and the nature of the amputation itself. The costs might be offset by the benefits of amputation in some cases but not in others. It is interesting to note that of the two would-be amputees featured in the *Complete Obsession* documentary, the person seeking amputation of a single leg was given psychiatric approval, while the person seeking to have both her legs amputated was denied psychiatric approval. And of course the costs are not always borne just by the patient; they are often also borne by the patient's family and by society as a whole.

There is ample room here for false consciousness. On the one hand, one can argue that wannabes have an overly rosy image of what life as an amputee involves. And certainly those wannabes who have become amputees have a motivation for thinking that their life is better than it really is. On the other hand, one could also argue that those of us who are able bodied have an overly pessimistic image of the lives of the disabled. As able-bodied individuals, we might be tempted to dwell on the harm that accompanies amputation and minimize what is gained by way of identification. Perhaps we are tempted to think that the effects of the surgery are worse than they are.

Repugnance

We believe that the arguments canvassed above establish a *prima facie* case for thinking that wannabes should have access to amputation, at least in those instances in which they suffer from BIID. However, we recognize that many people will continue to find the idea of voluntary amputation of a healthy limb objectionable, even when they acknowledge the force of these arguments. What motivates such reactions?

We suspect that much of this hostility derives from the sense of repugnance that is evoked by the idea that a person might wish to rid themselves of an apparently healthy limb. Dennis Canavan, the Scottish member of parliament who campaigned to prevent Robert Smith from carrying out such operations was quoted as saying: 'The whole thing is repugnant and legislation needs to be brought in now to outlaw this'.[29] Mr Canavan is surely not alone in having such a reaction. Wannabes evoke an affective response not dissimilar to that evoked by the prospect of kidney sales, bestiality, or various forms of genetic engineering. Even when a limb is severely diseased and must be removed in order to save the patient's life, the thought of amputation strikes many as distasteful at best.

Although they should not be dismissed, we think that such responses should be treated with a great deal of caution. A large number of morally benign practices—such as masturbation, inter-racial marriage, burial (and cremation) of the dead, organ selling, artificial insemination, tattooing and body piercing—have the ability to elicit disgust responses. Disgust responses can alert us to the possibility that the practices in question *might* be morally problematic, but they do not seem to be reliable indicators of moral transgression.[30]

Indirect Effects

We have explored three arguments for allowing self-demand amputation of healthy limbs: the argument from harm minimization, the autonomy argument and the therapeutic argument. We have suggested that these arguments have some force. But even if we are right about that, it does not follow that we ought to allow self-demand amputation of healthy limbs. One might hold that although these arguments are strong, their force is outweighed by reasons for not allowing such surgery.

In our view, the strongest such argument concerns the possible effects of legitimising BIID as a disorder. The worry is that giving official sanction to a diagnosis of BIID makes it available as a possible identity for people. To use Ian Hacking's term, psychiatric categories have a "looping" effect: once in play, people use them to construct their identities, and this in turn reinforces their reality as medical conditions.[31] Arguably, something like this has occurred in the case of Dissociative Identity Disorder (formerly multiple personality disorder): the explosion of diagnoses of DID might be due in part to the fact that people regard DID as a culturally sanctioned disorder. The very awareness of a disorder can contribute to its proliferation.

Could a similar effect occur for BIID? Is it likely that the inclusion of the disorder in the forthcoming DSM-V will generate an explosion of cases on the order of that seen in the study of dissociation? Perhaps, but there is reason to think that such fears are unwarranted. The desire for amputation of a healthy limb is at odds with current conceptions of the ideal body image. The preference for bodily integrity is deep-seated in normal human beings, and advertising does much to reinforce such norms. We therefore think it unlikely that the desire for amputation will proliferate.

Conclusion

In a world in which many are born without limbs, or lose their limbs to poisons, landmines, and other acts of man and God, it might seem obscene to legitimise the desire for the amputation of healthy limbs. But we have argued that, in the case of at least some wannabes, the limb in question is not as healthy as it might appear: in an important sense, a limb that is not experienced as one's own is not in fact one's own. Disorders of depersonalisation are invisible to the outside world: they are not observable from the third-person perspective in the way that most other disorders are. But the fact that they are inaccessible should not lead us to dismiss the suffering they might cause. Whether amputation is an appropriate response to this suffering is a difficult question, but we believe that in some cases it might be.[32]

Notes

1. K. SCOTT (2000) Voluntary amputee ran disability site. *The Guardian*, February 7.

2. G. FURTH and R. SMITH (2002) *Amputee Identity Disorder: Information, Questions, Answers, and Recommendations about Self-Demand Amputation* (Bloomington, IN, 1st Books).

3. M. GILBERT (2003) *Whole* U.S.A.

4. K. PHILLIPS (1996) *The Broken Mirror: Understanding and Treating Body Dysmorphic Disorder* (Oxford, Oxford University Press).

5. D. M. GARNER (2002) Body image and anorexia nervosa in T. F. CASH and T. PRUZINSKY (eds) *Body Image: A Handbook of Theory, Research, and Clinical Practice* (New York, The Guilford Press).

6. J. MONEY, R. JOBARIS, and G. FURTH (1977) Apotemnophilia: Two cases of self-demand amputation as paraphilia. *The Journal of Sex Research*, 13, 2, 115–125.

7. Furth & Smith op. cit.

8. The term 'body schema' is used in different ways by different authors. We are following Shaun Gallagher's usage. See S. GALLAGHER (1995) Body schema and intentionality in J. BERMÚDEZ, N. EILAN and J. MARCEL (eds) *The Body and the Self.* (Cambridge MA, M.I.T. Press) pp. 225–44 and S. GALLAGHER (2001) Dimensions of embodiment: Body image and body schema in medical contexts in S. K. TOOMBS (ed) *Handbook of Phenomenology and Medicine* (Dordrecht, Kluwer Academic Publishers) pp. 147–75.

9. S. GALLAGHER and J. COLE 1995 Body schema and body image in a deafferented subject, *Journal of Mind and Behavior*, 16, 369–90.

10. The term 'body image' is also used in different ways by different authors. Again, we follow Shaun Gallagher's usage of the term. See reference [8].

11. T. E. FEINBERG, L. D. HABER, and N. E. LEEDS (1990) Verbal asomatognosia, *Neurology*, 40, 1391–4; J. A. M. FREDERIKS (1985) Disorders of the body schema. In Clinical Neuropsychology in J. A. M. FREDERIKS (ed) *Handbook of Clinical Neurology*, rev. Series, No. 1 (Amsterdam, Elsevier); M. SIERRA and G. E. BERRIOS (2001) The phenomenological stability of depersonalization: Comparing the old with the new, *The Journal of Nervous and Mental Disorders*, 189, 629–636.

12. An account of such a case is described in O. SACKS (1985) The man who fell out of bed, in *The Man Who Mistook his Wife for a Hat* (New York, Touchstone).

13. O. SACKS (1991) *A Leg to Stand On* (London, Picador).

14. R. M. GARDNER and C. MONCRIEFF (1988) Body image distortion in ano-rexics as a non-sensory phenomenon: A signal detection approach, *Journal of Clinical Psychology*, 44, 101–107 and T. F. CASH and T. A. BROWN (1987) Body image in anorexia nervosa and bulimia nervosa: A Review of the literature, *Behavior Modification*, 11, 487–521.

15. C. ELLIOTT (2003) *Better Than Well: American Medicine Meets the American Dream* (New York, W.W. Norton & Company).

16. M. B. FIRST (unpublished) Desire for amputation of a limb: Paraphilia, psychosis, or a new type of identity disorder? Submitted.

17. R. BRUNO (1997) Devotees, pretenders and wannabes: Two cases of facti-tious disability disorder, *Journal of Sexuality and Disability*, 15, 243–260.

18. G. C. RIDDLE (1988) *Amputees and Devotees: Made for Each Other?* (New York, Irvington Publishers).

19. C. E. ELLIOTT (2000) A new way to be mad, *The Atlantic Monthly*, 286, 6, December.

20. Quoted in R. DOTINGA (2000) Out on a limb, *Salon*, August 29, 1.

21. AMERICAN PSYCHIATRIC ASSOCIATION (2000) *Diagnostic and Statisti-cal Manual of Mental Disorders, Text Revision*. Fourth Edition (Washington D.C., American Psychiatric Association).

22. For a feminist argument against the permissibility of cosmetic surgery see K. P. MORGAN (1991) Women and the knife: Cosmetic surgery and the colonization of women's bodies, *Hypatia* 6, 3, 25–53.

23. H. BOWER (2001) The gender identity disorder in the DSM-IV classifica-tion: a critical evaluation, *Australian and New Zealand Journal of Psychiatry*, 35, 1–8.

24. M. GARBER (1993) *Vested Interests: Cross-Dressing & Cultural Anxiety* (London, Penguin).

25. See J. OAKLEY (1992) Altruistic surrogacy and informed consent, *Bioethics*, 6, 4, 269–287.

26. Bruno op. cit. and Riddle op. cit.

27. See also ELLIOTT (2000) and (2003) op. cit. and F. Horn (2003) A life for a limb: Body integrity identity disorder, *Social Work Today*, Feb 24.

28. R. SMITHAND and K. FISHER (2003) Healthy limb amputation: ethical and legal aspects (letter), *Clinical Medicine*, 3, 2, March/April, 188.

29. Quoted in Dotinga op. cit.

30. See J. R. RICHARDS (1996) Nefarious goings on, *The Journal of Medicine and Philosophy*, 21, 375–416.

31. I. HACKING (1995) *Rewriting the Soul: Multiple Personality and the Sciences of Memory* (Princeton, Princeton University Press).

32. We are very grateful to Shaun Gallagher, Jonathan Cole, Michael First and an anonymous reviewer for their very useful comments on a previous ver-sion of this paper. We also thank Suzy Bliss for her valuable help.

Wesley J. Smith

 NO

Should Doctors Be Allowed to Amputate Healthy Limbs?

If you want to see why Western culture is going badly off the rails, just read the drivel that passes for learned discourse in many of our professional journals. The most recent example is "Amputees by Choice: Body Integrity Identity Disorder and the Ethics of Amputation," published in the current issue of the *Journal of Applied Philosophy* (Vol. 22, No. 1, 2005).

The question posed by the authors, Tim Bayne and Neil Levy, both Australian philosophy professors, is whether physicians should be permitted to amputate a patient's healthy limb because the patient is obsessed with becoming an amputee, an apparently newly discovered mental disorder that has been given the name "Body Integrity Identity Disorder" (BIID).

For people of common sense, the answer is obvious: NO! First, who but a severely mentally disturbed person would want a healthy leg, arm, hand, or foot cut off? Such people need treatment, not amputation. Second, physicians are duty bound to "do no harm," that is, they should refuse to provide harmful medical services to patients—no matter how earnestly requested. (Thus, if I were convinced that my appendix was actually a cancerous tumor, that would not justify my doctor acquiescing to my request for an appendectomy.) Finally, once the limb is gone, it is gone for good. Acceding to a request to be mutilated would amount to abandoning the patient.

But according to Bayne and Levy, and a minority of other voices in bioethics and medicine, the need to respect personal autonomy is so near-absolute that it should even permit doctors to cut off the healthy limbs of "amputee wannabes." After all, the authors write, "we allow individuals to mould their body to an idealized body type" in plastic surgery—a desire that is "more problematic than the desire for amputation" since cosmetic surgery "reinforces a very unfortunate emphasis on appearance over substance." Moreover, the authors claim in full postmodernist mode, just because a limb is biologically healthy, does not mean that the leg is real. Indeed, they argue, "a limb that is not experienced as one's own is not in fact one's own."

That this kind of article is published in a respectable philosophical journal tells us how very radical and pathologically nonjudgmental the bioethics movement is becoming. And lest you believe that such advocacy could never reach the clinical setting: Think again. Such surgeries have already been performed in the United Kingdom with no adverse professional consequence to the amputating physicians.

Even more worrisome, the current trends in American jurisprudence could one day legalize amputation as treatment for BIID. For example, in 1999, the Montana Supreme Court invalidated a law that required abortions to be performed in hospitals. But rather than limit the decision to that issue, the 6-2 majority opinion in James H. Armstrong, M.D. v. The State of Montana, imposed a radical and audacious medical ethic on the people of Montana, ruling: "The Montana Constitution broadly guarantees each individual the right to make medical judgments affecting her or his bodily integrity and health in partnership with a chosen health care provider free from government interference."

If indeed almost anything goes medically in Montana—so long as a patient wants it and a health care professional is willing to provide it—then it would seem that a physician could legally amputate a patient's healthy limbs upon request to satisfy a neurotic BIID obsession.

⚜

Yours Truly Taken to Task for Allegedly Inaccurate Article

I have heard from one of the authors of the journal article supporting the right of doctors to amputate healthy limbs for sufferers of a new mental health disorder known as Body Integrity Identity Disorder (BIID). He is unhappy with me. Neil Levy claims I misrepresented his and co-author Tim Bayne's work.

Levy wrote: "You write that we advocate 'abandoning the patient' by acceding to their request to amputate a healthy limb. First, as you fail to mention, we conclude that the question is difficult, but we think that 'in some cases' it 'might' be acceptable to accede. Second, you misrepresent our views by taking them out of context. You say that we write, 'in full post modernist mode, just because a limb is biologically healthy, does not mean that the leg is real.'" (Indeed, they argue, "a limb that is not experienced as one's own is not in fact one's own.") "If we had implied any such thing, we would deserve your mockery. But it should be clear, from even a cursory reading, that we intended to claim not that if the patient believes the limb is not theirs, it is not. We couldn't be claiming any such thing, because we distinguish between somatoparaphrenia, which is a delusion in which the patient denies ownership of the limb, and BIID, in which there are no false beliefs. The claim, rather, is that acknowledging ownership is normally a necesary condition for full ownership. Think of disowning a child. This is an act which does not alter the biological relationship, but alters the lived relationship. There is nothing 'postmodernist' about this. If you were familiar with norms in analytic philosophy you would hesitate to make such an accusation: no one is more vocal in denouncing fac-ile relativism about truth. Third, we do not advocate abandoning the patient. Once again, a careful reading of the article would indicate that amputation is recommended only as a last resort: so long as there is genuine and significant suffering and there is no alternative treatment that is effective. If there is such an affective treatment developed, then it is obviously preferable."

My response was as follows:

"Thank you for writing.

It was a 550 word opinion piece. It is very clear that the term abandon-ment was mine and not yours, as was the opinion and interpretation that cut-ting off a healthy limb would be an act of abandonment. I never claimed you believed in abandoning a patient.

I quoted you accurately about the healthy limb not being the patient's, an amazing statement in my view. Whether or not a patient "owns" the limb, does not make it any less real. And the point I was making is that autonomy is getting recklessly out of control in bioethics advocacy, and in jurisprudence as well, ergo the quoting of the Montana court case. I probably should have said that "as a last resort," you would permit amputation. But you would still allow amputation.

I certainly had no intention of misrepresenting your article. I don't believe I did. I believe the essence of what I wrote is true."

(I would also note that the abstract of the article, which the authors wrote, states that they argue, "BIID sufferers meet reasonable standards for rationality and autonomy: so as long as no other effective treatment for their disorder is available, surgeons ought to be allowed to accede to their requests," in other words, cut off healthy limbs.)

⋯◈⋯

"Choice" Gone Mad: Amputee Wannabes

We are witnessing the beginning of the public normalization of the pro-found mental illness known as Body Integrity Identity Disorder (BIID)—also known as "amputee wannabe" because its sufferers become obsessed with losing one or more limbs. A column published in *The Guardian* is an example: Susan Smith (not her real name) writes about wanting to have both legs amputated because **"the image I have of myself has always been one with-out legs."**

To achieve these ends, Susan harmed herself so that one leg would have to be removed. And now, she plans to do it again: **"Removing the next leg will not be any easier than the first; the pain will be horrendous. But I have no regrets about the path I have chosen. In fact, if I regret anything,** it is that I didn't do this sooner. For the first time in my life, I can get on with being the real me."

And here's the normalizing part: "I think BIID will stay taboo until people get together and bring it out. A hundred years ago, it was taboo to be gay in many societies, and 50 years ago the idea of transsexuals was abhorrent to most. I have tried to make the condition more understood but it is difficult to get a case out in the open by yourself. My psychiatrist went to a meeting last year in Paris, and many doctors there told her that they had operated on people who needed an amputation under mysterious circumstances, and how happy the person was when they woke up. It led them to believe that perhaps BIID is more prevalent than people think."

Something has gone terribly wrong with us at a profound and fundamental level. And deeper minds than mine need to figure out precisely what it is. Because, in the name of "being myself" we are moving toward normalizing mutilating surgery. Indeed, I have already attended a transhumanist conference where two Ph.D.s advocated that doctors be allowed to remove healthy limbs. And it has been suggested as worth considering in a professional journal article by Tim Bayne and Neil Levy. What next? Help people who want to cut themselves, slice themselves repeatedly? Or burn themselves, do it safely? Or what about kill themselves? Oh, that's right. It is already explicitly legal to help do that in Oregon, the Netherlands, Belgium, and Switzerland.

People like Susan need to be protected from harming themselves. We used to have the basic humanity and decency to understand that. But we have become so in the thrall of radical individualism, I wonder whether we still do. "Choice" is becoming a voracious monster.

CHALLENGE QUESTIONS

Is It Ethical to Support the Wish for Healthy Limb Amputation in People with Body Integrity Identity Disorder (BIID)?

1. Tattooing and body piercing are regarded by some people not as forms of bodily degradation, but rather as artistic personal expressions. What differentiates these procedures from the choice to undergo limb amputation in order to enhance one's sense of self and emotional well-being?
2. In some extreme cases of body integrity identity disorders, individuals have attempted to sever their own limbs. When such procedures fail, and the individual is left with a badly damaged limb, and a possibly medically dangerous condition, how should physicians respond?
3. Some would argue that a person has the moral right to alter his or her body in any way desired. What are the arguments for and against this notion?
4. What kind of psychological assessment and intervention would you recommend for a person requesting limb amputation?
5. Assuming that a surgeon agrees to amputate a limb of a person with BIID, should health insurance cover this operation? Why or why not?

Suggested Readings

Elliott, C. & Kramer, P. D. (2004). Amputees by choice. In *Better than well: American medicine meets the American dream* (208–236). New York: W. W. Norton.

First, M. B. (2005). Desire for amputation of a limb: Paraphilia, psychosis, or a new type of identity disorder. *Psychological Medicine, 35*(6), 919–928.

Henig, S. S. (2005, March 22). At war with their bodies, they seek to sever limbs. *The New York Times.*

Schramme, T. (2007). Should we prevent non-therapeutic mutilation and extreme body modification? *Bioethics.* Retrieved from http://www.blackwell-synergy.com/toc/biot/0/0.

ISSUE 15

Does Exposure to Media Violence Promote Aggressive Behavior?

YES: Nancy Signorielli, from *Violence in the Media: A Reference Handbook* (ABC-CLIO, 2005)

NO: Jonathan L. Freedman, from *Media Violence and Its Effect on Aggression: Assessing the Scientific Evidence* (University of Toronto Press, 2002)

ISSUE SUMMARY

YES: Professor of communication Nancy Signorielli asserts that research supports the position that media violence affects viewers by fostering aggression, causing desensitization to violence, and promoting fear.

NO: Psychologist Jonathan L. Freedman argues that the scientific evidence does not support the notion that exposure to TV and film violence causes aggression, desensitization, or fear.

In recent years, video games have caught the attention of the public because of various reports about violent and sexually explicit imagery contained in products sold to young people. The debate about the potential impact of exposure to aggressive or sexually explicit media has raged for decades, with social critics expressing great concern about the impact of movies and television shows in which violence has become almost normative. The question has been raised about whether such imagery desensitizes viewers, and possibly even promotes a tolerance for the most unacceptable of interpersonal behaviors.

Nancy Signorielli asserts that there is a large body of research that delineates three ways in which media violence may affect viewers; she contends that exposure to such imagery fosters aggression, desensitizes viewers to violence, and causes people to develop a "mean world syndrome" in which they come to believe that the world is a scary place. Signorielli discusses research that points to the fact that exposure to media violence leads to aggressive behavior in children, teens, and adults.

Jonathan L. Freedman claims that scientific evidence does not support the notion that exposure to media violence leads to aggression in children or adults.

Freedman contends that far fewer than half the research studies have found a causal connection between exposure to media violence and aggression, and that the research may be interpreted as showing that there is no causal effect. Freedman points out other factors relevant to this debate, such as the major decline in violent offenses over the past 10 years, the notion that violent media may just be exciting and arousing to people, the impact of exposure to real violence hasn't been sufficiently considered, and several of the studies conducted on media violence and its effects on aggression are methodologically flawed.

POINT

- Numerous controlled laboratory studies provide strong evidence that there is a causal relation between seeing violent media portrayals and the expression of subsequent aggression in children's behavior.

- Researchers have documented some compelling findings about childhood exposure to media violence and the development of aggression several years later. One longitudinal study of boys found that the amount of violence seen on television at age 8 was related to aggressiveness at age 18, as well as involvement in antisocial behavior (fights and spouse abuse) and criminal acts at age 30.

- In many representations of media violence, there is a lack of adequate context, as well as a failure to convey the message that "crimes does not pay." This may transmit the lesson that violence is not necessarily immoral, and that those characters who commit violence are not sorry for their actions and may not be punished for their transgressions. These messages could lead viewers, especially children, to learn and even accept aggressive behaviors.

- Exposure to media violence may cause desensitization; that is, viewers may become less sensitive to the violence they see and thus become willing to tolerate a more violent society.

- Research shows a solid and consistent base of evidence supporting the relationship between watching media violence and subsequent aggressive behavior for children, teens, and adults.

COUNTERPOINT

- When considering laboratory experiments, there is an important difference between violent and nonviolent media, in that violent media are generally more arousing and exciting. People who are aroused by provocative imagery tend to perform any activity more strongly than those less aroused. Thus, when viewers of violent films punch a punching bag more vigorously, this does not necessarily reflect heightened aggression.

- The pattern of evidence from research fails to support the hypothesis that exposure to media violence at a young age causes aggressive behavior later in life. Longitudinal and cross-national studies have produced more nonsupportive results than supportive ones.

- Films and television programs that contain violence are not designed to convey the message that violence is good or that people should engage in violent acts. They do not contain information that is likely to convince anyone of anything; they do not contain explicit messages in favor of aggression or violence. They are just entertainment. So it should not be surprising that they have no effect on aggressive behavior or on attitudes toward violence.

- There is little or no evidence for a desensitization effect, and there is some evidence that directly contradicts it.

- Perhaps it is not exposure to fictional media violence but rather exposure to real-world violence that children, as well as adults, may then imitate.

YES

Nancy Signorielli

What We Know about Media Violence

Who Is Involved?

. . . Any discussion of the amount of violence on television must examine the characters who are involved in violence—those who do the hurting and killing or are hurt and killed. CI [Cultural Indicators project] has shown that television violence illustrates and provides lessons about power. Violence shows who's on top and who's on the bottom, who gets hurt and who does the hurting, and who wins and who loses. These studies consistently find a power structure related to character demographics, with earlier studies showing women and minorities more likely to be hurt than to hurt others.

Research in the CI tradition consistently shows that during prime time, men are more likely than women to be hurt (victimized) or hurt others (commit violence) (Signorielli 1990). There have been some changes in these patterns, however, in the past thirty-five years. In the programs of the 1980s, men were slightly less likely to be involved in violence than in the programs of the 1970s. Fewer characters still were involved in violence between 1993 and 2002 (Signorielli 2003). Only one-third of the major and supporting characters were involved in violence during that period, and although more men than women were involved (38 percent of the men, compared to 27 percent of the women), whites and minorities were equally likely to be victimized or commit violence (about a quarter of both whites and minorities). During the 1990s, the ratios of hurting to being hurt changed from the patterns seen in the 1970s and 1980s for women but not for men. Today, for every ten male characters who hurt or kill, eleven are victimized, the same ratio found in the earlier analysis. For women, however, instead of sixteen women being victimized for each woman who hurts or kills, the odds are even—women are equally likely to hurt or kill as to be hurt or killed. Moreover, although whites are a little more likely to be victimized than hurt others, the odds for minority characters are even.

Although the NTVS [National Television Violence Study] did not generate a profile of all characters on television, it did examine the demographic characteristics of perpetrators (those who commit) and targets (victims) of violence. Most of the perpetrators (close to three-quarters) were men; only one in ten was a woman. Few perpetrators were categorized as heroes, and most were white.

Similarly, most of the targets were men (71 percent)—only 10 percent were women—and most were white (Smith, et al. 1998). W. James Potter and colleagues (1995), in looking at a composite week of evening programming (6 PM to midnight) on four networks, also found that television typically presents an unrealistic picture of serious aggression in regard to the race of those who commit the acts as well as those who are victimized. In short, television overrepresents both white perpetrators and white victims of aggression. Although the study by Potter and colleagues, the NTVS, and the CI reports differ in how they isolate characters' involvement in violence, the patterns are similar—more men than women and more whites than minorities. Similarly, studies conducted in the United Kingdom found that women were much less likely to be involved in violence and that the onscreen time devoted to female violence was considerably less than that devoted to male violence (Gunter et al. 2003).

Overall, it appears that the consensus of findings from studies of media content indicated that contemporary television programs may not adequately support or reinforce the lesson that "crime does not pay." The lack of adequate contexts for violent behaviors may transmit the lesson that violence is "sanitary," that it is not necessarily immoral, and that those characters who commit violence are not sorry for their actions and may not be punished for their transgressions—in short, there are few, if any, consequences for committing violence. From a social learning perspective, these messages could lead viewers, particularly children, to learn and even accept aggressive behaviors. Thus, the environment of violent entertainment in which many people, including children, spend most of their free time may be potentially harmful. Moreover, television's lack of realistic contexts for violence may signal that aggression and violence are acceptable modes of behavior. . . .

How Media Violence Affects Us

There are numerous ways media violence affects us. Potter (2003) differentiates effects that are immediate or short-term from those that are long-term. Researchers, including John Murray (2003) and Potter (2003), further delineate three ways in which media violence may affect viewers: fostering aggression, becoming desensitized to violence, and becoming fearful. Each of these effects, in turn, may have both short- and long-term consequences.

Aggression and Aggressive Behavior

One of the biggest concerns about media violence is that exposure to violent images will result in aggression and aggressive behavior. There is a sizable body of research that supports this position. Although . . . there is some disagreement with this statement, the number of researchers in this camp is rather small, and some have ties to the broadcast industry. The strength of the evidence led the American Psychological Association (1985) to conclude that one factor in the development of aggressive and/or antisocial behavior in children is a steady diet of real and/or mediated violence. Similarly, the 1982 report by the National Institute of Mental Health concluded that children and teens who watch violence on television tend to exhibit more aggressive behavior. The research evidence on which these conclusions were based comes from experimental studies, longitudinal studies, and meta-analyses (a particular type of analysis that simultaneously compares the statistical results from a large number of existing studies on the same topic).

Some of the earliest research on mediated violence was experimental in nature and found that filmed or televised (mediated) images affected behavior. Glenn Ellis and Francis Sekyra (1972) and O. Ivar Lovaas (1961) found that children exposed to media violence behaved aggressively shortly after seeing violence. Another study comparing violent and prosocial (positive messages) programs (Stein and Friedrich 1972) found that children who saw positive or prosocial programs (e.g., *Mister Roger's Neighborhood*) increased their helping behaviors, whereas those who saw violent images behaved more aggressively. Overall, numerous studies have found a causal relation between seeing violent portrayals and later aggressive behavior. L. Rowell Huesmann and Laurie Miller conclude: "In these well-controlled laboratory studies there can be no doubt that it is the children's observation of the scenes of violence that is *causing* the changes in behavior" (1994, 163).

Another strong line of evidence of long-term effects comes from studies conducted over several years (longitudinal studies), specifically the research of Leonard Eron and L. Rowell Huesmann. One study of young boys begun in the 1970s in New York state that was able to control for intelligence quotient (IQ), initial levels of aggressiveness, and social class found that the amount of violence seen on television at age eight was related to aggressiveness at age eighteen, as well as involvement in antisocial behavior (fights and spouse abuse) and criminal acts at age thirty (Huesmann and Miller 1994). Similar results were found in samples of youngsters in Chicago as well as children from other countries, including Finland, Poland, and Israel. These studies found that more aggressive children, compared to less aggressive children, watched more television, preferred programs that were more violent, and perceived mediated violence as closer to real life. The most recent study in this tradition (Huesmann, Moise-Titus, Podolski, and Eron 2003) found that watching violence, identification with same-sex aggressive characters, and a perception that television violence is realistic were related to adult aggression, regardless of how much aggression was exhibited as a child.

A particularly interesting and important longitudinal study (Joy, Kimball, and Zabrack 1986) was conducted in the late 1970s in three communities in Canada as part of a larger study by Tannis MacBeth (formerly Williams). While vacationing in Canada, MacBeth visited an area in which a new and more powerful transmission tower was being built that would have a major impact on television reception in the area. One town located in the valley, Notel, would receive television for the first time. Unitel, a town about 50 miles away that had been receiving one television channel, would increase its reception by a second channel with the new transmitter. The third community, Multitel, was located close to the U.S. border and received numerous television channels originating both in Canada and the United States. The researchers gathered data relating to aggression, gender roles, and academic achievement both before and two years after the installation of the more powerful transmitter. The results showed that the children in Notel exhibited more aggressive behavior (both verbal and physical) after the introduction of television. Aggressive behavior increased for both boys and girls, for children of different ages, and for those who had different initial levels of aggressiveness. Interestingly, this comprehensive study also found that after the introduction of television, children's gender role stereotyping increased and measures of academic success (e.g., reading levels) decreased (Williams 1986).

A recent cross-cultural study of twelve-year-old children (2,788 boys and 2,353 girls) from twenty-three different countries (funded by the United Nations Education, Scientific, and Cultural Organization, or UNESCO) found an interactive relationship between media violence and real violence such that "media can contribute to an aggressive culture" (Groebel 2001, 265). In short, these studies found that aggressive people, particularly those who live in more aggressive environments, use the media to confirm their attitudes and beliefs, which are then reinforced by media content. For example, the study found that one of the messages of aggressive content is that aggression is a good way to solve conflicts and that it is fun and provides status. Moreover, the study found that successful media figures, such as the Terminator (Arnold Schwarzenegger) and Rambo (Sylvester Stallone), had become cross-cultural heroes.

Another line of naturalistic research is the work of Brian Centerwall, MD (1989a; 1989b). Using an epidemiological approach, Centerwall examines relationships between the introduction of television in a society (e.g., the United States, Canada, and South Africa) and changes in homicide rates among the white population in these countries. In comparison with South Africa, where television was banned until 1975, Centerwall found that the white homicide rates in both the United States and Canada increased 90 percent between 1945 and 1975, whereas homicide rates for the white population in South Africa remained stable. These increases held despite the implementation of statistical controls for economic growth, urbanization, alcoholism, gun ownership, and so on. Moreover, in South Africa homicide rates in South Africa's white population increased by 56 percent between 1975, when television was introduced in the country, and 1983. Although most social scientists find Centerwall's research compelling, Elizabeth Perse (2001) notes that South Africa may not have been a good choice for comparison because it was a highly controlled and repressed society and had a higher homicide rate before the introduction of television. Moreover, Perse notes that Centerwall's method, a simple bivariate graphical analysis, does not dispel the possibility that the relationships may be due to a third, unmeasured variable. Nevertheless, many find that these data are very compelling in that they show convincing, statistically significant increases in homicide rates of the white population over time.

Another solid base of evidence about the detrimental effects of media violence comes from a number of meta-analyses, a statistical technique that analyzes findings from a large number of studies about a particular topic. The first meta-analysis (Andison 1977) examined sixty-seven separate studies (experiments, surveys, longitudinal) conducted between 1956 and 1996 that examined over 30,000 participants. This analysis found strong support for a relationship between watching media violence and subsequent aggression. An analysis of samples of children, teens, and adults in 230 separate studies found a positive relationship between antisocial behavior (behaving aggressively, rule breaking, etc.) and exposure to violent media in most of the studies (Hearold 1986). Similarly, Haejung Paik and George Comstock's (1994) meta-analysis of 217 studies found statistically significant and positive correlations between viewing and subsequent aggression in samples of adults, children, and teens. Meta-analyses thus show a solid and consistent base of evidence supporting the relationship between watching media violence and behaving aggressively.

Desensitization

A second major concern is that media violence may be related to increased desensitization; that is, viewers may become less sensitive to the violence they see and thus become willing to tolerate a more violent society (Murray 2003). Laboratory studies have shown that adults and children become callous and even punitive after watching violent images. Children in the third grade, for example, who either did not see mediated violence or were shown a short clip from a violent western, were then asked to monitor two younger children by listening to the noise of them playing through an intercom. As they listened to the children, it became apparent that their play had become physically aggressive (Drabman and Thomas 1974). The children who saw the violent episode took considerably longer to get adult help than those who did not see violence. Similarly, Daniel Linz, Edward Donnerstein, and Steven Penrod (1984) found that a group of college men who viewed violent "slasher" films for five consecutive days rated the films as less violent and degrading to women at the end of the week. Moreover, after watching these films and then watching a documentary about a trial for sexual assault, these young men were less sympathetic toward the rape victim than the group of young men who had not seen the slasher films. Similarly, Stacy Smith and Edward Donnerstein (1998) note that the more viewers see graphic media violence, the more they rate material they originally perceived as offensive or degrading as less offensive or degrading.

Desensitization is particularly a concern as the amount of viewing increases. Several studies have shown that those who watch more violent programming may become more desensitized. Victor Cline, Roger Croft, and Steven Courrier (1973) found that those who saw more graphic violent portrayals were more likely to become physiologically desensitized—in short, the images stopped having an impact. In some situations, however, desensitization may have positive outcomes. Repeated exposure to an initially frightening or threatening image or character (e.g., the Incredible Hulk, the Wizard of Oz) can reduce children's fears (Cantor and Wilson 1984). Humor also contributes to desensitization (Potter 1999). Emotionally disturbed children (e.g., those with attention deficit hyperactivity disorder) are especially vulnerable to media violence and desensitization. Tom Grimes, Eric Vernberg, and Teresa Cathers (1997) found that after watching television violence, children with emotional problems (compared to a matched group of children without these disorders) showed less concern for the victims of violence and believed that the media violence they saw characters commit was justified.

Fear

Media violence may be related to fear, in both the short and long terms. Joanne Cantor (2002) has studied fright as both a physiological and emotional reaction and found that children may become fearful after seeing violent media images. These reactions typically do not last very long, but it is possible for some to last for several days, months, or even longer. For example, Kristen Harrison and Cantor (1999) found that nine out of ten college students said that they had an intense fear reaction to a media depiction that lasted for a long time. Some of the things that evoke fear responses include injuries and dangers as well as deformities and/or distortions, such as monsters or ghosts. Several factors are likely to induce fear or fright reactions. Viewers who identify and/or empathize with the target of violence are likely to feel more fearful. Similarly, viewers who think the violence could happen to them often become more fearful. Although these reactions may be immediate and short-lived, there may be some long-term consequences. For example, children may become scared while watching a movie or program and perhaps hide their eyes or scream and have nightmares. Fear, however, differs by age. Young children typically are more fearful of images that are fantastic, threatening, and just look scary; older, children, however, are more fearful of more realistic dangers, things that could possibly happen to them.

There is also evidence of a generalized fear effect—the result of long-term exposure to violent media. Cultivation theory posits a positive relationship between watching more television and being fearful and exhibiting the "mean world syndrome." Studies testing this theory show that those who watch more television believe that there are more people employed in law enforcement, exaggerate the numbers of people involved in violence in a given week, overestimate their own chances of being a victim of violence, are more likely to believe they need more protection, and believe that, in general, the world is a mean and scary place in that most people "cannot be trusted" and are "just looking out for themselves" (Gerbner et al. 2002, 52). Although there is some criticism of this approach . . ., it is a position that takes into consideration the fact that the media are an ongoing facet of day-to-day life and that the influence of the media (cultivation) is "a continual, dynamic, ongoing process of interaction among messages, audiences, and contexts" (Gerbner et al. 2002, 49).

Cultivation, however, may be culturally determined. There is less evidence of fear-related cultivation effects in the United Kingdom. Mallory Wober (1978) reports no relationship between television viewing and notions of fear and violence. There are, however, several cultural differences that may explain the lack of relationship. First, as noted above, U.K. television is considerably less violent and U.S. imports make up only a small portion of available programming. Second, programming in the United Kingdom must follow the government's family viewing policy requirements. This policy ensures that programs with potentially objectionable content are scheduled later in the evening and that programs unsuitable for children cannot be shown before 9 PM. Moreover, in the United Kingdom televised films are given age-based ratings (Gunter, Harrison, and Wykes 2003). Similarly, in the Netherlands, Bouwman and Signorielli (1985) found only weak associations between viewing and perceptions of violence, mistrust, and victimization. Even though the Netherlands imports a considerable amount of U.S. programming and Dutch and U.S. programming provides similar messages about violence, many viewers choose to watch programs that are more "informational" in nature.

Nevertheless, some cultures have shown cultivation effects. For example, students in Australia who watched more U.S. crime/adventure programs had higher scores on the "mean world" and "violence in society" indices (Pingree and Hawkins 1981). Other analyses have found evidence of the cultivation of conceptions of sex roles and political orientations as well as violence. For example, in South Korea, watching U.S. television was related, for women, to more liberal perspectives about gender roles and family values. Among the male students, however, seeing more U.S. programming was related to exhibiting greater protectiveness of Korean culture and more hostility toward the United States (Kang and Morgan 1988). Overall, the findings from numerous studies conducted in the cultivation tradition show that if televised images are less homogeneous and repetitive than those seen in the United States, the results of cultivation analyses are less consistent and predictable (Gerbner et al. 2002).

Who Will Be Influenced?

The research discussed in this section can be interpreted in three different ways: (1) that media violence is inconsequential and people, including children, are not affected by these images, particularly what they see on television (e.g., Fowles 1999); (2) that media violence will affect some people some of the time (Potter 2003); and (3) media violence will always have a very negative impact (as believed, for example, by grassroots groups such as the National Coalition on Television Violence).

The evidence from numerous research studies indicates that the first and third interpretations are too extreme. The position that media violence is inconsequential has only a few supporters. For example, during the 1970s, when NBC was actively involved in a research program, Ronald Milavsky and others (1982) conducted a three-year longitudinal study (1970–1973) of 2,400 elementary school children and 800 teenage boys and reported no evidence of a relationship between television violence and aggressive behavior. A re-analysis of this data set, however, found a relationship between television violence and aggression (Turner, Hesse, and Peterson-Lewis 1986). Huesmann and Miller (1994) also interpret the NBC data as consistent with other research findings that support a relationship.

Similarly, the position that television violence always has a negative impact on people, particularly impressionable children, is also too extreme and again has very few supporters. The one group that has supported this outcome, the National Coalition on Television Violence . . . was founded in 1980 and has been active in both rating television programs for violence and assessing which companies advertise on the most violent programs. Although the lion's share of the research shows a relationship between viewing and behaving aggressively, media violence is only one of many potential causes of aggression and/or violence in people. For example, child abuse or living in an excessively violent neighborhood may also play a critical role in subsequent aggressive behavior. Consequently, it is unreasonable to say that television violence will always have negative effects on viewers.

The most reasonable argument to make in understanding the effects of violent media content is to say that not everyone is affected in the same way; indeed, the same person may respond to violence differently on different occasions. Violent media content may have large effects on a small number of adults and/or children or small effects on large numbers of viewers. The large, consistent body of literature points to a positive relationship between television violence and aggressive behavior. Moreover, even though findings may be modest in size, the relationship must be taken seriously because of the large numbers of children who watch television each day, largely unsupervised. Even though their aggressive behavior may not put society at risk, it still may have negative social and cognitive consequences, such as the alienation of their peers and teachers (Singer and Singer 1988).

There is, however, another potentially important consequence. Although many people are reluctant to admit that they or their children could be affected by media violence, they believe that others are affected. This perspective, called "third-person effects" (Davison 1983), is particularly illusionary because it allows people to believe that they (and their children) are immune from the effects of media, but their neighbors (and their children) are not. People tend to overestimate the media's effects on others while underestimating its effects on themselves. An example might be the person who claims not to pay attention to advertising and states that advertising does not influence his or her purchasing decisions, yet won't buy anything but brand-name products and typically wears brand-name clothing such as T-shirts from the Gap or Abercrombie and Fitch.

Potter (2003) believes that third-person effects constitute one of the "myths of television violence" mentioned in the title of his book. This myth is troublesome because people do not understand how they may be affected by media violence. Although most people do not copy violent behavior they see in the media (and if they did with any regularity, the world would be extremely chaotic), that violence has numerous long-term effects, including physiological and/or emotional habituation and the cultivation of fear and the belief that the world is mean. Another of Potter's myths is that "children are especially vulnerable to the risks of negative exposure to media violence" (2003, 67). Classifying this statement as a myth does not mean that children are not vulnerable, for indeed they may be particularly influenced by media violence. Rather, this myth underscores the third-person effects because it diminishes the fact that people of all age groups may be negatively influenced by media violence.

Finally, as cultivation theory postulates, the ultimate long-term effects of watching television violence may post threats for civil liberties and freedom. Cultivation studies have found that those who watch more television, compared to those who watch less, are more likely to overestimate their chances of being involved in violence, believe that fear of crime is an important personal problem, and assume that crime is rising. Those who spend more time watching television tend to believe that they are living in a mean and dangerous world and express feelings of alienation and gloom (Gerbner et al. 2002). Because violent images are almost impossible to avoid, those who watch more television may express sentiments of dependency and be willing to accept deceptively simple, strong, and hard-line political and religious postures, if these beliefs seem to promise to relieve existing insecurities and anxieties. From the perspective of cultivation theory, the overall long-term effects of television violence may be the ready acceptance of repressive political and social environments that could translate into a loss of personal liberties.

Conclusion

This large and solid body of research about media violence shows generally stable levels of violence on television and interesting relationships between media use and violence, particularly aggression. As in any field of research, throughout the years there have been numerous controversies about different findings and ways of conducting research. . . .

Note

Although recent surveys (Kaiser Family Foundation 1999; Annenberg Policy Research Center 2000) focused only on children ages eighteen and under, my personal experience (my college-age children, their friends, and students in my classes at the University of Delaware) indicates that video game playing does not end with graduation from high school and that earlier gender differences still prevail.

All references for articles included in *Taking Sides: Clashing Views in Abnormal Psychology, 6/e* can be found on the Web at **www.mhhe.com/cls**.

Jonathan L. Freedman

 NO

Summary and Conclusions

This review has considered in detail a great deal of research on the effects of exposure to media violence. Each study was described, analyzed, criticized, and evaluated. The previous sections summarized the results of each type of research. Several conclusions seem to be warranted.

First, the survey research, combined with the longitudinal studies, provides fairly good evidence that exposure to media violence—or perhaps only preference for more violent programs—is related to aggressiveness. Those who are exposed to more violence in the media and/or who prefer more violence in the media tend to be more aggressive than those who are exposed to or prefer less violence. The evidence for this is not entirely consistent, and the size of the relationship varies greatly from study to study. Nevertheless, most of the studies do find a correlation, and its magnitude seems to be between .1 and .2, although conceivably it is as high as .3. This means that between 1 percent and, at the very high end, 9 percent of the variation in aggression is predicted by exposure to media violence. This is not a big effect—especially at the low end—but it *is* a relationship, and if it were as high as 9 percent it would be a substantial one.

Of course, as explained in detail in this review, the existence of this relationship only raises the possibility that media violence causes aggression. There is a temptation to think that because there is a correlation, there must be a causal link. That is not correct. The correlation alone tells us nothing about causality: the relationship could be produced without any causal effect of media violence. All of the other research discussed in this review was designed to establish whether there is a causal link—whether exposure to violent media makes people more aggressive.

Second, the rest of the research does not demonstrate that exposure to media violence affects aggression. Some studies using each type of research have found some support for the causal connection, but far more have not found support. The largest group of studies are the laboratory experiments. Of these, 39 percent found results that were consistent with the causal hypothesis, and 41 percent obtained results that were not consistent with it and did not support it. Moreover, when studies that used questionable measures of aggression were eliminated, only 81 percent of the remaining experiments supported the hypothesis, whereas 55 percent did not and the rest produced mixed results. This is not a pattern of results that scientists expect when a hypothesis is correct, nor is it one that would cause them to accept the hypothesis.

There were some significant effects in the laboratory experiments; however, this should not be interpreted to mean that exposure to media violence does cause aggression but not always. The significant effects that did occur were probably due to factors other than the violent content of the programs used in the experiments. In particular, I suggest that the violent programs were almost always much more interesting and more arousing than the non-violent programs. Few of the experiments even tried to equate the two types of films, even though it should have been clear that this was a crucial problem that had to be solved. You cannot show one group a film of a prizefight and another group a film of canal boating and argue that the only difference between the two films is the amount of violence. Almost all the laboratory experiments suffered from this problem; this casts doubt on the interpretation of the results in terms of the amount of violence in the films.

The most obvious difference between the violent and non-violent films was that the former were usually more arousing and exciting. This presents a very serious problem, because it is well established that differences in arousal affect behaviour. People who are more aroused tend to perform any activity more strongly than those who are less aroused. Given a bag to punch, they will punch it harder; given something to squeeze, they will squeeze it harder; and given almost any activity, they will do more of it. In the experiments at hand, subjects were often given a doll to punch or a button to press or a dial to turn. If we knew nothing about the subjects except their level of arousal, we would certainly expect those who were more aroused to punch the doll, press the button, or turn the dial more than those who were less aroused. Since the violent film produced more arousal, that alone could explain the effects of the films.

Perhaps an even more important problem with the laboratory experiments is that almost all of them had strong demand factors that, in essence, gave the subjects permission to behave aggressively or even instructed them to behave aggressively. When people are brought into a laboratory, they are very sensitive to what the experimenter does. If he shows them a film, they will wonder why that film was chosen. If no good explanation is provided, they will assume that the experimenter has a reason. And if the film is a violent film, many if not most people will infer that the experimenter likes the film, or approves of violence, or wants them to behave aggressively. This inference will be strengthened when they are later given a chance to behave aggressively—not something they would ordinarily expect to do in a laboratory. Having drawn that inference, they will be more likely to behave aggressively (since that is apparently what the experimenter wants). In other words, simply because of demand pressures, subjects shown violent films are more likely to behave aggressively than those shown non-violent films.

Psychologists are well aware of the problem of demand factors and usually make great efforts to eliminate or at least minimize them in laboratory research. Yet for some reason, in this group of experiments very little effort was made to do so. As a result, demand factors alone could explain the differences in aggressiveness that sometimes occurred.

In sum, the laboratory experiments produced inconsistent results, with more of them being non-supportive than supportive. And the results that were obtained were, in my opinion, more likely due to factors other than the violence in the programs. In any case, I firmly believe that the laboratory experiments tell us little about how exposure to violence in the media affects people in the real world—which is presumably our main concern.

The field experiments were in some sense the strongest test of the causal hypothesis. They involved relatively long-term effects, and full-length movies or actual television programs rather than short excerpts. Also, they were conducted in more natural settings: the programs were viewed and the behaviours were observed in locations that were familiar to the subjects. Perhaps most important, they were experiments, so any significant effects would have causal implications. For all these reasons, the field experiments were the best hope of getting evidence to support the causal hypothesis.

The results were, in fact, even less supportive of the hypothesis than were the results of the laboratory experiments. Only three of eleven field experiments obtained even slightly supportive results—three of twenty-four if one counts all the separate experiments. Those who favour the causal hypothesis often cite the research by the Leyens/Parke group as providing strong support. I agree that two of these studies (but not the third) produced results that are consistent with the hypothesis. However, as I discussed earlier, these studies suffered from having too few independent groups and from employing statistical procedures that were without question inappropriate (as admitted by Leyens). Yet even if these studies had produced strong, consistent results supporting the causal hypothesis, they would have been swamped by those that found either no effect of media violence on aggression, or a reverse effect, or a mixture of effects with most being inconsistent with the causal hypothesis. Moreover, the studies that obtained supportive results involved very small samples of subjects, whereas many of those that obtained non-supportive results had quite large samples. Even more so than with the laboratory experiments, this is an extremely discouraging pattern of results for the causal hypothesis.

The rest of the research related to the causal hypothesis is non-experimental. This means that regardless of the results, it could never provide terribly strong evidence that exposure to media violence causes aggression. Nevertheless, since the ideal experiment cannot he conducted, scientists can try to build a case for a causal effect using other methods. In this context, I consider longitudinal studies extremely important. They provide information relevant to two predictions from the causal hypothesis. First, they show whether the correlations between exposure to violent media and aggression change with age. If the causal hypothesis is correct, the correlations should probably increase as children get older. Even if this is not absolutely required by the hypothesis, there is little question that increasing correlations with age would be consistent with the hypothesis and provide some support for it. However, the longitudinal studies found no evidence for such a pattern. I consider this to be inconsistent with the hypothesis. In any case, it certainly does not support it.

An even more important aspect of these studies is that they provide evidence as to whether early exposure to media violence is associated with increased aggression at a later age after early aggression is held constant. The reasoning underlying this prediction and the statistical analyses have been discussed earlier. The basic point is that if children are equally aggressive at age eight but watch different amounts of media violence, those who watch more should become more aggressive than the others two or seven years later. As noted before, this spreading apart in terms of aggressiveness is the major prediction from the causal hypothesis. This prediction is tested with multiple regression analyses (or similar statistical analyses) that hold aggression constant at age eight and look at the remaining relationship between violence exposure at age eight and aggression at the later age. If this relationship is positive and significant, it is consistent with and to some extent supports the causal hypothesis. If it is not significant, it is inconsistent with the causal hypothesis.

As with all of this research, the results have been mixed. The supportive results were for males on one measure in the twenty-two-year study; from the cross-national study, for boys and girls in the Israeli city sample, and considerably weaker effects for boys and girls in Poland and for girls in the United States; and for boys and girls combined in the later phase of the nursery school study. Some of these results are open to serious criticisms, so they are less clear than they might appear. Moreover, both the twenty-two-year study and the cross-national study produced more non-supportive results than supportive ones. So considering only the results that are most consistent with the causal hypothesis, they are not impressive.

But even if one were to accept these supportive results entirely, there are many more studies that obtained results that are inconsistent with the causal hypothesis. The twenty-two-year study found no effect for girls or for boys on two other measures; the cross-national study found no effect for boys or girls in Australia, for boys or girls in the Netherlands, for boys or girls in Finland, for boys or girls in the Israeli kibbutz sample, or for boys in the United States. The nursery school study found no effect in the first phase. And none of the other studies found any support for the hypothesis. Although this body of research provides some supportive evidence, it obviously did not produce the kind of consistent support that would give one confidence in the hypothesis. Rather, the pattern of evidence generally fails to support the hypothesis.

Some studies compared communities that had television with those that did not and looked for differences in aggression. This research is perhaps the most discouraging for the causal hypothesis. One study reported an increase in aggression after television was introduced, but it is a flawed study, the results were inconsistent, and there are many possible explanations for the result. None of the other studies provided any evidence in favour of the causal hypothesis; in fact, they provided some quite strong evidence against it.

Finally, there was a small group of studies using a variety of methods. These studies offer no support at all for the causal hypothesis, and several of them provide quite convincing evidence against it.

It should be obvious from the individual reviews that the results of the research have been generally non-supportive of the causal hypothesis. Some studies of each type found results that could be considered as supporting the hypothesis, but more found results that did not support it. What should we make of this pattern of results?

Science depends on consistency. Before a theory or hypothesis can be considered correct, the research testing it must produce results that support it with great consistency. Ideally, every single study will support the hypothesis. More realistically—especially when dealing with complex hypotheses and situations—we would probably consider a hypothesis to be supported as long as the great majority of the studies support it. If 90 percent of the studies obtain the results predicted by the hypothesis, we can be reasonably confident that the hypothesis is correct. We may wish to know why the others failed, but even if we cannot establish why, we will still accept the hypothesis. If the results are less consistent than that—if, say, only 70 percent support the hypothesis and 30 percent do not—we will be considerably less confident. We may feel that the hypothesis is probably correct, but we will have serious concerns about the failures. And if only 50 percent support the hypothesis, we will be very unlikely to believe the hypothesis is correct. We may still think there is some slight truth to the hypothesis, but it will be clear that the effects are unreliable, probably very weak, and perhaps not there at all. In fact, if the results are this inconsistent, our focus may well shift to explaining why there were any positive results. We may then look for problems in the research that produced the effects even though the hypothesis is incorrect. If we still believe in the hypothesis despite the inconsistency and the lack of support, that belief is based on faith and hope rather than on the scientific results.

Turning to the research on media violence and aggression, it should be clear that not one type of research provided the kind of supportive evidence that is ordinarily required to support a hypothesis. Not one found 90 percent supportive or 80 percent or 70 percent or even 50 percent. In fact, regardless of the method used, fewer than half the studies found results that supported the hypothesis— sometimes considerably fewer than half. The results of this research have sometimes been described as overwhelmingly supportive of the causal hypothesis. That is not correct. Rather, the research is discouraging for the hypothesis, with most of the research not supporting it. I conclude that the scientific research does not support the hypothesis that exposure to violent media causes aggression.

Third, the small body of research on desensitization has tested two quite different effects. There is some evidence that exposure to media violence causes habituation and therefore reduced responsiveness to further media violence. The results are rather weak and inconclusive, but the effect may be real. Regarding the more important effect on actual violence, three small-scale studies found some support for this, but the effect failed to replicate and other studies did not support it. I conclude that there is little or no evidence for a desensitization effect and there is some evidence that directly contradicts it.

Where does this leave us? On the one hand, we have considerable justification for rejecting the hypotheses. If they were correct, we should expect to see a pattern of results that consistently support them. We do not get that pattern, so the hypotheses are almost certainly incorrect. On the other hand, those who continue to believe in them can argue that the research is flawed, or that one should not expect perfect consistency, or even that the existence of some supportive results shows that the hypotheses are correct. This is not very good science, but it cannot easily be rejected.

However, those who believe in the hypotheses cannot argue that the research provides overwhelming or even strong support for them. I hope it is clear that the research does not support either hypothesis. After so much research, with many of the studies being of very high quality, if the hypotheses were correct, I believe that we would have found the evidence to support them.

Accordingly, this comprehensive review of the scientific evidence leads to two clear conclusions. First, despite the way it has sometimes been described, the research does not provide overwhelming support for either the causal hypothesis or the desensitization hypothesis. On the contrary, the evidence for both hypotheses is weak and inconsistent, with more non-supportive results than supportive results. Second, following from the first conclusion, exposure to media violence does not cause aggression, or if it does the effects are so weak that they cannot be detected and must therefore be vanishingly small. I would not make such a strong statement about the desensitization hypothesis, because there has been too little relevant research. Instead I would conclude that it is probably not true, but the case is not yet closed. . . .

Films and television programs that contain violence are not designed to convey the message that violence is good or that people should engage in violent acts. They do not contain information that is likely to convince anyone of anything; they do not contain explicit messages in favour of aggression or violence. They are just entertainment. The programs are not meant to be persuasive, just popular. So it should not be surprising that they have no effect on people's aggressive behaviour or on their attitudes toward violence.

What about *implicit* messages? Though most people would agree that the media almost never deliver a message that explicitly encourages violence, some people argue that violence in the media carries the implicit message that violence is acceptable. When Batman punches the bad guy, perhaps the message is that one must resort to violence to solve problems. When the Roadrunner turns the tables on the Coyote and blows him up, perhaps children are being taught to use violence against their enemies rather than other means of settling disputes. When Bruce Willis or the police or the Power Rangers use violence against terrorists or criminals or evil monsters, perhaps the implicit message is that only violence will work and therefore you (the viewer) should also be violent. Or maybe the message is not so much that violence works as that violence is acceptable or even desirable. If all these nice, honest, good people are committing acts of violence, maybe this says to the viewer that this kind of behaviour is all right. These messages—that violence is the only way to settle disputes, that violence is acceptable—might influence attitudes and behaviours. If viewers who get these messages accept them, we can expect their own attitudes toward violence to become more positive, and that they will be likely to become violent themselves.

There are several responses to this idea. First, I do not think these programs carry the message that violence is the only way to settle disputes, or that violence is generally acceptable. To the extent they convey any messages about violence, those messages are quite different from these. One possible message is that when a bad person or a bad monster or a bad animal starts a fight or commits a crime or threatens you or those you love, those who are entrusted with protecting society may have to use violence in return. In the great majority of all films and television programs containing violence, all or most of the violence committed by the good guys is committed by police or crimefighters or others who are allowed to use violence. And they use violence only after it has been used by the bad guys; the good guys almost never (perhaps never) start the fight. While we would prefer a society without any violence, few of us would deny the police (and mythical protectors of society) the right to use violence when necessary. It would be nice if the police and other good guys could be shown trying a little harder to talk the bad guys out of the fight, convincing them to give up, and so on. Still, it is not realistic to expect many criminals, terrorists, monsters, and so on to be convinced by talk of this kind to give up their weapons and stop doing whatever bad stuff they are doing. The fact is that there is violence in our society and often it is dealt with by violence of some sort. I do not believe that those who watch these programs are getting the message that violence is the only way to deal with problems. If they get any message at all along these lines, it is that we should all be thankful that the good guys—those who are there to protect us—can also use violence when necessary. They are certainly not getting the message that they, the viewers, should engage in violence. So there is no reason to expect their behaviour to be affected.

A somewhat different concern of those who worry about the effects of media violence is that aggression is shown as effective. If so, viewers may come to believe this and may accordingly behave more aggressively themselves. The authors of the National Television Violence Study (NTVS) are especially adamant on this point. They assert that when violence is not punished—or even worse, when it is rewarded—it is especially likely to make viewers more aggressive. As we have seen, there is no scientific evidence to support this assertion. Despite that, it is repeated over and over as if it were a known fact. Scientific evidence of causation aside, the NTVS provides a highly useful picture of what occurs on television. It found that television programs often contain violent acts that are not punished immediately. However, the same study shows that bad characters in serious shows are almost always punished eventually. Although the authors of the study are concerned about the lack of immediate punishment, I think the viewers all know that punishment is coming. Much of the tension in the stories we watch on television comes from wondering when and how the bad guys will get punished, but there is no question that in almost every program, in almost every story, the bad people who start the violence will get what they have coming to them. One could argue that television presents an unrealistic picture in this respect: criminals on TV get caught and punished far more often than they do in the real world. So if viewers learn anything, if they get any message, it is that violence committed for a bad or illegal reason in a serious context will be punished.

The other possible message from most of the programs is that it is a bad idea, not a good one, to be the one who first uses violence. In almost every television program that has violence, and in most films, the person who starts the fight (the bad guy) eventually loses. The authors of the study are concerned that good characters are rarely punished after using violence. Naturally! They are allowed to use violence when it is necessary, so they should not get punished. When Batman punches a crook, should Batman get hurt? When Bruce Willis fights criminals, should Willis lose? When police officers get in a shootout with criminals, should the police get punished? Obviously not. In fact, to the extent that crime fighter shows have any message, it is not that police officers should get punished for using violence, but that it is dangerous to be a police officer or anyone who fights crime. This does not teach anyone that it is okay to use violence or that violence will be rewarded—if anything, it teaches the opposite.

Some have argued that the media glamorize violence. Certainly, some heroes are violent and glamorous. This is true of many of the comic book heroes (Batman, Superman, Power Rangers, Wonder Woman) and the non-cartoon versions of these characters. It is also true of some other characters, such as James Bond. But many violent heroes are anything but glamorous. Bruce Willis in *Die Hard,* most police officers in cop shows, and so on get dirty, are often hurt, and are typically shown doing their jobs, which are important but not at all glamorous. In fact, one theme that runs through many of the more realistic shows is that law enforcement people have tough, dangerous jobs and are not appreciated enough by the public or by politicians. Is there any evidence that the supposed glamour of these violent characters has caused more people to apply for jobs in law enforcement? I doubt it. So I do not accept that, in general, violence has been glamorized in the media. I agree that it is not made as awful and ugly as it really is, but not that it has been made especially attractive. Therefore, I am not surprised that children have not been influenced by the glamour of violence to engage in it.

I cannot prove that media violence carries no message or that it does not glamorize violence. But I ask those who believe it does to think seriously about whether the programs and films they know really urge people, explicitly or implicitly, to engage in violence; or suggest that violence is glamorous. A few films and programs may do this, but I think any reasonable view of the full range of programs would show that they do not encourage viewers to be violent themselves. They certainly do not directly try to sell violence the way ads for products try to sell those products. I cannot think of one television program that contains the explicit message that viewers should go out and commit violence.

One reason why some people are so convinced that media violence causes aggression is that they think they have seen it happen themselves. They know that children in schoolyards are imitating the Power Rangers and other television heroes who engage in martial arts. They see children watch a violent program and then get involved in fighting. Since they have witnessed it first-hand, they are totally convinced. At a congressional hearing, a congressman said he did not need any scientific evidence to prove that media violence causes aggression. The reason was that he had come home recently and been met at the door by his young son aiming a karate kick at him. Q.E.D. What more evidence does anyone need?

I understand the power of personal experience. However, it is important to step back and try to figure out what the experience means. The congressman's story is a perfect example. I did not get a chance to respond to him, but

I would have said the following: Congressman, I assume that you and your son have a good relationship. I assume he did not harm you and that he did not mean to harm you. (If he meant to harm you, please get some professional help right away.) Congressman, your son was playing. He was not fighting; he did not hurt you; he was playing. He had probably seen someone on television doing karate kicks—or maybe he saw it in the schoolyard—and he was imitating them. Years ago, he might have pretended to punch you or to shoot you with a bow and arrow or with a gun. Would you have been as upset if he had put his fingers into the shape of a gun—as so many boys do—and said 'bang, bang'? Then I suppose you would have known he was playing, but it would have been the same thing. The precise behaviour is surely influenced by the media, but it is not aggression—it is play. You might not like that kind of play; you might prefer him to throw you a ball or do something really imaginative. If you want to complain that television does not foster imagination and creativity, you may have a point. But aggression? No.

Also, for those who have watched kids get into trouble after a violent program, maybe the effect is due entirely to the fact that they are excited. Violent programs tend to get kids aroused. When they are aroused, they engage in more active behaviour, and some of that may be aggressive. But it is the arousal that affects them, not the content of the show. Any show that aroused them would have had the same effect. There is even a study showing that kids are more aggressive after watching 'Sesame Street.' I can believe it. There is no aggression in the program. It is hard to imagine a more prosocial, educational, imaginative show. But it is a very active, lively, fast-paced show—that's one of the reasons children like it so much. If they are more aggressive after it, obviously it is not because of any aggressive content, but rather because of the arousal. Yes, children may be more aggressive after watching violent programs, but they may be equally aggressive after any action program or any program that is lively and exciting. You may prefer children to be quieter. I'm not so sure. I think it is probably good for them to get excited and aroused even if it sometimes leads to more trouble for the parents. Bored children can get into real trouble; interested, excited kids are probably better off in the long run. So don't blame media violence for increased action and sometimes increased aggression, unless you want to blame everything—movies, television programs, books, any arousing, exciting activity.

Another argument I hear is that since the advent of television, crime and aggression have increased. Supposedly the connection is obvious. I dealt with this at some length in my discussion of Centerwall's paper. The main point is that all sorts of things have changed since television was available, and these other changes are much more likely than television to have produced the increase in crime. I do not want to rehash these arguments, but I urge those who see a connection to keep in mind that there are explanations other than television violence. Let me add that both aggression and crime have been with us for a long time, since well before television and movies. There is no indication that in general, either aggressiveness or crime has increased since the invention of movies or television. Moreover, the homicide rates in the United States and Canada have gone through many cycles. What people tend to focus on is that the rate of violent crime—for homicide in particular—increased sharply from about 1965 to 1980. That's true. But the rate then levelled off, and has been dropping sharply since around 1992. The rate is now back to about what it was in the early 1970s, not much above its low point in the 1960s. It is the increase that makes some people think it must be due to television, because the increase came soon after the introduction and spread of television. However, an almost identical pattern—a sharp increase followed by a sharper decrease—occurred in the early part of this century, long before there was any television. The increase then was certainly not due to television, but rather to social factors of various kinds. If that earlier increase occurred in the absence of television, why think that the later increase was due to television? It makes no sense.

Then there is the recent decrease in violent crime. All of the studies indicate that television and films have just as much violence as they used to, or more, and that the violence is more graphic than ever. Also, violent video games started to become available and popular in the early 1990s and are now a major element in many children's lives. And I suppose the lyrics in popular music, especially rap music, are much more violent than they have ever been. Yet despite the continuing media violence, and the new violence in video games and music, the rates for homicide and other violent crimes have dropped seven years in a row. If media violence caused the increase, how can one explain the decrease? A more likely explanation is that media violence did not cause either the increase or the decrease; both of these were caused by major social forces.

Finally, it is important to remember that the research I have reviewed dealt almost exclusively with the effects of fictional or fictionalized programs and films. There has been almost no systematic research on the effects of exposure to real violence or to media coverage of real violence. Some ingenious work by Phillips (1979, 1982) suggests that watching prizefights may increase homicides and that hearing about suicides may cause an increase in suicides. This work has been criticized on methodological grounds, and in my earlier review I found many of the details of the results implausible. Phillips has answered the criticisms, and he may be right that highly publicized violent events of these kinds cause an increase in similar events. Although there is no systematic evidence to support it, many people believe that media coverage of horrific crimes causes some people to imitate those crimes. The killings at Columbine High School received an enormous amount of media attention and were followed by a number of similar attacks in other schools. It is possible that the later crimes were caused to some extent by coverage of the earlier one.

We do not know very much about the effects of coverage of actual violent events. However, I want to make it absolutely clear that this review does not deal with this issue. The lack of scientific support for the causal hypothesis relates entirely to fictional material. Indeed, I think it is likely that real violence and the coverage of real violence do affect aggression and crime. Children may imitate violence they observe directly. Both children and adults may be influenced by their knowledge that their society or their neighbourhood has a lot of violence. Moreover, it seems likely that repeated exposure to real violence, either directly or in the media, causes desensitization to subsequent real violence. I believe that when there is a murder on the front page of the newspaper everyday or as the lead story on the television news everyday, people are less shocked than when murders are rare events. Thus, both the causal hypothesis and the desensitization hypothesis may be correct with respect to real violence or media coverage of real violence, and perhaps that is what people should be worrying about.

Let me end by acknowledging again that to many people it seems self-evident that media violence causes aggression. I think I have shown in this comprehensive, detailed review that the scientific evidence does not support that view. Perhaps some of the arguments in this chapter will make it seem less obvious, and people will be willing to change their views. In any case, I hope that neither organizations nor individuals will ever again say that the evidence for a causal effect of media violence is overwhelming or that the case is closed. Perhaps people will even begin to accept the clear fact that the evidence does not support the notion that exposure to media violence causes aggression or desensitization to aggression.

All references for articles included in *Taking Sides: Clashing Views in Abnormal Psychology, 6/e* **can be found on the Web at www.mhhe.com/cls.**

CHALLENGE QUESTIONS

Does Exposure to Media Violence Promote Aggressive Behavior?

1. Some people would suggest that a child emulating a Power Ranger by doing a karate kick is an aggressive act. Others might see the act as playful. If you were conducting research in this area, how would you operationally define the difference between playful behavior and aggressive behavior?
2. To what extent do you believe that media violence encourages or glorifies violence? Provide an example or two of film images that might have led to subsequent violence in society?
3. If you were a clinician treating a child who enacts behaviors seen in violent media, what kind of intervention would you try to develop in an effort to reduce the child's aggressive behavior?
4. Imagine that you are a researcher studying the differential impact of exposure to media violence and exposure to real-world violence. How would you go about studying this difference?
5. It is well-known that video games have become increasingly violent in the past decade. How do you explain this trend?

Suggested Readings

Carter, C., & Weaver, C. K. (2003). *Violence and the media*. Philadelphia, PA: Open University Press.

Dahl, G., & DellaVigna, S. (2009). Does movie violence increase violent crime? *The Quarterly Journal of Economics, 124(2)*, 677–734.

Ferguson, C.J., & Kilburn, J. (2009). The public health risks of media violence: A meta-analytic review. *The Journal of Pediatrics, 154(5)*, 759–763.

Huesmann, L. R., Moise-Titus, J., Podolski, C., & Eron, L. D. (2003). Longitudinal relations between children's exposure to TV violence and their aggressive and violent behavior in young adulthood, 1977–1992. *Developmental Psychology, 39(2)*, 201–221.

Potter, J. W. (2003). *The 11 myths of media violence*. Thousand Oaks, CA: Sage Publications.

ISSUE 16

Would Legalization of Virtual Child Pornography Reduce Sexual Exploitation of Children?

YES: Arnold H. Loewy, from "Taking Free Speech Seriously: The United States Supreme Court and Virtual Child Pornography," *UNC Public Law Research Paper No. 02–17* (November 2002)

NO: Diana E. H. Russell and Natalie J. Purcell, from "Exposure to Pornography as a Cause of Child Sexual Victimization," in Nancy E. Dowd, Dorothy G. Singer, and Robin Fretwell Wilson, *Handbook of Children, Culture, and Violence* (Sage Publications, 2006)

ISSUE SUMMARY

YES: Professor of Law Arnold H. Loewy views the issue of virtual child pornography from a legal perspective, asserting that such material is a form of free speech that ought to be constitutionally protected. He also contends that legalizing virtual child pornography would reduce the extent to which real children would be exploited.

NO: Authors Diana E. H. Russell and Natalie J. Purcell express vehement objections to any forms of pornography involving images of children, asserting that Internet users with no previous sexual interest in children may find themselves drawn into a world in which the societal prohibition against adult–child sex is undermined.

Some consumers of Internet pornography have pushed the limits farther and farther in their pursuit of images that will excite, and possibly shock, their sensibilities. The ultimate taboo, sadly, involves pornography involving children. Few, if any, sane people would defend the exploitation of real children in order to serve the masturbatory fantasies of pornography consumers. However, some have argued that virtual forms of pornography might actually protect real children by accommodating the fantasies of adults who crave sexual images of children. Critics of child pornography in any form argue that permitting even virtual images of children in sexual situations violates a societal boundary and puts children at great risk of being victimized in real life.

Judicial decisions have come down on the side of the legality of virtual child pornography. In 2002, the U.S. Supreme Court (*Ashcroft v. The Free Speech*

Coalition) ruled that virtual child pornography is speech that is protected under the First Amendment and cannot be banned by child-pornography laws. The Ohio Supreme Court in 2007 ruled that pornographic images that are wholly faked, no matter how realistic, are legal.

Professor of Law Arnold H. Loewy argues that pornography is a form of free speech that is constitutionally protected. Pragmatically speaking, Loewy acknowledges that child pornography is a reality that is here to stay; he believes that legalizing virtual child pornography may actually reduce the number of children that are currently being exploited by what he calls a "perverted industry."

Authors Diana E. H. Russell and Natalie J. Purcell advocate the implementation of legal sanctions against child pornography as critically important deterrents to the exploitation of children. They believe that allowing sexual images in any form that involve children undermines the prohibition against adult–child sex and facilitates the proliferation of Internet sites on which such behaviors or desires are not considered deviant and where pedophiles and others interested in child pornography can feel more normal. The ultimate risk is that more children will be put at risk of sexual victimization.

POINT

- Pedophiles most likely obtain child pornography because they are attracted to children, rather than becoming attracted to children by looking at the child pornography they already possess.

- Unless all speech is free, no speech is free. Virtual child pornography is speech that ought to be constitutionally protected.

- It is neither intuitively obvious nor has it been proved that eliminating all virtual pornography would significantly reduce the incidents of pedophilia. Even if it could be proved that virtual child pornography caused significant net harm, it would not follow that the law should permit its suppression.

- Many things can be misused. If virtual pornography is to be suppressed because of its capacity to seduce children, we might as well suppress cartoons, candy, puppy dogs, and vans.

- If virtual child pornography is (or can be made) nearly identical to real child pornography, and only real pornography is unlawful, why wouldn't pornographers and consumers view the virtual content? Legalizing virtual child pornography may actually reduce the number of children that are currently exploited by this perverted industry.

COUNTERPOINT

- Internet users with no previous sexual interest in children may find themselves aroused by child pornography, which transforms children into sexual objects.

- Fear of legal sanctions is the most important factor in restraining potential and active molesters from abusing children.

- Some males who have never acted on their desire to have sex with a child may be ignorant or anxious about how to proceed with this. While such concerns could inhibit them from perpetrating such an act, child pornography removes this impediment by providing instructions for the sexual abuse of children.

- Many child molesters show pornography to children in order to arouse their sexual curiosity and to persuade children that they would enjoy certain sexual acts, and to convince them that what they are being asked to do is alright.

- Child pornography undermines the prohibition against adult–child sex. Even child pornography cartoons communicate its social acceptability.

YES

Arnold H. Loewy[1]

Taking Free Speech Seriously: The United States Supreme Court and Virtual Child Pornography

I. The Importance of Protecting Bad Speech

Few liberal democracies challenge freedom of speech in the abstract. Specific applications, however, are different. Many, who would never challenge freedom of speech in the abstract, balk at extending such protection to flag burners,[2] and Nazis.[3] Yet, the slightest reflection should reveal that unless all speech is free, no speech is free. No sensible government, including the most dictatorial, will ever prosecute good speech or even neutral speech.[4] Indeed, no democracy would even think of prosecuting ordinarily bad speech (*e.g.*, vote Republican).[5] It is only when we get to very bad speech that the government even thinks about prosecution. Thus, it is in those situations in which free speech is needed most. Hence, protection for Nazis, flag burners, and virtual child pornographers logically follows if we want to take free speech seriously.

But should we want to take it seriously if the cost of doing so is to give added protection for speech that we would all be better off without? One's first intuition is to say "no," and indeed that is the result regularly reached in European courts[6] and too frequently in American courts.[7] The reason that this should bother us is that it gives government the power to decide which speech can compete in the marketplace and which speech is dead on arrival.

While some of us might be happy to relegate flag burning, Nazis, and virtual pornography to the scrapheap of dead on arrival speech, few would say that about speech urging racial integration. Yet speech urging racial integration fifty years ago would have been thought highly offensive to much of the citizenry of a large number of communities (including Charleston, South Carolina) and would have been subject to prohibition under a standard that protects the dignitary interest of some against the speech of others. Thus, even though government may be correct about some types of speech it is better to deny government the power to suppress that speech than it would be to allow it to suppress speech that may turn out to be valuable (such as civil rights speech).[8] . . .

UNC Public Law Research Paper No. 02-17, November 2002. First published in the *First Amendment Law Review*. Copyright © 2002 by Arnold H. Loewy. Reprinted by permission.

II. Distinguishing Real Child Pornography

Real child pornography is rightly subject to prosecution. But the reason that it is so treated has nothing to do with the abhorrent nature, or intrinsic worthlessness, of the material. It can be prosecuted for the same reason that employment of child labor can be prosecuted. Just as child labor harms the children that manufacture the goods to be sold, so does child pornography. It would not be a defense to a child labor prosecution that employment of children was necessary to enhance the quantity or quality of the product produced. Similarly, it should be no defense that the finished product had some kind of literary or artistic merit. It is the use of a child in an explicit sexual performance that is rightly forbidden.[9]

Similarly, as the United States Supreme Court has suggested, morphed child pornography, that is images of a real child morphed to appear to be engaging in sexual activity, is enough like real child pornography that it should be treated as though it were real.[10] A morphed image does not harm a real child by making the picture, but it does harm the child by providing an unauthorized permanent and false record of the child's engaging in sexual activity.[11]

Apart from pornography that displays the image of a real child, actual or morphed, the objections to the material are similar to the objections to any kind of distasteful speech and should be subject to the same kind of scrutiny. In the remainder of this paper, I shall explain why none of the justifications generally advanced against virtual child pornography warrant its prohibition.

III. Virtual Pornography's Capacity to Harm Real Children

Proponents of criminalizing virtual pornography argue that there are two ways in which the material can harm real children. First, they argue that virtual child pornography can whet a pedophile's appetite, making it more likely that he will abuse real children. Second, it is argued that a pedophile can use a picture of what appears to be a real child enjoying her sexuality as a visual aid to persuade an innocent victim to engage in similar activity. I will treat these arguments separately.

As to the first argument, I question both its factual accuracy and its legal significance. As to its accuracy, it is undoubtedly true that many, if not most, pedophiles possess child pornography. It is quite another thing to assume that the pornography caused the pedophilia. More likely, it was the perpetrator's attraction to children that caused him to possess the pornography rather than vice versa.[12] Indeed, one does not have to approach a "Clockwork Orange"[13] scenario to find behavioralists employing child pornography for the purpose of curing pedophiles?[14]

I do not mean to argue that there has never been a pedophile who but for the pornography would not have committed his crime. But, that can hardly be the relevant standard. For one to sustain this justification, it would be necessary to establish that virtual child pornography (as opposed to real child pornography) has significantly increased pedophilia. To prove that five people who viewed virtual pornography committed an act of pedophilia that they otherwise would not have committed (assuming one could establish causation, which I doubt) would only tell half of the story. We would also have to know how many potential pedophiles had their appetites satiated by virtual child pornography, and therefore left real children alone.

To illustrate, three of the most heinous crimes in history were inspired respectively by the holy Bible[15], an Anglican High Church Service[16], and the movie the Ten Commandments.[17] Obviously nobody measures the worth of these sources by the worst thing that they inspired. To be sure, child pornography, virtual or otherwise, has undoubtedly done far more harm and far less good than the aforementioned sources. Nevertheless, it is neither intuitively obvious, nor has it been proven, that eliminating all virtual pornography from the face of the earth would significantly reduce the incidents of pedophilia.

More importantly, even if it could be proven that virtual child pornography caused significant net harm, it would not follow that the law should permit its suppression. One of the costs of free speech is the recognition that sometimes speech will do more harm than good. Even so, for the reasons already given,[18] it is better to allow it to cause whatever harm it may rather than allow the government the power to decide whether the book can be published at all. For example, the Turner Diaries were said to have been the inspiration for Timothy McVeigh's massacre at Oklahoma City. It would not be hard for a court to conclude that on a cost/benefit basis that book should be condemned. Indeed, it is hard for me to believe that the Turner Diaries did not do significantly more harm than good. Yet, I would vehemently oppose the government's power to remove it from the marketplace of ideas.

To further illustrate the wrongness of allowing judges (or legislators) to condemn a book based on its net harm, imagine a claim in the United States that the Qur'an should be banned because it was said to inspire the 9/11 terrorists. Would anybody feel comfortable leaving a good versus harm standard to American judges, most of whom are Christian, in regard to Islam's holiest book? I certainly would not, and thus conclude that even if virtual child pornography were conclusively shown to do more harm than good, the Supreme Court was correct in not allowing it to be eliminated.[19]

As to the argument that virtual pornography can be used to seduce children, Justice Kennedy, for the Supreme Court, got it exactly right when he noted that if virtual pornography is to be suppressed because of its capacity to seduce children, we might as well suppress "cartoons, video games, and candy."[20] And, I might add that he could have included bicycles, puppy dogs, and vans. The point, of course, is that many things, including but not limited to literature, can be misused. But, as the Court once succinctly put it: "We cannot reduce the entire adult population to reading only that which is fit for children."[21]

IV. Distinguishing Virtual from Real Child Pornography

By far the most powerful argument for punishing virtual child pornography is the difficulty of distinguishing it from the real thing. The argument is that virtual and real pictures look so indistinguishable that a person marketing real child pornography might argue either that the material is virtual (and you can't prove beyond a reasonable doubt that it isn't) or at least that the defendant believed that it was virtual. To the extent that this argument rests on a factually sound premise, it presents a very serious problem. If real child pornography is punishable, but virtual isn't, and you can't tell the difference, what's a government to do?

The good news is that, at least for now, that does not seem to be an insurmountable problem. Although defendants have argued that the material was virtual, it has never been a successful defense.[22] Furthermore, there is technology available that allows the government to take a picture apart, pixel by pixel, to determine its origin.[23] Thus, as with the erstwhile nuclear arms race, detection appears to be keeping up with technology.

To the extent that technology outstrips detection and one really cannot tell the difference, some type of burden of proof shifting device might be appropriate. Surely, the government should be able to argue that a picture that appears real can be treated as real in the absence of evidence that it isn't. Such a rule would differ from the one at issue in *Ashcroft,* where the statute allowed punishment even when it was clear that the picture was virtual.

As for the *scienter* issue, presumably it would take more than the defendant's word that he intended to transmit virtual pictures to create a reasonable doubt. If the Government proves that the pictures are real, a simple statement from the defendant that he thought they were virtual would be very unlikely to create a reasonable doubt.

V. Decriminalizing Virtual Pornography May Protect Real Children

It is certainly not immediately obvious that real children would be *better* off by allowing the sale of virtual pornography, yet that may in fact be the case. In an ideal world, nobody would want child pornography, real or virtual. Unfortunately, the world we live in is not ideal. Despite the efforts of all civilized governments to suppress child pornography, it is still with us. Why? Simply because the demand is there. If one accepts the unfortunate truth that the demand for child pornography exists despite these governmental efforts, there is little reason to believe that we will totally stamp it out.

On the other hand, if virtual child pornography is (or can be made) nearly identical to real child pornography and only the latter is unlawful, why wouldn't the pornographer sell only the former? Certainly most pornographers would love to avoid the risk of prison if their anticipated profit would not be compromised. And, from the consumer's perspective, a virtual picture would also shield him from prosecution.[24] Thus, there is good reason to believe that legalizing virtual child pornography may reduce the number of children that are currently exploited by this perverted industry. And so, the United States Supreme Court may well have rendered a decision that will ultimately protect children as well as it protects freedom of speech.

Notes

1. Graham Kenan Professor of Law: University of North Carolina School of Law.

2. See Chief Justice Rehnquist's impassioned dissent (joined by Justices White and O'Connor) in Texas v. Johnson 491 U.S. 397 at 421 (1989). See also Justice Stevens dissent at 436. After *Johnson,* Congress and the President again attempted to ban flag burning with the "Flag Protection Act of 1989" which the Supreme Court again overturned by a bare 5–4 majority in U.S. v. Eichman 496 U.S. 310 (1990).

3. See dissenting opinion of Judge Sprecher in Collin v. Smith 578 F. 2d 1197 at 1210 (1978). A recent European example with strong ramifications in the United States has been the case of La Ligue Contra Le Racisme et L' Antisemitisme v. Yahoo (tried in America as Yahoo v. LICRA. 169 F. Supp. 2d 1181 N.D. Cal. 2001). Here a French judge held that the act of displaying Nazi memorabilia itself violated French law (Article R645-1 Penal Code) and that the American web site Yahoo must comply with French law and not display Nazi memorabilia on its own, American site. Also see David Kretzmer, *Free Speech and Racism,* 8 Cardozo L. Rev. 445 (1987).

4. For example, "Blue is prettier then green." See Arnold H. Loewy, *Criminal Speech: Should Free Trade in Ideas be Absolute?,* 2 Crim. L. F. 117, 118 (1990).

5. Or if you don't like that one, try "Vote Democrat."

6. See, for example, Gay News, Ltd. v. United Kingdom 5 E. H. R. R. 123 (1982). Cf Jeremy Jones v. Fredrick Toben (No H97/120) dealing with section 18C of Australia's Racial Discrimination Act of 1975 that makes it a crime "to offend, insult, humiliate, or intimidate another person or group of people" based on "race, colour or national or ethnic origin."

7. See, e.g., the Supreme Court's willingness to uphold obscenity laws such as in Miller v. California 413 U.S. 15 (1973). See Loewy, *Obscenity, Pornography, and First Amendment Theory, supra* at note 2. See also the four justice dissent in Texas v. Johnson, *supra* at note 9. As I have said elsewhere "It is understandable that our President, Congress, legislators, and general populace who do not regularly study the First Amendment would initially condemn the *Johnson* decision. It is more difficult to rationalize the opinions of the Supreme Court dissenters who really ought to know better." Arnold H. Loewy, *The Flag-Burning Case: Freedom of Speech When We Need It Most,* 68 N.C. L. Rev. 165 at 172–173 (1989).

8. For a more detailed development of this point, see Arnold H. Loewy, *Freedom of Speech as a Product of Democracy,* 27 U. Rich. L. Rev. 427 (1993).

9. I put to one side the issue of whether the jurisdiction punishing the dissemination of child pornography is the one in which the pornography was made. I deal with the resolution of that issue elsewhere. See Arnold H. Loewy, *Obscenity, Pornography, and First Amendment Theory,* 2 Wm. & Mary Bill Rts. J. 471 at 480–482 (1993). Cited *supra* at note 2.

10. But did not hold. Justice Kennedy wrote that "Although morphed images may fall within the definition of virtual child pornography, they implicate the interests of real children and are in that sense closer to the images in *Ferber.*" Ashcroft v. Free Speech Coalition 122 S. Ct. at 1397.

11. Any doubt that such pictures can be harmful, sometimes when least expected, was dispelled by the recent Miss North Carolina dispute in the

Miss America contest. The winner's picture was taken unauthorizedly while she was changing clothes. The suggested presence of those pictures was enough to disqualify her.

12. See Eberhard Kronhausen & Phyllis Kronhausen, *Pornography and the Law,* (1959 and 1964 update). Also see studies done in Denmark, Sweden and the former West Germany concluding that the availability of sexually explicit material leads to less crime, not more. Reprinted in Marcia Pally, Sense and Censorship: The Vanity of Bonfires (Americans for Constitutonal Freedom 1991, vol. 2). Even opponents of pornography have long had to concede that there is "no substantial basis for the belief that erotic materials constitute a primary or significant cause or development of character defects or that they operate as a significant determanitive factor in causing crime and delinquency." President's Commission on Obscenity and Pornography (Bantam 1970) p. 243. See a similar concession in Lydia W. Lee, *Child Pornography Prevention act of 1996: Confronting the Challenges of Virtual Reality,* 8 S. Cal. Interdisc. L. J. 639 (1999).

13. A Clockwork Orange (Warner Brothers 1972). In this film, a criminal is repeatedly shown images of horrific violence and given a drug that makes him associate it with strong feelings of nausea. The character is released into the world unable to commit any violent acts or even to think violent thoughts.

14. See Lobitz, W.C. and LoPiccolo, J., *New Methods in Behavioral Treatment of Sexual Dysfunction,* J. Behav. Ther. & Exp. Psychiat. Vol. 3 pp. 265–71. See generally, Patricia Gillan, *Therapeutic Uses of Obscenity,* reprinted in Dhavan and Davies, Censorship and Obscenity (Martin and Robertson 1978).

15. Albert Fish was inspired to castrate and 'sacrifice' young boys by reading about sacrifices in the Bible. See Earl Finbar Murphy, *The Value of Pornography,* 10 Wayne L. Rev. 655,668 (1964).

16. John George Haigh was inspired by the procedures of the Anglican High Church Service to drink his victims' blood through straws and dissolve their bodies in acid baths. *Id.*

17. Heinrich Pommerenke was prompted by Cecil B. DeMille's film The Ten Commandments to rape, abuse, and slay women. *Id.*

18. *Supra,* section I.

19. Anybody who doubts this would do well to see the Hollywood satire "Pleasantville," which recounts the story of a town from the fifties where only sweetness and light is allowed. Anybody who dares to deviate from the approved "everything is perfect" mantra is dealt with harshly.

20. 122 S. Ct. at 1402.

21. Butler v. Michigan 352 U.S. 380 at 384.

22. At least as of April 16, 2002 when *Ashcroft* was decided. See 122 S. Ct. at 1406 citing Brief for Petitioners 37.

23. The technique is called "digital pixel examination." Reported in ABC News "Detecting Real Child Porn: New software tools spot doctored pictures." (April 22, 2002) Available at. . . .

24. The only reason that this might not happen is the dollar cost of producing virtual child pronography. This, of course, is a reason for the law to keep the cost of exploiting real children high. It is also a reason to decriminalize virtual pornography as the Supreme Court has done.

Diana E. H. Russell and
Natalie J. Purcell

 NO

Exposure to Pornography as a Cause of Child Sexual Victimization

Researchers almost universally agree that photographing children for child pornography constitutes child sexual victimization. We will argue in this chapter that a causal relationship exists between adult and juvenile males' exposure to child pornography—including computer-generated, written, and oral forms of pornography—and their perpetration of child sexual victimization. Because the theoretical work behind this model comes from the work of Diana Russell over decades, we describe this as "Russell's theory."

Because child pornography does not negatively affect all viewers to the same degree, some researchers conclude that mere exposure to this material cannot play a causal role in child sexual victimization. This is analogous to the tobacco industry's faulty claim that, since many smokers do not die of lung cancer, smoking does not cause lung cancer. Such reasoning is faulty. When there are multiple causes for a phenomenon, any one of them "may be a sufficient but not necessary condition for the occurrence of the effect or a necessary but not sufficient condition" (Theodorson & Theodorson, 1979, p. 40). In this sense of the term, we argue that exposure to child pornography causes child sexual victimization.

Although women have been known to sexually abuse both male and female children, males form the overwhelming majority of child pornography consumers and perpetrators of child sexual victimization. Therefore, Russell's three-factor causal theory focuses on male perpetrators. (The terms "man," "men," "male," or "males" in this chapter should be understood to include juvenile and adult males.)

Catharsis vs. Intensified Desire

According to the catharsis theory, the repeated exposure of males to pornography "leads to a steadily decreasing interest" in the material (Bart & Jozsa, 1980, p. 210). This exposure is frequently described as a "safety valve." As applied to child pornography, this theory assumes that repeated viewing of child pornography decreases viewers' desire for sex with children. Hence, according to this theory, viewers of child pornography should be less likely to sexually victimize children.

Zillmann and Bryant (1986) conducted an experiment based on 160 subjects.

These researchers found that the subjects' boredom after repeatedly viewing the same pornographic material motivated them to switch to viewing different and more extreme pornography, such as material involving the infliction of pain, violent pornography, and "uncommon or unusual sexual practices," including bondage, sadomasochism and bestiality (Zillmann & Bryant, 1986, p. 577).

Research aside, common sense and rationality unequivocally challenge the catharsis theory. Very few people would likely support a proposal to solve the problem of parents physically beating their children by having them watch movies that show parents battering and torturing their children. Why is it only in the case of misogynistic pornography that so many individuals—including a handful of researchers—believe that exposure dissipates the problem? The plain inconsistency and irrationality of the catharsis theory suffice to dismiss the notion that pornography serves as a "safety valve."

Pornography as a Cause of Child Sexual Victimization

The major objective of this chapter is to challenge the belief that exposure to child pornography is harmless and to demonstrate that exposure to child pornography can cause child sexual victimization in societies where this is proscribed.

Causal Factor IA: Viewing Child Pornography Predisposes Some Males, Not Previously So Disposed, to Sexually Desire Children

It is commonly believed that exposure to child pornography cannot create a desire for sexual contact with children in males for whom it did not previously exist. Most people prefer to believe that any man who becomes sexually interested in children must have been predisposed to this interest. The following . . . points present ways in which exposure to child pornography can cause sexual arousal in some males who were not previously sexually interested in children. These points demonstrate that "normal" heterosexual males can become sexually aroused by depictions of children.

By Sexualizing/Sexually Objectifying Children

Child pornography transforms children into sexual objects designed to appeal to pedophiles and non-pedophilic child molesters.

Child pornographers often direct the girls they photograph to get into sexual poses or to engage in masturbation or sexual intercourse like women in adult pornography. These sexualized pictures of girls (often acting as mini-adults) evoke a sexual response in some males who previously had no interest in sex with girls.

By Application of the Laws of Learning

While some may believe that only males who are sexually aroused by child pornography would search for it, O'Connell (2001) maintains that "All the evidence is that many people [males] at least browse in this area [of child pornography], if not actively downloading" Web site pictures (p. 7).

A classic experiment by Rachman and Hodgson (1968) demonstrates that male subjects can learn to become sexually aroused by seeing a picture of a woman's boot after repeatedly seeing women's boots in association with sexually arousing slides of nude females. The laws of learning that created the boot fetish can also presumably teach males who previously were not sexually aroused by depictions of adult–child sex, to become aroused after exposure to child pornography.

Masturbation to child pornography during or following exposure to it, reinforces the association between these images and sexual gratification. This constitutes what McGuire, Carlisle, and Young (1965) refer to as "masturbatory conditioning" (p. 185). These researchers hypothesized that "an individual's arousal pattern can be altered by directly changing his masturbatory fantasies" (Abel, Blanchard, & Becker, 1978, p. 192). Abel et al. (1978) have treated violent sexual perpetrators by conditioning them to masturbate and ejaculate to nonviolent consensual portrayals of sex.

Presumably, it is equally possible to change males' non-deviant sexual fantasies and behavior to deviant ones. Hence, when male Internet users with no previous sexual interest in children inadvertently find themselves looking at child pornography, or when curiosity prompts such males to deliberately search out child pornography, they may be surprised to find themselves aroused by sexualized pictures of children. If these male viewers masturbate while viewing sexual pictures of children, this presumably can be the beginning of a growing interest in sex with children. For example, Jenkins (2001) notes that some posts on the Web "suggest that individuals were 'converted' after discovering the material [child pornography]" (p. 106). Furthermore, repeated masturbation to these portrayals may result in increased arousal. The pleasurable experience of orgasm is an exceptionally potent reinforcer. Adult and child pornography are widely used by males as ejaculation material and thus are effective at constructing or reconstructing viewers' patterns of sexual arousal and expression.

By Males Who Have Become Habituated to Adult Pornography Seeking Different or More Extreme Forms of Pornography

It is important to recognize that males who frequently view adult pornography, persons Russell describes as pornophiles, can also become interested and sexually aroused by child pornography.

It seems reasonable to suppose that some of the males who become bored with ordinary adult pornography would opt to view child pornography since it qualifies as a "less commonly practiced sexual activity."

Causal Factor IB: Viewing Child Pornography Intensifies the Desire of Some Males Who Are Already Sexually Aroused by Children

By Increasing Males' Masturbatory Activity Thereby Reinforcing Their Desires for Sex with Children

When pedophiles and other males who desire sex with children are exposed to child pornography that corresponds to their specific preferences (e.g., the gender and age of the child), their sexual arousal intensifies.

Many males with a sexual interest in children deliberately use child pornography to intensify their sexual desire as a prelude to masturbation or the sexual abuse of children. Silbert and Pines (1993) report that a father in their study used to show "his friends pornographic movies to get them sexually aroused before they would rape" his 9-year-old daughter (p. 117–118).

In sum, the more pedophiles and child molesters masturbate to child pornography, the stronger their arousal to this material, and the more it reinforces the association between their fantasies and their desire to have sex with or sexually abuse children.

By Suggesting Exciting New Ideas for Having Sex with/Sexually Abusing Children

Jenkins (2001) notes that most pedophiles consider the old child pornography pictures still circulating on the Internet (which he refers to as "oldies") to be boring (p. 84). Consequently, "[a] common theme on the pedo boards is requests for material that is not readily available,"—that is, novel kinds of child pornography (p. 84). "The range of requests is bewilderingly perverse," according to Jenkins. "A few themes recur often and arouse real enthusiasm. By far the most common include calls for 'Black loli,' African or African American subjects. . . . Also in demand are incest pictures" (p. 85).

With regard to incestuous abuse, every conceivable relationship is portrayed in pictorial and written forms on the Internet—especially fathers having sex with their daughters. Rare forms of incestuous abuse are greatly overrepresented, including mother—son incest and female-on-female incestuous abuse. Many of the acts demonstrated or described in Internet pornography are portrayed as exciting and unconventional, providing viewers with new ideas for having sex with children.

By Providing Images and Models of Adult–Child Sex/Abuse for Males to Imitate

Child pornography provides models for males who already have a sexual interest in children. By seeing the different acts perpetrated on children (many of which elicit no negative responses and some of which appear to elicit positive responses or enjoyment), these "newbies" (a term used by many pedophiles) are provided with models that can shape and intensify their desires. Portrayals of child pornography showing only positive consequences for the perpetrators and the victims are particularly conducive to imitation. (However, for males who are sadistic, child pornography showing negative consequences for the victim is more likely to intensify sexual arousal and serve as a model to imitate.)

Several examples illustrate the use of pornography as a model for imitation.

Consider also the young girl who testified in the 1985 Government Commission on Pornography:

> My father had an easel that he put by the bed. He'd pin a picture on the easel and like a teacher he would tell me this is what you're going to learn today. He would then act out the pictures on me. (Attorney General's Commission on Pornography: Final Report, Vol. 1, 1986, p. 782)

Tim Tate (1990) provides another example, quoting Len, a pedophile who had molested several hundred young boys during his lifetime:

> Child pornography became important to me because I enjoyed it, fantasized and masturbated to it. It wasn't a safety valve, though. At the time I was looking at the magazine it was OK, I was fine . . . but you're not going to look at a magazine all day. So when I went out in the open I would see another pretty boy and find myself chatting him up. In the end I would put into practice what I had seen in the magazines. (p. 110)

By Creating a Desire for Increasingly More Extreme Forms of Child Pornography

Jenkins (2001) maintains that some viewers of child pornography become addicted, with an increasing "hunger for ever more illegal material" (p. 109). Newcomers to child pornography on the Internet may be "amazed and stimulated by the first few softcore pornographic images" they see (p. 109). However, these images "are all too likely to become routine," motivating the more frequent downloaders to turn "avidly to the harder-core sites" (p. 109).

Habituation is clearly an intrinsic feature in the escalation described by viewers of child pornography. Some child pornography users acknowledge that "involvement thus becomes a cumulative process" (Jenkins, 2001, p. 109). For example, one pedophile explained, "With this hobby we get bored after a while with the usual and we risk a bit to get new stuff or get actual experience. It's a natural progression" (p. 109).

In conclusion, it seems clear that exposure to child pornography often becomes an escalating problem; what may have begun as observation of seemingly nonviolent images of adult–child sexual abuse can lead to sexual interest in increasingly more hardcore and violent images of child sexual victimization.

Causal Factor II: Viewing Child Pornography Undermines Some Males' Internal Inhibitions against Acting Out Their Desires to Have Sex with/Sexually Victimize Children

Each component of Causal Factor II contributes to the undermining of moral beliefs that inhibit some males with a sexual interest in children from acting out their sexual desires.

By Sexualizing/Sexually Objectifying and/or Depersonalizing Girls

Exposure to child pornography plays a vital role in both creating a sexual interest in children in some males not previously so disposed and undermining some males' internal inhibitions against acting out their desire to have sex with children. Child pornography portraying girls in sexually provocative poses or happily engaged in sexual acts with other children or with adult men or women can convince those exposed to it that some children want and enjoy sex with adult males.

By Undermining the Prohibition against Adult–Child Sex/Victimization

Although legal ages of consent vary in different countries, adult–child sex is proscribed in most countries today.

Despite the prohibition in the United States, there are massive numbers of child pornography Web sites that promote adult–child sexual victimization through photographs, videos, or written stories. For example, an incest Web site titled "Golden Incest Sites!" lists 50 titles. . . . The pictures, stories, videos, and other material it makes accessible to interested Internet surfers can serve as highly suggestive models for viewers who may never before have thought of their daughters, sons, nieces, nephews, and other younger relatives in a sexual way. The ubiquity of incest pornography also conveys the popularity of such images, suggesting that large numbers of men must experience such desires.

The prevalence of child pornography sites, their content, and their positive portrayals of adult–child sexual abuse all serve to diminish the deviant nature of incestuous and extrafamilial child sexual abuse. This in turn enhances the likelihood that some men's internal inhibitions against acting out incestuous and extrafamilial child sexual victimization will be undermined.

It is also important to note two other ways in which the prohibition against adult–child sex is undermined by child pornography. First, the inclusion of many child pornography cartoons in mainstream men's magazines like Playboy and Penthouse communicates its social acceptability. Second, the boards on various sites allow visitors to form their own subcultural communities in which such behaviors or desires are not considered deviant and where pedophiles and others interested in child pornography can feel more normal. . . .

By Advocating, Legitimizing, and/or Normalizing Adult–Child Sex/ Victimization

The legitimatizing and normalizing of adults' sexual victimization of children in child pornography are two of the most frequently cited ways in which this material undermines some viewers' internal inhibitions. As Tate (1990) points out,

> All paedophiles need to reassure themselves that what they are doing or want to do is OK. It [child pornography] validates their feelings, lowers their inhibitions and makes them feel that their behaviour is pretty normal in the context of this pornography—they see other people doing it in the videos or the magazines and it reassures them. (p. 24)

Clearly, child pornography has the power "to reinforce both the paedophile's attraction to children and his self-justification process" (Tate, 1990, p. 110). Pedophiles also "use porn to convince themselves that their behavior is not abnormal, but is shared by others" (Calcetas-Santos, 2001, p. 59).

By Providing Specific Instructions on How to Sexually Victimize a Child

Some males who have never acted on their desire to have sex with a child may be ignorant or anxious about how to proceed with this. Such concerns can inhibit them from perpetrating such an act. Child pornography removes this impediment by providing instructions for the sexual abuse of children. Tyler, a detective sergeant in the San Bernardino, California, Sheriff's Department, testified in hearings on child pornography and pedophilia conducted by Senator Arlen Specter about a child pornography magazine that described "how to have sex with prepubescent children" (Child Pornography and Pedophilia, 1984, p. 33). During these hearings, Senator Specter also discussed a book titled How to Have Sex With Kids that described "how to meet children, how to entice them, how to develop a relationship with them, and how to have sex with them" (p. 30). Sexually explicit illegal material presumably demonstrates at what ages it is possible for adult males to penetrate young children anally and vaginally.

Presumably, pedophiles and child molesters in general find such instructions useful. Even when explicit instructions on how to sexually victimize a child are not provided in child pornography, this material always provides models that viewers may learn from and attempt to emulate.

Causal Factor III: Viewing Child Pornography Undermines Some Males' Social Inhibitions against Acting Out Their Desires to Have Sex with/Sexually Victimize Children

Child pornography undermines viewers' social inhibitions against sexually victimizing children. It does so in three distinct ways.

By Diminishing Fear of Disapproval

Potential or actual child molesters who look at or download child pornography on the Internet will quickly become cognizant of the enormous number of child pornography Web sites, videos, and chat rooms. This material makes it abundantly clear that there are many other viewers and collectors of child pornography as well as many others who act out their sexual attraction to children. As Jenkins (2001) states it, "He [the pedophile viewer] finds that he is not alone in his deviant interests" (p. 106). This revelation "helps support the notion that the boards [where individuals post messages] are safe space that one can visit at will, [and] where like-minded friends can reliably be found," thereby diminishing viewers' fear of universal disapproval for their sexual interest in children (p. 108).

Crimmins (1995) testified at the Senate Judiciary Committee Hearings on Child Pornography on the Internet that, "People who may have never acted on such impulses before, are emboldened when they see that there are so many other individuals who have similar interests" (p. 2). Furthermore, Jenkins (2001) argues that, "The more pedophiles and pornographers are attacked by law enforcement agencies, mass media, and anti-pedos, the greater the sense of community against common enemies" (p. 114). The knowledge that they have a support group of like-minded colleagues contributes to undermining the fear of disapproval for sexually victimizing children.

By Diminishing Fear of Legal and Social Sanctions

Fear of legal sanctions is the most important factor in restraining potential molesters from abusing children. The more effective potential molesters perceive the social sanctions to be, the less likely they are to become perpetrators. Fear of legal sanctions also serves to restrain active child molesters.

However, child pornography consistently communicates the false message that those who violate children are in no danger of being apprehended or facing other negative consequences. We have not seen any pictorial child pornography that shows a sexual predator being apprehended by the police or ending up in prison. The same applies to written child pornography stories, fantasies, lists of Web sites and videos, as well as child pornography in men's magazines. The outcomes of child sexual abuse are always positive for the perpetrators. Hence, exposure to child pornography gives would-be child molesters a false sense of immunity from legal sanctions, thereby undermining their social inhibitions against acting out their desires.

Contributory Factor IV: Viewing Pornography Undermines Some Children's Abilities to Avoid, Resist, or Escape Sexual Victimization

Some perpetrators use force to accomplish their acts of child sexual victimization. In these cases, children's abilities to avoid, resist, or escape sexual victimization are irrelevant. There are, however, cases where children's exposure to pornography undermines these abilities and permits sexual abuse to occur where it otherwise would not.

By Arousing Children's Sexual Curiosity and/or Desire

Showing pornography to boys and girls is a common seduction strategy of pedophiles who hope thereby to arouse children's sexual curiosity or sexual desire.

Pedophiles posing as young teenagers in Internet teen chat groups often send pornographic pictures or e-mail messages containing pornographic language to children. These predators use pornographic pictures to arouse the children's curiosity or sexual interest and manipulate them into meeting. These meetings typically culminate in the sexual victimization of the child or children.

Thus we conclude that exposure to child or adult pornography can arouse children's sexual curiosity or desire and thereby undermine their abilities to avoid, resist, or escape being sexually abused.

By Legitimizing and/or Normalizing Child Sexual Victimization for Children

Many pedophiles and child molesters show pornography to children "in order to persuade them that they would enjoy certain sexual acts" (Kelly, 1992, p. 119). Another motive is "to convince them that what they are being asked to do is alright." Showing them a picture "legitimizes the abuser's requests" (p. 119).

In the following example, an incestuous father's attempts to use pornography to normalize and legitimize having sex with his daughter were unusually persistent.

> The incest started at the age of eight. I did not understand any of it and did not feel that it was right. My dad would try to convince me that it was ok. He would find magazines articles or pictures that would show fathers and daughters or mothers, brothers and sisters having sexual intercourse. (Mostly fathers and daughters.) He would say that if it was published in magazines that it had to be all right because magazines could not publish lies. . . . He would say, "See it's okay to do because it's published in magazines." (Attorney General's Commission on Pornography: Final Report, Vol. 1, 1986, p. 786)

Child molesters also send pornography to the children they have targeted for sexual victimization to convince them "that other children are sexually active" (Hughes, 1999, p. 28). Showing children child pornography thus normalizes and legitimatizes adult–child sexual encounters in the minds of some children.

By Desensitizing or Disinhibiting Children

A child molester's step-by-step "grooming" of a child serves to gradually desensitize her or him to the culminating act of sexual abuse, which is his goal. He moves from befriending a child, to touching her or him, to introducing her or him to an X-rated video, slowly showing more of it "until the child is able to sit and watch the videos without becoming too uncomfortable" (Whetsell-Mitchell, 1995, p. 201). Juliann Whetsell-Mitchell concludes, "Variations on the grooming ['seduction'] process are many but the end result is desensitizing the child to engaging in sexual acts with the perpetrator, other children, or other adults" (p. 201).

By Creating Feelings of Guilt and Complicity, Thereby Silencing Children

When child molesters expose targeted children to pornography, the children often feel guilty and complicit, particularly if they found the material sexually exciting or masturbated to it. According to Scotland Yard, one of the five major ways that pedophiles use pornography is to "ensure the secrecy of any sexual activity with a child who has already been seduced" (Tate, 1990, p. 24). Child molesters can often silence their victims by telling them that their parents would be very upset to learn that they had watched pornography. Even without such warnings, children often fear that their parents will blame and punish them for having looked at this material. Children who are sexually abused following the exposure may feel complicit in the abuse and thus become even more motivated to remain silent. Ultimately, this reduces the likelihood that abused children will disclose the sexual abuse to their parents or others.

Conclusion

Despite the relative dearth of research, we believe we have provided sufficient evidence to substantiate Russell's theory. This theory explains how exposure to child pornography can create a sexual interest in children in some males who previously had no such interest. When sexual interest in children exists, exposure to child pornography can intensify sexual desires and undermine internal and social inhibitions against acting them out. Thus, exposure to pornography induces some men, who otherwise would not sexually abuse children, to become child molesters.

All references for articles included in *Taking Sides: Clashing Views in Abnormal Psychology*, 6/e can be found on the Web at www.mhhe.com/cls.

CHALLENGE QUESTIONS

Would Legalization of Virtual Child Pornography Reduce Sexual Exploitation of Children?

1. For decades the United States Supreme Court has debated the definition of pornography. In light of dramatic changes in public attitudes during the past two decades, what would be a reasonable definition of pornography in contemporary American society?
2. Federal and state laws regard the production and procuring of pornography involving children as criminal. Should other groups of people be added to the category of individuals who should be protected from exploitation for the purposes of pornography (e.g., developmentally disabled people, psychiatrically disturbed individuals, senile or demented persons)?
3. Debate has arisen regarding the extent to which pedophiles should be viewed as criminals or as psychologically disturbed individuals. How might this same debate apply to adults who claim that they are addicted to child pornography?
4. What kind of research study could be developed to assess the extent to which virtual child pornography increases or reduces the likelihood of sexual victimization of children?
5. The treatment of pedophiles occasionally involves an aversive therapy in which shock is applied when the adult becomes sexually aroused at the sight of an inappropriate image involving a child. What are the pros and cons of using virtual images in such an intervention?

Suggested Readings

Carr, J. (2003). *Child abuse, child pornography, and the Internet.* London: NCH.

Kleinhans, C. (2004). Virtual child porn: The law and the semiotics of the image. *Journal of Visual Culture, 3*(1), 17–34.

Luck, M. (2009). The gamer's dilemma: An analysis of the arguments for the moral distinction between virtual murder and virtual paedophilia. *Ethics and Information Technology, 11*(1), 31–36.

Peters, R. (March, 2004). *The link between pornography and violent sex crimes.* From http://www.moralityinmedia.org/.

Seto, M. C., & Eke, A. W. (2005). The criminal histories and later offending of child pornography offenders. *Sexual Abuse: A Journal of Research and Treatment, 17*(2), 201–210.

ISSUE 17

Must Mentally Ill Murderers Have a Rational Understanding of Why They Are Being Sentenced to Death?

YES: American Psychological Association, American Psychiatric Association, and National Alliance on Mental Illness, from "Brief for *Amici Curiae* American Psychological Association, American Psychiatric Association, and National Alliance on Mental Illness in Support of Petitioner," *Scott Louis Panetti v. Nathaniel Quarterman,* U.S. Supreme Court, No. 06-6407 (2007)

NO: Greg Abbott et al., from "On Writ of Certiorari to the United States Court of Appeals for the Fifth Circuit: Brief for the Respondent," *Scott Louis Panetti v. Nathaniel Quaterman,* U.S. Supreme Court, No. 06-6407 (2007)

ISSUE SUMMARY

YES: The American Psychological Association, the American Psychiatric Association, and the National Alliance on Mental Illness collaborated in the preparation of an *amici curiae* brief pertaining to the case of Scott Panetti, who was sentenced to death for murder. In this brief, The argument is made that mentally ill convicts should not be executed if their disability significantly impairs their capacity to understand the nature and purpose of their punishment or to appreciate why the punishment is being imposed on them.

NO: An opposing argument is made by Nathaniel Qarterman, who asserts that punishment for murder does not depend on the rational understanding, but rather on the convict's moral culpability at the time the crime was committed.

$\mathbf{T}$he complexity of the issue of executing the mentally ill received special scrutiny as a result of the case of Scott Panetti, which was heard by the U.S. Supreme Court in 2007. In 1992, Panetti murdered his mother-in-law and father-in-law while his wife and his daughter watched. Panetti, who had a lengthy history of mental illness and psychiatric hospitalizations, was sentenced to death. In 2003, Panetti petitioned the Texas state court to determine his competency for execution, but this court ruled him competent. When Panetti brought his case to a higher level, the federal district court found fault with the earlier ruling and summoned three psychologists and a psychiatrist, all of whom concurred that Panetti suffered from mental illness. The court ruled that Panetti was competent to be executed. Panetti's case then went to the Fifth Circuit, and the argument was put forth that a previous U.S. Supreme Court ruling (*Ford v. Wainwright*) required that Panetti not only be aware of the fact that he would be executed, but also that he have a rational understanding of *why*. Panetti asserted that he was being executed because he preached the gospel, not because of his murders.

The American Psychological Association, the American Psychiatric Association, and the National Alliance on Mental Illness submitted a brief, stating that individuals with psychotic conditions such as that of Panetti may experience delusions and a disrupted understanding of reality; also, they may be unable to connect events or understand cause and effect (i.e., the connection between murder and punishment).

Nathaniel Quarterman, director of the Texas Department of Criminal Justice, asserted that the court should reject the proposition that a murderer must possess a rational understanding of the reasons for execution, to render death an acceptable punishment under the Eighth Amendment of the Constitution (cruel and unusual punishment). Quarterman argued that capital punishment in such cases should not rest on whether or not a convict has rational understanding, but rather on the convict's moral culpability at the time the crime was committed by this person.

POINT

- Mentally ill convicts are not competent to be executed if they have a disability that significantly impairs their capacity to understand the nature and purpose of their punishment.

- Some psychiotic individuals cannot grasp the essential truth: that their impending execution is retribution for their crimes.

- The Eighth Amendment forbids the execution of individuals who are unaware of the punishment they are about to suffer *and why they are to suffer it.*

- Some psychiotic individuals like Panetti may possess the ability to comprehend facts about the subject of their delusions, but they are often unable to appreciate the personal significance of those facts or to reason about them in a logical way.

- The Fifth Circuit's approach permits the execution of severely delusional individuals even though they believe they are to be executed *for something other than their crimes,* notwithstanding the State's assertions to the contrary.

COUNTERPOINT

- Mentally ill convicts are incompetent to be executed only if, because of their illness, they lack the *capacity* to recognize that the punishment (1) is the result of having been convicted of murder and (2) will cause death.

- Retribution as a permissible theory of punishment depends not on the rational understanding that a convict may or may not have, but rather on the convict's moral culpability at the time of the crime.

- The Court should reject the proposition that a capital convict must possess a "rational understanding" of the reasons for execution to render death an acceptable punishment under the Eighth Amendment.

- The conceded objective of the *amici* APA is not simply avoiding the inhumanity of executing a person who is truly insane, but rather removing from death row as large a class of capital convicts as reasonably possible and thus exempting vast numbers of convicted murderers from execution.

- Requiring a "deep" or "meaningful" appreciation of the State's reasons for imposing the death penalty would create an even greater risk that the Court's test could be circumvented through malingering or abuse.

American Psychological Association, American Psychiatric Association, and National Alliance on Mental Health

Brief for Amici Curiae American Psychological Association, American Psychiatric Association, and National Alliance on Mental Illness in Support of Petitioner

The American Psychological Association is a voluntary, nonprofit, scientific and professional organization with more than 155,000 members and affiliates, and is the major association of psychologists in the nation.

The American Psychiatric Association, with more than 36,000 members, is the nation's leading organization of physicians who specialize in psychiatry.

The National Alliance on Mental Illness was founded in 1979 and is the nation's largest grassroots organization dedicated to improving the quality of life of persons living with serious mental illness and their families.

Members of *amici* are regularly called before courts to participate in competency hearings. *Amici* therefore have both pertinent expertise and a strong interest in the establishment of legal competency standards consistent with the best scientific knowledge about individuals suffering from mental illness.

In 2003, the American Bar Association established a Task Force on Mental Disability and the Death Penalty, which included mental health professionals who are members and representatives of *amici*. The Task Force was convened in light of this Court's decision in *Atkins* to address unresolved issues concerning application of the death penalty to persons suffering from impaired mental conditions. In 2005, the Task Force presented a series of recommendations.

[T]he Task Force identified several situations in which the death penalty should not be applied to individuals with mental illness. One category encompasses individuals who, though having been determined competent to stand trial and sentenced to death, suffer from a severe mental disorder or disability that renders them incompetent to understand the nature and purpose of the death penalty. This category would include, for example, individuals whose mental illness worsens in material respects after imposition of valid sentences.[1] Based on the Task Force Report *amici* and the American Bar Association recommended, in substantially similar form, that the death penalty should not be applied to such persons.[2]

Supreme Court, 2007.

Introduction and Summary of Argument

The Fifth Circuit, in this case and in *Barnard v. Collins*, 13 F.3d 871 (5th Cir. 1994), has adopted a very narrow construction of this Court's decision in *Ford*, a construction that permits the execution of individuals whose severe mental illness precludes them from understanding that the State is putting them to death as retribution for their crimes. The Fifth Circuit recognized that Scott Panetti suffers from schizoaffective disorder, a severe form of psychosis, and that as a direct result he "suffer[s] from paranoid delusions that his [sentence of] execution was the result of a conspiracy against him and not his crimes." *Panetti v. Dretke*, 448 F.3d 815, 819 (5th Cir. 2006). The court of appeals nevertheless deemed Panetti competent to be executed under *Ford*.

Amici respectfully submit that the Fifth Circuit's approach is inconsistent with the reasoning of the controlling opinions in *Ford*. Scientific knowledge about schizophrenia and schizoaffective disorder supports the conclusion that persons in Panetti's condition cannot rationally understand the reasons for their execution. Convinced of the reality of their delusions, they simply cannot grasp the essential truth: that their impending execution is retribution for their crimes. Where the prisoner cannot appreciate the reason, his execution cannot further the retributive purpose of the death penalty any more than if the prisoner, as in *Ford*, suffers delusions that he can never be executed at all. As explained further in this brief, for these reasons *amici* American Psychological Association, American Psychiatric Association, and the National Alliance on Mental Illness each has resolved that a prisoner is not competent to be executed if he "has a mental disorder or disability that significantly impairs his or her capacity to understand the nature and purpose of the punishment, or to appreciate the reason for its imposition in the prisoner's own case." *See, e.g.,* American Psychological Association Council of Representatives, APA Policy Manual: N. Public Interest (2001) (incorporating policy adopted by the Council of Representatives in February 2006), *available at.* . . . *Amici*'s approach, which is consistent with *Ford*, requires reversal of the Fifth Circuit here.

In Part I of this brief, *amici* explain that individuals who, like Panetti, suffer from severe psychotic disorders such as schizophrenia or schizoaffective disorder, frequently suffer from bizarre delusions that disrupt their understanding of reality. These delusional beliefs are genuine and often unshakeable, withstanding all attempts to introduce logic or contrary evidence. When they attach to the State's reasons for carrying out the mentally ill prisoner's execution, such delusions can deny the prisoner all rational understanding about "why" he is to be executed. In such a circumstance, proceeding with the execution would not further the purposes of the death penalty. In Part II, *amici* explain that mental health experts can assist the courts in identifying prisoners with mental illness who suffer delusions that preclude them from understanding the actual reasons for their execution. Mental health professionals routinely evaluate patients for the presence of delusional beliefs and generate reliable conclusions as to how those delusions impact the patients' ability to rationally understand information.

Argument

I. The Fifth Circuit's Interpretation of *Ford v. Wainwright* Fails to Protect a Class of Severely Mentally Ill Prisoners, in Contravention of the Purposes That Animated *Ford*

A. In Panetti *and* Barnard, *the Fifth Circuit Has Interpreted and Applied* Ford *Very Narrowly*

In 1986, this Court held that the Eighth Amendment forbids the execution of individuals suffering from mental illness that renders them incompetent. *Ford v. Wainwright*, 477 U.S. 399 (1986). The Court relied on common law to support its interpretation of the Eighth Amendment and identified several reasons why the execution of the insane is unacceptable in a civilized society. *Id.* at 409–410.[3] As one justification, the Court "seriously question[ed] the retributive value of executing a person who has no comprehension of why he has been singled out and stripped of his fundamental right to life." *Id.* at 409. Yet, while suggesting that the Constitution prevents the execution of a prisoner who lacks "comprehension of why he has been singled out" for death, the Court did not provide a substantive test for defining insanity in this context. Justice Powell attempted to do so, in a separate concurring opinion largely devoted to explaining his disagreements with the procedural protections set forth by the four-justice plurality. Justice Powell noted that "today, as at common law, one of the death penalty's critical justifications, its retributive force, depends on the defendant's awareness of the penalty's existence and purpose." *Id.* at 421 (Powell, J., concurring). Accordingly, he concluded that "the Eighth Amendment forbids the execution . . . of those who are unaware of the punishment they are about to suffer *and why they are to suffer it*." *Id.* at 422 (emphasis added). Justice Powell recognized that the Constitution requires, as a minimum before a prisoner may be deemed competent to be executed, that the prisoner be aware of both the fact that he will be put to death and the reason for that: society's retribution for his criminal acts.

In the case at bar, the Fifth Circuit . . . has ruled that the Constitution permits the execution of a severely delusional man who has no awareness of the true reason for his execution. In upholding Panetti's death sentence, the court of appeals expressly ruled that the Constitution does not bar the execution of an individual "suffer[ing] from paranoid delusions that his execution was the result of a conspiracy against him *and not his crimes*." *Panetti v. Dretke*, 448 F.3d 815, 819 (5th Cir. 2006) (emphasis added). Panetti understands that he has been found guilty of murder and faces execution, but holds the unequivocal and delusional belief that the State is using his crimes as a pretext, and that its real motivation is "to prevent him from preaching the Gospel." *Id.* at 816 (citing *Panetti v. Dretke*, 401 F. Supp. 2d 702, 709 (W.D. Tex. 2004)). Relying on *Barnard*, the court of appeals found Panetti's recognition of the State's *articulated* reason for his execution adequate to satisfy the standard set forth in Justice Powell's *Ford* concurrence, despite the court's recognition that Panetti's delusional thinking denies him awareness that the stated rationale is genuine. *Panetti*, 448 F.3d at 819 (noting that "Justice Powell did not state that a prisoner must 'rationally understand' the reason for his execution, only that he must be 'aware' of it").

B. Panetti Is Readily Identifiable as Suffering from Delusions That Commonly Accompany Schizophrenia and Schizoaffective Disorder

Scott Panetti is not an anomaly who by some odd quirk can correctly comprehend the fact of his execution and the State's explanation for it yet who breaks with reality when he ascribes the State's true motivation to a fantastical conspiracy or bizarre purpose. Rather, he is readily recognizable as belonging to the class of mentally ill persons who suffer from severe psychotic disorders that impede their cognitive functioning in some respects while leaving other aspects relatively unimpaired.[4] Such people may possess the ability to comprehend and understand facts about the subject of their delusions, but they are often unable to appreciate the personal significance of those facts or to reason about them in a logical way.

1. Individuals who suffer from delusions firmly hold false, illogical beliefs that cannot be corrected with reason and that interfere with their ability to interpret ordinary experiences.   In the scientific literature, individuals such as Panetti are commonly described as suffering from delusions: false beliefs that cannot be corrected by reasoning and that usually involve a misinterpretation of perceptions or experiences. Such delusions are often characterized by flaws in logical thinking that prevent those who suffer from them from making the right connections between ideas and from testing their beliefs about the world in ways that would enable them to determine the veracity of those beliefs.

Delusional thinking forms part of various psychotic disorders. A delusion has been defined as:

> A false belief based on incorrect inference about external reality that is firmly sustained despite what almost everyone else believes and despite what constitutes incontrovertible and obvious proof or evidence to the contrary. The belief is not, one ordinarily accepted by other members of the person's culture or subculture (e.g., it is not an article of religious faith). When a false belief involves a value judgment, it is regarded as a delusion only when the judgment is so extreme as to defy credibility.

American Psychiatric Association, *Diagnostic and Statistical Manual of Mental Disorders* 821 (4th ed. text rev. 2000) (hereinafter DSM-IV-TR).

Delusional thinking is a hallmark symptom of schizophrenia[5] and of related psychotic disorders, such as schizoaffective disorder.[6] It may also occur as a symptom of mood disorders such as depressive disorders or bipolar disorders.[7] It is particularly pronounced in what is known as the Paranoid Type of Schizophrenia. DSM-IV-TR 313-314. The essential feature of this type of schizophrenia is "the presence of prominent delusions or auditory hallucinations in the content of a relative preservation of cognitive functioning and affect." *Id.* at 313. Typically, persons with this condition suffer from delusions that are categorized as *persecutory* and/or *grandiose*. *Id.* A persecutory delusion, generally speaking, is a delusion whose theme involves a conspiracy or other form of malicious obstruction to thwart the individual's goals. *Id.* at 325. A grandiose delusion is one whose central theme involves the patient possessing a great yet unrecognized talent, sometimes accompanied by the belief that the patient has a special relationship with a prominent person or bears a special message from a deity. *Id.* The two types of delusions are often intertwined: persons experiencing persecutory delusions may reason that, as one textbook puts it, "they must be very important if so much effort is spent on their persecution." Robert Cancro & Heinz E. Lehmann, *Schizophrenia: Clinical Features*, in *Kaplan & Sadock's Comprehensive Textbook of Psychiatry* 1187 (7th ed. 2000).[8]

Psychotic disorders such as schizophrenia distort the mind in certain ways while leaving other functions generally intact. As noted above, an individual with paranoid schizophrenia may possess "a relative preservation of cognitive functioning." DSM-IV-TR 313. Yet such a person, plagued by a delusional psychotic disorder, may have no ability to apply his cognitive functions to test the veracity of the conclusions that he draws; while the *process* of a person's thinking appears normal, the *content* of the thoughts defies accepted reality. For example, a person who is under the delusion that he is the basketball player Michael Jordan may be unable to "test reality" in a way that would disprove his belief. Michael Jordan is tall, athletically gifted, widely recognized, and wealthy. Even after it is pointed out to the delusional person that he possesses none of these characteristics "and even if the person *agrees* that he does not" he may persist in his belief that he is in fact Michael Jordan.

Such persons may understand much of the world around them and have real intelligence. Yet their delusional thought process may consistently lead them to wildly incorrect results. As one psychiatry textbook explains:

> Disturbances of thinking and conceptualization are one of the most characteristic features of schizophrenia. The feature common to all manifestations of schizophreni[c] thought disorder is that patients think and reason . . . according to their own intricate private rules of logic. Schizophrenic patients may be highly intelligent, certainly not confused, and they may be painstaking in their abstractions and deductions. But their thought processes are strange and do not lead to conclusions based on reality or universal logic.

Cancro & Lehmann, *supra*, at 1189. Thus, a person suffering from schizophrenia or schizoaffective disorder may know that he has committed a crime; that the death penalty is imposed on persons who commit such crimes; and that the State has asserted he will be put to death because he committed that crime; and yet be absolutely and unwaveringly certain that his execution is not in fact a response to his crime but is instead an effort to prevent him from preaching the Gospel.

2. Panetti suffers from grandiose, persecutory delusions that disrupt his understanding of the purpose of his execution.   Based upon the record and findings in this case, Panetti clearly falls into this framework. He is not incoherent: the district court found that "at least some of the time, Panetti is capable of communicating, and apparently understanding, in a coherent fashion." *Panetti*, 401 F. Supp. 2d at 708. As one of the State's experts concluded, Panetti possessed a "capacity to understand the Bible, to understand history, movies." *Id.* Indeed, he represented himself at trial, cross-examined witnesses, and applied for subpoenas.

Yet, in the decade preceding his crime, Panetti was hospitalized with diagnoses that included schizophrenia, schizoaffective disorder, and bipolar disorder—all serious mental disorders that, in his case, were accompanied by psychotic symptoms such as auditory hallucinations and delusions of persecution and grandiosity. Pet. 3. While defending himself at trial, he exhibited a wide array of delusional behaviors. His cross-examination tended to be rambling and illogical, and he attempted to subpoena John F. Kennedy, Pope John Paul II, and Jesus Christ. Although Panetti knows that the State claims it intends to execute him for the murders that he committed, he believes in the words of one of the experts who examined him that "God had nullified it, God had forgiven him, God had wiped the slate clean." *Panetti*, 401 F. Supp. 2d at 707. And the district court credited testimony from one of the State's experts who concluded that:

> Panetti does not even understand that the State of Texas is a lawfully constituted authority, but rather, he believes the State is in league with the forces of evil that have conspired against him. [That expert's] testimony is consistent with that of Dr. Conroy, Dr. Rosin, and Dr. Silverman, each of whom testified Panetti believes the real reason he is to be executed is for preaching the Gospel.

Id. at 712; *see also id.* at 707 (Panetti suffers from "grandiosity and a delusional belief system in which he believes himself to be persecuted for his religious activities and beliefs"). As reflected in the findings and the testimony below, therefore, Panetti is able to draw some logical connections but suffers from textbook persecutory and grandiose delusions centered around religion that render him deeply disturbed and deny him any genuine understanding of the reason for his execution.

Although the record does not reflect the methods employed by the doctors who examined Panetti, it is likely that his delusional belief withstood all attempts to "test reality" by confronting him with contrary evidence. A person who is captive to such a delusion would likely be unconvinced by evidence that, for example (1) the State does not, in fact, seek to execute people for preaching the Gospel and (2) the State has certainly not sought to execute others whose preaching is heard by many more than Panetti's.[9]

C. Contrary to the Rationale of Ford, by Permitting the Execution of Prisoners Who Suffer from Psychotic Delusions, the Fifth Circuit's Approach Permits Executions That Do Not Further the Death Penalty's Retributive Purpose

Insisting that the death penalty must serve its core retributive purpose in every case, Justice Powell wrote in *Ford* that "the Eighth Amendment forbids the execution . . . of those who are unaware of the punishment they are about to suffer and why they are to suffer it." 477 U.S. at 422. In *Panetti*, the Fifth Circuit held that "'awareness,' as that term is used in *Ford*, is not necessarily synonymous with 'rational understanding.'" *Panetti*, 448 F.3d at 821. Accordingly, the court of appeals allowed the execution of an individual who believes that the State's expressed reason for his execution is merely a pretext for the true reason: to stop him from preaching Gospel. The Fifth Circuit's approach fails to recognize the force of the delusions that characterize psychotic disorders such as Panetti's, and thus, contrary to *Ford*, permits executions where the retributive purpose of the death penalty is not served.

As a simple linguistic matter, "awareness of why" a person is to suffer the death penalty might arguably be construed to include mere "awareness of *what the State has claimed as a reason*." But that circumscription of Justice Powell's test otherwise makes little sense. There are individuals, like Panetti, who know what the State says but believe just as surely that the State's claim is not true. The Fifth Circuit's approach permits the execution of such severely delusional individuals even though they believe they are to be executed for *something other than their crimes*, notwithstanding the State's assertions to the contrary.

The Fifth Circuit's standard makes some forms of severe delusion about one's impending execution matter, while others do not. For example, an individual capable of repeating back the State's stated reasons for the execution may not be executed if he believes that his execution is impossible (as in *Ford*), but may be executed if he considers it possible or certain but entirely misapprehends why the death penalty is actually being applied to him. Yet both individuals suffer from debilitating delusional thinking about their forthcoming execution and therefore the retributive purpose of the death penalty is not served in either circumstance. Indeed, Justice Powell plainly recognized that the prisoner's awareness of the "why" was as important to the legitimacy of the execution as his awareness of the "whether." Nor does it appear that the retributive purpose is served more fully when the State executes a person whose delusions cause him entirely to disbelieve the State's asserted rationale than when it executes one who cannot comprehend that rationale in the first place.

Indeed, of the various grounds articulated by the *Ford* majority, none supports privileging one sort of fundamental delusion about an impending execution over another. Whether the ground is that "the execution of an insane person simply offends humanity," 477 U.S. at 407, or that such an execution "provides no example to others," *id.*, or that "it is uncharitable to dispatch an offender into another world, when he is not of a capacity to fit himself for it," *id.*, or that "madness is its own punishment," *id.*, or that executing an insane person serves no retributive purpose, *id.*; *see also id.* at 422 (Powell, J., concurring), there is no reason to spare one individual beset by a delusion regarding whether death awaits or the State's purported reasons for imposing the penalty, yet to execute another individual plagued by a different yet equally irrational delusion regarding the same subject.

D. All Three Amici Have Adopted a Common Position on This Issue

For these reasons, with respect to competency to be executed, *amici* and the American Bar Association have respectively adopted substantively identical versions of a recommendation proposed by the Task Force on Mental Disability and the Death Penalty:

> If, after challenges to the validity of the conviction and death sentence have been exhausted and execution has been scheduled, a court finds that a prisoner has a mental disorder or disability that significantly impairs his or her capacity to understand the nature and purpose of the punishment, or to appreciate the reason for its imposition in the prisoner's own case, the sentence of death should be reduced to a lesser punishment.[10]

This recommendation, *amici* submit, draws the proper line between individuals who are competent to be executed and those who are not. The recommendation recognizes that it is impossible to draw a meaningful line among the myriad delusions that may fog an individual's understanding of his pending execution, or the reasons for it.

Specifically, under the recommendation, awareness of the "why" of an execution necessarily includes understanding the reason the death penalty is being applied in one's own case. The Report of the Task Force, which explains the reasoning that underlies each recommendation, stated that an offender who has been sentenced to die

> must "appreciate" its personal application in the offender's own case— that is, why it is being imposed *on the offender*. This formulation is analogous to the distinction often drawn between a "factual understanding" and a "rational understanding" of the reason for the execution. If, as is generally assumed, the primary purpose of the competence-to-be-executed requirement is to vindicate the retributive aim of punishment, then offenders should have more than a shallow understanding of why they are being executed.

Recommendation and Report on the Death Penalty and Persons with Mental Disabilities, 30 Mental & Physical Disability L. Rep. 668, 675 (2006). In short, it does not fulfill the retributive purpose of the death penalty to execute an individual, like Panetti, who has no rational understanding as to why the punishment is being imposed on him. For that reason, the Fifth Circuit's ruling should be reversed.[11]

II. Mental Health Professionals Can Reliably Identify the Nature and Extent of an Individual's Rational Understanding of an Impending Execution and Routinely Make Similar Assessments in Other Judicial Contexts

In the case at bar, the experts for the State and for the defense largely concurred in the most important aspects of their assessments. *Panetti v. Dretke*, 401 F. Supp. 2d 702, 707– 708, 712 (W.D. Tex. 2004) (all experts testified that Panetti possesses cognitive functionality with respect to certain topics and communications, yet suffers delusions, including the belief that he will be executed for preaching the Gospel). Disagreements were limited to the degree, and not existence, of Panetti's delusions pertaining to the reason for his impending execution, *Panetti v. Dretke*, 448 F.3d 815, 817 (5th Cir. 2006), and thus the parties' dispute has focused on the impact of Panetti's functional deficiencies on the ultimate question of "competence to be executed," which is a legal, not a scientific or medical, question.

Expert agreement in this area can be attributed to two factors: first, the underlying scientific and clinical concepts, the nature of psychotic delusions, and the concept of "rational understanding" are well established; second, when the diagnosis is made through an evaluation of the prisoner's currently presenting condition, no extrapolation is needed to assess the prisoner's condition at a remote time in the past.[12] Indeed, the expert consensus on Panetti's diagnosis is consistent with studies showing that mental health professionals using structured interviews and assessing present-oriented functional capacities typically have very high levels of agreement. *See, e.g.*, Gary B. Melton, *et al.*, *Psychological Evaluations for the Courts: A Handbook for Mental Health Professionals and Lawyers* 138 (2d ed. 1997). Thus, mental health experts can provide testimony that can meaningfully inform judicial decisions about competency to be executed with established procedures that have a record of producing reliable, consistent results.

Conclusion

Amici submit that the Fifth Circuit's competence for execution standard permits the execution of individuals who lack any meaningful understanding of the nature and purpose of their punishment, contrary to this Court's decision in *Ford*. *Amici* urge this Court to reverse the judgment of the Fifth Circuit.

Notes

1. Both parties have consented to the filing of this brief. No counsel for a party authored any part of this brief. No person or entity other than *amici* and their counsel made any monetary contribution to the preparation or submission of this brief.
2. In addition to the recommendation discussed in text, the Task Force presented, and *amici* and the ABA adopted, recommendations relating to persons with mental retardation and equivalent impairments of intellectual and adaptive functioning, persons who were mentally ill at the time of the offense, and persons not competent to seek or assist counsel in post-conviction proceedings. *See Recommendation and Report on the Death Penalty and Persons with Mental Disabilities*, 30 Mental & Physical Disability L. Rep. 668, 668 (2006).
3. *Amici* gratefully acknowledge the assistance of Richard J. Bonnie, J.D., Joel A. Dvoskin, Ph.D., Kirk S. Heilbrun, Ph.D., and Diane T. Marsh, Ph.D., in the preparation of this brief.
4. The term "appreciate" approximates the term "rationally understand." *See* Norman G. Poythress, *et al.*, *Adjudicative Competence: The MacArthur Studies* 112 (2002); *see also Martin v. Dugger*, 686 F. Supp. 1523, 1569–1573 (S.D. Fla. 1988).

5. Justice Powell concurred in parts one and two of Justice Marshall's opinion, 477 U.S. at 418, creating a majority for the holding that "the Eighth Amendment prohibits a State from carrying out a sentence of death upon a prisoner who is insane." *Id.* at 409.

6. *Amici* of course have not examined Panetti in person; rather, *amici* rely upon the facts as set forth in the record and on Panetti's prior mental health evaluations.

7. Schizophrenia is typically defined as encompassing two or more of the following five symptoms: (1) delusions; (2) hallucinations; (3) disorganized speech; (4) grossly disorganized or catatonic behavior; and (5) negative symptoms, *i.e.*, affective flattening (diminished emotional expressiveness), alogia (poverty of speech), or avolition (inability to initiate and persist in goal-oriented activities). DSM-IV-TR 299–301, 312.

8. Schizoaffective disorder essentially consists of schizophrenic symptoms coupled with, at some point, either a major depressive episode, a manic episode, or a mixed episode (*i.e.*, an episode in which the individual alternates between major depressive and manic symptoms). DSM-IV-TR 319–323.

9. *See generally* DSM-IV-TR 345–428; *see also id.* at 327 (discussing Mood Disorders With Psychotic Features).

10. It is important to distinguish delusional beliefs from beliefs that are merely wrong. An individual who believes that her husband is cheating on her may be mistaken, but her view may not be delusional, depending upon the facts that she adduces to support her belief. But, the individual who, in one reported case, based such a belief solely on the presence of a red car outside of her apartment, is clearly delusional. *See* Adolfo Pazzagli, *Delusion, Narrative, and Affects*, 34 J. of the Am. Acad. of Psychoanalysis & Dynamic Psychiatry 367, 370 (2006).

11. The record in *Barnard* is much more sparse than in *Panetti;* accordingly, it is difficult to assess the true nature of Barnard's delusions. Because the state court found that Barnard tended to blame his conviction on "a conspiracy of Asians, Jews, Blacks, homosexuals, and the Mafia," 13 F.3d at 876, it is likely that his beliefs would have withstood efforts to test reality by presenting him with evidence that (1) those five groups do not, in fact, work in concert, (2) there is no reason why those groups would have any motive to do him harm, and (3) most fundamentally, those groups do not control the judicial system, and thus did not bring about his conviction.

12. American Psychological Association Council of Representatives, APA Policy Manual: N. Public Interest (2001) (incorporating policy adopted by the Council of Representatives in February 2006), *available at . . . Mentally Ill Prisoners on Death Row: Position Statement*, American Psychiatric Association (2005), *available at . . .* The National Alliance on Mental Illness adopted an earlier version of this language. *Public Policy Platform of the National Alliance on Mental Illness* 50 (8th ed. 2006), *available at . . .* The ABA adopted a later version of this proposal with a different final clause. *Recommendation and Report on the Death Penalty and Persons with Mental Disabilities*, 30 Mental & Physical Disability L. Rep. 668, 668 (2006).

NO

On Writ of Certiorari to the United States Court of Appeals for the Fifth Circuit: Brief for the Respondent

Statement of the Case

A. The Crime

Scott Louis Panetti has led a troubled and violent life. Between 1981 and 1992, Panetti was hospitalized on multiple occasions and variously diagnosed with substance abuse and dependence, personality disorders, depression, chronic undifferentiated schizophrenia, and schizoaffective disorder. JA 339–41;1 Federal Petition for Writ of Habeas Corpus, No. 1:99-CV-00260 (W.D. Tex. Sept. 7, 1999) (hereinafter "Federal Petition") (Ex. 14). Although his doctors initially treated him only with therapy, they later placed him on medication, which proved effective in controlling his mental illness. *Id.*, at 462–63 (noting in 1986 that, while taking medication, Panetti "shows no evidence of thought disorder" and "was not paranoid in his attitude"), 466 (observing in 1990 that, after Panetti was stabilized on his medication, he displayed no evidence of "any delusions or any psychotic thinking, or any suicidal or homicidal ideations").

Panetti married his second wife, Sonja, in 1988, and they had a daughter the following year. 31.RR.61. In August 1992, Sonja separated from Panetti because of his drinking and physical threats. 31.RR.62. She took their daughter, then three years old, to live with her parents, Amanda and Joe Alvarado. 31.RR.60-61. Panetti later called to threaten Sonja and his in-laws, saying he would kill both her and the Alvarados or burn down their house. 31.RR.64. On September 2, 1992, in response to these threats, Sonja obtained a protective order against Panetti. 31.RR.65-66; 41.RR (SX 91).

Six days later, Panetti awoke before dawn, 33.RR.695, shaved his head, 31.RR.95-96, and dressed himself in camouflage, 33.RR.679. Arming himself with a rifle, a sawed-off shotgun, 33.RR.696, and several knives, 33.RR.706-07, Panetti drove to the Alvarados' house, 33.RR.696. When he arrived, Panetti broke his shotgun trying to shatter a sliding glass door near Sonja's bed. 31.RR.69; 33.RR.717. He chased Sonja out of the house and confronted her in the front yard, 33.RR.704, hitting her face with the butt of his rifle, 31.RR.73.

Although Sonja managed to retreat into the house and lock the front door, Panetti shot the lock off and cornered Joe and Amanda Alvarado in the

Supreme Court, 2007.

kitchen. 31.RR.42-43; 33.RR.705. He asked Sonja, who was standing in the adjoining hallway, who she would like to see die first. 31.RR.84. Using his rifle, Panetti then shot and killed Joe Alvarado. 31.RR.84. Sonja begged Panetti not to kill her mother, 31.RR.91, but Panetti pressed the rifle against Amanda Alvarado's chest and pulled the trigger, 32.RR.417-18, killing her and spraying Sonja and their daughter with blood, 31.RR.91. Then his rifle jammed. 31.RR.92.

Panetti grabbed Sonja and their daughter and walked them out to his Jeep. 31.RR.92-93. He drove them back to his bunkhouse, 31.RR.94, where he had them wash off the blood, 31.RR.96. When Sonja asked if she could go check on her parents, he responded: "I just shot your parents. No more mommy, no more daddy; get that through your head." 31.RR.96-97. He then forced Sonja to read the protective order aloud. 31.RR.97-98. Sonja asked Panetti if he planned to shoot her and her daughter. 31.RR.98. He replied that he had not yet decided. 31.RR.98.

At dawn, Panetti allowed both Sonja and their daughter to leave the bunkhouse, telling Sonja that he planned to stay there and "shoot two or three policemen" before taking his own life. 31.RR.101. Panetti surrendered to police that afternoon. 31.RR.241. Later the same day, Panetti confessed to the murders, recounting the details of the crime to police. 33.RR.692-737. When asked if he thought that his mental condition excused his behavior, Panetti replied, "it doesn't excuse me from any of that. You know, I made my bed and I'm going to lie in it. . . . I f***ed up. I feel a lot of remorse." 33.RR.734-35; see also JA 208.

Dr. Michael Lennhoff, a psychiatrist, interviewed Panetti several times at the local jail. Panetti stated that he had followed his drug regimen over the preceding year, but he later confessed that he had not taken his medication for one week before the murders. Federal Petition Ex. 14, at 431, 436. Although Dr. Lennhoff noted that Panetti exhibited genuine mental illness, he also concluded that "Panetti may have wanted to impress me with how mentally disturbed he is, perhaps in an exaggerated way." *Id.*, at 434. After a later meeting, Dr. Lennhoff felt that Panetti was "still trying to impress me as not having committed a deliberate crime." *Id.*, at 436.

B. Panetti's Exhaustively Affirmed Conviction and Sentence and the Rejection of His Alleged Incompetence to Stand Trial and to Waive Counsel

Panetti was charged with capital murder. 1.CR.8. The trial court appointed Dr. E. Lee Simes, a psychiatrist, to evaluate Panetti's competence for trial. JA 9. Dr. Simes noted that, despite Panetti's delusional thinking, "his overall story was quite consistent and insightful." JA 13. In particular, Dr. Simes observed that Panetti understood why he was facing capital-murder charges, the significance of those charges, and the significance of the punishment he might receive. JA 13. Panetti also displayed ability to process questions and information and to assist in his defense. JA 13. Dr. Simes concluded that Panetti was competent to stand trial. JA 13.

In April 1994, Panetti moved for a competence hearing. 2.CR.236-41. In the first trial-competence hearing, the jury deadlocked at four for incompetent, three for competent, and five undecided. 3.CR.295-96; 10.RR.379.2. At the second trial-competence hearing, the jury found Panetti competent to stand trial. 13.RR.206-07.

Eight months later, Panetti sent the trial judge a letter explaining that he had stopped taking all medication and, as a result, was "restored to sanity"; he had dismissed his attorneys; he felt competent to represent himself; he did not intend to "act like a lawyer" in his trial; and he would be able to prove that he was insane at the time of the murders. 3.CR.360. Panetti's attorneys then moved to withdraw as his counsel. 3.CR.363–64.

The trial court called a pretrial hearing to inquire further into Panetti's expressed desire to represent himself. 15.RR.5. The judge told Panetti that he personally did not want Panetti to represent himself, 15.RR.10, and asked Panetti's attorneys to confer privately with Panetti about waiving counsel, 15.RR.11. After this consultation, Panetti's attorneys reported that they did not think Panetti should represent himself, but that was his "clear intent." 15.RR.12–13. Panetti confirmed that he wanted to represent himself because he had the right to do so under Texas law and the United States Constitution, and that he was "fully aware" of the penalty for the charges against him. 15.RR.18. Panetti then executed a voluntary waiver of counsel. 3.CR.369. The district attorney informed the court that, because the State was "concerned about protecting the Defendant's rights," he did not want Panetti's attorneys to withdraw. 15.RR.24. When the court reexamined Panetti about his decision, Panetti replied, "I understand everything that's been going on today, sir. I do, however, feel a little bit insulted that I have been asked the same question so many times, Your Honor." 15.RR.25–28. The court held that Panetti had voluntarily and intelligently exercised his right to represent himself and then appointed standby counsel for Panetti. 15.RR.29–30.

At trial, Panetti entered a plea of not guilty by reason of insanity. 31.RR.24. In his rambling opening statement, Panetti informed the jury that he had been diagnosed with paranoid schizophrenia and manic depression in 1986, and that he believed only an insane person could prove the insanity defense. 31.RR.28–29. As Panetti explains in his brief, he exhibited bizarre and incoherent behavior throughout his trial. Panetti Br. 11–15. He did call as witnesses two psychiatrists who had previously treated him, 38.RR.1567–1616, and endeavored to establish through one that, when he did not take his medication, his mental illness could prevent him from distinguishing right and wrong, 38.RR.1574–75. The jury nonetheless found Panetti guilty of capital murder and sentenced him to death. 7.CR.1041–44; 38.RR.1685; 39.RR.102. The Texas Court of Criminal Appeals (CCA) affirmed Panetti's conviction and sentence, *Panetti v. Texas*, No. 72,230 (Tex. Crim. App. Dec. 3, 1997) (unpublished), and the Court denied certiorari, 525 U.S. 848 (1998) (Mem.). Panetti then filed a state habeas petition raising fourteen claims, including whether he was competent to stand trial and competent to waive counsel. State Petition for Writ of Habeas Corpus, No. 3310-A, at 3–4 (Tex. Crim. App. June 19, 1997). The CCA denied relief. (pp. 1–5)

In sum, one jury and four courts rejected Panetti's trial-incompetence claim; one court found him competent to waive counsel and four courts rejected his collateral challenge to that determination; and another jury and two courts rejected his insanity defense. No judge or jury has ever found him incompetent.

C. Panetti's Efforts to Prove Incompetence to Be Executed in State and Federal Court

Once an execution date was set, Panetti filed a motion in the state trial court under Texas Code of Criminal Procedure Article 46.05 asserting incompetence to be executed. JA 355. After concluding that Panetti had failed to make a substantial showing of incompetence, the state court denied his Article 46.05 motion, JA 355, and the CCA dismissed his appeal, *Ex parte Panetti*, No. 74,868 (Tex. Crim. App. Jan. 28, 2004) (*per curiam*) (unpublished).

Panetti then filed a habeas petition in federal district court, asserting that *Ford v. Wainwright*, 477 U.S. 399 (1986), prohibited his execution. JA 355–56. The district court granted a stay of execution and allowed Panetti an opportunity to present his renewed allegations to the state trial court. JA 357.

In response to Panetti's second Article 46.05 motion, the state court appointed two neutral experts, Dr. George Parker and Dr. Mary Anderson, to assess Panetti's competence to be executed. JA 59. After conducting a joint interview of Panetti, Drs. Parker and Anderson filed a report documenting their observations and conclusions. JA 70–76. This report reflects Panetti's hostility to Drs. Parker's and Anderson's questions, his tendency toward religious conversation, his attempted manipulation of the interview process, and his general refusal to cooperate with the court-appointed experts. JA 70–73, 75.

Because of Panetti's refusal to cooperate, Drs. Parker and Anderson also relied on several sources of collateral data—including prison records; letters that Panetti had recently written to friends and family; court documents, including documents relating to other competence determinations; discussions with prison staff; and another expert evaluation of Panetti—to help form their relevant opinions. JA 73–75. Based on these data and their personal observations, Drs. Parker and Anderson concluded that Panetti (1) "knows that he is to be executed, and that his execution will result in his death" and (2) "has the ability to understand the reason he is to be executed." JA 75.

In response, Panetti filed a detailed submission criticizing Drs. Parker and Anderson's methodology and contrasting their conclusions with those in a psychiatric evaluation that Panetti had previously presented to the court. JA 79–98. After considering that submission, the state court again denied relief under Article 46.05. JA 99.

Panetti then sought habeas relief in the federal district court, JA 375, which concluded that the state court's determination of Panetti's competence to be executed was not entitled to AEDPA deference because Panetti allegedly failed to receive constitutionally sufficient process, JA 359–61. After granting Panetti's motions for appointment of counsel, discovery, and funds for expert and investigative assistance, JA 358, the district court held an evidentiary hearing on competence, JA 362. At the hearing, Panetti presented expert testimony[.]" (pp. 5–7)

"All of the expert witnesses agreed that Panetti suffers from some degree of mental illness." Although some of the experts labeled this illness schizophrenia or schizoaffective disorder, *e.g.*, JA 144–45, 205, they were collectively unable to agree on a single diagnosis, see JA 239, 313.[1]

The experts did agree, however, that Panetti has the capacity to—and does, in fact—understand that he will be executed. JA 147–48, 207, 236, 243, 245.[2]

Further expert testimony established Panetti's specific understanding that he committed the murders. Indeed, Dr. Rosin testified that Panetti recounted details of his activity on the day of the murders and expressed sorrow for having committed the crime. JA 208; see also JA 148–49 (Dr. Conroy's testimony that Panetti believed that God had forgiven him for killing the Alvarados and had "wiped the slate clean"). Dr. Silverman testified to uncertainty about whether Panetti knows that he killed the Alvarados, but only because Panetti steadfastly refused to answer his questions on this topic. JA 221.

Several experts also concluded that Panetti's delusions created a false sense of the true reason for his execution. *E.g.*, JA 149, 156, 202, 209 (testimony from Drs. Conroy and Rosin that Panetti believes his execution was ordered to prevent him from preaching the Gospel). Importantly, however, these same experts testified that Panetti understands that the State's stated reason for his execution is punishment for capital murder. JA 157, 214.

Dr. Parker testified that portions of Panetti's responses to the experts execution-competence examinations could be attributed to malingering, see JA 241–43; see also, *e.g.*, JA 174, 177, 181 (noting additional reports of Panetti's suspected malingering in the past), and Drs. Parker and Anderson each specifically testified that Panetti has the capacity to understand the reason for his execution, JA 245, 247, 303–04. Both Dr. Parker and Dr. Anderson emphasized that Panetti was deliberately manipulative and uncooperative during his interview with them. JA 239–40, 244–46, 271, 300, 303, 312–14; accord JA 75. They based their ultimate conclusions on Panetti's overall cognitive functionality, as demonstrated through letters he wrote to friends and family, his logical responses to interview questions, and his ability to understand such things as history and movies. JA 242–43, 302–04.

Dr. Parker's suspicions of malingering were corroborated by evidence of psychiatric evaluations conducted in the two years following Panetti's capital trial. For example, Dr. Michael Gilhousen noted that loosening of Panetti's thought processes "appeared to be intentional on his part to create the impression of mental illness." JA 167, II-30. After another interview, Dr. Gilhousen described Panetti's behavior as "obviously manipulative and theatrical." JA 171-72, II-20. Another doctor expressed the belief that Panetti's switching among different voices was "contrived . . . to impress us or lead us to believe that he did have alter personalities." JA 170, II-41.

After hearing all the evidence, the federal district court made three factual findings. First, based on the expert's agreement, the court concluded that Panetti is aware that he will be executed. JA 372.

Second, the district court found that Panetti is aware that he committed both murders. JA 372. The court based this conclusion on Dr. Conroy's and Dr. Rosin's testimony that Panetti knows that he murdered the Alvarados. JA 372. Although the court recognized that Dr. Silverman's testimony cast doubt on this conclusion, the court discounted that testimony, noting that it was based on Panetti's limited responses during his interview with Dr. Silverman. JA 372.

Third, the district court found that Panetti understands the State's stated reason for execution. JA 372. The court based this finding on the testimony of Drs. Conroy and Rosin, and discounted Dr. Silverman's contrary testimony for the same reason. JA 372–73.

Additionally, the district court recounted Dr. Parker's and Dr. Anderson's assessments that "some portion of Panetti's behavior could be attributed to malingering," and it expressly concluded that, although all of the experts had agreed Panetti had "some degree" of mental illness, their testimony collectively "casts doubt on the extent of Panetti's mental illness and symptoms." JA 363.

Finally, the district court noted Dr. Cunningham's testimony that "suggests" that Panetti's delusions prevent him from understanding that Texas is a lawfully constituted authority and lead him to believe that the State "is in league with the forces of evil that have conspired against him," and it observed that this testimony was consistent with the testimony of Panetti's other experts. JA 373. The court made no finding, however, whether these delusions were genuine or the partial product of malingering, because the court deemed it irrelevant to the question of whether Panetti "knows the reason for his execution" within the meaning of the court of appeals's execution-competence test. JA 373.

Based on these factual findings, the district court concluded that Panetti is competent to be executed. JA 373. Although the court denied Panetti's habeas petition, it stayed his execution pending appeal, JA 373, and granted a certificate of appealability, *Panetti v. Dretke*, No. 04-CA- 042 (W.D. Tex. Nov. 4, 2004). The court of appeals affirmed the district court's denial of habeas relief, *Panetti v. Dretke*, 448 F.3d 815 (CA5 2006); JA 374–84, and the Court granted certiorari, JA 387.

Summary of the Argument

In devoting fully half of his brief to his statement of the case, Panetti endeavors to focus the Court's attention on his lengthy mental-health history, explaining that "incompetency runs like a fissure through every proceeding in this case." Panetti Br. 6. But that fissure has been mostly sealed once and for all by the conclusive determinations of state and federal courts repeatedly rejecting Panetti's direct and collateral challenges to adverse rulings on his insanity defense, his competence to stand trial, and his competence to waive counsel. For that reason, Panetti correctly concedes that, as a matter of law, he is now presumed competent to be executed. *Ibid.*

The state court, the district court, and the court of appeals have all concluded that Panetti has failed to overcome that presumption. The district court found as a factual matter that Panetti knows that he murdered the Alvarados, that he will be executed, and that the State's stated reason for executing him is that he committed two murders. Panetti has not challenged those factual findings on appeal." (pp. 7–11)

"Both Panetti's and his *amici's* proposed standards, which require that a convict rationally understand" the reasons for his execution, are fundamentally flawed. Given the inherent subjectivity and manipulability of such a standard, capital murderers could as a routine matter claim a lack of "rational understanding" through malingering or refusing to cooperate with experts." (p. 12) . . . "Finally, the retributive and deterrent interests served by the death penalty—focused primarily as they are on society at large rather than the capital murderer—do not demand the "rational understanding" that Panetti urges.

The Court should instead adopt a clear and objective test for execution competence. Specifically, the Court should hold that a mentally ill capital convict is incompetent to be executed only if, because of his illness, he lacks the *capacity* to recognize that his punishment (1) is the result of his being convicted of capital murder and (2) will cause his death. This standard controls for the malingering or uncooperative convict, is appropriately tailored to the execution stage of capital proceedings, and serves the twin goals of retribution and deterrence that justify capital punishment. Applying this standard, the Court should hold that Panetti is competent to be executed." (pp. 12–13)

Argument

II. Even If AEDPA Deference Does Not Apply, Panetti's Execution Does Not Violate the Eighth Amendment

Only if the Court concludes that the AEDPA does not bar habeas review should it reach Panettis claim that the court of appeals employed the wrong legal standard for execution competence. Although *Ford* held that the Eighth Amendment proscribes execution of the "insane," 477 U.S., at 409–10, the Court did not define "insanity" or otherwise delineate the constitutional threshold of competence to be executed, *id.*, at 418 (Powell, J., concurring in the judgment), a question which remains unresolved.

Before turning to the merits of that claim, two issues bear emphasis. **First**, there is no dispute that, under *Ford*, executing the insane violates the Eighth Amendment. Executing the insane was forbidden at common law, and it is forbidden today." (p. 19) . . . "And **second**, there is no dispute that, like many capital defendants, Panetti suffers from some degree of mental illness." (p. 19)

"The only legal question before the Court on the merits of this case is what is the definition of "insanity"—that is, what must a court find to conclude that a capital murderer is constitutionally incompetent to be executed." (p. 19)

"Although execution of the "insane" was deemed cruel and unusual in 1971, *Ford*, 477 U.S., at 406–08, the common law did not then draw fine distinctions in mental ability, and thus did not delineate any precise competence standard. Consequently, the standards of the common law are, at best, inconclusive. Likewise, a survey of modern state legislation offers indefinite guidance, as it yields no consensus at all on the mental faculty a capital murderer must possess at the time of his execution. Finally, in the exercise of its independent judgment, the Court should reject the proposition that a capital convict must possess a "rational understanding" of the reasons for his execution to render death an acceptable punishment under the Eighth Amendment. Such a standard is not tailored to the particular interests at stake in the postsentencing phase of capital proceedings, invites malingering and abuse, and is not necessary to advance the retributive and deterrent justifications for the death penalty.

For all of these reasons, the Court should reject Panetti's and his *amici's* proposed execution-competence standards." (pp. 20–21)

C. The Court Should Hold That the Appropriate Constitutional Standard for Competence to Be Executed is Whether a Defendant Has the Capacity to Recognize That His Punishment Is the Result of His Being Convicted of Capital Murder and Will Cause His Death. (p. 33)

"Both Panetti's and his *amici's* proposed execution-competence standards are deeply flawed. The State urges the Court to reject those proposals and instead adopt a clearer and more objective test. Specifically, the Court should hold that a mentally ill capital convict is incompetent to be executed only if, because of his illness, he lacks the *capacity* to recognize that his punishment (1) is the result of his being convicted of capital murder and (2) will cause his death.

The State's proposed standard—derived from *Ford* and the Court's Eighth Amendment jurisprudence—prevents the execution of the truly incompetent, while at the same time (1) incorporating essential safeguards against malingering and noncooperation with psychological examiners, (2) being specifically tailored to the postsentencing phase of capital proceedings, and (3) effectively advancing the modern penological interests behind the death penalty.

> 1. Because of the inherent uncertainties and subjectivity of psychiatric testing, and the risks of malingering and abuse, any standard for competence to be executed should be rigorous and clear." (pp. 33–34)

"The Court has often noted the difficulties that attend even the most skilled psychiatric diagnoses. "[P]sychiatrists disagree widely and frequently on what constitutes mental illness [and] on the appropriate diagnosis to be attached to given behavior and symptoms." *Ake v. Oklahoma*, 470 U.S. 68, 81 (1985). For that reason, "a particularly acute need for guarding against error inheres in a determination that 'in the present state of the mental sciences is at best a hazardous guess however conscientious.'" *Ford*, 477 U.S., at 412 (plurality op.) (quoting *Solesbee v. Balkcom*, 339 U.S. 9, 23 (1950) (Frankfurter, J., dissenting)). As Justice Powell explained,

> "Unlike issues of historical fact, the question of petitioner's sanity calls for a basically subjective judgment. And unlike a determination of whether the death penalty is appropriate in a particular case, the

competency determination depends substantially on expert analysis in a discipline fraught with 'subtleties and nuances.'" *Id.*, at 426 (Powell, J., concurring in the judgment) (quoting *Addington v. Texas*, 441 U.S. 418, 430 (1979)) (citations omitted).

Just last Term, the Court observed that the medical definitions of mental illness "are subject to flux and disagreement," and that such diagnoses "may mask vigorous debate within the profession about the very contours of the mental disease itself." *Clark v. Arizona*, 126 S.Ct. 2709, 2722, 2734 (2006). "[T]he consequence of this professional ferment," the Court noted, "is a general caution in treating psychological classifications as predicates for excusing otherwise criminal conduct." *Id.*, at 2734.

Not only are psychiatric diagnoses subjective and frequently conflicting, they are by their nature subject to change. *Atkins* and *Roper* were predicated on constant variables: if a defendant is fifteen or seventeen or twenty at the time of the crime, that age at that instant is fixed and unchanging; likewise, if an individual is of normal intelligence throughout his or her life, that person cannot be expected later to become mentally retarded. In contrast, if a person is sane yesterday and today, that does not mean he or she will be sane tomorrow. As Justice O'Connor cautioned in *Ford*, that mutability carries with it serious risks of malingering:

> "[T]he *potential for false claims and deliberate delay* in this context is *obviously enormous*. This potential is exacerbated by a unique feature of the prisoner's protected interest in suspending the execution of a death sentence during incompetency. By definition, this interest can *never* be conclusively and finally determined: Regardless of the number of prior adjudications of the issue, until the very moment of execution the prisoner can claim that he has become insane sometime after the previous determination to the contrary." 477 U.S., at 429 (O'Connor, J., concurring in part and dissenting in part) (citations omitted) (first two emphases added).[3]

Finally, unlike with age or retardation, capital murderers facing execution may have some ability to voluntarily choose to render themselves incompetent to be executed simply by ceasing to take their medication. Indeed, in the case at bar, the evidence indicates that Panetti's medication had been largely successful in controlling his mental illness, Federal Petition Ex. 14, at 462–63, but that he willingly chose to stop taking it, *id.*, at 431, 436; 3.CR.360.

> **Panetti's proposed "rational understanding" standard has no basis in the Court's precedent and would invite abuse."** (pp. 34–36)

a. A "rational understanding" inquiry would engraft Fifth and Sixth Amendment concerns on an Eighth Amendment test.

Although Panetti uses the phrase loosely, "rational understanding" is a specific term of art; it describes the core of several pre-sentencing competence tests. "Rational understanding" was introduced in *Dusky*, in which the Court defined the test for competence to stand trial as whether the defendant has "sufficient present ability to consult with his lawyer with a reasonable degree of rational understanding" and has "a rational as well as factual understanding of the proceedings against him." 362 U.S., at 402 (quotation marks omitted); see also *Godinez v. Moran*, 509 U.S. 389, 398 (1993) (concluding that the "rational understanding" test should also be used to measure a defendant's competence to plead guilty and to waive the right to counsel)." (p. 37)

"[A] "rational understanding" is necessary to ensure that defendants do not foolishly or mistakenly relinquish valuable constitutional rights. A defendant faced with such choices must be able to "understand the nature and object of the proceedings against him, to consult with counsel, and to assist in preparing his defense." *Drope*, 420 U.S., at 171.

But a capital convict, unlike a capital defendant, has substantially fewer rights, and there are no significant strategic choices left for him to make. See *Herrera v. Collins*, 506 U.S. 390, 399 (1993) (explaining that the presumption of innocence disappears after conviction and listing numerous constitutional rights that defendants enjoy but that convicts do not); *Barefoot v. Estelle*, 463 U.S. 880, 887–88 (1983) (discussing the "secondary and limited" nature of federal habeas proceedings); see also *Ford*, 477 U.S., at 421 (Powell, J., concurring in the judgment) (noting that, because the Court's decisions already recognize . . . that a defendant must be competent to stand trial, . . . the notion that a defendant must be able to assist in his defense is largely provided for"). Assuming that a convict is competent to be executed, only the remote possibilities of clemency or commutation—processes that call for no significant strategic decisions by a convict—can prevent the sentence from being carried out.

b.   Panetti's conception of "rational understanding" is far too expansive.

Panetti's argument is, in fact, even more aggressive than one for inclusion of only a pure "rational understanding" component. Although he invokes that phrase throughout his brief, the substantive requirement that Panetti asks the Court to incorporate is actually a version of the heightened "knowing and voluntary" requirement that the Court has held applicable, over and above the "rational understanding" competence component, with respect to a defendant's decision to plead guilty or to waive his right to counsel. *Godinez*, 509 U.S., at 400–01 & n.12; *Faretta v. California*, 422 U.S. 806, 835 (1975).

As *Godinez* explained, "knowing and voluntary" is not part of any competence test; it is an additional safeguard designed to ensure not merely that a defendant has the *capacity* to understand trial proceedings, but rather that he "*actually does* understand the significance and consequences of a particular decision and whether the decision is uncoerced." 509 U.S., at 401, n.12 (emphasis added)." (pp. 38–39)

"[R]equiring a "deep" or "meaningful" appreciation of the State's reasons for imposing the death penalty would create an even greater risk that the Court's test could be circumvented through malingering or abuse. See *supra* Part II.C.1." (p. 39)

"When viewed in light of the overall death-row population, Panetti's proposal is especially problematic. As a matter of common understanding, most individuals who commit heinous murders are, almost by definition, not entirely sane. Although estimates vary, some sources indicate that as many as 70 percent of death-row inmates suffer from some form of schizophrenia or psychosis. Nancy S. Horton, Restoration of Competency for Execution: Furiosus Solo Furore Punitur, 44 Sw. L.J. 1191, 1204 (1990) (citing Amnesty International, United States of America: the Death Penalty 108–09 (1987)); see JA 142 (expert testimony that most of the convicts in federal Bureau of Prisons hospitals are schizophrenic). Many, if not most, schizophrenics exhibit the type of delusional thinking that Panetti has been observed to exhibit. See Douglas Mossman, *Atkins v. Virginia: A Psychiatric Can of Worms*, 33 N.M. L. Rev. 255, 280 (2003); APA Br. 8 (noting that "[d]elusional thinking is a hallmark symptom of schizophrenia" (citing DSM-IV-TR 299–301, 312)).[4] Accordingly, Panetti's "rational understanding" requirement would be applied to a population that is, in significant part, delusional—and thus necessarily *irrational*. See APA Br. 9, n.11." (p. 40)

"[T]he introduction of Panetti's ill-defined—and inherently indefinite— "rational understanding" component would render the execution-competence standard substantially overinclusive. See Mossman, *supra*, at 289 ("Given the high rate of serious mental illness among homicide defendants, granting psychiatric exemptions could leave very few individuals eligible for the death penalty.").

Nor is this potential for exempting vast numbers of convicted murderers from execution an unintended consequence of Panetti's and his *amici*'s proposed test. Indeed, *amicus* APA is nothing if not candid, explaining that both its own position and the ABA's is that "an individual who is found incompetent to face the death penalty" should not have his sentence "merely suspended," but should "have his sentence *permanently commuted* to a non-capital punishment." APA Br. 17, n.15 (emphasis added). Thus, the conceded objective of these *amici* (and the predictable consequence of their proposed test) is not simply avoiding the inhumanity of executing a person who is truly insane, but rather removing from death row as large a class of capital convicts as reasonably possible.[5] (pp. 40–41)

Application of the State's proposed test will advance the modern penological interests behind the death penalty.

The Court has recently confirmed that retribution and deterrence are capital punishment's two predominant social purposes. *Roper*, 543 U.S., at 571 (citing *Gregg v. Georgia*, 428 U.S. 153, 183 (1976) (joint opinion of Stewart, Powell, and Stevens, JJ.)); accord *Atkins*, 536 U.S., at 318–19. As shown below, application of the State's proposed test will advance each of those interests.[6]

a. The State's test will further the retributive purpose of punishment.

Retribution aims either "to express the community's moral outrage or . . . to right the balance for the wrong to the victim." *Roper*, 543 U.S., at 571; see

Atkins, 536 U.S., at 319 (explaining that retribution is "the interest in seeing that the offender gets his 'just deserts' "). The Court has repeatedly emphasized the societal focus of retribution. See, *e.g., Thompson v. Oklahoma*, 487 U.S. 815, 836 (1988); see also *Schriro v. Summerlin*, 542 U.S. 348, 360 (2004) (Breyer, J., dissenting); *Gregg*, 428 U.S., at 183–84 (joint opinion of Stewart, Powell, and Stevens, JJ.). Panetti misunderstands the societal nature of retribution, erroneously equating it with vengeance. Panetti Br. 46 & n.33." (p. 43)

i. The retributive justification for punishment necessarily precedes any execution-competence analysis.

The viability of retribution as a permissible theory of punishment depends not on the "rational understanding" that a convict may or may not have, see *supra* Part II.C.2; cf. Panetti Br. 46, but rather on the convict's moral culpability at the time he committed his crime, *Enmund v. Florida*, 458 U.S. 782, 800–01 (1982) (reflecting that "personal responsibility and moral guilt" define a criminal's level of culpability and concluding that execution of one convict for murders that he did not personally commit failed to serve the retributive goal of punishment)." (p. 44)

[I]n the present context the question of culpability will already have been conclusively—and affirmatively—resolved. The issue is not whether the Constitution permits society to *impose* the death penalty on a criminal who was, for some reason, less culpable at the time of his crime, cf. *Roper*, 543 U.S., at 556, 578; *Atkins*, 536 U.S., at 306–08, 321, but rather whether an unquestionably valid death sentence may be *carried out* against a criminal who has subsequently become mentally ill, see *Ford*, 477 U.S., at 425 (Powell, J., concurring in the judgment). This is so because any convict to whom the execution-competence test is applied will necessarily have been adjudicated both sane at the time of his offense and competent to stand trial, removing any doubts about culpability that might in some cases arise from mental illness.

ii. There are substantial problems with the wholly personal view of retribution that Panetti advances." (pp. 44–45)

"Relying heavily on nonjudicial sources, Panetti asserts that retribution requires a condemned prisoner to have a subjective appreciation of the moral impropriety of his criminal conduct and to "suffer the anguish" of knowing the reason for his fate. Panetti Br. 45." (p. 45)

"Putting aside its lack of support in case law, there are significant problems with Panetti's mind-of-the-criminal approach. First, tailoring the execution competence test to the innermost thoughts of capital convicts would present substantial practical problems. It is difficult to imagine how anyone other than the convict himself could accurately assess whether he truly appreciates the magnitude of his moral wrong—at least with respect to a convict who is willing to lie about such things. And under Panetti's proposed test, it would be remarkably easy for a convict to feign his way out of a death sentence.

Second, allowing the execution-competence test to be shaped primarily by a personal, subjective view of the retributive rationale would prevent the execution of convicts who genuinely lack moral qualms about their crimes. It cannot be that amoral capital convicts should be excused from death sentences based on amorality alone. Yet Panetti's proposed standard would yield that result." (p. 46)

D. Under Both the State's Proposed Test and the Test That the Court of Appeals Applied, Panetti Is Competent to Be Executed. (p. 48)

Under the State's proposed test, Panetti could properly be held incompetent to be executed only if, because of mental illness, he lacked the capacity to recognize that his punishment (1) is the result of his being convicted of capital murder and (2) will cause his death. To the extent, this test varies from that applied by the court of appeals, any such variances are immaterial to the result because, as shown below, the record establishes that Panetti is competent to be executed under either standard.

First of all, it is undisputed that Panetti has the capacity to recognize that the punishment he faces is death. Indeed, the experts all agreed and the district court expressly found that, as a factual matter, "Panetti is aware he is to be executed," JA 363, 372; accord JA 373. Panetti did not oppose this conclusion in the district court, see JA 367, 372, did not challenge it in the court of appeals, and does not challenge it here. Therefore, Panetti is unquestionably "[]aware of the punishment [he is] about to suffer," JA 379 (quoting *Ford*, 477 U.S., at 422 (Powell, J., concurring in the judgment))" (p. 48–49).

The only question that remains is whether Panetti has the capacity to recognize that his punishment is the result of his being convicted of capital murder, or, under the court of appeals's analysis, whether he is aware of why he is to be executed, JA 379. The record establishes that Panetti passes each of these prongs as well.

Dr. Parker and Dr. Anderson each testified that Panetti has the capacity to understand that he is being executed for the murders of which he was convicted. JA 245, 247 (testimony of Dr. Parker), 303–04 (testimony of Dr. Anderson); accord JA 75 (joint report of Drs. Parker and Anderson), and the district court explicitly concluded that "[t]here is evidence in the record to support a finding that Panetti is *capable* of understanding the reason for his execution," JA 367. Again, Panetti does not challenge this conclusion. And under the State's proposed test, it is irrelevant that these witnesses "were unable to reach a formal conclusion that [Panetti] did, in fact, understand" the reason for his execution. JA 364. For the reasons already noted, it is the *capacity* to understand—rather than actual demonstration of understanding—that defines the minimal level of competence needed to satisfy this prong of the State's proposed test. See *supra* Part II.C.3.

And with respect to the court of appeals's test, the district court accurately noted that two of Panetti's own execution-competence experts testified that, "despite his delusions, Panetti understands [that] the State's stated reason for seeking his execution is for his murders." JA 366; see also JA 157 (testimony of Dr. Conroy); JA 214 (testimony of Dr. Rosin). Thus, not only did the district court explicitly find that "Panetti is aware he committed the murders that serve as the basis for his execution," JA 372, but the court further found that "Panetti understands the State's stated reason for executing him is that he committed two murders," JA 372.

The district court also correctly concluded that the alternative sense of "understand" embodied in Panetti's proposal did not match the court of appeals's standard. JA 369" (p. 49–50).

In sum, the record establishes that Panetti: (1) has the capacity to recognize that his punishment will cause his death (and does in fact does recognize this), and (2) has the capacity to recognize that his punishment is the result of his being convicted of capital murder (or, within the meaning of the court of appeals's test, is aware of why he is to be executed). Taken together, these facts conclusively establish Panetti's competence to be executed under both the court of appeals's test and the State's proposed test.

Conclusion

The judgment of the court of appeals should be affirmed. (p. 50)

Notes

1. Citations to the transcript of Panetti's capital-murder trial are noted as "RR" ("Reporters Record"). Citations to the States exhibits admitted into evidence during those proceedings are noted as "SX" ("State Exhibit"). Citations to the pleadings, orders, and motions filed in the trial court are noted as "CR" ("Clerk's Record"). Citations to the federal district court's hearing on execution competence are noted as "FH" ("Federal Hearing"). Citations to the joint appendix filed in this Court are noted as "JA."

2. Panetti incorrectly reports the final vote as nine-to-three in favor of incompetence. Panetti Br. 8, n.6. That vote occurred earlier in the deliberations. 3.CR.290.

3. Dr. Conroy noted that "the major portion of our population in our in-patient units in federal Bureau of Prisons hospitals are diagnosed with some form of schizophrenia," JA 142, and Dr. Silverman opined that most schizophrenics are competent to be executed, JA 227.

4. Lay testimony corroborated this point. Major Miller testified that Panetti cooperated with him in going over the State's pre-execution forms, JA 281, II-42–53, and demonstrated his understanding of the forms' questions about disposition of assets, choice of last meal, and the like. JA 287–88. Additional lay testimony reflected Panetti's demonstrated ability to communicate coherently—and politely—with prison staff. *E.g.*, 1 FH 193–96 (testimony of Terri Hill); 1 FH 200 (testimony of Victoria Williams)."

5. In so noting, Justice O'Connor echoed the concerns of Hale, who, some three centuries earlier, likewise urged courts to guard against the potential for "great fraud" concerning those claiming incompetence. 1 Hale, *supra*, at 35; Legal Historians Br. 15, n.8."

6. Indeed, one death-row study of a limited population noted that half of the profiled inmates exhibited delusional tendencies, which included persecutory delusions (*e.g.*, inmate's belief that he was target of a Jewish conspiracy). Barbara A. Ward, Competency for Execution: Problems in Law and Psychiatry, 14 Fla. St. U. L. Rev. 35, 39–40 & n.26 (1986) (citing Bluestone & McGahee, Reaction to Extreme Stress: Impending Death by Execution, 119 Am. J. Psychiatry 393, 393 (1962)). Other inmates in the study coped with their predicament through obsessive rumination, "thinking furiously about other things, such as appeals, religion, or philosophy." *Ibid.*

CHALLENGE QUESTIONS

Must Mentally Ill Murderers Have a Rational Understanding of Why They Are Being Sentenced to Death?

1. In murder cases in which the assertion is made that an individual's crime was attributable to mental illness, complex questions arise about how to assess the legitimacy of the accused person's psychiatric symptoms. If you were a member of a jury in such a case, what kind of evidence would you deem necessary so that a determination could be made about the accused person's psychological functioning?

2. In criminal cases involving mentally ill individuals, several debates have emerged about the condition of the accused within the context of the trial. A particularly thorny issue pertains to whether the accused should be taken off all antipsychotic medication for the trial, so that the court can see this individual in a nonmedicated state (possibly similar to the functional level at the time of the crime). Discuss the benefits and problems of this option.

3. Some proponents of the death penalty would argue that people who engage in violent murder should be executed, regardless of whether they are mentally ill, if for no reason other than ridding society of such people. Discuss the moral implications of this stance.

4. Forensic specialists have worked diligently for years to develop assessment measures to determine whether people accused of a crime are malingering (faking symptoms for an ulterior motive). If you were given the task of developing such an instrument, what kind of data would you look for?

5. Discuss the hypothetical situation in which a convicted murderer understands the nature of his crime but has no understanding of what the death penalty means or why it would be associated with the crime he had committed. Discuss the moral dilemmas inherent in a decision to execute such an individual.

Suggested Readings

Ackerson, K. S., Brodsky, S. L., & Zapf, P. A. (2005). Judges' and psychologists' assessments of legal and clinical factors in competence for execution. *Psychology, Public Policy, & Law, 11*, 164–193.

Saks, E. R., & Jeste, D. V. (2006). Capacity to consent to or refuse treatment and/or research: Theoretical considerations. *Behavioral Sciences & the Law, 24*(4), 411–429.

Shapiro, D. L. (2005). Ethical dilemmas in competency for execution evaluations. *Journal of Forensic Psychology Practice, 5*(4), 75–82.

Slobogin, C. (2006). *Minding justice: Laws that deprive people with mental disability of life and liberty.* Cambridge, MA: Harvard University Press.

ISSUE 18

Does Research Confirm That Abortion Is a Psychologically Benign Experience?

YES: Report of the APA Task Force on Mental Health and Abortion (Brenda Major, Mark Appelbaum, Linda Beckman, Mary Ann Dutton, Nancy Felipe Russo, Carolyn West), from *Report of the APA Task Force on Mental Health and Abortion* (American Psychological Association, 2008)

NO: Priscilla K. Coleman, from *Critique of the APA Task Force on Abortion and Mental Health* (2008). Available from: http://aaplog .octoberblue.com/wp-content/uploads/2010/02/Coleman-Critique- of-APA-Report.pdf

ISSUE SUMMARY

YES: The APA Task Force (TFMHA) reviewed the empirical literature and concluded that for women who have an unplanned pregnancy, the risk of mental health problems is no greater than the risk for women who deliver an unplanned pregnancy.

NO: Professor Priscilla K. Coleman contends that the TFMHA analysis of the evidence reflects politically motivated bias in the selection of studies, analysis of the literature, and the conclusions derived.

The term postabortion syndrome emerged in the 1980s to characterize detrimental psychological symptoms that may follow the experience of abortion. Over the past few decades several studies have been conducted in an effort to assess the psychological effects of undergoing an abortion. The American Psychological Association (APA) summarized the research, which culminated in a 1990 article in *Science* concluding that scientific studies did not point to adverse psychological effects from abortion, and in 2007, the APA appointed yet another task force to review the literature.

In the 2008 report, the Task Force on Mental Health and Abortion (TFMHA) reviewed the empirical literature and concluded that for women who have an unplanned pregnancy, the risk of mental health problems is no greater than the risk for women who deliver an unplanned pregnancy. In drawing this conclusion from the research, they highlight methodological problems inherent in the research that points to detrimental psychological effects following abortion.

Dr. Priscilla K. Coleman takes aim at the TFMHA report, asserting that it reflects an extensive, politically motivated bias in the selection of studies reviewed, analysis of the literature, and conclusions drawn. Dr. Coleman contends that bias is evident even in the choice of Task Force members, and she contends that the conclusion drawn in the report does not follow from the literature reviewed.

POINT

- The TFMHA evaluated all empirical studies published in English in peer-reviewed journals post-1989 that compared the mental health of women who had an induced abortion to the mental health of comparison groups of women ($N = 50$) or that examined factors that predict mental health among women who have had an elective abortion in the United States ($N = 23$).

- Caution must be exercised in drawing conclusions. For example, Ferguson et al. (2006) (1) did not measure wantedness of pregnancy, (2) used a comparison group of women who had never been pregnant, (3) used a small sample of 48, (4) did not control for number of prior abortions or births, and (5) conducted the study in New Zealand.

- A study by Gilchrist et al. (1995), which stood out for its methodological rigor, concluded that once psychiatric disorders prior to pregnancy were taken into account, the rate of total psychiatric disorder was no higher after termination of an unplanned pregnancy than after childbirth.

- Feelings of stigma, perceived need for secrecy, exposure to antiabortion picketing, and low perceived or anticipated social support for the abortion decision, negatively affected women's postabortion psychological experiences.

COUNTERPOINT

- The TFMHA conveniently restricts its review to studies conducted in the United States, thereby eliminating at least 40 studies, including a large Swedish study of 854 women in which rates of negative experiences were considerably higher than in previously published studies using more superficial assessments.

- The study by Ferguson et al. (2006) (1) was longitudinal, (2) included comprehensive mental health assessments, (3) had lower estimated abortion concealment rates than previous studies, (4) used a sample representing 80% to 83% of a group of 630 subjects, and (5) used extensive controls.

- The study by Gilchrist et al. (1995) has a number of ignored flaws: (1) the response rate is not reported; (2) there are few controls for confounding variables; (3) the study had a problematically high attrition rate; and (4) no standardized measures of mental health diagnoses were used.

- The power attributed to cultural stigmatization of women's abortion-related stress is unsupported, as there have been few well-designed studies that support this claim.

Report of the APA Task Force on Mental Health and Abortion

Executive Summary

The Council of Representatives of the American Psychological Association charged the Task Force on Mental Health and Abortion (TFMHA) with "collecting, examining, and summarizing the scientific research addressing the mental health factors associated with abortion, including the psychological responses following abortion, and producing a report based upon a review of the most current research." In considering the psychological implications of abortion, the TFMHA recognized that abortion encompasses a diversity of experiences. Women obtain abortions for different reasons; at different times of gestation; via differing medical procedures; and within different personal, social, economic, and cultural contexts. All of these may lead to variability in women's psychological reactions following abortion. Consequently, global statements about the psychological impact of abortion on women can be misleading.

The TFMHA evaluated all empirical studies published in English in peer-reviewed journals post-1989 that compared the mental health of women who had an induced abortion to the mental health of comparison groups of women ($N=50$) or that examined factors that predict mental health among women who have had an elective abortion in the United States ($N=23$). This literature was reviewed and evaluated with respect to its ability to address four primary questions: (1) Does abortion cause harm to women's mental health? (2) How prevalent are mental health problems among women in the United States who have had an abortion? (3) What is the relative risk of mental health problems associated with abortion compared to its alternatives (other courses of action that might be taken by a pregnant woman in similar circumstances)? and (4) What predicts individual variation in women's psychological experiences following abortion?

A critical evaluation of the published literature revealed that the majority of studies suffered from methodological problems, often severe in nature. Given the state of the literature, a simple calculation of effect sizes or count of the number of studies that showed an effect in one direction versus another was considered inappropriate. The quality of the evidence that produced those effects must be considered to avoid misleading conclusions. Accordingly, the TFMHA emphasized the studies it judged to be most methodologically rigorous to arrive at its conclusions.

The best scientific evidence published indicates that among adult women who have an *unplanned pregnancy* the relative risk of mental health problems is no greater if they have a single elective first-trimester abortion than if they deliver that pregnancy. The evidence regarding the relative mental health risks associated with multiple abortions is more equivocal. Positive associations observed between multiple abortions and poorer mental health may be linked to co-occurring risks that predispose a woman to both multiple unwanted pregnancies and mental health problems.

The few published studies that examined women's responses following an induced abortion due to fetal abnormality suggest that terminating a wanted pregnancy late in pregnancy due to fetal abnormality appears to be associated with negative psychological reactions equivalent to those experienced by women who miscarry a wanted pregnancy or who experience a stillbirth or death of a newborn, but less than those who deliver a child with life-threatening abnormalities.

The differing patterns of psychological experiences observed among women who terminate an unplanned pregnancy versus those who terminate a planned and wanted pregnancy highlight the importance of taking pregnancy intendedness and wantedness into account when seeking to understand psychological reactions to abortion.

None of the literature reviewed adequately addressed the prevalence of mental health problems among women in the United States who have had an abortion. In general, however, the prevalence of mental health problems observed among women in the United States who had a single, legal, first-trimester abortion for nontherapeutic reasons was consistent with normative rates of comparable mental health problems in the general population of women in the United States.

Nonetheless, it is clear that some women do experience sadness, grief, and feelings of loss following termination of a pregnancy, and some experience clinically significant disorders, including depression and anxiety. However, the TFMHA reviewed no evidence sufficient to support the claim that an observed association between abortion history and mental health was caused by the abortion per se, as opposed to other factors.

This review identified several factors that are predictive of more negative psychological responses following first-trimester abortion among women in the United States. Those factors included perceptions of stigma, need for secrecy, and low or anticipated social support for the abortion decision; a prior history of mental health problems; personality factors such as low self-esteem and use of avoidance and denial coping strategies; and characteristics of the particular pregnancy, including the extent to which the woman wanted and felt committed to it. Across studies, prior mental health emerged as the strongest predictor of postabortion mental health. Many of these same factors also predict negative psychological reactions to other types of stressful life events, including childbirth, and, hence, are not uniquely predictive of psychological responses following abortion.

Well-designed, rigorously conducted scientific research would help disentangle confounding factors and establish relative risks of abortion compared to its alternatives as well as factors associated with variation among women in their responses following abortion. Even so, there is unlikely to be a single definitive research study that will determine the mental health implications of abortion "once and for all" given the diversity and complexity of women and their circumstances. . . .

Summary and Conclusions

The empirical literature on the association between abortion and mental health has been asked to address four primary questions: (1) Does abortion cause harm to women's mental health? (2) How prevalent are mental health problems among women in the United States who have had an abortion? (3) What is the relative risk of mental health problems associated with abortion compared to its alternatives (other courses of action that might be taken by a pregnant woman in similar circumstances)? and (4) What predicts individual variation in women's psychological experiences following abortion? As discussed above, the first question is not scientifically testable from an ethical or practical perspective. The second and third questions obscure the important point that abortion is not a unitary event, but encompasses a diversity of experiences. That said, in the following section we address what the literature reviewed has to say with respect to the last three questions.

The Relative Risks of Abortion Compared to Its Alternatives

The TFMHA identified 50 papers published in peer-reviewed journals between 1990 and 2007 that analyzed empirical data of a quantitative nature on psychological experiences associated with induced abortion, compared to an alternative. These included 10 papers based on secondary analyses of two medical record data sets, 15 papers based on secondary analyses of nine public data sets, 19 papers based on 17 studies conducted for the primary purpose of comparing women who had first-trimester abortions (or an abortion in which the trimester was unspecified) with a comparison group, and 6 studies that compared women's responses following an induced abortion for fetal abnormality to women's responses following other reproductive events. These studies were evaluated with respect to their ability to draw sound conclusions about the relative mental health risks associated with abortion compared to alternative courses of action that can be pursued by a woman facing a similar circumstance (e.g., an unwanted or unintended pregnancy).

A careful evaluation of these studies revealed that the majority suffered from methodological problems, sometimes severely so. Problems of sampling, measurement, design, and analyses cloud interpretation. Abortion was often underreported and underspecified and in the majority of studies, wantedness of pregnancy was not considered. Rarely did research designs include a comparison group that was otherwise equivalent to women who had an elective abortion, impairing the ability to draw conclusions about relative risks. Furthermore, because of the absence of adequate controls for co-occurring risks, including systemic factors (e.g., violence exposure, poverty), prior mental health (including prior substance abuse), and personality (e.g., avoidance coping style), in almost all of these studies, it was impossible to determine whether any observed differences between abortion groups and comparison groups reflected consequences of pregnancy resolution, preexisting differences between groups, or artifacts of methodology. Given this state of the literature, what can be concluded about relative risks from this body of research?

One approach would be to simply calculate effect sizes or count the number of published papers that suggest adverse effects of abortion and those that show no adverse effects (or even positive effects) of abortion when compared to an alternative course of action (e.g., delivery). Although tempting, such approaches would be misleading and irresponsible, given the numerous methodological problems that characterize this literature, the many papers that were based on the same data sets, and the inadequacy of the comparison groups typically used. Given this state of the literature, the TFMHA judged that the best course of action was to base conclusions on the findings of the studies identified as most methodologically rigorous and sound.

Of the studies based on medical records, the most methodologically rigorous studies were conducted in Finland. The largest and strongest of these examined the relative risk of death within a year of end of pregnancy associated with abortion versus delivery (Gissler et al., 2004b). It demonstrated that the relative risk differs depending on how cause of death is coded. Compared to women who delivered, women who had an abortion had lower rates of direct pregnancy-related deaths (cause of death was directly related to or aggravated by the pregnancy or its management, but not from accidental or incidental causes) but higher rates of pregnancy-associated deaths (deaths occurring within one year from end of pregnancy, regardless of whether deaths are pregnancy-related). When therapeutic abortions were excluded from the category of pregnancy-associated deaths, however, this latter difference was not significant. Across both the Medi-Cal and Finland record-based studies, a higher rate of violent death (including accidents, homicide, and suicide) was observed among women who had an abortion compared to women who delivered. This correlational finding is consistent with other evidence indicating that risk for violence is higher in the lives of women who have abortions and underscores the importance of controlling for violence exposure in studies of mental health associated with pregnancy outcome.

With respect to the studies based on secondary analyses of survey data, the conclusions regarding relative risk varied depending on the data set, the approach to the design of the study, the covariates used in analyses, the comparison group selected, and the outcome variables assessed. Analyses of the same data set (the NLSY) with respect to the same outcome variable (depression) revealed that conclusions regarding relative risk differed dramatically depending on the sampling and exclusion criteria applied.

The strongest of the secondary analyses studies was conducted by Fergusson et al. (2006). This study was based on a representative sample of young women in Christchurch, NZ, was longitudinal (although Fergusson also reported concurrent analyses), measured postpregnancy/abortion psychiatric morbidity using established diagnostic categories, and controlled for mental health prior to the pregnancy in prospective analyses. Fergusson et al. compared women who terminated a pregnancy to women who delivered or had not been pregnant. The prospective analyses reported by Fergusson et al. are most informative. These analyses compared number of total psychiatric disorders among women who had an abortion prior to age 21 to number of total psychiatric disorders among women who had delivered a child by age 21 or among women who had never been pregnant by age 21, controlling for pre-pregnancy mental health and other variables that differed initially among the three groups. In these analyses, women who had one or more abortions prior to age 21 had a significantly higher number of total psychiatric disorders by age 25 than women who had delivered or had never been pregnant by age 21. This study thus suggests that women who have one or more abortions at a young age (<21) are at greater relative risk for psychiatric disorder compared to women who deliver a child at a young age or women who do not get pregnant at a young age.

There are several reasons why caution should be used in drawing the above conclusion from this study. First and most importantly, Fergusson et al. (2006) did not assess the *intendedness or wantedness* of the pregnancy. As noted earlier, approximately 90% of pregnancies that are aborted are unintended, compared to only 31% of those that are delivered (Henshaw, 1998). Thus, although these were young women, it is reasonable to assume that at least some of the women in the delivery group were delivering a planned and wanted child. Delivery of a planned and wanted child would be expected to be associated with positive outcomes and is not a viable option for women facing an unintended pregnancy. Second, the other comparison group used by Fergusson et al.—women who had never been pregnant—is not a viable option for women already facing an unintended pregnancy. Third, the prospective analyses were based on only 48 women who had abortions, an extremely small sample. Fourth, the study did not control for number of prior abortions or births. Fifth, the study focused on women who had one or more abortions at a young age (<21 years), limiting its generalizability to younger women; younger age has been linked in some studies to more negative psychological experiences following abortion (e.g., Major et al., 2000). Finally, this study was conducted in New Zealand, a country with more restrictive abortion regulations than those in the United States. Because the focus of APA is on mental health in the United States, it may thus be less useful as a basis for drawing conclusions about relative risks of abortion for US. women.

The TFMHA also reviewed and evaluated 19 papers based on 17 studies conducted tor the primary purpose of comparing women who had first-trimester abortions (or an abortion in which trimester was unspecified) with a comparison group on a mental health relevant variable. These studies varied widely in methodological quality and cultural context. Although most of the studies showed no significant differences between the psychological experiences of women who had an induced first-trimester abortion and women in a variety of comparison groups once important covariates (e.g., marital status, age) were controlled, most also were characterized by methodological deficiencies. These included problems of sampling, measurement, design, analyses, and inappropriate comparison groups. Thus, as a group, these studies also do not provide good answers to questions of relative risk or prevalence.

One study, however, stood out from the rest in terms of its methodological rigor. This study was conducted in the United Kingdom by the Royal College of General Practitioners and the Royal College of Obstetricians and Gynecologists (Gilchrist et al., 1995). It was longitudinal, based on a representative sample, measured postpregnancy/abortion psychiatric morbidity using established diagnostic categories, controlled for mental health prior to the pregnancy as well as other relevant covariates, and compared women who terminated an unplanned pregnancy to women who pursued alternative courses of action. In prospective analyses, Gilchrist et al. compared postpregnancy psychiatric morbidity (stratified by prepregnancy psychiatric status) of four groups of women, all of whom were faced with an unplanned pregnancy: women who obtained abortions, who did not seek abortion, who requested abortion but were denied, and who initially requested abortion but changed their mind. The researchers concluded that once psychiatric disorders prior to the pregnancy were taken into account, the rate of total reported psychiatric disorder was no higher after termination of an unplanned pregnancy than after childbirth.

This study provides high-quality evidence that among women faced with an unplanned pregnancy, the relative risks of psychiatric disorder among women who terminate the pregnancy are no greater than the risks among women who pursue alternative courses of action. What appears to be a discrepancy between the conclusions of this study and those of Fergusson et al. (2006) is likely due to differences in sampling and study design. First and most importantly, Gilchrist et al. (1995) restricted their study to women identified by their family doctor as having an "unplanned" pregnancy, whereas Fergusson et al. did not assess the intendedness of the pregnancy, as noted above.

Consequently, the comparison groups used by Gilchrist et al. are more appropriate for addressing the question of relative risk of negative psychological experiences following elective abortion *compared to other courses of action women in similar circumstances (i.e., facing an unplanned pregnancy) might take.* Second, the Gilchrist et al. study was not restricted to women who became pregnant at a young age; hence the sample is more representative of women who seek abortion. Third, differences in abortion sample size were dramatic. The prospective analyses by Gilchrist et al. were based on an abortion sample of 6,410 women, as compared to 48 in the Fergusson et al. study. Fourth, unlike the study by Fergusson et al., the Gilchrist et al. study controlled for number of prior abortions and births. For these reasons, the TFMHA had more confidence in arriving at conclusions about relative risk based on the findings of Gilchrist et al. Nonetheless, it should be noted that the abortion context in the United Kingdom may differ from that in the United States, weakening generalization to the U.S. context.

The TFMHA reviewed six studies that compared women's responses following an induced abortion for fetal abnormality to women's responses following other reproductive events. These studies were based on extremely small samples often characterized by high attrition rates and low response rates. Nonetheless, these studies suggest that terminating a wanted pregnancy, especially late in pregnancy, can be associated with negative psychological experiences comparable to those experienced by women who miscarry a wanted pregnancy or experience a stillbirth or death of a newborn, but less severe than those experienced by women who deliver a child with a severe abnormality. At least one study also suggests that the majority of women who make this difficult choice do not regret their decision (e.g., Kersting et al., 2005). As a group, these studies of responses to termination of a wanted pregnancy for fetal abnormality underscore the importance of considering the wantedness of the pregnancy, as well as the reason for and timing of the abortion, in studying its psychological implications. Interpretation of prevalence of psychological distress and relative risk is clouded when researchers lump together under the category of "abortion" women who abort a wanted pregnancy for reasons of fetal anomaly with women who have an elective abortion of an unplanned and unwanted pregnancy.

In summary, although numerous methodological flaws prevent the published literature from providing unequivocal evidence regarding the relative mental health risks associated with abortion per se compared to its alternatives (childbirth of an unplanned pregnancy), in the view of the TFMHA, the best scientific evidence indicates that the relative risk of mental health problems among adult women who have an unplanned pregnancy is no greater if they have an elective first-trimester abortion than if they deliver that pregnancy (Gilchrist et al., 1995).

The evidence regarding the relative mental health risks associated with multiple abortions is more equivocal. One source of inconsistencies in the literature may be methodological, such as differences in sample size or age ranges among samples. Positive associations observed between multiple abortions and poorer mental health (e.g., Harlow et al., 2004) also may be due to co-occurring risks that predispose a woman to both unwanted pregnancies and mental health problems.

Terminating a wanted pregnancy late in pregnancy due to fetal abnormality appears to be associated with negative psychological experiences equivalent to those experienced by women who miscarry a wanted pregnancy or experience a stillbirth or the death of a newborn.

Prevalence of Mental Health Problems Among U.S. Women Who Have an Abortion

A second question this literature has been used to address concerns the prevalence of mental health problems among women in the United States who have had an abortion. As noted at the outset of this report, research capable of adequately addressing this question requires at minimum: (1) a clearly defined, agreed upon, and appropriately measured mental health problem (e.g., a clinically significant disorder, assessed via validated criteria); (2) a sample representative of the population to which one wants to generalize (e.g., women in the United States); and (3) knowledge of the prevalence of the same mental health problem in the general population, equated with the abortion group with respect to potentially confounding factors. None of the studies reviewed met all these criteria and hence provided sound evidence regarding prevalence. Few of the U.S. studies assessed clinically significant disorders with valid and reliable measures or physician diagnosis. In those studies that did use clinically relevant outcome measures, sampling strategies were inadequate to address the question of prevalence in the larger U.S. population either because the samples were biased, highly selected, geographically restricted or failed to use appropriate sampling weights. Furthermore, because of the lack of adequate control for co-occurring risks, the extent to which the incidence of mental health problems associated with abortion was due to the procedure versus to potentially confounding factors, such as poverty, poorer prior mental health, etc., was impossible to establish.

Given these caveats, however, the prevalence of mental health problems observed among women in the United States who had a single, legal, first- trimester abortion for nontherapeutic reasons appeared to be consistent with normative rates of comparable mental health problems in the general population of women in the United States. Consider, for example, the overall prevalence of depression among women in the NLSY, a longitudinal national survey of a cohort of men and women aged 14–21 years in 1979. Among *all* women in the NLSY, irrespective of reproductive history and without controlling for any covariates, 22% met criteria for depression in 1992 (i.e., scored above the clinical cutoff on the CES-D). Among women who reported one abortion, the corresponding percentage was 23%. Among women who reported multiple abortions, however, the percentage was higher; 31% met criteria for depression (see Table). A similar pattern was reported by Harlow et al. (2004) in their study of a representative sample of women in the Boston metropolitan area.

To say that women *in general* do not show an increased incidence of mental health problems following a single abortion, however, does not mean that no women experience such problems. Abortion is an experience often hallmarked by ambivalence and a mix of positive and negative emotions is to be expected (Adler et al., 1990; Dagg, 1991). Some women experience beneficial outcomes, whereas others experience sadness, grief, and feelings of loss following the elective termination of a pregnancy. Some women experience clinically significant outcomes, such as depression or anxiety. However, the TFMHA reviewed no evidence sufficient to support the claim that an observed association between abortion history and a mental health problem was caused by the abortion per se, as opposed to other factors. As observed throughout this report, unwanted pregnancy and abortion are correlated with preexisting conditions (e.g., poverty), life circumstances (e.g., exposure to violence, sexual abuse), problem behaviors (e.g., drug use), and personality characteristics (e.g., avoidance style of coping with negative emotion) that can have profound and long-lasting negative effects on mental health.

Population estimates of proportion of all women and women identified as having been pregnant exceeding CES-D clinical cutoff score, National Longitudinal Survey of Youth: 1992.

Group (N)	CES-D>15
All women (unweighted N = 4401)	22%
No abortion ever	21%
Ever abortion	25%
One abortion	23%
Multiple abortions	31%
All women ever pregnant + (unweighted N = 3503)	23%
No abortion ever	23%
Ever abortion	25%
One abortion	22%
Multiple abortions	31%

Notes: + Includes pregnancies ending in miscarriages.
No covariates are controlled.

Differences in prevalence of mental health problems or problem behaviors observed between women who have had an abortion and women who have not may be primarily accounted for by these preexisting and ongoing differences among groups.

Predictors of Individual Variation in Responses Following Abortion

A third issue addressed in the literature on abortion and mental health concerns individual variation in women's psychological experiences following abortion. The TFMHA reviewed 23 papers based on 15 data sets that were based solely on samples of women who had abortions in the United States, but that otherwise met inclusion criteria. These noncomparison group studies typically focused on predictors of individual variation in response. They were of two major types: (1) prospective or concurrent studies that usually included preabortion measures of psychological adjustment and risk factors and one or more postabortion assessments of adjustment and (2) retrospective studies that assessed women's perceived reactions to the event and current level of psychological functioning several years after the abortion. The retrospective studies had serious methodological problems that made interpretation of their findings difficult. The prospective studies, despite limitations of high attrition, geographically limited samples, and potential confounds that were not measured, provided valuable information about sources of variation in individual women's psychological experiences and, to a more limited extent, mental health problems subsequent to abortion.

The most methodologically strong studies in this group showed that interpersonal concerns, including feelings of stigma, perceived need for secrecy, exposure to antiabortion picketing, and low perceived or anticipated social support for the abortion decision, negatively affected women's postabortion psychological experiences. Characteristics of the woman also predicted more negative psychological experiences after first-trimester abortion, including a prior history of mental health problems, personality factors such as low self-esteem and low perceived control over her life, and use of avoidance and denial coping strategies. Feelings of commitment to the pregnancy, ambivalence about the abortion decision, and low perceived ability to cope with the abortion prior to its occurrence also predicted more negative postabortion responses. Across studies, prior mental health emerged as the strongest predictor of postabortion mental health (Major et al., 2000). Type of abortion procedures, at least those used in the first trimester, did not appear to be related to postabortion psychological well-being or mental health.

In considering these risk factors, it is important to recognize that many of the same factors shown to be associated with more negative postabortion psychological experiences also predict more negative reactions to other types of stressful life events, including childbirth (e.g., low perceived social support, low self-esteem, low self-efficacy, avoidance coping). For instance, low perceived social support and low self-esteem also are risk factors for postpartum depression (Beck, 2001; Logsdon & Usui, 2001). Most risk factors are not uniquely predictive of psychological experiences following abortion. Women characterized by one or more such risk factors might be equally (or more) likely to experience negative psychological reactions if they pursued an alternative course of action (motherhood or adoption).

Conclusions and Future Research

Based on our comprehensive review and evaluation of the empirical literature published in peer-reviewed journals since 1989, this Task Force on Mental Health and Abortion concludes that the most methodologically sound research indicates that among women who have a single, legal, first-trimester abortion of an unplanned pregnancy for nontherapeutic reasons, the relative risks of mental health problems are no greater than the risks among women who deliver an unplanned pregnancy. This conclusion is generally consistent with that reached by the first APA task force (Adler et al., 1990).

This report has highlighted the methodological failings that are pervasive in the literature on abortion and mental health. This focus on methodological limitations raises the question of whether empirical science is capable of informing understanding of the mental health implications of and public policy related to abortion. Some policy questions cannot be definitively answered through empirical research because they are not pragmatically or ethically possible.

Other questions, however, are amenable to the methods of well-designed, rigorously conducted scientific research. For example, empirical research can identify those women who might be more or less likely than others to show adverse or positive psychological outcomes following an abortion. Well-designed research can also answer questions of relative risk and prevalence. What would this research look like?

Such research would use methods that are prospective and longitudinal and employ exacting sampling methods (including the use of sampling weights that allow proper generalization back to the populations to whom the conclusions are being applied). Careful attention would be paid to adequately assessing preexisting and co-occurring conditions such as marital status, domestic violence, age, socioeconomic status, parity, prior mental health, and prior problem behaviors as well as other situations that are known to be associated with both differential utilization of abortion and mental health problems. Importantly, comparison groups would be selected so as to be equivalent to the abortion group on all variables other than abortion history. Critical variables such as intendedness and wantedness of the pregnancy would be assessed, and abortion status verified objectively (not only through self-report). Careful use of covariance or similar adjustment techniques (applied to pre-defined covariates) would be employed. Precision of measurement (both in terms of specification of outcome measure and psychometric adequacy of the measurements) would also be guaranteed. Positive psychological responses and experiences as well as negative mental health would be assessed. Repeated assessment of responses over time would be made to assess relevant changes, positive and negative, in the trajectory of responses following abortion. Samples sufficiently large to guarantee adequate power to detect effects that are present would be used, and attention would be paid to effect-size estimation in addition to the simple reliance of null hypothesis statistical testing.

Research that met the above scientific standards would help to disentangle confounding factors and establish relative risks of abortion compared to its alternatives. Even so, there is unlikely to be a single definitive research study that will determine the mental health implications of abortion "once and for all" as there is no "all," given the diversity and complexity of women and their circumstances. Important agendas for future research are to further understand and alleviate the conditions that lead to unwanted pregnancy and abortion and to understand the conditions that shape how women respond to these life events, with the ultimate goal of improving women's lives and well-being.

Priscilla K. Coleman

 NO

Critique of the APA Task Force on Abortion and Mental Health

The charge of the APA Task Force on Abortion and Mental Health was to collect, examine, and summarize peer-reviewed research published over the last 17 years pertaining to outcomes associated with abortion.

Evidence described below indicates an extensive, politically motivated bias in the selection of studies, analysis of the literature, and in the conclusions derived by the Task Force. As opposed to bringing light to a complex literature, the misleading report carries enormous potential to hinder scientific understanding of the meaning of abortion in women's lives. The report should be recalled and at a minimum, the conclusion changed. There is sufficient data in the world's published literature to conclude that abortion increases risk of anxiety, depression, substance use, and suicide. At this juncture, the APA cannot be trusted to provide accurate assimilation of information.

Problematic Features of the Report Substantiated in this Critique
The conclusion DOES NOT follow from the literature reviewed
When comparing reviews of the literature there is selective reporting
Avoidance of quantification
Biased selection of Task Force members and possibly reviewers
Power attributed to cultural stigmatization in women's abortion-related stress is unsupported
Selection criteria resulted in dozens of studies indicating negative effects being ignored
Methodologically based selection criteria as opposed to geographic locale should have been employed and consistently applied
Shifting standards of evaluation of studies presented based on the conclusion's fit with a pro-choice agenda

The Conclusion (in Italics Below) Does Not Follow from the Literature Reviewed

"The best scientific evidence published indicates that among adult women who have an unplanned pregnancy the relative risk of mental health problems is no greater if they have a single elective first-trimester abortion than if they deliver that pregnancy."

From Priscilla K. Coleman, (August 13, 2008).

They also note "Rarely did research designs include a comparison group that was otherwise equivalent to women who had an elective abortion, impairing the ability to draw conclusions about relative risks."

They are essentially basing the final conclusion of the entire report on one study by Gilchrist et al. (1995), which has a number of ignored flaws. The three studies that I authored or co-authored with unintended pregnancy delivered as a comparison group indicated that abortion was associated with more mental health problems. A few flaws of the Gilchrist study are highlighted below:

1. The response rate was not even provided.
2. Very few controls for confounding third variables. The comparison groups may very well have differed systematically with regard to income, relationship quality including exposure to domestic violence, social support, and other potentially critical factors.
3. On page 247, the authors report retaining only 34.4% of the termination group and only 43.4% of the group that did not request a termination at the end of the study. The attrition rate is highly problematic as are the differential rates of attrition across the comparison groups. Logically, those traumatized are less likely to continue in a study.
4. No standardized measures for mental health diagnoses were employed and evaluation of the psychological state of patients was reported by general practitioners, not psychiatrists. The GPs were volunteers and no attempt was made to control for selection bias.

When Comparing Reviews of the Literature There Is Selective Reporting

A review of Bradshaw and Slade (2003) in the report ignores this statement from the abstract: "Following discovery of pregnancy and prior to abortion, 40–45% of women experience significant levels of anxiety and around 20% experience significant levels of depressive symptoms. Distress reduces following abortion, but up to around 30% of women are still experiencing emotional problem after a month."

Also ignored from Bradshaw and Slade (2003) is the following: "The proportion of women with high levels of anxiety in the month following abortion ranged from 19% [to] 27%, with 3–9% reporting high levels of depression. The better quality studies suggested that 8–32% of women were experiencing high levels of distress."

Coleman is quoted from a testimony given in South Dakota rather than quoting from the two reviews she has published in prestigious peer-reviewed journals.

There is a claim that other reviews such as those of Coleman and a very strong quantitatively based one by Thorp et al. (2003) are incorporated, but the conclusions of these reviews are avoided entirely.

Avoidance of Quantification

The authors of this report avoid quantification of the numbers of women likely to be adversely affected by abortion. This seems like an odd omission of potentially very useful, summary information. There is consensus among most social and medical science scholars that a minimum of 10% to 30% of women who abort suffer from serious, prolonged negative psychological consequences (Adler et al., 1992; Bradshaw & Slade, 2003; Major & Cozzarelli, 1992; Zolese & Blacker 1992). With nearly 1.3 million U.S. abortions each year in the U.S. (Boonstra et al., 2006), the conservative 10% figure yields approximately 130,000 new cases of mental health problems each year.

In the report, the authors note "Given the state of the literature, a simple calculation of effect sizes or count of the number of studies that showed an effect in one direction versus another was considered inappropriate." What??? Too few studies to quantify, but a sweeping conclusion can be made?

Biased Selection of Task Force Members and Reviewers

No information whatsoever is provided in the report regarding how the Task Force members were selected. What was done to assure that the representatives do not all hold similar ideological biases? What was the process for selecting and securing reviewers? How many were offered the opportunity? Did any decline? How was reviewer feedback incorporated into revising the document? . . . very minimally from this reviewer's vantage point. Disclosure of this information is vital for credibility and accountability purposes.

Power Attributed to Cultural Stigmatization in Women's Abortion-related Stress Is Unsupported

There are few well-designed studies that have been conducted to support this claim. In fact, many studies indicate that internalized beliefs regarding the humanity of the fetus, moral, religious, and ethical objections to abortion, and feelings of bereavement/loss often distinguish between those who suffer and those who do not (see Coleman et al., 2005 for a review).

Selection Criteria Resulted in Dozens of Studies Indicating Negative Effects Being Ignored

According to the report "The TFMHA evaluated all empirical studies published in English in peer-reviewed journals post-1989 that compared the mental health of women who had an induced abortion to the mental health of comparison groups of women ($N=50$) or that examined factors that predict mental health among women who have had an elective abortion in the United States ($N=23$)."

Note the second type of study is conveniently restricted to the U.S. resulting in elimination of at least 40 studies. As a reviewer, I summarized these and sent them to the APA. There is an insufficient rationale (cultural variation) for exclusively focusing on U.S. studies when it comes to this type of study.

Introduction of this exception allowed the Task Force to ignore studies like a large Swedish study of 854 women one year after an abortion, which incorporated a semi-structured interview methodology requiring 45–75 minutes to administer (Soderberg et al, 1998). Rates of negative experiences were considerably higher than in previously published studies relying on more superficial assessments. Specifically, 50–60% of the women experienced emotional distress of some form (e.g., mild depression, remorse or guilt feelings, a tendency to cry without cause, discomfort upon meeting children), 16.1% experienced serious emotional distress (needing help from a psychiatrist or psychologist or being unable to work because of depression), and 76.1% said that they would not consider abortion again (suggesting indirectly that it was not a very positive experience).

Methodologically Based Selection Criteria as Opposed to Geographic Locale Should Have Been Employed and Consistently Applied

If the Task Force members were interested in providing an evaluation of the strongest evidence, why weren't more stringent criteria employed than simply publication of empirical data related to induced abortion, with at least one mental health measure in peer-reviewed journals in English on U.S. and non-U.S. samples (for one type of study)? Employment of methodological criteria in selection would certainly have simplified the task of evaluation as well. Sample size/characteristics/representativeness, type of design, employment of control techniques, discipline published in, etc. are logical places to begin. I am shocked to not see the development of criteria that reflect knowledge of this literature.

Shifting Standards of Evaluation of Studies Presented Based on the Conclusion's Fit with a Pro-choice Agenda

There are numerous examples of studies with results suggesting no negative effects of abortion being reviewed less extensively and stringently than studies indicating adverse effects. Further the positive features of the studies suggesting abortion is a benign experience for most women are highlighted while the positive features of the studies revealing adverse outcomes are downplayed or ignored. All the studies showing adverse effects were published in peer-reviewed journals, many in very prestigious journals with low acceptance rates. Clearly then, the studies have many strengths, which outweigh the limitations.

The same standards and criteria are simply not applied uniformly and objectively in the text, and I could literally write pages and pages pointing out examples of this blatantly biased survey of the literature. A few examples are provided below:

a. The Medi-Cal studies are sharply criticized for insufficient controls; however with the use of a large socio-demographically homogeneous sample many differences are likely distributed across the groups. Moreover, the strengths of the study include use of actual claims data (diagnostic codes assigned by trained professionals), which eliminate the problems of simplistic measurement, concealment, recruitment, and retention, which all are serious shortcomings of many post-abortion studies. The authors of the Medi-Cal Studies also removed all cases with previous psychological claims and analyzed data using an extended time frame, with repeated measurements enabling more confidence in the causal question. . . .

b. Results of the Schmiege and Russo (2005) study are presented as a superior revision of the Reardon and Cougle (2002) study, yet none of the criticism that was publicly leveled against the former study on the BMJ website is described. I contributed to this Rapid Response dialogue, and I reiterate a few of my comments here: "The analyses presented in Table 3 of the article do not incorporate controls for variables identified as significant predictors of abortion (higher education and income and smaller family size). These associations between pregnancy outcome and depression are troubling since lower education and income and larger family size predicted depression (see Table 4). Without the controls, the delivery group, which is associated with lower education and income and larger families, will have more depression variance erroneously attributed to pregnancy resolution. Among the unmarried, white women, 30% of those in the abortion group had scores exceeding the clinical cut-off for depression, compared to 16% of the delivery group. Statistical significance is likely to have been achieved with the controls instituted. This group is important to focus on as unmarried, white women represent the segment of the U.S. population obtaining the majority of abortions. Failure to convey the most scientifically defensible information is inexcusable when the data set contains the necessary variables. I strongly urge the authors to run these analyses. Curiously, in all the comparisons throughout the article, the authors neglect to control for family size without any explanation."

c. Fergusson and colleagues' (2006) study had numerous positive methodological features: (1) longitudinal in design, following women over several years; (2) comprehensive mental health assessments employing standardized diagnostic criteria of DSM III-R disorders; (3) considerably lower estimated abortion concealment rates than found in previously published studies; (4) the sample represented between 80% [and] 83% of the original cohort of 630 females; and (5) the study used extensive controls. Variables that were statistically controlled in the primary analyses included maternal education, childhood sexual abuse, physical abuse, child neuroticism, self-esteem, grade point average, child smoking, history of depression, anxiety, and suicidal ideation, living with parents, and living with a partner. Very little discussion in the report is devoted to the positive features of this study and the limitations, which are few compared to most published studies on the topic, are emphasized.

d. Attrition as a methodological weakness is downplayed because the studies with the highest attrition rates (those by Major et al.) are also the ones that provide little evidence of negative effects and are embraced despite attrition as high as 60%. Common sense suggests that those who are most adversely affected are the least likely to want to think about the experience and respond to a questionnaire. Research indicates that women who decline to participate or neglect to provide follow-up data are more likely to be negatively impacted by an abortion than women who continue participating (Soderberg, Anderson, Janzon, & Sjoberg, 1997).

Suffice to say, there is clear evidence of bias in reporting and in keeping with the rather transparent agenda of discrediting studies showing negative effects regardless of their true methodological rigor.

I strongly recommended evaluating only studies that met stringent inclusion criteria and then summarizing the studies in table format in such a way that the reader can quickly note the strengths and limitations of every study in a non-biased manner. Picking and choosing particular criteria from a large assortment of methodological criteria to evaluate various studies is inappropriate, suggestive of bias, and obfuscates the informative literature that is currently available. Lack of uniform application of evaluation standards creates a warped perception of the relative contributions of the studies.

The following quote by the editors of the *Canadian Medical Association Journal* (CMAJ) would have been insightful to the Task Force members as they incorporated feedback and endeavored to produce a report in keeping with their charge of objective assessment: "The abortion debate is so highly charged that a state of respectful listening on either side is almost impossible to achieve. This debate is conducted publicly in religious, ideological and political terms: forms of discourse in which detachment is rare. But we do seem to have the idea in medicine that science offers us a more dispassionate means of analysis. To consider abortion as a health issue, indeed as a medical "procedure," is to remove it from metaphysical and moral argument and to place it in a pragmatic realm where one deals in terms such as safety, equity of access, outcomes and risk–benefit ratios, and where the prevailing ethical discourse, when it is evoked, uses secular words like autonomy and patient choice." (CMAJ, 2003. p. 93)

CHALLENGE QUESTIONS

Does Research Confirm That Abortion Is a Psychologically Benign Experience?

1. Reviews of the literature on psychological consequences of abortion, and critiques of these reviews, are labeled by many as politically biased. What steps would you recommend for assembling a task force that would be free from bias on this topic?
2. Imagine that you are a researcher with a large grant to study the psychological experiences of women following abortion. What variables would be especially important to consider in the design of such a study?
3. Imagine that you are a clinician who is consulting with a woman who is considering an elective abortion and asks for reading recommendations on the topic of what she might experience after going through the procedure. What considerations would influence the publications that you recommend?
4. Priscilla K. Coleman criticizes the TFMHA on the basis that the review was restricted to studies conducted in the United States. What are the pros and cons of covering research studies on this topic that were conducted in non-U.S. countries?
5. The TFMHA report contends that negative postabortion psychological experiences are more likely attributable to interpersonal concerns such as feelings of stigma and low perceived or anticipated social support for the abortion decision. How would you go about assessing the extent to which psychological difficulties following abortion are due to concerns about stigma rather than due to emotional distress about the experience itself?

Suggested Readings

Bazelon, E. (2007, January 21). Is there a post-abortion syndrome? *New York Times Magazine, 40*–47, 62, 66, 70.

Charles, V. E., Polis, C. B., Sridhara, S. K., & Blum, R. W. (2008). Abortion and long-term mental health outcomes: A systematic review of the evidence. *Contraception, 79,* 436–450.

Coyle, C. T., Coleman, P. K., & Rue, V. M. (2010). Preabortion counseling and decision conflict as predictors of subsequent relationship difficulties and psychological stress in men and women. *Traumatology, 16,* 16–30.

Fergusson, D. M., Horwood, L. J., & Boden, J. M. (2008). Abortion and mental health disorders: Evidence from a 30-year longitudinal study. *British Journal of Psychiatry, 193,* 444–451.

Grote, N. K., & Bledsoe, S. (2007). Predicting postpartum depressive symptoms in new mothers: The role of optimism and stress frequency during pregnancy. *Health and Social Work, 32,* 107–118.

Hess, R. F. (2006). Postabortion research: Methodological and ethical issues. *Qualitative Health Research, 16,* 580–587.

Major, B., Appelbaum, M., Beckman, L., Dutton, M., Russo, N., & West, C. (2009). Abortion and mental health: Evaluating the evidence. *American Psychologist, 64*(9), 863–890. doi:10.1037/a0017497.

Pedersen, W. (2008). Abortion and depression: A population-based longitudinal study of young women. *Scandinavian Journal of Public Health, 36,* 424–428.

Sit, D., Rothschild, A. J., Creinin, M. D., Hanusa, B. H., & Wisner, K. L. (2007). Psychiatric outcomes following medical and surgical abortion. *Human Reproduction, 22,* 878–884.

Steinberg, J., & Russo, N. F. (2008). Abortion and anxiety: What's the relationship? *Social Science and Medicine, 67,* 238–252.

Wright, A. A., & Katz, I. T. (2006). Roe versus reality—Abortion and women's mental health. *The New England Journal of Medicine, 355*(1), 1–9.

Contributors to This Volume

EDITOR

RICHARD P. HALGIN is a professor of psychology in the Clinical Psychology Program at the University of Massachusetts—Amherst. He is coauthor, with Susan Krauss Whitbourne, of *Abnormal Psychology: Clinical Perspectives on Psychological Disorders,* 6th edition (McGraw-Hill, 2010); and coeditor, with Whitbourne, of *A Casebook in Abnormal Psychology: From the Files of Experts* (Oxford University Press, 1998). His list of publications also includes more than 50 articles and book chapters in the fields of psychotherapy, clinical supervision, and professional issues in psychology. He is a board-certified clinical psychologist, and he has over three decades of clinical, supervisory, and consulting experience. At the University of Massachusetts, his course in abnormal psychology is one of the most popular offerings on campus, attracting more than 500 students each semester. He also offers this course annually at Amherst College. His teaching has been recognized at the university and national level: he was honored with the University of Massachusetts Distinguished Teaching Award and the Alumni Association's Distinguished Faculty Award and was also recognized by the Society for the Teaching of Psychology of the American Psychological Association.

AUTHORS

GREG ABBOTT was reelected as the 50th Attorney General of Texas on November 7, 2006. Prior to his election as attorney general, Greg Abbott served as a Justice on the Texas Supreme Court and as a State District Judge in Harris County.

LAURIE AHERN is the president of Mental Disabilities Rights International (MDRI). She worked for 10 years as a newspaper editor and investigative reporter. Ms. Ahern is the former cofounder and codirector of the federally funded National Empowerment Center, and former vice president of the U.S. National Association of Rights Protection and Advocacy. She has written and lectured extensively on psychiatric recovery and self-determination, and has won several awards and honors for her efforts to improve conditions for, and attitudes toward, people with psychiatric disabilities.

AMERICAN PSYCHIATRIC ASSOCIATION (APA) is an international society working to ensure that all persons with mental disorders receive humane care and effective, accessible psychiatric diagnosis and treatment. In addition to supporting the prevention, diagnosis, and treatment of mental illness and working toward greater funding for education and psychiatric research, the APA educates lawmakers about a variety of issues, including the insanity defense. http://www.psych.org/

AMERICAN PSYCHOLOGICAL ASSOCIATION (APA) aims to improve psychology as a science and as a profession. As the United States' representative of psychology, the APA aspires to advance education, health, and human welfare by liberally supporting all branches of psychology and psychological research, advancing research methods, and improving psychologists' conduct, education, and ethics standards. The APA also advocates for psychology at the federal level through three directorates: education, public interest, and science. The APA works with federal agencies when they reformulate legislation and regulations of psychological interest. http://www.apa.org

APA TASK FORCE ON MENTAL HEALTH AND ABORTION consisted of Brenda Major, Ph.D. (Chair), Mark Appelbaum, Ph.D., Linda Beckman, Ph.D., Mary Ann Dutton, Ph.D., Nancy Felipe Russo, Ph.D., and Carolyn West, Ph.D. The American Psychological Association (APA) is a 150,000-member scientific and professional organization that represents psychology in the United States. The mission of the APA is to advance the creation, communication, and application of psychological knowledge to benefit society and improve people's lives.

RITA J. ARCHAMBAULT is a member of the department of counseling and consultation at Arizona State University. Her professional interests include eating disorders in men and women, anxiety and mood disorders, and trauma resolution. She is a member of the International Association of Eating Disorders Professionals.

RUSSELL A. BARKLEY is a professor of psychiatry at the Medical University of South Carolina and research professor in the Department of Psychiatry at SUNY Upstate Medical Center. He has authored or edited numerous articles, books, and newsletters on attention deficit hyperactivity disorder and related topics, including *The ADHD Report* (newsletter), *Taking Charge of ADHD, Revised Edition: The Complete, Authoritative Guide for Parents* (Guilford, 2000), and *Child Psychopathology,* 2nd ed. (Guilford, 2003).

TIM BAYNE is currently a university lecturer in the Philosophy of Mind at the University of Oxford and a Fellow of St. Catherine's College. Bayne is interested in applied ethics, the philosophy of religion, and especially the philosophy of cognitive science. Some of Bayne's more recent works include *Delusions and Self-Deception: Affective Influences on Belief Formation* (2007), *Hypnosis and the Unity of Consciousness* (2006/7), and *Phenomenology and the Feeling of Doing: Wegner on the Conscious Will* (2006). http://www.philosophy.ox.ac.uk/members/timothy_bayne

DIANE L. BEARMAN works as a clinical health psychologist at the University of Minnesota Medical School. She sees patients with psychological issues related to both acute and chronic medical conditions. Her clinical interests include HIV/AIDS, coping with medical diagnoses, and effects of illness on family members and caregivers.

SAMUEL J. BRAKEL is the CEO and education director for the Isaac Ray Forensic Group, a group that provides psychological and forensic psychiatric services in its mission to attain justice and public safety. Attorney Brakel, author of *Law and Psychiatry in the Criminal Justice System* (2001), has faculty appointments at Rush Medical College and DePaul University College of Law and continues to publish widely in the area of mental health law.

PETER R. BREGGIN is the founder of the International Center for the Study of Psychiatry and Psychology, a nonprofit organization concerned with the impact of mental health and practice on individuals. His background includes teaching at Harvard Medical School and a faculty appointment to the Johns Hopkins University Department of Counseling. He is the author of many books, including *The Antidepressant Fact Book* (Perseus Books, 2001) and *Talking Back to Ritalin, Revised: What Doctors Aren't Telling You About Stimulants and ADHD* (Perseus Books, 2001).

LISA D. BUTLER is a senior research scholar in the department of psychiatry and behavioral sciences at Stanford University. Her research interests include risk and resiliency in trauma, dissociation, the psychological sequelae of traumatic experiences (including medical illnesses), trauma and memory, and cognitive processes in paranoia.

PRISCILLA K. COLEMAN is an associate professor of Human Development and Family Studies at Bowling Green State University. Her research interests focus on socioemotional development in early childhood, parenting issues, and the psychological effects of the abortion experience.

MARK A. COSTANZO is a professor of psychology and codirector of the Center for Applied Psychological Research at Claremont McKenna College. He has conducted research on various issues pertaining to the application of psychological science to the legal system. He is the author of *Just Revenge: Costs and Consequences of the Death Penalty.*

PETER COTTON a clinical and organizational psychologist, is an Honorary Research Fellow at the University of Melbourne, Australia. Cotton has worked as a workplace mental health specialist with the National Occupational Health & Safety Commission in Australia and has published widely in the field of occupational health and well-being.

JOHN M. DAVIS is Gillman Professor of Psychiatry and Research Professor of Medicine at the University of Illinois, Chicago. His research focuses on schizophrenic spectrum disorders, mood disorders, obsessive-compulsive disorder, premenstrual dysphoric disorder, and the biology of major mental illnesses.

GRANT J. DEVILLY is a professorial fellow at the University of Australia, Melbourne and president of the Australasian Society for Traumatic Stress. Devilly's current research focuses on the causes and treatment of posttraumatic stress disorder, and he has also conducted extensive research in the field of criminology, in which he has published extensively on the topics of sex-offending and crime victimization.

HEATHER DRAPER is a senior lecturer in biomedical ethics at the University of Birmingham Medical School, where she teaches medical students and postgraduate health care professionals on a wide range of health care ethics and law issues. Dr. Draper's research interests include the ethics of reproductive technology, tissue transplantation, and gender reassignment. She serves on several ethics advisory committees in the UK, and is a member of the Human Genetics Commission.

JONATHAN L. FREEDMAN is a professor of psychology at the University of Toronto. He is the author of many articles on media violence, including "Effect of Television Violence on Aggressiveness" (1984), "Television Violence and Aggression: What Psychologists Should Tell the Public" (1992), and "Violence in the Mass Media and Violence in Society: The Link Is Unproven" (1996).

ELLEN GERRITY is an assistant professor of psychiatry at Duke University and coeditor of *The Mental Health Consequences of Torture*. She is the associate director of the UCLA-Duke University National Center for Child Traumatic Stress, and has focused her professional work for many years on topics pertaining to trauma and violence.

DAVID H. GLEAVES is an associate professor in the department of psychology at Texas A&M University. His research interests include dissociative disorders and the psychopathology of eating disorders. Gleaves is the recipient of the 1999 Pierre Janet Award for Writing Excellence and the 1996 Morton Prince Award, both from the International Society for the Study Dissociation.

JAMES B. GOTTSTEIN is a psychiatric rights lawyer from Anchorage, Alaska, where he has practiced law for over 25 years. Gottstein is the president of numerous organizations, including the Law Project for Psychiatric Rights (PsychRights), which he cofounded in 2002; Peer Properties, Inc., which he cofounded in 2002 to offer peer-run housing for mentally ill people in bad living situations; Soteria-Alaska, Inc., an organization that offers noncoercive and mostly nondrug alternatives to psychiatric hospitalization, which he cofounded in 2003; and CHOICES, Inc., which he also cofounded in 2003 to make available peer-run services that particularly support the right of people to choose whether or not to take psychiatric drugs. Gottstein has also been a member of the board of directors for the National Association for Rights Protection and Advocacy since 2005, acting as president in 2006, and he has been on the board of directors of the International Center for the Study of Psychiatry and Psychology since 2006. http://psychrights.org/about/Gottstein.htm

KIRK M. HUBBARD has served in administrative and clinical positions in the Veterans Administration Hospital in Hampton, VA, and has held adjunct faculty positions at Eastern Virginia Medical School and the College of William and Mary. Dr. Hubbard served as a psychologist supporting field operations and as director of Behavioral Sciences Research for the CIA.

MATTHEW ISRAEL is a psychologist who currently serves as director of the Judge Rotenberg Center (JRC), which he founded in 1971 as the Behavior Research Institute. Dr. Israel studied psychology under the late B.F. Skinner as an undergraduate, graduate student, and a postdoctoral fellow at Harvard University. In the 1960s, he was involved in several initiatives using behavioral interventions with disturbed children. JRC is a special needs school in Canton, Massachusetts, serving individuals from the age of 3 through adulthood. For nearly four decades, JRC has provided education and treatment to emotionally disturbed individuals with conduct, behavioral, emotional, and/or psychiatric problems, as well as to individuals with developmental delays and autistic-like behaviors.

THE JUDGE ROTENBERG CENTER (JRC) is a special needs school in Canton, Massachusetts serving ages 3-adult. For nearly 40 years JRC has provided education and treatment to emotionally disturbed students with conduct, behavior, emotional, and/or psychiatric problems and developmentally delayed students with autistic-like behaviors.

LEON R. KASS chaired the President's Council on Bioethics from 2002 until 2005. After earning his M.D. (1962) and Ph.D. in biochemistry (1967), both at Harvard, he went on to teach at St. John's College, Annapolis, MD, the Kennedy Institute of Ethics at Georgetown University, and, since 1976, has taught undergraduate students at the University of Chicago. Kass has written numerous articles, books, and essays, including *Life, Liberty, and the Defense of Dignity: The Challenge for Bioethics* (2002).

JOHN F. KIHLSTROM is a professor in the Department of Psychology at the University of California, Berkeley and a member of the Institute of Cognitive and Brain Sciences, the Institute of Personality and Social Research, and the Center for Health Research. Kihlstrom developed the Study of the Human Ecology of Memory project to study the links between memory in psychology and other social sciences. He has written numerous articles on self-knowledge, social cognition, and the study of unconscious mental life.

ADAM J. KOLBER is a professor at the University of San Diego School of Law, where he writes and teaches bioethics, criminal law, and neuroethics. In addition to running the "Neuroethics & Law Blog," Kolber has published such works as "A Matter of Priority: Transplanting Organs Preferentially to Registered Donors," *Rutgers Law Reviews*, and "Standing Upright: The Moral and Legal Standing of Humans and Other Apes," *Stanford Law Review*. He was named a Jurisdynamics Idol in August of 2006. http://www.sandiego.edu/usdlaw/faculty/facprofiles/kolberaj.php; http://jurisdynamics.blogspot.com/2006/08/adam-kolber-jurisdynamic-idol.html

NEIL LEVY is a principal research fellow at the University of Melbourne's Australian Research Council Special Research Centre for Applied and Public Ethics. Levy's numerous writings include *On the Competence of Substance Users to Consent to Treatment Programs* (2006), *Autonomy and Addiction* (2006), *Cognitive Scientific Challenges to Morality* (2006), and *The Case for Physician-Assisted Suicide: How Can It Possibly Be Proven?* (2006). http://www.onlineopinion.com.au/author.asp?id=1414; http://www.findanexpert.unimelb.edu.au/researcher/person8720.html

SCOTT O. LILIENFELD is a professor of psychology at Emory University and a clinical psychologist. He conducts research on the causes and assessment of personality disorders (especially psychopathic personality), scientific thinking and its application to psychology, and philosophical psychology.

ARNOLD H. LOEWY is a professor of Criminal and Constitutional Law at the Texas Tech University School of Law. Loewy graduated first in his class at Boston University, where he received his bachelor's degree in 1961 and his Doctor of Jurisprudence degree in 1963. After earning his Master of Laws degree from Harvard University in 1964, Loewy went on to teach at the University of North Carolina School of Law for 38 years, and then at the University of Connecticut School of Law for four years, before joining the Texas Tech University School of Law faculty in 2006. Loewy chaired the criminal justice section of the Association of American Law Schools in 1993, and has spoken to the International Society for the Reform of Criminal Law on the topics of criminal speech (1990), virtual child pornography (2002), and "Systematic Changes to Reduce the Conviction of the Innocent" (2006). http://www.law.ttu.edu/lawWeb/faculty/bios/Loewy.shtm

M. BRINTON LYKES is a professor of community-cultural psychology at Boston College and the associate director of the Boston College Center for Human Rights and International Justice. Her scholarly activities have focused on a range of social issues such as political violence, humanitarian aid, reparations, and mental health.

ROBERT MATHIAS has worked for numerous federal and state government agencies as well as nonprofit organizations. He has researched and written extensively about science and health-related issues and has served as a science writer and editor for *NIDA NOTES*, a publication of the National Institute on Drug Abuse that examines recent research findings about drug abuse.

MENTAL DISABILITIES RIGHTS INTERNATIONAL (MDRI) is an international human rights organization dedicated to human rights and full participation in society of people with disabilities. MDRI documents human rights abuses, supports the development of disability rights advocacy, and promotes international awareness and oversight of the rights of people with disabilities.

JEFFREY T. MITCHELL earned his Ph.D. in human development from the University of Maryland, where he is currently a clinical associate professor of emergency health services. He is also president emeritus of the International Critical Incident Stress Foundation (ICISF). He developed critical incident stress management after serving several years as a firefighter/paramedic. Mitchell has written or coauthored a number of books, including *Critical Incident Stress Debriefing: An Operations Manual for CISD, Defusing and Other Group Crisis Intervention Services,* and many articles about crisis intervention.

MICHAEL MONTAGNE has investigated the social and cultural aspects of psychedelic drug use for more than 25 years. His research has also focused on the role of meaning, symbolism, and metaphors in depression and the use of antidepressant medications. He is currently the Rombult Distinguished Professor of Pharmacy and Associate Dean at the Massachusetts College of Pharmacy and Health Science.

NATIONAL ALLIANCE ON MENTAL ILLNESS (NAMI) is dedicated to eliminating mental illness and improving the lives of mentally ill persons and their families. NAMI takes a strong stance on public policy issues that affect the mentally ill and their loved ones. The alliance supports the insanity defense, favoring both volitional and cognitive standards. http://www.nami.org/

NATIONAL INSTITUTE ON DRUG ABUSE (NIDA) was established in 1974 and became part of the National Institutes of Health, Department of Health and Human Services, in October 1992. Since then, it has been a federal focal point for research on drug abuse and addiction. NIDA's aim is to use the power of science to analyze drug abuse and addiction. NIDA addresses the most fundamental and essential questions about drug abuse, from detecting and responding to emerging drug abuse trends, and understanding how drugs work in the brain and body, to developing and testing new treatment and prevention approaches.

NATIONAL INSTITUTE OF MENTAL HEALTH (NIMH) is one of the 27 constituents that comprise the National Institutes of Health (NIH). The NIH is part of the U.S. Department of Health and Human Services, as well as the federal government's primary organization for behavioral and biomedical research. The NIMH is the lead government research agency for behavioral and mental disorders. http://www.nimh.nih.gov/index.shtml

THE PRESIDENTIAL COMMISSION FOR THE STUDY OF BIOETHICAL ISSUES advises the President on bioethical issues that may emerge from advances in biomedicine and related areas of science and technology. The

Commission works with the goal of identifying and promoting policies and practices that ensure scientific research, health care delivery, and technological innovation are conducted in an ethically responsible manner.

NATALIE J. PURCELL, who holds a Master's in Public Administration, works as a professional in the nonprofit sector, and as a sociopolitical activist associated with Amnesty International. http://www.amazon.com/Death-Metal-Music-Politics-Subculture/dp/0786415851

NATHANIEL QUARTERMAN is the director of the Texas Department of Criminal Justice (TDCJ) Correctional Institutions Division, a position he has held since 2006. Quarterman started working as a correctional officer for the TDCJ in 1984. In 2003, Quarterman was appointed the position of deputy director for the Correctional Institutions Division's Prison and Jail Management. As the TDCJ Correctional Institutions Division's director, Quarterman supervises 106 TDCJ facilities, which house roughly 151,000 offenders. http://www.tdcj.state.tx.us/mediasvc/connections/JulAug2006/agency_v13no6.html

ROBERT RESNICK has served as a professor of psychology at Randolph-Macon College since 1996. He is also a licensed and board-certified clinical psychologist. Dr. Resnick was the president of the American Psychological Association from 1995 to 1996, and has received numerous awards and distinctions for his research and contributions to the field of psychology. His publications and presentations include the areas of attention deficit/hyperactivity disorder and health policy.

JUNE RIEDLINGER is a naturopathic physician at Integrative Holistics in the Boston area, and an adjunct associate professor at the Massachusetts College of Pharmacy and Health Sciences. In 1985 she testified about the therapeutic effects of MDMA and later coauthored several articles on MDMA. Reidlinger has most recently been working in the field of complementary and alternative medicine, offering educational programs on topics relating to psychedelic drugs and MDMA.

WILLIAM N. ROBINER is a professor in the Department of Medicine at the University of Minnesota. He is a diplomate in Health Psychology through the American Board of Professional Psychology and is former Chair of the Psychology Standards Committee of the University of Minnesota Hospital. Dr. Robiner's clinical and research interests include AIDS, anxiety disorders, sexuality, and psychotherapy.

ERIC ROSENTHAL is the founder and executive director of Mental Disabilities Rights International (MDRI), and is also vice president of the United States International Council on Disability. He has served as a consultant to the World Health Organization, UNICEF, and the U.S. National Council on Disability. Mr. Rosenthal has won awards for his human advocacy efforts on behalf of people with disabilities.

DIANA E. H. RUSSELL, who holds a Ph.D. in Social Psychology from Harvard, has spent the last 25 years exploring the topic of sexual violence against women and girls. She is a leading expert in her field, having written many books and articles on the topics of pornography, rape, the misogynist murder of women, and incest. Her writings include *The Epidemic of Rape and Child Sexual Abuse in the United States* (2000) and *The Trials & Tribulations of Publishing a Book Attacking Porn* (1999). Russell has won numerous awards, being named to the Veteran Feminists of America's Honor Roll for American Writers in 2002, and receiving the American Humanist Association's "Humanist Heroine" award in 2001. Russell has spoken publicly on television and radio shows, including *Oprah Winfrey* and *National Public Radio*. http://www.dianarussell.com/

SALLY SATEL is a practicing psychiatrist and lecturer at the Yale University School of Medicine as well as a resident scholar for the American Enterprise for Public Policy Research. She examines mental health policy as well as political trends in medicine. Some of her publications include *The Health Disparities Myth, and One Nation under Therapy,* which she coauthored with Christina Hoff Sommers.

NANCY SIGNORIELLI is a professor of communication at the University of Delaware. Professor Signorielli is a member of the National Communication Association and the International Communication Association, the Broadcast Education Association. In 1993, she testified before the U.S. House Energy and Commerce committee's subcommittee on telecommunications and finance oversight hearings on television violence and its impact on children. Her publications include "Prime-Time Violence 1993–2001: Has the Picture Really Changed?" in *Journal Broadcasting & Electronic Media* (2003), and "Aging on Television: Messages Relating to Gender, Race, and Occupation in Prime-Time," also in *Journal of Broadcasting & Electronic Media* (2004).

STEVEN M. SMITH is a professor in the department of psychology at Texas A&M University. Smith's research interests involve human memory, particularly recovered and false memories, memory blocks, and eyewitness memory. He is the author of many articles on blocked and false memories and was the recipient of a National Science Foundation grant concerning memory functions.

WESLEY J. SMITH left his full-time law practice in 1985 to work in public advocacy and pursue a writing career, and was named one of the nation's top professional thinkers in bioengineering by the *National Journal* in 2004. Smith is an award-winning author, having written or coauthored eleven books, including *Culture of Death: The Assault on Medical Ethics in America*, which was named the 2001 Best Health Book of the Year, a *Consumer Guide to a Brave New World* (2005), and his recently updated *Forced Exit: Euthanasia, Assisted Suicide, and the New Duty to Die* (2006). Smith works as a special consultant for the Center for Bioethics and Culture and as an attorney for the International Task Force on Euthanasia and Assisted Suicide; he is also a senior fellow at the Discovery Institute. Smith runs a well-read Web Log titled "Secondhand Smoke," a log defending the importance and exceptional moral value of human life. http://www.wesleyjsmith.com/blog/

DAVID SPIEGEL is professor and associate chair of Psychiatry an Behavioral Sciences at Stanford University School of Medicine. He is the author of over 280 research papers, chapters in scientific journals, and books. His work focuses on psychosomatic research and treatment, specifically within the field of oncology.

TRADITIONAL VALUES COALITION (TVS), founded in 1980 by Reverend Louis P. Sheldon, is "the largest nondenominational, grassroots church lobby in America." TVC focuses on issues such as marriage, religious liberties, pornography, education, family tax relief, and what the Coalition calls "the right to life," and "the homosexual agenda." The organization emphasizes "the restoration of the values needed to maintain strong, unified families," providing information on these topics to Christians and pastors.

JAMES L. WERTH, JR. holds a Ph.D. in counseling psychology and is an Associate Professor of psychology at the University of Akron. His research examines the professional, legal, and ethical issues of counseling psychology, particularly pertaining to end-of-life decisions. He has published numerous books and articles, including *Psychosocial Issues Near the End of Life: A Resource for Professional Care Providers* and *Contemporary Perspectives on Rational Suicide*.

KELLEY WINTERS is the founder of GID Reform Advocates as well as a writer on issues of transgender medical policy. Winters is the author of *Gender Madness in American Psychiatry: Essays from the Struggle for Dignity* (2008), and her articles have appeared in a number of books and journals. She is also on the advisory board for TransYouth Family Advocates and the Matthew Shepard Foundation.

KIMBERLY S. WRIGHT is a clinical psychologist who practices in Tempe, Arizona.

ROGERS H. WRIGHT is a past president of the Division of Clinical Psychology of the American Psychological Association, and cofounded the Council for the Advancement of the Psychological Professions and Sciences (CAPPS). Dr. Wright is a fellow of the American Psychological Association.

PATRICK ZICKLER has served as a consultant for the National Research Council of the National Academy of Sciences. He has written extensively on scientific research in medicine and has been in a major editorial role for *NIDA NOTES*, a publication of the National Institute on Drug Abuse that examines recent research findings about drug abuse.